U0887126

高等学校教材

国际物流双语

第2版
Second Edition

International Logistics

陈 艳 主编
刘 艳 周海霞 副主编

化学工业出版社
·北京·

内容简介

《国际物流》（双语）（第2版）是为培养我国国际物流业所需的既能熟练掌握国际物流专业知识，又能熟练运用专业英语从事国际物流具体业务的复合型人才而专门编写的双语教材，同时也能帮助具备一定英语基础并初步具有国际物流专业知识的专业人员提高国际物流专业英语水平，利用英语直接从事国际物流的实际工作和研究工作。

《国际物流》（双语）（第2版）共分13章，每章包括三个部分。第1部分是课文，该部分用中英文全面系统地阐述了国际物流领域的各个重要环节；第2部分是词汇和术语，该部分紧扣课文，提供与课文内容相关的常用词汇和专业术语；第3部分是练习，既有中文练习又有英文练习，便于读者自学。

本书可作为高等院校物流管理、物流工程以及相关专业的学生学习国际物流理论与实务的教材，也可作为从事国际物流工作人员的参考书。

图书在版编目（CIP）数据

国际物流：英、汉/陈艳主编. —2版. —北京：化学工业出版社，2023.6（2024.9重印）
高等学校教材
ISBN 978-7-122-43243-8

Ⅰ.①国… Ⅱ.①陈… Ⅲ.①国际物流-高等学校-教材-英、汉 Ⅳ.①F259.1

中国国家版本馆CIP数据核字（2023）第058668号

责任编辑：陶艳玲　　文字编辑：丁　瑞
责任校对：宋　夏　　装帧设计：韩　飞

出版发行：化学工业出版社（北京市东城区青年湖南街13号　邮政编码100011）
印　　装：大厂聚鑫印刷有限责任公司
787mm×1092mm　1/16　印张23½　字数580千字　2024年9月北京第2版第2次印刷

购书咨询：010-64518888　　售后服务：010-64518899
网　　址：http://www.cip.com.cn
凡购买本书，如有缺损质量问题，本社销售中心负责调换。

定　　价：**69.00元**

前 言

Preface

本书自2016年8月出版以来，因其知识框架完整、内容新颖实用且中英文对照等特点，受到了众多院校师生及学者的关注和认可，至今已经9次印刷，并在全国90余所院校推广应用。本次修订主要基于以下几个原因。

第一，随着互联网与国际物流领域的深度融合以及跨境电子商务时代的到来，国际物流课程必须与时俱进，适应“互联网+”的时代背景以及跨境电商时代提出的新要求。因此，有必要紧跟形势发展，对本书进行修改和补充。

第二，随着“一带一路”倡议的推进，国际物流领域产生了一些新的国际合作模式和物流运作方式，尤其值得一提的是，中欧班列的蓬勃发展对全球互联互通以及全球贸易便利化发挥了重要的推动作用，因此有必要对国际物流领域的一些新形势和新模式进行介绍和探讨。

第三，《国际贸易术语解释通则2020》（Incoterms 2020）已于2020年1月1日正式生效，因此，本书中所涉及的相应内容也必须随之修订。

第四，在本书第1版的使用过程中，广大读者、专家、学者也不断地向出版社和作者本人反馈了许多建设性的修改建议。

为了更好地紧跟国际物流的最新发展形势，作者对本书进行了修订，主要修订内容如下：

(1) 基于国际物流系统的网络特征，在第2章中新增三节内容介绍构成国际物流网络的物流节点和物流通道，即国际主要海运航线和国际主要港口，国际主要空运航线和航空机场以及国际物流其他运输线；

(2) 第3章内容基于国际贸易术语解释通则的最新版（Incoterms 2020）进行了相应的更新；

(3) 增加了第12章跨境电子商务物流，以便读者系统了解跨境电商物流的重要环节、运作、运营方式以及政府监管模式；

(4) 增加了第13章国际物流信息技术，以便读者系统地了解互联网、大数据、云计算、物联网等先进信息网络技术在国际物流领域的推广应用；

(5) 第7章中增加了一节介绍中欧班列，可使读者全面了解中欧班列的发展背景和运营现状，以及中欧班列对推进国际物流合作和全球互联互通的重要意义。

修订后的教材主要体现以下特点：一是紧跟国际物流领域发展的最新形势，主要表现在对国际贸易术语解释通则最新版Incoterms 2020所涉及知识的修正，中欧班列、跨境电商物流以及最新物流信息技术等内容的增加；二是完善了第1版中不足的地方；三是突出了应用性和操作性。

本书由陈艳任主编，刘艳、周海霞任副主编，参编人员有杨煜、王田田。本书编写过程中，多位专家为本书审稿并提供了修改意见和指导，在此表示感谢！

本书修订过程中，参考借鉴了国内外出版社出版的一系列相关著述，在此一并向这些著作及论文的作者表示由衷的感谢。由于作者水平有限，尽管竭力编写和修正，仍难免存在不足之处，恳请专家和读者多多指正，以便在下次修订时加以完善，渐臻善境。

“国际物流（双语）”在线课程在智慧树网站已开课多个学期，欢迎读者前往参考。

为便于英语学习，书中各章的词汇和术语配有诵读录音，可扫码播放。

编者

2023 年 7 月

第1版前言

Preface to the first edition

20 世纪 80 年代以来，信息技术以及网络技术的迅猛发展和广泛普及，极大地推动了国际间的经济合作与交流，世界经济、金融走向一体化，为生产、贸易服务的物流也因此从国内延伸至国外，从而诞生了国际物流这一新的物流形式。进入 21 世纪后，随着经济全球化趋势的日益增强，国际物流获得了突飞猛进的发展，在国际经济中处于举足轻重的地位。近年来，随着“一带一路”倡议的推进，我国国际物流业迎来了全新的发展机遇，国际物流量空前增长，国际物流产业呈现出欣欣向荣的景象。然而，国际物流在中国还是一门新兴学科，国际物流产业也刚刚起步，其科学理论和技术应用的普及程度还很低，教育和培养大批的国际物流专业人才，已经成为中国现代物流业发展的当务之急。由于国际物流所涉及的业务领域十分广阔且涉外性强，如订单处理、运输、仓储、包装、供应商管理、多式联运等具体的业务，在这些业务操作中会用到大量的专业词汇及专业英语知识，所以国际物流专业人才应是既掌握国际物流专业知识和技术，又具备扎实的国际物流英语基础和较强的英语语言应用能力的复合型专业人才。随着全球经济一体化程度的加深，摆在高校教育面前的一个迫切任务就是如何应对全球经济一体化的要求，培养更多能将专业知识和英语语言能力有机结合，融会贯通的复合型专业人才。正是基于此目的，我们组织编写了这本双语教材。

目前我国有关国际物流的教材较多，其中中文教材占到多数；另有少数以英文为主，只提供少量中文注释或中文阐述的国外原版影印教材或专业英语教材，没有做到中英文完全对照。基于此，本书将突出中英文对照的双语特色，旨在一定程度上弥补当前国际物流双语教材的缺乏。本书力求以中英文对照的方式来介绍国际物流的理论知识和实务操作，结构完整，内容全面，操作性强，集中反映了近年来国际物流领域的最新发展，使读者能够用已掌握的英语来系统学习国际物流专业知识。全书共分 12 章，每章包括 3 个部分。第一部分是课文，该部分用中英文全面系统地阐述了国际物流领域的各个重要环节。第二部分是词汇和术语，该部分紧扣课文，提供与课文内容相关的常用词汇和专业术语。第三部分是练习，该部分充分体现了教材的双语特点，既有中文练习又有英文练习，便于读者自学。

本书可作为高等院校物流管理、物流工程及相关专业学习国际物流专业理论知识的教材和国际物流行业从业人员的职业培训教材；也可作为物流工程硕士生课外的辅助读物及从事物流研究与教学人员的参考用书；还可作为社会上一些对国际物流感兴趣的人士的参考读物。

本书由陈艳策划并主编，刘艳、周海霞和郝国英为副主编。编写队伍多年来从事国际物流、物流与供应链管理、物流专业英语等的教学和研究，承担多项双语教学改革项目，积累了较为丰富的教学经验。

在本书编写过程中，编写人员参阅了大量国内外论著，得到了大量丰富的资料，并从中引用了不少经典的概念。编者在本书最后将主要参考文献列出。在此，谨向各位国际物流研究的专家、学者致以诚挚的谢意。

由于本书编写时间紧、任务重，加之作者水平有限，难免出现疏漏之处，真诚希望广大读者批评指正。

编者

2016 年 8 月

目 录
Contents

Chapter One Introduction to International Logistics 国际物流概述

Chapter Two International Logistics System and International Logistics Network 国际物流系统与国际物流网络

Chapter Three Fundamental Knowledge on International Trade 国际贸易基础知识

Chapter Four International Cargo Warehousing 国际货物仓储

Chapter Five International Maritime Transport Logistics 国际海运物流

Chapter Six International Air Transport Logistics 国际空运物流

Chapter Seven International Land Transport Logistics 国际陆运物流

Chapter Eight International Container Transport and Multimodal Transport Logistics 国际集装箱运输和多式联运物流

Chapter Ten International Cargo Insurance 国际货物保险

Chapter Eleven International Freight Forwarder 国际货运代理

Chapter Twelve Cross Border E-commerce Logistics 跨境电子商务物流

Chapter Thirteen Information Technology Applied in International Logistics 国际物流信息技术

Chapter One

Introduction to International Logistics
国际物流概述

Part A Text 课文

1.1 Brief Introduction to International Logistics

1.1.1 Definition of International Logistics

In the past 20 years, with the development and integration of global capital market, the progress of information and communication technologies has created a growing global market. That is, the originally segmented national or regional markets have gradually evolved into an integrated global market. Corresponding to the continuous development of market globalization, the trend of global economic integration is constantly growing, which has enabled economic and trade activities to cross the boundaries of countries and/or regions and directly promoted the development of international logistics. International logistics has gradually become one of the most concerned issues for all countries around the world.

International logistics refers to the flow or transfer of goods (including raw materials, work in process and finished products) and articles (including postal items, exhibits, and aid, etc.) between different countries and regions. International logistics can be interpreted both narrowly and broadly. From the narrow side, international logistics mainly refers to trade logistics which includes all the logistical activities necessary to conclude an international trade transaction, such as transportation, warehousing, packaging, material handling, processing, customs clearance, insurance, inspection and quarantine, etc. And broadly interpreted, international logistics includes both trade logistics and non-trade logistics. Non-trade logistics means those logistical activities not for commercial purposes, such as cross-border international mails and parcels, international exhibits, international aid, international public welfare activities, etc.

Particularly, the concepts of international logistics can be better understood from the following aspects:

Firstly, international logistics is the extension of domestic logistics, which conducts logistical activities across national boundaries and includes all the operations related to material management and material transportation. From this perspective, international logistics is also known as "international big circulation" or "big logistics".

Secondly, international logistics is an integral part of international trade, which emerges and grows with the development of international trade and international division of labor. Due to the further specialization of labor, there is no country which is capable of assuming all professional division of labor. Therefore, international exchange has become increasingly frequent, which has greatly promoted the international flow and transfer of goods and/or materials and has inevitably led to the evolution of international logistics. The essence of international logistics is to achieve the effective flow of goods and/or materials across various counties and regions and to promote the optimal deployment of world resources and the development of regional economy by utilizing international logistics networks, facilities and technologies on the basis of the principles of international division of labor and collaboration.

Thirdly, the ultimate purpose of international logistics is to better serve international trade and multinational operation. In specific, it attempts to transfer the goods and/or materials from the supplying place to the demanding place by selecting the optimal transportation modes and routes at lowest risks and costs. As far as a particular country is concerned, it is through the well-organized international logistical processes that goods can be delivered, in high quality and efficiency, at low costs and risks, to the hands of foreign customers and also goods and materials can be transported to its domestic market efficiently and effectively to satisfy the requirements of its economic and social development.

1.1.2 Features of International Logistics

Compared to domestic logistics, international logistics has a bigger scope, a longer cycle, more uncertainties, more required documents and higher logistical requirements. In particular, it has the following major features:

Firstly, it involves more links and has a longer cycle. Besides the common links such as transportation, warehousing, packing, material handling and information management, etc., international logistics includes some special links because it conducts logistical activities across national boundaries. For instance, when goods and/or materials are shipped into or out of a country's customs territory, the links of commodity inspection and customs clearance are required. Since goods in international transportation are exposed to greater risk of being damaged or lost, the exporter or the importer is supposed to arrange insurance for the goods.

Secondly, it is much more complicated than domestic logistics. The complexity is mainly generated from the significant differences of logistical regulations, infrastructures and technologies among different countries and regions. In most cases, international logistics uses the combination of various transportation modes, thus increasing the complexity of transportation. Another factor that greatly contributes to the complexity is the sheer amount of documentation required for international logistical operations. While domestic logistical operations can generally be completed by using only an invoice and a bill of lading, international logistical operations require substantial documentation regarding order contents, transportation, financing and government control.

Thirdly, it is often in exposure to greater risks. Typically, international logistics is faced with a lot of uncertainties because of its long cycle, complicated links and cross-border operations. In addition to some common logistics risks (such as accidents, damages, carelessness of tally, natural losses, contract risks), international logistics is also confronted with high political, economic and natural risks. Political risks mainly refer to the risks incurred by political reasons such as the instability of a country or region (including wars, strikes, or social unrest) and the change of the political and economic relationship between countries or regions, which may lead to logistical interrupts, transport delays, cargo damages and other losses. Under current international monetary system, national currency exchange rates often vary with the transaction situation of international financial market and fluctuate greatly, leading to the instability of the relative value of settlement currency in international logistics. For example, shipping companies usually levy additional currency devaluation surcharge to cover the loss of profit incurred by the fluctuation of currency exchange rates. Natural risks refer to the risks incurred by natural calamities including earthquakes, tsunamis, storms and other natural disasters, which often result in transportation accidents and logistics service breakdowns.

1.1.3 Links of International Logistics

Since international logistics is the further extension of domestic logistics, it includes all the logistical links of domestic logistics, such as transportation, warehousing, material handling, processing, packing and information processing, etc. In addition, international logistics generally involves some special links necessary for the implementation of commodity inspection, customs clearance, cargo insurance, international settlement and other relevant procedures.

(1) Basic Links

1) Transportation: It refers to the physical movement of goods from a point of origin to a point of consumption and can involve raw materials being brought into production process and finished goods being delivered to the customer. As it fulfills the physical flow of goods and often occupies a large portion of the total cost, transportation always assumes a significant role in many logistics systems. Enterprises, no matter large companies or SMEs (small and medium sized enterprises), usually appoint designated managers in charge of the planning, organizing and controlling of transportation processes.

2) Warehousing: Warehousing is often referred to the storage of goods/materials. Broadly interpreted, this definition also includes a wide range of facilities and locations that provide warehousing. Thus, warehousing can include the storage of iron ore in open fields; the storage of finished goods in production facilities; and the storage of raw materials, parts or components, and finished goods while they are in transit.

3) Material handling: Material handling is concerned with the movement of raw materials, work in process or finished products into or out of logistics facilities as well as their short-distance movement within the facilities.

4) Packing: It is mainly concerned with protecting the products in the course of shipment and storage. Another role of packing is to make products look appealing to customers, which facilitates the promotion of sale.

5) Information management: It is what links all areas of logistics system together. The growth of reasonably priced computers and software has put sophisticated management information system within the reach of even the smallest organizations. To offer secure and reliable logistics service, logistics companies are greatly dependent on the accurate and timely transfer of information among various links and parties of international logistics.

(2) Special Links

1) Customs Clearance: When goods are shipped into and out of a country's customs territory, consignees or consignors, or their agents are required to make customs declaration. They need to fill out the forms named "Customs Declaration for Imports and Exports" with the attached documents required by Customs for examination. The customs declaration is an activity that must be carried out when the goods flow into or out of the customs territory of a country. It is regarded as mandatory regulatory measures for international trade. Since goods in international logistics are definitely transported into or out of the customs territories of different countries, customs declaration is one of the indispensable links of international logistics.

2) Cargo Insurance: Due to long distance, multiple handling and storage activities, and various kinds of unpredictable risks during international logistics transportation, cargo transportation insurance needs to be effected by the buyer or the seller in order to reduce the losses arising from the cargo damage or loss. Free from Particular Average (F. P. A.), With Particular Average (W. P. A.), and All Risks are the three basic insurance coverages of marine transportation insurance provided by People's Insurance Company of China (PICC).

3) International Settlement: The payment of international trade is quite complex. The commonly used settlement modes include remittance, collection and letter of credit.

1.1.4 Relationship between International Logistics and International Trade

Firstly, international logistics provides fundamental supports for international trade. At the stage of signing an international trade contract, shipping terms must be stipulated clearly. Then, goods should be transported across customs territories from the supplying place to the specified demanding place in strict accordance with the stipulations of shipping terms. It is only through the well-organized process of international logistics that the cost-effective physical movement of products can be completed when the title to the products is transferred from the seller to the buyer. Without international logistics, neither the physical movement of products nor the creation of value in the form of products can be completed.

Secondly, the development of international trade has raised new requirements to international logistics. With the development of production and the continuous growth of international trade volume, the competition in the international trade market is becoming more and more fierce. Businesses have attached more importance to the quality, speed and cost of transportation as well as the delivery time. The new trends and features of international trade have put forward new requirements to the operation of international logistics. They are as follows:

1) Quality Requirements: With the change of international trade structure, the goods under international trade have switched from traditional primary products and raw materials to intensely processed products of high-value. Thus, high quality logistics services are required so as to protect the value of products in transit. In addition, diversified customer demands in international markets have led to the trend of small-lot, multi-species logistics, driving the development of lean and diversified international logistics.

2) Safety Requirements: International logistics has the features of wide geographical span, long cycle, and complicated links. And it is subject to various natural and political factors including weather, geographical conditions, political situations, wars, strikes, etc. Thus, when making decisions on the routes and modes of international logistics transportation, firms should take into account such factors as weather, geographical, political and economic conditions of countries and regions along the route.

3) Efficiency Requirements: In order to accelerate international logistics process, large-scale specialized logistics equipment, including specialized shipping vessels, handling equipment, berths, etc., needs to be applied on the basis of the full consideration of the features of cargoes.

4) Cost Requirements: International logistics always involves many complicated links and lasts a long period of time. There is great potential for controlling and reducing the total costs by reengineering the processes of international logistics.

5) Information Requirements: Information is the only driver which facilitates both the acceleration of logistics process and the cost saving of the entire logistics system. The trend of information in international logistics requires that EDI declaration, electronic inspection and quarantine and electronic space booking be widely used.

1.1 国际物流概述

1.1.1 国际物流的定义

在过去的 20 年里，随着全球资本市场的成长和整合，信息和通信技术的进步创造出一个正在成长的全球市场，即传统分割型的国家或区域市场正在逐渐演变成一个统一的全球市场。与市场全球化的不断发展相对应，全球经济一体化的趋势不断增强，从而促使经济与贸易跨越了国与国、地区与地区的界限，直接推动了国际物流的演进。国际物流已经逐渐成为世界各国普遍关注的问题之一。

国际物流是指货物（包括原材料、半成品和制成品等）及物品（包括邮品、展品、捐赠物资等）在不同国家（地区）间的流动或转移。我们可以从狭义和广义两个角度来理解国际物流。狭义的理解是国际物流即贸易物流，是指与国际贸易活动相关的物流活动，如运输、仓储、包装、装卸搬运、流通加工、报关、保险、检验检疫等活动。而广义的理解是国际物流包含贸易物流和非贸易物流两大部分。非贸易物流是指不以商业为目的的物流活动，如跨越国界的国际邮件及包裹、国际展品、国际援助物资、国际间公益活动等。

具体来说，国际物流的内涵还可以从以下几个方面来理解。

第一，国际物流是国内物流的延伸和进一步扩展，是跨国界的、范围扩大了的物流活动，包括全球范围内与物料管理以及物资运送相关的所有业务环节。所以，国际物流又称为“国际大流通”或“大物流”。

第二，国际物流是国际贸易活动的重要组成部分，是伴随着国际贸易和国际分工合作形成的。基于国际分工的专业化程度加深，任何国家都不可能包揽一切专业分工。因此，国际交流日益频繁，这就推动了国际间的商品和物资的流动，也必然带来了国际物流的演进。国际物流的实质就是根据国际分工协作的原则，依照国际惯例，利用国际化的物流网络、物流设施和物流技术，实现商品和物资在国际间的高效合理流动，以促进区域经济的发展和世界资源的优化配置。

第三，国际物流的总目标是为国际贸易和跨国经营服务。具体而言，即选择最佳的运输方式和路径，以最低的风险和费用，将货物和/或物料从供给地运至需求地。就某个具体的国家而言，只有合理地组织国际物流活动，才能将国外客户所需要的商品高效率、高质量、低成本地送到，同时也可将本国需要的商品及物料高效、便宜地运至国内，以满足国内经济和社会发展的需要。

1.1.2 国际物流的特点

与国内物流相比，国际物流涉及的空间跨度更大，物流周期更长，不确定性更多，所需的单证更多以及物流操作方面的要求更高。具体而言，国际物流具有如下特点：

第一，物流作业环节多，周期长。国际物流业务需要跨越国界，在全球范围内进行运作。与一般物流相比，国际物流不仅需要运输、仓储、包装、装卸搬运、信息管理等一般的物流环节，还需要某些特殊的环节。例如，货物运出和运入关境都要进行检验检疫、报关清关等必需的海关过境程序。由于国际运输途中的货物遭遇损坏或灭失的风险较大，因此出口商或进口商应办理相关的国际货物保险。

第二，物流作业复杂。其复杂性主要来源于不同国家和地区在物流法律法规、物流基础设施和物流技术等方面的显著差异。在大多数情况下，国际物流采用多种运输方式的组合，从而提高了运输的复杂程度。另一个大大增加其复杂性的因素是国际物流运作所需的大量单证。国内物流业务一般只需一张商业发票和海运提单就可以完成，而国际物流业务则需要关于订单、运输、融资和政府监管的大量单证。

第三，物流过程具有高风险性。国际物流因其完成周期较长，物流作业复杂以及跨国界运作，存在许多不确定性。除了存在一般性物流风险（如意外事故、不可抗力、作业损害、理货检验疏忽、货物自然损耗、合同风险）外，国际物流还面临着政治、经济和自然等方面的更高的风险。政治风险主要指所经过国家的政局动荡，如罢工、动乱或战争，以及国与国之间、地区与地区之间的政治、经济关系的变化等原因造成物流过程中断、运输延迟、物流流程延长以及货物损害甚至丢失等。在现行国际货币体系下，各国货币汇率往往会随着国际金融市场的交易情况而变化，波动较大，导致国际物流中结算货币的相对价值不稳定。例如，航运公司通常会征收额外的货币贬值附加费，以弥补货币汇率波动造成的利润损失。自然风险是指地震、海啸、风暴等自然灾害所带来的风险，这些自然灾害往往会导致运输事故和物流服务中断。

1.1.3 国际物流环节

由于国际物流是国内物流的进一步延伸，所以国际物流包含了国内物流中的所有物流基本业务环节如运输、仓储、包装、装卸搬运、流通加工信息处理等。除此之外，国际物流还包含了商品检验、报关、运输保险、国际结算等特殊业务环节。

(1) 基本业务环节

1）运输：产品从产地到消费地的实体移动过程，包括将原材料运至生产过程以及将成品递送至消费者手中。因为运输完成了产品或物料的实体流动过程且在物流总成本中占据较大比例，运输在许多物流系统起着极为重要的作用。无论大公司还是中小型企业，往往会任命一个专职经理负责运输的规划、组织和控制。

2）仓储：仓储通常指的是货物/物料的储存。广义地说，它还包括能提供仓储的各种各样的设施和场所。因此，仓储可以包括在露天场地存储铁矿石，在生产工厂存储产成品以及运输途中货物（原材料、部件以及产成品）的存储。

3）装卸搬运：将原材料、在制品或产成品移入或移出物流设施以及它们在设施内的短距离移动。

4）包装：是指采用一定包装技术在运输以及仓储过程中保护产品。包装的另一作用在于增加产品的吸引力以促进销售。

5）信息管理：通过信息管理将物流系统的所有环节连成一个整体。计算机以及应用软件价格的渐趋合理使得小企业也能借助功能强大的信息管理系统进行物流系统所有环节信息的收集、加工和处理。为了能提供安全可靠的物流服务，物流企业需极大地依赖国际物流各环节以及各参与方之间准确及时的信息传递。

(2) 特有业务环节

1）报关：报关是指货物在进出关境时，由进出口货物的收、发货人或其他代理人按照海关的规定格式填报《进出口货物报关表》，随附海关规定交验的单证，向海关办理报关手续。报关是货物进出入一国关境时必须进行的一项活动。由于国际物流项下的货物必然需要出入不同国家的关境，所以报关是国际物流不可缺少的特有业务环节之一。

2）国际货物运输保险：国际物流运输距离长，装卸保管次数多，在物流过程中可能会遇到难以预测的各种风险，因此为了减少货物灭损而产生的损失，必须对国际物流中的货物办理运输保险。我国海洋运输的基本险别分为平安险、水渍险和一切险三种，由中国人民保险公司承保。

3）国际结算：国际物流活动中的结算支付方式较为复杂。一般使用的结算支付方式有汇付、托收和信用证。

1.1.4 国际物流与国际贸易的关系

首先，国际物流是实现国际贸易的保障。在签订国际贸易合同时，需明确规定运输条款。合同签订后，需严格按照运输条款的规定，将货物从供应地越过关境运至指定的需求地。只有通过精心组织国际物流，当产品的所有权从卖方转移到买方时，产品的实体移动才能高效地完成。没有国际物流，无论是货物的实体移动，还是体现为产品形式的价值创造，都无法完成。

其次，国际贸易的发展对国际物流提出了新的要求。随着世界各国生产的发展和国际贸易额的不断增长，国际贸易市场竞争越来越激烈，企业对运输质量、交货时间、运输速度以及运输费用更加重视。国际贸易出现的新的趋势和特点，对国际物流在质量、安全、效率、经济和信息化方面提出了更新、更高的要求。

1）质量要求：国际贸易结构正在发生巨大的变化，传统的初级产品、原料等逐步让位于高附加值、精密加工的产品，因此，需要高质量的国际物流服务来保障在途商品。此外，国际贸易需求的多样化还造成了物流的多品种和小批量化，从而要求国际物流向精细化、多样化发展。

2）安全要求：国际物流涉及的国家多，地域辽阔，在途时间长，易受气候、地理条件等自然因素和政局、罢工、战争等社会政治因素的影响。在组织国际物流，选择运输方式和运输路径时，应密切注意所经区域的气候条件、地理条件，还需注意沿途所经国家或地区的政治局势、经济状况等，以防这些人为因素和不可抗拒的自然力造成的货物灭失和损害。

3）效率要求：应充分考虑货物的特性，采用与之相适应的巨型专用货船、专用泊位以及大型机械专用运输设备等，以加快国际物流进程。

4）成本要求：国际物流环节多，备运期长。通过对国际物流过程的流程再造/业务重组，控制和降低物流总成本还具有很大潜力。

5）信息化要求：信息是唯一一个既能加快国际物流速度，又能降低物流系统总成本的驱动力量。国际物流领域的信息化趋势要求广泛采用 EDI 通关、电子检验检疫以及电子订舱等。

1.2 Development of International Logistics

1.2.1 Evolution of International Logistics

Since its emergence, international logistics has experienced three important stages:

(1) Beginning stage: 1950s—1980s

After World War Ⅱ, international economic exchanges further extended and became increasingly active. Especially in the late 1970s, international trade became very huge in volume. Under this circumstance, systematic logistics appeared. With the increased volume of international trade, large-scale logistics came into being and large-scale logistics equipment was invented, such as 200-thousand-ton oil tanker, 100-thousand-ton ore ship, etc. In the 1970s, international containers and international container vessels developed rapidly, which satisfied the requirements of transporting medium-sized and small-sized cargoes. Major scheduled liners of international shipping routes all put container vessels in use, which greatly improved the service level of international logistics.

(2) Developing stage: 1980s—1990s

In the 1980s, with the changes of customer requirements in a new era, international logistics focused on solving the challenges raised by “small-lot, high-frequency, multi-types” logistics. Many new technologies and methods appeared and were put in use. In the case that international logistics volume ceased to increase, the automation and mechanization of logistics were greatly improved. With the application of logistics information system and EDI system, international logistics moved to a new developing stage. Information enabled the development of logistics to move towards the direction of lower cost, better service and leaner operation. This trend became more prominent in international logistics than in domestic logistics. Almost every functional area of international logistics depended greatly on information. Accurate and timely transfer of information became the cornerstone in any logistics system. It can be concluded that in 1980s and 1990s international logistics entered the era of logistics information.

(3) Flourishing stage: 1990s—now

The concepts and roles of international logistics have been widely acknowledged by governments around the world and many countries have begun to take measures to promote smooth international logistics. Doing business with global trading partners definitely requires international or even global logistics activities, including international logistics facilities, logistics technology, logistics service, cargo transportation, packaging and distribution processing. Almost every country around the world has extensively implemented bold exploration of the theories and practices of international logistics. There is a global consensus: State-less logistics should be carried out under the framework of the whole world. Only through the extensive cooperation among countries in the field of international logistics, the prosperity of world economy can be achieved. Nowadays, with the wide application of high-tech approaches, including network technologies, bar code and radio frequency, and satellite positioning system, etc., in the area of international logistics, the trend of information has been more prominent and the level of logistics service has been significantly improved. Leading logistics companies have invested heavily in the construction and improvement of logistics information system. It can be argued that the twenty-first century will be a blooming era of international logistics owing to the wide application of information and intelligence.

1.2.2 Hurdles of International Logistics

Although economic globalization has laid the solid foundation for the smooth operation of international logistics, there are some hurdles which may impede the further development of international logistics. These unfavorable factors can be divided into three categories: market entry barriers, international market risks and non-standardized barrier of logistics infrastructure and facilities.

(1) Market entry barriers

Market entry barriers include market entry restriction, information insufficiency and tariff barrier. Market entry restriction means using legislation or judicial practices to restrict the entry of import commodities into a country's domestic market. For example, Japan has applied "local retailer's voting system" to limit the entry of foreign commodities. Under this system, whether imported products are allowed to sell in the Japanese market or not is completely at the discretion of local retailers.

The hurdle of information insufficiency can also be called as information asymmetry barrier. As far as foreign enterprises are concerned, it is quite difficult for them to obtain adequate information relating to market size, competition status as well as import procedures and required documents. Since different countries have different policy orientations, the corresponding import procedures and documents may differ greatly. In many cases, the lack of information often leads to defective documents. Consequently, shipments will be postponed or even be detained, which not only leads to logistics process interrupts but also sometimes incurs clients' claims.

In addition, in order to protect their domestic markets and local enterprises, some countries use both tariff and non-tariff barriers to restrict international trade. To a certain extent, these measures increase the difficulties and costs of international logistics operations. For example, in response to a country's restrictions on the volume of import goods, some importers often use bonded warehouses to keep stocks. Although this measure helps to reduce tariff expenses, it definitely increases the complexity and costs of the entire logistics process.

(2) International market risks

Under the global environment, the prices of international trade commodities are greatly influenced by exchange rate fluctuations, thus affecting the time distribution of logistics demands. For example, distributors selling German auto parts in the US would make replenishments of parts as late as possible to reduce inventory investment if the Euro against the U. S. dollar is in the decreasing period. Otherwise, keeping more inventory of parts would generate cost savings on parts procurement. Therefore, exchange rate fluctuations affecting the prices of international trade commodities actually increase the complexity of international logistics operations. In response to this, manufacturers have to extend the lead time of inventory and transportation.

(3) Non-standardized barrier of logistics infrastructure and facilities

Nowadays, significant differences still remain in logistics infrastructures and facilities among different countries or regions. Although in recent years the degree of container standardization has been raised, huge differences of measurement, capacity, weight and track specification of transport vehicles still remain. Unless standardization is achieved, the cost and duration of international logistics will definitely increase.

1.2.3 New Trends of International Logistics

Since 1990s, the trend of economic globalization and the pattern of international purchasing, producing and distributing have brought about the consequent internationalization of logistics industry. Without the aid of smooth international logistics, international trade will never expand and it is quite difficult to achieve multinational production and global purchasing. In this century, the further growth of world economy will boost the development of international logistics. The new trends of international logistics are as follows:

Firstly, multinational companies (multinationals) are becoming the major users and drivers of international logistics. Nowadays, multinational operation has occupied a dominant position in the world economy. The features of multinational operation and the complexity of its logistics are directly reflected in the requirements of international logistics. Currently, the requirements of multinationals have occupied over 75% of international cargo volume. The internal trade and technology trade within multinationals impact the growth of world economy in terms of quantity and quality. Consequently, the internal transportation of multinationals has greatly increased. Over the past two decades, multinational company has revised its previously localized focus—manufacturing and marketing its products in individual countries, and now instead it typically sources materials and components on a world basis for global production. Different global pipelines of multinationals have influenced the direction of international cargo flows, the deployment of shipping routes as well as the size and specification of facilities. Furthermore, multinationals have established much closer relationship with international logistics firms and have become the major clients of global carriers. The implementation of multinational's global strategy has increased the volume of international logistics and will definitely depend on the further development and improvement of international logistics.

Secondly, the operation of international logistics will be deeply incorporated into global supply chain. In today's increasingly fierce competition, business firm needs to focus on its core business whilst collaborating with its upstream and downstream companies and participating in supply chain alliance that is composed of excellent suppliers, manufacturers, wholesalers, retailers, logistics providers and related service providers of financing, insurance, information and consulting, etc., so as to maintain its survival and development. The international operation of each firm requires that international logistics be incorporated into the entire global supply chain.

Thirdly, the service scope of international logistics will continue to expand and integrated service providers (ISP) will occupy the leading position. Two traditional logistics service providers are transportation and warehousing specialists. Integrated service providers focus on marketing a range of logistics services that include all work necessary to accommodate customers, ranging from order entry to product delivery. In many situations transportation and warehouse services are augmented by a wide range of tailored logistics services. These customized services are typically described as value-added services. The common name used throughout industry to describe ISPs is Third-Party and Fourth-Party logistics service providers. In a general sense, Third-Party Logistics (TPL), also known as asset-based ISPs, own and operate transportation equipment and warehousing buildings. In contrast, Fourth-Party Logistics (FPL), also known as non-asset-based ISPs, specialize in providing comprehensive information services that facilitate supply chain management.

Fourthly, international logistics will fully enter a new stage of development focusing on automation, digitization and intelligence. With the wide application of various advanced information, telecommunication and recognition technologies, including Internet, Internet of Things, POS, GIS, GPS, and Radio Frequency Identification (RFID) and so on, in the field of international logistics, all functional areas of logistics have been vastly enhanced. More and more modern logistics technologies, including intelligent transportation, automatic guided vehicle, stacking robot, unmanned forklift truck, automatic sorting system, have been applied and consequently the level of automatic and intelligent logistics has been significantly improved.

Finally, green logistics and green supply chain will be one of the dominant global trends. In the year ahead, the environment will increasingly become the focus of attention. A range of companies is already preparing environmental accounts as an appendix to their annual reports. A number of companies are becoming certified based on environmental standards such as ISO 14000. More and more companies have started to probe more deeply into the substances and materials used to manufacture their products in order to reduce adverse environmental impacts. Greening logistics and supply chain are becoming global consensus. China has implemented substance restrictions along with labeling, marking and testing requirements for electronic products by legislation. Japan and Korea have expanded chemical substance laws. In the US, numerous people have proposed State legislative initiatives to require end-of-life take-back. Mexico and Canada have updated hazardous waste laws to include loosening import/export laws on viable recyclables. Brazil, Argentina, Paraguay, and Uruguay have proposed "Policy on Environmental Management of Waste and Discarded Product Liability" for electronics waste management.

1.2 国际物流的发展

1.2.1 国际物流的发展历程

自产生以来，国际物流的发展大致经历了以下三个阶段。

(1) 起步阶段：20世纪50—80年代

第二次世界大战以后，国际间的经济交往得到扩展且越来越活跃，尤其在20世纪70年代以后，国际贸易从业务量来讲已经非常巨大，交易水平和质量要求也越来越高，系统物流就是在这个时期进入到国际领域。20世纪60年代开始形成了国际间的大数量物流，在物流技术上出现了大型物流工具，如20万吨的油轮、10万吨的矿石船等。20世纪70年代，国际集装箱及国际集装箱船发展很快，很好地满足了运输中、小件杂货的需求。开行国际航线的大班轮公司都投入了集装箱船，使得物流服务水平获得了很大提高。

(2) 发展阶段：20世纪80—90年代

20世纪80年代，伴随新时代人们需求观念的变化，国际物流着力于解决"小批量、高频度、多品种"的物流，出现了不少新技术和新方法。在物流量基本不继续扩大情况下出现了"精细物流"，物流的机械化、自动化水平不断提高。伴随物流信息系统和电子数据交换(EDI)系统的应用，国际物流的发展进入了一个新的阶段。信息使物流向更低成本、更高服务以及更精细化方向发展。这种趋势在国际物流中更为凸显。国际物流的所有功能领域都在很大程度上依赖信息（支撑）。准确及时的信息传递已成为各物流系统的重要基石。可以说，20世纪80年代、90年代国际物流已进入了物流信息时代。

(3) 繁荣阶段：20世纪90年代至今

这一阶段国际物流的概念和重要性已为各国政府所普遍接受，并开始采取措施努力促进国际物流的顺利进行。贸易伙伴遍布全球，必然要求物流国际化，即物流设施国际化、物流技术国际化、物流服务国际化、货物运输国际化、包装国际化和流通加工国际化等。世界各国广泛开展国际物流理论及实践方面的大胆探索。人们已经形成共识：物流无国界，只有广泛开展国际物流合作，才能促进世界经济繁荣。如今，网络技术、条码技术以及卫星定位系统得到了普遍应用，这些高科技手段在国际物流中的应用，极大地提高了物流的信息化和物流服务水平。各大物流企业纷纷投入巨资用于物流信息系统的建设。可以说，21世纪将是国际物流信息化高度发展的时代。

1.2.2 国际物流发展的阻碍

虽然经济全球化为国际物流的顺利运行奠定了坚实的基础，但仍存在一些阻碍国际物流进一步发展的障碍。这些不利因素可以分为三类：市场进入壁垒、国际市场风险和物流基础设施设备的非标准化障碍。

(1) 市场进入壁垒

市场进入壁垒包括市场进入限制、信息不充分、关税和非关税壁垒等。市场进入限制往往是通过立法或司法实践来限制进口商品进入一国的国内市场。例如，日本实施“当地零售商投票”制度来限制外国商品进入其国内市场，即进口商品是否能进入日本当地市场完全由当地零售商投票决定。

信息不充分障碍也称为信息的不对称障碍。对于外国企业来说，有关市场规模、竞争状况以及进口程序和所需单证等信息往往难以掌握充分。由于不同国家有不同的政策取向，所以进口业务和有关单证的差异很大。在许多情况下，信息的缺失往往导致单证有瑕疵，结果是，货物装运延迟或货物被扣押。这将导致物流流程的中断，甚至引发客户索赔。

此外，为保护本国市场和企业，一些国家还通过关税和非关税壁垒来限制国际贸易，也在一定程度上增加了国际物流运作的难度和成本。例如，为应对某国对商品进口数量的限制，有些进口商会使用在保税仓库里建立库存的方法。这种策略虽然减少了关税费用，但却增加了国际物流活动的复杂性及其成本。

(2) 国际市场风险

在全球环境下，国际贸易商品价格受汇率变动的影响很大，从而影响着物流需求的时间分布。例如，经营德国汽车零配件的美国销售商在欧元对美元的汇率下降时，会尽量推迟(从德国采购）补货，以减少库存投资。然而，当欧元对美元的汇率处于上升期时，更多地储备零配件反而能节约采购成本。因此，汇率波动影响国际贸易商品价格，从而增加了国际物流运作的难度，为此，厂商不得不延长存货和运输的提前期。

(3) 物流基础设施设备的非标准化障碍

世界各国在运输和装卸搬运设备、仓库设施和港口设施以及通信系统等方面存在着很大的差异。尽管近年来提高了集装箱标准化程度，但在全球运输设备中，运输工具的尺寸、能力、重量和轨道规格等方面依然存在着较大的差异，当其未被标准化时，国际物流的费用和时间势必会增加。

1.2.3 国际物流的新趋势

20 世纪 90 年代以来，全球经济化浪潮以及国际化采购、国际化生产、国际化销售格局的形成，伴随而来的是国际化物流。没有顺畅的国际物流，国际贸易不会扩大，跨国生产和全球采购也难以实现。21 世纪全球经济将进一步增长，伴随着经济增长的物流国际化将会得到更大的发展，其发展趋势可以归纳为以下几个方面：

首先，跨国公司将成为未来国际物流的主要需求者和推动力。当今跨国公司的生产和经营在全球经济中占有举足轻重的地位。跨国公司的生产经营特性及其物流的复杂性从国际物流的需求上直接反映出来。目前，国际贸易总量中 75％的国际货运量都来自跨国公司。跨国公司的技术贸易和内部贸易从数量和质量上左右着世界经济的增长。因此，跨国公司内部运输大量增加。在过去的 20 年里，跨国公司改变了原来的本土化经营策略，即本国生产和本国销售，开始在世界范围内采购原材料及零部件从事全球化生产。跨国公司不同的购销渠道和货源影响着国际运输货流的走向、航线的配置以及设施的规模和规格。此外，跨国公司与国际物流（运输）企业的关系比以往更为密切，大型跨国公司已经成为全球承运人的主要揽货目标。跨国公司全球战略的实施，使得国际物流量加大，跨国公司的全球战略必然依赖国际物流的发展和完善。

其次，国际物流的运作将深度融入全球供应链管理。在当今日益激烈的商业竞争中，企业只有在发挥核心竞争力的同时，与自己的上下游企业紧密协作，参加由优秀的制造商、供应商、批发商、零售商、物流企业以及相关的金融、保险、信息、咨询等企业组成的供应链联盟，才能维持生存和发展。（供应链上）各企业的国际化运营均要求国际物流的运作融入全球供应链管理中。

第三，国际物流服务范围将进一步扩大，一体化物流服务提供商将占据主导地位。以前，物流公司主要提供运输和仓储两种专业化服务。一体化服务提供商向客户提供一系列满足其需求的服务，包括从订单处理直至产品发货的所有环节。在很多情况下，系列化、专业化服务的出现大大扩展了运输和仓储服务领域的范围。我们通常把这种专门为客户定制的服务称为增值服务。一体化服务提供商在行业中通常被称为第三方或第四方物流提供商。第三方物流往往利用自有的运输设备和仓储设施来从事经营，而第四方物流主要提供改善供应链管理的集成信息服务。

第四，国际物流将全面进入信息化、自动化和智能化发展阶段。随着各种先进信息、通信、网络及识别技术的广泛应用，如互联网、物联网、销售时点技术（POS）、地理信息系统（GIS）、全球定位系统（GPS）以及射频识别技术（RFID）等，大大增强了物流各个环节的功能。除了智能交通运输外，无人搬运车、机器人堆码、无人操作叉车、自动分拣系统等现代物流技术大大提高了物流自动化和智能化的水平。

最后，绿色物流和绿色供应链将成为世界性发展趋势。未来一段时期，环境将成为日益关注的焦点。有些企业开始在发布企业年度报告时增加了环保报告。还有一部分企业开始努力获得 ISO 14000 环境管理系列国际认证。越来越多的企业开始对生产其产品所用的原材料和物质进行深入研究以减少对环境的不利影响。绿色物流和绿色供应链已经成为全球共识。中国通过法律对电子产品的材料及其标签、标记、测试要求都做了限制。日本和韩国扩大了法律对化学物质的限制范围。在美国，许多人建议国家立法要求企业在产品使用寿命结束后对其进行回收。墨西哥和加拿大更新了危险废物法，从法律上对可循环产品的进出口放宽限制。巴西、阿根廷、巴拉圭和乌拉圭在电子废料管理方面提出了“针对废料及废弃产品责任的环境管理政策”。

Part B Vocabulary and Terminology 词汇和术语

international logistics 国际物流
domestic logistics 国内物流
international trade 国际贸易
multinational company 跨国公司
economic globalization 经济全球化
tariff 关税
exchange rate 汇率

lean logistics 精细物流
information asymmetry 信息不对称
tariff barrier 关税壁垒
non-tariff barrier 非关税壁垒
lead time 前置时间，提前期
remittance 汇付
collection 托收
letter of credit 信用证
raw materials 原材料
work-in-process 半成品，在制品
finished products 产成品
international division of labor 国际分工
documentation 单证
transportation 运输
warehousing 仓储
material handling 装卸搬运
packing（packaging） 包装
information management 信息管理
replenishment 补货
global supply chain 全球供应链
upstream and downstream companies 上下游企业
integrated service providers 一体化服务提供商
third-party logistics service providers 第三方物流服务提供商
fourth-party logistics service providers 第四方物流服务提供商
green logistics 绿色物流
green supply chain 绿色供应链

Part C Exercise 练习

Ⅰ. Answer the following questions.

1. What is the background for the development of international logistics?
2. How do you define international logistics?
3. In what aspects does international logistics differ from domestic logistics?
4. Why is international logistics more complicated than domestic logistics?
5. What is the relationship between international logistics and international trade?
6. What are the basic links of international logistics? What special links does international logistics include?
7. What are the major barriers for international logistics?
8. Why are the multinationals becoming the major users and drivers of international logistics in future?
9. Please describe the trend of Green Logistics and Supply Chain.

Ⅱ. Judge whether the following statements are true or false.

1. Logistics only manages the transportation of the finished goods to the buyer.

2. Global organization normally looks at the whole world as one potential market-sourcing, manufacturing, researching, raising capital, and selling wherever the job can be done best.

3. Countries are becoming closer and closer because of the success in logistics.

4. Fulfilling customer needs in the USA or Europe requires the same skills and resources as satisfying buyers in India or China.

5. The whole world is becoming more and more competitive due to the growth in logistics activity.

6. Two traditional logistics service providers are transportation and inventory specialists.

Ⅲ. Translate the following passages into Chinese.

1. Two major phases in the movement of materials are important. The first phase is inbound materials management which means the timely movement of raw materials, parts, and supplies into and through the firm. The second phase is outbound distributions, which involves the movement of the firm's finished products to its customers. Stationary periods (storage and inventory) are included. The basic aim of logistics management is the effective coordination of both inbound and outbound phases to achieve given level of customer service at the lowest total cost.

2. Integrated service providers focus on marketing a range of logistics services that include all work necessary to accommodate customers, ranging from order entry to product delivery. In many situations the foundation of transportation and warehouse services was augmented by the performance of a wide range of special services. These customized services are typically described as value-added services. The common name used throughout industry to describe ISPs is third-party and fourth-party logistics service providers.

Ⅳ. Translate the following passages into English.

1. 在当今日益激烈的商业竞争中，企业只有在发挥核心竞争力的同时，与自己的上下游企业紧密协作，参加由优秀的制造商、供应商、批发商、零售商、物流企业以及相关的金融、保险、信息、咨询等企业组成的供应链联盟，才能维持生存和发展。

2. 国际物流中有众多的参与方：买方、卖方、承运人、中间商，有时还有政府。在产品经由多个国家从供应商向顾客的实体移动过程中，国际物流通过实体运输、信息交流以及库存管理等物流活动创造产品的空间和时间效用，实现了价值增值。

Chapter Two

International Logistics System and International Logistics Network 国际物流系统与国际物流网络

Part A Text 课文

2.1 Objectives and Structure of International Logistics System

2.1.1 Definition of International Logistics System

Compared with domestic logistics system, international logistics system is much more complicated and integrated. In essence, it is an organic system with specific functions and consists of some interacting and interdependent elements, including goods to be transported, handling and packing equipment, transportation vehicles, storage facilities, related personnel, etc.

2.1.2 Objectives of International Logistics System

The ultimate purpose of logistics management is to provide space and time utilities during the transfer of the title to the product from the seller to the buyer. To be specific, logistics system attempts to realize the following 5S objectives:

1) Service: This objective means that the delivery of goods should be fulfilled without the phenomena of stock-out and cargo damage or loss, meanwhile at lowest possible costs.

2) Speed: it emphasizes that the delivery should be rapid and timely at customer's desired time and place.

3) Space saving: It means to make full use of storage space by using Automated Storage and Retrieval System (AS/RS) and related handling and stacking equipment.

4) Scale optimization: It refers to applying economies of scale to logistics to cut down logistics costs. For example, consolidation and break-bulk operations in cross-docking distribution centers can greatly reduce transportation cost as well as inventory cost.

5) Stock: This objective is mainly concerned with setting appropriate level of inventory in order to fulfill the customer orders at minimum inventory investment.

Besides the above 5S objectives, international logistics system should also serve international trade and multinational operation by means of selecting the optimal transportation modes and routes to transport the goods in right quality and quantity, at lowest possible risks and costs, from the supplying places to the demanding places.

2.1.3 Structure and Mode of International Logistics System

The structure of international logistics system refers to the interrelating way of the components or subsystems that constitute international logistics system. From the aspect of structure, international logistics system is a multi-structured complicated system that not only contains stable and dynamic structures but also includes time and space structures. It is an integrated system with time and space sequence and is composed of multiple stereoscopic subsystems.

In terms of spatial structure, the international logistics system is composed of nodes, lines and planes, which interlace to form an international logistics network. In terms of functional structure, each link of international logistics such as transportation, warehousing, packing, material handling, processing, inspection and customs clearance, is a stereoscopic subsystem with specific functions and is made up of physical elements including organizers, goods, carriers, routes and information, etc. According to specific requirements of different consignments, those related subsystems are incorporated into an integrated system in an orderly manner.

Although international logistics is a complicated system containing a wide range of links, it basically has the same three functions, namely input, transformation and output, as those of domestic logistics system. It is through input and output functions that international logistics system accomplishes the exchanges with its external environment and adapts itself to the outside world.

2.1 国际物流系统的目标和结构

2.1.1 国际物流系统的定义

与国内物流相比，国际物流是个更为庞大而复杂的集成系统。它是由需运输的产品、包装设备、装卸搬运设备、运输工具、仓储设施、相关人员等若干相互制约的动态要素构成的、具有特定功能的有机整体。

2.1.2 国际物流系统的目标

物流管理的最终目的是在产品从卖方转移至买方的过程中创造出空间和时间效用。具体而言，物流系统要实现以下五项目标。

1）优质服务：货物递送不发生缺货、货损及货物丢失，且费用尽可能低。

2）迅速及时：按用户指定的时间和地点迅速及时地送达。

3）节约空间：利用立体仓库和有关的物流机械以充分利用仓储空间。

4）规模适当：在物流领域内利用规模经济来降低物流成本，如交叉转运配送中心内的集装和拆散作业大大降低了运输及库存成本。

5）合理库存：合理设置库存水平，以最小的库存投入满足客户订单需求。

在上述 5 项目标的基础上，国际物流还要为国际贸易和跨国经营服务，选择最佳的运输方式与路径，以尽可能低的风险和成本，保质、保量地将货物从供应地运至需求地。

2.1.3 国际物流系统的结构和模式

国际物流系统的结构是指构成国际物流系统的要素或子系统之间相互联系的方式。国际物流系统是一个既有静态也有动态结构、既有时间也有空间结构的多重结构复杂系统。它是由多个立体型的子系统连接而成的具有时空序列的总系统。

从空间结构上讲，国际物流系统由点、线、面构成，这些点、线、面交错形成国际物流网络。从功能结构上讲，运输、仓储、包装、装卸搬运、流通加工、报检报关等国际物流环节都是由组织者、货物、承运人、路线和信息等实体要素结合而成的具有特定功能的立体子系统。这些立体型的子系统又按照不同的具体需要连接成先后有序的总系统。

虽然国际物流包含各种各样的业务环节，是一个极其复杂的系统，但是与国内物流系统一样，国际物流系统也具有输入、转换及输出三大功能。通过输入和输出系统，国际物流完成了与外界环境的交换，并不断调整自身以适应外部环境。

2.2 International Logistics Network

International logistics network is formed by connecting international logistics nodes with international logistics channels. It is an organic whole which contains the physical network of logistics composed of multiple "nodes" for receiving and delivering goods and the "links" between them, as well as the accompanying network of information flow. To put it another way, international logistics network consists of three parts: international logistics nodes, international logistics links and logistics information network. The former two belong to the physical network of international logistics (Figure 2.1), and the latter belongs to the invisible network of international logistics information.

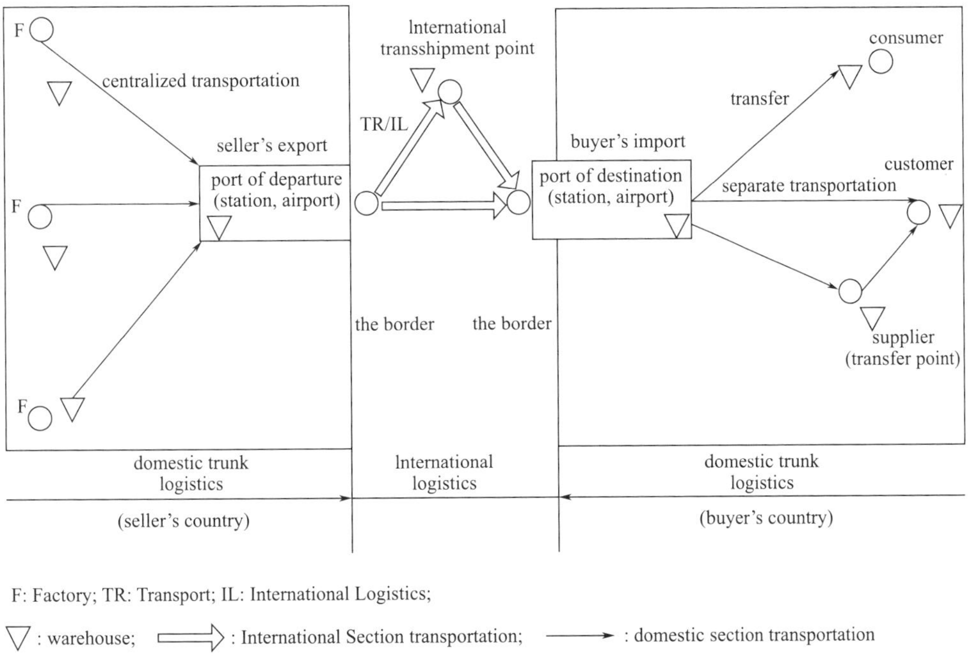

Figure 2.1 Physical network of international logistics

2.2.1 International Logistics Nodes

Logistics node is the nodule or the connection point of logistics lines/channels in logistics network, which plays a critical role in logistics system as well as in logistics network. All logistical activities in logistics system are carried out either on the lines or at the nodes. The activities implemented on the lines are mainly transportation, including aggregate shipments, line haul and distribution transportation, etc. Other functional activities of logistics, such as packaging, loading and unloading, storage, sorting, assembling, and processing, are completed at the nodes. Moreover, logistical activities on logistics lines are actually organized and connected by logistics nodes. Without nodes, movement of goods or materials on logistics lines would be paralyzed.

International logistics nodes refer to those logistics facilities engaged in international logistics activities, such as ports, international logistics centers, bonded areas, bonded warehouses, free trade zones (free ports), export processing zones, storage and transportation centers and other transshipment, distribution or storage sites. International logistics cargoes are received and delivered through these warehouses and logistics centers, and stored and kept in these nodes to achieve the time utility of international logistics system, overcome the time discrepancy between production and consumption, and promote smooth operations of international trade system.

According to the main functions, international logistics nodes can be divided into the following four categories.

1) Transshipment nodes: Referring to the nodes whose main function is to connect different modes of transportation, such as freight depots, marshalling yards, railway stations, freight yards, airports, ports, docks, etc.

2) Storage nodes: Referring to the nodes that take the storage of goods as the main function, such as storage warehouses, transit warehouses, port warehouses, etc.

3) Circulation processing nodes: Referring to the ones whose major functions are to organize the physical movement of goods in the logistics system, and to conduct packaging, sorting, measurement, assembling, marking, commodity inspection and other operations according to specific requirements, such as circulation warehouses, circulation centers, distribution centers, etc.

4) Comprehensive nodes: Referring to the multi-functional international logistics nodes, such as international logistics centers, export processing zones, international logistics parks, free trade zones, etc. In a comprehensive node, a variety of transformation activities can be achieved, thus making international logistics services more precisely catered to demands and greatly simplifying the international logistics system.

2.2.2 International Logistics Links

International logistics links refer to the transportation lines connecting multiple nodes for receiving and delivering cargo, such as various sea routes, railway lines, air routes and sea-land-air intermodal routes. These international logistics links are the materialized form of the movement (transportation) track of inventory. There are many links between each pair of nodes to represent various transportation services of different transportation routes. Each node indicates that the inventory flow is temporarily stagnant, and its purpose is to help realize a more effective movement.

Essentially, international logistics link is also the path of international logistics material flow. It mainly includes international shipping routes, international air routes, international railway transportation lines and continental bridges, international oil pipelines, etc.

2.2.3 International Logistics Information Network

The information transfer between all the nodes and along the routes constitutes the information flow of international logistics. And the transfer and processing of information between all nodes and links constitutes the information network system of international logistics. The connection as well as the completion of all business activities in international logistics network rely heavily upon the information network system. As mentioned above, international logistics is a complex operation system composed of many links, multiple layers and several subsystems. There are many involved links and nodes in the entire logistics process, and there is always a quite long distance between two nodes. To achieve the effective operation of the whole system and the seamless connection between all logistical activities, it is vital to ensure that the timely and accurate transfer of information is conducted. Therefore, the efficiency of information network directly impacts the overall effectiveness of international logistics operation.

2.2 国际物流网络

国际物流网络是由国际物流节点和国际物流通道连接而成的，是由多个收发货的“节点”和它们之间的“连线”所构成的物流实体网络，以及与之相伴的信息流网络构成的有机整体。因此，国际物流网络由三个部分组成：国际物流节点、国际物流通道和国际物流信息网络，前两者属于有形的国际物流实体网络（见图 2.1），后者属于无形的国际物流信息网络。

2.2.1 国际物流节点

物流节点是物流网络中连接物流线路的结节之处/连接点，在物流系统及物流网络中居于非常重要的地位。物流系统中的全部物流活动都是在线路和节点进行的。在线路上进行的活动主要是运输，包括集货运输、干线运输以及配送运输等；而其他物流活动，如包装、装卸、保管、分拣、配货、流通加工等则是在物流节点上完成的。而且，物流线路上的物流活动实际上也是靠节点来组织和联系的。如果没有节点，物流线路上的运动将会陷入瘫痪。

国际物流网络“节点”是指那些从事国际物流活动的物流节点，如口岸、国际物流中心、保税区、保税仓库、自由贸易区（自由港）、出口加工区、储运中心等中转、集散或储存场所。国际贸易商品或者物品通过这些仓库和物流中心的收进发出，并在这些节点中存放保管，来实现国际物流系统的时间效用，克服生产时间和消费时间上的分离，促进国际贸易系统顺利进行。

根据其主要功能，国际物流节点可分为以下四类。

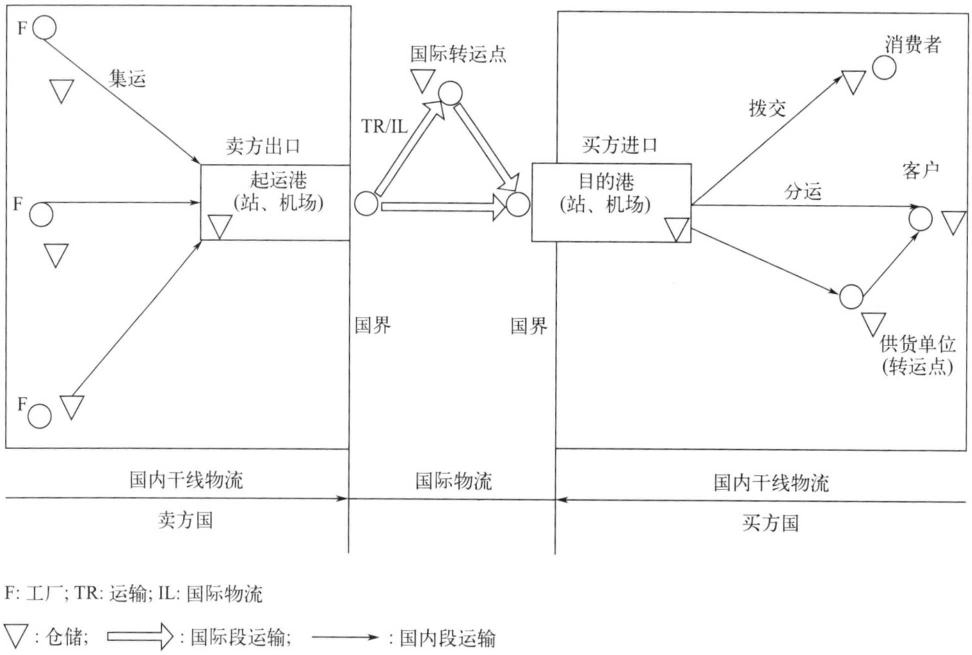

图 2.1 国际物流实体网络

1）转运型节点。指以连接不同运输方式为主要功能的节点，如货站、编组站、车站、货场、机场、港口、码头等。

2）储存型节点。指以存放货物为主要功能的节点，如储备仓库、中转仓库、口岸仓库等。

3）流通加工型节点。指以组织货物在系统中流动为主要功能，并根据具体需要对货物施加包装、分割、计量、组装、刷标志、商品检验等作业的节点，如流通仓库、流通中心、配送中心等。

4）综合性节点。指多功能的国际物流节点，如国际物流中心、出口加工区、国际物流园区、自由贸易区等。在一个综合性节点中实现多种转换活动，使国际物流服务更加精准，也大大简化了国际物流系统。

2.2.2 国际物流连线

国际物流连线是指连接国内外众多收发货节点间的运输线，如各种海运航线，铁路线，飞机航线及海、陆、空联运航线。这些国际物流连线是库存货物的移动（运输）轨迹的物化形式；每一对节点间都有许多连线以表示不同的运输线路、不同产品的各种运输服务；各节点表示存货流动暂时停滞，其目的是为了更有效地移动。

国际物流连线实质上也是国际物流流动的路径。它主要包括国际海运航线、国际空运航线、国际铁路运输线与大陆桥、国际主要输油管道等。

2.2.3 国际物流信息网络

国际物流各节点之间以及各线路上的信息传递构成信息流，所有物流节点和线路之间的信息传递及处理构成了国际物流的信息网络系统。国际物流网络中所有业务活动的衔接和完成都在很大程度上依赖于信息网络系统。前文述及，国际物流是由多环节、多层次、多个子系统构成的复杂运作系统。整个物流过程中的线路和节点非常多，且节点之间的空间距离通常很远，要保证整个系统的有效运转，使各业务环节之间无缝衔接，就必须保证信息传递的及时、准确，因此，信息网络的效率直接影响着国际物流运作的总体效率。

2.3 Functional Subsystems of International Logistics System

2.3.1 Transportation Subsystem

Transportation refers to the physical movement of goods and materials from a point of origin to a point of consumption. Transport plays an essential role in the development of economic resources on a national or global scale. Goods and materials are transported from the areas where they have low utilities to the places where they have high value. In this sense, transportation creates the space utility to the goods. This enables transportation to be the core subsystem of international logistics. It is a work of strong timeliness, wide involved aspects, long distance and complicated processes and more risks.

During the process of international cargo transportation, various types of transportation modes can be used. According to different transportation vehicles and routes, there are the following eight major types of international cargo transportation:

(1) Marine Transport (Ocean Shipping)

Marine transport is the most widely used form of transportation in international trade as well as the most efficient form in terms of energy. It still has the attraction of being the cheapest transportation mode for delivering large quantities of goods over long distance. As far as foreign trade is concerned, goods transport is mostly (over 2/3 of world trade in volume terms) done by ocean vessels. Concerning operation modes, it can be divided into liner shipping/liners and chartering/tramps. They will be explained in detail later in this book.

(2) Railway Transport

Railway is capable of attaining relatively high speed with large quantities and it is safe, punctual, relatively cheap, and less influenced by weather.

(3) Airway Transport

It is the quickest transportation mode with the advantages of low risks of cargo damage and pilferage, savings in packing cost and insurance expense. The chief disadvantage is the limited capacity of air freight, which makes it to be the most expensive transportation mode. It is also subject to the influence of weather. However, it is suitable for those goods that are of time pressing (fresh goods), small quantities of emergency cargo as well as precious goods or light cargoes, etc.

(4) Road Transport

Road transport is a modern means of transportation. It can not only ship in and out Import & Export goods directly at the border, but also plays the role of consolidating and distributing cargoes at ports, railway stations and airports.

(5) Inland Waterway Transport

Inland waterway transport is an important component of water transport, which acts as the linkages between inland areas and coastal areas and plays an important role in the transportation and distribution of import and export goods.

(6) Pipeline Transport

Pipelines are used for transporting commodities, such as crude oil and gas, long distances over land and under the sea. Rising fuel costs make pipeline transport an attractive economic alternative to other forms of transport in certain circumstances. Safety in transferring flammable commodities is another important consideration.

(7) Postal Transport

According to international trade practices, the seller fulfills the duty of delivery upon he delivers the parcel to the post office, pays off the postage, and gets the receipt. The post office is responsible for the delivery of the goods to the destination, and the consignee is supposed to go to the post office for picking up his goods. It is a kind of international door-to-door transport based on the international postal network. Because of its convenience and low cost, it is one of the frequently used transport modes in international trade, especially for cross-border e-commerce logistics.

(8) International Combined Transport

International combined transport means the conveyance of cargo includes at least two modes of transport by which the goods are carried from the place of dispatch to that of destination on the basis of a combined transport or a multimodal transport contract. Under this method, the container is used as an intermedium and the entire transport is actually the combination of multiple stages of marine, air and land transport.

Each transport mode has its own advantages, disadvantages, application scope as well as economical transport mileage. In order to smoothly complete international cargo transport, comprehensive factors should be taken into account, including nature and quantity of the goods shipped, shipping distance, urgency of needs, transportation costs, weather and natural conditions, political situations, etc., when making decisions on the transport mode.

2.3.2 Warehousing Subsystem

The major function of warehousing in logistics is to overcome time difference between production and consumption, thus creating the time utility during the transfer of goods. International logistics warehousing and international logistics transportation are known as the two pillars of international trade and international logistics. It not only refers to the storage of import and export trade commodities, but also includes a series of logistical work such as processing, sorting, packing, marking, assembling and so on.

The storage and processing activities in international warehousing subsystem enable goods to be in a relatively stagnant stage in the process of circulation. This is because the circulation of foreign trade commodities is actually an ongoing process from decentralization to centralization and then from centralization to decentralization. For example, large quantities of export goods are firstly collected from multiple origins or plants and then transported to the loading ports (or railway stations, airports) for export. In some cases, these commodities need temporary storage before being shipped out. In order to ensure smooth commodity exchanges and well satisfy export requirements, a certain amount of storage must be held. In other cases, export commodities need such logistical work as sorting, assembling, re-processing or re-packaging, etc. before being shipped out, so as to meet special requirements of ultimate customers. In addition, as for commodities with the features of seasonal supply or seasonal demand, seasonal inventory may need to be held.

In the past decade, the storage of goods in Bonded Warehouses has become one of the main forms of international warehousing. Due to its convenient service and great flexibility, Bonded Warehouse plays a critical role in promoting the development of international trade, especially the processing trade. A bonded warehouse, or bond, is a building or other secured areas in which dutiable goods may be stored, manipulated, or undergo manufacturing operations without payment of tariff. Therefore, many foreign firms use bonded warehouses to implement storage and other necessary activities to cut down costs of customs duties and warehousing.

2.3.3 Packaging Subsystem

Packaging is the technology of enclosing or protecting products for distribution, storage, sale, and use. It is an integral link of modern logistics, generally being considered as the final point of production and the starting point of logistics. Packaging has now become more and more important in competing for overseas markets. One of its basic purposes is to protect the product. This is important because the product may have to withstand a lot of handling during transportation between the manufacturing plant and the ultimate user. The second purpose of packaging is to make the product look appealing to the buyer. Products packed in an attractive way to catching the consumer's eyes will definitely facilitate the sale. Other common purposes of packaging are to provide information about the product inside, make it easy to carry the product, and provide convenience in using the product. When considering the packaging of export products, business firms ought to link packaging organically with warehousing and transportation and make an overall plan so as to achieve the integration of these three logistics stages. That is to say, when starting to pack the products, firms should consider whether or not the packing will facilitate the storing, transporting as well as loading and unloading of commodities.

2.3.4 Material Handling Subsystem

Material handling operation often refers to the short distance transfer of goods. Although it is not as independent as other logistical work in logistics system, material handling is the vital linkage between warehousing and transportation. The major function of material handling is to ensure the continuity of logistics activities. It is of great importance to accelerate international logistics process and cut down logistics costs that material handling operations, including loading, unloading, receiving, checking, moving, re-packing, etc., are conducted effectively. Common material handling equipment mainly includes three-dimensional shelves, automatic pelletizer, automatic guided vehicle (AGV), conveying equipment, sorting system, lifting equipment (hoist or elevator), etc.

2.3.5 Inspection and Customs Declaration Subsystem

Inspection and Customs Declaration are two special operations of international logistics system. On the one hand, in order to guarantee that the quality and quantity of delivered goods as well as packaging conditions are in strict accordance with the stipulations of international trade contracts, inspection terms must be included in trade contracts. On the other hand, since goods and/or materials in international logistics are typically needed to be shipped into or out of the customs territories of several countries, almost every country around the world requires that I&E goods or materials as well as transportation vehicles go through Customs Declaration formalities in order to safeguard its state sovereignty and economic interests. Usually, the goods or materials shall be checked and released only by Customs upon the presentation of the seal of inspection authority affixed on the customs declaration forms.

2.3.6 Information Management Subsystem

Information reflects the real state of international logistics activities and therefore it serves as the solid foundation of planning, managing and coordinating international logistics activities. International logistics information management subsystem contains various types of information relating to demands, shipping, financing, documentation and so on. The main functions of information subsystem are to properly collect, transfer and process information in all stages of international logistics. Accurate and timely transfer of information is the cornerstone of international logistics management. In today's increasingly fierce international market, many countries have strengthened information management of international logistics system and raised it to the level of national strategies. Some advanced information technologies such as EDI, bar code, RFID, GPS, GIS, etc., have been widely applied in international logistics information management, which has not only improved international logistics service level but also cut down the total costs of international logistics system.

2.3 国际物流系统的功能子系统

2.3.1 运输子系统

运输是指产品和物料从供应地到需求地的实体移动。它对于本国经济资源以及世界经济资源的开发利用起到了重要作用。运输将商品及物料从使用价值低的地区运至使用价值高的地区，从而创造了商品的空间效用。国际货物运输是国际物流系统的核心子系统，具有时间性强、涉及面广、路线长、环节多以及风险大等特点。

在国际货物运输中，涉及的运输方式很多，根据所使用的运输工具和运输路线，主要分为以下八种方式。

(1) 海洋运输

海洋运输是国际贸易运输中采用最广泛的一种形式，从能源来讲也是最有效的形式。对于长途运输大批量货物，它还具有作为一种廉价运输方式的吸引力。就国际贸易而言，大多数的国际贸易运输（2/3 以上）都是由海洋运输来完成的。按照运营方式，海洋运输可以分为班轮运输和租船运输。

(2) **铁路运输**

铁路运输具有货运量大、速度快、安全可靠、运输成本低、运输准时和受气候影响较小等特点。

(3) **航空运输**

航空运输是最快的运输方式，优点是交货迅速、货损率低以及节省包装、储存、保险等费用；主要缺点是运量小，运费昂贵，易受气候影响。因而，它适用于一些时效性强、体轻而贵重、量少而急需的货物运输。

(4) **公路运输**

公路运输是一种现代化的运输方式，它不仅可以在边境将进出口货物直接运进或运出，而且也是车站、港口和机场进出口货物集散的重要手段。

(5) **内河运输**

内河运输是水上运输的重要组成部分，它是连接内陆腹地与沿海地区的纽带，在进出口货物的运输和集散中起着重要的作用。

(6) **管道运输**

管道运输是利用管道输送石油、天然气等商品的一种运输方式，这种管道运输线路长、一般埋于海底。油价的不断上涨，使得管道运输越来越受青睐，此外，对于运输易燃物品，管道运输安全可靠。

(7) **邮包运输**

根据国际贸易惯例，卖方在将包裹送到邮局、付清邮费并取得收据后，即完成义务。邮局负责将货物送至目的地，收货人要去邮局取货。它是一种以国际邮政网络为基础的国际门到门运输。其便利性和成本低的特点，使其成为国际贸易中常用的运输方式之一，尤其是跨境电商物流。

(8) **国际多式联运**

国际多式联运是在集装箱运输的基础上产生和发展起来的一种综合性的连贯运输方式。它一般是以集装箱为媒介，把海、陆、空多种传统的单一运输方式有机地结合起来，形成一种国际间的连贯运输。

上述各种运输方式各有其优缺点，适合不同种类、不同距离的货物运输。为了顺利地完成国际货物运输，应对货物的性质、运量的大小、运距的长短、需要的缓急、运输费用的高低、气候及自然条件以及国际政治形势等因素充分考虑来做运输方式的选择决策。

2.3.2 仓储子系统

物流中的仓储作业主要是克服商品使用价值在供需时间上的差异，从而创造商品的时间价值。国际物流仓储同国际物流运输一样，都是国际贸易和国际物流不可缺少的环节。国际物流仓储不仅包括对外贸商品的储存保管，而且还包括出口加工、拣选、整理、包装、刷唛、备货、组装、配送和发运等一系列工作。

国际物流仓储子系统中的储存、保管和加工等作业使商品在其流通过程中处于一种相对停滞状态，这是因为外贸商品的流通是一个由分散到集中，再由集中到分散的源源不断的流通过程。如外贸商品从多个生产厂或产地被集中运送到装运港（或铁路车站、机场），以备出口，有时需临时存放一段时间，再装运出口，是一个集和散的过程；为了保证不间断的商品往来，满足出口需要，必须有一定量的周转储存；有些商品需要在出口前进行整理、组装、再加工、再包装等。此外，对于某些出口商品在产销时间上的背离，例如，季节性生产但常年消费的商品和常年生产但季节性消费的商品，则必须留有一定数量的季节储备。

近十年来，保税仓库存储作业已经成为国际物流仓储的主要形式。由于服务性强以及灵活性大，保税仓库对于促进国际贸易尤其是加工贸易的发展起到了重要作用。保税仓库是经海关核准的专门存放保税货物的专用仓库。特定的进口货物，在进境后尚未确定内销或复出的最终去向前，可以暂缓缴纳进口税，在保税仓库内存储，并进行包装、分级分类、加刷唛码、分拆、拼装等简单加工，不得进行实质性加工。因此，很多外国企业利用保税仓库来进行货物存储以降低关税和存储费用。

2.3.3 包装子系统

包装是指因配送、储存、销售和使用等环节所需而包封或保护产品的技术。它是现代物流中不可或缺的一环，一般被认为是生产的终点和物流的起点。在争夺海外市场的过程中，包装变得越来越重要。包装的基本功能之一是保护产品。这一点很重要，因为从制造工厂到最终用户的运输过程中，产品必须经历若干次的搬运。包装的第二个功能是使产品的外观能取悦买家。能够吸引消费者眼球的包装能很好地促进销售。包装的另几个常见功能是提供产品信息、便于产品的携带以及方便产品的使用。在考虑出口商品包装设计时，应将包装与仓储、运输有机联系起来统筹考虑，全面规划，实现“包、储、运一体化”。即商品开始包装时，企业就要考虑该包装方式是否方便存储、保管、运输、装卸商品。

2.3.4 装卸搬运子系统

装卸搬运是指短距离的商品搬移。尽管它是物流系统中的辅助性业务环节，但却是仓储作业和运输作业的重要桥梁和纽带。它的主要功能是保证商品运输和保管的连续性。搞好商品的装船、卸船、商品进出库以及在库内的搬移、清点、换装等装卸搬运作业，对于加快国际物流进程以及降低物流成本有着非常重要的意义。常见的装卸搬运设备主要包括立体货架、自动堆垛机、自动导向车、出入输送设备、分拣系统、升降设备（提升机或升降机）等。

2.3.5 检验和报关子系统

检验和报关是国际物流中的两大特殊环节。一方面，为了确定交货品质、数量和包装条件等是否符合合同规定，在国际贸易买卖合同中，一般都订有商品检验条款。另一方面国际物流往往是跨越关境的物品流通，为了维护国家主权和经济利益，各国海关都对进出口货物实施必要的监督管理。在我国，海关一律凭报关地检验检疫机构签发的通关单验放货物。

2.3.6 信息管理子系统

国际物流信息是国际物流活动的反映，也是组织、调节和控制国际物流活动的依据。国际物流信息管理子系统涉及客户需求、运输、融资、单证等各种信息。信息管理子系统的主要功能是正确采集、传递和处理国际物流所有环节的信息。准确而及时的信息传递是国际物流管理的重要基石。随着国际市场竞争的日趋激烈，世界各国日益加强了对国际物流系统中信息流的管理，并将其提升到国家战略的高度。先进的信息技术，如电子数据交换、条形码、射频标签、全球卫星定位、地理信息系统等，已经广泛应用于国际物流信息管理，既提升了国际物流服务水平又降低了国际物流总成本。

2.4 Shipping Routes in International Logistics

2.4.1 Shipping Routes and Influencing Factors

Under the restriction of natural conditions such as bay, tidal current, wind direction, water depth and distance from the earth's surface, certain paths that can be navigated by ships in the seas of the world are called routes. Among the available routes, according to the limitations of subjective and objective conditions, the operating route selected by the shipping carrier to maximize economic benefits is called the shipping route.

The formation of shipping routes mainly depends on the following factors:

1) Safety factors: Referring to various phenomena in nature that should be considered when determining the shipping route, such as wind direction, wave, tide, water flow, reef, ice flow, etc., which may affect the safety of ship navigation.

2) Freight factors: Referring to the main direction and volume of cargo flow along the route. Freight factors mainly impact the operating incomes of shipping companies.

3) Port factors: Referring to port facilities and conditions affecting berthing and loading& unloading of ships, such as the water depth of the port, freezing period, port usage fees, etc..

4) Technical factors: Referring to technical factors that need to be considered when a ship sails. For instance, suppose that the earth is oval, it is necessary to sail along a maximum arc of the earth, which will make the distance between the two places the shortest, and short sailing distance can save both time and cost. Choosing this route is the most advantageous in operation.

In addition, international political situation, as well as changes in tariff laws, economic policies and navigation policies of countries along the routes, will affect the profits shipping companies can obtain in the future, and will also influence the shipping companies' choice of shipping routes.

2.4.2 Classification of Shipping Routes

(1) divided by the operation mode of the ship

According to the operation mode of the ship, shipping routes are divided into regular routes and irregular routes.

Regular routes use fixed ships that sail on fixed routes and berth at fixed ports, so regular routes are also called liner routes. The routes frequently used in liner shipping are called scheduled routes. The continuous and stable round-trip supply of ports along the route is a prerequisite for opening regular routes.

Compared with regular routes, irregular routes refer to the use of unfixed ships, sailing on unfixed routes and berthing at unfixed ports. Non-scheduled routes are very flexible, and most of them are operated by charter shipping, which mainly aims at the transportation market of most big-batch and low-priced goods.

(2) divided by distance

According to the distance, shipping routes are divided into ocean routes, near-ocean routes and coastal routes.

Ocean routes refer to trans-oceanic shipping routes. And near-ocean routes usually refer to the sea routes from domestic ports to ports of neighboring countries, while coastal routes refer to sea transportation lines between domestic coastal ports.

2.4.3 Major Shipping Routes in the World

Currently, the busiest shipping routes in the world include the North Atlantic route, the North Pacific route, the Suez Canal route and the Panama Canal route.

(1) North Atlantic Route

The North Atlantic route is a transportation route between North America and Western Europe, which is named after its crossing the northern Atlantic Ocean. This route starts from the east coast of North America in the west, crosses the Atlantic and English Channel via Newfoundland in the north and reaches Western Europe. Its branch lines are scattered on both sides of Europe and the United States, and the route connects the two most developed industrial regions in the world. Both sides have two-fifths of the world's ports and 80% of the ocean freight volume, making it the busiest international freight route in the world. There are many world-famous ports along the North Atlantic route, such as Hamburg, Rotterdam, Antwerp, London, Liverpool and Marseille in Europe; Alexandria, Monrovia, port Harcourt and Cape Town in Africa; New York, Philadelphia, Baltimore, New Orleans and Houston in North America; Maracaibo, Rio DE Janeiro and Buenos Aires in South America. The disadvantages of this route lie in that there are dangerous winds and waves in winter, and there are threats of fog and iceberg, which may affect shipping safety. Therefore, business tries to avoid taking the North Atlantic route in winter when carrying out international logistics.

(2) North Pacific Route

Located between Asia, Oceania, Antarctica and North and South America, the Pacific Ocean is the largest ocean among the four oceans on the earth. It is also the deepest ocean with the most islands and coral reefs, which is of great significance in international traffic. The Panama Canal in the east and the Malacca Strait in the southwest, the shortcuts from the Pacific Ocean to the Atlantic Ocean and the Indian Ocean respectively, are the main waterways in the world. More than 30 countries coast this route, with 1/2 of the world's population and many excellent ports. The Pacific route accounts for about a quarter of the world's cargo volume and three-tenths of the world's turnover, ranking second only to the North Atlantic route. The North Pacific route is the route between the west coast of North America and the Far East and Southeast Asia, mainly because it crosses the north of the Pacific Ocean. The main ports along the North Pacific Route include the ports located in the Far East such as Tokyo, Yokohama, Kawasaki, Hong Kong and Nagoya, Osaka, Kobe, Vladivostok, the East Port, Nakhodka, Busan, Inchon, etc.; and Chinese ports including Dalian port, Qinhuangdao port, Tianjin port, Qingdao port, Lianyungang port,

Shanghai port, Ningbo port, Guangzhou port, Hong Kong, etc.; and other important Asian ports such as Manila, Haiphong, Ho Chi Minh City, Bangkok, Singapore and so on.

(3) Suez Canal Route

The Suez Canal route is a route connecting Asia and Europe, named after its passing through Suez Canal. It is also known as Asia-Europe route, and is one of the busiest shipping routes in the world. The route starts from western and southern European ports in the west, enters the Mediterranean Sea via Gibraltar Strait, enters the Red Sea via Suez Canal, and then enters the Indian Ocean. After entering the Indian Ocean, it is divided into two roads. Ports eastward to the Far East are the main routes between Europe and Asia while ports southward to Australia are the main routes between Europe and Australia. This route greatly shortens the voyage from Europe to Asia. More than 20, 000 ships pass through Suez Canal every year, carrying about 300 million tons of oil annually, mainly oil tankers. Oil transportation from the Middle East to Western Europe accounts for more than 60% of the total canal volume.

(4) Panama Canal Route

Located in the middle of the American continent, Panama Canal connects the narrowest point of the isthmus of North and South America. It is a lock canal with six locks connecting the Pacific and Atlantic oceans and also it is a route connecting ports between the Pacific Ocean and the Atlantic Ocean. Its opening greatly shortens the voyage between the two oceans and has become the busiest canal in the world. Located in the central region of the Republic of Panama, the Panama Canal is the world's second man-made Grand Canal, opened to navigation in 1920. Because the water level at both ends of the canal is not equally high, the canal is a lock canal. It is 81. 3 kilometers long, takes nine hours for ships to pass through the canal and can handle 76, 000-ton ships. About 15, 000 ships pass through Panama Canal every year, carrying about 180 million tons of cargo annually.

2.4 国际物流海运航线

2.4.1 航线及影响因素

世界各地水域在海湾、潮流、风向、水深以及地球表面距离等自然条件限制下，可以供船舶航行的一定路径，称为航路。承运人在可供通行的航路中，根据主客观条件的限制，为达到经济效益最大化而选定的营运航路叫做海运航线。

海运航线的形成主要取决于下列因素。

1）安全因素：指确定航线时应考虑自然界的种种现象，如风向、波浪、潮汐、水流、暗礁及流冰等，这些都可能影响船舶航行的安全。

2）货运因素：指航线沿途货物的主要流向及流量。货运因素主要影响航运公司的经营收益。

3）港口因素：指影响船舶靠泊和装卸的各种港口设施和条件，如港口的水深、冰冻期、港口使用费等。

4）技术因素：指船舶航行时在技术上需要考虑的因素。例如，因地球为椭圆形，所以必须循着一个最大地球弧线来进行航行，这样就会使得两地间的距离达到最短，距离短就可以节省时间和费用，（船公司）选择这样的航线在经营上是最为有利的。

此外，国际政治形势，以及沿途国家的关税法令、经济政策、航行政策等的变化也会影响到航运公司未来所能获得的利润水平，进而影响航运公司对海运航线的选择。

2.4.2 海运航线的分类

(1) 按船舶经营方式划分

按船舶经营方式，航线分为定期航线和不定期航线。

定期航线使用固定的船舶，按照固定的船期，航行固定的航线，靠泊固定的港口，因此定期航线也叫做班轮航线。班轮运输经常使用的航线就叫做定期航线。航线沿途港口持续稳定的往返货源是开辟定期航线的先决条件。

不定期航线是相对于定期航线而言的，是指使用不固定的船舶，以不固定的船期，航行不固定的航线，停泊不固定的港口。不定期航线非常灵活，大多是以租船方式经营，主要针对大多数大宗低价货物的运输市场。

(2) 按航程远近划分

按航程远近，航线分为远洋航线、近洋航线和沿海航线。

远洋航线指跨越大洋的海运航线，近洋航线通常指本国各港口至邻近国家港口的海上航线，沿海航线则指本国沿海各港口间的海上运输线。

2.4.3 世界主要海运航线

目前世界上最繁忙的海运航线包括北大西洋航线、北太平洋航线以及苏伊士运河航线和巴拿马运河航线等。

(1) 北大西洋航线

北大西洋航线为北美与西欧间的运输线，因其横跨大西洋北部而得名。这条航线西起北美的东部海岸，北经由纽芬兰横跨大西洋的英吉利海峡到达西欧，它的支线散布于欧、美两岸，航线连接世界两个工业最发达的地区，两岸拥有世界 2/5 的港口、80%的海洋货运量，是世界上最繁忙的国际货运航线。北大西洋沿岸港口繁多，如欧洲的汉堡、鹿特丹、安特卫普、伦敦、利物浦、马赛等港口，非洲的亚历山大、蒙罗维亚、哈科特、开普敦等港口，北美洲的纽约、费城、巴尔的摩、新奥尔良、休斯敦等港口，南美洲的马拉开波、图巴兰、里约热内卢、布宜诺斯艾利斯港口。这条航线的缺点是冬季有险恶的风浪，且有浓雾和冰山的威胁，会影响航运安全，因此设计组织国际物流的时候，应尽量避免冬季走北大西洋航线。

(2) 北太平洋航线

太平洋位于亚洲、大洋洲、南极洲、南北美洲之间，是地球四大洋中最大的一个海洋，同时也是最深和岛屿、珊瑚礁最多的海洋，在国际交通上有着相当重要的意义。东部的巴拿马运河和西南部的马六甲海峡，分别是太平洋通往大西洋和印度洋的捷径，是世界的主要航道。该航线沿岸有 30 多个国家，居住着世界上约 1/2 的人口，拥有许多优良的港口。太平洋航线的货运量约占世界的四分之一，周转量占世界的十分之三，居世界第二位，仅次于北大西洋航线。北太平洋航线为北美西海岸与远东、东南亚之间的航线，主要因其横跨太平洋的北部而得名。北太平洋航线沿岸有东京港、横滨港、川崎港、名古屋港、大阪港、神户港、符拉迪沃斯托克港、东方港、纳霍德卡港、釜山港、仁川港等远东港口；还有位于我国的大连港、秦皇岛港、天津港、青岛港、连云港港、上海港、宁波港、广州港、香港港等，以及马尼拉港、海防港、胡志明市港、曼谷港、新加坡港等亚洲重要港口。

(3) 苏伊士运河航线

苏伊士运河航线是连接亚洲与欧洲的航线，因其通过苏伊士运河而得名，又称亚欧航线，是世界上最繁忙的航线之一。该航线西起西欧、南欧各港，经直布罗陀海峡入地中海，通过苏伊士运河进入红海，然后再进入印度洋。进入印度洋以后分为两路，东至远东的各个港口，为欧洲、亚洲之间的主要航线，南至澳大利亚的各个港口，为欧洲和澳洲之间的主要航线。这条航线大大缩短了从欧洲到亚洲的航程，每年通过这条运河的船舶数量达到两万多艘，年运量达到三亿吨左右，其中主要是油轮，从中东运往西欧的石油占运河总运量的60%以上。

(4) 巴拿马运河航线

巴拿马运河位于美洲大陆的中部，连接南北美洲的地峡最窄处，是一条设有6座船闸的沟通太平洋和大西洋的船闸式运河，是连接太平洋和大西洋之间各个港口的航线，它的开通大大缩短了两大洋之间的航程，已经成为世界上最繁忙的运河之一。巴拿马运河位于巴拿马共和国中部地区，是世界上第二条人工大运河，于1920年通航。由于运河两端的水位不一样高，所以该运河是船闸式运河。它全长81.3千米，船舶通过运河一般需要9个小时，可以通航76000吨级的轮船。每年通过运河的船舶大约是1.5万艘次，年货运量约1.8亿吨。

2.5 International Maritime Port

2.5.1 Types of Maritime Port

There are many kinds of maritime ports, mainly including commercial ports, military ports, fishing ports, etc. A commercial port mainly refers to the port that provides supplies (fuel, materials, etc.), ship maintenance and other corresponding services for incoming and outgoing ships, and it is a hub for marine transportation and inland transportation. Due to the important position of maritime transportation in international trade and international logistics, modern commercial port often needs to provide goods storage, processing, assembly, manufacturing and transshipment. Therefore, modern port is not only the center of the comprehensive transportation system of sea, land and air, but also the center of production and processing. Port size is usually measured by port throughput. The classification of commercial ports is introduced below.

1) According to geographical location, ports can be divided into bay ports (gulf harbor), estuary harbors and inland ports. Bay port refers to the port that is bordering on the bay and located in the estuary, such as Dalian port and Qinhuangdao port in China. Estuary harbor refers to the port which is located at the estuary of the river, such as Shanghai port, London port, Calcutta port, etc. Inland port refers to the port along the inland river. It plays an important role in inland water transportation. It is generally connected with the seaport, such as Nanjing port, Hankou port, etc.

2) According to port function, ports can be divided into storage ports, transshipment ports and stopover ports. Storage ports are generally located at the crossroads between land and water, providing convenient transportation and being industrial and commercial centers. Generally speaking, the port of storage has complete port facilities, which is conven-

ient for the storage and transshipment of goods. It is a distribution hub of inland and port cargoes. Transshipment port is generally located at the junction of waterway traffic, which transfers land goods out by sea and ships seaborne goods in by land, mainly for transshipment business. Stopover port means that the port is located at the critical point of the waterway and is the only place that the ships pass through. If necessary, passing ships may stop here for a short time to add fuel, food or fresh water before continuing their voyages.

3) According to port development project, ports can be divided into natural ports and artificial ports. The natural conditions of the bay of the natural port meet the needs of the commercial port. In addition to adding necessary equipment on water or on shore to meet the needs of ship berthing and cargo handling, the natural geographical and climatic conditions such as channel and depth of the harbor can be fully used. By contrast, the harbor area of the artificial port is completely excavated from the land.

4) According to the impact of tide on the port, ports can be divided into open ports and closed ports. An open port is the port built directly on an open bay or near the coast. Its characteristics lie in that the water area in the port is directly connected with the sea surface and the port water level changes little. Owing to these, ships can enter and exit the port at any time without being affected by tide. Closed port, also known as tidal range port, refers to the port built on or near the coast greatly affected by tide. In order to solve the problem that ebb tide affects the entry and exit of ships, a gate is usually built in the port to keep the water level in the port at a certain depth, which facilitates the entry and exit of ships. Otherwise, when the tide is low, the water level of the port becomes shallow, and large ships are easily stranded.

5) According to national policies, ports are divided into domestic ports and international ports. A domestic port refers to the port exclusively used by domestic ships for domestic trade. Foreign ships are not allowed to enter domestic ports except for natural disasters or some accidents and special permits. An international port, also known as open port, refers to the commercial port that is opened in accordance with treaties or decrees to facilitate international trade. Any foreign ship sailing in the international route is allowed to enter and exit the port after going through necessary procedures, but it must accept the supervision of local shipping authorities and customs.

2.5.2 Major International Seaports

At present, major seaports in the world include Rotterdam in the Netherlands, Marseille in France, London in the UK, Hamburg in Germany, Antwerp in Belgium, New York, Los Angeles and San Francisco in the US, Kobe and Yokohama in Japan, Singapore, Busan in South Korea and a series of Chinese ports as well. In recent years, Chinese ports have developed rapidly, accounting for more than half of the world's top ten ports, which will be detailed in the next heading.

1) Rotterdam Port. Rotterdam port is located in the lower Rhine River port area in the southwest of the Netherlands, covering an area of more than 1 million square kilometers with a total length of 42 kilometers. It is one of the top ten container ports in the world and

one of the ports with the largest throughput in the world. The port is located at the crossroads of land and water transportation in Europe, and is the cargo distribution center of the Netherlands and the European Economic Community. About 1/4 of the import and export goods of the European Economic Community are transshipped through the port, so Rotterdam port is also known as the "Gateway to Europe". The development goal of Rotterdam port is to build a safe, efficient, comprehensive and clean zone for port and industrial complex. Its service feature is the one-package service of storage, transportation and sales. Its main functions include bulk cargo transfer, storage of crude oil and chemical products, as well as oil refining.

2) New York Harbor. New York harbor, also called Port of New Jersey, is located at the mouth of the Hudson River in southeast New York State on the east coast of North America, bordering on the Atlantic Ocean. It is the largest seaport in the US and one of the largest natural deep-water ports in the world, with an annual throughput of more than 100 million tons. New York Harbor has a total shoreline of more than 1200 kilometers, mainly composed of the lower Hudson River, Long Island Sound and the waters west of Stat knee Island. It covers an area of about 3840 square kilometers, with more than 700 square kilometers of water and more than 1000 square kilometers of land. It has more than 430 deep-water berths between 9 and 14. 6 meters as well as 37 container terminals. It is the largest port in the world.

3) Port of New Orleans. The port of New Orleans is located in the south of the United States, on the Mississippi River in Louisiana. It is one of the largest ports in the United States, with an annual throughput of more than 100 million tons. The port is not only a shipping port, but also a distribution center for inland waterway transportation. It is a combined transportation center for American land transportation, inland waterway transportation and sea transportation. The total length of the port terminal is 40 km, with more than 280 deep water berths ranging from 8. 8 to 12. 2 meters.

4) Port of Houston. The Port of Houston is one of the largest ports in the United States as well as in the world. Located on the north shore of the Gulf of Mexico, it is one of the largest petroleum processing centers in the world, mainly exporting petroleum and its products, as well as cotton and wheat, with an annual throughput of more than 100 million tons.

5) Antwerp Port. The port of Antwerp is the largest port in Belgium, the trade center of northern Europe, and one of the world's famous ports, with an annual throughput of about 100 million tons. As a result of the improvement of the waterway, 100000-ton ships can enter its waterway, and ships with a draft of 14 meters can enter and exit the port freely. This port is the main export port of European steel and its steel throughput ranks first in the world.

6) Port of Hamburg. Hamburg port is the largest port in Germany, accounting for half of Germany's exports, the second largest port in Europe, and one of the largest free ports in the world. It is located at the confluence of the Elbe River and its tributaries, the Ulster River and the Beale River, 110 kilometers away from its mouth, and is called the "port of

two seas and three rivers". The two seas are the North Sea, the Baltic Sea, while the three rivers are the Elbe, The Ulster and the Bille. Actually, it is a meeting point for Europe's north-south east-west shipping routes. Hamburg port covers an area of more than 100 square kilometers, with more than 700 berths and storage stacks of more than 1 million square meters. It has the largest berths in the world, and its berths are about 11 meters deep, which can be directly reached by seagoing ships. The facilities in the port are very advanced, with a high degree of mechanization and automation. There are more than 300 international shipping lines connected with the world's major ports, always known as Germany's gateway to the world, with an annual throughput of about 60 million tons.

7) London Port. London Port is the largest port in the UK. It is located in the lower reaches of the Thames River, 88 kilometers away from the mouth of the river. The maximum water depth is 14 meters, and the average tidal range is 6 meters. The 200000-ton seagoing vessel can enter and exit the port directly, with an annual throughput of more than 50 million tons. The port of London has a draft depth of 6m at high and low tide, which requires locks to control it.

8) Kobe Port. Kobe port is Japan's largest seaport, located on the northwest shore of Osaka Bay, covering an area of 463 hectares, with 239 berths of all sizes, capable of docking 250 seagoing vessels at the same time, and has 13 routes to more than 120 countries. Kobe port is Japan's largest container port, with an annual throughput of 150 million tons.

9) Singapore Port. The port of Singapore is the main port of the Republic of Singapore. It is located in the southern tip of the Malay Peninsula and the mouth of the Strait of Malacca and often compared to the throat of the Pacific Ocean and the Indian Ocean. As early as the 13th century, the Port of Singapore was an international trade port, and now it has developed into a world famous entrepot port and free port, as well as a world-famous container port. The port covers an area of 583 square kilometers, including parts of the Johor Strait and Singapore Strait. The total length of the port is more than 13 kilometers, with more than 200 berths. The port of Singapore has 250 international routes connecting more than 370 ports around the world. The natural conditions of the port are very superior, especially the suitable depth, and thus ships with a draft of about 13 meters can enter the port and berth smoothly. The harbor waters are spacious, with few storms and no freezing periods. The port of Singapore ranks the third in the world in terms of oil refining capacity. Every year, about 40000 to 50000 ships pass through the port of Singapore, mainly transporting oil, grain and ore. The port of Singapore has an annual throughput of over 100 million tons.

2.5.3 Major Chinese Shipping Ports

China has a coastline of more than 18000 kilometers, with many excellent seaports along the coast. At present, there are more than 190 large and small ports. Among them, there are 26 ports with an annual throughput of more than 1 million tons. China's major foreign trade ports include Dalian port, Qinhuangdao port, Tianjin port, Qingdao port, Lianyungang port, Shanghai port, Xiamen port, Guangzhou port, Shenzhen port, Hong Kong port, Kaohsiung port, and Keelung port. Among them, Shanghai port, Ningbo Zhoushan Port, Shenzhen port, Guangzhou port, Qingdao port, Hong Kong port and Tianjin Port are among the top 10 container ports in the world in 2020.

1) Shanghai Port. Shanghai port is adjacent to the East China Sea and located near the mouth of the Yangtze River. The port area covers 36 square kilometers and the port depth is more than 10 meters. Currently, it has 87 berths of 10000-ton class and its annual cargo throughput accounts for about 1/3 of the total throughput of all ports in China. It is the largest port in China and one of the ten billion ton ports in the world. It has economic and trade contacts with more than 170 countries and regions in the world. The main import and export goods of Shanghai port are iron and steel, grain, coal, petroleum, chemical fertilizer, timber and some non-bulk goods.

2) Dalian Port. Dalian port is located in Dalian Bay at the southern tip of Liaodong Peninsula. The harbor is wide and deep, with an average depth of 9 meters. It is free from freezing and silt. It is a natural harbor that can be navigable in four seasons. The port is mainly for petroleum and petroleum products, as well as coal, timber and grain. The grain transshipment terminal of Dalian port is the largest modern and professional bulk grain center in China and even in the Far East.

3) Qinhuangdao Port. Qinhuangdao port is located in the northwest of Bohai Bay, where the wind is gentle and the waves are low. The water depth is 6.5～12.5 meters. There are 17 berths in the whole port area, which are divided into oil, coal and general cargo operation areas. The crude oil operation area has a special dock, which can simultaneously dock 15, 000 to 30, 000 tons of tankers. There are two oil pipelines, directly connecting Daqing and Beijing. The coal operation area has mechanized equipment system and two special railways are laid inside, namely Beijing-Qinhuangdao railway and Datong-Qinhuangdao railway, which mainly transport coal. The port accounts for 80% of the country's annual coal shipments, of which 60%～70% are delivered to Japan. With an annual throughput of more than 60 million tons, the port has become the world's largest coal port and China's largest energy exporting port.

4) Tianjin Port. Tianjin port is located in the west of Bohai Bay. It is not only the gateway to the capital Beijing, but also an important international trade port in the north of China. Tianjin Port is located at the mouth of Haihe River and in the center of Western Bohai Bay. It is one of the starting points of the eastern end of the Eurasian Land Bridge. It has the shortest distance from the Bohai Rim, North China, northwest China and other inland regions, with a vast economic hinterland. Tianjin Port has a total area of 200 square kilometers, a total length of berth shoreline of 14443 meters, and a berth capacity of 104 million tons. Tianjin Port consists of three major ports: Beijiang, Nanjiang and Haihe ports. Beijiang port area mainly deals with containers and non-bulk cargo, Nanjiang port area mainly deals with liquid bulk cargo and dry bulk cargo, and Haihe port area mainly deals with small ships of less than 5000 tons. Tianjin port is the largest grain importing port, the second largest coal loading port and the largest coke exporting port in China.

5) Qingdao Port. Qingdao Port is located in Jiao Zhou Bay, Shandong Peninsula. The port is not frozen or silt, and there are 68 berths, among which 29 berths are 10000-ton ones. The average water depth is 3～10 meters, and the deepest depth can reach 50 meters. It can dock 200000-ton cruise ships, and the container terminal can receive and unload fifth-generation large container ships.

6) Hong Kong Port. Hong Kong is located outside the Pearl River Estuary and in the center of the Asia-Pacific region. It is one of the three natural fine harbors in the world. The superior conditions and appropriate location make it an internationally famous transit port and free trade port. Its main port area, Victoria Harbor, covers an area of 5000 hectares and has an average depth of 12 meters. It can harbor 100 large vessels at the same time. Hong Kong's shipping industry has been booming, making Hong Kong Port a major hub in the global supply chain.

2.5 国际海运港口

2.5.1 港口的类型

港口有很多种，主要包括商港、军港、渔港等，其中商港主要指供商船停靠进行客货运输，为往来船舶提供（燃料、物料等）供给、船舶维修等相应服务的港口，它是海上交通和内陆交通联系的枢纽。由于海洋运输在国际贸易及国际物流当中的重要地位，所以现代化的商港除了具备货物集散作用之外，往往还需要提供货物的储存、加工、组装、制造以及转运等。由此可见，现代化的港口不但是海陆空综合运输体系的中心，同时也是生产加工中心。港口规模的大小一般是以港口吞吐量来衡量。下面介绍商港的分类。

1）按照地理位置不同，港口可分为海湾港、河口港和内河港。海湾港指濒临海湾、又据海口，如我国的大连港、秦皇岛港等。河口港是指位于河流入海口处的港口，如上海港、伦敦港、加尔各答港等。内河港是指位于内河沿岸的港口，它在内河水运中扮演着重要的角色，一般与海港有航道相通，如我国的南京港、汉口港等。

2）按照港口的功能，港口可分为存储港、转运港和经停港。存储港一般地处水陆联络的要道，交通十分方便，同时又是工商业中心。一般来讲，存储港的港口设施完备，便于货物的存储、转运，是内陆和港口货物集散的一个枢纽。转运港一般位于水路交通衔接处，将陆运货物集中转由海路运出，又可将海运货物转由陆路运入，主要办理转运业务。经停港指该港口地处航道的要冲，为往来船舶的必经之地，途经船舶有需要时可在此作短暂停泊，以便添加燃料，补充食物或淡水，再继续航行。

3）按照港口的开发工程，港口可分为天然港和人工港。天然港的海湾自然条件符合商港的需要，除了添置水上或岸上各种设备，以应船舶停泊及货物装卸搬运之需外，基本上可以利用港湾的航道、水深等天然地理气候条件。相较而言，人工港的港湾停泊地区，则完全依靠人工从陆地上开挖而成。

4）按照潮汐对港口的影响，港口可分为开敞港和闭合港。开敞港指港口直接建在一个开敞的海湾上或者是海岸的附近。其特点是港口内水域同海面直接相联，港口水位变化较小，船舶可以随时进出港口，不受潮汐影响。闭合港又称潮差港，指港口建在受潮汐影响比较大的海岸上或海岸附近。为解决退潮影响船舶出入港口的问题，一般在港口会修建一个闸门，使港口内的水位保持一定的深度，以利于船舶出入港口。否则，退潮时港口的吃水变浅，大船容易搁浅。

5）按照国家政策，港口可分为国内港和国际港。国内港指为了经营国内贸易、专供本国船舶出入的港口。外国船舶除了自然灾害或一些意外事故以及特许之外，不得任意驶入国内港口。国际港又称开放港，指为了方便国际贸易，依照条约或法令予以开放的商港，任何航行于国际航线的外籍船舶，经办理必要手续后都准许进出该港口，但是必须要接受当地渔政机关和海关的监督。

2.5.2 世界主要港口

目前世界上主要的港口包括荷兰的鹿特丹港，法国的马赛港，英国的伦敦港，德国的汉堡港，比利时的安特卫普港，美国的纽约港、洛杉矶港、旧金山港，日本的神户港、横滨港，新加坡的新加坡港，韩国的釜山港，以及中国的一系列港口。近年来，中国港口发展迅速，全球前十大港口中中国港口占了半席以上，下一部分会详细介绍。

1）鹿特丹港。鹿特丹港位于荷兰西南部莱茵河下游港区，面积约 100 万平方千米，码头总长 42 千米，是世界十大集装箱港口之一，也是世界上吞吐量最大的港口之一。该港口位于欧洲的水陆交通要冲，是荷兰和欧洲经济共同体的货物集散中心，欧洲经济共同体大约有 1/4 的进出口货物都是经由该港进行中转，因此鹿特丹港又有“欧洲门户”之称。鹿特丹港的发展目标是建成一个安全、高效、综合和清洁的港口和工业综合区，其服务特点是储、运、销一条龙，主要功能包括散货中转、原油和化工产品的储存以及炼油业等。

2）纽约港。纽约港也叫新泽西港，位于北美东岸的纽约州东南的哈德逊河口，濒临大西洋，是美国第一大海港，也是世界上最大的天然深水港之一，年吞吐量达到一亿吨以上。纽约港的港区岸线总长 1200 多千米，主要由哈德逊河下游、长岛海峡以及斯塔滕岛西面的水域组成，港区面积约 3840 平方千米，水域 700 多平方千米，陆域 1000 多平方千米，水深 9～14.6 米的深水泊位 430 多个，集装箱码头 37 个，是世界上港区面积最大的港口。

3）新奥尔良港。新奥尔良港位于美国南部，路易斯那州密西西比河畔，是美国最大的港口之一，年吞吐量一亿吨以上。该港既是海运港口，也是内河航运的集散地，是美国陆、河、海的一个联运中心。港口码头的总长有 40 千米，有 280 多个深水泊位，水深在 8.8～12.2 米。

4）休斯敦港。休斯敦港是美国也是世界大港之一，位于墨西哥湾北岸，是世界最大的石油加工中心之一，主要输出石油及其制品，还有棉花、小麦，年吞吐量一亿吨以上。

5）安特卫普港。安特卫普港是比利时最大的港口，是北欧北部的贸易中心，同时也是世界著名的港口之一，它的年吞吐量也在一亿吨左右。由于航道的改善，十万吨级的船舶可进入航道，吃水 14 米的船舶可以自由地进出。这个港口是欧洲钢铁的主要输出港，它的钢铁吞吐量居世界第一位。

6）汉堡港。汉堡港是德国第一大港口，出口量占德国的 1/2，是欧洲第二大港口，也是世界最大的自由港之一。它位于易北河及其支流阿尔斯特河和比勒河的汇合处，距河口 110 千米，有“两海三河之港”的称呼。两海指北海、波罗的海，三河指易北河、阿尔斯特河和比勒河，是欧洲南北东西航线的一个交汇点。汉堡港面积约 100 平方千米，有 700 多个泊位，共有仓储堆栈 100 多万平方米，是世界上泊位最多的港口，其泊位水深 11 米左右，海轮可以直达。港内设备非常先进，机械化、自动化程度非常高，有 300 多条国际海运航线和世界各主要港口联系，素有德国通向世界门户之称，年吞吐量在 6000 多万吨左右。

7）伦敦港。伦敦港是英国第一大港，它位于泰晤士河下游，距河口 88 千米，最大水深

14 米，潮差平均 6 米，20 万吨级的海轮可直达，年吞吐量 5000 多万吨。伦敦港涨潮和退潮时吃水深度 6 米，需要水闸进行控制。

8）神户港。神户港是日本最大的海港，位于大阪湾西北岸，面积 463 公顷，大小泊位 239 个，可同时停靠 250 艘海轮，有 13 条航线，通往 120 多个国家。神户港是日本最大的集装箱港，港口年吞吐量在 1.5 亿吨。

9）新加坡港。新加坡港是新加坡共和国的主要港口，位于马来半岛南端、马六甲海峡海口，扼太平洋、印度洋的咽喉，从 13 世纪开始就是国际贸易港口，目前已经发展成为世界著名的转口港和自由港，也是世界著名的集装箱港。港区面积达 583 平方千米，包括柔佛海峡和新加坡海峡的部分水域，码头总长超过 13 千米，泊位 200 多个，国际航线达到 250 条，可连接世界 370 多个港口。港口自然条件非常优越，水深适宜，吃水在 13 米左右的船舶可顺利的进港靠泊。港口水域宽敞，很少有风暴，无冰冻期。新加坡港炼油能力居世界第三，每年进出新加坡港口的船舶大约有 4 万～5 万艘，主要运输石油、粮食及矿砂，港口年吞吐量一亿吨以上。

2.5.3 中国主要海港

中国拥有海岸线 18000 多千米，沿海有很多优良的海港，目前约有大小港口 190 多个。其中，年吞吐量在 100 万吨以上的港口有 26 个。我国主要的外贸港口有大连港、秦皇岛港、天津港、青岛港、连云港港、上海港、厦门港、广州港、深圳港、香港港、高雄港和基隆港。其中，上海港、宁波舟山港、深圳港、广州港、青岛港、香港港和天津港跻身 2020 年全球十大集装箱港口。

1）上海港。上海港濒临东海，位于长江入海口附近，港区面积 36 平方千米，港口水深达 10 米以上，现在万吨级的码头泊位有 87 个，年货物总吞吐量大约占全国各港口总吞吐量的 1/3。它是我国最大的港口，也是世界十大亿吨港口之一，与世界 170 多个国家和地区有经济贸易往来。上海港进出口的主要货物有钢铁、粮食、煤炭、石油、化肥、木材及一些杂货等。

2）大连港。大连港位于辽东半岛南端的大连湾内。港阔水深，平均水深达到 9 米，不冰冻、不淤泥，是四季都可以通航的天然良港。该港口主要运输石油及石油制品，还有煤炭、木材和粮食等。大连港的粮食中转码头，是我国乃至远东地区最大的现代化专业散粮中心。

3）秦皇岛港。秦皇岛港位于渤海湾西北部，风小浪低，不冻不淤。水深 6.5～12.5 米，全港泊位有 17 个，分为油、煤、杂货三个作业区。原油作业区有专用码头，可同时停靠 1.5 万～3 万吨级别的油轮作业，有两条输油管道，直连大庆和北京。煤炭作业区有机械化装运系统，铺设有北京至秦皇岛、大同至秦皇岛两条专用铁路，主要以运送煤炭为主。该港口煤炭的年运量占全国的 80%，其中 60%～70%是运往日本的。港口年吞吐量达到 6000 多万吨，已成为世界最大的煤炭港和我国最大的能源输出港。

4）天津港。天津港位于渤海湾西侧，是首都北京的门户，也是我国北方重要的国际贸易港。天津港位于海河的入海口，渤海湾西部的海湾中心，是亚欧大陆桥东端起点之一，与环渤海、华北、西北等内陆地区的距离最短，经济腹地辽阔。天津港总面积 200 平方千米，泊位岸线总长 14443 米，泊位能力为 1.04 亿吨。天津港包括北疆港区、南疆港区和海河港区三大港区。其中北疆港区以集装箱和件杂货作业为主，南疆港区以液体散货和干散货作业为主，海河港区以 5000 吨级以下的小型船舶的作业为主。天津港是我国最大的粮食进口港，是我国第二大煤炭装船港和最大的焦炭出口港。

5）青岛港。青岛港位于山东半岛的胶州湾，港口不冻不淤，现有泊位 68 个，其中万吨级泊位 29 个，平均水深在 3～10 米，最深处可达 50 米，可以停靠 20 万吨级的巨型油轮，集装箱码头可以接卸第 5 代大型集装箱船。

6）香港港。香港港位于珠江口外侧，地处亚太中心，是世界航道的一个要冲。港区内港阔水深，风平浪静，是世界三大天然良港之一。优越的条件和适中的位置使它成为国际上著名的中转港和自由港。主要港区维多利亚港占地 5000 公顷，平均水深 12 米，可同时停泊 100 艘大型巨轮。香港的航运业发展一直非常蓬勃，已成为全球供应链上的主要枢纽港。

2.6 International Airports and Air Routes

This section mainly introduces important international airports and air routes. Currently, the world's air transport has formed a global network and several crucial hubs.

2.6.1 Major International Airports

Major airports in Asia are Beijing, Shanghai, Tokyo, Hong Kong, Manila, Bangkok, Singapore, Jakarta, Rangoon, Kolkata, Mumbai, New Delhi, Karachi, Tehran, Beirut and Jeddah. Europe's main airports are London, Paris, Frankfurt, Zurich, Rome, Vienna, Berlin, Copenhagen, Warsaw, Moscow, Bucharest and Athens and Lisbon. Major airports in North America include New York, Washington, Chicago, Montreal, Atlanta, Los Angeles, San Francisco, Seattle, Vancouver, and Honolulu on the Pacific Ocean. Major airports in Africa are Cairo, Kashmu, Nairobi, Johannesburg, Brazzaville, Lagos, Algiers, Dakar. And main airports in Latin America include Mexico City, Caracas, Rio de Janeiro, Buenos Aires as well as Santiago and Lima.

2.6.2 Major International Cargo Airports

The world's leading cargo airports include Chicago Airport in the US, Frankfurt Airport in Germany, Schiphol Airport in the Nethelands, Heathrow Airport in the UK, Charles de Gaulle Airport in France, Narita Airport in Japan, Kai Tak Airport in Hong Kong China and so on. These cargo airports are modern and highly specialized large-scale international hubs of air transport, handling more than 100000 tons of air transport cargo annually. In addition, these airports have modern navigation equipment, enough runways and huge passenger and cargo centers. Especially, the development of cargo freight enables each international airport to be equipped with modern full-cargo terminals and warehouses dedicated to the transportation of goods, greatly improving the efficiency of cargo handling.

2.6.3 Major International Air Routes

An aircraft flying in the air must have access suitable for aircraft navigation. An air traffic line that connects two or more locations for scheduled and irregular flights is the air route. The world's busiest air routes are mainly the following.

1) North Atlantic air route between Western Europe and North America. This route mainly connects Paris, London, Frankfurt, New York, Chicago, Montreal and other air

transport hubs.

2） Air route from Western Europe to the Middle East to the Far East. This route connects major airports in Western Europe to airports in the Far East such as Hong Kong，Beijing and Tokyo，and passes through important airports such as Athens，Cairo，Tehran，Karachi，New Delhi，Bangkok and Singapore.

3） North Pacific air route from the Far East to North America. This route is from Beijing，Hong Kong，Tokyo and other airports over the North Pacific Ocean，all the way to Vancouver，Seattle，San Francisco，Los Angeles and other airports on the west coast of North America，and it can be extended to airports on the east coast of North America.

In addition，there are important international air routes from North America to South America，from Western Europe to South America，from Western Europe to Africa，from Western Europe to Southeast Asia to Australia and New Zealand，and from the Far East to Australia and New Zealand，and from North America to Australia and New Zealand. From the above-mentioned international air routes and major airports，it can be seen that the world's air transport has formed a global transport network and a number of transport hubs.

2.6.4 China's Air Transport Industry

China's air transport industry is still a growing young sector. China's international trade air cargo business began in the middle of the 1950s and has been opened up to Russia，Mongolia，Laos，Myanmar，North Korea，Vietnam，Cambodia，Japan，Pakistan，France，Iran，Romania，Albania，Egypt，Ethiopia，Yugoslavia，Switzerland，Germany，Philippines，United Arab Emirates，Iraq，Thailand and the United States，Britain，Australia and other countries. At present，the main route distribution network of Civil Aviation Administration of China （CAAC） consists of Beijing route network，Guangzhou route network and Shanghai route network. China's international air routes to all parts of the world mainly include the routes from China to the United States，from China to Canada，from China to Japan，from China to Australia，from China to Europe，from China to Africa，from China to Middle East and from China to Southeast Asia. According to the data disclosed，at the 40th General Assembly of the International Civil Aviation Organization （ICAO） (held in Montreal on September 24，2019)，the total turnover of China's civil aviation has ranked second in the world for 14 consecutive years，contributing more than 20% to the world's civil aviation growth.

2.6 国际航空运输机场及空运航线

本节主要介绍重要的国际航空运输机场以及空运航线。目前，世界航空运输已形成了一个全球性的运输网和若干运输枢纽。

2.6.1 国际重要航空站

世界各大洲重要的航空站主要有亚洲的北京、上海、香港、东京、马尼拉、曼谷、新加坡、雅加达、仰光、加尔各答、孟买、新德里、卡拉奇、德黑兰、贝鲁特和吉达。欧洲的主要机场有伦敦、巴黎、法兰克福、苏黎世、罗马、维也纳、柏林、哥本哈根、华沙、莫斯科、布加勒斯特以及雅典和里斯本等。北美洲的主要机场包括纽约、华盛顿、芝加哥、蒙特利尔、亚特兰大、洛杉矶、旧金山、西雅图、温哥华，以及位于太平洋上的火奴鲁鲁。非洲的机场有开罗、喀什穆、内罗毕、约翰内斯堡、布拉柴维尔、拉各斯、阿尔及尔和达喀尔。拉丁美洲的机场包括墨西哥城、加拉加斯、里约热内卢、布宜诺斯艾利斯还有圣地亚哥和利马。

2.6.2 国际重要货运机场

世界主要的航空货运机场有美国的芝加哥机场、德国的法兰克福机场、荷兰的希普霍尔机场、英国的希斯罗机场、法国的戴高乐机场、日本的成田机场、中国香港的启德机场等。这些机场都是现代化、专业化程度高的大型国际货运空中枢纽，每年的货运量都在数10万吨以上，这些机场有现代化的导航设备，有足够的跑道和庞大的客货运中心，尤其是货运的发展，使得每个国际机场都备有现代化的全货机码头和仓库专门用于货物的运输，大大地提高了货机的装卸效率。

2.6.3 国际重要空运航线

航空器在空中飞行必须有适合航空器航行的通路，经过批准而开辟的，连接两个或几个地点进行定期和不定期航空运输业务的航空交通线就是空运航线。世界上最繁忙的空运航线主要有以下几条。

1）西欧到北美间的北大西洋航空线。这条航线主要连接巴黎、伦敦、法兰克福、纽约、芝加哥、蒙特利尔等航空枢纽。

2）西欧到中东再到远东的航空线。这条航线连接西欧各主要机场，一直到中国的香港、北京，日本的东京等机场，并且途经雅典、开罗、德黑兰、卡拉奇、新德里、曼谷、新加坡等一些重要的航空站。

3）远东到北美间的北太平洋航线。这条航线是从北京、香港、东京等机场经过北太平洋的上空，一直到北美西海岸的温哥华、西雅图、旧金山、洛杉矶等机场的航空线，并且可继续延伸到北美东海岸的机场。

此外还有北美到南美的航线、西欧到南美的航线、西欧到非洲的航线、西欧到东南亚到澳新的航线以及远东到澳新、北美到澳新等重要的国际航空线。从这些主要的国际航线及世界重要的航空站，可以看出世界航空运输目前形成了一个全球性的运输网和若干运输枢纽。

2.6.4 中国航空运输业

我国航空运输业属于处于成长期的行业。我国国际贸易航空货运业务开始于20世纪50年代中期，先后开辟了飞往俄罗斯、蒙古、老挝、缅甸、朝鲜、越南、柬埔寨、日本、巴基斯坦、法国、伊朗、罗马尼亚、阿尔巴尼亚、埃及、埃塞俄比亚、前南斯拉夫、瑞士、德国、菲律宾、阿拉伯联合酋长国、伊拉克、泰国及美国、英国、澳大利亚等国家的航线。目前中国民航主要航线分布网是由以北京为中心的航线网、以广州为中心的航线网以及以上海为中心的航线网组成。我国通往世界各地的国际航线主要有中国至美国的航线、中国至加拿大的航线、中国至日本的航线、中国至澳大利亚的航线、中国至欧洲各国的航线、中国至非洲各国的航线、中国至中东各国的航线以及中国至东南亚各国的航线。据国际民用航空组织（简称国际民航组织，英文简称ICAO）第40届大会（2019年9月24日蒙特利尔召开）披露的数据，中国民航总周转量连续14年位居世界第二位，对世界民航增长贡献率超过20%。

2.7 Other International Logistics Transport Lines

2.7.1 Main Railway Transport Lines in International Logistics

There are four major railway transport trunk lines in the world. They are as follows.

(1) The Trans-Siberian Railway

The Trans-Siberian Railway starts from Vladivostok, Russia in the east, passes through Boli, Chita, Irkutsk, Novosibirsk, Omsk, Chelyabinsk, Gubyshev, and ends in Moscow, with a total length of more than 9300km.

Other railways connected to the eastern end of the Trans-Siberian railway are: ①Vladivostok-Chongjin port-Hamhung-Pyongyang Railway; ② Dalian-Shenyang-Changchun-Harbin-Chita Railway; ③ Guangzhou-Changsha-Wuhan-Zhengzhou-Beijing-Datong-Ulan Bator-Ulan-ude Railway.

Main railways connected to the western end of the Siberian railway are: ① Moscow-St. Petersburg-Helsinki-Stockholm-Oslo Railway; ② Moscow-Warsaw-Berlin-Cologne-Brussels-Paris Railway; ③Moscow-Rostov-Tbilisi-Zolfa-Tehran Railway.

Trade between China and CIS (the Commonwealth of Independent States) countries, Eastern European countries and Iran is mainly carried out through the Trans-Siberian Railway.

(2) Main Railways Connecting the East and West Oceans in Canada

There are two main railways connecting the east and west oceans in Canada.

Firstly, Port Rupert-Edmonton-Winnipeg-Quebec (namely Canadian National Railway).

Secondly, Vancouver-Calgary-Winnipeg-Sundby-Montreal-St. John-Halifax (namely Canadian Pacific Railway).

(3) Major Railways Connecting the East and West Oceans in the US

There are four major railways connecting the two oceans in the United States.

Firstly, Seattle-Spokane-Bismarck-St. Paul-Chicago-Detroit (namely Northern Pacific Railway).

Secondly, Los Angeles-Albuquerque-Kansas City-St. Louis-Cincinnati-Washington-Baltimore (namely Santa Fe Railway).

Thirdly, Los Angeles-Tucson-Paso-Houston-New Orleans (namely Southern Pacific Railway).

Fourthly, San Francisco-Ogden-Omaha-Chicago-Pittsburgh-Philadelphia-New York (namely Union Pacific Railway).

(4) Middle East-Europe Railway

Middle East-European railway starts from Basra in Iraq, running westward through Baghdad, Mosul, Muslim MIA in Syria, Adana, Konya and Erskishir in Turkey to Justridar on the east bank of the Bosporus Strait, crosses the Bosporus bridge to Istanbul to connect the Balkan railway, extends further westward through Sofia, Belgrade and Budapest to Vienna and connects the central and Western European railway networks.

2.7.2 Main Land Bridges in International Logistics

Land bridge refers to the transcontinental railway connecting the sea with the sea. At present, the widely used land bridges are the Siberian Land Bridge, the New Eurasian Land Bridge and the North American Land Bridge (including American Land Bridge and Canadian Land Bridge).

(1) Siberian Land Bridge

The Siberian Land Bridge (SLB) connects the Pacific Far East with the Baltic Sea, the coast of the Black Sea and the Atlantic coast of Western Europe, making it the longest land bridge in the world. For more than ten years, the western end of this land bridge has been extended from Britain to the whole European continent and Middle East countries including Western Europe, Central Europe, Eastern Europe, Southern Europe and Northern Europe. And its eastern end extends not only to Japan, but also to South Korea, the Philippines, Mainland China and Hong Kong. From Western Europe to the Far East, the transport distance via this land bridge is 13000km, which is about 1/2 shorter than the sea route through the Cape of Good Hope and 1/3 shorter than the sea route through the Suez Canal. At the same time, the freight is 20%~25% lower, and the transportation time can be saved by 3~5 days.

(2) New Eurasian Land Bridge

The New Asia-Europe Land Bridge (A-E. Land Bridge) starts from Lianyungang of China in the east, passes through Longhai Railway, Lanzhou-Xinjiang Railway and Beijiang Railway, leaves Alashan Pass and finally arrives at Rotterdam of the Netherlands. It is 10800 km long and passes through China, Kazakhstan, Russia, Belarus, Poland, Germany and the Netherlands. Covering more than 30 countries and regions, it shortens 2000 kilometers than the Siberian land Bridge, saves about 30% of freight, and shortens transportation time by about 60% compared with sea transportation.

(3) North American Land Bridge

In addition to the Siberian Land Bridge and the New Eurasian Land Bridge, there are also the American Land Bridge, the American Mini-land Bridge, the American Micro-land Bridge or Semi-land Bridge in international cargo land Bridge transport. American Land Bridge is a part of the North American Land Bridge, the first road bridge from the Far East to Europe. The paths of American Mini-land Bridge are: Far East or West Coast of the US-East Coast of the US or ports of Mexico Gulf-destination. This Mini-land Bridge avoids the detour through the Panama Canal, and can enjoy preferential freight rate of railway container train, thus reducing the cost and shortening the route. The transportation mode is sea-rail. The American Micro-land Bridge is shorter than the American Mini-land bridge by distance, using only part of the land bridge.

2.7.3 Main Oil Pipelines in International Logistics

The world pipeline network is unevenly distributed, mainly concentrated in North America and Europe. The United States (with more than 300000 kilometers of oil pipelines) and CIS (the Commonwealth of the Independent States) countries (with a total length of more than 200000 kilometers) have the most developed pipeline transportation. In addition to the United States and CIS countries, Canada (with more than 35000 kilometers of oil pipelines), Western Europe, the Middle East and other countries and regions also have well-developed pipeline networks. The main oil pipelines in the world are as follows.

(1) Russian "Friendship" Oil Pipeline

It is one of the longest and largest oil pipelines in the world, with a total length of 9912km, a pipe diameter of 426—1220mm, a pipeline working pressure of 4. 9—6. 28MPa, and an annual crude oil transport capacity of more than 100 million tons. The pipeline starts from Samara, Russia, and passes through 8 Russian states. The entire pipeline is sealed and its pumping stations adopt advanced automation management technology. The pipeline also divides a branch line to Lithuania and Latvia to transport Russian Siberian oil to the Eastern and Western European countries. It was completed in 1973.

(2) The Alaska Oil Pipeline

It runs from Prudhoe Bay in Alaska to Valdez and is the world's first oil pipeline to reach the Arctic Circle. Most of the pipeline passes through permafrost. More than half of the main line is erected on the ground and insulated with foamed plastic. There are relatively perfect anti earthquake and pipeline protection measures. The total length of the pipeline is 1200km, the pipe diameter is 1220m, the working pressure of the pipeline is 8. 2MPa, and the annual oil transport capacity is 12000 tons.

(3) American Colonier Refined Oil Pipeline

The American Colonier refined oil pipeline has the longest length, the widest pipe diameter and the largest throughput in the world. The pipeline was commissioned in 1963. The pipeline begins in Houston, Texas, and ends in Linden, New Jersey. When it was put into operation in 1963, the total length of the trunk line was 2460km. After several expansions, the total length of the trunk line was more than 4600km by the early 1980s, with four pipe diameters of 750mm, 800mm, 900mm and 1000mm. The pipeline system transports refined oil products from refineries in the coastal area of the Mexico Gulf in the southern United States to the industrial areas in nearly 10 states in the southeast and east of the US, of which about 50% is transported to New York port. The whole pipeline system is connected with 10 big oil receiving points and more than 280 oil delivery points, conveying more than 100 types and grades of light oil products such as gasoline, kerosene, diesel, etc.. The system adopts sequential transportation mode. The delivery lot of one type of oil shall not be less than 4000 cubic meters, and the cycle period of one group of oil shall be 10 days. Delivery order has been basically finalized as: high quality gasoline-conventional gasoline-turbine fuel-kerosene-diesel-unleaded gasoline. The pipeline adopts computer centralized management and control system.

(4) Arab-Italian Gas Transmission Pipeline

The 2506km pipeline, with an annual capacity of 12. 5 billion cubic meters, connects Algeria to Italy and was put into operation in 1983. It is the first intercontinental gas pipeline connecting Africa and Europe. It is also the first deep-water pipeline crossing the Mediterranean, creating a world record for laying pipelines on the seabed with a water depth of 600m.

(5) Saudi Arabia East-West Oil Pipeline

The pipeline was started in 1969 and put into operation in 1983. The pipeline crosses the central region of Saudi Arabia, and the whole pipeline is under centralized control, with a total length of 1202km. The pipeline is composed of two parallel pipelines with a pipeline transportation capacity of about 4.8 million barrels/day.

2.7 国际物流其他运输线

2.7.1 国际物流主要铁路运输线

国际主要铁路运输干线有以下 4 条。

(1) 西伯利亚大铁路干线

西伯利亚大铁路干线东起俄罗斯的海参崴（符拉迪沃斯托克）经伯力、赤塔、伊尔库茨克、新西伯利亚、鄂木斯克、车里雅宾斯克、古比雪夫，止于莫斯科，全长 9300 多千米。

与西伯利亚大铁路干线的东端相连接的其他干线有：①海参崴（符拉迪沃斯托克）—清津港—咸兴—平壤铁路；②大连—沈阳—长春—哈尔滨—赤塔铁路；③广州—长沙—武汉—郑州—北京—大同—乌兰巴托—乌兰乌德铁路。

与西伯利亚大铁路干线的西端相连接的干线有：①莫斯科—圣彼得堡—赫尔辛基—斯德哥尔摩—奥斯陆铁路；②莫斯科—华沙—柏林—科隆—布鲁塞尔—巴黎铁路；③莫斯科—罗斯托夫—第比利斯—卓勒法—德黑兰铁路。

我国与独联体、东欧国家及伊朗之间的贸易，主要通过西伯利亚大铁路干线进行。

(2) 加拿大连接东西两大洋的铁路干线

加拿大连接东西两大洋的铁路干线主要有 2 条。

其一，鲁珀特港—埃德蒙顿—温尼伯—魁北克（加拿大国家铁路）；

其二，温哥华—卡尔加里—温尼伯—散德贝—蒙特利尔—圣约翰—哈利法克斯（加拿大太平洋大铁路）。

(3) 美国连接东西两大洋的铁路干线

美国连接东西两大洋的铁路干线主要有 4 条。

其一，西雅图—斯波坎—俾斯麦—圣保罗—芝加哥—底特律（北太平洋铁路）；

其二，洛杉矶—阿尔布开克—堪萨斯城—圣路易城—辛辛那提—华盛顿—巴尔的摩（圣菲铁路）；

其三，洛杉矶—图森—帕索—休斯敦—新奥尔良（南太平洋铁路）；

其四，旧金山—奥格登—奥马哈—芝加哥—匹兹堡—费城—纽约（联合太平洋铁路）。

(4) 中东—欧洲铁路干线

中东—欧洲铁路干线始于伊拉克的巴士拉，向西经巴格达、摩苏尔、叙利亚的穆斯林米亚，土耳其的阿达纳、科尼亚、厄斯基色希尔至博斯普鲁斯海峡东岸的于斯屈达尔，过博斯普鲁斯大桥至伊斯坦布尔，接巴尔干铁路，向西经索非亚、贝尔格莱德、布达佩斯至维也纳，连接中、西欧铁路网。

2.7.2 国际物流主要大陆桥

大陆桥是指把海与海连接起来的横贯大陆的铁路。目前广泛使用的大陆桥有西伯利亚大陆桥、新亚欧大陆桥和北美大陆桥(包括美国大陆桥和加拿大大陆桥)。

(1) 西伯利亚大陆桥

西伯利亚大陆桥把太平洋远东地区与波罗的海、黑海沿岸及西欧大西洋岸连接起来，为世界最长的大陆桥。十几年来，这条大路桥运输路线的西端已从英国延伸到了包括西欧、中欧、东欧、南欧、北欧的整个欧洲大陆和中东各国，其东端也不只是到日本，而是延伸到了韩国、菲律宾、中国等。从西欧到远东，经大陆桥运输的路程为13000千米，比经过好望角的海运航线缩短约1/2的路程，比经苏伊士运河的海运航线缩短约1/3的路程，同时，运费要低20%~25%，运输时间也可节省3~5天。

(2) 新亚欧大陆桥

新亚欧大陆桥东起中国的连云港，经陇海线、兰新线、北疆铁路，出阿拉山口，最终抵达荷兰的鹿特丹，全长10800千米，途经中国、哈萨克斯坦、俄罗斯、白俄罗斯、波兰、德国、荷兰7国，辐射30多个国家和地区，比西伯利亚大陆桥缩短2000千米，节省运费约30%，与海运相较，缩短运输时间60%左右。

(3) 北美大陆桥

除西伯利亚大陆桥、新亚欧大陆桥外，国际货物运输大陆桥还有美国大陆桥、美国小陆桥、美国微型路桥或半路桥。美国大陆桥是北美大陆桥的组成部分，是从远东至欧洲水陆联运线中的第一条路桥。美国小陆桥路线为：远东或美国西海岸—美国东海岸或墨西哥湾港口—目的地。这条小陆桥路线避免了绕道巴拿马运河，可以享受铁路集装箱专用列车优惠运价，从而减低了成本，缩短了路径，其运输方式为海-铁。美国微型路桥比美国小路桥又缩短了一段运输距离，只用了部分路桥。

2.7.3 国际物流主要输油管道

世界管道运输网分布很不均匀，主要集中在北美和欧洲，美国(输油管道超过30万公里)和独联体各国(总长20多万公里)的管道运输最为发达。除美国和独联体国家外，加拿大(输油管道超过3.5万公里)、西欧、中东等国家和地区的管道网也很发达。世界主要的输油管道如下。

(1) 俄罗斯"友谊"输油管道

它是世界上距离最长、口径最大的输油管道之一，总长为9912km，管径为426~1220mm，管道工作压力为4.9~6.28MPa，年输原油量超过1亿吨。该输油管道的起点位于俄罗斯萨马拉州，途经俄罗斯8个州，全线密封输油，其泵站采用先进的自动化管理技术。该输油管道还分出一条通往立陶宛和拉脱维亚的支线，将俄罗斯西伯利亚的石油输往东欧和西欧国家，于1973年完工。

(2) 美国阿拉斯加输油管道

它从美国阿拉斯加州的普拉德霍湾直至瓦尔迪兹，是世界上第一条深入北极圈的输油管道。该管道大部分线路经过冻土地带，半数以上干线采用地上架设，采用泡沫塑料保温，有比较完善的抗地震和管线保护措施。管道总长为1200km，管径为1220m，管道工作压力为8.2MPa，年输油量1.2万吨。

(3) 美国科洛尼尔成品油管道

美国科洛尼尔成品油管道是世界上最长、管径最大和输送量最大的成品油管道系统。这一管道于1963年投产。管道起点在美国得克萨斯州的休斯敦，终点在新泽西州的林登。1963年投产时，干线总长2460千米，经多次扩建，至20世纪80年代初，干线全长4600

多千米，管径有 750mm、800mm、900mm、1000mm 四种。这一管道系统把美国南部墨西哥湾沿海地区的许多炼油厂生产的成品油输往美国东南部和东部近 10 个州的工业地区，其中约有 50%输送到纽约港。整个管道系统联系着 10 个大的接油点和 280 多个交油点，输送的油品有汽油、煤油、柴油等 100 多个牌号和品级的轻质油品。该系统采用油品顺序输送方式。一种油品的交运批量规定不少于 4000 立方米，一组油品的循环周期为 10 天。输送顺序已基本定型为：优质汽油-常规汽油-透平燃料-煤油-柴油-不含铅汽油。管道采用电子计算机集中管理控制系统。

(4) 阿意输气管线

该输气管道总长为 2506km，年输气量达 125 亿立方米，由阿尔及利亚连通到意大利，1983 年投产。它是第一条连接非洲与欧洲的洲际输气管道，也是第一条穿越地中海深水管道，创建了在水深 600m 的海底铺设管道的世界纪录。

(5) 沙特阿拉伯东西输油管道

该输油管道于 1969 年动工，1983 年投产。该管道横贯沙特阿拉伯中部地区，管道全线集中控制，全长 1202 千米。管道由两条并行管线组成，管输能力约 480 万桶/日。

Part B Vocabulary and Terminology 词汇和术语

international logistics system 国际物流系统
space utility 空间效用
time utility 时间效用
scale economies, economies of scale 规模经济
liner 班轮
charter 租船
consignee 收货人
door-to-door transportation 门到门运输
international multimodal transport 国际多式联运
import and export trade commodities 进出口贸易商品
sorting 整理
marking 刷唛
assembling 组装
processing 流通加工
bonded warehouse 保税仓库
customs territory 关境
electronic data interchange (EDI) 电子数据交换
bar code technology 条形码技术
global satellite positioning system (GPS) 全球卫星定位系统
shipping route 海运航线
air route 空运航线

Part C Exercise 练习

Ⅰ. Answer the following questions.

1. What is the ultimate purpose of logistics system?

2. Please explain in English what objectives international logistics system attempts to achieve.

3. What is the structure of international logistics system?

4. Describe the major types of international logistics transportation.

5. What kind of role does packing play in international logistics system?

6. Why is information management subsystem of paramount importance in international logistics system?

7. What are the busiest shipping routes in the world?

8. Please briefly introduce the North Pacific Route.

9. How can seaports be categorized according to port function?

10. Briefly describe the composition of international logistics network.

Ⅱ. Decide whether the following statements are true or false.

1. Warehousing is often the single largest cost in the logistics system.

2. The major function of transportation is to create the time utility of products.

3. Packaging performs two basic roles—marketing and logistics.

4. Information is the vital link between the entire logistical process and the firm's supplier.

5. Material handling often refers to the storage of products.

6. The strategic placement of warehouses can assist firms in improving customer service levels.

Ⅲ. Translate the following passages into Chinese.

Transportation decisions have an impact on the functional costs of finance, production and marketing. In the absence of a total-cost approach to the transportation decision, a company may use a mode of transportation that has a low transportation rate. The use of a low cost method of movement may minimize transportation costs, but it does not guarantee the minimization of total logistics costs. Low-cost transportation usually is associated with slow service, which means higher warehousing and inventory costs and lower customer service level.

Ⅳ. Translate the following sentences into English.

1. 国际物流信息子系统的主要功能是采集、存储和加工国际物流和商流的信息情报。准确而及时的信息传递是国际物流管理的重要基石。

2. 企业如果没有采用系统观念的话，物流通常表现为一系列分散在企业各个部门中的相互孤立、互不协调的活动，且每个部门都有各自不同的预算、目标以及绩效评价系统。

3. 物流中的仓储作业主要是克服商品使用价值在供需时间上的差异，从而创造商品的时间价值。国际物流仓储不仅包括外贸商品的储存保管，而且还包括出口加工、拣选、整理、包装、刷唛、备货、组装、配送和发运等一系列工作。

4. 由于海洋运输在国际贸易及国际物流当中的重要地位，所以现代化的港口除了具备货物集散作用之外，往往还需要提供货物的储存、加工、装配、制造以及转运等。由此可见，现代化的港口不但是海陆空综合运输体系的中心，同时也是生产加工中心。

Chapter Three

Fundamental Knowledge on International Trade
国际贸易基础知识

Part A Text 课文

International logistics is an important part of international trade, and they are inseparably interconnected and develop together. Many practices in international trade need logistics services. For this reason, this chapter makes introduction to international logistics related trade terms, international conventions of trade terms, trade procedure in import and export, international trade methods, and etc.

国际物流是国际贸易的重要组成部分，它们相辅相成，共同发展。由于国际贸易的许多业务贯穿于国际物流过程中，为了便于理解国际物流业务，特设此章专门介绍与国际物流密切相关的国际贸易术语、贸易术语的国际惯例、进出口交易程序以及国际贸易方式等国际贸易基础知识。

3.1 Introduction to International Trade

International trade has long history and has been playing a significant part in human society development. In the context of rapid global economy development and deepened economic connection between countries, promoting international trade has become a main way for a country to strengthen its role in international economy.

3.1.1 Classification of International Trade

By the objects traded, international trade can be classified into three domains, namely goods import and export, technology import and export, and international service trade. Goods import and export is called tangible trade, whereas technology import and export, together with international service trade, are called intangible trade. Tangible trade accounts for a substantial part of international trade and therefore is the fundamental and most important part. The categories of tangible trade are listed below.

(1) Classification by the Direction Goods are Transferred

1) Export trade: domestic goods leaving customs frontier.

2) Import trade: foreign goods entering customs frontier.

3) Transit trade: goods from a country passing through host country's territory and being delivered to other countries without change of original conditions of the goods.

(2) Classification by Countries Involved

1) Direct trade: The direct deal of goods between consuming and producing countries. When goods are directly sold from producing countries to consuming countries, it is called direct export on the part of producing countries and direct import on the part of consuming countries.

2) Indirect trade: The goods transaction being made between producing countries and consuming countries via a third country. It is called indirect export on the part of producing countries and indirect import on the part of consuming countries.

3) Transit trade: In an indirect trade, what the third country commits is transit trade.

(3) Classification by Exchange Settlement Means

1) Trade by free settlement: currency is used as settlement means in international trade.

2) Barter trade: goods after evaluation are used to settle the transaction in international trade.

3.1.2 International Trade Contract and Contract Implementation

International trade involves commodity transaction; however, nation crossing makes it riskier. For this reason, the conclusion and implementation of international trade contracts is critical in safeguarding the rights and interests of the purchaser and seller. Apart from the purchaser and seller, interested parties also include companies in the fields of transportation, insurance, finance, and so on, their rights and obligations in international trade being defined in trade contracts too. Therefore, international trade contract is the most important and fundamental contract in international trade activities. Once the contract takes effect, the interested parties are legally protected on their rights and supervised and bound on their obligations. For that reason, the provisions concerning goods, transportation, insurance, and claim indemnity, etc., must be clearly and explicitly defined in the contract.

It needs to be noted that the conclusion and performance of international trade contract must be in accordance with norms of law. The law based on could be from the country that is most closely connected to the contract or chosen by interested parties. Furthermore, international trade convention, as one of the main origins of international trade law as well as relative bilateral or multilateral treaties entered by parties involved in the contract, could be also followed by as norms. Currently, the most globally influential international trade conventions and international treaties are INCOTERMS (*International Rules for the Interpretation of Trade Terms formulated by International Chamber of Commerce, with International Commercial Terms for short*), UCPDC (*Uniform Customs and Practice for Documentary Credit*), and CISG (*United Nations Convention on Contracts for the International Sale of Goods*) formulated by ICC (The International Chamber of Commerce).

Once taking effect, the contract should be implemented. And all the parties concerned should perform their respective obligations strictly in accordance with the contract. No parties should modify or terminate the contract without authorization, and the corresponding legal responsibility should be assumed should any party breach the contract.

Contract and credit honoring is the main principle for China to develop international trade. In import and export, one party should perform his duty of payment and goods pickup when the other fulfills the delivery on terms.

3.1.3 Procedures of Import

In principle, China conducts importation under FOB term, using L/C as settlement means. In this context, the process of Chinese importation generally has three stages.

(1) Preparation Preceding Importation

The following should be done in this stage: market investigation, import cost estimation, import planning, import license application, foreign exchange arrangement, contact with overseas parties via import/export company or import department if the company is a licensed import/export company, import scheme specification, choice of market, timing and counter party of import.

(2) Negotiation and Contract Conclusion

Different negotiation methods are to be adopted according to the types of imported goods. Business correspondence is used in the import of common goods, whereas in the case of key material import, oral negotiation is necessary. The negotiation will generally run through the process of inquiry, offer, counter-offer and acceptance, in which inquiry and offer are inevitable.

When agreement is reached after repeated negotiation, a written contract is needed. The content of an import contract is similar to that of an export contract in that both include basic terms such as quality, quantity, packing, price, shipment, insurance, payment, commodity inspection, as well as claim and arbitration. There are two types of contract, purchasing agreement and confirmation of purchasing, both having equal legal effect. Confirmation of purchasing is used in common import, whereas formal purchasing agreement should be signed in the case of substantial quantity or complex transaction. Two originals of the contract should be signed by seller and purchaser, each retaining a copy, as the basis for contract performance and handling of dispute.

(3) Contract Performance

An importer should conduct the following activities to perform import contract: issuance of foreign payment guarantee (usually by means of L/C), entrance of transportation agreement, insurance application, documents examination, payment, customs declaration, goods reception and inspection, and claim pursuance with certificate of inspection and quarantine and other documents should goods be detected by the inspection and quarantine agency questionable in quality, quantity or else. Furthermore, payment should be settled and other expenses be paid to domestic ordering company when a third-party import company is involved.

3.1.4 Procedures of Export

In principle, China conducts exportation under CIF or CFR terms, regularly using L/C as settlement means. In this context, the process of Chinese exportation generally has three stages.

(1) Preparation

Before exportation, export plan should be compiled and submitted for approval from department in charge and source of goods be determined according to the plan. Meanwhile, international market investigation should be conducted in the following aspects:

1) Import country's political, economic, and foreign trade condition for sake of market choosing;

2) The production, consumption, trade, and price of relative commodity in international market in order to understand pricing and trade terms of the commodity to be exported;

3) The political attitude held by related clients towards China and their creditworthiness, operation domain and capability.

On the base of the investigation, exporter should make export scheme, determine the means of settlement and promotion strategy, develop client relationship and promotion network, and carry out advertisement.

(2) Negotiation and Contract Conclusion

Export negotiation could take the form of business correspondence, appointing representatives to conduct negotiation, or inviting foreign companies or representatives to Chinese trade fairs and conducting negotiation personally. It involves the work of inquiry, offer, counter-offer and acceptance before final agreement is achieved, sometimes repeated negotiations is necessary. Once the deal is made, the parties should sign written sale contract, which could be in the form of confirmation of sale when common goods are to be exported in small amount. The contract is used as basis of performance and dispute settlement.

(3) Contract Performance

The following activities are involved in the performance of a contract:

1) Preparing goods in accordance with contract.

2) Urging the importer to issue L/C if it is used as settlement means; preparing goods after the reception, investigation and confirmation of L/C according to contract terms and regulations in UCPDC; timely notifying the purchaser of making modification to the L/C if it is found to be discrepant or unacceptable.

3) Handling goods inspection and arranging insurance, consignment, customs declaration and shipment under the term of CIF/CIP.

4) Once the shipment is done, issuing shipment notification, filling in documents according to the requirement of L/C, and submitting the documents to banks for negotiation and settlement within the period of L/C validity.

5) Lodging a claim, requiring arbitration, or even filing a lawsuit in the event of breach or dispute.

3.1 国际贸易概述

国际贸易有着悠久的历史，并在人类社会发展中起着重要的作用。随着世界经济的迅猛发展，各国（地区）间经济联系的加深，国际贸易已成为世界各国努力成为世界经济舞台中重要一员的主要手段，进而决定了各国在世界经济结构中所处的地位。

3.1.1 国际贸易分类

国际贸易从其内容构成看主要分为货物进出口、技术进出口和国际服务贸易三大块。其中，货物进出口称为有形贸易，技术进出口和国际服务贸易称为无形贸易。目前，在世界各国的国际贸易活动中，有形贸易占有相当大的比重，是国际贸易中最基本、最主要的部分。其主要分类如下。

(1) 按货物转移方向分类

1）出口贸易：本国货物离开关境。

2）进口贸易：外国货物进入关境。

3）过境贸易：别国出口货物通过本国国境，未经加工改制，在基本保持原状条件下运往另一国的贸易活动。

(2) 按贸易参加国分类

1）直接贸易：货物消费国与货物生产国直接买卖货物的行为，称为直接贸易。货物从生产国直接卖给消费国，对生产国而言，是直接出口；对消费国而言，是直接进口。

2）间接贸易：货物生产国与货物消费国通过第三国进行的货物买卖行为，对生产国和消费国而言都称为间接贸易。其中，对生产国是间接出口；对消费国是间接进口。

3）转口贸易：在间接贸易中，第三国所从事的就是转口贸易。

(3) 按结汇工具分类

1）自由结汇贸易：在国际贸易中，以货币作为清偿工具。

2）易货贸易：在国际贸易中，以货物经过计价作为清偿工具。

3.1.2 国际贸易合同及合同履行

国际贸易属商品交换的范畴，但由于其跨国界的特性使国际贸易具有强烈的国际性和巨大的风险性，因此订立和履行国际贸易合同对买卖双方当事人权益的维护关系重大。同时国际贸易中的每笔交易除了买卖双方当事人之外，还涉及运输、保险、金融等部门，关系错综复杂，各部门在国际贸易中的权利和义务均需以国际贸易合同为准加以确定。因此国际贸易合同是国际贸易活动中最重要、最基本的合同。合同一旦生效，合同当事人的权利就受到法律的保护，同时义务也将受到法律的监督和约束。也正因为如此，合同中必须清楚地载明有关货物标的、运输、保险、索赔等各项条款，做到明确无误。

值得一提的是，国际贸易合同的订立和履行，必须符合法律规范，方能受到法律保护并受法律约束。一般以与合同有最密切联系的国家的法律或允许由当事人选择合同适用的法律为依据。另外，作为国际贸易法律的主要渊源之一的国际贸易惯例和合同当事人所在国缔结或参加的有关双边或多边国际公约也是国际贸易合同应当遵循的规范。目前，在全球影响最大的国际贸易惯例和相关国际公约包括由国际商会制定的《国际贸易术语解释通则》《跟单信用证统一惯例》和《联合国国际货物销售合同公约》等。

一项有效合同生效后，履行合同是合同当事人按照合同规定履行各自义务的行为，任何一方不得擅自变更或者解除合同，任何一方的责任违约，都将因此而承担相应的法律责任。

"重合同、守信用"是我国开展国际贸易的重要原则，也是履约的基本准则。无论是进口还是出口，在一方按质、按时、按量履行交货义务的同时，也要求另一方切实履行付款、取货的义务。

3.1.3 进口交易程序

我国进口贸易原则上应按FOB价格条件成交，支付条件大多为信用证方式，基于上述情况，我国进口贸易程序大致分为以下三个阶段。

(1) 进口交易前的准备阶段

进口交易前的准备工作主要有市场调查、进口成本估算、编制进口计划；申请进口许可证，落实用汇资金；用货部门根据国家批准的进口计划或地方批准的进口项目，选择进出口公司或安排其进口部门（有自营进出口权的企业）开展对外联系工作，制定具体进口方案，安排订购市场、订购时间和选择交易对象等。

(2) 进口交易洽商和签订进口合同阶段

根据进口物资的不同种类采用不同的洽商方式。进口一般物资，可采用函电洽商方式；进口重点物资，包括技术转让内容则需采用口头谈判方式进行洽商。交易洽商一般要经过询盘、发盘、还盘和接受几个环节，其中发盘和接受是必不可少的两个环节。

买卖双方通过反复洽商达成交易后，需签订书面合同。进口合同与出口合同的内容基本相同，合同的基本条款包括商品的品质、数量、包装、价格、装运、保险、支付、检验、索赔及仲裁等由双方商妥的内容。合同的形式主要有购货合同和购货确认书两种，二者具有同样的法律效力。一般进口交易多使用购货确认书，数量较大或交易条件复杂者，则使用正式购货合同。书面合同正本一式两份，经买卖双方签署后各保留一份，作为履约和处理争议的依据。

(3) 履行进口合同阶段

进口方履行进口合同，需要做好以下各项工作：办理对外付款保证手续（一般为开立信用证）；与运输部门订立运输合同；办理保险、审单、付款、清关、接货和验收；经检验检疫机构检验发现货物质量、数量或其他方面有问题时，须依据相关检验检疫证书和其他单据对外进行索赔。同时，还需与国内订货单位结算货款和其他费用。

3.1.4 出口交易程序

我国出口贸易原则上应按CIF或CFR价格条件成交，支付条件大多数使用信用证方式，在上述情况下，我国出口交易程序大致分以下三个阶段。

(1) 出口交易前的准备阶段

出口交易前要编制出口计划，报有关主管部门批准，根据下达的计划落实货源。同时，要做好国际市场的调查，调查内容包括：

1）调查进口国（地区）政治、经济、对外贸易方面的情况和特点，以便正确选择销售市场；

2）调查有关商品在国际市场的生产、消耗、贸易、价格，以便正确掌握出口商品的价格及交易的其他条件；

3）调查有关客户对我国的政治态度、资信度、经营范围和能力等。

在调查的基础上，制定商品出口经营方案，确定收汇方式和推销策略，建立客户关系和推销网，开展广告宣传及办理商标注册等。

(2) 出口交易洽商与签订出口合同阶段

出口交易洽商可采用函电磋商方式，或派人到国外洽谈交易，或邀请外商参加我国的交易会，由双方当面磋商。一般需经询盘、发盘、还盘和接受等环节，有时需多次来往磋商才能达成交易。交易达成后，应签订销售合同，成交金额不大的一般货物可签订简化格式的售货确认书，将交易洽谈达成一致的内容以书面形式固定下来，作为履约和处理争议的依据。

(3) 履行出口合同阶段

履行出口合同的主要工作如下。

1）根据合同备妥货物。

2）如采用信用证方式收汇的交易则需向买方催开信用证，在收到信用证后，根据合同条款规定及《跟单信用证统一惯例》的规定进行审查，在确认无误后，方可备货。如发现不符又不能接受时，应及时通知买方改证。

3）办理商品检验、CIF（或 CIP）下办理保险、托运、报关和装运。

4）货物装运后，应发装运通知并按信用证要求缮制单据，在信用证有效期内，交银行议付和结汇。

5）如果在履约中出现问题，产生争议，可能需要索赔与理赔、仲裁或诉讼。

3. 2 Trade Terms

Trade Terms are specified terms composed of words or abbreviations in foreign letters used in international trade to indicate price component and relevant risk, obligation and expense allocation in commodity delivery. In quotation and contract signing, trade terms are inevitably used when it comes to price, therefore, trade terms are also called price terms.

Trade terms have been developing from long term trade practice and playing significant role in simplifying negotiation content, shortening dealing process, and reducing related expenses, which greatly promotes the development of international trade.

3. 2. 1 International Conventions of Trade Terms

Early in 19th century, trade terms were already used in international trade. However, there was no standard explanation to various trade terms. Later, some commercial organizations and academic institutions made explanations to trade terms and relative rules, some of which are widely acquainted, acknowledged and accepted in law and business community and thereby become international trade conventions.

The conventions of international trade terms are general practices and customs formed in international trade with stable and widely accepted contents, which, different from law, are not legally binding, except when a party concerned admits and applies them to business practice. For a long time, it is the law and conventions that underlie international trade.

(1) The Warsaw Oxford Rules 1932

The Warsaw Oxford Rules 1932 revised by the International Law Association mainly deals with CIF trade terms and specifically demonstrates the obligation allocation between the parties under CIF contract.

(2) The Revised American Foreign Trade Definitions 1941

In 1919, nine commercial organizations in USA formulated The U. S. Export Quotation and Abbreviations, which was revised in 1941 and thereby called The Revised American Foreign Trade Definitions 1941. The revision explains 6 trade terms and becomes influential in American countries. Since the explanations to trade terms, especially the ones to FOB terms are different from those given in other international conventions, one should be alert when dealing with countries in America.

(3) Incoterms

The ICC published the first set of international conventions explaining trade terms in 1936, namely Incoterms 1936, with eight revisions and supplements following in 1953, 1967, 1976, 1980, 1990, 2000, 2010, and 2020 in order to adapt to the need of international trade practice in different periods. The latest version of 2020 was published on September 10, 2019 and took effect on January 1, 2020 with rules defining the responsibilities of buyers and sellers for the delivery of goods under sales contracts. They are the authoritative rules for determining how costs and risks are allocated to the parties.

So far, among the above mentioned 3 international conventions, the latest Incoterms 2020 is the most versatile, the most widely applied and influential one. In view of internal transaction happening in some big regional trading blocks, Incoterms 2020 is also applicable to domestic sales.

3.2.2 Classification of Trade Terms

Incoterms 2000 explains 13 trade terms, using 4 letters as their codes and arranging the terms in an ascending order of seller's responsibility and the distance between delivery place and seller's premises. The terms are classified into four groups, namely E, F, C, and D. Incoterms 2010 made some revisions, where DDU, DAF, DES, and DEQ were removed whereas DAT and DAP were added to the terms. Incoterms 2010 classifies the terms into two groups according to the suitable mode of transport, one group suitable for any mode of transport (including EXW, FCA, CPT, CIP, DAT, DAP, and DDP) and the other only suitable for sea and inland waterway transport (including FAS, FOB, CFR, and CIF). With respect to Incoterms 2020, there came 7 Key changes among which DAT Incoterm 2010 was replaced by DPU, own transport rather than 3rd party transport is allowed in FCA, DAP, DPU and DDP, and Bill of Lading with an 'on board' notation should be issued by carrier in FCA.

The classification of Incoterms 2020 is shown in Figure 3.1, where the terms are classified into two groups according to the suitable mode of transport.

However, for convenience, we still introduce the terms using the classification adopted in Incoterms 2000.

(1) Term E

Group E is a term of departure and only includes term EXW (Ex Works … Named Place), meaning that the sellers make the goods available at their premises, or at another named place.

(2) Term F

Group F represents the terms under which main freight is unpaid, sellers are responsible for delivering the goods to the carrier nominated by the buyers. It involves 3 terms:

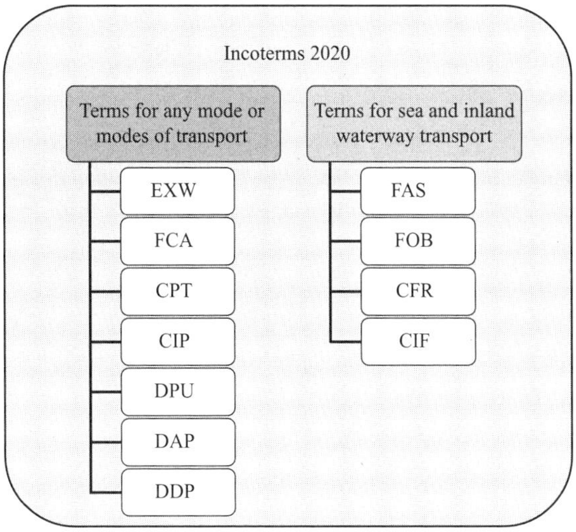

Figure 3.1 Classification of Incoterms 2020

1) FCA: Free Carrier…Named Place

2) FAS: Free Alongside Ship…Named Port of Shipment

3) FOB: Free On Board…Named Port of Shipment

(3) Term C

Group C represents the terms under which main freight is paid, which includes:

1) CFR: Cost and Freight…Named Port of Destination

2) CIF: Cost, Insurance and Freight…Named Port of Destination

3) CPT: Carriage Paid to…Named Place of Destination

4) CIP: Carriage and Insurance Paid to…Named Place of Destination

Under group C terms, sellers are responsible for arranging shipping contract and paying for the delivery of goods to named port or place. Under CIF and CIP, the sellers also need to apply for goods transport insurance and pay for the premium. They will have to bear the risk of loss of or damage to goods and extra expenses incurred before goods are loaded on board the ship at port (under CFR and CIF) or before the goods are handed over to the carrier at the place of shipment (in CPT and CIP), and transfer the risks to the buyers the moment goods get on board the vessel or are handed over to the carrier.

(4) Term D

Group D represents the terms of arrival, which includes:

1) DDP: Delivered Duty Paid…Named Place of Destination

2) DPU: Delivery at Place Unloaded…Named Place of Destination

3) DAP: Delivered At Place…Named Place of Destination

The sellers are responsible for shipping the goods to a named port or place and assuming all expenses and risks incurred.

3.2.3 Primary Trade Terms

In the 11 trade terms, FOB, CFR and CIF are typical port to port delivery method only applicable to ocean and inland water transportation, which are most widely used and thereby also called common trade terms. However, the three terms mentioned above fail to meet the new requirements in the context of diversified international transport methods and container centered multi-modal transport development. Accordingly, FCA, CPT and CIP came into being, which are applicable not only to single transport model such as railway, road, air, ocean, and inland water transportation, but also to container multi-modal transport. They are world widely used for their advantages of door-to-door delivery.

In the following text, introduction is made concerning the main obligations of the two parties under FOB, CFR, CIF and the corresponding FCA, CPT, and CIP.

(1) FOB (Free On Board)

FOB means that the seller delivers the goods on board the vessel nominated by the buyer at the named port of shipment. The risk of loss of or damage to the goods transfers from the seller to the buyer when the goods get on board the vessel, and the buyer bears all costs from the moment onward. The FOB term requires the seller to clear the goods for export. The obligations of the seller and the buyer are as follows:

1) Seller's Obligation

① Produces the goods and commercial documents as required in the sales contract.

② Arranges export clearance if stipulated in the sales contract.

③ Makes the goods available to the buyer after loading them on the vessel at the named port of shipment.

④ Assumes all risks to the goods (loss or damage) only up to the point they have been delivered onto the vessel at the named port, place, and time stipulated in the sales contract.

⑤ Seller must advise the buyer of the location and time that goods have been delivered onto the named vessel.

⑥ Seller has to provide the buyer with proof of delivery to the carrier or transport documents.

2) Buyer's Obligation

① Buyer must pay for the goods as per the sale contract.

② Buyer must obtain all commercial documentation, licenses, authorizations, and import formalities at his own risk and cost.

③ Buyer must take delivery of the goods after they have been delivered by the seller onto the vessel at the named port of origin.

④ Buyer must assume all risks and responsibility for the goods from the time the goods have been delivered onto the vessel to delivery into the buyer's warehouse or other specified location. Buyer pays for all costs of transportation, insurance, import customs and duty fees, and all other formalities and charges related to the transportation of the shipment from the time the goods have been delivered onto the vessel. This includes all costs relating to loss of or damage to the goods or non-delivery from the time the goods have been delivered onto the vessel.

⑤ Buyer would accept the seller's proof of delivery to the carrier or transport documents.

3) Attentions

① the explanation differences from that defined by USA

a. In USA, FOB term is interpreted as a means of delivery on any transport vehicle. Revised American Foreign Trade Definitions 1941 divided FOB terms into 6 categories, among which only FOB Vessel "named port of shipment" is similar to that interpreted in Incoterms 2020.

b. When it comes to customs clearance, USA regulates that the seller should render the buyer, only at the buyer's request and expense, assistance in obtaining the export documents issued, which is different from Incoterms 2020 in that the latter requires the seller to conduct customs clearance and undertake the corresponding expense.

For the above reasons, Chinese foreign trade companies, when negotiating or signing contract with USA or other American traders in the light of FOB terms, should put the word "Vessel" after FOB, demonstrate the named port, and clarify the seller's responsibility to get export license and pay for all export duties and taxes and other expenses.

② Loading on board charges

Buyer prefers shipping by chartering in the case of bulk commodity transaction agreed under FOB terms. He should negotiate with the seller on who should bear loading charges such as stowage and trimming fee and specify the provisions in the contract. He would usually attach additional clauses after FOB terms, which makes FOB variations possible.

a. FOB liner terms: all the loading charges constitute part of freight and is borne by the party who pays for the freight (i. e. the buyer), as happens in liner service.

b. FOB under tackle: the seller is only responsible for transferring goods to the buyer under the hook of the designated ship, with the loading charges after the lifting of the goods borne by the buyer.

c. FOB stowed: the seller is responsible for loading the goods into the cabin and paying for the loading charges including stowage fee. Stowage fee refers to the expenses paid for settlement, organization, leveling and separation of goods in the cabin.

d. FOB trimmed: the seller is responsible for loading the goods into the cabin and paying for the loading charges including trimming fee. Trimming fee refers to the expenses paid for smoothing and organizing of bulk commodity in order to keep the ship from tilting and hull damage.

In many standard contracts, FOB stowed and trimmed (FOBST) is used to indicate that the seller bears all the loading fees. This is applicable to the situation where the seller is responsible for loading in the case of chartering.

The above-mentioned FOB variations only differ in who should bear the loading fees, but this does not influence the nature of FOB, where risk is transferred from the moment goods are put on board the ship.

(2) CIF Cost, Insurance & Freight (named port of destination)

CIF involves the seller, within the stipulated time of shipment, handing over the goods onto the ship to named port of destination at the port of departure and timely notifying the buyer of the shipment. The seller should pay for all charges incurred before the goods get on board the vessel and take the risk of loss and damage, be responsible for insurance application and charting arrangement or cargo space booking, and paying for insurance premium and shipment fees from port of departure to port of destination.

In contrast with FOB, CIF lays heavier obligations on the seller by requiring him to arrange insurance and transportation and pay for corresponding fees. Under CIF, the obligations of the seller and the buyer are as follows:

1) Seller's obligation

① Within the stipulated time of shipment, the seller hands over the required goods onto the ship to the port of destination and timely gives notice that goods have been delivered on board.

② Settles export formalities and obtains export license or other approvals needed.

③ Arranges chartering or cargo space booking and pays for the freight to the port of destination.

④ Buys insurance from the delivery point to (at least) the destination port. Incoterms 2020 requires 'Institute Cargo Clause C' [ICC(C)] insurance cover under CIF. The insurance shall cover, at a minimum the price provided in the contract, plus 10% (i. e. 110% of the price).

⑤ Bears all the expenses and risks arising before the goods get on board the vessel.

⑥ Provides commercial invoice, insurance policy, and shipment documents indicating the shipment of cargo to the port of destination, or equivalent electronic documents.

2) Buyer's obligation

① Settles import formalities and obtains import license and other approvals needed.

② Bears all the expenses and risks arising after the goods are put on board the vessel.

③ Makes payment upon documents.

3) Attentions

① CIF contract adopts symbolic delivery: Different from actual delivery, under symbolic delivery the seller delivers when he completes loading at designated place on time and submits all documents required to the buyer. The seller doesn't have to guarantee the actual arrival of the goods. The seller delivers goods and the buyer makes payment, both upon documents; for this reason, the transaction is also known as sale by documents. To the contrary, actual delivery requires the seller to make real and true handover of the goods to the buyer or a named party at designated time and place and guarantee the arrival of the goods.

CIF is a shipment contract where the seller only guarantees loading of the goods and submission of documents, but not the arrival of goods, not to say the risk taking after the goods get on board, which makes it a typical symbolic delivery. The moment the seller timely submits qualified documents, the buyer must make payment despite any damage to or loss of the goods onward. Therefore, in CIF negotiation, the seller should keep alert on trap clauses requiring seller to guarantee the arrival of the goods or committing payment against arrival. However, the buyer is entitled not to pay on arrival of qualified goods if the seller doesn't submit the required documents. What should also be clarified is that the seller must perform his obligation of goods delivery except the submission of documents which is only a prerequisite of getting paid. If the goods delivered fail to meet requirement, the buyer is entitled to reject the goods and claim reimbursement even after payment.

Thus, the documents are of great importance in CIF, which clearly define when and where a seller should submit what documents. Generally, for purpose of foreign exchange receipt, the seller would submit the documents required as soon as possible once the goods is delivered. However, things would be different if payable at usance is agreed upon, where the seller is not anxious in documents submission and consequently the buyer is deprived of his right of reselling the goods by reselling the documents. Therefore, it is deemed an implied obligation in international trade that the seller should submit the documents required as soon as possible.

② Who bears discharging expenses: similar to FOB, the parties should make it clear in the contract on who should pay for cargo discharging at destination port when chartering is used to bulk commodities in a CIF contract. Usually, additional provisions are attached after CIF terms, which make some CIF variations possible:

a. CIF liner terms: the discharging expense is on the party who pays for shipment (i. e. the seller), same as settled in liner.

b. CIF ex ship's hold: the buyer handles the discharging and is responsible for discharging expense till the goods are settled to the port.

c. CIF ex tackle: the seller is responsible for discharging expense from the moment the goods are hooked from cabin floor to alongside the ship till the goods is unhooked.

d. CIF landed: the seller is responsible for discharging the cargo to land and the payment incurred.

CIF variations only illustrate who bears discharging expense, without changing place of delivery or risk allocation in a CIF contract.

③ Special interpretation in USA: The CIF in USA defines named destination, generally referring to port of destination, any port or inland location at destination, making it applicable in larger scope.

(3) CFR

Under CFR, seller must deliver the goods at port of shipment and put them on the ship to the named port of destination within time of shipment as stipulated in the contract, and make timely notification to the buyer of the shipment. In addition, the seller should bear all expenses and risk of loss of or damage to the goods arising before the goods get on board and be responsible for chartering or cargo space booking, and paying for freight on the arrival of goods at port of destination as well.

CFR makes basically the same division of obligation to the parties as in CIF and adopts the same method with CIF in who should bear discharging expense. However, it differs from CIF in that the cargo insurance application and premium payment are the responsibilities of the buyer. The seller should timely notify the buyer of the shipment for the latter to arrange cargo insurance, failing to do so will incur risk assumption in the transportation by the seller.

The above mentioned three terms are applicable to ocean and inland water transportation, with same risk allocation but different obligation division, formality arrangement and expense payment on the part of seller and buyer. The relationship between the three terms is shown in Figure 3.2.

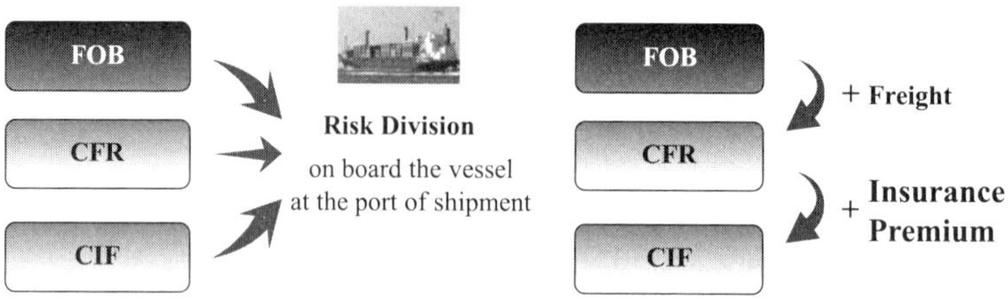

Figure 3.2 Relationship between FOB, CFR and CIF

(4) FCA

In FCA, the seller delivers after he completes export customs clearance, puts goods under the supervision of a named carrier at designated time and place, and submits commercial invoice or equivalent electronic documents required. The expenses incurred and the risk of loss and damage are on the seller till the goods are put under the supervision of the carrier; whereas the transportation, all the charges and risks incurred afterwards are transferred to the buyer. The buyer is responsible for timely advising the seller of the carrier's name, delivery time and place, arranging import customs clearance formalities, receiving goods, and making payment as stipulated in the contract.

There are some issues to be noticed in the use of FCA.

1) Delivery place and method: FCA is applicable to all transport means; accordingly, delivery places such as railway depot, departure airport, container port, and named delivery place vary depending on mode of transport which should be specified in the contract. Whatever mode of transportation is adopted, containerized or not, the seller's obligation of delivery is done as long as he loads the goods onto the conveyance of the carrier nominated by the buyer or his agent at named place, or puts the goods under the carrier's supervision at a place other than his own locale, even without unloading the goods from his conveyance.

2) Risk transfer and expenses bearing: in FCA, the point used to allocate expenses and transfer risk is when the seller delivers the goods to the carrier. The moment the seller delivers the goods to the carrier in negotiated way at required time, the risk is transferred to the buyer, the latter bearing the expenses incurred afterwards. On the premise that the buyer timely notifies the seller of shipment issue, the seller should arrange export customs clearance formalities and pay for customs fees, duties, taxes and other fees. If the buyer fails to nominate a carrier/agent or notify the seller, or the agent fails to take over the goods, the cargo risk and expenses should be borne by the buyer since the delivery date agreed upon or the date delivery period expires.

3) Issuance of Bill of Lading with an 'on board' notation: in the past, carriers have frequently refused to issue a Bill of Lading with a notation to the seller if they have received the goods from an intermediary transport (such as a truck), instead of directly from the seller, which is one of the reasons many sellers prefer FOB. To encourage exporters of containerized goods to use the term of FCA, provisions have been made to the Incoterms® 2020

to state that, if agreed in the contract, the buyer should instruct the carrier to issue a transport document stating that the goods have been loaded- i. e. , a Bill of Lading with an 'on board' notation.

(5) CPT

Under CPT, the seller concludes a transportation contract, pays for the freight till goods arrive at named destination, bears all the risk and expenses before the goods are put under the supervision of first carrier, timely notifies the buyer of the shipment, arranges export customs clearance formalities, and submits required documents or equivalent electronic documents as well. The buyer should bear all the expenses and risks the moment the first carrier takes over the goods, arrange cargo insurance and pay for insurance premium, receive and discharge the goods at destination, and receive documents and make corresponding payment as stipulated in the contract.

The following application issues should be given enough attention in the use of CPT:

1) Time of shipment and named place at destination should be specified in the contract, so that the seller could choose carrier and perform transportation.

2) Seller's duty to notify the buyer of the goods delivery should be expressly indicated in the contract, in order that the buyer arranges insurance after shipment. This helps in settling possible disputes in the future.

3) When the buyer is to decide the time of shipment and destination, it is extremely essential to indicate in the contract that he is responsible for making notification to the seller. Failing to do so or late notification for reason of market fluctuation may result in late shipment on the part of the seller. In this case, the buyer should bear the risk and extra expenses incurred since the agreed date of departure or the date when time of shipment expires.

(6) CIP

Under CIP, the seller, apart from taking the responsibility same as regulated in CPT, should arrange insurance covering the risk of loss and damage happening in the transportation and pay for insurance premium.

Similar to CIF, the seller doesn't necessarily guarantee the arrival of goods and the delivery is done once the seller hands over the goods to the carrier as required in the contract. Furthermore, when buying insurance, it should be assured that the minimum insured amount which covers 110 percent of the contract value is required.

FCA, CPT, and CIP have developed from FOB, CFR, and CIF, with basically same principle of obligation division, but there are differences in the following aspects:

1) Applicable to different transportation mode: FOB, CFR and CIF are only applicable to water transport, while the other three to all transport modes including multi-modal transport.

2) The point used to define delivery and divide risks: FOB, CFR and CIF use board of the ship at shipment port to define delivery and divide risk, while the other three use delivery of goods to the carrier (the first carrier in the case of multi-modal transport) as division line.

3) Different allocation of handling expenses: under FOB, CFR and CIF, the seller

should pay for all expenses incurred before the goods get on board; however, he has to pay for the regular freight till the goods arrive at port of destination under CFR and CIF. In FOB contract, it should be defined who bears loading charges, while under CFR and CIF who pays for discharging is clarified. Seller pays for expenses incurred before the delivery of goods to carrier under FCA, therefore, loading charges should be included in the transportation contract and undertaken by the buyer. The seller under CPT and CIP needs to pay for the freight, which includes charges for loading and discharging, till the goods are shipped to place of destination.

4) Different shipment document submitted: under FOB, CFR and CIF, the seller should submit Ocean Bill of Lading, while in FCA, CPT and CIP, the document could be Railway Bill, Roadway Bill, Parcel Post Receipt, or Combined Transport Documents (CTD), depending on the mode of transport. It is worth to be noticed that Incoterms 2020 regulates the issuance of bill of lading with an "on board" notation by carrier to seller in FCA.

5) Different insurance cover with CIF: Incoterms 2020 requires an upgraded 'Institute Cargo Clause A' [ICC (A)] insurance cover under CIP. ICC (A) indicates its insurance coverage by covering all risks other than "exclusions". It is equivalent to All Risks as in the China Insurance Clauses, but its coverage is wider.

3.2.4 Other Five Trade Terms

(1) EXW——Ex Works (named place of delivery)

The seller makes the goods available at their premises, or at another named place. This term places the maximum obligation on the buyer and minimum obligation on the seller. The Ex Works term is often used when making an initial quotation for the sale of goods without any other costs included.

EXW means that a buyer bears the risk for bringing the goods to their final destination. The seller does not load the goods on collecting vehicles or clear them for export, or even though he does load the goods, he does so at buyer's risk and cost. If the parties agree that the seller should be responsible for loading of goods on departure and bearing the risk and cost incurred, it must be made clear by adding explicit wording to this effect in the contract of sale.

There is no obligation on either the seller or buyer to arrange a contract of carriage, the buyer may sell the goods on to his own customer for collection of goods from the original seller's warehouse. However, in common practice, the buyer arranges the collection of the freight from the designated location, and is responsible for clearing the goods through Customs and completing all the export documentation.

(2) FAS——Free Alongside Ship (named port of shipment)

The seller delivers when the goods are placed alongside the buyer's vessel at the named port of shipment. This means that the buyer has to bear all costs and risk of loss of or damage to the goods from that moment. The FAS term requires the seller to clear the goods for export at his own cost.

(3) DPU——Delivered at Place Unloaded (named place of destination)

Due to problems in the interpretation of the term "terminal" in DAT Incoterms 2010 (Delivered at Terminal) rule, in Incoterms 2020 the DPU rule was created to replace DAT. It is because the destination terminal was often confused with the customs terminal. In DPU, the seller is responsible for arranging carriage and for delivering the goods, unloaded from the arriving means of transport, at the named place which should be specified precisely. There are no restrictions on the named place, for example, it can be a transport hub, a warehouse or the buyer's depot. Risk transfers from seller to buyer when the goods have been unloaded. This is the only rule that requires the seller to unload the goods in order to complete delivery. The buyer is responsible for import clearance and any applicable local taxes or import duties.

(4) DAP——Delivered at Place (named place of destination)

Incoterms 2020 defines DAP as 'Delivered at Place'. It means that the seller delivers when the goods are placed at the disposal of the buyer on the arrival of named conveyance ready for unloading at the named place of destination. Under DAP terms, the risk transfers from seller to buyer from the point of destination mentioned in the contract of delivery.

Once goods are ready for shipment, necessary packing is carried out by the seller at his own cost, so that the goods can reach their final destination safely. All necessary legal formalities in the exporting country are completed by the seller at his own cost and risk to clear the goods for export.

After arrival of the goods in the country of destination, the customs clearance in the importing country needs to be completed by the buyer at his own cost and risk, including all customs duties and taxes. However, any delay or demurrage charges are to be borne by the seller.

Under DAP terms, freight and any terminal expenses are paid by seller up to the agreed destination point. Necessary discharging cost at final destination has to be borne by seller too.

(5) DDP——Delivered Duty Paid (named place of destination)

Under DDP, seller is responsible for delivering the goods to the named place in the country of the buyer, and pays for all costs in doing so including import duties and taxes. The seller is not responsible for unloading however. This term places the maximum obligation on the seller and minimum obligation on the buyer. No risk or responsibility is transferred to the buyer until delivery of the goods at the named place of destination.

The most important consideration for DDP terms is that the seller is responsible for clearing the goods through customs in the buyer's country, including both paying duties and taxes, and obtaining necessary authorizations and registrations from the authorities in that country. Unless the rules and regulations in the buyer's country are very well understood, DDP terms can be of great risk to seller and should be used with caution.

The text above introduces the customs clearance in the 11 terms of Incoterms 2020. In those terms, the seller is responsible for export clearance and the buyer for import clearance, except in EXW and DDP, wherein the buyer and the seller are respectively to arrange export clearance and import clearance. The expenses involved in the terms include: ① cargo

Table 3.1 Comparison of Incoterms 2020 Rules

Term	Freight Collect Terms				Freight Prepaid Terms						
	EXW	FCA	FAS	FOB	CPT	CFR	CIF	CIP	DPU	DAP	DDP
	Ex Works (Place)	Free Carrier (Place)	Free Alongside Ship(Port)	Free On Board(Port)	Carriage Paid To (Place)	Cost and Freight(Port)	Cost Insurance& Freight(Port)	Carriage& Insurance Paid To (Place)	Delivered at Place Unloaded (Place)	Delivered at Place(Place)	Delivered Duty Paid (Place)
Transfer of Risk	At Buyer's Disposal	On Buyer's Transport	Alongside Ship	On Board Vessel	At Carrier	On Board Vessel	On Board Vessel	At Carrier	At Named Place Unloaded	At Named Place	At Named Place
Cost Allocation											
Loading at origin	Buyer	Seller	Seller	Seller	Seller	Seller	Seller	Seller	Seller	Seller	Seller
Export customs declaration	Buyer	Seller	Seller	Seller	Seller	Seller	Seller	Seller	Seller	Seller	Seller
Carriage to port of export	Buyer	Buyer/seller	Seller	Seller	Seller	Seller	Seller	Seller	Seller	Seller	Seller
Unloading from truck in port of export	Buyer	Buyer	Seller	Seller	Seller	Seller	Seller	Seller	Seller	Seller	Seller
Loading on vessel/airplane in port of export	Buyer	Buyer	Buyer	Seller	Seller	Seller	Seller	Seller	Seller	Seller	Seller
Carriage (sea/air) to port of import	Buyer	Buyer	Buyer	Buyer	Seller	Seller	Seller	Seller	Seller	Seller	Seller
insurance	Buyer	Buyer	Buyer	Buyer	Buyer	Buyer	Seller	Seller	Seller	Seller	Seller
Unloading in port of import	Buyer	Buyer	Buyer	Buyer	Buyer/seller	Buyer	Buyer	Buyer/seller	Seller	Seller	Seller
Loading on truck in port of import	Buyer	Buyer	Buyer	Buyer	Buyer/seller	Buyer	Buyer	Buyer/seller	Seller	Seller	Seller
Carriage to place of destination	Buyer	Buyer	Buyer	Buyer	Seller	Buyer	Buyer	Seller	Seller	Seller	Seller
Import customs clearance	Buyer	Buyer	Buyer	Buyer	Buyer	Buyer	Buyer	Buyer	Buyer	Buyer	Seller
Import duties and taxes	Buyer	Buyer	Buyer	Buyer	Buyer	Buyer	Buyer	Buyer	Buyer	Buyer	Seller
Unloading at destination	Buyer	Buyer	Buyer	Buyer	Buyer	Buyer	Buyer	Buyer	Seller	Buyer	Buyer

related expenses (e. g. freight, insurance premium, packing and examination fees); ②customs clearance expenses (e. g. export permits, customs formalities charges for import and export, transit transport, customs duty and tax); ③other charges.

Other changes in Incoterms 2020 compared to Incoterms 2010 include cost allocation and permission of seller/buyer's own means of transport.

Costs became quite a problem with Incoterms 2010 with some parties. In some cases, carriers were changing their pricing, so sellers were often faced with new back charged terminal handling charges. Incoterms 2020 now provides much more details around costs and clearly states which costs are allocated to each party.

Under Incoterms 2010 it was assumed that all transport would be undertaken by a third-party transport provider. Updates to Incoterms 2020 allow for the provision of the buyer or seller's own means of transport. This recognizes that some buyers and sellers are using their own methods of transport, including trucks or planes, to make the delivery.

- This allows for the buyer's own means of transport under the FCA rule;
- This allows for the seller's own means of transport under DAP, DPU and DDP.

Table 3. 1 summarizes the differences between terms in Incoterms 2020.

3. 2 贸易术语

贸易术语（Trade Terms）是在国际贸易中，用以表示商品的价格构成，以及商品交接过程中有关风险、责任和费用划分问题的以文字或外文缩写字母组成的专门用语。由于对外报价和签订合同时，涉及价格问题时都离不开贸易术语，因而亦称之为价格术语（Price Terms）。

贸易术语是在长期的贸易实践中产生的，并随着国际贸易的发展而发展变化。贸易术语的出现对于简化交易洽商的内容、缩短成交的过程、节省业务费用等都具有重要的作用，因此，贸易术语的运用促进了国际贸易的发展。

3. 2. 1 贸易术语的国际惯例

早在 19 世纪初，在国际贸易中已开始使用贸易术语。但是，最初对各种贸易术语并无统一的解释。后来，某些商业团体，学术机构为了消除分歧，有利于国际贸易的发展，曾先后作过关于贸易术语的解释和制订规则。有些解释和规则为较多国家的法律界和工商界所熟悉、承认和接受，成为有关贸易术语的国际贸易惯例。

国际贸易术语的国际惯例，是在国际贸易实践中逐渐形成的内容较为固定的贸易习惯和一般做法，它不同于法律之处在于不具有强制性，只有当事人承认并在实际业务中采用时，才对当事人有约束力。长期以来，国际贸易就是在法律和惯例的基础上进行的。

(1) 1932 年华沙-牛津规则

国际法协会修订的《1932 年华沙-牛津规则》。该规则主要说明 CIF 贸易术语，对 CIF 合同的买卖双方各项责任划分的阐述较为具体。

(2) 1941 年美国对外贸易定义修正本

1919 年，美国九个大商业团体制定了《美国出口报价及其缩写条例》，1941 年作了修改，并改称《1941 年美国对外贸易定义修正本》。该修正本对六种贸易术语作了解释，在美洲国家有较大的影响。由于它对贸易术语的解释，特别是对 FOB 术语的解释，在某些方面与其他国际惯例的解释有所不同，在与美洲地区国家进行交易时，应予特别注意。

(3) 国际贸易术语解释通则

国际商会(ICC)于1936年首次公布了一套解释贸易术语的国际规则，名为《1936年国际贸易术语解释通则》(简称Incoterms 1936)。为了适应不同时期国际贸易实践的需要，曾先后于1953年、1967年、1976年、1980年、1990年、2000年、2010年和2020年对该通则作了八次修订和补充。最新版即Incoterms 2020于2019年9月10日发布，并于2020年1月1日起生效，其规则界定了买卖双方根据销售合同交付货物的责任。这些是确定费用和风险如何分配给各方的权威性规则。

目前，上述三种与贸易术语有关的国际惯例中，Incoterms 2020是包括内容最多、适用范围最广、影响最大的贸易术语国际惯例。鉴于一些大的地区性贸易区块的内部交易，Incoterms 2020也适用于国内贸易。

3.2.2 贸易术语的分类

Incoterms 2000共解释了13种贸易术语，分别以三个字母的符号作为13种贸易术语的代码，并将13种贸易术语按卖方责任由小到大、交货地点与卖方所在地距离由近到远进行排列，按各种术语的共同特点分别归类，分成E、F、C、D四组。而Incoterms 2010对此进行了修改，在D组中删除了DDU、DAF、DES和DEQ，而增加了DAT和DAP两个术语。Incoterms 2010将这些术语依照其适用的运输模式分成两类，一类适用于所有运输模式(包括EXW、FCA、CPT、CIP、DAT、DAP和DDP)，另一类仅适用于海运及内河运输(包括FAS、FOB、CFR和CIF)。Incoterms 2020有7个关键变化，其中DAT Incoterms被DPU取代，FCA、DAP、DPU和DDP中允许自有运输而不仅是第三方运输，FCA中承运人应签发装船批注提单。Incoterms 2020按其适合的运输方式分类可见图3.1。

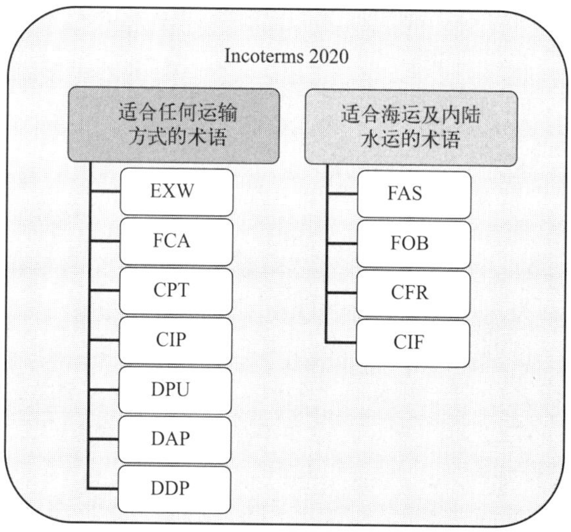

图3.1 Incoterms 2020术语分类

然而，方便起见，我们仍然按照Incoterms 2000的分类方法对术语进行介绍。

(1) E组

E组为启运术语，只有一个术语。

EXW(Ex Works…Named Place)工厂交货……指定地点。

(2) F组

F组为主运费未付术语，卖方应负责将货物交给由买方指定的承运人。包括以下三个术语：

1）FCA（Free Carrier…Named Place）货交承运人……指定地点。

2）FAS（Free Alongside Ship…Named Port of Shipment）船边交货……指定装运港。

3）FOB（Free On Board…Named Port of Shipment）船上交货……指定装运港。

(3) C组

C组为主运费已付术语，包括以下四个术语。

1）CFR（Cost and Freight…Named Port of Destination）成本加运费……指定目的港。

2）CIF（Cost，Insurance and Freight…Named Port of Destination）成本加保险费和运费……指定目的港。

3）CPT（Carriage Paid to…Named Place of Destination）运费付至……指定目的地。

4）CIP（Carriage and Insurance Paid to…Named Place of Destination）运费、保险费付至……指定目的地。

C组术语的卖方必须负责订立运输合同，并支付到合同规定的目的港或目的地的正常运费。其中CIF和CIP的卖方尚需负责投保货物运输险并支付保险费。卖方还需承担货物在装运港装上船（CFR，CIF）或在发货地将货物交给承运人接管（CPT，CIP）之前，货物的灭失或损坏以及额外增加费用的风险，并于货物装上船或交付承运人接管时转移给买方。

(4) D组

D组为到达术语，包括以下三种术语。

1）DDP（Delivered Duty Paid…Named Place of Destination）完税后交货……指定目的地。

2）DPU（Delivery at Place Unloaded…Named Place of Destination）卸货地点交货……指定目的地。

3）DAP（Delivered At Place…Named Place of Destination）指定地点交货……指定目的地。

按这类术语，卖方必须负责将货物运送到约定的目的港或目的地，并承担货物交到目的港或目的地为止的一切费用和风险。

3.2.3 主要的贸易术语

在11种贸易术语中，FOB、CFR和CIF是典型的“港至港”的交货方式，仅适用于海洋与内河运输，是采用最早和最普遍的贸易术语，亦称常用贸易术语。随着国际物流运输方式的多样化以及以集装箱为主体的多式联运的发展，上述三种贸易术语已不能适应发展需要。FCA、CPT和CIP不仅适用于铁路、公路、航空、海洋和内河等单一的运输方式，同时也适用于集装箱多式联运，并以“门到门”交货方式的优势，在世界范围内得到普遍采用。

以下对FOB、CFR和CIF以及对应的FCA、CPT和CIP等六种贸易术语下买卖双方的主要义务和运用注意事项等逐一介绍。

(1) FOB

FOB亦称“离岸价”，FOB是指卖方在指定的发货港将货物交至买方指定的船上，并承担在此之前货物灭失或损坏的风险，而此后的成本则由买方承担。这一术语要求卖方办理货物的结关。买卖双方的义务如下。

1）卖方义务

① 按合同约定生产商品并提供商业单据。

② 如果合同中有规定则安排出口通关手续。

③ 在指定的发货港将货物装上船。

④ 承担指定的时间于指定的港口、地点将货物装上船之前的一切风险。

⑤ 向买方告知将货物装上指定船只的地点及时间。

⑥ 向买方提供货发承运人的证明或运输单据。

2）买方义务

① 买方必须按照合同进行付款。

② 买方必须安排全部商业单据、许可、批准，办理进口手续，并承担相应风险及成本；

③ 当货物在指定港口由卖方交上船之后，买方需接收货物。

④ 在货物交至船上之后，直到被送入买方仓库或其他特定地点之前的这段时间内，买方承担全部的风险和责任。买方需支付全部的运输、保险、进口清关和关税，以及其他手续所产生的成本，承担货物交至船上之后产生的运杂费。这包括了货物运至船上之后而产生的与货物损失或货交不到有关的一切成本。

⑤ 买方接收卖方提交的货交承运人证明或运输单据。

3）运用时的注意事项

① 与美国对 FOB 术语的解释存在差异

a. 美国对 FOB 术语解释为在任何一种运输工具上交货。《1941 年美国对外贸易定义修正本》将 FOB 术语分为六种，其中，只有“指定装运港船上交货”与 Incoterms 2020 所解释的 FOB 术语相近。

b. 在结关手续方面，美国规定卖方只是在买方请求并承担费用的情况下，协助买方取得出口证件。这与 Incoterms 2020 中要求卖方自行出口结关并承担相应费用的解释不同。

因此，我外贸企业在与美国和其他美洲国家出口商按 FOB 术语洽谈进口业务，签订合同时，应在 FOB 术语后加注“Vessel”字样，并列明装运港名称，同时应明确由卖方负责取得出口许可证，支付一切出口税及费用。

② 装船费用的负担。按 FOB 条件成交的大宗商品，买方通常采用租船运输。买卖双方对包括理舱费和平舱费在内的装船费用由谁负担需进行洽商，并在合同中作具体规定，通常是在 FOB 术语之后列附加条件，从而产生了以下 FOB 的变形。

a. FOB liner terms（班轮条件）。指所有装船费用如同以班轮运输那样，全部加在运费里，由支付运费的一方（买方）负担。

b. FOB under tackle（吊钩下交货）。指卖方仅负责将货物交到买方指派船只的吊钩所及之处，从货物起吊开始的装船费用由买方负担。

c. FOB stowed（FOBS，包括理舱费）。指卖方负责将货物装入船舱并负担包括理舱费在内的装船费用。理舱费是指货物进入舱底后，对其进行安置、整理和垫隔所支付的费用。

d. FOB trimmed（FOBT，包括平舱费）。指卖方负责将货物装入船舱并负担包括平舱费在内的装船费用。平舱费是指为保证航行时船身平稳和不损坏船身结构，对大宗散装货物进行削平、整理所支付的费用。

在许多标准合同中，还采用 FOB stowed and trimmed（FOBST，包括理舱和平舱费）

来表示卖方负担所有装船费用，适用于租船运输下由卖方负责装船作业的情形。

上述FOB的变形只是用以表明装船费用由谁负担，并不改变FOB的性质，即以货装置船上为界划分风险及交货地点。

(2) CIF

CIF亦称“到岸价”，是指卖方必须在合同规定的装运期内在装运港将货物交至运往指定目的港的船上，装运后及时通知买方。卖方需承担货物装上船为止的一切费用和货物灭失或损坏的风险，并负责办理货运保险和租船或订舱，支付保险费和从装运港到目的港的运费。

与FOB相比，CIF卖方责任加重，需增加办理保险与运输，并支付相应费用。买卖双方主要义务如下。

1）卖方义务

① 在合同规定的装运港和装运期内，将符合合同规定的货物交至运往指定目的港的船上，并及时向买方发出装船通知。

② 办理货物出口手续，取得出口许可证或其他核准书。

③ 租船或订舱，并支付至目的港的运费。

④ 购买从交货点（至少）到目的港的保险。Incoterms 2020 要求CIF下卖方购买“Institute Cargo Clause C”［ICC（C）］保险。保险金额应至少涵盖合同价格另加成10%（即合同价格的110%）。

⑤ 承担货物在装运港装上船为止的一切费用和风险。

⑥ 提供商业发票、保险单和货物运往目的港的通常运输单据或等同的电子单证。

2）买方义务

① 办理进口手续，取得进口许可证或其他核准书。

② 承担货物在装运港装货上船后的一切费用和风险。

③ 按合同规定付款赎单。

3）运用时的注意事项

① CIF合同采用象征性交货。象征性交货是针对实际交货而言的，是指卖方只要在约定地点按期完成装运，并向买方提交合同规定的各项单据就算完成交货义务，无需保证到货。所以卖方凭单交货，买方凭单付款，这样的交易也被称为单据买卖。实际交货则要求卖方在规定的时间、地点将符合合同规定的货物真实地交给买方或其指定人，保证安全到货。

CIF合同属装运合同性质，卖方只要保证装船交单，既不保证到货，也不承担货物装上船之后的风险，是一种典型的象征性交货。只要卖方如期提交合格的单据，即使货物运输途中发生损坏或灭失，买方也必须付款。因此，在CIF合同的谈判中，要防止出现要求卖方保证到货或以到货作为付款条件的陷阱条款。反之，如果卖方交单不符，即使合格货物安全到达，买方仍有权拒付货款。还需要澄清的是卖方交单只是其获得货款的前提条件，他仍然要履行交货义务。如果卖方提交的货物不符合要求，买方即使已经付款，仍有权拒收货物并追偿已付款项。

由此可见，单据在CIF合同的重要性。在合同中明确规定卖方在什么时候、什么地方提交什么单据是十分必要的。一般地，出于及时收汇的愿望，卖方会在货物付运后尽快交单。但双方同意远期付款时，卖方就不会急于去交单。这样会使买方丧失在运输途中以转卖单据方式转售货物的权利。所以国际上有卖方应尽快交单的默示责任。

② 卸货费用的负担。与FOB相类似，如大宗货物CIF合同使用租船运输，在目的港由

谁来支付卸货费，买卖双方应在合同中订明。一般也采用在 CIF 术语之后列附加条件，由此产生以下 CIF 的变形条件。

a. CIF liner terms（班轮条件）。指卸货费用按班轮条件处理，由支付运费的一方（卖方）负担。

b. CIF ex ships hold（舱底交货）。由买方自行启舱，负担将货物从舱底起吊卸到码头的卸货费用。

c. CIF ex tackle（吊钩交货）。由卖方负担将货物从舱底吊至船边卸离吊钩为止的费用。

d. CIF landed（卸到岸上）。卖方负责将货卸到岸上，并负担由此引起的费用。

CIF 的变形也只是说明卸货费负担问题，不改变 CIF 的交货地点和风险划分界限。

③ 美国的特殊解释。美国定义的 CIF 是指定的目的地，泛指目的港和目的地的任何港口和内陆地点，因而适用范围更广。

(3) CFR

CFR 亦称“到岸价”，卖方必须在合同规定的装运期和装运港将货物交至运往指定目的港的船上，并及时通知买方。承担货物装至船上为止的一切费用和货物灭失或损失的风险，并负责租船或订舱、支付货物抵达目的港的正常运费。

CFR 与 CIF 合同中关于买卖双方义务的划分基本相同，而且 CFR 合同在解决卸货费负担问题上所采用的方法也与 CIF 一致。两者不同之处仅在于：CFR 合同下，货运保险手续由买方自行办理，并支付保险费。但卖方在装船后需及时向买方发出装船通知，以便买方能及时办理货运保险，否则卖方须承担因买方未及时办理保险而货物在运输途中可能出现的风险。

上述三种适用于海洋和内河运输的贸易术语，就买卖双方而言，在风险划分上是一致的，主要区别在于双方承担的责任、办理的手续和支付的费用不同。三种术语的关系如图 3.2 所示。

图 3.2 FOB、CFR 及 CIF 关系

(4) FCA

FCA 是由卖方办理货物出口结关手续，在指定时间和地点把货物交给买方指定的承运人监管，同时提交商业发票或等同的电子单据，就算完成交货义务。卖方承担货物交由承运人监管为止的一切费用和货物灭失或损坏的风险；而买方要自费办理运输，承担货交承运人后的一切费用和风险，并将有关承运人名称、交货时间与地点及时通知卖方，办理进口结关手续，按合同规定收取货物和支付货款。

运用 FCA 时需注意以下问题。

1) 交货地点和方式：由于 FCA 适用于各种运输方式，它的交货地点也要因运输方式而异，通常要在合同中作明确规定。如铁路货运站、启运机场、集装箱码头、指定交货点等。无论采用哪一种运输方式，也不区别集装箱货与非集装箱货，卖方只要在指定的交货地点将货物装上买方或其代理指定的承运人提供的运输工具，或卖方在其处所以外交货点将货物置于买方指定的承运人监管之下，甚至无需将货卸离卖方的运输工具，就算完成向承运人交货的义务。

2）风险转移与费用承担：对FCA合同双方来说，风险转移与费用承担的分界点是在卖方向承运人交付货物时。当卖方按合同规定的时间，以约定的方式向承运人交付货物时起，货物风险转移至买方，并由买方承担货物交付时起的与货物有关的费用。鉴于出口结关手续由卖方办理，因而由卖方而非买方承担出口支付的海关费用、关税、捐税和其他费用。但这是以买方及时而充分地通知卖方运输事宜为前提的。如果买方未指定承运人或代理人，或代理人未接管货物，或未通知卖方，则货物风险及费用从约定交付日或约定交付期届满日起由买方承担。

3）承运人签发带有装船批注的提单：以往，如果承运人从中间运输工具（例如卡车）而非直接从卖方收到货物，则承运人经常拒绝向卖方签发带有批注的提单，这也是很多卖家更喜欢选择FOB的原因之一。为鼓励集装箱货物的出口商使用FCA条款，Incoterms 2020做出了规定，如双方在合同中达成协议，则买方应指示承运人签发一份运输文件以说明货物已装船，即装船批注提单。

(5) CPT

CPT术语下，卖方订立运输合同，支付货物运至指定目的地的运费，承担货交第一承运人接管前的一切风险和费用，交货后及时通知买方，办理出口清关手续，并提供约定的各项单证或等同的电子单证；买方则应承担货交第一承运人接管时起的一切费用和风险，办理货运保险和支付保险费，在目的地接卸货物，并按合同规定领取单证和支付货款等。

运用CPT术语应注意的问题。

1）合同中要明确装运期和目的地指定地点，以便卖方选定承运人和实施运输。

2）为保证卖方运输与买方投保的衔接，明示卖方及时通知买方货已交付的责任，有助于日后纠纷的妥善解决。

3）在允许买方确定装运时间或目的地时，订明买方负有对此及时通知卖方义务的条款也十分必要。当买方因市场波动等原因不通知或延迟通知致使卖方无法按时装运时，由此产生的风险及额外费用由买方承担，时间始于规定的启运日或装运期届满之日。

(6) CIP

CIP术语是指卖方除具有CPT术语相同的义务外，还须对货物在运输途中灭失或损坏的买方风险取得货物保险，订立保险合同，并支付保险费。

与CIF相似，CIP合同也属装运合同，卖方按运输合同要求向承运人交付货物后，交货义务完成，无需保证到货。此外，购买保险时，最低保险金额为合同金额的110%。

FCA、CPT和CIP三种贸易术语是从FOB、CFR和CIF这三种传统术语发展而来的，其责任划分的基本原则是相同的，但也有区别，主要表现在以下几个方面。

1）适用的运输方式不同：FOB、CFR和CIF仅适用于水上运输方式，而FCA、CPT和CIP则适用于包括多式联运在内的各种运输方式。

2）交货和风险转移地点不同：FOB、CFR和CIF的交货地点及风险转移地均以装运港装货上船为准。而FCA、CPT和CIP则需提前到货交承运人（多式联运时为货交第一承运人）为界。

3）装卸费用负担不同：FOB、CFR和CIF的卖方承担货物在装运港装货上船为止的一切费用，CFR和CIF的卖方还需支付到目的港为止的正常运费。FOB合同中，需明确装船费由何方负责，CFR 和 CIF 合同则要确定卸货费由何方支付。而涉及水上运输的 FCA 的卖方费用承担提前到货交承运人为止，所以装卸船的费用自然包含在运输合同中由办理运输的买方支付。至于 CPT 和 CIP 的卖方则需支付向后延伸到目的地为止的运费。

4）提供的货运单据不同：FOB、CFR 和 CIF 术语下，卖方一般应向买方提交海运提单，而 FCA、CPT 和 CIP 术语则需视运输方式而不同，有铁路运单、公路运单、邮包收据和多式联运单据等多种选择。值得注意的是 Incoterms 2020 规定 FCA 下承运人需对卖方签发装船批注提单。

5）保险险种与 CIF 不同：Incoterms 2020 要求 CIP 下保险险别升级至英国伦敦保险业协会制定的协会货物条款［ICC（A）］。ICC（A）采用承保“除外责任”之外的一切风险的方式来表明该险种的承保范围。它相当于中国保险条款中的一切险，但其责任范围更为广泛。

3.2.4 其他五种贸易术语简介

（1）EXW——工厂交货

EXW 是指卖方在他的工厂或指定地点将货物提供给买方即履行了交货义务。采用这一术语，买方承担的责任最大，而卖方承担的责任最小。当采用不加成本的初始报价时，常常采用工厂交货条件。

EXW 条件下，买方承担将货物运至终点的风险。卖方无需将货装上买方指派的任何收取货物的运输工具，也不办理出口结关手续，即使卖方负责装货上船，其风险和成本也由买方承担。如果双方约定由卖方负责在始发港将货物装船，并承担装船风险及成本，则应在销售合同中追加明确的说明。

卖方没有义务签订运输合同，买方亦是如此——买方可能将货物出售给顾客，让其到原始卖方的仓库处取货。然而，在实践当中，买方安排于指定地点取货，负责办理通关手续，并安排全部出口单据。

（2）FAS——船边交货（指定装运港）

FAS 是船边交货（指定装运港）。指卖方在指定装运港将货物交到船边，即完成交货。自货物交付起，买方必须承担货物灭失或损坏的一切风险和所有费用，同时要求卖方办理出口结关手续和承担相应费用。

（3）DPU——卸货点交货（指定目的地）

由于 DAT Incoterms 2010（在终端交付）规则中对术语“终端”的解释存在问题，于是 Incoterms 2020 中创造了 DPU 规则以取代 DAT。这是因为目的地终端经常与海关终端混淆。在 DPU 中，卖方负责安排运输，到达合同明确的指定地点，从运输工具上卸货并交货。指定地点没有限制，例如可以是交通枢纽、仓库或买方仓库。货物卸载后，风险从卖方转移到买方。这是唯一要求卖方卸货才能完成交货的规则。买方负责进口清关和任何适用的地方税或进口关税。

（4）DAP——指定地点交货

Incoterms 2020 将 DAP 定义为：当载货的运输工具抵达指定的目的地准备卸货并交由买方处置时，卖方即为交货。在 DAP 条件下，货物运达运输合同指定的目的地后，风险由卖方转移至买方。

货物准备运送时，卖方需对货物进行必要的包装并承担成本，如此货物得以安全抵达目的地。卖方负责安排货物出口结关的一切必要的法律手续并承担相应的成本及风险。

表 3.1 Incoterms 2020 规则的对比

术语	运费到付				运费预付						
	EXW	FCA	FAS	FOB	CPT	CFR	CIF	CIP	DPU	DAP	DDP
	Ex Works (Place)	Free Carrier (Place)	Free Alongside Ship(Port)	Free On Board(Port)	Carriage Paid To (Place)	Cost and Freight(Port)	Cost Insurance& Freight(Port)	Carriage& Insurance Paid To (Place)	Delivered at Place Unloaded (Place)	Delivered at Place(Place)	Delivered Duty Paid (Place)
风险转移时点	交由买方	至买方运输工具	船舷	船上	交由承运人	船上	船上	交由承运人	指定地点卸货	指定地点	指定地点
成本分配											
启运地装车	买方	卖方	卖方	卖方	卖方	卖方	卖方	卖方	卖方	卖方	卖方
出口报关	买方	卖方	卖方	卖方	卖方	卖方	卖方	卖方	卖方	卖方	卖方
运至出口港	买方	买/卖方	卖方	卖方	卖方	卖方	卖方	卖方	卖方	卖方	卖方
于出口港卸货	买方	买方	卖方	卖方	卖方	卖方	卖方	卖方	卖方	卖方	卖方
于出口港装船/飞机	买方	买方	买方	卖方	卖方	卖方	卖方	卖方	卖方	卖方	卖方
海/空运至进口港	买方	买方	买方	买方	卖方	卖方	卖方	卖方	卖方	卖方	卖方
保险	买方	买方	买方	买方	买方	买方	卖方	卖方	卖方	卖方	卖方
于进口港卸货	买方	买方	买方	买方	买/卖方	买方	买方	买/卖方	卖方	卖方	卖方
于进口港装车	买方	买方	买方	买方	买/卖方	买方	买方	买/卖方	卖方	卖方	卖方
运至目的地	买方	买方	买方	买方	卖方	买方	买方	卖方	卖方	卖方	卖方
进口清关	买方	买方	买方	买方	买方	买方	买方	买方	买方	买方	卖方
进口关税	买方	买方	买方	买方	买方	买方	买方	买方	买方	买方	卖方
于目的地卸货	买方	买方	买方	买方	买方	买方	买方	买方	卖方	买方	买方

货物抵达进口国之后，买方需安排进口国的清关工作并承担相应成本及风险，包括关税。然而，DAP之下产生的拖延及滞期费也由卖方承担。

DAP条件下，货到指定的目的地之前的运输费及终点费用由卖方缴纳，且卖方也要承担终点站必要的卸货成本。

（5）DDP——完税后交货（指定目的地）

卖方负责将货物运送到买方所在国的指定地点并支付货至终点的全部成本，包括进口关税，然而其不负责卸货。这一条件使卖方风险最大化而买方风险最小，直至货物抵达指定目的地之前，买方都不必承担任何风险和责任。

DDP条件下最重要的一点是，卖方须负责在买方所在国的货物清关工作，不仅要缴纳关税，还要获得该国主管部门的批准并进行登记。在不十分了解买方所在国的规定的情况下，卖方采取DDP将是十分危险的，因而应慎用。

前文介绍了Incoterms 2020规则下11种术语的清关手续，除EXW与DDP这一对应的术语分别由买方办理出口结关和卖方办理进口清关外，其他术语均是卖方办理出口结关，买方办理进口清关。11种术语涉及的费用主要有：①与货物有关的费用，如运费、保险费、商品包装及检验费；②进出口清关费用，如办理出口许可证、货物进出口及过境运输的海关手续费、海关关税及其他费用；③额外费用等。

与Incoterms 2010相比，Incoterms 2020还发生了其他变化，包括成本分配和允许卖方/买方使用自己的运输工具。

使用Incoterms 2010时，某些方面的成本成为一个相当大的问题。在某些情况下，承运人改变他们的定价，因此卖家经常面临新的终端处理费。Incoterms 2020提供了更多有关成本的详细信息，清楚地分配了每一方要承担的成本。

Incoterms 2010假定所有运输将由第三方运输商承担。而Incoterms 2020允许买方或卖方的自有运输方式，从而认可了一些买家和卖家使用他们自己的运输工具，包括卡车或飞机来交付货物，这意味着：

在FCA规则中，允许买方使用自己的运输工具；

在DAP、DPU和DDP规则中，允许卖方使用自己的运输工具。

表3.1对Incoterms 2020规则进行了对比。

3.3 Major Forms of International Trade

3.3.1 Exclusive Sales

Exclusive Sale involves an exporter (client) by way of agreement granting one foreign customer or company exclusive right to trade one commodity or one type of commodities in a certain area and within a time limit. Different from unilateral individual export, exclusive sales involve exclusive sales agreement preceding sales agreement.

Exclusive sales agreement is an indenture concluded by supplier/exporter and dealer to define their legal relationships. The content of the agreement could be simplified or complex depending on the characteristics of the commodity, the sale territory, and the parties' intention. The rights and obligations of the two parties are defined in the agreement. The sales contract should also be in consistency with the provisions in exclusive sales agreement. The following contents are usually parts of the exclusive sales agreement.

1) The name of the agreement, the date and venue of conclusion of the agreement.

2) The preamble of the agreement, in which relationship between exclusive distributor and client are clarified as principal to principal.

3) The scope of the commodity, which must be defined in the agreement, for reasons of different types of commodity or different trademark and specification of the same type.

4) The sales territory, the determination of which involves considering factors such as the scale and capability of exclusive distributor, the sales network under the control of the distributor, the nature and type of the commodity, market differentiation, topographic position of the sales territory, and so on.

5) The sales duration, also called validity period. In China's export, exclusive sales duration, which is usually one year, is clearly defined in the agreement. In other countries, however, specified duration is not regulated but termination or renewal clause is involved.

6) Franchise. Franchise refers to the exclusive right of the distributor's to purchase and sell the commodity, which is a key provision of the agreement. It includes exclusive selling right and exclusive purchasing right. The former entitles the distributor to exclusively sell one commodity in regulated territory and duration, with exporter's responsibility of not selling directly to other customers in that territory. The latter provides that the distributor is liable for purchasing commodity from the exporter, not anybody else.

7) The quantity and amount, which is equally binding to both parties. According to this provision, the distributor has the responsibility of purchasing required quantity and value of commodity from the exporter, the latter, on the other hand, must export the same quantity and value to the distributor. A minimum purchase value is usually defined.

8) Pricing method. One-time pricing could be adopted within the duration, with settlement made at a fixed price defined in the agreement. This method is in less usage for risk of price fluctuation. The other method is batch pricing in the agreed duration, which is more widely used for reason of drastic price fluctuation. And a regular price negotiation is also acceptable.

9) Other obligations of distributor. In many exclusive sales agreements, the distributor is required to conduct advertising and propagate, to make market research, and to safeguard the rights and interests of the supplier.

3.3.2 Agency

Agency involves an agent, at the authorization of a principal, entering into contract with a third party or conducting other legal activities on behalf of the principal, with principal directly sharing consequent rights and assuming corresponding obligation.

The agent service in international trade regulates independent agent conducting business in the name and at the cost of the principal within the agreed duration and territory. In international commodity transaction, agent could be classified into three categories.

1) General Agent

A general agent is legally authorized to represent principal on all kinds of commercial or sometimes even noncommercial activities. They are empowered to act on the basis of agreements reached with the principal they represent and to appoint sub-agents and share their commission.

2) Exclusive agent (also called Sole Agent)

Exclusive agent is one that within certain duration and territory exclusively represents the principal to conduct relative business provided in the agreement. No other agent should be named in the same territory by the principal.

3) Commission Agent

Within the same duration and territory, the principal may designate several agents to act in his name, and no exclusive right is regulated. The commission agent, after successfully conducting activities within authorization, collects commission from the principal.

Agent could also be classified as sales agent, purchasing agent, shipment agent, insurance agent, advertisement agent, bidding agent, law agent, and so on.

3.3.3 Consignment

Consignment means that the exporter will send the goods for sale to a foreign consignment place and entrust the local agent to sell the goods locally on behalf of the consignor according to the conditions stipulated in the consignment agreement, while the ownership of the goods still belongs to the consignor. The exporter of goods is known as the "consignor" and the agent entrusted with the custody and care of the goods is known as the "consignee". On sales of the goods, the consignee settles the sales revenue with the consignor and gets commission as stipulated in the consignment contract.

The features of consignment lie in that:

1) The relationship between the two parties is that of principal and agent, not that of buyer and seller.

2) The consignor shall bear all the costs and risks of the consigned goods before the sale, including those in transit and after the arrival of the goods at the consignment place.

3) The consignee is not responsible for damage of goods during transport.

4) Goods are sold at the risk of consignor with profit or loss distributed to the consignor only.

A consignor who consigns goods to a consignee only transfers the right of possession, not ownership, of the goods. The consignor retains the title to the goods before they are sold. If the consignee converts the goods to a use not contemplated in the consignment agreement, such as selling them without consignor's permission and keeping the proceeds of the sale, the crime of embezzlement has been committed.

3.3.4 Invitation to Tender & Submission of Tender

An invitation to tender (ITT, often called tender for short) is a special procedure for generating competing offers from different bidders looking to obtain an award of business activity in works, supply, or service contracts. It is usually preceded by a pre-qualification questionnaire (PQQ). Submission of Tender, also called bidding, is a recognized way of competing with other businesses for a contract. The tendering company examines and compares bid proposals from different businesses to choose the firm with the best overall proposal. Tender and bidding are two sides of a trade method.

Four steps are contained in a tender and bidding, namely tender, bidding, bid opening and evaluation, and contract signing.

(1) Tender

International tender includes open tender and restricted tender. Open tender, also called competitive tender or public tender, is open to all qualified bidders in which the sealed bids are opened in public for scrutiny and winning bid is chosen on the basis of price and quality.

Restricted tenders, restricted calls for tenders, or invited tenders are only open to selected prequalified vendors or contractors. Tender notice is not publicized but only rendered to a few clients according to previous business relations established and their information. Restricted tenders are widely used in the purchasing of professionalized high technology equipment. The bidding companies invited are those equipped with rich experience, advanced facility, and good reputation.

(2) Bidding

The bidder needs to prepare book of tender after acquisition of and careful study on the tender documents. The book of tender is in essence an offer made before specific bid opening date. In a book of tender, all key contents to be agreed upon by tenderee and bidder in the contract should be listed. Any recall of the book, change of quotation or material modification to the content is forbidden within tender validity. Therefore, the bidder should deal with great caution, taking comprehensive factors into consideration.

To prevent the bidder from withdrawing or rejecting to sign contract, the tenderee usually requires the bidder to provide a portion of contract amount or certain amount of money as deposit. Once a winning bidder is chosen, other bidder's deposit is immediately refunded. The popular practice in international tender and bidding is to adopt performance bond or standby letter of credit in lieu of deposit.

Book of tender should be delivered to tenderee or a named recipient prior to the deadline of tender submission, any delay would be deemed invalid. Conventionally, the bidder can request in writing the modification to or withdrawing of the book. The withdrawn book of tender will be neglected in bid opening and the deposit won't be confiscated.

(3) Bid opening and evaluation

Public bid opening and non-public bid opening are two approaches, which should be decided in bidding announcement.

Public bid opening is unsealing and inspection of sealed bids received in response to an invitation to bid, at an advertised place in presence of anyone who may care to attend. Bids may be read aloud if requested by a member of the audience. In non-public bid opening, however, the most favorable winning bidder is selected by the tenderee himself after comprehensive consideration, without the presence of the bidder. In modern international bidding, the price quotation is not the only consideration. However, in international competitive bidding loaned by World Bank, the bidder with the lowest quotation must be acknowledged as the winning bidder. If all bids proposed are considered dissatisfactory, a failed tender and bidding could be announced.

(4) Signing of contract

A letter of acceptance is sent and contract signing date and place are arranged once the winning bidder is decided. The winning bidder should provide performance security to replace the bidding deposit to guarantee his performance of the contract.

3.3.5 Counter Trade

Counter trade means exchanging goods or services which are paid for, in whole or part, with other goods or services, rather than with money. A monetary valuation can however be used in counter trade for accounting purposes. Counter trade also occurs when countries lack sufficient hard currency, or when other types of market trade are impossible. There are six main variants of counter trade: barter, switch trading, counter purchase, buyback, off-set, and compensation trade.

3.3.6 Barter

Barter is trading in which goods or services are exchanged without the use of cash. Resorted to usually in times of high inflation or tight money (also used when foreign exchange is scarce or the country is kicked out of the SWIFT system), barter is now a common form of trading in deals such as offering to buy surplus goods in exchange for advertising space or time. Advent of internet has transformed bartering from largely person-to-person to mainly business-to-business exchange, where items for daily cross border barter range from steel to paper, and et al.

3.3.7 Buyback Trade

Buyback occurs when a firm builds a plant in a country, or supplies technology, equipment, training, or other services to the country and agrees to take a certain percentage of the plant's output as partial payment for the contract.

3.3.8 Counter Purchase

Counter purchase, also called reciprocal or parallel trade, means sale of goods and services to one company in another country by a company that promises to make a future purchase of a specific product from the same company in that country. Two independent but interconnecting contracts are singed, one stipulating that the importer purchases commodity from exporter at spot exchange, the other providing that the exporter in the former contract guarantees future purchase from the counter party within certain period of time.

3.3 国际贸易主要方式

3.3.1 包销

包销指出口人（委托人）通过协议把某一种商品或某一类商品在某一个地区和期限内的经营权给予国外某个客户或公司的贸易做法。包销同通常的单边逐笔出口不同，它除了当事人双方签有买卖合同外，还须在事先签有包销协议。

包销协议是供货人和经销人订立的确立双方法律关系的契约，其内容的繁简可根据商品的特点、经销地区的情况以及双方当事人的意图加以确定。采用包销方式，买卖双方的权利与义务是包销协议所确定的。两者签订的买卖合同也必须符合包销协议的规定。通常包销协议包括下列主要内容。

1）包销协议的名称、签约日期与地点。

2）包销协议的前文。通常在前文条款中，明确包销商——委托人之间的关系是本人与本人的关系（principal to principal）即买卖关系。

3）包销商品的范围。委托人（出口人）经营商品的种类繁多，即使是同一类或同一种商品，其中也有不同的牌号与规格。因此，在包销协议中，双方当事人必须约定包销商品的范围。

4）包销地区。包销地区是指包销商行使销售的地理范围。确定包销地区的大小，要考虑的因素主要有：包销商的规模及能力、包销商所能控制的销售网络、包销商品的性质及种类、市场的差异程度、包销地区的地形位置等。

5）包销期限。包销期限即协议的有效期，可以长也可以短。在我国的出口业务中，往往在签订包销协议时明确规定期限，通常为一年。其他国家市场的习惯做法，在包销协议中不规定期限，只是规定中止条款或续约条款等。

6）专营权。专营权是指包销商行使专卖和专买的权利，这是包销协议的重要内容。专营权包括专卖权和专买权。前者是委托人（出口人）将指定的商品在规定的地区和期限内给予包销商独家销售的权利。出口人负有不向该区域内的客户直接售货的义务。后者是包销商承担向出口人购买商品，而不得向第三者购买的义务。

7）包销数量或金额。包销协议中除规定上述内容外，还应规定包销商在一定时期内的经销数量或金额。此项数量与金额对协议双方均有同等的约束力。有时在协议中规定数量与金额，则包销商必须承担向出口人购买规定数量和金额的义务，出口人必须承担向包销商出口上述数量和金额的责任。包销数额一般采用最低承购额的做法。

8）作价办法。包销商品可以在规定的期限内一次作价，结算时以协议规定的固定价格为准。这种方法由于交易双方要承担价格变动的风险，故采用较少；另一种做法是在规定的包销期限内分批作价，由于国际商品市场的价格变化多端，因此采用分批作价较为普遍。当然，也可由双方定期地根据市场情况加以确定。

9）包销商的其他义务。在许多包销协议中，往往要求包销商要负责做好广告宣传、市场调研和维护供货人权益等工作。

3.3.2 代理

代理是指代理人（Agent）按照委托人（Principal）的授权，代表委托人与第三人订立合同或做出其他法律行为，而由委托人直接享有由此而产生的权利与承担相应的义务。

在国际贸易中的代理业务是以委托人为一方，独立的代理人为另一方，在约定的时间和地区内，以委托人的名义与资金从事业务活动。国际货物买卖中的代理可以从不同角度分类，按委托人授权的大小可分为以下三种。

(1) 总代理

总代理（General Agent）是委托人在指定地区的全权代表，他除了有权代表委托人从事买卖合同的签订、货物的处理等商务活动外，还可进行一些非商业性的活动。他有权按与委托人签订的协议行事，有权指派分代理，并可分享分代理的佣金。

(2) 独家代理

独家代理（Sole Agent or Exclusive Agent）是在指定地区和期限内单独代表委托人行事，从事代理协议中规定的有关业务的代理人。委托人在该地区内，不得委托其他代理人。

(3) 一般代理

一般代理（Agent）又称佣金代理（Commission Agent），是指在同一地区和期限内委托人同时委派几个代理人代表委托人行为，代理人不享有独家专营权。佣金代理完成授权范围内的事务后按协议规定的办法向委托人计收佣金。

代理按行业性质和职责分类，又可分为销售代理、购货代理、货运代理、保险代理、广告代理、投标代理、诉讼代理等多种类型，这里不再赘述。

3.3.3 寄售

寄售是指出口商将准备销售的货物送抵国外寄售地，委托当地的代理人/代销人按照寄售协议规定的条件代替委托人在当地进行销售，而货物的所有权仍属于委托人。其中，出口商被称为寄售人，而被委托以托管或照看货物责任的一方则被称为受托人。寄售货物售出后，受托人按寄售协议规定的方式与委托人结算货款并获得其佣金。

寄售的特点在于：

1）合同双方是委托人与代理人的关系，而非买卖双方关系。

2）寄售货物售出前的一切风险与费用，包括运输途中以及寄售货物在寄售地的所有费用和风险，均由寄售人/委托人承担。

3）在运输或其他过程中对寄售商品造成的损坏，受托人不予负责。

4）寄售商品出售的风险由委托人承担，连同利润与损失也只归于委托人。

委托人将商品交予受托人寄售，仅是转移了商品的占有权而非所有权。委托人在寄售商品售出前仍拥有商品的所有权。如果受托人未按寄售协议而将商品转作他用，如将其私自销售并且保留销售收入，则此时受托人犯有侵占罪。

3.3.4 招标和投标

招标（Invitation to Tender，ITT）是从不同的想从工程、供应和服务中获得回报的投标人处获得竞争性报价的特定过程。招标通常在资格预审和调查之后展开。投标是与其他企业竞争以获取合同的一种方式。招标单位对不同企业的竞标方案进行审查和对比，以选择方案总体最佳的公司。招标与投标是贸易方式的两个方面。

招标投标业务基本上包括四个步骤：招标、投标、开标评标和签约。

(1) 招标

国际招标主要有公开招标和选择性招标两种。公开招标也叫竞争性招标或公共招标，对所有的符合条件的投标人开放，封好的标书被当众打开以供审查，并依据投标价格与质量从中选择。

选择性招标也叫邀约式招标，仅对所选择的符合条件的供应商或承包商开放。这可能是不公开发布招标通告，只是根据以往的业务关系和情报资料，向少数客户发出招标通知。非公开招标多用于购买技术要求高的专业性设备或成套设备，应邀参加投标的企业通常是经验丰富、技术装备优良，在该行业中享有一定声誉的企业。

(2) 投标

投标人首先要取得招标文件，认真分析研究之后，编制投标书。投标书实质上是一项有效期至规定开标日期为止的发盘，内容必须十分明确，中标后与招标人签订合同所要包含的重要内容应全部列入，并在有效期内不得撤回标书、变更标书报价或对标书内容做实质性修改。因此，投标人必须综合各种因素慎重考虑。

为防止投标人在投标后撤标或在中标后拒不签订合同，招标人通常都要求投标人在投标时提供一定比例或金额的投标保证金。招标人决定中标人之后，未中标的投标人已缴纳的保证金即予退还。现今国际招标投标业务中一般都以银行保函或备用信用证代替保证金。

投标书应在投标截止日期之前送达招标人或其指定的收件人，逾期无效。按照一般的惯例，投标人在投标截止期之前，可以书面提出修改或撤回标书。撤回的标书在开标时不予宣读，所缴纳的投标保证金也不没收。

(3) 开标评标

开标有公开开标和非公开开标两种方式，招标人应在招标通告中对开标方式做出规定。

公开开标是指招标人在规定的时间和地点当众启封投标书，投标人都可参加，监视开标，标书内容可应观众要求大声宣读。非公开开标则是由招标人经综合考虑后自行选择最有利的投标人，而投标人本人不必参加。在现代国际招标业务中，中标与否不完全取决于报价的高低。但在世界银行贷款项目的国际竞争性招标中，招标人必须接受标价最低的产品或服务。如果招标人认为所有的投标均不理想，可宣布招标失败。

(4) 签约

招标人选定中标人之后，要向其发出中标通知书，约定双方签约的时间和地点。中标人签约时要提交履约保证金，取代原投标保证金，用以担保中标人将遵照合同履行义务。

3.3.5 对销贸易

对销贸易是指用货物或服务而非钱财部分或全部地去交换其他货物或服务。然而在会计处理上可以采用货币进行估价。如果有的国家缺乏硬通货币，或者不允许其他的市场交易方式，则也可能采用对销贸易。主要的对销贸易方式有六种，即易货贸易、转手贸易、互购贸易、回购贸易、抵消贸易及补偿贸易。

3.3.6 易货贸易

易货贸易是指相互交换商品或服务，而非以现金结算。易货贸易通常在高通胀或银根紧缩时采用（外汇紧缺或者被踢出 SWIFT 系统时也用），但目前也被当作常用的贸易方式得以应用，如提出购买对方剩余产品以换取广告空间。因特网的出现使易货贸易从人与人的交易向企业对企业的交易转换，而跨越国境的日常交易的范围也从钢铁到纸张等不一而足。

3.3.7 回购贸易

回购贸易是指一方在一个国家建立工厂，或提供技术、设备、培训或其他服务给该国家，并同意收购该工厂所生产的一定比例的产品作为部分的合同款项的方法。

3.3.8 互购贸易

互购贸易（Counter Purchase），又称互惠贸易（Reciprocal Trade）和平行贸易（Parallel Trade），是指一家公司出售产品和服务给其他国家的另一公司并承诺于将来从该公司购买一定数量的特定产品。即双方签订两份既独立又有联系的合同：一份是约定先由进口的一方用现汇购买对方的货物；另一份则由先出口的一方承诺在一定期限内购买对方的货物。

Part B Vocabulary and Terminology 词汇和术语

EXW (Ex Works…Named Place) 工厂交货

FCA (Free Carrier…Named Place) 货交承运人

FAS (Free Alongside Ship…Named Port of Shipment) 船边交货

FOB (Free on Board…Named Port of Shipment) 船上交货

CFR (Cost and Freight…Named Port of Destination) 成本加运费

CIF (Cost, Insurance and Freight…Named Port of Destination) 成本加保险费和运费

CPT (Carriage Paid to…Named Place of Destination) 运费付至

CIP (Carriage and Insurance Paid to…Named Place of Destination) 运费、保险费付至

DDP (Delivered Duty Paid…Named Place of Destination) 完税后交货

DPU (Delivery at Place Unloaded…named place of destination) 卸货地点交货

Bill of Lading with an on board notation 装船批注提单

DAP (Delivered At Place…Named Place of Destination) 指定地点交货

FOB liner terms FOB 班轮条件

FOB under tackle FOB 吊钩下交货

FOB stowed FOB 包括理舱费

FOB trimmed FOB 包括平舱费

payable at usance 远期付款

contract of carriage 运输合同

demurrage charges 滞期费

exclusive sales 包销

general agent 总代理

sole agent/exclusive agent 独家代理

commission agent 佣金代理

consignment 寄售

consignor 委托人

consignee 受托人

transit trade 转口贸易

invitation to tender 招标

submission of tender 投标

book of tender 投标书

tenderee 招标人

bidder 投标人

performance bond 履约保函

standby letter of credit 备用信用证

barter 易货贸易

counter trade 对销贸易
switch trading 转手贸易
compensation trade 补偿贸易
offset 抵消贸易
counter purchase 互购贸易
spot exchange 现汇

Part C Exercise 练习

Ⅰ. Answer the following questions.

1. What is the key procedure of import?

2. What are the main trade terms related international conventions?

3. What are the differences between the group of FOB, CFR and CIF and the group of FCA, CPT and CIP?

4. What is exclusive sales? What content should be included in an exclusive sales contract?

5. Please briefly describe the basic steps of tender and bidding.

6. How do you define consignment and its features?

Ⅱ. Tell whether the following statements are true or false.

1. Incoterms 2020 defines 13 international trade terms.

2. Under FOB, the buyer assumes all risks to the goods (loss or damage) up to the point they have been delivered onto the vessel at the named port.

3. EXW term places the maximum obligation on the buyer and minimum obligation on the seller.

4. When currency is used as settlement means in international trade, we call it trade by free settlement.

5. CIF contract adopts actual delivery, meaning the delivery by the seller at the arrival of the goods.

Ⅲ. Translate the following passages into Chinese.

1. Submission of Tender, also called bidding, is a recognized way of competing with other businesses for a contract. The tendering company examines and compares bid proposals from different businesses to choose the firm with the best overall proposal. Tender and bidding are two sides of a trade method.

2. Open tender, also called competitive tender or public tender, is open to all qualified bidders in which the sealed bids are opened in public for scrutiny and wining bid is chosen on the basis of price and quality. Restricted tenders, restricted calls for tenders, or invited tenders are only open to selected prequalified vendors or contractors. Tender notice is not publicized but only rendered to a few clients according to previous business relations established and their information.

3. With respect to Incoterms 2020, there came 7 Key changes among which DAT Incoterm was replaced by DPU, own transport rather than 3rd party transport is allowed in

FCA，DAP，DPU and DDP，and Bill of Lading with an 'on board' notation should be issued by carrier in FCA.

Ⅳ. Translate the following passages into English.

1. 国际贸易术语的国际惯例，是在国际贸易实践中逐渐形成的内容较为固定的贸易习惯和一般做法，它不同于法律之处在于不具有强制性，只有当事人承认并在实际业务中采用时，才对当事人有约束力。

2. CIF合同条件下，卖方需承担货物装上船为止的一切费用和货物灭失或损坏的风险，并负责办理货运保险和租船或订舱，支付保险费和从装运港到目的港的运费。

3. 寄售是指将货物送抵代理人处进行销售，而货物的所有权仍属于送货人。代理人根据送货人的指示代其销售货物。其中，送货人被称为委托人，而被委托以托管或照看货物的一方则被称为受托人。

Chapter Four

International Cargo Warehousing 国际货物仓储

Part A Text 课文

4.1 Brief Introduction to International Cargo Warehousing

The storage of a commodity puts it into a condition of short or long stoppage, which is an indispensable and necessary part in commodity circulation. In international trade and transnational operation, the commodity is collectively transported from producer or supplier to port of shipment. Sometimes short-time storage is needed before shipping for export, which makes international logistics warehousing necessary. This kind of warehousing mainly happens in free trade zone or bonded warehouse; for this reason this chapter will also introduce bonded system and bonded warehouse.

4.1.1 Significance of International Logistics Warehouse

Warehousing plays significant role in national economy and international commodity production, distribution, exchange, and consumption. In another word, it possesses very important position in national and worldwide commodity production and circulation. International logistics warehousing not only performs storage of import and export goods, but also conducts processing, selecting, assorting, packing, preparing, assembling and shipping of the goods. Besides, warehouse operator should also provide information on change of quantity of goods, the duration of storage, turnover period and etc. to related parties, find problems underlying and assist interested parties to resolve the problems.

(1) Coordinating Time Difference between Production and Consumption

For many products, time and regional difference is great from their production to consumption. To solve this problem, products must be stored in warehouse, which creates time effect for products.

(2) Safeguarding Quality of Internationalized Commodity

From production to circulation, commodity is inspected in their quality in the warehouse. In this way, unqualified goods or goods in lower quality are excluded from entering market. Warehousing safeguards quality of goods in two ways: quality inspection during storage and examination before outbound delivery.

(3) Products Processing

With the development of modern logistics, warehousing, apart from storing and safeguarding goods, provides more and more value-added services, e. g. sorting, selecting, organizing, processing, simple assembling, packing, la beling, and goods preparing. These services closely bind warehousing and production process together and corresp ondingly add value to the goods.

(4) Adjusting Price of International Commodity

Warehousing plays its role in adjusting price of international commodity in that it can overcome great contradiction between supply and demand, as well as adjust supply and demand relationship and consequently the price difference.

(5) Adjusting the Inadequacy of Shipping Capacity

Shipping conveyances vary in their shipping capacity, which may lead to imbalance. Warehousing of foreign trade goods could alleviate congested ship or port and offset the weakness of inland transport in its loading capacity.

(6) Decreasing Damage to and Shortage of Goods in International Logistics

In import and export, the depot in the port or airport needs to check the goods and their packing, and stow and unitize goods to pallet. Some goods even need bagging and binding. After inbound handling, imported goods need to be assorted, tallied, and deconsolidated. Goods could be temporarily stored in the depot to avoid damage, should delay arises for reason of late customs clearance, inspection and quarantine procedures or bad weather. Depot also provides services of stacking, assorting and packing should any inexplicit marks or mixed packing be found out.

To summarize, international warehousing is an indispensable part of international logistics. Strengthening warehousing management is one important way to shorten circulation cycle and decrease circulation expenses.

4.1.2 Classification of International Logistics Warehouse

(1) Classification by Function of Warehouse in International Logistics

1) Port Warehouse: It refers to the type of warehouse which is characterized by short storage period and fast turnover of goods. This type of warehouse is mostly built in large scale in coastal port city where export goods are centralized. It functions as a storage place for commodities to be shipped for export or those to be distributed in import. Therefore, it is also called transfer shed.

2) Transshipment Depot: Most of transshipment depots are built in between mass production area and port of shipment, e. g. railway and highway station, river port, big and middle sized cities with centralized production, and transportation hub where goods are distributed concentratedly. The function of it is to store and transship goods flowing through the depot.

3) Processing Warehouse: This type of warehouse is characterized as combining storage and processing of export goods. Apart from goods storage, it also provides processing

services such as goods selection, sorting, labeling, assembling, packing, and repacking, in order to meet the need of international market.

4) Storage Warehouse: This type is usually used for storage of goods to be exported, reserved materials for foreign aid, reserved goods in export business and so on. The goods in storage warehouse need to be inspected and maintained regularly.

(2) Classification by Management System

1) Private Warehouse: The warehouse equipped with administration staff from the company and managed by the company itself. Compared with public warehouse, private warehouse has the following advantages for a company.

① Stronger Control over Goods. The company can perform stronger control over the goods as the goods' owner due to its management right over the warehouse. Before the transit of goods to customer, the company has direct responsibility for the goods and together the right of direct control. This can coordinate the storage function of warehouse with the overall distribution system of the company.

② More Flexible Management. This flexibility has nothing to do with the change of storage space, but refers to the fact that the company, as the owner of the warehouse, can make reasonable design and layout of the warehouse according to its requirement and goods characteristics. For those highly specialized products, professional storage and handling technique and equipment are needed, which could hardly be provided in public warehouse. In such cases, a company must have its own private warehouse.

③ Lower Cost for Long-Term Storage. If utilized efficiently for a long run, the cost of private warehouse will be lower than that of public warehouse. That leads to economies of scale, meaning a reduction in cost of unit goods if private warehouse is used to store large quantity of goods for longer period. If the utilization rate of private warehouse is lower than 75 percent, the economies of scale formed is not sufficient to recover the cost incurred by holding the warehouse. In that case, the company should consider using public warehouse.

④ Better Image for the Company. Holding private warehouse helps the company to establish a good image of going concern in front of public. Customers may think of the company as a stable, reliable, and consistent supplier, which helps increasing competitiveness.

However, private warehouse is not applicable to every company, for it has its disadvantages.

Firstly, fixed storage capacity and cost of holding private warehouse will occupy funds for a long time. Once completed, the warehouse's fixed storage capacity is hard to be altered, no matter how much storage space the company actually needs. When the need for space declines, the company still has to bear the cost of unused space; however, when extra space is needed, private warehouse no longer suffices. Apart from that, private warehouse is restricted in its location and structure. The size and location of market, customer's preference and location of suppliers often change; consequently, the company will lose many business opportunities if its warehouse cannot meet this change for reason of fixed structure and limited services provided.

Secondly, many companies find it hard to construct their private warehouse for its high cost. Private warehouse means a long-term risky investment and is hard for sale due to its specialization. Therefore, companies should be discreet in their decision of building private warehouse.

2) Public Warehouse: The warehouse to which the company has no ownership but must pay for the use of it. The operation of the warehouse is the responsibility of the staff appointed by exterior company. The expenses rising from storage of goods in public warehouse all belong to variable cost, i. e. the expenses are proportional to handling capacity of goods.

The advantages of using public warehouse lie in that:

① From financial perspective, a company doesn't have to make capital investment, thus avoiding financial risk from that. With public warehouse, the company need not make any investment on warehousing facility or equipment, but only pays comparatively lower rental for the services provided.

② Extra storage need could be satisfied at peak of a company's inventory. For most companies, level of inventory often changes for seasonal or promotional reasons or others. By using public warehouse, the company's need for storage space at different time could be met, especially when inventory comes to a peak, for the company could adjust storage space by increasing or surrendering space according to actual inventory level. In contrast, a private warehouse has fixed capacity, which may lead to shortage of space in boom season but idled space during off season. Meanwhile, the cost of using public warehouse varies with the storage quantity of goods, making storage cost easily accessible to managers.

③ Using public warehouse helps to avoid management hardship. Training of workers and management are issues any warehouse will have to face, especially for seasonal products or products needing special handling. However, by using public warehouse, this problem could be easily resolved.

④ The economies of scale brought about by public warehouse helps to decrease storage cost for cargo owner. Public warehouse may achieve economies of scale which is almost unachievable to private warehouse. It stores inventory in large quantity for many companies, which greatly increases utilization rate of space and thus reduces unit cost of storage. Economies of scale makes it possible for public warehouse to adopt more efficient handling equipment and thus provide better service to client. Furthermore, realizing economies of scale is conducive to LCL operation and bulk transport, and therefore decreases transport cost for cargo owners.

⑤ Public warehouse makes a company's operation more flexible. If owning or for long-term leasing a warehouse, a company may find it burdensome when it plans to change the location of the warehouse. However, by using public warehouse, the company can easily change location of the warehouse when market, mode of transport, sale of products or financial situation changes, for contract of using public warehouse is usually a short-term one. And the company doesn't need to alter number of workers for reason of inventory changes. In addition, the company could enter into or terminate leasing contract in accordance with the contribution of a warehouse to the overall distribution system, its cost and quality of service provided, and so on.

⑥ Using public warehouse makes it easier for a company to master its storage and handling cost. Business will get charges documents for storage each month from public warehouse and thus clearly acknowledge storage and handling cost incurred, which is helpful in forecasting and controlling cost at various inventory level.

However, public warehouse also has its defects.

First of all, it will increase a company's packing cost. In public warehouse, various products in different type and nature are stored, which may cause interact with each other. Consequently, protective packing is necessary when using public warehouse, resulting in higher packing cost.

Secondly, public warehouse makes it harder for a company to conduct inventory control. Despite the mutual obligation by cargo owner and warehouse operator, the loss to the cargo owner for reasons of theft and so on is much higher than what is compensated by the warehouse. Therefore, when it comes to inventory control, using public warehouse incurs higher risk than private warehouse.

Thirdly, using public warehouse has the risk of revealing business secret.

3) Contract warehouse: The warehouse or warehouse areas a third-party logistics company uses to provide specialized logistics services to specific clients, the service relation of which is realized in the form of contract. Contract warehouse has been developed from public warehouse. Many companies in logistics developed countries are using contract warehouse or third-party warehouse.

Different from general public warehouse, contract warehouse provides professional, efficient, economic and accurate logistics services for advanced design and the ability to satisfy high standard and specialized handling requirement. In its nature, contract warehouse reflects a partner relation between manufacturer and warehouse company. For this reason, contract warehouse could provide specialized space, personnel, equipment, and other services.

Contract warehouse provides limited number of cargo owners with services such as storage, unloading, LCL operation, assorting, consolidated storage in transit, inventory control, transport arrangement, information provision and other services required by cargo owner. It is obvious that contract warehouse not only provides service of storage but covers a complete set of logistics services.

The advantages of contract warehouse include:

① Helping a company to efficiently use resources. Compared with private warehouse, contract warehouse can solve seasonal storage to seasonal production companies. For instance, it can provide storage service to products whose boom seasons are respectively in winter and summer, e. g. , down jackets and air conditioners. Due to professionalization, management specialists are able to provide more innovative distribution concept and more effective ways to reduce cost, which is helpful in efficiency increase.

② Helping a company to broaden its market. Contract warehouse broadens a company's market coverage through its well-equipped web system. Because of strategic site selection and specialized facility and services by contract warehouse, the cargo owner can get the same storage management and other logistics services at warehouses located at different sites. The company can directly control its private centralized storage facility and utilize contract warehouse as well to reduce labor cost and expand market.

③ Helping a company to test its new market. When launching product promotion or introducing new products, a company could use contract warehouse for short term to test market demand to its products. When the company intends to enter a new market, it will spend a long time to establish a set of distribution facility. However, by using contract warehouse, it can utilize existing facility to serve customers.

④ Helping a company to reduce transport cost. Contract warehouse handles large quantity of goods from different owners and conducts mass transport after LCL operation, which greatly reduces transport cost.

Despite all the advantages, contract warehouse has its shortcomings, among which, loss of direct control over logistics activities are the biggest concern of a company. There is little control from cargo owner over the operation and personnel of contract warehouse, which becomes the biggest obstacle for companies producing high-valued goods to choose contract warehouse.

(3) Classification by Performance of Products and Technique and Equipment of Storage

1) General Warehouse: Used in the storage of industrial or agricultural products without special storage requirement. It takes the largest proportion of warehouses.

2) Specialized Warehouse: Used to store a specific category of goods with its high quality maintenance technique and storage equipment to safeguard the quality of goods.

3) Special Commodity Warehouse: For storage of goods with special nature that require specialized storage equipment, e.g., hazardous chemicals, perishable goods, petroleum, and some medical commodity. This type of warehouse is equipped with specialized facilities, such as cold storage, thermal insulation library, and dangerous cargo warehouse.

Apart from those, there is also bonded warehouse. A bonded warehouse is one that is supervised and controlled by Customs and specifically used for storage of imported goods with duties unpaid. Bonded warehouse will be introduced in next section.

4.1.3 Reasonable Positioning of International Logistics Warehouse

Reasonable positioning of international logistics warehouse is significant in rationally distributing and transporting export goods, speeding goods circulation, decreasing times of transit, reducing logistics expenses, and increasing service level. The network construction of international logistic warehouse develops with development of industrial and agricultural production and expansion of circulation scale of goods.

(1) Positioning Principles

1) Forecasting foreign trade circulation volume (i. e. Quantity of export and import goods) on the basis of proportional relation between development of industrial and agricultural production and circulation scale of goods for foreign trade.

2) Managing relationship between storage and purchasing, sale, distribution and transportation of goods; clarifying storage or transit volume of foreign trade goods after ex-

cluding commodity of direct shipment and distribution.

3) Managing proportional relation between storage volume, constructional area and actual use area of the warehouse and acknowledging warehouse capacity data needed.

4) Understanding estimated turnover times of inventory.

(2) Influential Factors

1) National industrial and agricultural production layout. The development of industrial and agricultural production lays foundation for commodity export. The international logistics warehouse storing these commodities should be located in big and middle sized cities or centralized industrial production area, which makes nearby acquisition and storage available.

2) Foreign trade development. Logistics warehouse network layout should satisfy the need of foreign trade business, upon which size, type, layout and development direction of the warehouse are determined.

3) Economic regionalization and reasonable commodity flow. Warehouse positioning must take into consideration of economic regionalization and reasonable commodity flow, which helps to better design warehouse network and reduce logistics cost.

4) Transport condition of international logistics. Convenient transport and storage of export goods relies on smooth transport which helps in speeding circulation of commodity.

The location of international logistics warehouse should be close to: producer of export goods, supplier and export commodity production base, transport hub, central city, port, station, airport, consumption area (i. e. importers), etc. When setting up a foreign trade warehouse, one should also consider the following factors:

① Availability of electricity, coal, gas, water, fuel oil and heat.

② Emission condition of waste gas, water, and residue.

③ Abatement condition of smoke, noise, and vibration.

④ Good geological conditions and non-earthquake region.

⑤ Special condition requirement for specialized warehouse.

⑥ Fire and pollution proof condition and safe and hygienic environment.

4.1 国际物流仓储概述

商品的储存和保管使商品在其流通过程中处于一种或长或短的相对停留状态，这种停留不是可有可无的，而是商品从生产过程到消费过程中所必需的。国际贸易和跨国经营中的商品从生产厂家或供应部门被集中运送到装运港口，有时需临时存放一段时间，再装运出口，这就涉及国际物流货物仓储业务。由于这种仓储主要是在各国的保税区和保税仓库进行的，因此本章也会涉及各国保税制度和保税仓库建设等方面内容。

4.1.1 国际物流仓储的意义

仓库在各国的国民经济中，在国际间的生产、分配、交换、消费过程中，或者说在一国范围和世界范围的商品生产和商品流通过程中，都有着十分重要的地位和作用。国际物流货物仓库不仅担负着进出口货物保管存储的任务，而且还担负着出口货物的加工、挑选、整理、包装、备货、组装和发运等一系列的任务。另外，仓库还要根据库存商品货件变化和库存时间的长短、周转的快慢等资料，及时向有关单位提供信息，发现问题，并协助解决之。

（1）调整商品在生产和消费之间的时间错位

由于许多商品在生产和消费之间都存在着时间间隔与地域差异，所以为了克服商品供需的时间差异，必须设置仓库将这些商品储存于其中，这种仓储服务创造了商品的时间效应。

（2）保证进入国际市场的商品质量

商品从生产领域进入流通领域的过程中，通过仓储环节，对即将进入市场的商品在仓库进行检验，可以防止质量不合格或质量低下的商品进入市场。

通过仓储来保证商品的质量主要有两个关键环节：一是商品入库保管期间的质量检查；二是商品出库前的检验检查。

（3）延伸生产特性的加工业务

随着现代物流的发展，仓储在提供一般的货物储存和保管服务的基础上，为物流活动提供越来越多的增值服务项目，例如，分拣、挑选、整理、加工、简单的装配、包装、加标签、备货等活动，使仓储过程与生产过程更有机地结合在一起，从而增加了商品的价值。

（4）调节国际市场上商品的价格

国际商品的仓储业务可以克服国与国之间巨大的供求矛盾，并以储存调节供求关系，调整由于供求矛盾而造成的价格差异。所以，仓储还具有调节商品价格的作用。

（5）调节内外运输工具载运能力的不平衡

在各种运输工具中，由于其运载能力差别很大，容易出现极其不平衡的状态，外贸商品无论出口还是进口，进行一定的仓储皆可以减少压船、压港，弥补内陆运输工具运载量的不足。

（6）减少国际物流中的货损货差

在货物进出口过程中，无论是港口还是机场的库场在接收托运货物时，需要检查货物及其包装，并根据货物性质、包装进行配载、成组装盘（板），有的货物还需在库场灌包、捆绑。进口货物入库后还需进行分票、点数、分拨。一旦发生因海关、检验检疫手续的延误，或因气象原因延误装船、交付、运输等，货物可暂存在库场，避免货损发生。在货物装卸过程中，若发现货物标志不清、混装等则可入库整理，这时库场又可提供暂时堆存、分票、包装等方面的业务。

总之，国际仓储业务是国际物流业务中不可缺少的重要环节之一。随着国际贸易的发展，加强仓储管理是缩短商品流通时间、节约流通费用的重要手段。

4.1.2 国际物流仓库的分类

（1）按仓库在国际物流中的用途分类

1）口岸仓库：口岸仓库的特点是商品储存期短，商品周转快。这类仓库大都设在商品集中的发运出口货物的沿海港口城市，仓库规模大。主要储存口岸和内地对外贸易业务部门收购的出口待运商品和进口待分拨的商品。因此，这类仓库又称为周转仓库。

2）中转仓库：中转仓库也称转运仓库。其特点是大都设在商品生产集中的地区和出运港口之间。例如，铁路及公路车站，江河水运港口码头附近，商品生产集中的大、中城市和商品集中分运的交通枢纽地带。其主要职能是储存、转运经过口岸出口的商品。

3）加工仓库：加工仓库的特点是将出口商品的储存和加工结合在一起。除商品储存外，还兼营对某些商品的挑选、整理、分级、包装、改装等简单的加工业务，以适应国际市场的需要。

4）储存仓库：储存仓库的商品储存期较长，主要用于储存待销的出口商品、援外的储备物资、进口待分拨、出口业务需要的储备商品等。这类仓库所储存的商品要定期检查，加强商品养护。

(2) 按仓库管理体制分类

1) 自有仓库：自有仓库是指企业自己拥有仓库管理权，自己配备管理人员、自己从事仓库管理业务。相对于公共仓库来说，企业利用自有仓库进行仓储活动具有以下优势。

第一，可以更大程度地控制仓储。由于企业对自有仓库拥有管理权，所以企业作为货主能够对仓储实施更大程度的控制。在产成品移交给客户之前，企业对产成品负有直接责任并可直接控制。这种控制使企业易于将仓储的功能与企业的整个分销系统进行协调。

第二，自有仓库的管理更具灵活性。这里的灵活性并不是指能迅速增加或减少仓储空间，而是指由于自有仓库下，企业就是仓库的所有者，所以可以按照企业的要求和产品的特点对仓库进行合理的设计与布局。特别是对于一些高度专业化的产品而言，往往需要专业的保管和搬运技术、设备，而公共仓库难以满足这种要求。因此，这样的企业必须选择自有仓库。

第三，长期仓储时，自有仓库的成本低于公共仓库。如果自有仓库得到长期的充分利用，自有仓库的成本将低于公共仓库的成本。这是由于长期使用自有仓库保管大量货物会降低单位货物的仓储成本，在某种程度上说这也是一种规模经济。如果企业自有仓库的利用率较低，一般而言若低于75%，说明自有仓库形成的规模经济不足以补偿自有仓库的成本，则应转向公共仓库。

第四，可以为企业树立良好形象。当企业将产品储存在自有仓库时，会给客户一种企业长期持续经营的良好印象，客户会认为企业经营十分稳定、可靠，是产品的持续供应者，这将有助于提高企业的竞争优势。

并不是任何企业都适合拥有自己的仓库，因为自有仓库也存在以下缺点。

一是自有仓库固定的容量和成本使得企业的一部分资金被长期占用。不管企业对仓储空间的实际需求如何，自有仓库一旦建成后其容量就是固定的，不能随着需求的增加而扩大或减小。当企业对仓储空间的需求减少时，仍需承担自有仓库中未利用部分的成本；而当企业对仓储空间有额外需求时，自有仓库却无法满足。另外，自有仓库还存在位置和结构的局限性。如果企业只能使用自有仓库，则会由于数量限制而失去战略性优化选址的灵活性；市场的大小及位置、客户的偏好以及供应商的位置等会经常变化，如果企业在仓库结构和服务上不能适应这种变化，企业将失去许多商业机会。

二是由于自有仓库的成本高，所以许多企业因资金问题而难以修建自有仓库。自有仓库是一项长期、有风险的投资，并且因其专业性强而难以出售。而企业将资金投资于其他项目可能会得到更高的回报。因此，投资建造自有仓库的决策要非常慎重。

2) 公共仓库：公共仓库是指企业没有仓库管理权，通过付费才可以使用的仓库。仓库由外部企业配备管理人员和设备，负责日常仓库业务。与公共仓库相关的仓储费用全部属于变动成本，即费用多少与使用仓库的吞吐量大小成正比。

利用公共仓库进行仓储活动的优点如下。

① 从财务角度上看，最重要的原因是企业不需要资本投资，可以避免资本投资的财务风险。公共仓库不要求企业对其设施和设备做任何投资，企业只需支付相对较少的租金即可得到仓储服务。

② 可以满足企业在库存高峰时大量额外的库存需求。大多数企业由于产品的季节性、促销活动或其他原因而导致存货水平变化，利用公共仓库，则没有仓库容量的限制，从而能

满足企业在不同时期对仓储空间的需求，尤其是库存高峰时大量额外的库存需求。公共仓库使企业可以根据实际的存货水平通过多租场地或退租在短时间内调整仓库空间。而自有仓库在仓容上则具有很大的刚性，在库存高峰时仓容有可能不够，而在淡季时又会导致一定的闲置。同时，使用公共仓库的成本将直接随着储存货物数量的变化而变动，从而便于管理者掌握仓储成本。

③ 使用公共仓库可以避免管理上的困难。工人的培训和管理是任何一类仓库所面临的一个重要问题，尤其是对于产品需要特殊搬运或具有季节性的企业来说。而使用公共仓库则可以避免这一困难。

④ 公共仓库的规模经济可以降低货主的仓储成本。公共仓库会产生自有仓储难以达到的规模经济。由于公共仓库为众多企业保管大量库存，与自有仓库相比，大大提高了仓库的利用率，降低了存货的单位储存成本；另外，规模经济还使公共仓库能够采用更加有效的物料搬运设备，从而提供更好的服务；最后，公共仓库的规模经济还有利于拼箱作业和大批量运输，降低货主的运输成本。

⑤ 使用公共仓库时企业的经营活动更加灵活。如果自己拥有或长期租赁仓库，那么当需要设立仓库的位置发生变化时，原来的仓库就变成了企业的负担。由于公共仓库的合同是短期的，当市场、运输方式、产品销售或企业财务发生变化时，企业能灵活地改变仓库的位置；另外，企业不必因仓库业务量的变化而增减员工；再有，企业还可以根据仓库对整个分销系统的贡献以及成本和服务质量等因素，临时签订或终止租赁合同。

⑥ 便于企业掌握保管和搬运成本。当企业使用公共仓库时，由于每月可以得到仓储费用单据，可以清楚地掌握保管和搬运的成本，有助于企业预测和控制不同仓储水平的成本。

使用公共仓库进行仓储活动也有如下的缺点。

第一，增加了企业的包装成本。公共仓库中储存了各种不同种类的货物，而各种不同性质的货物有可能互相影响，因此，企业使用公共仓库时必须对货物进行保护性包装，从而增加包装成本。

第二，增加了企业控制库存的难度。企业与仓库经营者都有履行合同的义务，但盗窃等对货物的损坏给货主造成的损失将远远大于货主得到的赔偿。因此在控制库存方面，使用公共仓库将比使用自有仓库承担更大的风险。

另外，公共仓库还有可能会泄露有关的商业机密。

3）合同制仓库：所谓合同制仓库是指第三方物流企业为特定客户提供专门物流服务的仓库或仓库区域，双方通过合同建立服务关系。合同制仓库是由公共仓库演变而来的。在物流发达的国家，越来越多的企业转向利用合同仓库或称第三方仓库。

合同制仓库不同于一般公共仓库。合同制仓库能够提供专业化的高效、经济和准确的物流服务，因为合同制仓库的设计水平更高、并且符合特殊商品的高标准、专业化的搬运要求。从本质上说，合同制仓库是生产企业和仓储企业之间建立的伙伴关系。正是由于这种伙伴关系，合同制仓储公司与传统仓储公司相比，能为货主提供特殊要求的空间、人力、设备和特殊服务。

合同制仓储公司只为数量有限的货主提供专门物流服务，其中包括存储、卸货、拼箱、货分类、在途混合、存货控制、运输安排、信息和货主要求的其他服务。由此可见，合同制仓库不仅仅只是提供存储服务，而且还可为货主提供一整套物流服务。

合同制仓库的优势如下。

① 有利于企业有效利用资源。合同制仓库比自有仓库更能有效处理季节性产业普遍存在的

产品的淡、旺季存储问题。例如，合同制仓储企业能够同时为销售旺季分别在冬季和夏季的企业进行合同仓储，如羽绒服与空调器。另外，由于合同仓库的管理具有专业性，管理专家能提供更具创新性的分销理念和降低成本的方法，因此有利于物流系统发挥功能，从而提高效率。

② 有利于企业扩大市场。合同制仓储能通过设施齐全的网络系统扩大企业的市场覆盖范围。由于合同制仓储企业具有战略性选址的设施与服务，因此，货主在不同位置的仓库得到的仓储管理和一系列物流服务都是相同的。企业在保持对集中仓储设施直接控制的同时，利用合同制仓库来降低直接人力成本、扩大市场的地理范围。

③ 有利于企业进行新市场的测试。企业在促销现有产品或推出新产品时，可以利用短期合同制仓储来考察产品的市场需求。当企业试图进入一个新的市场区域时，要花很长时间建立一套分销设施。然而通过合同仓储网络，企业可利用这一地区的现有设施为客户服务。

④ 有利于企业降低运输成本。由于合同制仓库处理不同货主的大量产品，因此经过拼箱作业后可大规模运输，这样大大降低了运输成本。

尽管合同制仓库具有以上优势，但也存在一些不利因素，其中对物流活动失去直接控制是企业最担心的问题。由于企业对合同制仓库的运作过程和雇佣员工等控制较少，因此这一因素成为产品价值较高的企业利用合同制仓库的最大障碍。

(3) 按存储商品的性能及技术设备分类

1) 通用仓库：它是用以储存一般没有特殊要求的工业品或农用品的仓库。在各类对外贸易仓库中占比重最大。

2) 专用仓库：它是专门用于储存某一类商品的仓库。在保养技术和保管设备方面能保证商品的质量安全。

3) 特种仓库：它是用于存储具有特殊性质，要求使用特别保管设备的商品，一般指化学危险品、易腐蚀品、石油及部分医药商品等。这类仓库配备有专门的设备。如冷藏库、保温库、危险品仓库等。

除了以上类别，还有保税仓库。保税仓库是根据有关法律和进出口贸易的规定，专门保管国外进口而暂时未缴纳进口税的商品的仓库，由海关统一进行监督和管理。保税仓库有关内容将在下一节专门介绍。

4.1.3 国际物流仓库的合理布局

国际物流货物仓库的合理配置，对外贸商品储备的合理分布、组织合理运输、加速国际物流货物流转速度和减少中转次数、降低物流费用和提高服务水平等都具有重要意义。国际物流货物仓库建设是随着工农业生产的发展和外贸商品流通规模的扩大而不断发展的。

(1) 国际物流货物的布局原则

1) 根据工农业生产发展与外贸商品流通规模之间的比例关系，预测掌握好相应期间的外贸商品流通量（即出口商品收购量和进口商品采购量）。

2) 处理好商品储存与商品收购、销售、调拨运输之间的比例关系，扣除直运、直拨等不经仓库环节的商品量，弄清计划期外贸商品的储存量或中转量。

3) 要掌握好外贸商品储存量与仓库建筑面积和实际使用面积之间的比例关系，掌握实际需要的仓库容积数据。

4) 了解计划期库存商品预计的周转次数。

(2) 制约国际物流货物仓库分布的综合因素

1) 一个国家的工农业生产布局。工农业生产发展了才会有大量商品出口，而储存这些出口商品的国际物流货物仓库应建设在大、中城市及出口工业品生产较集中的地区，确保就近收购、就近储存。

2）进出口业务发展。国际物流货物仓库网点布局应满足进出口购销业务发展需要，确定国际物流货物仓库建设的规模、类型、分布及发展方向。

3）经济区划和商品合理流向。国际物流货物仓库网点布局还应考虑经济区划和商品合理流向，做好国际物流货物仓库网点布局，降低物流费用。

4）国际物流运输条件。只有交通运输通畅了，外贸商品的流通才能近运、近储，快速将外贸商品发送出去，实现外贸商品的快速流转。

具体的一个国际物流货物仓库的选址应要求尽量靠近以下地点：出口商品生产厂、供货单位以及外贸专用出口商品生产基地；交通运输枢纽；中心城市；口岸、车站、机场；消费地，即进口厂家等。建立一个外贸仓库还必须考虑：

① 提供“六供”条件：供电、供煤、供气、供水、供油、供热。

② 排出废气、废水、废渣的条件。

③ 消除烟尘、噪声、震动等自然条件。

④ 地质条件差、震区等地不能建立外贸仓库。

⑤ 特殊外贸专用仓库的建立应有特殊的条件要求。

⑥ 要求具有防火、防污和环境安全卫生等条件。

4.2 Bonded Warehouse and Free Trade Zone

4.2.1 Bonded Warehouse

Bonded warehouse is the most typical in bonded system and has strong service function and great flexibility. Consequently, it is considered to be an important part of international logistics warehousing. As bonded warehouse is approved by the customs for the storage of bonded goods and other goods that have not gone through customs formalities, it belongs to the type of specialized warehouse. Besides, imported goods stored in the bonded warehouse are authorized to be modified, graded, sampled, mixed, and reprocessed in the warehouse. These goods are exempt from duty if re-exported, but subject to import duty if sold in domestic market. In this regard, bonded warehouses fall into the category of processing warehouses mentioned above. The administration to bonded warehouse in China is based on *Administrative Rules of the Customs of the People's Republic of China Concerning the Bonded Warehouse and Goods* promulgated by the General Administration of Customs.

(1) Definition of Bonded Warehouse

The development of international trade promoted the diversification of mode of trade, e.g., re-export of imported materials and accessories after processing and assembling, compensation trade, transit trade, futures trade. If tariff and taxes are levied upon imported goods, the cost of cargo will be higher when they are re-exported, which hinders development of foreign trade. The establishment of bonded warehouse, however, could help to promote processing trade and encourage foreign capital investment.

Bonded warehouse is one that is approved by customs authority to specifically store bonded goods. It is equipped with security facility for storage and stack of goods, perfect warehouse management system, detailed warehouse account book and professional management personnel trained and approved by the Customs. The bonded duration for foreign goods is no longer than 2 years, during which, goods owner may find appropriate timing for sale. Once sale is made, Customs clearance formalities such as duty payment could be arranged. If sale is not realized within 2 years, goods could be transshipped to other countries without duties payment.

(2) Goods Permitted for storage in Bonded Warehouse

China's Customs supervision system mainly focuses on bonded warehouse system. Bonded warehouse is approved and supervised by the Customs. The bonded warehouse is confined to store the following goods:

1) Goods permitted by the Customs to import but suspended for formality of import duty. These include pre-imported goods to meet project and production need or others. These goods are stored in bonded warehouse, among which the picked-up portion is cleared and the remaining returned with duty unpaid. This category of goods also includes those having no finalized flow direction or handling decision due to market variation in importing country. If situation allows actual import, these goods are levied tariff and other duties. In this case the taxation on importers is postponed to when the goods are sold.

2) Goods needing technical processing for import. Some goods need to be altered in their decoration and size of packing or other processing before they become suitable for sale in importing country, which could be completed in bonded warehouse. When meeting the requirements of importing country, the goods could be taxed and sold, or else they should be returned without taxation.

3) Goods for re-export after processing on buyer-supplied materials. To some buyer-supplied material processing business, the processing is completed in free trade zone or bonded warehouse. For reason of re-export, these goods are allowed to be stored in bonded warehouse without taxation.

4) Goods of temporary storage for transit. Some goods need to be transited for reasons of impossible sales in importing country, favorable transit condition of the bonded warehouse, or difficult direct export to a third country. These goods could be stored in bonded warehouse.

Bonded warehouse is suitable to both import and export goods.

(3) Types of Bonded Warehouse

1) Specialized Bonded Warehouse: Warehouse approved by the Customs and operated and used by enterprises with right of foreign trade.

2) Public Bonded Warehouse: Comprehensive bonded warehouse approved by the Customs, which is an economic entity with legal personality. This type of warehouse usually doesn't trade commodities but only serves owners of bonded goods.

3) Bonded Factory: A whole factory or specialized workshop under supervision of the Customs that specifically conducts processing of imported materials and assembling of imported parts.

4) Customs Supervised Warehouse: Storing goods or luggage entering territory but not

picked up yet or goods having no complete documents or formalities and thus not cleared by the Customs and needed to be supervised in Customs Supervised Warehouse. The other type of Customs supervised warehouse is export supervised warehouse, which stores goods that have been successfully traded and paid but temporarily not allowed by the Customs to leave territory.

4.2.2 Free Trade Zone

Free trade zone is a specified region and warehouse established, approved, and supervised by the Customs. Foreign goods are not taxed in the Zone or when they are re-exported. However, when they enter the market of the country where the Zone is located, Customs clearance should be conducted and tariffs be paid. Foreign goods could be stored, assorted, consolidated, processed, and exhibited in the Zone.

In 1990, China, learning from international practice, founded her first Free Economic Zone, Shanghai Waigaoqiao Free Trade Zone. Free trade zone is a result of China's comprehensive opening-up strategy in 1990s, the founding of which is to improve investment environment and attract foreign capital. Till now, free trade zone has the greatest opening degree in China and plays significant role in promoting both regional and national economy. The Zone has particular advantages in attracting foreign capital and conducting export processing, international trade, transit trade and warehousing.

Since 1980s, a key trend of Free Economic Zone is that it abandoned the traditional mode possessed by free trade port, free trade zone and export processing zone, evolving from playing simplex function to performing multiple and comprehensive functions. Free Economic Zone not only pays attention to foreign trade and export processing, but introduces finance, insurance and travel into the Zone. China's free trade zone exhibits the same trend with worldwide Free Economic Zone, fortifying China's foreign trade and developing export processing, warehousing, finance and insurance as well.

4.2 保税仓库与保税区

4.2.1 保税仓库

保税仓库是保税制度中应用最为广泛的一种形式，具有较强的服务功能和较大的灵活性，对于促进国际贸易和加工贸易的开展起到了重要作用。因此，它是国际物流货物仓储一个非常重要的部分。由于保税仓库是指经海关批准设立的专门存放保税货物及其他未办结海关手续货物的仓库，所以属于专用仓库一类。而且，储存于保税仓库内的进口货物经批准可在仓库内进行改装、分级、抽样、混合和再加工等，这些货物如再出口则免缴关税，但如果进入国内市场销售则须补缴进口关税。就这点而言，保税仓库属于前面提到的加工仓库一类。我国海关对保税仓库管理的基本依据是海关总署颁布的《中华人民共和国海关对保税仓库及所存货物的管理办法》。

(1) 保税仓库的概念

随着国际贸易的不断发展，贸易方式日益多样化，如进口原材料、配件进行加工装配后复出口、补偿贸易、转口贸易、期货贸易等。如果进口时要征收关税，必然会加大货物的成本，不利于发展对外贸易。建立保税仓库后，有利于推动加工贸易的开展，鼓励外国企业在本国投资。

保税仓库是指经海关批准专门用于存放保税商品的仓库，具备专门储存、堆放商品的安全设施，健全的仓库管理制度和详细的仓库账册，配备经海关培训认可的专职管理人员。外国货物的保税期一般最长为两年。这期间，经营者可以找到最适当的销售时机，一旦实现销售，再办理关税等通关手续。如果两年之内未能销售完毕，则可再运往其他国家，保税仓库所在国不收取关税。

(2) 保税仓库允许存放的货物范围

我国海关监管制度中，主要是保税仓库制度，保税仓库也是由海关批准并由海关监管的。我国规定，保税仓库制度允许存放的货物范围如下。

1）缓办纳税手续的进口货物。这主要包括由于进口国工程或生产需要以及其他种种原因而造成的预进口货物，储存在保税仓库内，随需随提的部分办理通关手续，剩余的货物免税退运。也包括因进口国情况变化、市场变化，而暂时无法决定去向的货物，或是无法做出最后处理的进口货物，这些情况下都需要将货物存放一段时间。如果条件变化，需要实际进口，再缴纳关税和其他税费，这就使进口商将纳税时间推迟到货物实际内销的时间。

2）需做进口技术处置的货物。有些商品到货后，由于不适于在进口国销售，需换包装装潢、改包装尺寸或做其他加工处理，则可进入保税仓库进行这一技术处置，待到符合进口国的要求再内销完税，不符合的则免税退返。

3）来料加工后复出的货物。对有些来料加工业务，也是在保税区或保税仓库完成的。由于这些货物完成加工后复出口，所以可免税存放于保税仓库。

4）不内销而过境转口的货物。有些货物或内销无望而转口，或在该区域存放有利于转口，或无法向第三国直接进口而需转口，货物则可存放于保税仓库中。

保税仓库在国际物流中，不仅适于进口货物，也可用于出口货物。

(3) 保税仓库的类型

1）专业型保税仓库：这是由有外贸经营权的企业，经海关批准而建立的自管自用的保税仓库。

2）公共保税仓库：这是具有法人资格的经济实体，是经海关批准建立的综合性保税仓库。这类保税仓库一般不经营进出口商品，只为国内外保税货物持有者服务。

3）保税工厂：这是整个工厂或专用车间在海关监督管理下，专门生产进料加工、进件装配复出口产品的工厂。

4）海关监管仓库：海关监管仓库主要存放已进境而所有人未来提取的货物或行李物品，或者无证到货、单证不齐、手续不完备以及违反海关规程，海关不予放行，需要暂存海关监管仓库等候海关处理的货物。海关监管仓库的另一种类型是出口监管仓库，专门存储已对外成交，并已结汇，但海关批准暂不出境的货物。

4.2.2 保税区

保税区又称保税仓库区，是海关设置的或经海关批准注册的、受海关监管的特定地区和仓库群。国外商品存入保税区内，可以暂时不缴纳进口税；若再出口，也无需缴纳出口税；若要进入保税区所在国的国内市场，则要办理报关手续，缴纳进口税。进入保税区的国外商品，可以在保税区内进行储存、分类、混装、加工、展览等。

1990 年，经国务院批准，我国借鉴国际通行做法，按照自由贸易区模式建立了中国第一个自由经济区——上海外高桥保税区。兴建保税区是我国 20 世纪 90 年代实行全方位开放战略的新产物，其设立的目的是改善投资环境和吸引外资。保税区是我国目前开放度最大的地区，对所在地区的区域经济和全国经济的发展都起着重要的作用。建区后的这几年中，保税区在发挥招商引资、出口加工、国际贸易、转口贸易和仓储等功能，带动区域经济发展等方面显示出独特的优势。

20 世纪 80 年代以来，自由经济区发展的一个重要特点是突破传统的自由港、自由贸易区、出口加工区的模式，由原来的单一功能向着多功能综合型方向发展，它们不仅重视对外贸易，也重视出口加工，并把金融、保险、旅游等第三产业引入自由经济区。在这一点上，我国保税区和世界自由经济区的发展趋势是一致的。在大力发展对外贸易的同时，各保税区纷纷开展出口加工、仓储、金融、保险等业务，努力走出一条有中国特色的工贸结合的综合型自由之路。

4.3 Basic Procedures for International Cargo Warehousing Operations

Warehousing management is an important part of international logistics management, which directly influences the operation efficiency of international logistics. In the following part, management on warehousing and bonded warehouse will be introduced.

4.3.1 Warehousing Management

(1) Warehouse Receipt and Its Management

Warehouse receipt is a legal document issued by warehouse keeper after acceptance of cargo proving the delivery of a quantity of goods to the warehouse for safekeeping. The Receipt is a certificate upon which the obligation of warehouse keeper, cargo owner, and consignee is allocated and stored goods are returned by warehouse keeper. It is a legal obligation of the warehouse keeper to issue the Receipt to show the acceptance of the cargo listed in the Receipt. At the expiration of storage or other pickup time agreed by the keeper, the holder of the Receipt submits the Receipt to the warehouse keeper; upon check of document, the latter arranges formality of goods pickup.

(2) Entry of Cargo

The entry of cargo to warehouse is the process of cargo acceptance, which includes pickup, unloading, handling, tallying, inspection, organization and stacking of goods and arrangement of entry formality. Based on business procedure, it has steps of acceptance preparation, cargo acceptance, inspection, and warehouse entry.

1) Acceptance preparation: Arranging allocation of goods, organizing necessary personnel and equipment, and preparing corresponding documents.

2) Document examination and cargo tallying and acceptance: Examining entry documents and carefully tallying goods against the documents; rejecting and returning the goods or storing them in certain place after recording should any wrong delivery be detected. Any shortage of or damage to the goods must be recorded in detail on delivery note or on note of mistake, which should be signed by both parties.

3) Filling in warehousing warrant: Filling in warehousing warrant and establishing file

of entry by warehouse keeper.

4) Handling by classification: Moving qualified goods to selected location by their quantity and type listed in the warehouse warrant. Import goods are stacked in order of entry and export goods in order of arrival at port and hatch allotted.

5) Issuing documents: Including the issuance of goods acceptance note, warehouse warrant and warehouse receipt. Warehouse keeper should count and record in-store goods as required.

(3) Pickup of Cargo

Pickup of cargo includes four ways: proprietary shipping line pickup, pickup at station/port, pickup at owner's, and warehouse reception.

1) Proprietary shipping line pickup: Transited goods are directly shipped by train to proprietary shipping line of the warehouse.

2) Pickup at station/port: In port pickup, the consignee hands over the originals of Bill of Lading to the shipping company in exchange for Delivery Order. After completing the formalities of customs declaration and tax payment, the consignee can pick up the goods from the designated warehouse upon Delivery Order.

3) Pickup at owner's: Goods are picked up from site of cargo owner upon trust of consignor.

4) Warehouse reception: Goods are delivered directly to the warehouse. Warehouse keeper or inspector receives goods from the shipper and complete transfer procedure.

(4) Inspection of Cargo

1) Inspection preparation: Determining storage place, pile shape and manner of safekeeping; preparing materials for stacking, covering and padding, handling equipment and personnel, and inspection tools; understanding inspection certificate and related materials.

2) Document examination: Including Inward Notice, purchasing agreement provided by depositor, Quality certificate, Container Load Plan (CLP), Weight Memo, Specification, Sales Delivery Detail Report, Drawings, Laboratory Test Report provided by supplier.

3) Inspection and acceptance: Including inspection on quantity, type, packing and quality of goods as well as quantity of packing. If any non-compliance in respect of the type, specification, quantity or weight of the goods occurs, or any damage, mustiness or contamination to the package rises, comment should be made on the waybill. Warehouse keeper should fill in cargo acceptance record upon result of inspection.

(5) Safekeeping of Cargo

1) On floor storage: leveling the goods on the floor.

2) Pallet on floor storage: storing the goods in pallet on the floor.

3) Stacking on floor storage: stacking the goods directly on the floor, which is suitable to bulk cargo.

4) Pallet stacking: stacking goods on the pallets which are piled up on the floor.

5) On rack storage: stacking the goods on racks.

(6) Exit of Cargo

Exit of cargo includes seven steps including warehouse receipt examining, checking and bookkeeping, goods picking and goods preparing, centralized handling, exit reexamining and goods dispatching, outbound order filling, and site and file clearing.

1) Warehouse receipt examining: upon the Outward Notice by depositor or receipt holder, warehouse keeper must examine the receipt.

2) Checking and bookkeeping: Once legitimacy and authenticity of the warehouse receipt is testified, the accountant should check the storage of goods. According to items listed in the certificate, he should make record on cargo storage book, write off corresponding storage, comment on outbound certificate, take back warehouse receipt, and issue Outbound Order which is delivered to warehouse keeper for goods picking and preparing.

3) Goods picking and preparing: After reexamining Outbound Order and certificate, the warehouse keeper should check the goods by storage location and pick goods according to the items listed in the certificate. Goods preparing is to prepare goods to be delivered on time, quality and quantity.

4) Centralized handling: centralizing the cargo from the same owner for handling in order not to make wrong or shortage shipment.

5) Exit reexamining and goods dispatching: To avoid wrong exit of goods, reexamining should be made immediately after goods preparation. Then warehouse operator transfers the type and quantity of goods listed in Delivery Order to consignee.

6) Outbound order filling: After the transfer of goods, warehouse keeper should fill in Outbound Order with actual quantity and date of dispatching, sign the Order and submit it to cargo owner together with related certificates for purpose of charges settlement.

7) Site and file clearing: Site clearance is made to storeroom, storage site, equipment and tools; file clearance refers to organizing documents concerning goods delivery, storage, shortage and stack position and put them away for safekeeping and later use.

4.3.2 Management on Bonded Warehouse

Bonded warehouse management/bonded warehousing refers to the storage of bonded goods in the bonded warehouse approved by the customs. Bonded warehousing will be directly monitored by the customs. Therefore, the difference between bonded warehousing and general warehousing is that the Customs has great supervision over bonded warehousing, and the Customs requires to be able to grasp the real-time status of goods in the whole storage cycle.

(1) Supervision over Cargo in Bonded Warehouse by the Customs

1) Storage of goods: As required by the Customs, bonded warehouse is established independently and used for specific goods other than non-bonded cargo. The Customs is entitled to appointing personnel to the warehouse any time for storage and account book examination. Personnel (s) might be stationed in the warehouse if needed.

2) Processing of goods: Goods are not allowed to be processed in bonded warehouse. Any altering to and marks on the packing or others should be approved and supervised by the Customs.

3) Usage of goods: Goods stored in bonded warehouse are bonded goods under supervi-

sion of the Customs. Without approval of the Customs and related formalities, they are not allowed to be sold, picked up, delivered, changed, mortgaged, transferred, or used for other purpose.

4) Pickup of goods: Cross Customs or warehouse pickup of bonded goods is generally not allowed; it has to be registered in the Customs should cross customs pickup be needed.

(2) Business Conducted in Bonded Warehouse

1) Storage, handling, transit, distribution, packing and labeling of goods.

2) Arrangement of Customs formalities.

3) Delivery and transport of goods.

4) Selection of import goods source and new trading channels for importers.

5) Provision of platform for exporters to exhibit their goods in international market, as well as new trading approach.

6) Service of operation. The services provided include supervising condition of shipment, providing shipment and other commercial information, preparing various shipping documents, providing cargo tracing report, handling of containers and so on.

7) Assembling of mechanical parts, alteration and repacking of cargo.

4.3 国际物流货物仓储业务基本程序

仓储管理是国际物流管理业务中的一项重要内容，其管理水平的高低将直接影响到国际物流业务运作的效率。下面重点讲述仓储管理业务和保税仓库管理业务。

4.3.1 仓储管理业务

(1) 仓单及其管理和使用

仓单是保管人在接受仓储货物后签发的表明一定数量的保管货物已经交付仓储保管的法律文书，它是确定保管人和仓单持有人、提货人责任和义务的依据，是仓储保管人凭以返还保管物的凭证。签发仓单是仓储保管人的法律义务，这表明保管人已接受了仓单上所记载的仓储货物。仓单由保管人提供，在保管期满或者经保管人同意的提货时间，仓单持有人向保管人提交仓单，经保管人核对无误后，保管人给予办理提货手续。

(2) 货物的入库业务

货物入库业务即收货过程，包括货物的接运、卸货、搬运、清点、验收、整理、堆码、办理入库手续等。按其业务程序可以分为收货准备、货物接运、货物验收、货物入库等几个环节。

1) 收货准备：根据入库货物情况提前安排货位，组织必需的人力、机力，做好文件单证准备。

2) 核对凭证，点收货物：货物运抵仓库后，首先要检验货物入库凭证，然后按入库凭证对货物进行仔细核对。如果发现送错，应拒收退回，或进行清点并另行存放，做好记录；如发现差错、破损等，必须在送货单上详细注明或出具差错、异状记录，批注时要经双方签证。

3) 填制入库单证：仓管员填写入库单，建立入库档案。

4) 分类搬运：验收合格的入库商品，按入库单开制的数量和品种集中，分批送到预定的货位。进口货按入库顺序，出口货物按到港顺序和配舱顺序堆码。

5）凭证签发：凭证签发是货物入库办妥收货业务的签证手续。包括货物到库接收的凭证签发、货物入库后的凭证签发和仓单的签发。对入库货物应按照要求进行详细记录和统计。

（3）货物接运

货物接运分为四种方式，即专用线接运，车站、码头提货，自提入库，库内接货。

1）专用线接运：专用线接运是铁路部门将转运的货物直接运送到仓库内部专用线的一种接运方式。

2）车站、码头提货：车站提货时，收货人向车站出示“铁路运单正本”即可提货。码头提货时，收货人用正本提单向船公司换取提货单，向海关办理抵关纳税手续后，可凭提货单从指定仓库提取货物。

3）自提入库：到货主单位提取货物，这是仓库受托运方的委托，直接到货主单位提货的一种形式。

4）库内接货：这是直接送达仓库的一种供货方式，当货物到达后，保管员或验收员直接与送货人办理接收工作，当面验收并办理交接手续。

（4）货物验收

1）验收准备：应提前确定存放地点、垛形和保管方法；准备堆码苫垫所需材料和装卸搬运机械、设备及人力；准备相应的检验工具；搜集和熟悉验收凭证及有关资料。

2）核对证件：证件包括存货单位提供的入库通知单、订货合同等；供货方面提供的质量证明书或合格证、装箱单、磅码单、说明书、发货明细表、图纸、化验单等。

3）验收：包括数量检验，品种验收与实物核对、包装验收、商品的内在质量和包装的数量验收等。在验收过程中，如果发现品种、规格不符，件数或重量溢短，包装破损、潮霉、污染和其他问题时，要在运单上批注。验收后，填写“货物验收记录”。

（5）货物保管

货物保管通常包括以下方法。

1）地面平放式：将保管物品直接平放在地面上。

2）托盘平放式：将保管物品直接放在托盘上，再将托盘平放于地面。

3）直接堆放式：将货物在地面上直接码放堆积。

4）托盘堆码式：将货物直接堆码在托盘上，再将托盘堆码放在地面上。

5）货架存放式：将货物直接码放在货架上。

（6）货物出库

仓储货物出库业务流程包括审核仓单、核对登账、配货、备货、集中搬倒、出库复核和发货、填单销账、现场清理和归案七个环节。

1）审核仓单：仓库接到存货人或仓单持有人出库通知后，必须对仓单进行核对。

2）核对登账：审核仓单的合法性和真实性以后，仓库货物会计要核对货物储存情况。核对无误后，可根据凭证所列各项内容，登入货物保管账，核销储存量，并在出库凭证上批注，收回仓单，签发仓库货物出库单，交仓库保管员查对配货。

3）配货、备货：保管员对仓库会计转来的货物出库凭证复核无误后，按其所列项目内容和凭证上的批注，到货位对货，核实后进行配货。备货是根据规定，按时、按质、按量地准备好应交的货物。

4）集中搬倒：要把一个货主一次出库货物尽量集中一起，避免抓药式捡货装车造成错装、漏装。

5）出库复核并发货：为了保证出库货物不出差错，备货后应立即进行复核。复核完成后，仓储管理人员按提货单上所记载的有关货物的品种、数量点交给提货人。

6）填单销账：货物交点以后，保管员应在出库单上填写实发数、发货日期等内容，并签名。将出库单和有关证件资料及时交送货主，以便货主办理费用结算。

7）现场和档案的清理：现场清理包括库房、场地、设备和工具等。档案清理指一批货物发完后，应根据出入库情况，将收发、保管、溢缺数量和垛位安排等资料整理好，存入商品保管档案，妥善保存，以备日后查用。

4.3.2 保税仓库管理

保税仓库管理/保税仓储指的是在海关核准的保税仓库里存放保税货物的仓储行为。保税仓储会受到海关的直接监控，因此保税仓储与一般仓储的不同之处在于海关对保税仓储的监管力度很大，海关要求能够掌握货物全储存周期的实时状态。

(1) 海关对保税仓库货物监管的主要内容

1）货物的存放：海关要求保税仓库必须独立设置，专库专用，保税货物不得与非保税货物混放。海关可随时派员进入保税仓库检查货物储存情况，查阅有关仓库账册，必要时可派员驻库监管。

2）货物的加工：规定在保税仓库中不得对所存货物进行加工。如果需对货物进行改变包装、加刷唛头等整理工作，应向海关申请核准并在海关监管下进行。

3）货物的使用：保税仓库所存货物，属于海关监管的保税货物，未经海关核准并按规定办理有关手续任何人不得出售、提取、交付、调换、抵押、转让或移作他用。

4）货物的提取：公共保税仓库的保税货物，一般不得跨关区提取和转库存取，只能供应本关区内的加工贸易企业按规定提取使用。必须跨关区提取的，加工贸易企业应事先在海关办理登记备案。

(2) 保税仓库的管理业务项目

1）货物的存储、装卸、中转、分发、包装、贴标签。

2）办理货物的各种海关手续。

3）货物收发和集疏运输手续。

4）为进口客商选择进口货物的场所和新的交易渠道。

5）为出口客商提供产品在国际市场的展示窗口和新的贸易途径。

6）提供经营管理服务。监督船运状态，提供船运和各种商业信息；准备各种运输文件；定期提供货物跟踪报告；对集装箱的一些操作等。

7）进行机械零部件组装、货物修复、整型、分改包装。

4.4 International Cargo Packing

4.4.1 Significance of Packing

Packing has the function of protecting quality and quantity of goods in circulation. In international trade, appropriate packing helps in the storage, safekeeping, transport, handling, tallying, sale and security guard of the goods, as well as selection and carrying by customers. Well packaged goods in themselves attract customers. In addition, packing to some extent reflects production, technology and culture level of a country.

When designing packing of goods, a company should comprehensively integrate packing storage, handling and transport of goods. That is to say, packing should take into consideration the convenient storage and speedy transport in order to reduce logistics cost.

4.4.2 Basic Requirement on Goods Packing

(1) Scientificity, Firmness and Security

The material and design of packing must make it scientific and firm. The packing should not only fit characteristics of the goods but be suitable to long-distance transport, various transport mode and weather condition in order to safeguard the quality and quantity of the goods.

(2) Foreign market satisfaction

The material and design of packing should conform to sale and consumption habit in foreign market and abide by regulations on packing and decoration by import countries in order to expand export.

(3) Labor, material and freight saving

When choosing material and improving packing, a company should consider saving of material and reduction of logistics cost and freight.

4.4.3 Types of Packing

Internationally traded cargo is classified into three categories: nude cargo, bulk cargo and packed cargo. The packing is classified into transport packing and sales packing by their function in commodity circulation.

(1) Transport packing

Transport packing is also called outer packing, which is used for purpose of quality and quantity protection and convenient transport, storage, checking, tallying and distribution of goods. It includes single piece packing and collective packing.

1) Single piece packing: Goods being put into a smaller vessel by piece or pieces according to their form and characteristics. In single piece packing, enough consideration should be given to material fitness and structure and shape of the packing, as well as temperature, humidity and port facility in different countries or regions, together with performance, characteristics, and shape of goods. The single piece packing can be classified by its appearance, texture and material. When classified by appearance, the frequently used packages are wrappage, box, bucket and bag. When it comes to texture of package, there are soft, semi-rigid and rigid package. By the material used, we have packages that are made of paper, metal, wood, plastic, cotton and linen, pottery product of bamboo, willow, straw and glass.

2) Collective packing: Referring to the collection of some single pieces into a bigger package or vessel. In this case, the package includes:

① Container: Reusable cubic box made of metal sheet such as steel and aluminum. It is a package of goods and at the same time a part of conveyance. The most frequently used shipping containers are respectively in size of 8ft×8ft×20ft and 8ft×8ft×40ft.

② Flexible container: It is a wrappage woven of synthetic fiber or composite material whose mouth could be tightened. It is suitable for bucket packed or bag packed goods, with each container holding 1～1.5 tons of cargo.

③ Pallet: A pad put under a piece or a set of goods. To prevent falling of goods from pallet, goods are usually firmly bundled to the pallet with thick liner board, shrinkable film, and stretchable film. Usually a pallet has a capacity of 1～1.5 tons of goods.

(2) Sales packing

Also called small packing or inner packing, sales packing faces consumers in commodity retail.

Except decoration and literal statement, bar code is also printed on sales packing. Supermarkets in many countries use bar code technique to perform automatic scan and settlement, thus products are forbidden to access supermarket without bar code on the package even though they are brand name products. Some countries even stipulate that products without bar code be not allowed import. In this context, in April 1991, China joined EAN International who assigned 690, 691 and 692 as our country code. Correspondingly, goods with bar code starting with these three numbers are goods made in China.

4.4.4 Marks on Packing

Marks on packing are simple figures and letters printed on outer package of goods.

(1) Shipping Mark

Shipping mark is made up of a simple geometric figure, together with some letters, numbers, and simple words. It makes goods easily recognizable. The content of shipping mark includes code of consignor and consignee, name and code of destination, and number of piece and batch. Sometimes country of origin, number of contract, number of license, weight (gross and net) and size (length, width and height) are attached too.

To unify and simplify shipping marks, UNECE Working Party on Facilitation of International Trade Procedures, with the support of International Organization for Standardization (ISO) and International Cargo Handling Coordination Association (ICHCA), formulated and recommended a set of standard shipping marks. The marks include: abbreviated name of consignor and consignee in English, number of reference (e.g. number of B/L, order and invoice), destination, and number of pieces.

(2) Indicative Mark

Indicative mark is used to propose some requests on handling and storage of fragile, damageable or perishable goods by the usage of some simple but striking figures or words according to the performance and characteristics of goods. Examples are This Side Up, Handle with Care, To Be Protected from Heat, Heave Here, Open from This Side, Use No Hooks, and Fragile and so on.

(3) Warning Mark

It is mark on outer packing used to strengthen security measures in the transport, storage and handling of hazardous goods with purpose of protecting the safety of goods and personnel. For hazardous articles such as Explosives, Inflammable, Spontaneously Combustible, Dangerous When Wet, Poison, Corrosive, Oxidizing Material, and Material Radioactive, explicit and obvious warning marks should be printed on shipping package.

4.4.5 Neutral Packing and Designated Brand Packing

At present, the use of neutral packing or designated brand packing in the sales packing of some export commodities has become a more commonly used packaging method in many trade practices, mainly to break the tariff or non-tariff barriers of some importing countries and regions, and sometimes to meet the special needs of commercial transactions, such as entrepot trade. In addition, neutral packaging can also help manufacturers improve the competitiveness of their export products to expand sales and earn more foreign exchange.

(1) Neutral Packing

This is a packing without country or place of origin or name of producer printed on the commodity or its exterior/interior packing, not even brand, trademark, or any letters. Neutral packing includes no brand packing and designated brand neutral packing. For the former, there is neither name of origin or producer, nor brand or trademark on the packing; Whereas for the latter, only brand or trademark designated by the buyer is printed on the packing, without name of origin or producer.

The usage of neutral packing becomes a regular practice in international trade to overcome tariff barrier, quota restriction, and other discriminative import limitation measures adopted by some countries or regions.

(2) Designated Brand Packing

Designated brand packing involves seller printing brand or trademark designated by the buyer on the commodity or its packing upon request of the buyer. Supermarkets, department stores and specialty stores in many countries print their own trademarks or brands on their commodities or on the packing for sale in order to enhance their popularity and exhibit value of the commodities. Many exporters, for purpose of utilizing buyers' operation capability and business reputation, are willing to accept this method to raise commodity price and expand sales. In China, exporters can accept printing trademarks designated by the buyer for long-term stable purchasing order.

4.4.6 Green Packing

With the increasing deteriorate resource scarcity and environment pollution, environment protection becomes a new international issue. Some countries use packing as one of their non-tariff barriers out of their support of environment protection or their own economic benefit. For instance, the German Packaging Federation banns the usage of PVC as packing material; Italy forbids foreign exporters to use PVC as blister package since 1990; and Korea requires sellers of imported household electrical appliances to recycle poly-foams in the packing since 1993. Therefore, green packing should be given enough attention in international trade.

Since 1980s, industrialized countries began to follow principles of 3R, meaning Reduce, Reuse and Recycle, which was strengthened in 1990s by the addition of 1D, meaning Degradable. In 1990s, China introduced Green Packing, which is in accordance with the principle of 3R and 1D. Green Packing should at least meet the requirements of material, resource and energy saving, degradable disposals, less or no pollution to environment, and being harmless to environment and human being.

4.4 国际物流货物包装

4.4.1 商品包装的重要意义

商品包装是保护商品在流通过程中品质完好和数量完整的重要举措。在国际贸易中，经过适当包装的商品，有利于储存、保管、运输、装卸、计数、销售和防止盗窃等工作的进行，有利于消费者的挑选和携带。包装良好的商品，还有利于吸引顾客，扩大销路，增加销售，多创外汇。此外，商品的包装还在一定程度上反映出一个国家的生产水平、科学技术和文化艺术水平。

在考虑出口商品包装设计和具体作业过程时，应把包装、储存、搬运和运输有机联系起来，统筹考虑，全面规划，实现现代国际物流所要求的“包、储、运一体化”，即从开始包装就考虑方便的储存、快速的运输，以降低物流费用，符合现代物流的系统化要求。

4.4.2 商品包装的基本要求

(1) 科学、牢固、安全

包装的用料和设计必须科学、牢固，既符合商品的特性，又适应国际贸易长途运输，适应各种不同的运输方式和沿途气候条件变化的要求，从而保护商品的品质安全和数量完整。

(2) 适合国外市场的需要和规定

包装的用料和设计，应力求适应国外市场的销售习惯和消费习惯，适应进口国家对于包装、装潢的合理规定，以利于扩大出口商品的销路。

(3) 省工、省料、省运费

在选用材料与改进包装等方面，都要从节约物料、降低成本及节省运费的角度考虑。

4.4.3 包装的种类

进入国际贸易的商品，可以分为三类，即裸装货（Nude Cargo）、散装货（Bulk Cargo）和包装货（Packed Cargo）。

国际贸易中的商品包装，按其在流通过程中作用的不同，可以分为运输包装和销售包装两种。

(1) 运输包装

运输包装又称大包装或外包装，它的作用主要在于保护商品的品质和数量，便于运输、储存、检验、计数、分拨。运输包装的方式主要有两种：单件运输包装和集合运输包装。

1）单件运输包装：单件运输包装是指根据商品的形态或特性将一件或数件商品装入一个较小容器内的包装方式。制作单件运输包装时，要注意选用适当的材料，并要求结构造型科学合理，同时还应考虑不同国家和地区的气温、湿度、港口设施和不同商品的性能、特点、形状等因素。单件运输包装的种类很多：按照包装外形来分，习惯上常用的有包、箱、桶、袋等；按照包装的质地来分，主要有软性包装、半硬性包装和硬性包装；按照制作包装所采用的材料来分，一般常用的有纸质包装，金属包装，木制品包装，塑料包装，棉麻制品包装，竹、柳、草制品包装，玻璃制品包装和陶瓷包装。

2）集合运输包装：主要是指将一定数量的单件商品组合成一件大的包装或装入一个大的包装容器内。集合运输包装的种类如下。

① 集装箱（Container）：集装箱一般由钢板、铝板等金属制成，多为正方形，可以反复使用周转，它既是货物的运输包装，又是运输工具的组成部分。目前国际上最常用的海运集装箱规格为 8 英尺×8 英尺×20 英尺和 8 英尺×8 英尺×40 英尺两种。

② 集装包、袋（Flexible Container）：集装包是用合成纤维或复合材料编织成抽口式的包，适于装载已经包装好的桶装和袋装的多件商品。每包一般可容纳 1～1.5 吨重的货物。

③ 托盘（Pallet）：托盘是在一件或一组货物下面所附加的一块垫板。为防止货物散落，需要用厚箱板纸、收缩薄膜、拉伸薄膜等将货物牢固包扎在托盘上，组合成一件“托盘包装”。每一托盘的装载量一般为 1～1.5 吨。

（2）销售包装

销售包装又称小包装或内包装。它是随着商品进入零售环节和消费者直接见面的包装，实际是一种零售包装。

在销售包装上，除附有装潢画面和文字说明外，有的还印有条形码的标志。由于许多国家的超级市场多使用条形码技术，进行自动扫描结算，如商品包装上没有条形码，即使是名优产品也不能进入超级市场。有的国家甚至规定商品包装上无条形码标志的即不予进口。为了适应国际市场的需要和扩大出口，1991 年 4 月，我国正式加入了国际物品编码协会，该会分配给我国的国别号为“690”“691”“692”。凡标有“690”“691”“692”条码的商品，即表示为中国产品。

4.4.4 包装的标志

包装标志是指在商品外包装上刷制的简单图形和文字。

（1）运输标志（Shipping Mark）

运输标志，习惯上称为“唛头”，它通常是由一个简单的几何图形和一些字母、数字及简单的文字组成，其作用主要是便于识别货物。

运输标志的主要内容有收、发货人的代号；目的地的名称或代号；件号、批号。此外，有时根据需要还列有原产国名称、合同号、许可证号、重量（毛重和净重）以及尺码（长、宽、高）等内容。

鉴于运输标志的内容、繁简不一，联合国欧洲经济委员会简化国际贸易程序工作组，在国际标准化组织和国际装卸协调协会的支持下，制定了一套标准的运输标志向各国推荐使用。该运输标志包括收货人或买方的英文缩写字母或简称；参考号，如运单号、订单号或发货票号；目的地；件号。

（2）指示性标志（Indicative Mark）

根据商品的性能和特点，用简单醒目的图形或文字对一些容易破碎、残损、变质的商品，提出某些在装卸搬运操作和存放保管条件方面的要求和注意事项，可用指示性标志。例如，“此端向上”“小心轻放”“怕火”“由此吊起”“由此开启”“勿用手钩”“易碎”等。

(3) 警告性标志（Warning Mark）

警告性标志是针对危险货物，为了在运输、保管和装卸过程中，使有关人员加强防护措施，以保护物资和人身的安全而加在外包装上的标志。

凡包装内装有爆炸品、易燃物品、自燃物品、遇水燃烧物品、有毒品、腐蚀性物品、氧化剂和放射性物品等危险品，应在运输包装上刷写清楚明显的危险品警告标志。

4.4.5 中性包装和定牌包装

目前，某些出口商品中的销售包装采用中性包装或定牌包装已经成为许多贸易实务中比较常用的包装方法，主要是为了打破某些进口国家和地区的关税或非关税壁垒，有时也是为了适应商业交易的特殊需要如转口贸易。此外，中性包装还能帮助生产厂商提高出口产品的竞争能力以扩大销售从而赚取更多外汇。

(1) 中性包装

中性包装是指在商品上和内外包装上不注明生产国别、地名和生产厂商的名称，也不注明商标或牌号，甚至没有任何文字的包装。中性包装包括无牌中性包装和定牌中性包装。前者是指包装上既无生产地名和厂商名称，又无商标、品牌；后者是指包装上仅有买方指定的商标或品牌，但无生产地名和出口厂商的名称。

采用中性包装，是为了打破某些进口国家和地区实行的关税壁垒、配额限制和其他一些限制进口的歧视性措施。目前，某些出口商品使用中性包装已成为国际贸易中的一种习惯做法。

(2) 定牌包装

定牌包装是指卖方按买方要求在其出售的商品或包装上标明买方指定的商标或牌号。当前，世界许多国家的超级市场、大百货公司和专业商店，对其经营出售的商品，都要在商品上或包装上标有本商店使用的商标或品牌，以扩大本店知名度和显示该商品的身价。许多国家的出口厂商，为了利用买方的经营能力及其商业信誉和品牌声誉，以提高商品售价和扩大销路，也愿意接受定牌生产。在我国出口贸易中，一般对于国外大量的长期的稳定的订货，可以接受买方指定的商标。

4.4.6 绿色包装

随着环境资源的日益稀缺和环境污染的不断恶化，环保已成为新的国际焦点，国际贸易中货物及货物的包装同样涉及环保问题。一些国家出于对环保事业的支持，也出于对自己经济利益的保护，将包装也列入限制进口的非关税壁垒之一。如德国包装联盟禁止使用PVC包装材料；意大利1990年起通知外国出口商不能使用PVC片作泡罩包装；韩国从1993年起要求进口家电制品的销售商负责收回其产品包装中的泡沫塑料。所以，在国际贸易的过程中要考虑到这一趋势的存在，预先采取适当的对策。

关于绿色包装，工业发达国家早在20世纪80年代叫做“3R”原则，即减量化（reduce）、重复使用（reuse）和再循环（recycle），90年代又增加了一个“1D”，即可降解（degradable）。我国从20世纪90年代初开始出现“绿色包装”的提法，这与工业发达国家对包装提出的“3R”和“1D”原则是一致的。按照上述定义和原则，绿色包装至少应当符合以下要求：尽量节省材料、资源和能源；废弃物能降解，不污染或少污染环境；对环境和人体健康无害等。

Part B Vocabulary and Terminology 词汇和术语

warehousing 仓储
contract warehousing 合同制仓储
bonded warehouse 保税仓库
free trade zone 保税区
bonded goods 保税商品
neutral packing 中性包装
designated brand 定牌
sorting 分拣
port warehouse 口岸仓库
transfer shed 周转仓库
transship warehouse 中转仓库
private warehouse 自有仓库仓储
public warehouse 公共仓库
LCL operation 拼箱作业
economies of scale 规模经济
general warehouse 通用仓库
specialized warehouse 专用仓库
special commodity warehouse 特种仓库
thermal insulation library 保温库
cold storage 冷藏库
compensation trade 补偿贸易
transit trade 转口贸易
futures trade 期货贸易
warehouse receipt 仓单
waybill 运单
hand-over list 交接清单
warehouse warrant 入库单
delivery note 送货单
proprietary shipping line pick-up 专用线接运
pickup at station/port 车站、码头提货
pickup at owners 自提入库
warehouse reception 库内接货
delivery order 领货凭证，提货单
bill of lading 提货单
inward notice 入库通知单
container load plan (CLP) 装箱单

weight memo 磅码单
sales delivery detail report 发货明细表
laboratory test report 化验单
cargo acceptance record 货物验收记录
outward notice 出库通知单
outbound order 出库单
nude cargo 裸装货
bulk cargo 散装货
packed cargo 包装货
single piece packing 单件运输包装
collective packing 集合运输包装
container 集装箱
flexible container 集装包
UNECE：the United Nations Economic Commission for Europe 联合国欧洲经济委员会
UNECE Working Party on Facilitation of International Trade Procedures 联合国欧洲经济委员会简化国际贸易程序工作组
International Organization for Standardization/ISO 国际标准化组织
International Cargo Handling Coordination Association（ICHCA） 国际货物装卸协调协会

Part C Exercise 练习

Ⅰ. Answer the following questions.

1. Please briefly describe the significance of international logistics warehousing.
2. Describe the meaning of bonded warehouse.
3. What is the basic operation procedure of international logistics warehousing?
4. What is the significance of packing in international logistics and the principles to follow?

Ⅱ. Tell whether the following statements are true or false.

1. International logistics warehousing only performs storage of import and export goods.
2. Most of transshipment depots are built in between mass production area and port of shipment，e. g. railway and highway station and river port.
3. Private warehouse management is more flexible in that the storage space is more easily to be changed.
4. Free trade zone is a specified region and warehouse established，approved and supervised by the Customs.
5. Packing is classified into transport packing and sales packing by their function in commodity circulation.
6. To save logistics expenses，package doesn't have to be green in international market.

Ⅲ. Translate the following passages into Chinese.

1. Free trade zone is a specified region and warehouse established, approved, and supervised by the Customs. Foreign goods are not taxed in the Zone or when they are re-exported. However, when they enter the market of the country where the Zone is located, Customs clearance should be conducted and tariffs be paid.

2. Warehouse receipt is a legal document issued by warehouse keeper after acceptance of cargo proving the delivery of a quantity of goods to the warehouse for safekeeping. The Receipt is a certificate upon which the obligation of warehouse keeper, cargo owner, and consignee is allocated and stored goods are returned by warehouse keeper. It is a legal obligation of the warehouse keeper to issue the Receipt to show the acceptance of the cargo listed in the Receipt.

3. Neutral packing is a packing without country or place of origin or name of producer printed on the commodity or its exterior/interior packing, not even brand, trademark, or any letters. Neutral packing includes no brand packing and designated brand neutral packing. For the former, there is neither name of origin or producer, nor brand or trademark on the packing; Whereas for the latter, only brand or trademark designated by the buyer is printed on the packing, without name of origin or producer.

Ⅳ. Translate the following passages into English.

1. 公共保税仓库是具有法人资格的经济实体，是经海关批准建立的综合性保税仓库。这类保税仓库一般不经营进出口商品，只为国内外保税货物持有者服务。

2. 海关监管仓库主要存放已进境而所有人未来提取的货物或行李物品，或者无证到货、单证不齐、手续不完备以及违反海关规程，海关不予放行，需要暂存海关监管仓库等候海关处理的货物。

3. 仓单是保管人在接受仓储货物后签发的表明一定数量的保管货物已经交付仓储保管的法律文书，它是确定保管人和仓单持有人、提货人责任和义务的依据，是仓储保管人凭以返还保管物的凭证。

Chapter Five

International Maritime Transport Logistics

国际海运物流

Part A Text 课文

The delivery of goods， in international trade， is one of the most important steps. This is because in international trade where an exporter and an importer are always located far apart， the goods under the international trade contract have to go a long distance and sometimes change several carriers in transit before they finally reach the importer. In international business， it is one of the basic tasks for the exporter to deliver the goods to the buyer or named carrier or agreed conveyance after the contract has been signed， according to the stipulations of the contract relating to latest shipment date， port of loading， delivery place， partial shipments and transshipment， etc.

In international trade practices， there are many methods to deliver the goods purchased， such as ocean transport， railway transport， air transport， inland waterway transport， road transport， postal transport， pipeline transport， land bridge transport and international multi-modal transport and so on. The buyer and seller can decide which method will be the most appropriate for goods to be transported according to goods nature， consignment quantity， transit journey， cargo value， delivery time， natural conditions and so on.

As far as foreign trade is concerned， goods transport is mostly （over 2/3 of world trade in terms of volume） done by ocean vessels. Marine transport has always been a dominant transport mode in international logistics because of its obvious advantages of large volume and low cost. In this chapter， we will fully discuss its main features， operation modes and required shipping documents.

国际货物运输是国际贸易的一个重要组成部分，因为买卖双方所在地往往相隔甚远，国际贸易项下的货物从卖方国家转移到买方国家，必须通过运输来实现，有时甚至需要多次转运才能到达进口商手中。在一笔具体的进出口交易中，在买卖合同签订以后，按照合同有关最迟装运期、装货港、交货地点、分批装运和转运等的规定，将货物运交买方或承运人或指定的运输工具是卖方的基本义务。

国际贸易运输有多种方式：海洋运输、铁路运输、航空运输、江河运输、邮政运输、公路运输、管道运输、大陆桥运输以及由各种运输方式组合的国际多式联运等。买卖双方应根据商品特点、数量大小、路程远近、价值大小、时间长短、自然条件等因素商定应采用的运输方式。由于具有运量大、运费低的突出优势，海洋运输一直是国际物流货物运输中应用最为普遍的主导运输方式。这一章将详细介绍海洋运输的特点、主要经营方式以及重要的货运单据。

5.1 General View of Marine Transport

5.1.1 Definition and Features of Marine Transport

Marine transport is the most widely used form of transportation in international trade. Currently, goods transport is mostly (over two-thirds of world trade and 90 percent of China's import and export trade in terms of volume) done by ocean vessels. Compared with other transport modes, it has the following major features.

(1) Large volume

The carrying capacity of marine transport is much stronger than that of any other transport mode, including railway transport, road transport and air transport. With the continuous improvement of shipbuilding technology, the carrying capacity of the ship is still increasing. The load of a 10000-ton vessel is equal to those of 250～300 railway wagons.

(2) Low freight

Since marine transport usually carries large quantities of cargoes and has a quite long voyage, the transportation cost per ton of cargo is relatively low. Ocean freight of per ton of goods is equal to the 1/5 of railway freight and the 1/10 of road freight and the 1/25 of air freight.

(3) Strong transport capacity

Marine transport uses natural waterways and is not restricted by tracks and roads. Therefore, it has a stronger transport capacity compared with railway transport and road transport.

Marine transport has traditionally faced two drawbacks. Firstly, it is slow, with speeds at sea averaging 15knots (26km/h). More recent ships can travel at speeds between 25～30knots (45～55km/h). But it is still relatively slow compared with other transport modes. Secondly, delays often occur in the processes of loading and unloading at ports. Frequently, it takes quite a few days to conduct loading and unloading as far as break-bulk cargo is concerned. These two drawbacks are particularly restrictive where goods have to be moved over short distances or where shippers require rapid deliveries. However, technical improvements tend to blur the distinction between bulk and break-bulk cargo, as more and more break-bulk cargoes are transported by collective packing such as pallets and containers.

5.1.2 Maritime Freight

Generally, maritime freight is divided into container cargo and bulk cargo, and the latter is divided into dry bulk cargo and liquid cargo.

(1) Bulk cargo

Bulk cargo refers to the freight, either dry or liquid, that is not packaged such as minerals (oil, coal, iron ore) and grains. It often requires the use of specialized ships such as oil tankers as well as specialized transshipment and storage facilities. Conventionally, this kind of cargo has a single origin, destination and client. Bulk cargo can be divided into dry bulk cargo and liquid cargo. Dry bulk cargo refers to various raw materials and bulk cargo, mainly including coal, grain, various kinds of ores, steel, building materials, chemical fertilizer, wood and so on. Liquid cargo refers to bulk liquid goods such as crude oil, refined oil, chemicals and liquefied gas.

(2) container cargo

At present, most common industrial products and consumption goods (such as fruits, refrigerated and frozen food, etc.) are typically loaded in containers to realize rapid transportation in a standardized form.

(3) Break-bulk cargo

Break-bulk cargo refers to general cargo that has been packaged in some way with the use of cartons, bags, boxes, drums, etc. This type tends to have numerous origins, destinations and clients. Before containerization, economies of scale were difficult to achieve with break-bulk cargo as the loading and unloading processes were very labor and time consuming. Maritime shipping is dominated by bulk cargo. With the wide application of container technology, break-bulk cargo transport has been replaced by container transport.

5.1.3 Cargo Ships

Cargo ships employed around the world can be categorized into the following types:

(1) Bulk carriers

Bulk carriers are ships designed to carry specific commodities, and are differentiated into liquid bulk and dry bulk vessels. They include the largest vessels afloat. The largest tankers, the Ultra Large Crude Carrier (ULCC) are up to 500000 deadweight (dwt) tons, with the more typical size being between 250000 and 350000 tons. The largest dry bulk carriers are around 350000 tons, while the more typical size is between 100000 and 150000 tons. The emergence of liquefied natural gas technology enabled the maritime transport of natural gas with specialized ships.

(2) General cargo ships

General cargo ships are vessels designed to carry break-bulk cargoes. The traditional general cargo ships were less than 10000 dwt tons because of extremely slow loading and unloading. More recently, these vessels have been replaced by container ships because the latter can conduct loading and unloading more efficiently.

(3) Container ships

Container ships (sometimes spelled containerships) are cargo ships that carry all of their load in truck-size intermodal containers, in a technique called containerization. They are the common means of commercial intermodal freight transport and now carry most seagoing break-bulk cargoes. Container ship's capacity is measured in Twenty-Foot Equivalent Unit

(TEU). Today, about 90 percent of break-bulk cargo worldwide is transported by container ships, and modern container ships can carry nearly 20000 TEU. Container ships now rival crude oil tankers and bulk carriers as the largest commercial vessels on the ocean.

(4) Roll-on-roll-off (Ro-Ro) vessels

Ro-Ro vessels are designed to allow cars, trucks and trains to be loaded directly on board. Originally appearing as ferries, these vessels are used on deep-sea trade and are much larger than typical ferries. The largest are the car Ro-Ro vessels that transport vehicles from assembly plants to the main markets.

Bulk carriers can operate on a regular schedule between two ports or on a voyage basis. In the latter case, the ship may haul cargoes between different ports based on demand. General cargo vessels operate on liner services, in which the vessels are employed on a regular scheduled service between fixed ports of call or as tramp ships where the vessels have no fixed schedules and move between ports based on cargo availability.

5.1 海上运输

5.1.1 海上运输的定义和特征

海洋运输是国际贸易中最广泛使用的运输方式。目前，国际贸易总运量中的2/3以上以及我国进出口货运量的90%都是通过海洋运输方式运输的。与其他运输方式相比，海洋运输主要有以下特点。

(1) 运量大

海洋运输的运载能力要远远高于铁路运输、公路运输和航空运输。随着现代造船技术的不断提高，船舶的运载能力也不断增大。一艘万吨船舶的载重量相当于250～300个火车车皮的载重量。

(2) 运费低

海洋运输运量大、航程远，分摊到每吨货物的运输成本相对较小。一吨货物的海洋运费仅相当于铁路运费的1/5、公路汽车运费的1/10和航空运费的1/25。

(3) 通过能力强

海洋运输利用的是天然航道，且不受道路和轨道的限制，因此其通过能力比公路运输和铁路运输等要大。

海洋运输一直有两个缺陷。它的速度慢，平均时速为15节（即26公里/小时）。近来航行速度虽已提高到25～30节（即45～55公里/小时），但是较其他运输方式而言，海运的速度还是较慢。其次，港口的装卸过程常常出现延误，特别是件杂货的装卸，常常需要数天时间才能完成。这些缺点在货物的短距离运输或货主要求快速送达服务的情况下更为明显。然而，包装技术的进步使得散货运输和件杂货运输的区别变得模糊，因为越来越多的件杂货采用托盘和集装箱等的集装模式来运输。

5.1.2 海上货运

海上货运一般分为集装箱和散货两大类，后者又分为干散货和液态货两类。

(1) 散货

散货是指没有经过包装的固体或液体，如矿物（油料、煤炭、铁矿石）和粮食等。这些货物的运输常常需要使用专用船舶，比如油轮或其他专用装运设备和存储设施。通常一批散货的产地、目的地和客户都是单一的。散货又可分为干散货和液态货两类。干散货是指各种原材料以及大宗散货，主要包括煤炭、谷物、各种矿石、钢材、建材、化肥、木材等等。液态货是指原油、成品油、化学品、液化气等散装液体货物。

(2) 集装箱

目前，大多数常见的工业产品和消费品（如水果、冷藏和冷冻食品等）通常用集装箱装载，以实现标准化的快速运输。

(3) 件杂货

主要是指那些使用袋、盒、箱、或桶进行包装的货物。货物可能有不同的产地、目的地和客户。在运输集装箱化之前，件杂货难以实现规模效应，因为其装卸过程非常耗时耗力。随着集装箱技术的广泛应用，件杂货运输已经被集装箱运输所取代。

5.1.3 货船

(1) 散货船

散货船是为装载特别的散装货物而设计的，有液货船和干散货船两大类。它们可称为海上最大型的船舶。最大的一种油轮—特大型油轮，其最高载重能达到 50 万吨，一般油轮的载重在 25 万吨～35 万吨之间。最大的干散货船容量约为载重 35 万吨，载重 10 万吨～15 万吨的散货船更为常见。因为液化天然气技术的出现，现在已经可以使用特殊的船舶在海上进行天然气的运输。

(2) 杂货船

杂货船用于运输件杂货。传统杂货船的载重量不超过 1 万吨，这是因为装卸件杂货速度非常慢（件杂货包装不统一，多用人力装卸，装卸效率很低）。近来这些船已被集装箱船取代，因为集装箱船能更有效率地完成装卸作业。

(3) 集装箱船

集装箱船是指专门用来装运集装箱的船舶，即利用集装箱化技术将所有货物装入卡车尺寸的多式联运集装箱内进行运输。集装箱船运输是国际多式联运的重要组成，目前海运货物中的绝大部分件杂货都是由集装箱船来进行运输。集装箱船的装载能力以 TEU（Twenty Equivalent Unit 的缩写，又称 20 英尺换算单位）来衡量。如今，世界范围内 90%的件杂货都是通过集装箱船来运输，现代集装箱船的装载能力已达到 20000TEU，并已超越油轮和散货船成为海上最大型的船舶。

(4) 滚装船

滚装船的特殊设计使小轿车、卡车和火车能直接驶上船舶。滚装船最早以渡轮的形式出现，目前主要用于远洋运输，比普通的渡轮要大得多。最大的滚装船常用于批量运载汽车，航行在汽车装配厂和汽车销售地之间。

散货船可能按固定的时间表在两个港口之间，也可能以航次为基础来开展运输。在第二种情况下，散货船根据特定的需求在不同港口之间进行货物运输。杂货船可能是以班轮的方式运营，即船舶按固定的船期表在固定的挂靠港之间提供运输服务，或者以不定期租船的方式运营，也就是说船舶航行没有固定的船期表，航程中停靠什么港口取决于货运需求。

5.2 Practices of International Maritime Transport Logistics

5.2.1 Shipping Services

The maritime shipping industry offers two major types of service: liner service and tramp service.

(1) Liner Service / Regular Shipping Liner Service

A liner is a vessel with regular sailing and arrival on a stated schedule between a group of fixed ports of call. The main features of liners usually include:

Firstly, the liners have regular sailing routes, ports of call, schedules and comparatively fixed freight, which is the basic feature of liners.

Secondly, the ship owner usually leases part of shipping space instead of the whole ship.

Thirdly, the carrier is responsible for loading and unloading operations, i. e., Gross Terms.

Fourthly, the B/L drawn by the shipping company plays the role of the shipping contract between the carrier and the shipper. The rights and obligations of the carrier and the shipper are based on the B/L issued by the shipping company.

Currently, the international shipping market offers three types of liner service, namely, conference lines, non-conference lines and non-vessel operating common carriers (NVOCC).

1) Conference Lines: A shipping conference is a group of shipping lines operating in any particular route under agreement to provide a scheduled service with a common tariff and a fixed itinerary of ports of call. The purpose of shipping conference is to eliminate price competition among member lines and reduce outside competition by trying to capture most of the traffic for member lines through loyalty arrangements with shippers. The main advantages of the conference system to shippers are the stability of freight rate and the regularity of service. However, the disadvantages are obvious. Rates are usually high and do not fluctuate according to supply and demand as in tramp service. Rules and procedures are inflexible.

2) Non-conference Lines: In recent years, along most international routes, non-conference lines have posed a challenge to the conference system. This is attributable to the development of containerization and the emergence of many independent carriers. As a result, along some routes, the conference lines have been forced to come to terms with the non-conference lines with regard to rates, terms and conditions of service.

3) Non-vessel Operating Common Carrier (NVOCC): An NVOCC is a carrier who operates a regular scheduled service. He does not own or operate the vessels by which sea transport is provided. Although the NVOCC is a carrier in his relationship with actual shipper, he is a shipper in his relationship with the actual carrier. He assumes the role of a principal and performs several functions. He bears responsibilities for ocean carriers, both conference and non-conference lines. He renders a useful service by providing groupage or consolidation service, particularly to small shippers who do not have much bargaining power in

negotiating freight rates with the carriers.

(2) Tramp Service / Charter Service

Tramp service has no fixed itinerary or schedule and is operated on any route according to supply and demand. It is first in one trade and then in another, always seeking those ports where there is a demand at the moment for shipping space. The shipper charters the ship from the shipowner and uses it to carry the goods. Tramp vessels are usually chartered at negotiated rates, particularly when the quantity of the goods is large. Tramp service falls into the following three kinds.

1) Voyage charter: The voyage charter is one for the carriage of goods from one specified port to another, or for a round trip. It includes single voyage charter, return voyage charter and successive voyage charter. According to the route stipulated in the charter party, the shipowner is responsible for delivering the goods to the port of destination and for managing the ship as well as bearing all the expenses. Under voyage charter, payment for the charterer is usually based on an agreed rate per ton for a "full and complete cargo". Should the charterer fail to provide sufficient cargo to fill the ship, he is liable for what is termed dead freight, a prorate payment for the space not used. A voyage charter also stipulates the number of days, known as lay days, for loading and unloading. Should these stipulated days be exceeded, the charterer is liable for a demurrage charge for each day in excess, and conversely the charterer is entitled to obtain dispatch money from the ship owner for each day not taken up. The liability of the shipowner is to provide a ship that is seaworthy and to avoid unjustifiable deviation en route. Under a voyage charter, the shipowner retains the operational control of the vessel and is responsible for all the operating expenses such as port charges, bunkers, taxes and so on.

2) Time charter: The shipowner provides a designated manned ship to the charterer, and the charterer employs the ship for a specific period against payment of hire. What concerns the charterer most is the period, not the voyage. The chartering may be for a period of one year or several years. During the period of chartering, the ship is managed, deployed and used by the charterer. Meanwhile, the charterer should bear the fuel expenses, port expenses, loading & unloading expenses incurred by loading, unloading, stowing and trimming. The shipowner should bear the wages and provisions of the crew, and be responsible for seaworthiness during the period of chartering and the expenses incurred and the vessel insurance premium.

3) Demise charter: Demise charter, also called bare-boat charter, means that the vessel is put at the disposal of the charterer for a long period of employment without any crew. Therefore, demise charter essentially belongs to time charter, but there are some differences: as to time charter, during the period of chartering, the shipowner provides the charterer with the crew, while as to bare-boat charter, the shipowner only provides the charterer with a bare-boat, and the charterer is supposed to employ the crew and pay the crew's wages and provisions, ship's maintenance and stores, etc., by himself, apart from those expenses he is responsible for under the time charterer.

5.2.2 Ocean Freight Rates

Ocean freight rates can be broadly divided into liner freight rates and tramp rates. Liner freight rates are fixed by shipping conference liners and other liner operators. They are related more to the costs of operation and remain comparatively steady over a period of time. Tramp rates fluctuate with market conditions of supply and demand. In a boom period, tramp rates rise, while in a period of recession they decline.

The freight of liners is a freight charges the consignors pay to the liner companies for the carriage of cargo. Although the principles on which the liner freight rates are fixed have not been clarified by shipping conference liners or operators, it is apparent that the cost of providing such service will cover actual costs and a margin profit. The total costs of providing the liner service consist of fixed costs and variable costs. Fixed costs include costs of officers and crew, insurance expenses, repairs and maintenance, stores, administrative costs, interests, and depreciation. Variable costs involve cost of fuel, loading and unloading expenses, and port costs.

In practice, the freight of liners comprises basic freight charges and additional charges. Additional charges are the charges the consignors pay to the liner companies to cover their additional costs for the carriage of cargoes under certain special circumstances. Additional charges, if there is any, are also stated in the liner's freight tariff in the way of a certain percentage of the basic freight charges or certain amounts of charges.

$$\text{Freight} = Fb + \sum S$$

Fb——Basic freight

S——Surcharge

The standards for calculating the basic freight rates of liners are stipulated as follows:

① According to gross weight, i. e. , weight ton, which is indicated by "W" in the liner's freight tariff. Heavy cargo is usually charged on this basis. Internationally, besides M/T (Metric Ton, each equaling 1000 kilograms), British Long Ton (L/T) and American Short Ton (S/T) are also used nowadays. One weight ton is to be considered as one M/T or one Long Ton (1016kg) or one Short Ton (907.18kg)。

② According to volume, i. e. , measurement ton, which is indicated by "M" in the liner's freight tariff. It is 40 cubic feet or one cubic meter that constitutes one measurement ton. Typically, light cargoes are charged on this basis.

③ According to value of the cargo, i. e. , a certain percentage of FOB price, which is indicated by "A. V. " (Ad Valorem) in the liner's freight tariff. Usually, a percentage between 1% and 4% is charged on the value of such goods as gold, silver, precious stones, valuable drawings and paintings.

④ According to gross weight or volume, i. e. , choosing the higher rate between the two standards, which is indicated by "W/M" in the freight tariff.

⑤ According to gross weight or volume or A. V. , i. e. , at the discretion of the carrier, choosing the highest rate of the three, which is indicated by "W/M or A. V. " In this case, it is up to the carrier to decide to charge whichever of the three that produces the highest freight rate.

⑥ According to gross weight or volume, and then adding a certain percentage of cargo value, which is indicated by "W/M plus A. V." in the freight tariff.

⑦ According to the number of the cargo. For example, freight for shipping trucks or live animals is calculated on per truck or per head. Minimum freight is as per B/L.

⑧ According to the temporary/interim or special agreement entered into between the shipowner and the consignor.

Based on different draftsmen, liner's freight tariff can be divided into four kinds:

(a) Shipping Conference Freight Tariff.

(b) Liner Company Freight Tariff.

(c) Consignor Freight Tariff.

(d) Freight Tariff of Both Parties.

The main surcharges are shown as follows:

(a) Heavy lift additional.

(b) Long length surcharge.

(c) Direct additional.

(d) Transshipment surcharge.

(e) Port congestion surcharge.

(f) Port surcharge.

(g) Bunker adjustment factor (BAF).

(h) Optional fees.

(i) Alternation of destination surcharge.

(j) Deviation surcharge.

In addition to the above-mentioned surcharges, ice surcharge, currency adjustment factor, fumigation surcharge, etc., are sometimes included.

5.2.3 The Way to Calculate the Liner Freight Rates

1) First translate the English name of the commodity, and determine the class and basis of basic freight rate.

2) Determine the basic freight rate and the relative surcharges in the liner's freight tariff according to the class, the sea route and port of destination.

3) The freight per freight ton is obtained by adding various additional surcharges to the basic freight rate.

4) Total freight is obtained by multiplying the freight per freight ton by total freight tons.

$$\text{Freight Per Freight Ton} = \text{basic freight rate} + \sum \text{rate of surcharge}$$

$$\text{Total freight amount} = \text{freight tons of the goods} \times \text{freight per freight ton}$$

Here is an example to illustrate how to calculate the liner freight rate.

A Chinese trading company exports 100 cases of remote-controlled model cars from Shanghai to Singapore. The dimensions and gross weight of each case are 60cm × 50cm × 30cm and 80kg. According to the Scale of Commodity Classification, the basis for remote controlled model cars is M and the class is 10. From the Basic Freight Rate by Class (in US$) From Shanghai to Singapore, we know that the basic freight rate is USD$ 70 per freight ton and bunker adjustment factor (BAF) is the surcharge which is 20% of the basic freight rate. How much is the total freight?

Step 1: Determine the class and basis of basic freight rate

Scale of Commodity Classification		
commodity	basis	class
…	…	…
Toys, Electrically operated	M	10
Toys, Wooden, Metal, Plush	M	8
…	…	…

Step 2: Determine the basic freight rate and surcharge

Basic Freight rate by Class(in US$) From Shanghai		
Class	Port of Destination	
	Bangkok	Singapore
…	…	…
9	50.00	65.00
10	55.00	70.00
* Bunker Adjustment Factor 20%		

Step 3: Calculate volume

$$\text{Basis} = M = 0.6 \times 0.5 \times 0.3 \times 100 = 9\text{m}^3$$

Step 4: calculate total freight

$$\text{Total Freight} = \text{Total Freight Tons} \times (\text{Basic Rate} + \text{Surcharge})$$
$$= 9 \times (70 + 70 \times 20\%) = \text{US\$ } 756$$

5.2.4 Charter Party

The charter party is a contract concluded between the shipowner and the charterer when the latter charters the ship from the former. It stipulates the rights and obligations of the two parties. The main terms in the charter party include the interested parties, name and flag of the ship, description and quantity of the shipments, time of chartering, freight, loading and unloading expenses, time limit of loading and unloading, demurrage and dispatch money.

The freight may be stipulated in the charter party as follows:

① Freight can be paid in advance.

② Freight can be paid after the goods have arrived at the port of destination.

③ Part of freight is paid in advance, the rest of which is paid after the goods have arrived at the port of destination.

Before the charterer pays off freight and other charges, the shipowner is entitled to refuse to deliver the good. This kind of right is called lien.

When discussing the problem of which party will be responsible for the charges of loading and unloading, both the shipowner and the charterer should make it very clear in the charter party. There are four methods to be used to stipulate the expenses of loading and unloading:

① The shipowner bears gross terms.

② The shipowner is free in (F. I.).

③ The shipowner is free out (F. O.).

④ The shipowner is free in and out (F. I. O.).

The time of loading and unloading will affect the turn-over rate of the ship, and thus will affect the interests of the shipowner. Therefore, it is the main clause specified in the charter party. The time limit of loading and unloading may be indicated by:

① Fixed days.

② Efficiency of loading and unloading.

③ Customary quick dispatch.

During the time limit of loading and unloading, in case the charterer does not finish the work of loading and unloading, in order to compensate the shipowner for his losses, the charterer should pay a certain amount of fine for the exceeding time. This is the so-called demurrage.

During the time limit of loading and unloading, in case the charterer finishes the work of loading and unloading ahead of schedule, the shipowner shall pay a certain amount of bonus to the charterer. This is the so-called dispatch money.

5.2.5 Shipping Documents

The documents commonly used in the carriage of goods by sea are bills of lading, sea waybills, manifests, shipping notes, delivery orders, and mate's receipts.

A bill of lading by itself is not a contract of carriage as it is signed only by the carrier. However, it provides evidence of the contract of carriage. It serves as a receipt for goods delivered to the carrier. Additionally, the bill of lading serves as a document of title to the goods enabling the goods to be transferred from the shipper to the consignee or any other party by endorsement. See Appendix 5-1 Ocean Bill of Lading for details.

A sea waybill is the replacement for the traditional ocean bill of lading. The sea waybill is a non-negotiable document made out to a named consignee who is allowed, upon proper identification, to claim the goods without presenting the waybill.

A cargo manifest provides information regarding cargoes on board. A freight manifest gives information regarding freight rates, surcharges, rebates, and so on. The manifest is prepared by the carrier's agent, but the freight forwarder has to handle it while dealing with Customs and port authorities.

A shipping/booking note is issued by a shipper to a carrier requesting allocation of shipping space. It is a commitment on the part of a shipper to truthfully report the consignment and serves as the basis for the preparation of a bill of lading.

A shipping order (shipping permit) is issued by the shipping company to a shipper with confirmed space booking, authorizing the receiving clerk (cargo checker) at the container terminal or at the dock to receive a specified amount of goods from the named shipper. The shipping order typically contains the number of space booking, name and address of the shipper, the Customs declaration agent or freight forwarder, vessel and voyage number, sailing time, delivery day and location, Customs closing date, and number and type of packages. See Appendix 5-2 Shipping Order for details.

A delivery order is issued by the carrier or his agent to enable the consignee or his forwarding agent to take delivery of cargo (import cargo) from a vessel.

A mate's receipt is a receipt issued by the carrier (actually, the mate of the shipping vessel) in the acknowledgement of the goods received on board. And the mate's receipt is subsequently exchanged for the bill of lading. See Appendix 5-3 Mate's Receipt for details.

5.2 国际海运物流实务

5.2.1 航运服务

海运行业提供两种主要航运服务：班轮运输服务和租船运输服务。

（1）班轮运输服务

班轮运输，亦称定期船运输，是指船公司按照公布的船期表在特定的航线上，以既定的挂靠港顺序，进行规则的反复的航行和运输的一种船舶经营方式。班轮运输主要有下列特点。

第一，有固定航线、固定挂靠港、固定船期和相对固定的运费率。这是班轮运输的基本特点。

第二，船方通常出租部分舱位，而不是全部舱位。

第三，承运人/船方管装管卸，有关装卸费均包括在运费内，即船方负责装卸。

第四，承运人和托运人双方的权利、义务及责任豁免以船公司签发的提单条款为依据。

目前，国际航运市场提供三种班轮运输服务，即班轮公会运输、非班轮公会运输和无船承运人。

1）班轮公会运输：班轮公会是按预定的船期表在特定的航线上从事运营的班轮公司的组织，具有共同的费率表、固定的挂靠港。班轮公会运输的目的是消除会员公司之间在海运运价上的竞争，通过与托运人之间达成的忠诚协议为会员争取大量货源，以减少外部竞争。班轮公会运输体系对于托运人而言，具有稳定的运费率和定期的运输服务等好处。然而，其缺点也显而易见。运费率通常很高，且运费率不像租船运输那样随供求关系的变化而变化，其规则和程序也不太灵活。

2）非班轮公会运输：近年来，出现在大多数国际航线上的非班轮公会运输，对班轮公会运输体系构成了挑战，这是由于集装箱运输的发展以及众多独立承运人的出现。结果，班轮公会被迫在运价、运输条件等方面，与非班轮公会航运公司达成协议。

3）无船承运人（NVOCC）：无船承运人是从事定期营运的承运人，但不拥有或实际运营海上运输所需的船舶。虽然无船承运人在与实际托运人的关系中是承运人，但是在与实际承运人的关系中无船承运人充当的是托运人的角色。他担任着委托人的角色，履行多项职能，可提供班轮公会以及非班轮公会航线运输服务。他主要向货主/托运人提供诸如拼箱、集运等的实用服务，特别是对那些在海运价格谈判方面没有多大议价能力的小货主。

(2) 租船运输

租船运输，亦称不定期船运输，是指既没有固定的船期表，也没有固定的航线和挂靠港的运输。哪里有货，就向哪里开航，哪里装船最好就去哪里接货，总是开向那些有装运需求的港口。特别是当货物数量较大时，托运人/货主通常从船东手中租船来装运货物，租船运输的运费率一般由双方协商而定。国际上使用的租船方式有三种：定程租船、定期租船和光船租船。

1）定程租船：定程租船又称程租船或航次租船，指租船人按照航程租赁全部舱位，由船舶所有人负责将货物运至指定目的港。定程租船就其租赁方式的不同可分为：单程租船（又称单航次租船）、来回航次租船以及连续航次租船。在定程租船情况下，租船人常常按议定的每吨货舱满载费率支付费用。如果他不能使船只装满而产生部分空舱，租船人也必须按船舱满载时的载重吨来支付运费。定程租船还规定了装卸货物的受载日期。如果受载日期超过租船合同规定，租船人需要为超期天数支付滞期费（滞期费率×超期天数）。反之，如果在受载期内提前完成装卸，船东需要支付给租船人速遣费（速遣费率×提前天数）。船东的责任是保证船舶的适航性，并避免航途中不必要的绕航。在航次租船中，船东仍保有对船舶的控制，并负责港口使用费、燃油、税费等所有的营运费用。

2）定期租船：船东将配备好船员的指定船舶提供给租船人/承租人，在约定的期限内，由租船人掌控船舶的营运并支付租金。租船时间可以是一年或数年。在租船期间，货船的经营、管理和使用都由租船人/承租人负责。同时，由装卸货物、平仓理舱等引起的燃油费、港口费、装卸费也都由承租人负担。船东则负责支付船员的工资，并保证船舶在租用期间的适航性以及支付船舶的保险费。

3）光船租船：光船租船是指租船人/承租人在一定租期内取得对特定船舶的控制，且由承租人自行配备船员。因此光船租船也是定期租船的一种，所不同的是：在定期租船方式下，船东不仅提供货船，还负责配备船员和支付船员工资，而在光船租船方式下，船东只是把一艘空船（没有船员）租赁给承租人使用，且承租人除支付定期租船下的租金及费用外，还得负责自行配备船员，支付船员工资，以及船舶的维修供给等。

5.2.2 海运运费率

海洋运输运费率（即海运运价）可大致分为班轮运费率和租船/不定期船运费率。班轮运费率是由班轮公会和其他的班轮营运人确定的，它们多与运营成本密切相关，在一段时间内保持相对稳定。租船运费率随市场供求情况而波动。在营运旺季，租船运费率会上升，而在淡季则会下降。

班轮运费是发货人因班轮公司为其运输货物而向班轮公司支付的运费。虽然班轮公会或班轮经营人对班轮运费率的确定原则并不公开，但很显然，班轮运费应覆盖实际运输总成本和预期利润。总成本包含固定成本和可变成本两部分。固定成本包括船员工资、保险费、维修和保养费、物料费、管理费用、利息以及折旧。可变成本则包括燃料费、装卸费和港口使用费等。

实际上，班轮运费包括基本运费和附加运费两部分。附加运费是发货人在某些特殊情况下支付给班轮公司的额外运费。如果有附加运费的话，会在班轮公司运价表中以基本运费的一定百分比或某一固定金额的形式标明。

$$班轮运费=Fb+\sum S$$

式中 Fb——基本运费

S——附加运费

班轮基本运费率的计算标准规定如下。

① 按货物毛重计收，即以重量吨为计算单位计收运费，在班轮公司运价表中用“W”表示。重量较大的货物（即重货）一般适用这种标准。此外，除了国际标准单位公吨外，有时还会采用长吨（英制）和短吨（美制）。一重量吨为一公吨（1000千克）或一长吨（1016千克）或一短吨（907.18千克）。

② 按货物体积计收，即以尺码吨为计算单位计收运费，在运价表中用“M”表示。一尺码吨为1立方米或40立方英尺。通常重量较轻的货物（即轻泡货物）适用这种标准。

③ 按商品的价格计收，如按其FOB价的一定百分比来计收运费，称为从价运费，在运价表中用“A. V.”或“Ad Val”表示。此项标准适用于高价值商品，如金、银、宝石和贵重字画等，百分比一般为1%～4%。

④ 船公司选择按货物毛重或按货物体积两种标准中运价高的那种标准来计收运费，在运价表中用W/M表示。

⑤ 船公司选择按货物毛重或按货物体积或按从价运费三种标准中运价高的那种标准来计收运费，在运价表中用“W/M or AV.”表示。

⑥ 船公司选择按货物毛重或按货物体积两种标准中运价高的那种标准，再加上货物价格的一定百分比，在运价表中用“W/M plus A. V.”表示。

⑦ 按货物的件数计收。如卡车按每辆（Per Unit）、活牲畜按每头（Per Head）计收，最低运费按“每份提单”（Per B/L）计收。

⑧ 按船主与托运人之间临时签订的协议计收运费。

基于不同的起草人，班轮运费可分为四种：

(a) 航运公会运价表；

(b) 班轮公司运价表；

(c) 货方运价表，如中租表；

(d) 双边运价表，如中远表。

班轮公司向发货人征收的主要附加运费如下：

(a) 超重附加费；

(b) 超长附加费；

(c) 直航附加费；

(d) 转船附加费；

(e) 港口拥挤费；

(f) 港口附加费；

(g) 燃料附加费；

(h) 选港费；

(i) 变更港口附加费；

(j) 绕航附加费。

除了上述提到的附加运费外，还有冷冻附加费、币值调整附加费、熏舱附加费等。

5.2.3 班轮运费计算方法

1) 首先译出商品的英文名称，确定该商品所属的等级以及基本运费率的计算标准。

2）根据商品等级、海运航线和目的港，在班轮运价表查出基本运费率及相关的附加运费率。

3）在基本运费率的基础上加上各种附加费率，即为该商品的每运费吨运费。

4）将每运费吨运费乘以总运费吨（重量吨或尺码吨），可得总（班轮）运费。

$$每运费吨运费=基本运费率+\sum 附加费率$$

$$总（班轮）运费=每运费吨运费\times 总运费吨$$

下面举例说明如何计算班轮运费。

一家中国贸易公司从上海向新加坡出口 100 箱遥控模型玩具车。每箱尺寸及毛重为 60cm×50cm×30cm，80kg。根据商品分类表，可查得遥控模型车基本运费率的计算标准为 M，等级为 10。查班轮运价表（美元），可得：从上海运到新加坡的基本运费率是每运费吨 70 美元；附加费是燃油附加费（BAF），为基本运费率的 20%。请问总运费为多少？

第一步：确定该商品所属的等级以及基本运费率的计算标准。

Scale of Commodity Classification		
commodity	basis	class
…	…	…
Toys, Electrically operated	M	10
Toys, Wooden, Metal, Plush	M	8
…	…	…

第二步：确定基本运费率和附加费率。

Basic Freight Rate by Class(in US$) From Shanghai		
Class	Port of Destination	
	Bangkok	Singapore
…	…	…
9	50.00	65.00
10	55.00	70.00
* Bunker Adjustment Factor 20%		

第三步：计算总运费吨。

$$总运费吨=M\times 100=0.6\times 0.5\times 0.3\times 100=9m^3$$

第四步：计算总运费。

$$总运费=总运费吨\times(基本运费率+\sum 附加费率)=9\times(70+70\times 20\%)=756 美元$$

5.2.4 租船合同

租船合同是租船人和船舶所有人/船东之间所订立的载明双方权利、义务的契约。主要条款包括有关当事人、船名和货船标识、装运货物的名称和数量、租期、运费、装卸费、装卸时限、滞期费率、速遣费率。

租船合同中有关运费的规定如下。

① 运费预付；

② 运费到付，即货物到达目的港后再支付运费；

③ 部分运费预付，剩下部分运费待货物抵达目的港后再支付。

在租船人付清运费之前，船主有权拒绝装运货物，这叫留置权。

在签订租船合同时，租船人和船东应充分协商并在合同中载明装卸费用由哪方承担，主要有以下四种规定方法：

① 船方负责装船和卸船，承担全部的装卸费用，等同于班轮条件；

② 船方管卸不管装，即船方只承担卸船费用；

③ 船方管装不管卸，即船方只承担装船费用；

④ 船方不管装卸，即租船人自行装船、卸船，并承担所有的装卸费用。

装卸时间影响装卸费用，进而影响船方的利益，因此装卸时间也是租船合同的主要条款。关于装卸时间，有以下三种规定方法：

① 在一定天数内装卸完毕；

② 按照规定的装卸速度进行装卸；

③ 按惯常的速度进行装卸。

在规定的装卸时限内，如果租船人没有完成货物的装卸工作，租船人必须向船东支付一定金额的罚款，这就是滞期费。

在规定的装卸时限内，如果租船人提前完成货物的装卸工作，船东会向租船人支付一定金额的奖励，即速遣费。

5.2.5 货运单据

海上货物运输常用的单证包括海运提单、海运单、舱单、托运单、装货单、提货单和大副收据。

海运提单本身不是运输合同，因为它只由承运人一方签署。但它是海上运输合同的证明。提单是货物交付给承运人的收据。另外，提单可作为物权凭证，使提单可通过背书，将货物的所有权从托运人转让给收货人或者其他人。详见附录 5.1。

海运单是传统海运提单的替代。海运单是不可流通的单据，且指定收货人，该收货人在提供了身份证明后，无须出示海运单即可实现提货。

货物舱单提供已装船货物的必要信息，包括运费、附加费、折扣等。货物舱单是由承运人代理（船代）准备的，但是货运代理（货代）必须持货物舱单才能办理海关及港口相关手续。

托运单是托运人签发给承运人的要求其分配舱位的申请。托运单是托运人向承运人提出的正式托运申请，也是缮制提单的重要依据。

装货单（装船单）是指海运承运人/船公司接受了托运人的托运申请后签发给托运人以确认订舱成功，并命令集装箱堆场或码头的理货员接受托运人货物且将其装船的单据。装货单通常包括订舱号、托运人的名称及地址、报关代理或货代、船名、航次、发货日期及地点、结关日期以及包装数量和方式。详见附录 5.2。

提货单是由承运人或其代理签发给收货人或其代理的单证，使后者能够从船上提取货物（前提是向船公司交出全部正本海运提单）。

大副收据由船上的大副签发，对货物已装船的事实以及货物装船的真实状况进行确认，并后续用以换取正式海运提单。详见附录 5.3。

5.3 Bill of Lading

As mentioned above, the bill of lading is one kind of the shipping documents. Because of its important role and wide application, this section focuses on bill of lading. The Bill of Lading (B/L) is a type of document that is issued by the carrier to acknowledge the receipt of a shipment of goods. The B/L defines the terms and conditions of the carriage of cargo by sea. Definitions of B/L vary from country to country. Broadly, the B/L has been defined as a receipt for good shipped on board a vessel, signed by the carrier (or his agent) contracting to carry them, and stating the terms on which the goods were delivered to and received by the ship. It is not the actual contract of carriage, but forms excellent evidence of the terms of the transportation contract.

5.3.1 Functions of Bill of Lading

Marine bills of Lading perform a number of functions. Generally, it is a receipt for goods shipped, a document of title to the goods, and evidence of the terms of a contract of affreightment.

A bill of lading is a receipt issued by the carrier indicating that an identifiable consignment of goods has been received by him for shipment, or actually loaded on board his ship. The bill of lading as a receipt will show the quantity and condition of the cargo loaded, the ship's name, ports of lading and destination, date of shipment, and so on.

A bill of lading is a document of title to the goods. The possession of a bill of lading is equivalent in law to the possession of the goods. The lawful holder (bona fide holder) of B/L is able to obtain delivery of goods at the port of destination and during transit the goods can be sold merely by endorsing the B/L.

Additionally, the B/L provides evidence of the contract of carriage between the carrier and the shipper because the terms of the B/L cover the terms of the contract of carriage.

5.3.2 Contents of Bill of Lading

A bill of lading contains not only a full description of the consignment, but also a lot of other information. It quotes the shipper and the carrying vessel, the ports of loading and destination, the freight rate, the name of consignee (unless the B/L is order B/L), and the date of shipment, which is very important from a contractual point of view. It may also contain other terms and conditions. Some bills of lading are marked "Freight Prepaid", when a shipper is selling the goods under CIF or CFR. Others may allow transshipment, which means that the cargo may be transferred from one ship to another at some intermediate ports. It is often important to a shipper that his bill of lading should be "clean" rather than "dirty", that is, the carrier (shipping company) has not made any unfavorable remarks about the quantity or condition of the cargo actually shipped. This is because the shipper's Letter of Credit may insist on clean B/L, just as it may insist on "on board B/L" as opposed to "received for shipment B/L".

5.3.3 Drawing up Marine Bills of Lading

A marine Bill of lading can be drawn up in a variety of ways, but it is nearly always prepared on a pre-printed form. This form may relate to specific or general cargo trade. Whatever its form, a bill of lading may contain some main elements, such as quantity of shipment, description of cargo, date of B/L, names of the shipper and consignee, ports of loading and discharge, name of the vessel, terms and conditions of carriage, and payment of freight.

A shipper's agent, in fact, may be given the task of drawing up the bills of lading. If these bills are subsequently required for Letter of Credit (L/C) transactions, it is useful that the agent be supplied with appropriate details of the L/C so that all the relevant information can be included in the wording.

The main parties to a bill of lading are the Shipper, Consignee, Notify Party and Carrier. The Shipper is a person, usually the exporter, who sells the goods to foreign customers. The Consignee refers to the person entitled to take delivery of the goods. The Carrier is a person or company who has concluded a contract with the shipper for carriage of the goods. The Notify Party is the party that the carrier must notify when the goods arrive at the port of destination. The carrier issues an Arrival Notice informing the Notify Party about the cargo discharge point, number of packages, and other information.

It is important to date bills of lading correctly, and as per the date on which the cargo is actually loaded. Cargo quantity and condition should also be adequately and correctly described in the bills of lading. Relevant comments should be entered in the mate's receipts, and therefore in the bills of lading.

Bills of Lading are usually made out in a full set of more than one original, usually 1-3 originals. Any original can be used for taking delivery of goods. Therefore, the buyer asks the seller for the full set of Bills of Lading. The shipper may ask for several extra copies for his files. One copy of the Bills of Lading is kept for the ship. The other copies are sent to the exporter or directly to his bank. The originals of the Bills of Lading are used for payment. They are passed on to the importer/buyer in the importing country. Then the Bs/L and the other shipping documents are presented to the shipping company when the ship arrives. The shipping company can then compare the original Bs/L with the copy on the ship. In this way, the importer can show his legal right to the goods and take delivery of goods later.

5.3.4 Classification of Bill of Lading

There are several types of Bills of Lading which are categorized in different ways.

(1) On board B/L and received for shipment B/L

According to whether the goods are loaded or not, the B/L can be classified into on board B/L and received for shipment B/L. An on board B/L is evidence that the goods have been loaded on board a certain ship/vessel. It commences with the wording "Shipped in apparent good order and condition". According to general foreign trade practices, only on board B/L is accepted by banks for payment under a L/C transaction.

A received for shipment B/L is an evidence given by a carrier that the goods have been received, waiting for shipment, but have not yet been actually loaded on a particular ship. The goods are not on board the ship, but somewhere on the docks or at the warehouse under the shipping company's control. A received for shipment B/L does not indicate the actual date of loading. When payment is arranged under L/C, the terms of L/C usually do not allow the acceptance of such kind of B/L for negotiation.

(2) Clean bill and foul/unclean bill

According to whether there are remarks of the carrier or not, the B/L falls into two kinds: clean B/L and foul B/L.

A clean B/L shows that the goods have been shipped on board, in apparent good order and condition, and there are no unfavorable remarks about the conditions or packing of the cargo from the shipping company. This kind of B/L is called "clean" or "unclaused". Usually, the words "apparent good order and condition", "clean on board" or the like are indicated on the B/L. A clean B/L confirms that the goods have not suffered apparent or outside damage and there does not seem to be any defect in the packing. By issuing a clean B/L, the carrier admits his full liability of the cargo described in the B/L under the law and his contract. This type of B/L is much favored by banks for financial settlement purpose.

A foul B/L, also named as unclean B/L, dirty B/L or claused B/L, is the opposite of the clean B/L. It is generally marked "insufficiently packed", "wet by rain", "packed in damaged condition", "unclean", "foul", etc. There are many recurring types of such clauses as inadequate packaging, wet or stained cartons, damaged crates, missing safety seal, one carton short, etc. This type of B/L is usually unacceptable to a bank. But not all Bills of lading which are noted are unclean B/L.

The following three kinds of noted B/L are not regarded as unclean Bs/L.

① The notes do not indicate clearly that the goods or packing are unsatisfactory, e. g. "old carton" or "old drum", etc.

② The purpose of the note is to emphasize that the carrier shall not be responsible for the risks resulting from the quality of the goods or packing.

③ The purpose of the note is only to deny that the carrier has any knowledge of the content, quantity, volume, quality or technical specifications of the goods.

(3) A straight B/L, An order B/Land A blank B/L

According to whether it is transferable or not, the B/L is divided into three kinds: straight B/L, order B/L and blank B/L.

A straight B/L is made out so that only the named consignee at the destination is entitled to take delivery of the goods under the B/L. The consignee is designated by the shipper. Therefore, the carrier has to hand over the goods to the named consignee in the "consignee" column of the B/L, not to any other party in possession of the B/L. This kind of B/L is not transferable. The shipper cannot transfer the B/L to a third party by endorsement. Therefore, the kind of B/L is of very restricted application. When the goods are shipped on a non-commercial basis, such as samples or exhibits, materials in aid, or when the goods are extremely valuable, a straight B/L is generally issued.

An order B/L indicates that the B/L is made out by filling in "to order" or "to order of…any person (e. g. to order of shipper, to order of the issuing bank, etc.) " in the "consignee" column of the B/L, which can be transferred/negotiated after endorsement. Thus, it is a negotiable document and sometimes called transferable B/L. It is because of its negotiability that it is commonly used in international trade.

A blank B/L is also called open B/L or bearer B/L. It refers to the B/L in which the name of a definite consignee is not mentioned. The column of "consignee" on the B/L is left blank, with neither the name of the consignee nor the phraseology of "to order" filled in. This kind of B/L can be transferred/negotiable without endorsement. In some cases, the words "to bearer" appear in the column of "consignee" and any holder of the B/L can take delivery of the goods under the B/L. That is to say, the ownership of the goods passes when the B/L is handed over to anyone. This type of B/L is very risky and seldom used.

(4) A direct B/L, A transshipment B/L, A through B/L

According to the mode of transport, the B/L can be divided into the following three kinds.

A direct B/L is referred to the consignment carried to the port of destination directly without transshipment.

A transshipment B/L is issued by a carrier when there is no direct shipping service between the port of loading and the port of destination, and the carrier arranges to tranship the goods at intermediate ports at his expense. This kind of B/L usually bears such a clause-"Transshipment to be made".

A through B/L is issued when the entire voyage involves more than one carrier, the ocean shipment forms only part of the complete journey, and thereafter the goods need to be transported by other land or sea carriers. The first carrier issues the through B/L and collects the freight for the entire voyage, and arranges transshipment and forwarding of the goods at the intermediate ports. The shipper prefers this kind of B/L because the trouble of dealing with other carriers by himself can be avoided.

(5) A long form B/L, A short form B/L

According to the contents of the B/L, the B/L can be divided into two forms: Long Form B/L and Short Form B/L.

A long form B/L refers to the B/L on the back of which all the detailed terms and conditions about the rights and obligations of the carrier and the consignor are listed as an integral part of the B/L. It is more frequently used.

A short form B/L is a document which omits the terms and conditions on the back of B/L.

(6) A freight prepaid B/L, A freight to be collected B/L

According to the time for payment of freight, the B/L can be divided into two types.

A freight prepaid B/L means that all the freight is paid by the consignor when B/L is issued by the carrier and "Freight Prepaid" is marked on the B/L.

A freight to be collected B/L refers to the B/L on which "Freight Collect" is marked. That is to say, the freight is paid after the goods arrive at the port of destination.

(7) A Liner B/L, A charter party B/L

According to the type of the carrying vessel, the B/L can be classified into a liner B/L and a charter party B/L.

(8) Other types of B/L

Besides the above-mentioned types of B/L, there are some other types, such as container B/L, on deck B/L, stale B/L, groupage B/L, ante-dated B/L, advanced B/L and so on.

Ante-dated Bill of Lading refers to the B/L issued by the carrier at the request of the shipper after the goods are loaded on board, and the issuance date of the B/L is earlier than the actual date of shipment. Besides, advanced Bill of Lading refers to a document which is issued when goods are not all loaded or not loaded at all. These two types of B/L are actually frauds and willful misrepresentations. The issuance of ante-dated B/L or advanced B/L may cause harms of breaking B/L system, disturbing transaction security, and increasing risks of the carrier. Therefore, ante-dated and advanced B/L should be effectively prevented to avoid and eliminate the B/L fraud behavior.

5.3 海运提单

前文提及，提单是海洋运输单据中的一种，因其地位重要且用途广泛，这一节就提单进行专门介绍。提单是承运人签发的用来确认收到货物的一种单据。海运提单明确规定了货物海上运输的条款和条件。提单的定义因国而异。从广义上讲，提单是货物装船的收据；它由海运承运人（或其代理）签字，上面载有货物送到船上以及被船方接收的条款。提单虽不是实际的运输合同，却是海洋运输合同条款的充分证明。

5.3.1 海运提单的作用

海运提单具有多种功能。总体而言，提单是货物装船的收据，是货物所有权凭证，是货物运输合同条款证明。

提单是承运人签发的有关承运人已接管提单所明确记载的货物或已将货物装船的证明。提单作为货物装船的收据，将显示所装货物的数量和状况、船名、装货港、目的港、装船日期等详细信息。

提单是货物所有权凭证。在法律上，对提单的所有权等同于对提单项下货物的所有权。提单的合法持有人（善意持有人）可以在目的港提取货物，且在运输途中只要通过合法背书货物就可以进行出售。

此外，提单是货物运输合同条款证明。提单条款涵盖了货物海洋运输合同条款。

5.3.2 海运提单的内容

提单不只包含货物的详细说明，它还包含许多其他的有用信息。提单提供了发货人的姓名和运载船舶的船名、装运港及目的港、运费率、收货人姓名（除非是指示提单）以及装船日期，从合同的观点来看，装船日期极为重要。提单也可能包含其他一些条款。在发货人按CIF 或 CFR 贸易术语出售货物时，提单上会注明“运费预付”。有些提单允许转船，转船的意思是货物可在一些中转港从一艘船转到另一艘船上。对发货人来说，有一点非常重要：提单应是“清洁”的，而不能是“不清洁”的；也就是说，船公司对实际装运货物的数量及状况等没有任何不良批注。其原因在于发货人的信用证往往会要求必须提交清洁提单，就像要求提交“已装船提单”而非“备运提单”一样。

5.3.3 海运提单的缮制

缮制海运提单的方法多种多样，但几乎都是预先印制好的。格式可能因贸易方式差异（特殊贸易或一般贸易）而有所不同。不论格式如何，提单的主要内容大同小异，例如货物的数量、货物确切的品名和状态、提单的签发日期、托运人和收货人的名称、装货港和卸货港、船名、货物运输的条款和条件以及运费的支付。

实际上，承运人会委托港口的代理（船代）制作提单，如果以后的信用证交易也需要使用提单，应向船代提供有关信用证的详细资料，这样在提单的措辞中就可以包含所有的相关信息。

提单的主要当事人有托运人、收货人、被通知方和承运人。发货人即向国外销售货物的出口商。收货人是指有权提取提单项下货物的人。承运人是指与托运人订立货物运输合同并承担运输业务的个人或公司。被通知方是指货物到达目的港时承运人会向其发出货物到港通知的当事人。承运人签发货物到港通知，目的是向被通知方提供有关卸货地点、包装件数和其他方面的信息。

正确地标注提单日期是很重要的，提单日期应是货物实际的装船日期。货物的数量和真实状况也应在提单上充分和正确地进行描述。大副收据上的所有批注都应一字不差的填写在提单上。

全套海运提单可能有1份以上的正本，常见有1～3份正本。任何一份正本都可以作为提货凭证，因此买方应向卖方索要全套正本提单。卖方（即发货人/出口商）可以要求船公司多签发几份副本以便存档；船方保留一份副本提单，其他的几份副本送交给出口商或直接给其银行。正本海运提单是可转让的，信用证业务中出口商需在信用证有效期内向议付行提交全套正本提单以及信用证规定的其他相关单证以办理议付、获取货款，接着全套正本提单及其单据被传递到开证行及进口国的买方手中。当货船抵达目的港时，买方（即收货人/进口商）或其代理拿着全套正本提单及其他相关单据到船公司办理提货。船公司将正确背书的可转让正本提单与船上留存的副本提单进行仔细比对。如果一致的话，进口商就可以行使对提单项下货物的所有权，向船公司交出全套正本提单以换取提货单，后续凭提货单进行进口通关并提取货物。

5.3.4 海运提单的种类

根据不同的方法，海运提单可分为如下几种类型。

(1) 已装船提单和备运提单

根据货物是否装船，提单可分为已装船提单和备运提单。已装船提单是表明货物已装上开往目的港的运输船只的提单，它的正面通常标有“货已装船”字样，一般还有“货物装运情况良好”的条款。按照国际贸易惯例，在信用证业务下，银行只接受已装船提单。

备运提单是船方签发的表明货已收到，但还没实际装上船的证明。因此，货物能否在比较短的时间内发运或装运上船尚未确定，它的正面通常有“货已收待运”的字样。很显然，这种提单没有已装船提单的价值大。当以信用证方式付款时，信用证上的条款通常不允许银行接受备运提单来办理议付。

(2) 清洁提单和不清洁提单

根据海运提单上有无承运人/船公司的不良批注，提单可分为两种：清洁提单和不清洁提单。清洁提单表明货物已装上运输船只，表面状况良好，并且上面没有船公司对装船货物状况或包装的不良批注。这种提单被称为“清洁提单”或“无条款提单”。通常，提单上会标有“外观良好”“已清洁装船”或类似字样。清洁提单证明货物没有受到内在或外在损伤，包装也没有任何缺陷。签发清洁提单意味着海运承运人/船公司承认它将按法律和合同对提单中描述的货物负完全责任。清洁提单对银行有利，因为它便于结算。

当提单被批注了某些不利于货主/托运人的批语时，如“包装不充分”“覆盖物陈旧并有污点”“雨淋”“包装破损”“不清洁”“污浊”等语句时，它就称为“不清洁”提单。类似的语句有很多，例如：包装不合适，机械保护不当，包装箱受潮、有污点，包装箱破损，缺少安全密封，一箱缺失等。不清洁提单在信用证业务中将不被银行所接受。

但是，根据国际航运公司的解释，含有下列性质批注的提单不应视为不清洁提单。

① 批注未明确表示货物或包装的“不清洁状况”，如仅批注“旧箱”或“旧桶”等。

② 批注意在强调承运人对货物或其包装性质所引起的风险不承担责任。

③ 批注意在表明承运人不知道货物的内容、重量、容量、质量或技术规格，对所引起的风险不承担责任。

(3) 记名提单、指示提单和不记名提单

按照提单是否可以转让，可将提单分为三种：记名提单、指示提单和不记名提单。

开具记名提单，意味着只有目的地的记名收货人才能提取提单项下的货物。托运人/货主指定了记名收货人，因此承运人只能将货物交给提单中收货人一栏里载明的收货人，不能交给持有提单的任何第三方。记名提单是不能通过背书实现转让的，因此这种提单的应用范围有限，常用于非商业目的货物运输，如样品、展品、援助物品以及贵重物品等。

指示提单是指在提单的收货人一栏内填写“凭指示”或“凭某人指示（如凭托运人指示，凭开证行指示等）”，并经背书就可转让的提单，故又称为“可转让提单”。由于指示提单可通过正确背书实现转让，具有很好的流通性，所以国际经贸业务经常使用指示提单。

不记名提单是指提单的收货人一栏空着不填，即没有指明任何收货人，既没有收货人的名称，也没有“凭指示”字样。有时会在收货人一栏填有“来人”字样。空白提单是可以转让的，且不需要通过背书就可转让，这意味着空白提单的任何持有人都可获得提单项下货物的所有权。因此，这种提单风险很大，一般极少使用。

(4) 直达提单、转船提单和联运提单

根据运输分式，提单可分为以下三种。

直达提单是指海运船舶不需中途换船而直接驶往目的港卸货所签发的提单。

当装运港与目的港之间没有直达的海运服务，且船主准备在中转港自己付费将货物转船时，船公司会签发转船提单。这种提单通常有“将转船……”这样的条款。

联运提单是指货物需经海运和其他运输方式联合运输时，由第一程承运人所签发的包括全程运输的提单。第一承运人签署联运提单并收取整个航程的运费，并负责在中转港的转船事宜。托运人更愿意选择联运提单，因为可以避免自己与多个承运人打交道的麻烦。

(5) 全式提单和略式提单

根据提单内容的繁简程度，可将提单分为全式提单和略式提单两种。

全式提单又称繁式提单，是指提单背面列有承运人和托运人双方权利、义务的详细条款的提单。

略式提单又称简式提单，是指提单略去了背面条款内容，只列有提单正面的必须记载事项的提单。

(6) 运费预付提单和运费到付提单

根据运费支付时间，提单可分为两种。

运费预付提单是指运费已由托运人预付，承运人签发提单时，在提单上注明“运费预付”的字样。

运费到付提单是指提单上注明“运费到付”字样的提单，即运费在货物运抵目的港后支付。

（7）班轮提单和租船提单

根据船舶营运的方式，提单可分为班轮提单和租船提单。

（8）其他类型的提单

除了上述提单外，还有其他一些种类的提单，如集装箱提单、舱面提单、过期提单、成组提单、倒签提单和预借提单。

倒签提单指的是指承运人应托运人的要求在货物装船后签发的，提单（签发）日期早于实际装船完毕日期的提单。预借提单指的是提单在货物尚未全部装船时，或者货物虽然已经由承运人接管但尚未开始装船的情况下签发的提单。提单一旦被倒签或者预借，都属于欺诈和故意歪曲事实行为，从而带来破坏提单制度、扰乱交易安全、增加承运人风险等的危害。因此，应有效防止提单的倒签和预借，以避免和消除提单欺诈行为。

Part B Vocabulary and Terminology 词汇和术语

bulk cargo 散货
break-bulk cargo 件杂货
bulk carrier 散货船
general cargo ship 杂货船
container ship 集装箱船
Roll on-Roll off（RORO）vessel 滚装船
Liner/Regular Shipping Liner 班轮运输
Shipping by Chartering 租船运输
voyage charter 航次租船
time charter 定期租船
demise charter/bare-boat charter 光船租船
freight tariff，tariff 运价表
Charter Party 租船合同
demurrage 滞期费
dispatch 速遣费
shipping documents 装运单据
Bill of Lading（B/L） 海运提单
Sea Waybill 海运单
Cargo Manifest 货物舱单
Shipping Note，Booking Note（B/N） 托运单
Shipping Order（S/O） 装货单/装船单
Delivery Order（D/O） 提货单
Mate's Receipt（M/R） 收货单，大副收据
on board Bill of Lading 已装船提单
received for shipment Bill of Lading 备运提单
clean Bill of Lading 清洁提单

unclean Bill of Lading, foul Bill of Lading 不清洁提单
straight Bill of Lading 直达提单
order Bill of Lading 指示提单
blank Bill of Lading 空白提单
through Bill of Lading 联运提单
transshipment Bill of Lading 转船提单
contract of carriage 运输合同
document of title 物权凭证
insufficient packing 包装不良；包装不固
negotiable document 可转让单据
Notify Party 通知方
on board 在船上
port of lading 装货港
shipping company 海运公司，船公司
tramp service 不定期船运输，租船运输
shipping conference 班轮公会
conference lines 班轮公会航线，班轮公会航运公司
scheduled service 定期航运
non-conference line 非班轮公会航线，非班轮公会航运公司
common carrier 公共承运人
non-vessel operating common carrier (NVOCC) 无船承运人

Part C Exercise 练习

Ⅰ. Answer the following questions.

1. What kind of role does transportation play in the logistics system?
2. What are the advantages of ocean shipping?
3. What is shipping by liner?
4. Please explain charter service and its major forms.
5. What is clean on board Bill of Lading?
6. Please tell the functions of Bill of Lading.
7. What are the major kinds of Bill of Lading according to different ways of filling in the space of "consignee" in B/L?
8. What is Delivery Order?

Ⅱ. True or false.

1. A Bill of Lading is a transport contract in which the shipping company promises to transport the goods received to the destination.
2. An order Bill of Lading is negotiable after being endorsed.
3. When you transport your goods by a time charter, you have to pay for loading and unloading.
4. When the ship-owner speeds up his ship and arrives at the destination at an earlier

date than is stipulated, he can obtain dispatch money from the shipper.

5. When the charterer fails to load or unload the goods within the stipulated period of time, he has to pay demurrage to the ship-owner.

6. An international freight forwarder should have knowledge of international trade.

7. Conferences lines do not provide a scheduled service.

8. A delivery order is issued by the carrier to enable a shipper to load the cargo.

9. Tramps move from port to port without following a fixed route.

Ⅲ. Choose the right answer from the four choices below.

1. Ships that do not sail on regular routes or do not have regular schedules are called (　　).

A. liners　　B. tramps　　C. charters　　D. NVOCCs

2. (　　) is the list of current freight rates issued by a shipping conference.

A. Tariff　　B. Schedule　　C. Manifest　　D. Shipping note

3. (　　) is a document signed by the mate of a ship as proof that the goods specified in the document have been loaded onto his ship.

A. Delivery order　　B. Shipping note　　C. Mate's receipt　　D. Manifest

4. Which of the following terms refers to a person or company that carries goods from place to place? (　　)

A. shipper　　B. charterer　　C. operator　　D. carrier

5. Which of the following is the amount of money payable under a contract for the carriage of goods by sea? (　　)

A. delivery　　B. endorsement　　C. freight　　D. receipt

Ⅳ. Translate the following passages.

1. A shipping conference is a group of shipping lines operating on any particular route under agreement to provide a scheduled service with a common tariff and a fixed itinerary of ports of call. The purpose of a shipping conference is to eliminate price competition among member lines and reduce outside competition by trying to capture most of the traffic for member lines through loyal arrangement with shippers.

2. A NVOCC is a carrier who operates a regular scheduled service. He does not own or operate the vessels by which sea transportation is provided. Although the NVOCC is carrier in his relationship with the actual shipper, he is the shipper in his relationship with the actual carrier.

3. Chartering is a business of providing employment for a vessel and arranging suitable sea transport for a variety of commodities. The term Charter Party is employed to describe contacts relating to the use of vessels owned or controlled by others. The three principal methods of chartering a tram ship are voyage charter, time charter, and bare-boat charter.

Ⅴ. Translate the following sentences into English.

1. 总体而言，提单是货物装船的收据，是货物所有权凭证，是货物运输合同条款证明。

2. 班轮运输是指船公司按照公布的船期表在特定的航线上，以既定的挂靠港顺序，进行规则的反复的航行和运输的一种船舶经营方式。

3. 清洁提单是提单上没有任何关于货物外表状态不良批注的提单，表明承运人在接收货物时，货物的外在状态良好。国际贸易合同和信用证一般都规定卖方必须凭清洁提单向银行结汇。

附录 5.1 Ocean Bill of Lading 海运提单

Ocean Bill of Lading
海运提单

托运人 Shipper		B/L No. 中国对外贸易运输总公司 北京 BEIJING 联 运 提 单 COMBINED TRANSPORT BILL OF LADING **RECEIVED** the foods in apparent good order and condition as specified below unless otherwise stated herein. THE Carrier, in accordance with the provisions contained in this document: 1)undertakes to perform or to procure the performance of the entire transport form the place at which the goods are taken in charge to the place designated for delivery in this document, and 2) assumes liability as prescribed in this document for such transport One of the bills of lading must be surrendered duty indorsed in exchange for the goods or delivery order	
收货人或指示 Consignee or order			
通知地址 Notify Address			
前段运输 Pre-carriage by	收货地点 Place of Receipt		
海运船只 Ocean Vessel	装货港 Port of Loading		
卸货港 Port of Discharge	交货地点 Place of Delivery	运费支付地 Freight payable at	正本提单份数 Number of original Bs/L

标志和号码 Marks and Nos.	件数和包装种类 Number and kind of packages	货 名 Description of goods	毛重(公斤) Gross weight(kgs.)	尺 码(立方米) Measurement(m^3)
以上细目由托运人提供 ABOVE PARTICULARS FURNISHED BY SHIPPER				

运费和费用 Freight and charges	IN WITNESS where of the number of original bills of Lading stated above have been signed, one of which being accomplished, the other(s) to be void.	
	签单地点和日期 Place and date of issue	
	代表承运人签字 Signed for or on behalf of the carrier	
		代 理 as Agents

海运提单（背面）

1. DEFINIYIONW The term "Shipper" occurs hereinafter. It shall be deemed to include also Receiver, Consignee. Holder of this Bill of Lading and Owner of the goods.

2. JURISDICTION All disputes arising under and in connection with this Bill of Lading shall be determined by the court in the People's Republic of China.

3. DEMISE CLAUSE If the ship is not owned by or chartered by demise to the corporation by whom this Bill of Lading is issued (as may be the case notwithstanding anything that appears to the contrary) this Bill of Lading shall take effect only as a contract with the Owner or demise charterer as the case may be as principal made through the agency of the said corporation who act as agents only and shall be under no personal liability whatsoever in respect thereof

4. HAGUE RULES This Bill of Lading shall have effect in respect of Carrier's liabilities, responsibility, rights and immunities subject to the Hague Rules contained in the International Convention for the Unification of Certain Rules Relating to Bills of Lading 1924.

5. PACKING AND MARKS The Shipper shall have the goods properly packed accurately and clearly marked before shipment. The port of destination of the goods should be marked in letters of 5cm high, in such a way as will remain legible until their delivery.

6. OPTIONAL STOWAGE (1) The goods may be stowed by the Carrier in containers or similar articles of transport used to consolidate goods (2) Goods stowed in containers other than flats, pallets, transportable tanks or similar articles of transport whether by the Carrier or the Shipper, may be carried on or under deck without notice to the Shipper. Such goods whether carried on or under deck shall participate in general average.

7. DECK CARGO. PLANTS AND LIVE ANIMALS Cargo on deck, plants and live animal are received, handled, carried, kept and discharged at Shipper's or Receiver's risk and the Carrier shall not be liable for loss thereof or damage thereto.

8. FREIGHT (1) Freight and charges shall be deemed earned on receipt of the goods by the Carrier and shall be paid by the Shipper and non-returnable in any event. Freight payable at destination together with other charges is due on arrival of the goods at the place of destination and shall be paid before delivery of the goods. (2) For the purpose of verifying the freight basis, the Carrier reserves the right to have the goods and the contents of containers, trailers or similar articles of transport inspected in order to ascertain the weight, measurement, value or nature of the goods. In case the particulars of the goods furnished by the Shipper are incorrect, the Shipper shall be liable and bound to pay to the Carrier a sum either five times the difference between the correct freight and the freight charged or to double the correct less the freight charged, whichever sum is the smaller, as liquidated damages to the Carrier.

9. LIEN The Carrier shall have a lien on the goods and any documents relating thereto for all sums payable to the Carrier under this Bill of Lading and for general average contributions to whomsoever due and for the cost of recovering the same, and for that purpose shall have the right to sell the goods by public auction or private treaty without notice to the Shipper. If on sale of the goods, the proceeds fail to cover the amount due and the cost incurred, the Carrier shall be entitled to recover the deficit from the Shipper.

10. TIME BAR, NOTICE OF LOSS In any event the Carrier shall be discharged from all liabilities under this Bill of Lading unless suit is brought within one year after the delivery of the goods or the date when the goods should have been delivered. Unless notice of loss of or damage to the goods and the general nature of it be given in writing to the Carrier at the place of delivery before or at the time of the removal of the goods into the custody of the person entitled to delivery thereof under this Bill of Lading, such removal shall be provided evidence of the delivery by the Carrier of the goods as described in this Bill of Lading. In the case of any actual or apprehended loss or damage the Carrier and the Shipper shall give all reasonable facilities to each other for inspecting and tallying the goods.

11. THE AMOUNT OF COMPENSATION (1) When the Carrier is liable for compensation in respect of loss of or damage to the goods, such compensation shall be calculated by reference to the invoice value of the goods plus freight and insurance premium of paid. (2) Notwithstanding clause 4 of this Bill of Lading the limitation of liability under the Hague Rules shall be deemed to be RMB. ￥700 per package or unit. (3) Higher compensation may be claimed only when, with the consent of the Carrier, the value for the goods declared by the Shipper which exceeds the limits laid down in this clause has been stated in this Bill of Lading and extra freight has been paid as required. In that case the amount of the declared value shall be substituted for that limit. Any partial loss or damage shall be adjusted pro rata on the basis of such declared value.

12. LOADING, DISCHARGING AND DELIVERY The goods shall be supplied and taken delivery of by the owner of the goods as fast as the ship can take and discharge them, without interruption, by day and night. Sundays and Holidays included, notwithstanding any custom of the port to the contrary and the owner of the goods shall be liable for all losses or damages incurred in default thereof. Discharge may commence without previous notice. If the goods are not taken delivery of by the Receiver in due time from alongside the vessel, or if the Receiver refuses to take delivery of the goods, or in case there are unclaimed goods, the Carrier shall be at liberty to land such goods on shore or any other proper places at the sole risk and expense of the Shipper or Receiver, and the Carrier's responsibility of delivery of goods shall be deemed to have been fulfilled. If the goods are unclaimed during a reasonable time, or wherever the goods will become deteriorated, decayed or worthless, the Carrier may, at his discretion and subject to his lien and without any responsibility attaching to him, sell, abandon or otherwise dispose of such goods solely at the risk and expense of the Shipper.

13. LIGHTERAGE Any lighterage in or off ports of loading or ports of discharge shall be for the account of the Shipper or Receiver.

14. FORWARDING, SUBSTITUTE OF VESSEL, THROUGH CARGO AND TRANSHIPMENT If necessary, the Carrier may carry the goods to their port of destination by other persons or by rail or other means of transport proceeding either directly or indirectly to such port, and to carry the goods or part of them beyond their port of destination, and to transship and forward same at Carrier's expense but at Shipper's or Receiver's risk. The responsibility of the Carrier shall be limited to the part of the transport performed by him on the vessel under his management.

15. DANGEROUS GOODS, CONTRABAND (1) The Shipper undertakes not to tender for transporting any goods which are of a dangerous, inflammable, radio-active, and/or any harmful mature without previously giving written notice of their nature to the Carrier and marking the goods and the container or other covering on the outside as required by any laws or regulations which may be applicable during the carriage. (2) Whenever the goods are discovered to have been shipped without complying with the subclause (1) above or the goods are found to be contraband or prohibited by any laws or regulations of the port of loading, discharge or call or any place or waters during the carriage, the Carrier shall be entitled to have such goods rendered innocuous, thrown overboard or discharged or otherwise disposed of at the carrier's discretion without compensation and the Shipper shall be liable for and indemnify the Carrier against any kind of loss, damage or liability including loss of freight, and any expenses directly or indirectly arising out of or resulting from such shipment. (3) If any goods shipped complying with the subclause (1) above become a danger to the ship or cargo, they may in like manner be rendered innocuous, thrown overboard or discharged or otherwise disposed of at the Carrier's discretion without compensation except to general average, of any.

16. REFRIGERATED CARGO (1) The Shipper undertakes not to tender for transportation any goods which require refrigeration without previously giving written notice of their nature and particular temperature range to be maintained. If the above requirements are not complied with, the Carrier shall not be liable for any loss of or damage to the goods howsoever arising. (2) Before loading goods in any insulated space, the Carrier shall, in addition to the Class Certificate, obtain the certificate of the Classification Society's Surveyor or other competent person, stating that such insulated space conveyor or other competent person fit and safe for the carriage and preservation of refrigerated goods. The aforesaid certificate shall be conclusive evidence against the Shipper, Receiver and/or any Holder of Bill of Lading. (3) Receivers have to take delivery of refrigerated goods as soon as the ship is ready to deliver, otherwise the Carrier shall land the goods at the wharf at Receiver's or Shipper's risk and expense.

17. TIMBER Any statement in this Bill of Lading to the effect that timber has been shipped "in apparent good order and condition" does not involve any admission by the Carrier as to the absence of stains, shakes, splits, holes or broken pieces, for which the Carrier accepts no responsibility.

18. BULK CARGO As the Carrier has no reasonable means of checking the weight of bulk cargo, any reference to such weight in this Bill of Lading shall be deemed to be for reference only, but shall constitute in no way evidence against the Carrier.

19. COTTON Description of the apparent condition of cotton or cotton products does not relate to the insufficiency of or torn condition of the covering, nor to any damage resulting therefrom, and Carrier shall not be responsible for damage of such nature.

20. OPTIONAL CARGE The port of discharge for optional cargo must be declared to the vessel's agents at the first of the optional ports not late than 48 hours before the vessel's arrival there. In the absence of such declaration the Carrier may elect to discharge at the contract of carriage shall then be considered as having been fulfilled, Any option must be for the total quantity of goods under this Bill of Lading.

21. GOODS TO MORE THAN ONE CONSIGNEE Where bulk goods or goods without marks or goods with the same marks are shipped to more than one Consignee, the Consignees or Owners of the goods shall jointly and severally bear any expense or loss in dividing the goods or parcels into pro rata quantities and any deficiency shall fall upon them in such proportion as the Carriers, his servants or agents shall decide.

22. HEAVY LIFTS AND OVER LENGTH CARGO Any one piece or package of cargo which exceeding 2000 kilos or 9 meters must be declared by the Shipper in writing before receipt by the Carrier and/or length Clearly and durably on the outside of the piece or package in letters and figures not less than 2 inches high by the Shipper. In case of the Shipper's failure in his obligations aforesaid, the Shipper shall be liable for loss of or damage to any property or for personal injury arising as a result of the Shipper's said failure and shall indemnify the Carrier against any kind of loss or liability suffered or incurred by the Carrier as a result of such failure.

23. SHIPPER-PACKED CONTAINERS. ETC. (1) If a container has not been filled, packed or stowed by the Carrier, the Carrier shall not be liable for any loss of or damage to its contents and the Shipper shall cover any loss or expense incurred by the Carrier, of such loss, damage or expense has been cause by negligent filling, packing or stowing of the container; other contents being unsuitable for carriage in container; or the unsuitability or defective condition of the container unless the container has been supplied by the Carrier and the unsuitability or defective condition would not have been apparent upon reasonable inspection at or prior to the time when the container was filled, packed or stowed. (2) The provisions of the sub-clause (1) above also apply with respect to trailers, transportable tanks, flats and pallets which have not been filled, packed or stowed by the Carrier.

24. WAR, QUARANTINE, ICE, STRIKES, CONGESTION, ETC. Should it appear that war, blockade, pirate, epidemics, quarantine, ice, strikes, congestion and other causes beyond the Carrier's control would prevent the vessel from safely reaching the port of destination and discharging the goods thereat, the Carrier is entitled to discharge the goods at the port and the contract of carriage shall be deemed to have been fulfilled. Any extra expenses incurred under the aforesaid circumstances shall be borne by the Shipper or Receiver.

25. GENERAL AVERAGE General average shall be adjusted in Beijing in accordance with the Beijing Adjustment Rules 1975.

26. BOTH TO BLAME COLLISION If the carrying ship comes into collision with another ship as a result of the negligence of the other ship and any act, neglect or default in the navigation or the management of the carrying ship, the Shipper undertakes to pay the Carrier, or, where the Carrier is not the Owner and in possession of the carrying ship, to pay to the Carrier as trustee for the Owner and/or demise charterer of the carrying ship, a sum sufficient to indemnify the Carrier and/or the Owner and/or demise charterer of the carrying ship against all loss or liability to the other or non-carrying ship or her Owners insofar as such loss or liability represents loss of or damage to his goods or any claim whatsoever of the Shipper, paid or payable by the other or non-carrying ship or her Owners to the Shipper and set-off, recouped or recovered by the other or non-carrying ship or her Owners as part of their claim against the carrying ship or her Owner or demise charterer or the Carrier. The foregoing provisions shall also apply where the Owners, operations, or those in charge of any ship or ships or objects, other than, or in addition to, the colliding ships or objects, are at fault in respect to a collision, contact, stranding or other accident.

27. U. S. A. CLAUSE Notwithstanding any other term hereof the Carriage of Goods by Sea Act 1936 of the United States of America shall have been affect subject to in respect to carriage of goods to and from the United States of America. If any provision of this Bill of Lading be invalid under the Carriage of Goods by Sea Act 1936, such provision shall, to the extent of such invalidity, but no further, be null and void.

附录 5.2 Shipping Order 装货单

中国外轮代理公司

CHINA OCEAN SHIPPING AGENCY

装 货 单

SHIPPING ORDER

托运人

Shipper ______________________________

编号 No. ______________________ 船名 S/S ______________________

目的港

For ______________________

兹将下列完好状况之货物装船后希签署收货单

Receive on board the undermentioned goods apparent in good order and condition and sign the accompanying receipt for the same

标记及号码 Marks & Nos	件　数 Quantity	货　名 Description of Goods	重量公斤 Weight Kilos	
			净重 Net	毛重 Gross

共计件数(大写)

Total Number of Package in Writing

____

日期 Date ______________________ 时间 Time ______________________

装入何舱 Stowed ______________________ 实收 Received ______________________

理货员签名 Tallied by ______________________ 经办员 Approved by ______________________

附录 5.3 Mate's Receipt 收货单

中国外轮代理公司

CHINA OCEAN SHIPPING AGENCY

收 货 单

MATE'S RECEIPT

托运人
Shipper ____________________

编号
No. ____________________

船名
S/S ____________________

目的港
For ____________________

兹将下列完好状况之货物装船后希签署收货单

Receive on board the undermentioned goods apparent in good order and condition and sign the accompanying receipt for the same

标记及号码 Marks & Nos	件 数 Quantity	货 名 Description of Goods	重量公斤 Weight Kilos	
			净重 Net	毛重 Gross

共计件数(大写)

Total Number of Package in Writing

____

日期
Date ____________________

时间
Time ____________________

装入何舱
Stowed ____________________

实收
Received ____________________

理货员签名
Tallied by ____________________

大副
Chief Officer ____________________

Chapter Six

International Air Transport Logistics 国际空运物流

Part A Text 课文

6.1 Introduction to Air Transport

6.1.1 Definition to Air Transport

Air transport is one of the youngest forms of transport, and without doubt, it continues to make a major contribution to the exploitation of world resources. International air transport provides fast and convenient transport services for long-distance logistics, or accelerates international logistics through combined transport with other modes of transport. Compared with ocean transport, cargo volume of air transport is quite small. But due to its outstanding advantages, air transport plays an increasingly important role in international logistics. Air transport is usually used to transport small quantities of light goods with high requirements on delivery time and high value, such as small-sized urgent goods, valuables, precise instrument, electronic and high-tech products, fresh goods (flowers, fruits and seafood, etc.) and first-aid materials. Moreover, air cargo is more varied and expensive than sea cargo.

In the following, we will cover such aspects of international air transport as the advantages, disadvantages, service modes, document required, and freight rate.

6.1.2 Advantages and Disadvantages of Air Transport

First of all, there are many advantages of air transport. The main advantages are stated as below.

① High speed and quick transit. The route of air transport is not very much restricted by ground conditions. It typically flies directly between two points and thus makes a shorter route. The longer the route is, the quicker air freight transit will be.

② Simplified documentation system. One document, namely Air Waybill (AWB), is used throughout the air freight transit and is interchangeable between IATA (International Air Transport Association) accredited airlines.

③ Reliable and high-quality service.

④ Low risks of damage and pilferage, generating great cost savings on insurance and packing and reducing the amount of capital tied up in transit as well.

Besides the advantages mentioned above, there may be some other advantages. It is ideal for palletized consignments and a wide range of consumer-type cargoes. Compared with major seaports, major airports worldwide tend to be located in the center of commercial/industrial areas. In addition, the worldwide network of air transport is more extensive than that of ocean transport and airlines offer more frequent flights than shipping liners do.

Although air transport has a number of advantages, it has some disadvantages which go as follows.

① Limited carrying capacity and quite a few restrictions on the weight and measurement of acceptable cargo.

② High freight.

③ Susceptible to weather conditions.

6.1 航空运输概述

6.1.1 航空运输的定义

航空运输是一种现代化的运输形式，虽然起步较晚，但毫无疑问它对于世界资源的开发利用做出了重要的贡献。国际航空运输为长距离的物流提供了快速、便捷的运输服务，或者通过与其他运输方式的联运，加快了国际物流的速度。虽然与海洋运输相比，航空货运量较小，但是由于它的优点突出，它在国际物流中的地位和作用越来越重要。航空运输通常用于运输小批量、重量较轻的、递送时间要求高、货值高的货物，如小件急需品、贵重物品、精密仪器、电子产品和高科技产品、鲜活商品（鲜花、水果和海鲜等）以及急救品等。而且，相比海运货物，空运货物种类更为多样，价值也更昂贵。

6.1.2 航空运输的优势和劣势

首先，航空运输具有如下的主要优势。

① 运送速度快。航空线路不受地面条件限制，一般可在两点间直线飞行，航程比地面短得多，而且航程越长，快速的特点就越明显。

② 简化了单证要求。在整个航空运输过程中，只需一份单据即航空运单，且航空运单在所有 IATA（国际航空运输协会）注册登记的航空公司间可以通用。

③ 可靠安全且运输质量高。

④ 货物受损及被盗的风险小，节省了包装、保险费用，也减少了在途库存的资金占压。

除了上述主要优点外，航空运输的优点还体现为：适合运输托盘化、客户化包装的货物；全球许多重要的机场都位于商业或工业区域的中心以及全球航空运输网络覆盖面越来越广，航空公司能比班轮公司提供更为频繁的航班服务等。

虽然航空运输具有许多优点，但它也存在如下缺点。

① 装载的货运量有限，而且在货物体积以及重量上有较多的限制。

② 运费高昂。

③ 易受气候的影响等。

6.2 Modes and Document of Air Transport

6.2.1 Modes of Air Transport

Generally speaking, there are four major modes of air transport: scheduled airline, chartered carrier, consolidation, and air express service.

(1) Scheduled airline

Scheduled airline service means that the aircraft flies regularly between a group of fixed airports. The scheduled airline has a fixed timetable, a fixed route, and fixed airports of departure and destination. It is usually a mixed passenger and freight transport, and in some cases, airlines use flights for only carrying cargoes. It is suitable for the delivery of urgently needed goods, fresh goods and in-season commodities, because the flight has a fixed timetable and flying route and thus is relatively punctual.

(2) Chartered carrier

In this mode, an airline leases a flight to one charterer or multiple charterers. That is to say, a flight can be fully chartered by one charterer or be jointly chartered by several charterers. In the case that the quantity of one charterer's consignment is less than a full aircraft load, multiple charterers can jointly charter an aircraft to optimize the carrying capacity of the aircraft.

(3) Consolidation

Consolidation means the assembly of small parcels of cargoes from several consignors at one point of origin intended for several consignees at another point of destination, dispatching the parcels as one consolidated consignment to the consolidator's agent at the destination and finally delivering them to their respective consignees. Consolidation is a useful method that will reduce transportation cost without increasing inventory investment. Consolidation mode is shown as Figure 6.1.

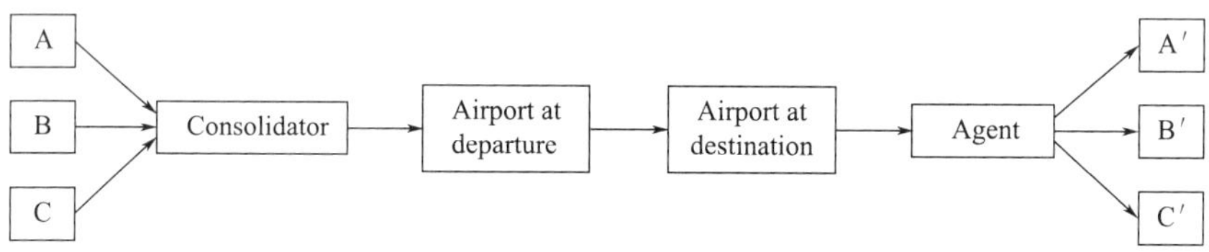

Figure 6.1 Consolidation mode

Usually, air freight forwarder acts as the consolidator and consolidate cargoes from different shippers under one Master Air Waybill (MAWB) and airline companies must give all cargoes under the same MAWB with the same treatment. But not all cargoes are suitable for consolidation, such as valuable products, live animals, diplomatic mails and dangerous cargoes. Forwarders who act as consolidators deliver full-container-load (FCL) cargo composed of some individual less-than-container-load (LCL) consignments to the carrier (airline company) to take advantage of the low FCL freight rates. As a consolidator, the freight forwarder will provide a service in his own name and issue a House Air Waybill (HAWB) to each actual shipper/consignor. In consolidation transport, the freight forwarder acts as a sort of wholesaler by buying large amounts of plane space which are sold out in retail to his customers, i. e. , actual consignors. To the individual consignors, the consolidator is a carrier while in his relationship with the actual carrier (airlines), he is a consignor. The individual consignors and consignees do not deal directly with the actual carrier.

This mode is more popular because of its cheaper freight and more convenience. Consideration can benefit all concerned parties, e. g. , exporter/shipper, carrier and forwarder. For exporters/shippers, they get the benefit of a freight rate lower than they would have normally paid to the airline company. It is particularly beneficial to small shippers who do not have enough bargaining strength to negotiate air freight rates with the airline company. Also, shippers find it advantageous to deal with a freight forwarder who is able to provide consolidation service to a wide range of destination instead of his own approaching several airline companies. Besides, consolidation can also benefit a carrier. A carrier does not have to handle individual consignments, which results in considerable savings in paperwork and time. And there is more intensive utilization of aircraft's carrying capacity because the consolidator typically offers FCL cargoes. Additionally, a carrier does not have to take the risk of freight payments by individual shippers as this is taken care of by the forwarder.

(4) Air express service

Air express service is provided by the business that specializes in this service due to its close cooperation with airlines. Its specific operations include: After the Courier company sends the specially-assigned person to pick up the goods from the consignor, the goods will be shipped by the earliest flight. Upon arriving at the destination, the goods will be picked up by the specially-assigned person at the airport and directly delivered to the consignee after completing customs formalities. Goods of emergency are normally delivered in air express service. It is also named as "door to door" service, or even "desk to desk" service, whose freight is the highest.

The characteristics and application scope of each mode are illustrated in the Table 6. 1.

Table 6. 1 The characteristics and application scope of each mode

Types of service	Characteristics	Scope of application
Scheduled airline	Small volume, expensive freight, fixed schedule, fixed route, fixed points of departure and destination	It is suitable for delivery of urgently needed goods, fresh goods and in-season goods.
Chartered carrier	Relatively lower freight, large volume, longer delivery time than the scheduled airline, restrictions by governments, restricted landing sites	It is suitable for delivery of a large volume of goods.
Consolidation	Low freight, handled by air freight forwarders, providing convenience for both consignors and consignees, facilitating early settlement of exchange	It is suitable for delivery of general cargoes.
Air express service	Fastest delivery, safe and reliable service, fast query, highest freight	It is suitable for delivery of urgently needed goods and documents

6. 2. 2 Document of Air Transport—Air Waybill

The Air Waybill (AWB) is the key document in air transport. The Air Waybill, also called consignment note, is a document used for the carriage of goods by air issued by the carrier to the consignor.

Air Waybill has the following features:

① It is an actual contract of carriage between the carrier (airline company) and the shipper (the consignor or air freight forwarder under consolidation service).

② It is a receipt from the carrier acknowledging the receipt of the consignment from the shipper.

③ The Air Waybill is an internationally standardized document that is mostly printed in English and in the official language of the country of departure, which facilitates the on-carriage of goods going through 2 or 3 airlines in different countries to the final destination.

The Air Waybill is the most important document for a batch of air freight goods. An air waybill is also used for freight calculation, customs declaration and specific information on handling a shipment. Essentially an air waybill is non-negotiable, that is, the goods must be sent to the consignee titled in the AWB. Each shipment has an air waybill. For consolidated shipments, individual air waybills, called the House Air Waybills (HAWB), are also combined into a Master Air Waybill (MAWB) for the consolidated shipment.

Generally, in China, the AWB consists of 12 pages, including 3 originals, 6 copies and 3 additional copies. They are sent to various interested parties, such as the shipper, consignee, issuing carrier, second carrier (if applicable), third carrier (if applicable), airport of destination, airport of departure, etc. Different pages are in different colors. The three originals are held/retained separately by the shipper, the carrier and consignee.

The page marked "Original 1 (For the carrier) " is retained by the carrier for filing and accounting purposes. It is signed by the shipper and given back to the carrier.

The page marked "Original 2 (For the consignee) " is to be sent with the consignment and delivered to the consignee titled in the AWB at the destination. This original is signed by both the carrier and the shipper.

The page marked "Original 3 (For the shipper) " is the original that would normally be presented by the shipper to the negotiating bank under documentary Letter of Credit. This is signed by the carrier and sent back to the shipper.

According to the issuer of the AWB, air waybills can be categorized into two types: Master Air Waybill (MAWB) and House Air Waybill (HAWB). All AWBs issued by airlines are called MAWBs. It is a contract signed between the airline and the shipper. Each shipment of air transport has its corresponding MAWB. As for consolidation service mode, HAWB is also required. The HAWB is a document evidencing the handing over and taking over of cargoes between air freight forwarder and the actual shipper/consignor. The air freight forwarder first issues its own HAWB to the individual consignors. But normally, the format of HAWB is pursuant to that of airline's MAWB. In a HAWB, the information about the shipper and consignee reflects the real/actual shipper and consignee. After taking over cargoes from actual shippers, the forwarder consolidates cargoes from different shippers and then hands them over to an airline company. In connection, an evidencing document between the forwarder and the airline company is necessary, and this document is called MAWB. The MAWB has recorded the main information of cargoes to be shipped by air. It defines the relationship between the forwarder/consolidator and the airline company as the shipper to the carrier. Therefore, under the mode of consolidation, actual shippers do not need to deal with the airlines.

6.2 航空运输的方式和单据

6.2.1 航空运输的方式

航空运输主要有如下四种经营模式。

(1) 班机运输

班机运输方式是指在固定的开航时间、固定的航线、固定的始发站、目的站和途经站飞行的运输方式。通常是客货混合型飞机，一些大的航空公司有时也会开辟全货机航班运输。班机运输适用于运送急需品、鲜活商品以及节令性商品，因为班机具有定时、定航线、定点等特点。

(2) 包机运输

包机运输可分为整包机和部分包机两种。整包机指航空公司或航空货运代理公司按照约定的条件和费率，将整架飞机租给租机人，从一个或几个航空站装运货物至目的地。部分包机指由几家航空货运公司或发货人联合包租一架飞机或者由航空公司把一架飞机的舱位分别租给几家航空货运公司装载货物，它主要用于托运装不满一整架飞机，但货量又较大的货物运输。

(3) 集中托运

集中托运又称集拼业务，是指集中托运人将多个托运人/发货人发往同一目的地的若干批小票货物集拼成一批大票货物向航空公司办理托运，货物到达目的站后由集中托运人在目的地的代理统一进行提货报关后分拨给各实际收货人。集中托运是在不增加库存投资的情况下降低运输成本的有效方法。集中托运业务如图 6.1 所示。

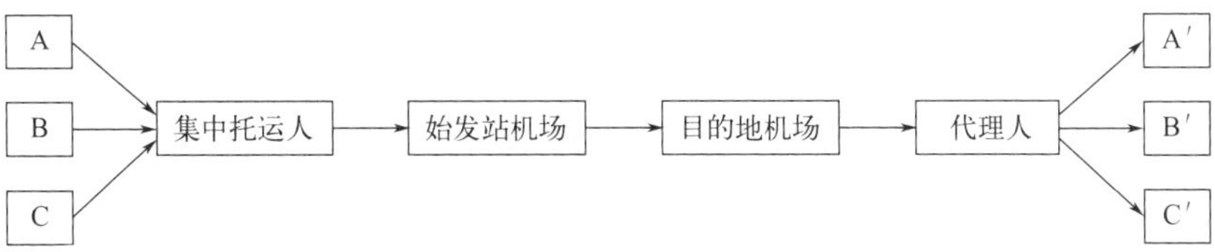

图 6.1 集中托运业务

集中托运通常把属于不同托运人的货物整合在一个总运单下，即填写一份总运单向航空公司办理托运送至同一目的地，而航空公司则必须对所有在同一总运单下的货物给予相同的处理。但并不是所有的货物都适合集中托运，如贵重货物、活动物、外交信件、危险货物等。作为集中托运人的货运代理（航空货运代理），将由小票/散箱货物集拼而成的大票/整箱货物交付给承运人，以获得便宜的整箱运费。作为集中托运人，货运代理将以自己的名义向单个实际发货人/货主提供服务，并签发航空分运单。在集中托运业务中，货运代理扮演着批发商的角色，它向航空公司购买的是大量的飞机货舱空间，然后再零售给他的客户。对于单个实际托运人/发货人来说，集中托运人是其承运人，而在集中托运人与实际承运人（航空公司）的关系中，集中托运人是托运人。实际托运人/发货人以及收货人不直接与实际承运人打交道。

集中托运业务由于能提供更低的运费以及更多的便利而广受欢迎。它能使所有相关方从中获益，如出口商和托运人、承运人以及货代等等。对于出口商和托运人来说，他们能从集中托运人那里获得一个比他们自己向航空公司托运时低得多的运费率。这对那些在与航空公司协商运价时没有讨价还价优势的中小货主尤其有利。此外，集中托运非常有利于托运人，他们只需与一家能提供整合服务的货运代理打交道，省去了与几家航空公司打交道的时间和精力。此外，集中托运也可以使承运人受益。承运人不需要处理单独的小票/散箱货物，这可以节省大量的单证工作和时间。而且，由于集中托运人托运的都是整箱货物，所以大大提高了航空运输的装载能力和效率。此外，承运人不必承担个别发货人不支付运费的风险，因为在集中托运业务下是货运代理与实际货主发生直接业务关系，该风险自然也由货运代理来承担。

（4）航空快递

航空快递是由快递公司与航空公司合作，向货主提供的快递服务。其业务包括：由快递公司派专人从发货人处提取货物后以最快航班将货物发运，飞抵目的地后，由专人接机提货，办妥进关手续后直接送达收货人，称为“门到门服务”，甚至“桌到桌服务”。这是一种最为快捷也最为昂贵的运输方式，特别适用于急需药品、贵重物品、紧急文件等的传送。

表 6.1 列出了各种航空运输方式的特点及适用范围。

表 6.1 各种航空运输方式的特点及适用范围

运输类型	特点	适用范围
班机运输	运量较小，运价较贵，航期固定，具有定时、定航线、定点等特点	适用于运送急需物品、鲜活商品以及节令性商品
包机运输	运费低，运量较大，但运送时间比班机长。受各国政府限制，包机的活动范围比较小，降落地点受到限制	适用于批量较大的商品
集中托运	主要优势为运费低；主要由航空货运代理提供和组织；为货主和收货人提供方便；有助于提早结汇	适用于一般商品
航空速递	运输快捷，服务安全可靠，查询快，运费昂贵	急需物品、急救药品、紧急文件等

6.2.2 航空运输单据——航空运单

空运单据，也称为航空运单，是航空运输中的核心单据，是用来证明货物已由承运人通过航空运输送至收货人的货运单据。

航空运单具有如下特点。

① 航空运单是托运人/发货人与承运人/航空公司之间签订的航空运输协定；

② 航空运单是航空公司开给托运人的表明已收到托运货物的收据；

③ 航空运单通常按国际标准用英语和起运地官方语言印制，这样方便途中经由 2～3 个不同国家中转至目的地。

对于空运货物来说，航空运单是最重要的文件。它既是承运人与托运人之间的运输协议，又是航空运输的货运接收凭据。航空运单也用于运费计算、海关报关，它还包含处理货物的具体信息。航空运单是不可转让的，即货物必须交付给航空运单上标明的记名收货人。每批货物都有航空运单。对于集中托运业务，集中托运人（航空货运代理）会给各小票货物的实际货主签发航空分运单，然后集中托运人再将小票货物合并为集运货物向航空公司办理托运，由航空公司签发一份航空主运单给集中托运人。

在我国，一套航空运单共有 12 联（包括 3 份正本，6 份副本和 3 份额外副本）以交给不同的当事人，包括托运人、收货人、第一承运人、第二承运人（如果有的话）、第三承运人（如果有的话）、目的地机场、起飞机场以及其他（如果需要的话）。每一联的颜色都不同。三份正本分别由托运人、承运人以及收货人留存。

第一份正本（承运人联），由托运人签署并返给承运人，供承运人保存作为运输契约凭证。

第二份正本（收货人联），由承运人与托运人共同签署，连同货物一起运至目的地交给航空运单的记名收货人，作为收货人核收货物的依据。

第三份正本（托运人联），由承运人签署后返给托运人，以便于跟单信用证业务下的托运人将其提交给议付行以办理议付、收取货款。

根据航空运单的签发人，航空运单可分为航空主运单（MAWB）和航空分运单（HAWB）两类。航空公司签发的运单都称为航空主运单，它是航空公司和托运人之间签订的运输契约/合同。每批空运货物都有其对应的航空主运单。空运的集中托运业务还需要航空分运单。航空分运单是证明航空货运代理（空运货代）和实际托运人/发货人之间货物移交和接管的文件。首先，空运货代签发自己的航空分运单，不受航空公司的限制。但通常情况下，航空分运单的格式要与航空公司签发的航空主运单的格式相一致。航空分运单中关于托运人及收货人的信息反映了实际的托运人和收货人。航空货运代理在接收实际托运人/货主的货物后，将来自不同托运人的小票货物合并集装成一大票货物，然后作为托运人将其交给航空公司申请托运。因此，货代和航空公司之间需要签订一份证明文件，即航空主运单。MAWB 记录了所运载大票货物的主要信息，将货代和航空公司之间的关系定义为托运人与承运人的关系。因此，在集中托运业务中，实际的托运人不需要与航空公司打交道。

6.3 Air Cargo Charges and Rates

Deciding on a pricing policy for air freight presents airlines with many difficulties because freight consignments vary greatly in shape, size, and weight, which must be taken into account in the price structure. Moreover, it is difficult to do so since many costs do not vary proportionately with consignment size. Cost of documentation is fixed for almost any size of consignments and costs of ground handling on a per kg basis are generally much lower for large consignments than for small ones. Costs also vary according to commodity type. Some items such as hazardous goods and valuable cargoes need special handling, which incurs extra costs. These costs must be covered as far as possible from the shippers. Freight consignments vary in density, so airlines must decide whether charging should be based on weight, on volume or on a mixture of the two, with high-density cargoes charged on weight and low-density ones on volume.

6.3.1 Calculation of Air Freight

(1) Basic concepts

① Rate. Rate refers to the amount charged by the carrier (s) for the carriage of a unit goods (TACT Rules 1.5) from the airport of departure to the airport of destination.

② Weight Charge/Air Freight. Weight Charge, also named as air freight, refers to the air transportation fee that an airline company should charge for transporting a consignment of goods from the airport of origin to the airport of destination. This charge is calculated based on the applicable freight rate and the chargeable weight of each shipment. Each consignment means the cargo using the same air waybill.

③ Other charges. They are charges charged by the carriers, agents or other authorities in connection with the carriage of goods by air.

(2) Chargeable Weight

It means the weight which is used in calculating the air freight of the cargo. The weight of the goods can either be the actual gross weight of the goods, or be the volumetric weight of the goods, or be the weight at the higher weight cut-off point.

① Actual Gross Weight. The weight of the goods including the packaging of the goods is called the Actual Gross Weight of the goods. As for high-density cargo, the actual gross weight may generally be the chargeable weight due to the limitation of the maximum take-off full weight of the aircraft and the available cargo load.

② Volume Weight. In accordance with the rules of IATA, the volume of the cargo converted into a certain proportion of the weight, is called Volume Weight. In general, for low-density cargo (light-foam cargo), the Volume Weight may be chargeable weight due to the limitation of space in the cargo hold. Generally speaking, no matter whether the shape of the goods is regular cuboid or cube, the longest, widest and highest three sides should be calculated in centimeters when calculating the volume of goods. The length, width and height of the decimal part is rounded to the whole, and the standard of Volume Weight conversion is 1kg per $6000cm^3$. The formula is as follows.

$$\text{Volume weight (KGS)} = \text{cargo volume} / 6000cm^3$$

③ Weight of the higher weight cut-off point. Generally, the chargeable weight is the higher of the Actual Gross Weight of the goods or the Volume Weight of the goods. However, when the air freight of the goods is lower at the lower rate of the higher weight cut-off point, the starting weight of the higher weight cut-off point shall be taken as the chargeable weight.

IATA stipulates that 0.5kg shall be the minimum unit for the chargeable weight of international cargo. If the mantissa is less than 0.5kg, it shall be 0.5kg. If the weight is above 0.5kg but less than 1kg, then the weight shall be counted as 1kg.

For example: 103.001kg→103.5kg

103.501kg→104.0kg

When the same Air Waybill is used for shipment of two or more pieces of goods for which the freight can be calculated at the same rate of the same category, the chargeable weight shall be the higher of the total actual gross weight and the total volumetric weight of the goods. As mentioned above, the higher weight cut-off point weight may also be the chargeable weight for the cargo.

(3) Minimum Charge

Minimum Charge means the minimum amount of aviation charges for carrying the cargo from the airport of departure to the airport of destination. The air freight of the goods, calculated on the basis of the applicable rate and its chargeable weight, shall be higher than the Minimum Charge.

6.3.2 Air Freight Rates

At present, international air freight rates are divided into agreed freight rates and International Air Transport Association (IATA) Tariff according to the ways of formulation. Agreed freight rates are used when an agreement is signed between the airline company and the shipper. The shipper guarantees to annually deliver a certain amount of goods to the airline company, and the airline company provides a certain freight discount to the shipper. IATA Tariff means the freight rates published by IATA on the TACT (The Air Cargo Tariff). IATA freight rates can be divided into published direct freight rates and non-published direct freight rates according to the form of publication. Among them, published direct freight rates include General Cargo Rate (GCR), Specific Commodity Rate (SCR), Class Rate (CR) and Unit Load Device Rate. Non-published direct freight rates include Construction Rate and Combination of Rates and Charges.

(1) General Cargo Rate (GCR)

The General Cargo Rate (GCR) refers to the freight rate applicable to the transport of general goods other than the freight rate for graded goods and designated goods. The Rates are published in TACT Rates Books Section 4.

Generally, GCR is divided into several cut-off points according to the weight of the goods. For example, "N" refers to the Normal General Cargo Rate, which refers to the GCR under 45kg. At the same time, GCR is also announced "Q45", "Q100", "Q300" and other different weight cut-off point freight rate. Here, "Q45" refers to GCR above 45kg (including 45kg), and so on. "Q" is used to express GCR with different weight cut-off points above 45kg.

It is worth noting that the air freight of the cargo calculated on the basis of the chargeable weight and the applicable rate shall not be lower than the Minimum Charge published on the freight data.

Here are two examples to illustrate the calculation of air freight.

Example 1:

A carton of clothing is shipped by air transport from Beijing to Tokyo. Its gross weight is 28.4kg and its volume size is 82cm×48cm×32cm. Please calculate the airfreight of the goods.

The published air freight rates are as follows:

BEIJING		CN	BJ
Y. RENMINBI		CNY	KGS
TOKYO	JP	M	200.0
		N	38.67
		45	29.04

Volume: 82cm×48cm×32cm=125952cm^3

Volume Weight: 125952cm^3÷6000cm^3=20.99kgs=21kgs

Gross Weight: 28.4kgs

Gross Weight > Volume Weight, thus choose Gross Weight

Chargeable Weight: 28.4→28.5kg

Applicable Rate: GCR N 38.67CNY/KG

Weight Charge: 28.5×38.67=1102.1 > Minimum Charge 200

Therefore, the air freight of goods should be CNY1102.1.

Example 2:

There is one shampoo sample weighing 5.3 kg which needs to be shipped from Shanghai to Osaka, Japan. Please calculate the airfreight as per the following published air freight rates.

SHANGHAI		CN	SHA
Y. RENMINBI		CNY	KGS
OSAKA	JP	M	200.0
		N	30.22
		45	22.71

Gross Weight: 5.3kgs

Chargeable Weight: 5.3→5.5kgs

Applicable Rate: GCR N 30.22CNY/KG

Weight Charge: 5.5×30.22=166.21

Minimum Charge: 200.00

200>166.21

Thus, the air freight of goods should be the Minimum Charge CNY200.00.

(2) Specific Commodity Rate (SCR)

The Specific Commodity Rates are always lower than GCR, but they are only applicable to the those named types of cargo. IATA has worked with major airlines to develop a special catalogue of designated commodities, which defines more than 5000 kinds of commodities applicable to SCR in international air transport services.

(3) Class Rate (CR)

Class Rates are a further supplement to GCR, and are applied by most airlines. Under Class Rates, commodities are offered a discount of freight rate. But it is often the case that surcharges will be imposed on most goods that suit Class Rates.

(4) Unit Load Device Rate

Unit Load Device Rates can offer a lower unit rate, actually relative to General Cargo Rates. They are available for all types of consignments, irrespective of commodity type. However, the low rates are only available for the consignments that are prepackaged into an aircraft Unit Load Device (ULD) and can be loaded directly into the aircraft. When Unit Load Device Rates are applied, a ULD (an aircraft pallet or a container) is used as "pivot weight". ULD acts as a minimum charge, with the shipper required to pay for this weight even if he is unable to fill a ULD with his cargo.

6.3 航空运费

航空货运定价决策给航空公司带来了巨大挑战，由于空运货物在外形、尺寸及重量等方面往往存在较大差异，所以在制定航空运价时必须考虑周全。而且，空运的许多成本并非随着货物尺寸成比例地变化，因此做到考虑周全十分困难。对于几乎所有尺寸的空运货物，单证成本是固定的；对于大批量货物而言，以每公斤为单位计算的地面装卸成本要比小批量货物低得多。成本也会随着商品类型的变化而变化。例如，危险品和贵重货物都需要一些特殊处理，因此会产生附加成本。对于这些附加成本，航空公司必定会尽可能多地从托运人处得到补偿。空运货物在密度上往往也有差异，因此航空公司必须确定航空运费到底是按货物重量计收还是按货物体积计收，或者混合计收，即高密度的货物按其重量计收运费，低密度货物则按其体积计收运费。

6.3.1 航空运费的计算

(1) 基本概念

① 运价。运价是指承运人对所运输的每一重量单位货物所收取的自始发地机场至目的地机场的航空费用。

② 航空运费。货物的航空运费是指航空公司将一票货物自始发地机场运至目的地机场所应收取的航空运输费用。该费用根据每票货物所适用的航空运价和货物的计费重量计算而得。每票货物是指使用同一份航空运单的货物。

③ 其他费用。其他费用是指由承运人、代理人或其他部门收取的与航空货物运输有关的费用。

(2) 计费重量

计费重量是指用以计算货物航空运费的重量。货物的计费重量或者是货物的实际毛重，或者是货物的体积重量，或者是较高重量分界点的重量。

① 实际毛重。包含货物包装在内的货物重量，称为货物的实际毛重。由于飞机最大起飞全重及货舱可用载荷的限制，一般情况下，对于高密度货物，将其实际毛重作为计费重量。

② 体积重量。按照国际航协规则，将货物的体积按一定的比例折合成的重量，称为体积重量。由于飞机货舱空间的限制，一般对于低密度的货物即轻泡货物，将其体积重量作为计费重量。一般而言，不论货物的形状是否为规则的长方体或正方体，在计算货物体积时，均应以最长、最宽、最高的三边的厘米长度来计算。长、宽、高的小数部分按四舍五入取

整，体积重量折算的标准为每 $6000cm^3$ 折合 1kg。公式为：

$$体积重量(kgs)=货物体积\div 6000cm^3$$

③ 较高重量分界点的重量。一般地，计费重量采用货物的实际毛重与货物的体积重量两者中的较高者。但当货物按较高重量分界点的较低运价计算的航空运费较低时，则将此较高重量分界点的起始重量作为货物的计费重量。

国际航协规定，国际货物的计费重量以 0.5kg 为最小单位，重量尾数不足 0.5kg 的，按 0.5kg 计算；0.5kg 以上不足 1kg 的，按 1kg 计算。

例如：103.001kg→103.5kg

103.501kg→104.0kg

当计算使用同一份运单的两件或两件以上适用相同运价的货物的航空运费时，其计费重量规定为：计费重量为货物总的实际毛重与总的体积重量两者较高者。同上所述，较高重量分界点重量也可能成为货物的计费重量。

(3) 最低运费

最低运费是指一票货物自始发地机场至目的地机场航空费用的最低限额。

货物按其适用的航空运价与其计费重量计算所得的航空运费，应与最低运费相比，然后取高者作为航空运费。

6.3.2 航空运价

目前，国际航空运价按制定的途径划分，主要分为协议运价和国际航协运价。协议运价用于航空公司与托运人签订协议的情况，托运人保证每年向航空公司交运一定数量的货物，航空公司则向托运人提供一定的运价折扣。国际航协运价是指国际航协 IATA 在 TACT (The Air Cargo Tariff) 运价资料上公布的运价。按照运价公布的形式划分，IATA 运价可分为公布直达运价和非公布直达运价。其中，公布直达运价包括普通货物运价 GCR、指定商品运价 SCR、等级货物运价 CR 和集装货物运价；非公布直达运价包括比例运价和分段相加运价。

(1) 普通货物运价 GCR

普通货物运价是指除了等级货物运价和指定商品运价以外的适用于普通货物运输的运价。该运价公布在 TACT Rates Books Section 4 中。

通常，普通货物运价根据货物重量不同，分为若干个重量分界点运价。例如，“N”表示标准普通货物运价，是指 45kg 以下的普通货物运价。同时，普通货物运价还公布有“Q45”“Q100”“Q300”等不同重量分界点的运价。这里，“Q45”表示 45kg 以上（包括 45kg）货物的运价，以此类推。对于 45kg 以上的不同重量分界点的普通货物运价均用“Q”表示。

用货物的计费重量和其适用的普通货物运价计算而得的航空运费不得低于运价资料上公布的最低运费标准。

下面用两个例子来说明空运货物运费的计算。

示例 1：

一箱衣服从北京空运到东京，毛重 28.4kg，体积 82cm×48cm×32cm。请计算其航空运费。

公布的运价如下：

BEIJING Y. RENMINBI		CN CNY	BJ KGS
TOKYO	JP	M	200.0
		N	38.67
		45	29.04

解：体积：82cm×48cm×32cm＝$125952cm^3$

体积重量：$125952cm^3$÷$6000cm^3$＝20.99 kg＝21kg

毛重：28.4kg

由于毛重＞体积重量，所以选择毛重作为计费重量

计费重量：28.4→28.5kg

查运价表可得适用费率为：GCR N 38.67CNY/KG

航空运费：28.5×38.67＝1102.1 元＞最低 200 元

因此，货物的航空运费应为 1102.1 元人民币。

示例 2：

有一份洗发水样品重 5.3 公斤，需要从上海运往日本大阪。请按照以下公布的运价计算航空运费。

SHANGHAI Y. RENMINBI		CN CNY	SHA KGS
OSAKA	JP	M	200.0
		N	30.22
		45	22.71

解：毛重：5.3kg

计费重量：5.3→5.5kg

查运价表可得适用费率为：GCR 30.22 元/千克

航空运费：5.5×30.22＝166.21 元

由于最低运费为 200，200＞166.21，所以该货物的航空运费取最低运费，应为 200 元人民币。

(2) 指定商品运价 SCR

指定商品运价总是比普通货物运价的费率低，但仅适用于指定的商品类型。IATA 与知名航空公司共同制订了专门的 SCR 商品目录，对国际空运服务中 5000 多种可适用 SCR 的商品进行了定义。

(3) 等级货物运价 CR

等级货物运价进一步对普通货物运价进行了补充，并且被大部分航空公司使用。等级运价下，对某些商品给予了折扣运价，不过会对大多数商品征收附加费。

(4) 集装货物运价

集装货物运价能提供低的单位运价，实际上是相对普通货物运价而言的。集装货物运价适用于所有类型的货物，但前提是货物应预先装妥于集装板或集装箱内且可直接装入飞机。对于集装货物运价，以集装单元（一集装板或一集装箱）作为一个基准重量来计收运费，即

便是货物不能装满一个集装板或一个集装箱，货主也要按照一个集装单元来支付运费。

Part B Vocabulary and Terminology 词汇和术语

air transport 航空运输
IATA 国际航空运输协会
scheduled airline 班机运输
chartered carrier 包机运输
consolidation 集中托运
air express service 航空快递
Air Waybill（AWB） 航空运单，空运单
General Cargo Rates（GCR） 普通货物运价
Minimum Charge 最低运价
Class Rates 等级运价
Specific Commodity Rates（SCR） 指定商品运价
Unit Load Device Rate 集装货物运价
airline 航空公司
air freight 空运货件
Master Air Waybill（MAWB） 航空主运单
House Air Waybill（HAWB） 航空分运单

Part C Exercise 练习

Ⅰ. Answer the following questions.

1. What kinds of consignment is air transport normally used for?
2. What are the disadvantages of air transport?
3. What are the four major modes of air transport?
4. Please explain the meaning and advantages of consolidation service.
5. Please tell the features of Air Waybill. Is Air Waybill a document of title?

Ⅱ. Decide whether the following statements are true or false.

1. The Air Waybill is a contract for transportation between the carrier and the shipper.
2. House Air Waybills are often accompanied by a Master Air Waybill for consolidated shipments.
3. Each consignment is identified by an AWB number.
4. The House Air Waybill is issued by the airline to the actual shippers.
5. An Air Waybill may have more than ten copies that will only be sent to the consignee.

Ⅲ. Translate the following sentences into Chinese.

1. The Air Waybill（AWB） is the most important document for a batch of air freight

goods. It is both a contract for transportation between a carrier and a shipper (or an agent for a shipper) and a receipt acknowledging the receiving of the air cargo.

2. In addition to the routine of arranging for pickup and delivery, booking the shipments on flights, and filling out Air Waybills, a freight forwarding agent is also involved in such problems as tracing lost or strayed shipments and dealing with claims on damaged shipments.

Ⅳ. Translate the following sentences into English.

1. 国际航空运输具有许多优势，例如快速运送、单据简单、服务可靠且质量高、几乎无包装成本、可降低物流成本等。航空运输的关键文件是航空运单。在大多数情况下，航空运输由航空货运代理安排，而不是由航空公司来安排。

2. 集中托运能使所有相关各方获益，例如出口商/托运人，承运人以及货运代理人。对于出口商/托运人来说，他们可以从低于正常情况下支付给承运人（航空公司）的运价中获益，尤其对于那些规模和实力较小的托运人而言，他们没有与航空公司讨价还价的能力。此外，发货人还发现了集中托运服务的另一好处，即航空货运代理集中托运服务所提供的目的地范围更广，省去了发货人自己联系多家经营不同航线的航空公司所带来的麻烦。

Chapter Seven

International Land Transport Logistics
国际陆运物流

Part A Text 课文

7.1 International Railway Transport Logistics

Railway transport is a major mode of transport in terms of shipping capacity, only followed by marine transport. It is capable of achieving high speed and is more economical especially if it provides a complete train load for a shipper or on a regular basis. Besides, it is rarely affected by bad weather and can endure all the year-round work. However, it is confined to railroads and therefore less flexible. Formalities of railway transport are more convenient than those of marine transport.

7.1.1 Service Characteristics of Railway Transport

Railway service is available in almost every major metropolitan center in the world. However, the railway network is not nearly as extensive as the highway network in most countries because it is limited to fixed track facilities. As a result, railway transport, like air, water, and pipeline transport, provides terminal-to-terminal service rather than point-to-point service for most shippers.

Railway transport generally costs less (on a weight basis) than air and road transport. For many shipments, railway transport does not compare favorably with air transport on loss and damage ratios. It has disadvantages compared to road transport in terms of transit time and service frequency. Trains travel on timetables, but departures are less frequent than those of road carriers. If a shipper has strict arrival and departure requirements, railway transport is usually at a competitive advantage compared to road transport.

Railway transport falls into three kinds:

① Domestic railway transport.

② International railway transport between two countries.

③ International railway through transport.

The New Eurasian Land bridge, starting from Lianyungang of China and ending in Rotterdam of Holland, is as long as 10900 kilometers. It is the fastest and cheapest transport passage connecting the Asian Pacific region with the whole Europe. Alashan port in Xinjiang Province is a world-renowned west bridgehead of New Eurasian Land Bridge in China.

7.1.2 Definition and Advantages of International Railway through Transport

International railway through transport means that during cargo transit through two or more countries by rail, just one Railway Bill is issued and all the countries participating international railway through transport act as a uniform carrier and assume joint liability when handling the entire carriage of goods without the involvement of the shipper and the consignee.

The major advantages of International Railway through Transport are as follows.

(1) Simplifying the procedures and providing great convenience for both consignors and consignees

According to the stipulations of the International Union of Railways, Agreement on International Railway Through Transport of Goods and the International Convention Concerning Carriage of Goods by Rail, the goods belonging to the exporting country may be transported directly to the place of destination as long as the carrier issues a Railway Bill at the place of departure.

Although goods need to be transported through several countries and loaded and unloaded multiple times during the entire transport, consignors only need to go through one-time shipping procedures at the station of departure and then the goods can be directly transported to the station of destination. There is no need for consignors or consignees to repeatedly go through complicated shipping procedures at each frontier station, which provides great convenience for both parties.

(2) Making full use of the advantages of railway transportation in international trade

Railway transport has advantages in its security, low cost, punctuality, and invulnerability to weather. After the implementation of International Railway through Transport, the railways of all participating countries are connected and integrated into a huge international railway transport network. Based on this network, consignors can take full advantage of railway transport and choose appropriate transportation routes according to the nature and quantity of goods, which can not only expedite the delivery but also cut down the related expenses.

(3) Facilitating early settlement

After completing shipping formalities of export goods at the place of dispatch, consignors can present the evidence of Railway Bill together with other commercial documents to the negotiating bank to make early settlement. There is no need for consignors to wait for the actual arrival of goods at the destination. In this way, not only can consignors get the payment of goods safely, but also the turnover of capital is accelerated.

China's railway transport falls into two kinds: International Railway Transport and Railway Transport to Hong Kong and Macao with Railway Bill (RWB) and Cargo Receipt (C/R) separately.

The main transport documents are the Railway Bill and its duplicate. The Railway Bill is the transportation contract binding upon the carrier from the place of departure to the place of destination. It is delivered to the consignee after the freight of railway transport and other charges have been paid off. The consignor may make exchange settlement with the bank against the duplicate of Railway Bill.

The Railway Bill (RWB) comprises five joint duplicated pages.

The first page (the original RWB) as well as the fifth page (the arrival notice), are delivered together with the goods to the consignee for him to take delivery and pay relative charges.

The third page is the copy RWB to the consignor for him to effect negotiation with the bank.

The rest two pages are to railway stations for transport arrangement.

In Railway Transport to Hong Kong and Macao, Cargo Receipt (C/R) is used as a transport document after the export goods have been loaded and dispatched. The freight forwarder will issue a C/R to the consignor for him to effect negotiation with the bank.

7.1.3 Operations of Railway Transport

The railways can be typified as large organizations with substantial investments in fixed equipment (e.g., tracks). Considerable efforts are therefore devoted to obtain maximum productivity from the facilities through attention to such matters as engineering design and operational performance. In addition, management tasks in railways must take account of the need to obtain a satisfactory return on the vast amount of capital invested. Thus, attention is focused on such matters as:

① Cost reduction through efficient management practices;

② Revenue raising by concentrating on tasks that are performed efficiently and by changing rates which encourage efficient use of railway resources.

Rail freight transport operations involve three distinct processes:

① Loading and unloading;

② Assembly;

③ Line haul.

Unless trains are operated in fixed units, it is necessary to undertake an assembly process, i.e., wagons have to be sorted into trains. This can be the most significant source of waste and inefficiency in the railway industry. Thus, it is important to understand the activities required in this process.

Although the following summary relates to the American situation, it generally reflects the process involved in the carriage of freight by rail from origin to destination:

① The shipper places an order for a wagon.

② The yard office receives the order and selects a wagon.

③ The wagon is inspected to ensure that it is in sound condition.

④ The wagon or a group of wagons will be moved to the terminal.

⑤ The loaded wagon (s) is (are) moved to an assembly yard (classification yard).

⑥ The wagon is coupled with other wagons having similar destinations to form a train.

⑦ The completed train undertakes the line haul movement, during which it may be necessary to pass through intermediate classification and interchange yards.

⑧ On arrival at its destination, the train is broken up in another classification yard and then the wagons are delivered to their respective terminals.

⑨ Goods are unloaded and the wagon is released.

7.1.4 China Railway Express to Europe

Since Chinese President Xi Jinping advocated the construction of the "Belt and Road" and the revival of China's "Silk Road", China's trade with Russia, Belarus, Central Asia and European countries has developed rapidly. The development of commerce requires the support of logistics development which calls for heavy investment in logistics infrastructure. This resulted in the inception of China Railway Express. China Railway Express, or CR Express, is the most visible part of the OBOR ("One Belt, One Road") initiative that connects Asia with Europe. This railway transportation was initiated to enhance trade and shipping overland by train, to boost trade between China and countries participating in the "Belt and Road" initiative. CR Express handles international rail transport of containers based on fixed train numbers, fixed routes, fixed schedules and full-time operation.

Since the first CR Express line, Yuxinou express (from Chongqing, China to Duisburg, German) was successfully launched on March 19, 2011, CR Express has expanded its business to 151 cities in 22 European countries by May 2021, covering the distribution network of Europe.

The CR Express has laid out three transportation corridors from west, mid and east of China, with the western corridor extending from Central and Western China via Alashankou (Khorgos) to Europe, the mid Corridor starting from North China to Europe by Erlianhot, and the Eastern Corridor from the coastal areas of Southeast China to Europe via Manzhouli (Suifenhe). The initiation of the CR Express has strengthened commercial and trade connection with European countries and has become the mainstay of international logistics land transportation.

The significance of China Railway Express in international logistics is as follows:

Firstly, CR Express provides a strong transportation guarantee for "Belt and Road" construction. Featured by short distance, fast speed, high safety, as well as greening, and low impact from natural environment, CR Express has become the mainstay of land transportation in international logistics. The logistics organization of the Express is increasingly mature, the economic and trade connection between countries along the lines are becoming more active, and the cooperation between railways, ports, customs and other departments between countries is getting closer. These favorable conditions will further facilitate the role of CR Express in transiting Silk Road from the original "business road" to an "economic belt" for industry and population agglomeration.

Secondly, by running highly frequent CR Express trains and constructing comprehensive international inland-ports, inland cities have access to convenient passages and ports connecting overseas market, making inland cities comparable to coastal areas in terms of international logistics. More and more trade-oriented industries are moving inland, causing the centralization of logistics bases for cross border e-commerce in free trade zones such as Zhengzhou. This has narrowed the economic gap between the central and western regions and coastal cities and enabled these regions to participate in international trade and international division of labor, which consequently has promoted local economic development and foreign communication.

Although CR Express service has not been in operation for a long time, its main advantages are outstanding.

1) time and cost saving. The average transport time from Chinese seaport cities to European coastal cities by ocean shipping is 35～42 days, while that of CR Express is only 11～15 days. Although the transportation price of CR Express is much higher than that of ocean shipping, the cost is about the same as by sea considering shorter time and reduced wastage. When compared to air transport, CR Express is obviously much cheaper, costing only 1/6 or even 1/8 of the price in air transport.

2) stable running. Less constrained by weather and environmental impact, railway transportation provides more stable transportation services than sea/air transportation. Run with fixed train numbers, by fixed routes, at fixed schedules and full-time operation, CR Express undoubtedly becomes a competitive alternative for international shipment.

3) convenient customs clearance. To address the problem of complicated and time-consuming customs clearance, a digital port system code-named 95306 was put into use in July 2020 by China's railway system to enable comprehensive information-sharing and paperless customs declarations among countries along the routes. After the application of "95306 digital port", the traditional customs clearance method is shifting to information interconnection and close coordination between railway and customs. Manual declarations and paper documents were eliminated, as a result, cargo owner can complete customs declarations and railway route alteration at home. Consequently, the port convenience and customs clearance efficiency have significantly increased, shortening customs clearance time from half a day to less than 30 minutes or even a few minutes. Meanwhile, in the process of data exchange with neighboring country's railway companies, the Chinese standard and language identification were introduced for the first time, and a Chinese and foreign code dictionary was established, which realized the automatic translation of Chinese and foreign information. The application of the new system shortens the stay time of CR Express at a port and lowers the cost of customs clearance.

Despite CR Express's rapid development , its operating mode is primarily point-to-point (direct transportation between source and destination of goods) rather than an optimized network. CR Express faces issues such as insufficient cargo supply, lower load factor, unsatisfactory profit margin, and high pressure on governmental subsidy. These issues have seriously weakened its economic efficiency and international competitiveness in long-distance cross border transportation and has thereby restricted its development.

7.1 国际铁路运输物流

就运输能力而言，铁路运输是仅次于海洋运输的主要运输方式。它能够高速、经济地实现货物的长距离运输，特别是能向托运人提供定期的整车装载大批量长途货运服务。此外，铁路运输受恶劣天气的影响较小，且能全年运营。然而，铁路运输的运营必须预先建好铁路等必要基础设施，不像海运可以利用天然航道，因此这方面的灵活性较海运而言稍差。不过，铁路运输的手续却要比海运简便得多。

7.1.1 铁路运输的特点

铁路运输遍布世界各地的主要都市，然而铁路运输线路并不如公路线路分布广阔。跟空运、水运、管道运输一样，铁路运输受限于固定的铁路线，提供的是“端至端”（“运输终端”到“运输终端”）运输服务，不能提供“点至点”或者“门到门”运输服务。

铁路运输通常比空运的运费低得多，但空运的货损率和货物丢失的概率都比铁路运输低。跟公路运输相比，铁路运输的货物交接效率较低（运送时间和运送频率两方面来看）。铁路运输按时刻表运行，不过发车频次不如公路运输多。如果货主在发货和到货时间上要求较高的话，铁路运输则更有竞争优势。

铁路运输有三种：

① 国内铁路运输。

② 国与国之间的铁路运输。

③ 国际铁路货物联运。

亚欧大陆桥从中国的连云港起，到荷兰的鹿特丹止，全长10900公里。它是连接亚太地区和整个欧洲的最快和最便宜的运输通道。新疆阿拉山口岸现已成为位于中国的世界著名的亚欧大陆桥西桥头堡。

7.1.2 国际铁路联运的定义和优势

国际铁路货物联运是指在两个或两个以上国家铁路运送中，使用一份运输单据，并以连带责任办理货物的全程运送，在一国铁路向另一国铁路移交货物时，无需发货人、收货人参加。

国际铁路货物联运的主要优势如下。

(1) 简化手续、方便发货人和收货人

根据“国际铁路联盟”“国际铁路货物联运协定”和“国际铁路货物运送公约”的规定，只要承运人在起运地车站签发铁路运单，出口货物就可以直接运往目的地车站。虽然货物在全程运送中要经过多个国家，涉及多次交接甚至多次换装等作业，但发货人只需在始发地/起运地车站办理一次性托运手续即可将货物运抵目的地车站，发货人或收货人无需在国境站重复办理托运的烦琐手续，从而大大方便了发货人和收货人。

(2) 便于在国际贸易中充分利用铁路运输的优势

铁路运输具有成本低、连续性强、风险小和不易受天气变化影响等优势。实行国际铁路联运后，参加联运的联运国铁路联成一体并形成一个巨大的国际铁路运输网络。发货人可以根据货物的特点及运输要求，充分利用铁路运输优势来选择运输路径，这样既可加快货物送达速度，又能节省费用支出。

(3) 有助于提早结汇

发货人利用国际铁路联运办理完出口货物的托运手续后，即可凭承运人开具的铁路运单和其他商务单证办理结汇，而无需等到货物运抵目的地。这样，既能保证发货人安全收取货款，又加速了资金周转。

我国铁路运输分为国际铁路运输和港澳铁路运输两种，分别使用铁路运单和货物收据作为运输单证。

铁路运输的主要运输单据是铁路运单及其副本。铁路运单是对承运人有全程（从发货地到目的地）约束力的运输合同。在付清铁路运费和其他费用后，铁路运单随货物运至目的地一起交付给收货人。而托运人/货主凭铁路运单副本到银行办理议付，结算货款。

一套铁路运单由五联组成。

第一联（运单正本）和第五联（到货通知）随货物一起运至目的地交给收货人，收货人凭运单正本提取货物并支付相关费用。

第三联是给发货人的运单副本，以便发货人提交银行办理议付和货款结算。

其余两联交给火车站以安排铁路运输。

在港澳铁路运输中，货物收据用作运输单证。出口货物装车发运后，货运代理将签发货物收据给发货人，以便发货人与银行进行议付结算。

7.1.3 铁路运输业务

铁路运输的典型特点在于固定设施（铁轨等）方面的大量投资，因此也希望通过关注工程设计以及运营绩效来实现设施方面的最大生产率。

此外，铁路运输运营管理还要考虑前期的巨大投资能否获得满意的投资回报，因此其管理重点如下。

① 通过有效的管理实现成本降低；

② 通过专注于作业效率的提升来增加营业收入以及不断变化利率来实现资源的高效利用。

铁路运输实务主要包括以下三个具体过程。

① 装车和卸车；

② 组装或组配（在铁路编组站进行）；

③ 干线运输。

除了那些由固定车皮组成并运营的火车之外，通常的铁路运输都需要火车的组装过程，即将车皮组装成火车。该过程也是铁路运输行业浪费和低效之源。因此理解该过程中需要包含哪些具体作业显得非常重要。

尽管下面的实务操作主要参照的是美国的具体实践，却能普遍反映货物通过铁路运输实现从货源地到目的地的整个运送过程：

① 发货人向铁路部门提出要车申请，列明具体托运要求；

② 铁路编组站审核后接受托运申请，并根据发货人托运要求选择合适的铁路车皮；

③ 对所选车皮进行检查以保证它处于良好状态；

④ 将一节车皮或一组车皮运至铁路站等待装车；

⑤ 将装车完毕的车皮运至装配场；

⑥ 将装车完毕的车皮和其他发往同一目的地或目的地方向的车皮组装在一起形成整列火车；

⑦ 整列火车进行长途干线运输，途中可能需要停靠一些分类站及转运站以卸下或搭载一些货物；

⑧ 到达目的地后，整列火车将在编组站或分类站进行拆分，装有不同货主货物的车皮将被运到各自的终点站；

⑨ 将货物卸下车皮，车皮回到空车状态等待下一次装车。

7.1.4 中欧班列

自习近平主席倡导“一带一路”建设、重振中国“丝绸之路”以来，中国与俄罗斯、白俄罗斯、中亚和欧洲国家的贸易发展迅速。商业的发展需要物流发展的支撑，物流的发展需要物流基础设施的大力投资，中欧班列应运而生。中欧班列是“一带一路”项目中连接亚洲和欧洲的最引人注目的部分。这条铁路旨在加强双向铁路贸易，以促进中国与参与“一带一路”倡议国家之间的贸易。该班列按照固定车次、线路、班期和全程运行时刻承接集装箱国际铁路联运业务。

自 2011 年 3 月 19 日首列中欧班列（重庆—杜伊斯堡，渝新欧国际铁路）成功开行以来，截至 2021 年 5 月，中欧班列已通达欧洲 22 个国家的 151 个城市，物流配送网络覆盖欧洲。

中欧班列规划了西中东 3 条通道运行线：西部通道由中国中西部经阿拉山口（霍尔果斯）出境，中部通道由中国华北地区经二连浩特出境，东部通道由中国东南部沿海地区经满洲里（绥芬河）出境。中欧班列的开通加强了与欧洲国家的商业贸易联系，成为国际物流陆路的运输骨干。

中欧班列对于国际物流的重要意义体现为以下两点。

首先，中欧班列为“一带一路”建设提供了强力运输保障。中欧班列以其运距短、速度快、安全性高、绿色环保、受自然环境影响小的优势，已经成为国际物流中陆路运输的骨干方式。中欧班列物流组织日趋成熟，班列沿途国家经贸交往日趋活跃，国家间铁路、口岸、海关等部门的合作日趋密切，这些有利条件，为铁路进一步发挥国际物流骨干作用，在“一带一路”倡议中将丝绸之路从原先的“商贸路”变成产业和人口集聚的“经济带”起到重要作用。

其次，通过高频率的中欧班列和完备的国际陆港，内陆城市拥有了连接海外的便利大通道和口岸，使内陆城市在国际物流上有了与沿海地区相类似的条件。越来越多的贸易导向型产业向内陆转移，跨境电商的物流基地向郑州等自贸区内聚集，这缩小了中西部地区与沿海城市的经济差距，使这些城市也能参与到国际贸易和国际分工中，促进了本地的经济发展和对外交流。

尽管中欧班列开行时间并不长，但却展现出如下的优势。

1）节省时间和成本。中国海港城市到欧洲沿海城市的海运平均运输时间为 35～42 天，而中欧班列仅为 11～15 天。虽然中欧班列的运输价格远高于海运，但考虑到更短的时间和减少的浪费，成本与海运差不多。与空运相比，中欧班列显然要便宜很多，成本仅为空运价格的 1/6 甚至 1/8。

2）运行稳定。受天气和环境影响较小，铁路运输提供的运输服务比海/空运输更稳定，加之固定的车次、路线、时刻表和全时运营，中欧班列成为国际物流的一个有力的竞争选择。

3）通关便捷。为解决通关烦琐、耗时长的问题，中国铁路系统于 2020 年 7 月投入运行代号为“95306”的数字口岸系统，实现沿线国家信息全面共享和无纸化报关。“95306 数字口岸”上线运用后，改变了传统通关方式，实现铁路与海关部门信息互联互通、高度协同作业，取消了人工申报和纸质单据，货主足不出户即可完成海关申报、铁路流向变更等手续。口岸便利化程度和通关效率显著提升，从申报到海关放行的时间由原来的半天左右缩短至30分钟以内，最快只需几分钟。同时，在与周边国家铁路公司数据交换过程中，首次引入中文规范、语言标识，建立了中外文代码字典，实现了中外文信息的自动翻译。新系统的运用减少了中欧班列的口岸停留时间及通关成本。

尽管中欧班列发展迅速、势头强劲，但其运营模式主要是点对点（起源地到目的地之间的直接运输），而不是优化的运输网络。中欧班列还面临货物供应不足、载货率低、利润率低、政府补贴运营压力大等问题。这些问题严重削弱了其在长途跨境运输方面的经济性和国际竞争力，从而制约了其发展。

7.2 International Road Transport Logistics

7.2.1 Brief Introduction to Road Transport

In a country's transportation system, road transportation occupies an important position, while in international transportation, road transportation is also frequently used because of its flexibility and door-to-door service, such as between European countries. Roads are the most convenient way of transporting goods even to the interior parts of the world. Highway transport has expanded rapidly since the end of World War Ⅱ. To a significant degree, the rapid growth of the motor carrier industry has resulted from high speed coupled with door-to-door operation.

In comparison to railway transport, road transport has relatively less fixed investment in terminal facilities and operates on publicly financed and maintained roads. Although the costs of license fees, user fees, and tolls are considerable, these expenses are directly related to the number of trucks and miles operated. The variable cost per mile for motor carriers is high because a separate power unit and driver are required for each trailer or combination of tandem trailer. Labor requirements are also high because of driver safety restrictions and need for substantial dock labor. Truck operations are characterized by low fixed costs and high variable costs. In comparison to railways, motor carriers more efficiently handle small shipments moving short distances.

The trucking industry is not without problems. The primary difficulties relate to costly equipment replacement, maintenance, safety, driver shortages, driver hours-of-service regulations, and dock labor wages. Although accelerating labor rates influence all modes of transport, road transport is labor-intensive, causing high wages a major concern. To counteract this trend, motor carriers have placed a great deal of attention to improved line-haul scheduling, computerized billing systems, mechanized terminals, tandem operations that haul two or three trailers with a single power unit, and participation in coordinated multimodal transport systems.

7.2.2 Types of Road Transport

The types of road transport operators can be classified into: scheduled operators, chartered operators, own account operators, and freight forwarder.

(1) Scheduled Operators

Scheduled operators engage in cargo road transport business and attempt to satisfy the requirements of road transport for the whole society. Its major operation modes include: ①it operates on a regular schedule and route regardless of the loads; ②vehicles are spread out at regular routes on the basis of demand without fixed schedules; ③vehicles are spread out in fixed areas based on demand.

(2) Chartered Operators

Such services or supplemental modes have neither fixed schedules nor designated routes. The shipper may charter the entire vehicle in order to transport the goods between specific points of origin/destination.

(3) Own Account Operators

Own account operators refer to the corporations who undertake their in-house, or own account, transport services. Tailored customer service and economic factors are the main reasons for this type of transport activity.

(4) Freight Forwarder

In this mode, the forwarder contracts to move goods from one place to another, making all the arrangements of road transport for the cargo owner. It may also provide a package of services including rail transport, storage and distribution functions in addition to arranging road transport. The freight forwarders themselves control neither the sources of goods nor the vehicles of transport. They work as middlemen for both shippers and motor carriers, mainly earning commissions. Some freight forwarders are specialized in collecting LTL (Less than Truck Load) consignments from cargo owners and assembling them into TL (Truck Load) consignments. And then the forwarders consign TL cargoes to the motor carrier in the name of the shipper, earning the difference between LTL freight and TL freight.

7.2.3 CMR (Convention de Merchandises Par Routes)

In the contract of carriage of goods by road, the rights, duties and responsibilities of road carrier may be discussed under Convention de Merchandises Par Routes (CMR) and national laws. The CMR convention is the convention on contracts for international carriage of goods by road that was adopted in 1956, and that generally governs international transport of goods by road. The CMR convention has been ratified only by countries in Europe. And road transport in the countries outside Europe is to a great extent governed by national laws and ordinances, which vary from country to country. However, it is of benefit to forwarders outside Europe to be aware of CMR as they will then understand the legal regime applicable to movement of cargo when land transport in Europe forms part of the intermodal transport system.

Under CMR convention, the carrier is responsible for:

① the acts and omissions of his agents and servants or other persons of whose services he makes use of; and

② loss or damage to goods occurring between the time he takes possession of the goods and the time of delivery as well as for any delay in delivery.

However, the carrier is relieved of liability if loss, damage or delay is due to:

① any wrongful act or neglect of the consignor;

② inherent vice of the goods; or circumstances that he could not avoid and the consequence of which he was unable to prevent.

The carrier shall not be relieved of liability by reason of defective condition of vehicle used by him in order to perform the carriage, or by reason of the wrongful act or neglect of the person from whom he may have hired the vehicle or of the agents or servants of the latter.

7.2.4 TOFC and COFC

Trailer-on-flatcar (TOFC) or container-on-flatcar (COFC) services offer the economy of railway transport combined with the flexibility of road transport. Truck trailers or chassises carrying containers are driven directly onto railway flatcars by the motor tractor. At the destination terminal, they are separated from the train and delivered to the consignee.

Although technically there are differences, most logistics executives refer to TOFC and COFC as piggyback service. The trailer or container will be directly driven by the tractor on the railway flat car, and then the tractor removes the trailer or container and leaves. After that, it is by the railway transport that the line haul movement between two or more railway stations is conducted. At an intermediate or destination station, a truck or tractor can be connected to the trailer or container loaded with conversion equipment, that is, converted into a trailer transport. And finally, road transport completes the terminal transport to the consignee. Piggyback service thus combines the low cost of line-haul railway transport with the flexibility and convenience of road transport.

7.2 国际公路运输物流

7.2.1 公路运输简介

在一个国家的运输系统中，公路运输占据重要地位；且在国际运输中，公路运输也因其灵活性和门到门服务等优势被频繁使用，比如欧洲各国之间。公路运输是最方便的运输方式。二战后高速公路得到迅速扩展，公路运输的高速发展得益于它能高效地实现门到门运输。

与铁路运输相比，公路运输用于终端设施的固定投资相对较少，并且车辆可以在公共投资养护的公路上行驶。虽然用于执照费、养路费及过路过桥费的开支也很可观，但是这些开支都是与车辆的数量、行驶的实际里程密切相关的。因为每辆拖车或每辆双节拖车的组合都需要一个独立的动力单元和司机，因此汽车承运人每英里的可变成本就显得相对较高。运输必须保障司机安全，并且需要大量的装卸工，所以汽车运输对人力的需求也较高。较低的固定成本与较高的可变成本便是公路运输的运营特点。与铁路运输相比，公路运输非常善于高效地处理小批量的短途货运业务。

公路运输也存在一些问题，主要是高昂的设备更替、维修费用，安全驾驶问题，驾驶员短缺，驾驶员连续驾驶时间的限制，装卸工的工资等。尽管提高劳动效率对每种运输方式都有影响，而公路运输属于劳动密集型，并且司机工资的逐年升高使得提高公路运输运营效率尤为重要。为了提高效率，公路运输采取了很多措施，如采用优化的长途干线运输计划，电子计费系统，机械化终端，一个牵引车后挂2～3个挂车，以及加入国际多式联运等。

7.2.2 公路运输的主要运营方式

公路运输的运营方式主要有以下几种。

(1) 定期运输服务

定期运输服务提供专业的社会化汽车货运业务，其经营方式有以下3种：①不论货载多少，在固定路线上按固定的时间表行驶；②在固定路线上视货载情况派车行驶，没有固定的时间表；③在固定的区域内根据货载需要派车行驶。

(2) 租车运输服务

这种运输服务既没有固定的时间表也没有指定的运输路线。按照承托双方签订的运输契约在货源地、目的地及其他中转地之间运送货物。与之签订契约的一般都是一些大的工矿企业，常年运量较大且较稳定。

(3) 自用运输

自用运输指工厂、企业、机关等自己购置汽车并雇佣司机，专门运送自己的物资和产品，一般不对外承揽业务。

(4) 汽车货运代理

在这种模式下，汽车货运代理负责根据合同将货物从一个地方运送到另一个地方，为货主安排所有的公路运输。它还可提供除安排公路运输服务外的包括铁路运输、存储和配送功能在内的一揽子服务。汽车货运代理本身既不掌握货源，也不掌握运输车辆。它作为托运人和公路运输承运人之间的中间人，赚取的是佣金。有些货代专门从货主那里收集零担货物将其拼装成整车货物。然后货代以托运人的名义将整车货物交给公路运输承运人（托运），从而赚取零担运输和整车运输之间的运费差额。

7.2.3 国际公路货物运输合同公约

在公路运输合同中，公路承运人的权利、义务及责任在国际公路货物运输合同公约和国内立法中有详细论述。国际公路货物运输合同公约（CMR）1956年被采用，而且通常被用来调整国际公路运输。CMR公约仅被欧洲国家认可，而欧洲以外国家的公路运输很大程度上是受其国内的法律法规制约，各国的规定又不尽相同。然而，欧洲以外的货运代理了解该公约也是有益的，因为当他们作为多式联运经营人组织国际多式联运，且欧洲的陆路运输构成了该多式联运的一部分时，他们可以更好地了解货物运输所适用的法律体制。

据CMR约定，公路承运人应就以下状况负责：

① 承运人的代理人，受雇人和其他人的作为和不作为；

② 自他接管货物到交付期间发生的灭失、损害和延迟交付。

但如果货物的灭失和损害是由以下原因所致，承运人可免责：

① 发货人的任何违法行为或过失造成的；

② 货物固有缺陷，以及发生了承运人难以避免且不可预见的情形。

对于由于运输车辆的不良状态或由于承运人已租用其车辆的人或他的代理人的错误行为或过失造成的损失，承运人不应免责。

7.2.4 驮背运输

TOFC 和 COFC 是两种驮背运输方式。驮背运输是一种将公路运输的灵活性和铁路运输的经济性相结合的运输方式。(牵引车)将卡车挂车或载有集装箱的底盘车直接开上铁路平板车，到达目的地后跟火车分离，交付给收货人。

尽管技术上不尽相同，大部分物流经理把 COFC 和 TOFC 均称为驮背运输。由牵引车将挂车或载有集装箱的底盘车直接开上铁路平板车，停妥摘挂后牵引车离去，由铁路运输完成接下来的两个或更多铁路站之间的长途干线运输。在中途转运站或目的站，卡车或牵引车可以跟装载了转换设备的集装箱连接，即转换成甩挂运输，由公路运输完成到收货人处的末端运输。驮背运输兼具铁路运输的低成本和公路运输的便捷灵活的优点。

Part B Vocabulary and Terminology 词汇和术语

CMIC Agreement On International Railroad through Transport of Goods 国际铁路货物联运协定（简称《国际货协》）

TOFC trailer-on-flatcar 平板车载运拖车驮背运输

COFC container-on-flatcar 平板车载运集装箱驮背运输

piggyback service 驼背运输服务

International Railway Through Transport 国际铁路联运

rail transport 铁路运输

road transport (or motor transport) 公路运输

line haul 长途运输、干线运输

CMR (Convention de Merchandises Par Routes) 国际公路货物运输合同公约

China Railway Express, or CR Express 中欧班列

"Belt and Road" Initiative "一带一路"倡议

Part C Exercise 练习

Ⅰ. Answer the following questions according to the text.

1. What kind of role does rail transport play in the national economy?
2. What is the relationship between rail transport and road transport?
3. What does CMR refer to?
4. Why should freight forwarders outside Europe have knowledge of CMR?
5. Please explain the advantages of CR Express.

Ⅱ. Multiple choice questions.

1. Road transport undertakes ( )

A. the local collection and distribution　　B. line haul

C. the domestic economy　　D. rail transport

2. The CMR convention generally governs ( ).

A. carriage of goods by sea
B. carriage of goods by air
C. international transport of goods by road
D. long distance transport

3. Which countries have ratified the CMR convention? ( )

A. countries outside Europe
B. developed countries
C. developing countries
D. countries in Europe

4. Road transport in the countries outside Europe is to a great extent governed by ( ).

A. the CMR convention
B. international laws
C. national laws
D. the same rules

Ⅲ. 案例分析

某货运代理受货主委托为其安排货物出口工作。在货物从内地往港口的运输过程中，由于汽车动力紧张，该货运代理以自己名义雇用了一辆货运车辆承运，结果承运该货物的汽车连同货物一起下落不明。请回答下列问题：

1. 货运代理人在选择公路承运人时有无不当，为什么？

2. 作为公路承运人，应如何加强对所雇用司机的管理？

Ⅳ. Translate the following passages into Chinese.

CR Express provides a strong transportation guarantee for "Belt and Road" construction. Due to its short distance, fast speed, high safety, as well as greening, and low impact on natural environment, CR Express has become the backbone of land transportation in international logistics. The logistics organization of the express is becoming more mature, the economic and trade exchanges of countries along the lines are becoming more active, and the cooperation between railways, ports, customs and other departments between countries is getting closer. These favorable conditions will further play the role of the CR Express as a backbone in international logistics and in Chinese "Belt and Road" Initiative.

Ⅴ. Translate the following sentences into English.

1. 国际铁路货物联运不涉及其他运输方式的参与，因而在具备一般铁路运输优点的基础上，该种运输形式在国际运输的连贯性、持续性等方面有其特有的优势，货物甚至可以不经换装就可实现长距离的陆上跨国运输而运抵目的地。

2. 与铁路运输相比，公路运输承运人用于终端设施的固定投资相对较少，并且公路运输使用的是由政府投资且养护的公路。

3. 铁路运输具有成本较低、运输连续性强、运输风险小和不易受气候条件影响等优势。

4. 国际铁路货物联运是涉及多个国家铁路运输的一种国际联合运输形式。由于要考虑各参加国铁路的设备条件、运输组织方式及其相关的法规制度，所以该项业务的复杂性增大，特别是有关国际联运的规章条款既繁多又复杂，在办理国际联运时，其货物、车辆及有关票据单证都必须符合有关规定和一些国家的具体要求。

Chapter Eight

International Container Transport and Multimodal Transport Logistics

国际集装箱运输和多式联运物流

Part A Text 课文

8.1 Introduction to International Container Transport

8.1.1 Definition

Container, in a literal sense, is a kind of tremendous holder with sort of intensity (most containers are made of steel now) for cycling and is easy to be mechanically operated. Container transport is a method of distributing merchandise in a unitized form adopting an inter-modal system which provides a possible combination of sea, road and other modes of transport. As a major form of group transport, container transport, due to its large loading capacity, can often connect ships, trains, automobiles, aircraft and other means of transportation together, thus reducing nearly half of the transport cost and becoming an increasingly popular transport in international trade.

8.1.2 Types and Specifications of Container

The International Standard Organization (ISO) has established 3 series, 13 classes standard specifications from 1A to 3A, among which the most frequently used types are Type 1A (8feet × 8feet × 40feet), Type 1C (8feet × 8feet × 20feet) and Type 1AA (8feet × 8.6feet × 40feet) of the first series of ISO. When calculating the circulating quantity of container, we often take the 20-foot container (Type 1C, 8feet × 8feet × 20feet) as a measuring unit, i.e. TEU (Twenty-foot Equivalent Unit) to indicate it, meaning "being equal to a 20-foot unit". The following two are the most frequently used container types, referred to as 20ft container (20 GP, meaning 20 General Purpose) and 40ft container (40 GP):

(1) ISO 20-foot dry freight container

L6.06m × W2.44m × H2.59m (20ft × 8ft × 8ft6in)

Internal Volume: 5.69m × 2.13m × 2.18m

Net load: ≤17.5 metric ton

This kind of container is generally used for shipping heavy cargo. The gross weight of the cargo is generally not allowed to exceed 17.5 metric tons, and the volume of cargo can be approximately 24～26 cubic meters.

(2) ISO 40-foot dry freight container

L12.19m×W2.44m×H2.59m (40ft×8ft×8ft6in)

Internal Volume: 11.8m×2.13m×2.18m

Net load: ≤22 metric ton

This kind of container is generally used for shipping light cargo. The gross weight of the cargo is generally not allowed to exceed 22 metric tons, and the volume of the cargo can be approximately 54 cubic meters.

8.1.3 Cargo Handing Over of Container Transport

(1) Types of Container Goods

1) Full Container Load (FCL)

The FCL consignments are packed into the container as one unit by the consignor for shipment. This means is adopted when the goods are of a container load or many containers' load. Except that some consignors have their own containers, others generally rent a certain number of containers and then the empty containers are sent to consignors' plants or warehouses. Under the customs official's supervision, consignors pack the goods into the containers. And after locking and sealing up the containers, consignors hand over the containers to the carriers and get the Dock Receipt (D/R) in exchange for Bills of Lading (B/L) or other shipping documents.

2) Less than Container Load (LCL)

LCL stands for less than container load or partial container load as opposite to FCL. As for the consignment that cannot meet the volume or load requirements of a container, the cargo owner/shipper usually delivers the goods to the carrier's Port Container Freight Station or Inland Container Depot. And then the carrier assembles the goods of multiple owners into full containers according to the nature, flow direction and weight of the goods, and then transports them to the Container Yard (CY).

(2) Container Cargo Delivery Mode

FCL/FCL—receipt of a whole container, delivery of a whole container, one consignor and one consignee.

FCL/LCL—receipt of a whole container, delivery of loose cargo, one consignor and several consignees.

LCL/FCL—receipt of loose cargo, delivery of a whole container, several consignors but one consignee.

LCL/LCL—receipt of loose cargo, delivery of loose cargo, several consignors and consignees.

(3) Container Cargo Delivery Place

The FCL and LCL consignments are delivered from different locations. There are three delivery sites of container cargo.

Door: the factory or warehouse of the consignor/consignee; usually door is the handover site of FCL cargo.

Container Yard (CY): CY is the handover site of FCL cargo. The CY is the delivery (or receipt) of a whole container from (or at) the shipper's or the forwarder's (or the consignee's) Contain Yard or premises.

Container Freight Station (CFS): CFS is the handover site of LCL cargo. The CFS is the delivery (or receipt) of loose cargo from (or at) the carrier's Container Freight Station.

8.1 国际集装箱运输概述

8.1.1 定义

集装箱又称"货箱""货柜"。按字面含义解释，它是一种大型货物"容器"，必须具有一定的强度（集装箱现今多为钢制），专供周转使用，且便于机械操作。所谓集装箱运输的概念就是将一定数量的单件货物装入按标准规格特制的集装箱内，并以该箱作为运送单位的一种现代化运输方式。它适用于各种运输方式的单独运输和不同运输方式的联合运输。集装箱这种成组运输因其装载量大，往往又能将船舶、火车、汽车、飞机等各种运输工具衔接在一起，从而降低近一半的运输成本，因而成为一种新型的现代化运输方式。

8.1.2 集装箱的种类和规格

国际标准化组织（ISO）制定了从1A到3A的3个系列、13个等级的集装箱标准规格，其中最常用的类型是ISO第一个系列中的1A型（8英尺×8英尺×40英尺）、1C型（8英尺×8英尺×20英尺）和1AA型（8英尺×8.6英尺×40英尺）。在计算集装箱的流通量时，我们通常以20英尺集装箱（1C型，8英尺×8英尺×20英尺）为计量单位，称为TEU（俗称"标箱"），意为"20英尺相当单位"。下面是两种最为常用的集装箱类型，简称20尺货柜（20GP，即20英尺普柜）和40尺货柜（40GP）：

(1) ISO20英尺干货集装箱

长6.06m×宽2.44m×高2.59m

内部体积：5.69m×2.13m×2.18m

净载重：不超过17.5公吨

这种集装箱一般配装重货，配货毛重一般不允许超过17.5吨，能容纳货物体积约为24～26立方米。

(2) ISO40英尺干货集装箱

长12.19m×宽2.44m×高2.59m

内部体积：11.8m×2.13m×2.18m

净载重：不超过22公吨

这种集装箱一般配装轻泡货，配货毛重一般不允许超过22吨，能容纳货物体积约为54立方米。

8.1.3 集装箱运输的货物交接方式

(1) 集装箱货物的分类

1）整箱货：这种装箱方式是指货主自行将货物装入集装箱后，以整箱为单位向承运人办理托运。这种情况是货主有足以装满一个或几个整箱的货源时所采用的装箱方式。除一些有实力的货主自备集装箱外，一般都是货主向承运人或集装箱租赁公司租用一定数量的集装箱。当空箱运到货主的工厂或仓库后，在海关人员的监督下，由货主把货物装入箱内，加锁铅封后交给承运人并取得场站收据，凭以换取海运提单或其他运输单据。

2）拼箱货：LCL代表相对于整箱货而言的拼箱货。对于托运量达不到一个集装箱容积或负荷量要求的货物，通常由货主/托运人先将货物交到承运人的码头集装箱货运站或内陆集装箱货运站，然后由承运人根据货物的性质、流向、重量等将多个货主的货物拼装成整箱货，再运至集装箱堆场。

(2) 集装箱货物的交接方式

FCL/FCL——整箱交，整箱接；一个发货人，一个收货人。

FCL/LCL——整箱交，拼箱接；一个发货人，多个收货人。

LCL/FCL——拼箱交，整箱接；多个发货人，一个收货人。

LCL/LCL——拼箱交，拼箱接；多个发货人，多个收货人。

(3) 集装箱货物交接地点

集装箱运输的整箱货与拼箱货是在不同的场地集中分拨。集装箱运输有三个主要的货物交接地点。

门：发货人或收货人的工厂或仓库，一般在门口处完成整箱货的交接。

集装箱堆场CY：集装箱堆场是整箱货的交接地点。CY方式是指从托运人或其货代（或收货人）的堆场、货场或营业场所交付或接收整箱货。

集装箱货运站CFS：集装箱货运站是专门集中交接拼箱货的场所。CFS方式是指从承运人的集装箱货运站接收或交付散装货物，亦即拼箱货。

8.2 Procedures of International Container Transportation

8.2.1 Procedures of Container Transportation of Export Goods

In terms of container transport, although different ports around the world may have different working practices, common procedures of container transport of export goods by sea are as follows:

(1) Space Booking

Upon the receipt of Letter of Credit, the exporter should contact the shipping company or its agent for space booking and prepare for the shipment in accordance with the shipping terms of export contract. In this step, the Booking Note (B/N) should be made out and presented to the shipping company.

(2) Acceptance of Space Booking

After carefully checking the B/N, the shipping company accepts the application of space booking and then the Shipping Order (S/O) is issued and sent to the shipper or his freight forwarder. With the S/O, the shipper or forwarder can apply for Customs Declaration. And the shipping company or its agent makes Booking List according to booking notes and sends them respectively to container terminals, including Container Yards and Container Freight Stations, so as to prepare for the distribution of empty containers and the interchange of heavy containers.

(3) Distribution of Empty Container

Typically, the shipper can get the empty FCL containers from the designated dock CY or inland CY and handle the procedure of Equipment Interchange Receipt (EIR). But the empty LCL containers are distributed by the mutually agreed CFS.

(4) Packing of LCL Cargo

The consignor sends LCL cargo to the CFS. CFS is responsible for counting, packing, sealing and making packing list in accordance with the B/N, D/R as well as other instructions of the shipping company and finally moving heavy containers to dock CY.

(5) Delivery of FCL Cargo

The shipper or his forwarder is responsible for counting, packing, sealing the container and delivering the sealed container to dock CY. The operators of CY accept the container on the basis of Booking List, Dock Receipt and container EIR.

(6) Obtaining B/L

The consignor or his forwarder can get the B/L from the shipping company or its agent by presenting signed CY Dock Receipt. Upon the receipt of B/L, the consignor can apply to the bank for settlement formalities.

Figure 8.1 illustrates the major procedures of container transport of export goods by sea.

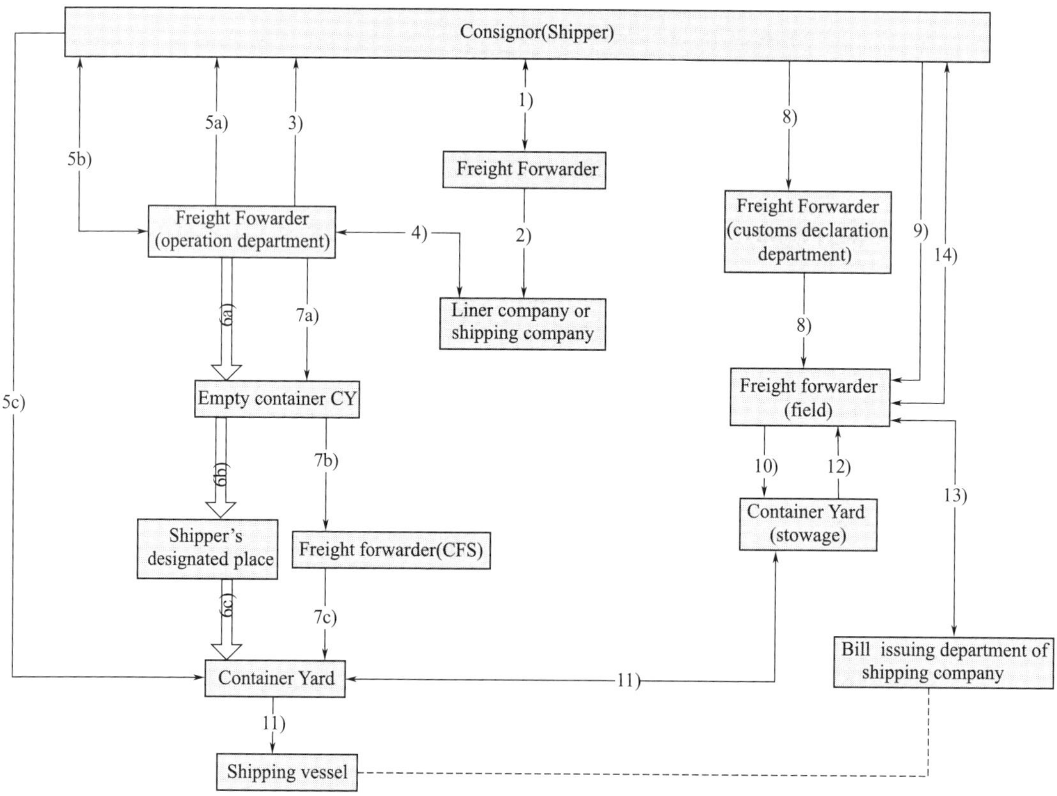

Figure 8.1 Procedures of container transport of export Goods by sea

In specific, there are the following steps:

1) The consignor establishes principal-agent relationship with a freight forwarder;

2) The consignor makes out the Booking Note and entrusts the freight forwarder to book shipping space from the shipping company in due time;

3) The freight forwarder informs the consignor of the shipping information or returns the Booking Receipt to the consignor;

4) The freight forwarder applies for containers and gets EIR (Equipment Interchange Receipt, EIR), which is an essential document for getting empty containers from the shipping company or its agent;

Remarks: The following work is to pick up empty containers, pack them, make packing list or container load plan (CLP), and hand over the heavy containers loaded with goods. There are three ways to do this work (5a, 5b; 6a, 6b, 6C; 7a, 7b, 7C in Figure 8.1). In practice, only one of the three is selected.

5) FCL-CY: The consignor picks up empty container(s) after receiving EIR from the forwarder, packs the container(s) and makes CLP (Container Loading Plan), and then sends FCL container(s) to CY in due time;

6) FCL-Door: The forwarder picks up empty container(s), sends container(s) to the place designated by the consignor, packs the container(s) and makes CLP, and then delivers FCL container(s) to CY;

7) LCL-CFS: The consignor sends LCL goods to the CFS of the forwarder. The forwarder picks up empty container(s), packs the container(s) and makes CLP, and then delivers load container(s) to CY;

8) The freight forwarder, authorized by the consignor, conducts the formalities of commodity inspection and customs declaration;

9) The consignor can also conduct the formalities of commodity inspection and customs declaration by himself;

10) The freight forwarder forwards the relevant documents to CY for loading;

11) Loading department makes the shipment plan and conducts loading activities with the confirmation of the shipping company for shipment;

12) After the goods are loaded on the vessels, original D/R is issued;

13) The freight forwarder can get the B/L or other relevant documents by presenting the original D/R;

14) The freight forwarder delivers the B/L and other documents to the consignor.

8.2.2 Procedures of Container Transport of Import Goods

Container transport of imported cargo involves inquiry on shipping date, import service contract conclusion, space booking, cargo tracing, charges payment for exchange of documents, customs declaration and inspection application, goods pickup, and empty container return, and so on.

(1) Procedures under FOB (see Figure 8.2)

1) The consignee establishes the principal-agent relationship with a freight forwarder;

2) The freight forwarder gets relevant documents ready before space booking;

3) The freight forwarder makes out cargo list, conducts space booking from shipping company who then makes confirmation on space booking;

4) The freight forwarder notifies the consignor and the forwarder's agent at the port of shipment;

5) The shipping company arranges the arrival of the vessel at the port of shipment;

6) The consignor delivers his cargo to the shipping company and acquires relevant shipping documents after lading;

7) The consignee and consignor complete their dealing formalities and acquire relative documents and certificate respectively;

8) The freight forwarder needs to be informed of shipping condition, collect and keep relative documents;

9) The freight forwarder timely arranges documents for import and completes relative formalities;

10) The goods enter the warehouse or depot after discharge at the arrival of the vessel;

11) The freight forwarder takes delivery of goods with Delivery Order after conducting the import declaration;

12) The freight forwarder transfers the goods to the consignee, and returns the empty containers to Container Yard.

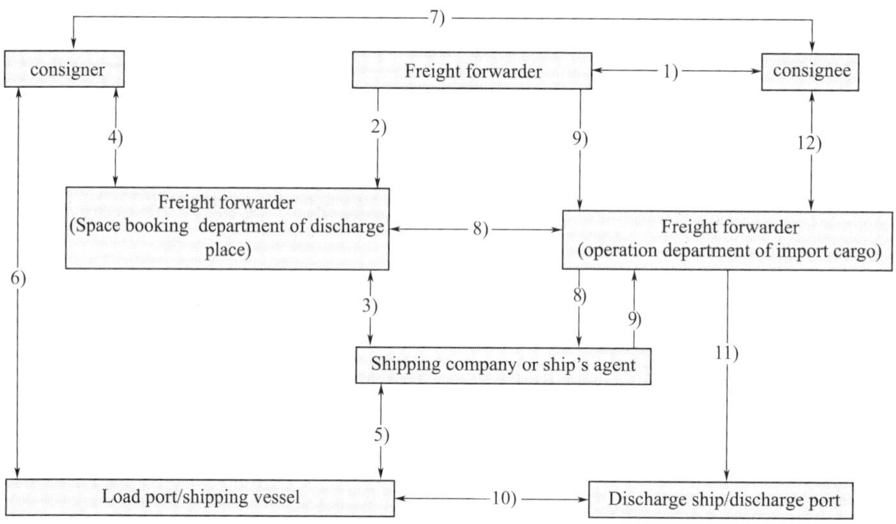

Figure 8.2 Procedures of container transport of import goods under FOB

(2) Procedures under CFR & CIF (see Figure 8.3)

1) The consignee establishes the principal-agent relationship with a freight forwarder;

2) The shipping company signs Bill of Lading to the consignor after shipment;

3) The consignor sends the Shipping Advice to the consignee;

4) The freight forwarder needs to be informed of the shipping condition, collect and keep the relevant papers and documents;

5) The freight forwarder timely arranges documents for import and completes relative

formalities;

6) The goods enter the warehouse or depot after discharge at the arrival of the vessel;

7) The freight forwarder takes delivery of goods with Delivery Order after conducting the import declaration;

8) The freight forwarder transfers the goods to the consignee, and returns the empty containers to Container Yard.

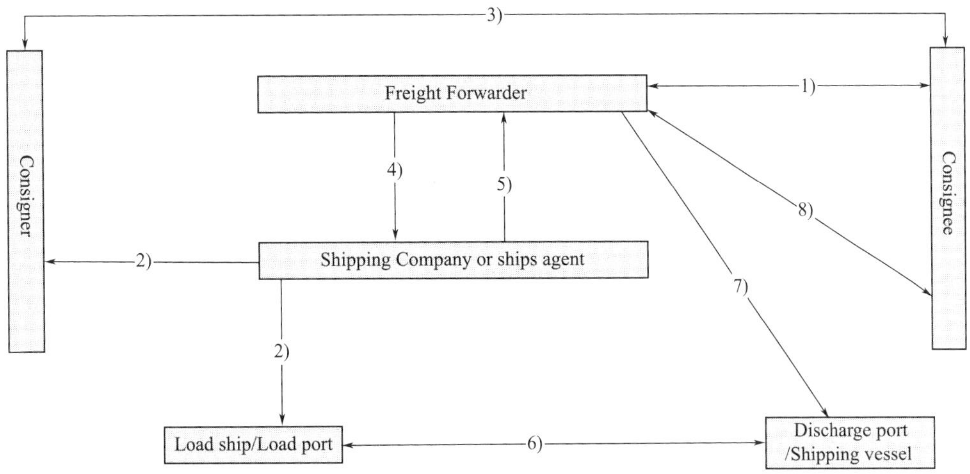

Figure 8.3 Procedures of container transport of import goods under CFR、CIF

8.2 国际集装箱运输业务流程

8.2.1 集装箱海运出口业务流程

在实际操作中，世界各港口的操作习惯不尽相同，但集装箱海运出口业务基本都包括以下几个环节。

(1) 订舱

收到信用证后，出口商必须马上与船公司或其代理（船代）联系订舱，并按照出口合同的装船要求准备装运。在这个环节中，需要填写托运单。

(2) 接受托运申请

船公司或船代在接到托运申请后应审核托运单，确认无误后签发装货单，然后将装货单退还给货主或其货运代理。货主或其货代即可持装货单，向海关办理货物出口报关手续。而船公司或其船代则在承运货物后，根据托运单缮制订舱清单，分送集装箱装卸作业区的集装箱码头、堆场和货运站，以准备空箱的发放和重箱的交接事宜。

(3) 发放空箱

除货主自备整箱外，通常整箱货使用的空箱由发货人凭船方提供的提箱单到指定的码头集装箱堆场（或内陆集装箱堆场）领取空箱，并办理设备交接单手续，拼箱货使用的空箱从双方议定交接货物的集装箱货运站领取。

(4) 拼箱货装箱

发货人将拼箱货交至集装箱货运站，由货运站根据订舱单、场站收据和船方的其他指示负责装箱、加封并制作装箱单，然后将重箱运至码头堆场。

(5) 整箱货交接

整箱货交接指的是由发货人或其货运代理负责装箱并将已加海关封志的整箱货运至码头堆场（或内陆堆场），堆场作业员根据订舱清单、场站收据及集装箱交接单接收货物。

(6) 换取提单

发货人或其货运代理凭集装箱堆场签署的场站收据可向船公司或其代理换取正式海运提单，并据此向银行结汇。

图 8.1 列出了集装箱海运出口业务的主要流程。

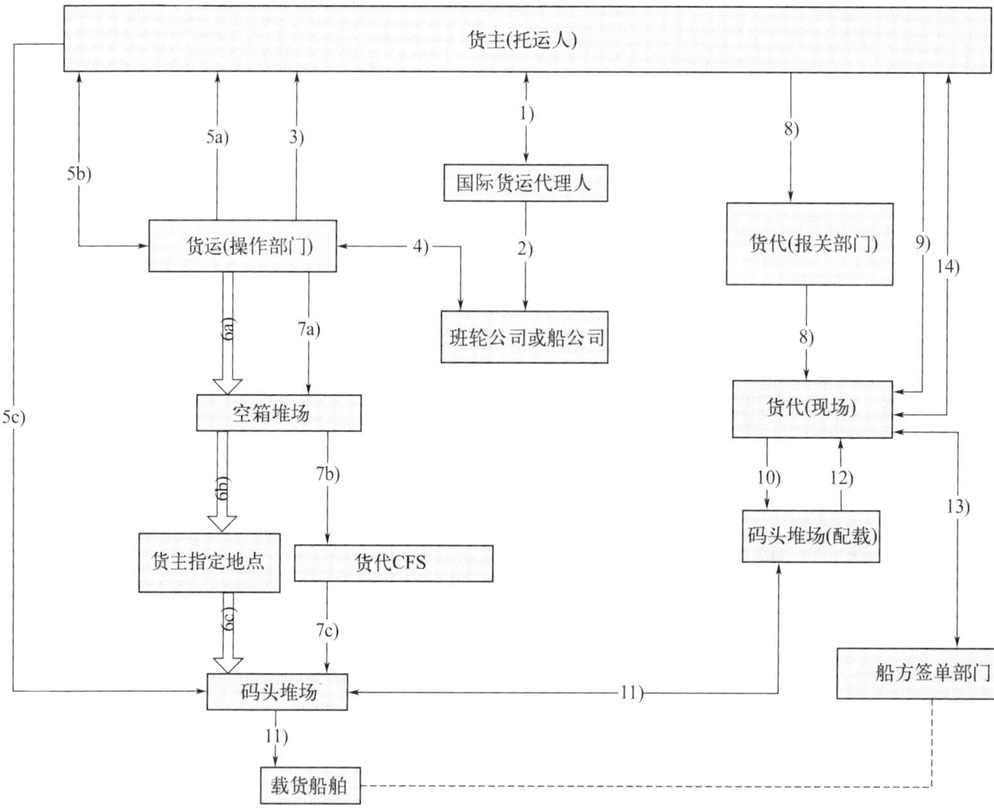

图 8.1 集装箱海运出口业务流程图

具体而言，有以下步骤。

1) 货主与货代建立货运代理关系；

2) 货主填写托运单，货代及时订舱；

3) 订舱后，货代将有关订舱信息通知货主，或者将“配舱回单”转交货主；

4) 货代向船公司或船代申请用箱，取得设备交接单 EIR 后，就可以凭 EIR 到空箱堆场提取所需要的集装箱。

注：随后的工作是提取空箱，装箱并制作集装箱装箱计划单（container load plan，CLP)，交接装有货物的重箱。该工作有以下三种方式（图 8.1 中分别用 5a、5b；6a、6b、6c；7a、7b、7c 来表示），实践中只选其中一种。

5) 货主“自拉自送”方式（FCL-CY）：货主先从货代处取得 EIR，然后自行提取空箱，装箱后制作 CLP，并按要求及时将重箱送码头堆场等待装船；

6) 货代上门装箱方式（FCL-Door）：货代负责提取空箱，到货主指定地点进行装箱并制作 CLP，然后将重箱送码头堆场等待装船；

7）货主送货至货代 CFS，货代负责装箱方式（LCL-CFS）：货主将拼箱货送到货代 CFS，货代提取空箱，并在 CFS 装箱，制作 CLP，然后将重箱送到码头堆场等待装船；

8）货主委托货代进行报检报关，办妥有关手续后将单证交货代；

9）货主也可自行报检报关，办妥有关手续后将单证交货代；

10）货代将办妥手续后的单证交码头堆场配载；

11）配载部门制作装船计划，经船公司确认后实施装船作业；

12）货物装船后可以取得场站收据 D/R 正本；

13）货代凭 D/R 正本到船方签单部门换取正本海运提单及其他单据；

14）货代将正本提单等单据交给货主。

8.2.2 集装箱海运进口业务流程

集装箱海运进口业务包括进口船期查询、签订进口合同、订舱、货物跟踪、付费换单、报关报检、提取货物以及空箱回运等多个环节。

(1) FOB 条件下的业务流程（见图 8.2）

1）收货人与货代建立货运代理业务；

2）货代办理订舱业务前要落实货单齐备；

3）货代缮制货物清单后，向船公司办理订舱手续，船公司进行订舱确认；

4）货代通知发货人，并通知货代自己在装运港的代理人；

5）船公司安排载货船舶抵达装货港；

6）发货人将货物交给船公司，货物装船后发货人取得有关运输单证；

7）发货人与收货人之间办理交易手续及单证；

8）货代需要掌握船舶动态，收集、保管好有关单证；

9）货代及时办理进口货物的单证及相关手续；

10）船舶抵达卸货港，货物入库、进场；

11）货代办理货物进口报关等手续后凭提货单到现场提货；

12）货代将货物交给收货人，并将空箱返还给空箱堆场。

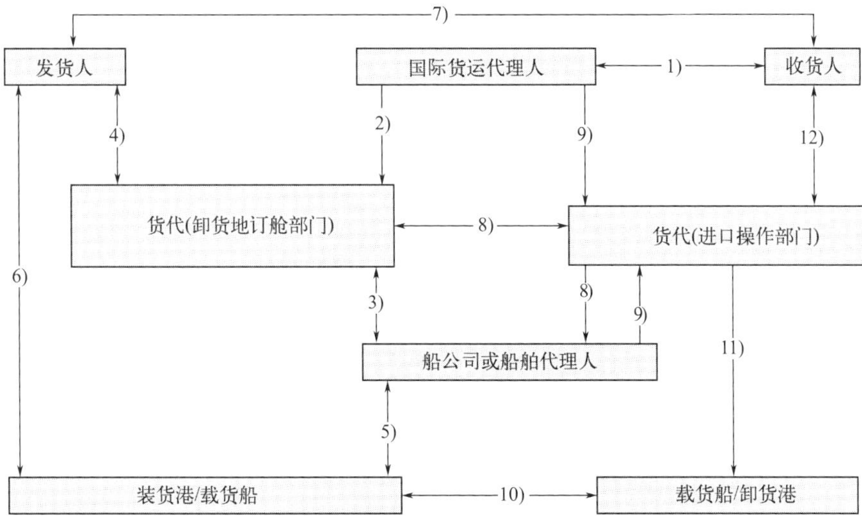

图 8.2 FOB 条件下整箱货进口业务流程图

（2）CFR、CIF 条件下的业务流程（见图 8.3）

1）收货人与货代建立货运代理关系；

2）船公司装船，装船后签发提单给发货人；

3）发货人向收货人发出装船通知；

4）货代需掌握船舶动态，搜集、保管好有关单证；

5）货代及时办理进口货物的单证及相关手续；

6）船舶抵达卸货港后进行卸货，货物入库、进场；

7）货代办理货物进口报关等手续后凭提货单到现场提货；

8）货代将货物交接给收货人，并办理空箱回运到空箱堆场等事宜。

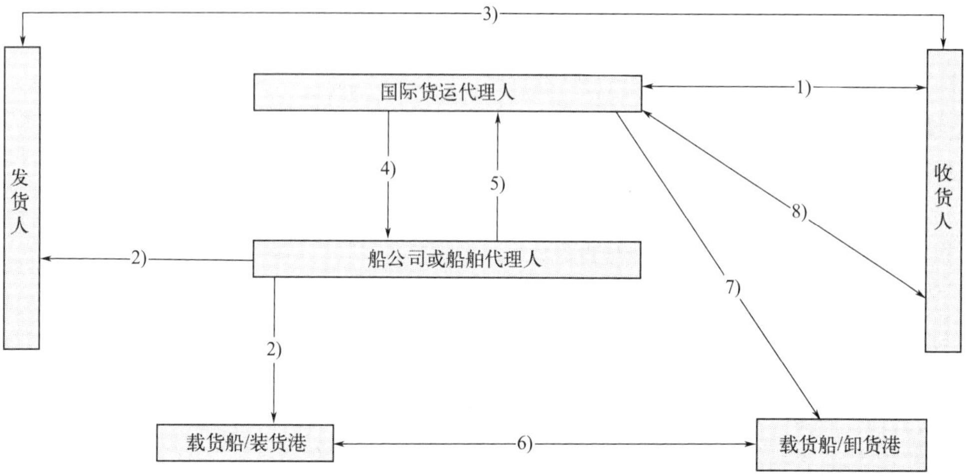

图 8.3　CFR、CIF 条件下整箱货进口业务流程图

8.3　International Multimodal Transport（IMT）

8.3.1　Definition of IMT

International multimodal transport is the most widely used form of container transport in the field of international logistics. International multimodal transport means the carriage of goods by at least two different modes of transport on the basis of a multimodal transport contract from a place in one country at which the goods are taken in charge by the Multimodal Transport Operator（MTO）to a place designated for delivery situated in a different country. Under the conventional system of segmented transport，the consignor is required to enter into several separate contracts with carriers of different transport stages，the liability of each carrier being limited to the carriage performed by him. The consignor or his freight forwarder，if necessary，has to handle the warehousing of the goods at any transshipment point.

MTO is who arranges the complicated multimodal transportation of goods from door to door and assumes contractual responsibility throughout the entire carriage，irrespective of whether he is an actual carrier for one stage of the whole transport process.

The development of multimodal transport is closely related to the "container revolution" in the 1960s and 1970s; as of 2011, container transport has been the most important multimodal transport mode. However, it is important to remember that multimodal transport is not equivalent to container transport as multimodal transport is feasible without any form of container. The MTO assures the supplier (and the buyer) that their goods will be effectively handled.

8.3.2 Advantages of International Multimodal Transport

Multimodal transport has the following advantages.

(1) Minimizing time loss at transshipment points

Multimodal transport, which is planned and coordinated as a single operation, minimizes the loss of time and the risk of loss, pilferage and damage to cargo at transshipment points. The Multimodal Transport Operator (MTO) maintains his own communication links and coordinates interchange and onward carriage smoothly at transshipment points.

(2) Providing faster transit of goods

The faster transit of goods made possible under multimodal transport reduces the disadvantages of long-distance from markets and the tying-up of capital.

(3) Reducing the burden of documentation and formalities

The burden of documentation and other formalities connected with segmented transport is reduced to a minimum.

(4) Saving costs

The cost savings resulting from these advantages are usually reflected in the unified and economical Through Freight Rate charged by the MTO and also in the lower cost of cargo insurance.

(5) Establishing only one agency to deal with

The consignor only needs to deal with the MTO in all matters relating to the transportation of his goods, including the settlement of claims for loss of goods, or damage to them, or delay in delivery at the destination.

(6) Reducing cost of export

The inherent advantages of International Multimodal Transport help to reduce the cost of exportation and improve exporters' competitive advantages in the international market.

8.3.3 Types of IMT

Currently, different types of multimodal transport operations involving different combinations are taking place. These are sea/air, air/road, rail/road/inland waterways-sea-rail/road/inland waterways, mini bridges, land bridges, piggyback and sea train.

Sea/air combines in itself the economy of sea transport and the speed of air transport. The economic benefit of this combination favors high value items such as electronics, electrical goods, computers, photographic equipment, etc.

In air/road, road transport is now increasingly used for trucking air freight over long distances, sometimes across national boundaries, to connect the main bases of airlines operating line haul services such as transpacific, transatlantic and inter-continental transport.

Rail/road/inland waterways-sea-rail/road/inland waterways mode is in common use when goods have to be moved by sea from one country to another and one or more inland modes of transport such as rail, road or inland waterways have to be used for moving goods from an inland center to the seaport in the country of origin or from the seaport to an inland destination.

A mini-bridge involves the movement of containers, under a Through Bill of Lading issued by an ocean carrier, by a vessel from a port in one country to a port in another country and then by rail to the railway station of another port city in the destination country.

A land bridge system concerns itself with shipment of containers overland as part of a sea-land or a sea-land-sea route. In this case, the railways are paid a flat rate by the ocean carrier who issues the Through Bill of Lading. This system is in operation for the movement of containers on certain important international routes.

Piggyback is a system of unitizing multimodal land transportation of transport by road and rail. It combines in itself the speed and reliability of rail on long trunk hauls with door-to-door flexibility of road transport for collection and delivery.

Sea train is another innovation in the multimodal transport system involving the use of rail and ocean transport. It is similar to the Roll-on-Roll-off system, except that train wagons instead of cars are driven directly onto the ro-ro vessel in order to link geographically fragmented rail systems by sea.

8.3 国际多式联运

8.3.1 国际多式联运的定义

国际多式联运是目前集装箱运输在国际物流领域最广泛采用的一种形式。国际多式联运是指按照国际多式联运合同，以至少两种不同的运输方式，由多式联运经营人将货物从一国境内的接管地点运至另一国境内指定交付地点的货物运输。传统的分段运输方式下，发货人需要跟每段承运人订立运输合同，承运人只对自己区段内的运输负责；发货人或其货代还需要负责转运节点的货物仓储。

多式联运经营人按照多式联运合同负责“门到门”的全程运输，无论他是否是全程某段运输的实际承运人，他都对全程运输承担承运人的义务，也享有承运人的权利。

国际多式联运的发展与二十世纪六七十年代“集装箱革命”紧密相连。到2011年，集装箱运输已经成为最重要的运输方式。然而，多式联运并不等同于集装箱运输，即便没有使用集装箱，也可开展多式联运。多式联运经营人确保货物的全程运输安全、高效。

8.3.2 国际多式联运的优点

1）缩短转运环节的时间：统一计划和运作的多式联运可以降低转运环节的货损货差，节省时间。由一个多式联运经营人对整个运输全程负责。

2）提高运输效率：多式联运下，更快的货物运输能减少远离市场和资金占压的不利条件。

3）简化制单和结算手续：将各分段运输的制单和结算手续降到最少。

4）节约成本：多式联运实行单一费率，节约了运杂费用和保险费用。

5）仅和一个运输代理建立委托关系：发货人委托多式联运经营人运输货物，多式联运经营人负责处理全程运输中的一切问题，比如货物灭失、货损、延期交付的索赔。

6）降低出口成本，提高出口商的国际竞争力。

8.3.3 国际多式联运的组合方式

当前，已出现多种多式联运的组合方式，有海/空、陆/空、铁路/公路/内河-海洋-铁路/公路/内河、小陆桥、陆桥、驮背运输和海/铁联运等。

海空联运兼具海运的经济性和空运的快捷性。海空联运适合运输高价值的商品，比如电子电器产品、计算机和照相设备等。

在陆空联运中，公路运输越来越多地用于长距离运输空运货物，有时需要跨越国界，以连接经营长途货运服务如跨太平洋、跨大西洋和洲际运输的航空公司的主要机场。

当货物需要通过水运从一个国家运往另一个国家时，铁路/公路/内河-海洋-铁路/公路/内河是常用的联运方式。必须使用铁路、公路或内河运输中的一种或多种运输将货物从内陆生产中心运往原产国港口或从港口运往内陆目的地。

小陆桥运输是指以国际标准规格集装箱为容器，使用一份由海洋运输承运人签发的联运提单，将货物从一国港口运往另一国港口，再通过铁路转运至目的国另一港口城市的铁路站。

陆桥运输是将集装箱货物通过横贯大陆的铁路运输将海港连接起来的运输方式。陆桥运输将集装箱的大陆运输作为海/陆联运或海—陆—海运输的一部分。在这种情况下，由海运承运人签发全程联运提单，且向铁路支付与海洋费率一样的统一运费率。这一联运被用于某些重要国际物流线路的集装箱运输。

驮背运输是一种公路和铁路联合的运输方式，货运挂车或集装箱直接开上火车车皮，到达目的地再从火车车皮上开下。它使用铁路作为长途干线运输工具，而用公路运输实现门到门的末端短途运输。

海上火车是多式联运系统的另一项创新，是将铁路和海运组合使用。它类似于滚装船系统，区别是将火车车皮而不是汽车直接开上渡轮，从而把在地理上分割开的铁路系统通过海洋运输连接起来。

Part B Vocabulary and Terminology 词汇和术语

TEU Twenty-Foot Equivalent Unit 20英尺标准箱

FCL Full Container Load 整箱货

LCL Less than Container Load 拼箱货

EIR Equipment Interchange Receipt 设备交接单

Packing List 装箱单

Container Loading Plan (CLP) 集装箱装箱计划单

D/R Dock Receipt 场站收据

IMT International Multimodal Transport 国际多式联运

MTO Multimodal Transport Operator 多式联运经营人
CY Container Yard 集装箱堆场
CFS Container Freight Station 集装箱货运站
Land Bridge 大陆桥运输
Mini-bridge 小陆桥运输

Part C Exercise 练习

Ⅰ. Answer the following questions according to the text.

1. What is container?
2. What are the major types of container goods?
3. What are the main container cargo delivery modes?
4. What is International Multimodal Transport?
5. What are the advantages of International Multimodal Transport?

Ⅱ. Please choose the best answer.

1. Another innovation in the multimodal transport system involving the use of rail and ocean transport is called ( ).

A. sea train B. air freight C. sea/air D. road

2. A transport system of utilized multimodal land transportation of transport by road and rail is called ( ).

A. land bridge B. piggyback C. sea train D. Mini-bridge

3. The multimodal transport system involving the use of rail and ocean transport is ( ).

A. land bridge B. Mini-bridge C. sea train D. sea/air

4. The system combining in itself the economy of sea transport and the speed of air transport is ( ).

A. Mini-bridge B. Sea/train C. Land bridge D. sea /air

5. Which of the following is not one of the multimodal transport's advantage? ( )

A. Saving cost B. Proving the fast transit of goods
C. Reducing the cost of export D. Issuing a landing permit

Ⅲ. Translate the following passages into Chinese.

Currently, different types of multimodal transport operating different combinations are taking place. There are sea/air, air/road, rail/road/inland waterways-sea-rail/road/inland waterways, mini bridges, land bridges, piggy back and sea train.

Sea/air combines in itself the economy of sea transport and the speed of air transport. The economy of this combination makes it suitable to high value items like electronics, electrical goods, computers and photographic equipment. In air/road, road transport is now being increasingly used for trucking air freight over long distances, sometimes across national boundaries, to connect with the main bases of airlines operating long haul services such as transpacific, transatlantic and intercontinental transport.

Rail/road/inland waterways-sea-rail/road/inland waterways road is in common use when goods have to be moved by sea from one country to another and one or more inland modes of transport such as rail, road or inland waterways have to be used for moving goods from an inland center to the seaport in the country of origin or from the seaport to an inland destination. Mini-bridge involves the movement of containers, under a through bill of lading to a port in another country and then by rail to a second port city in the second country, terminating at the rail carrier's terminal in the second port city.

Ⅳ. Translate the following passages into English.

1. 订舱委托是发货人或其货运代理根据贸易合同或信用证条款的规定，在货物托运前的一定时间内，填写货物托运单或订舱单，向船公司或其代理申请订舱的过程。

2. 船公司或其代理公司（船代）在接到托运申请后，应审核托运单并与订舱单核对，确认无误后，在装货单上签章，然后将装货单退还给货主或货运代理人。货主或货运代理即可持装货单，向海关办理货物出口报关手续。

3. 货代向船公司或船代领取集装箱设备交接单到指定集装箱堆场领取空箱，并到货主存货地点进行装箱封箱后，将集装箱整箱货物连同集装箱装箱单、设备交接单送到码头，码头将船公司或船代提供的装货清单及集装箱装箱单送海关供海关监管装船。

Chapter Nine

Inspection and Clearance 国际物流报检报关

Part A Text 课文

9.1 Commodity Inspection

Import and export commodity inspection refers to the inspection and appraisal of the quality, specification, health, safety and quantity of import and export goods by the inspection institution established by the state or an independent institution registered with the government, and the issuance of certificates. It covers the inspection of quality, quantity, packing, safety, hygiene, place of origin, etc. of the goods. Commodity inspection is a necessary step in executing an I&E contract. It plays an important role in Import and Export business. Commodity inspection testifies the accordance of the quality, quantity, packing, etc. of the delivered goods with the requirements specified in the I&E contract. It also testifies the accordance of the quality, quantity, packing, etc. of the delivered goods with the legal and administrative regulations of the importing country. In case of damage to the goods in transit, inspection certificates are necessary for the exporter or importer to claim compensation against the insurance company, shipping company or other concerned parties.

9.1.1 Basic Concepts of Import and Export Inspection

(1) Commodity inspection institutions

There are two major types of inspection bodies: governmental and non-governmental. Governmental inspection bodies such as the Food and Drug Administration (FDA) in the US specialize in the inspection of particular merchandise, including food, drugs, etc. The international inspection of commodity is mainly undertaken by nongovernmental bodies which have the same legal status as notary organizations. Notable bodies are Societe General De Surveillance S. A. (SGS) in Switzerland, Underwriters laboratory (UL) in the US, Lloyd Surveyor in the UK, BV in France and Marine Surveyor& Sworn Measurers Association in Japan.

China's Entry-Exit commodity inspection and quarantine is carried out by governmental inspection body-General Administration of Quality Supervision, Inspection and Quarantine of the People's Republic of China (AQSIQ). It is a ministerial administrative organ directly under the State Council of the People's Republic of China. It is in charge of national quality, Entry-Exit commodity inspection, Entry-Exit health quarantine, Entry-Exit animal and plant quarantine, Import-Export food safety, certification and accreditation, standardization as well as administrative law-enforcement.

(2) Commodity inspection certificates

Inspections certificates are documents issued by inspection institutions. Upon inspection of the quality, quantity or packing, etc. of the goods, certificates may be issued up to the requirements of the applicant. In I&E business, inspection certificates may be required for customs clearance, payment negotiation or related claims. The most commonly used inspection certificates are listed as follows: Inspection Certificate of Quality/Weight/Quantity/Packing; Veterinary Certificate; Health Certificate; Disinfection Certificate; Certificate of Origin; Generalized System of Preferences Certificate of Origin Form A; Inspection Certificate of Value; Inspection Certificate on Damaged Cargo; Inspection Certificate on Tank or Hold.

(3) Inspection standards

The commodity inspection authorities shall conduct inspection according to the following standards.

The inspection shall be performed according to the standards specified by laws and administrative regulations. These standards are compulsory.

In the absence of compulsory standards, the inspection shall be performed according to the standards agreed upon in transaction contracts. If the trade is conducted against the sample, the inspection shall be performed according to the sample provided.

In case that compulsory standards are lower than the standards agreed upon in transaction contracts, the inspection shall be conducted according to the standards stipulated in transaction contracts.

In the absence of compulsory standards, and inspection standards are either not agreed upon or agreed upon unclearly in the contract, the inspection shall be conducted according to the standards of the manufacturing country, relevant international standards or the standards designated by the state inspection agency.

(4) Stipulation on the place and time of inspection

There are four commonly used ways of stipulating the place and time of inspection in the contract.

① To make inspection in the exporting country. This means that inspection at the seller's factory or at the port of shipment/loading is final. Buyer can reinspect the goods at the port of destination, but normally he cannot claim for compensation. And thus, this means is favorable to the seller.

② To make inspection in the importing country. This means that inspection carried out at the port of destination is final. Obviously, this arrangement is favorable to the buyer.

③ To make weight inspection at the port or place of shipment, whereas quality inspection at the port or place of destination.

④ To make inspection in the exporting country and make re-inspection in the importing country. It means after inspection at the port of shipment, the buyer retains the right to re-inspect and claim for compensation. Apparently, it is favorable to both sides. Therefore, this way is frequently used in international trade practices.

9. 1. 2 Procedures of Inspection and Quarantine

As for import commodities that are subject to inspection by the inspection authorities as stipulated in the foreign trade contract, upon their arrival, the consignees or their agents (i. e. freight forwarders) should apply to the inspection authorities at the arrival port in due time. Survey reports or inspection certificates shall be issued to the applicants after inspection. These commodities shall be checked and released by Customs upon presentation of the special seal of the inspection authorities stamped on the customs declaration forms.

As for export commodities which are subject to inspection as stipulated in the contract or by laws, the exporters or their agents should apply for inspection before shipment. If the export commodities are proved up to the standards, the inspection authorities shall stamp a special seal on the customs declaration forms or issue inspection certificates for the exporters to clear the goods through Customs. If vessels and containers are used for carrying perishable goods, such as cereals, oils, foodstuffs, and frozen products for exportation, the carrier or container stuffing organization should apply for inspection of the holds or tanks and containers to inspection authorities to make sure that the declared holds or containers conform to the technical condition for shipping.

Entry-exit commodity inspection and quarantine generally undergo the following steps illustrated by Figure 9. 1.

The scope of entry-exit inspection and quarantine includes the following types of goods:

1) Legal inspection of the commodities, including animals, plants and their products, which are listed in the "Entry-exit Goods Catalogue for Inspection and Quarantine by Entry-exit Inspection and Quarantine Institutions" and are subject to inspection as stipulated in other international conventions, laws and regulations;

2) Inspection of the functions and usages of packages for carrying export dangerous goods;

3) Inspection of the holds or tanks and containers for carrying perishable goods, such as cereals, oils, foodstuffs, and frozen products;

4) Inspection of transport vehicles, packaging materials, bedding materials and feeding tools used for carrying animals and plants;

5) Animal vaccine, serum, diagnosticum and waste of plants and animals;

6) Health quarantine of export food;

7) Imported food, food additives, food containers, packaging materials and food equipment.

9. 1. 3 Keynotes on Handling the Inspection of Import Commodities

When handling the inspection of import commodities, the following points should be

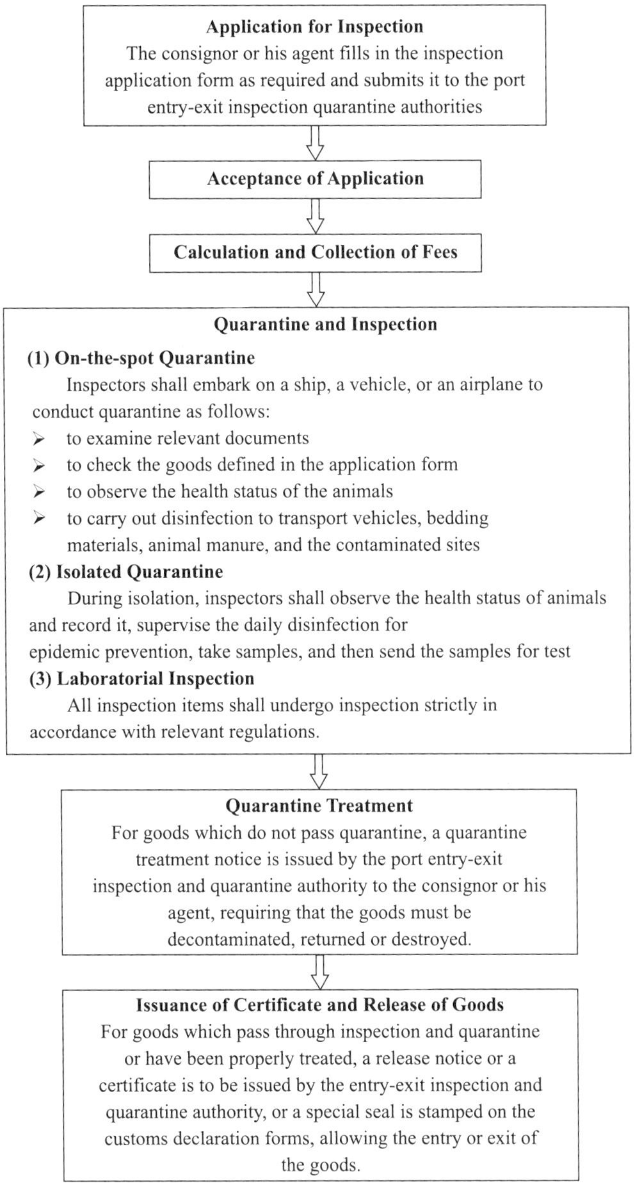

Figure 9. 1 Procedures of entry-exit commodity inspection and quarantine

noted:

1) Documents required for the inspection and quarantine of import commodities:

foreign trade contract;

commercial invoice;

Bill of Lading or Air Waybill, Railway Bill, etc. ;

packing list and weight note;

import permits;

inspection and quarantine report and certificate of origin issued by the exporting country.

2) The inspection procedures should be accomplished before the time limit for claims prescribed in the I&E contract.

3) For import crucial commodities or complete sets of equipment, in accordance with the terms agreed upon in the contract, the importers can conduct preliminary inspection and supervision before shipment in the exporting country. If necessary, the inspection institutions may appoint their inspectors to take part in such inspection.

9.1.4 Keynotes on Handling the Inspection of Export Commodities

When handling the inspection of export commodities, the following points should be noted:

1) Documents required for the inspection and quarantine of export commodities are:

Sales Contract (or Sales Confirmation);

Letter of Credit;

License (export commodity quality certification, hygiene registration certificate);

Factory inspection list.

2) The inspection procedures should be completed before the date of shipment. Therefore, it is stipulated in China that the exporter submit the application form to the inspection institution at least seven days before the date of shipment.

3) The export commodities, which pass through inspection and quarantine and for which inspection certificates have been issued by the inspection institution, should be applied for customs clearance and shipped out of the country within a certain time limit. Otherwise, they will have to be reinspected before shipment. The time limit usually varies for different goods and will be stated in the inspection certificates.

4) The export commodities included in the List of Commodities shall be checked and released by Customs upon presentation of inspection certificates issued by inspection authorities or the special seal of the inspection authorities stamped on the customs declaration forms.

9.1.5 Animal and Plant Quarantine

According to the "Law of the People's Republic of China on Import and Export Commodity Inspection" and its implementation regulations, "Law of the People's Republic of China on Entry and Exit Animal and Plant Quarantine" and its implementation regulations, "Frontier Health and Quarantine Law of the People's Republic of China" and its implementation rules, "Food Safety Law of the People's Republic of China" and other related laws and regulations, the following animals and plants must undergo Animal and Plant Quarantine.

1) Animals and plants, animal and plant products and other quarantine objects for import.

2) Export or transit goods.

3) Containers, packages and dunnage used for carrying animals and plants, animal and plant products and other quarantine objects.

4) Means of transportation from epidemic areas.

5) Old and disused vessels entering the country for salvage purposes.

6) Goods or articles subject to quarantine in accordance with the provisions of relevant laws, administrative regulations, international treaties or trade contracts.

It should be noted that the following animals and plants are prohibited from entering China:

1) Pathogenic micro-organisms (including seed of bacteria and viruses) of animals and plants, pests and other harmful organisms.

2) Related animals and plants, animal and plant products and other quarantine objects from countries or regions with the outbreak of animal or plant epidemic.

3) Animal carcasses and soil.

9.1 商品检验检疫

进出口商品检验是指由国家设立的检验机构或向政府注册的独立机构，对进出口货物的质量、规格、卫生、安全、数量等进行检验、鉴定，并出具证书的工作。商品检验是履行进出口合同的必要步骤，在进出口业务中起着重要的作用。商品检验一是确保所交付货物的质量、数量、包装等符合进出口合同的有关规定；二是确保所交付货物的质量、数量、包装等与进口国法律法规的要求相一致。此外，如果发现货物损坏，进出口商可凭商检证明向保险公司、船公司或其他相关方提出索赔。

9.1.1 进出口商品检验检疫的相关概念

(1) 商品检验机构

目前，世界各国有两种主要的商检机构：官方机构和非官方机构。美国食品药品监督管理局（FDA）等官方机构专门对特定商品进行检查，如食品、药品等。国际贸易中的商品检验主要由非官方机构承担，这些机构具有公证机构的法律地位。著名的非官方商检机构有瑞士通用公证行、美国保险人实验室、英国劳合氏公证行、法国船级社和日本海事鉴定协会。

中国出入境商品检验检疫由官方机构——国家市场监督管理总局（AQSIQ）负责执行。国家质量监督检验检疫总局是中华人民共和国国务院直属部级行政机关，负责国家质量管理、出入境商品检验、出入境卫生检疫、出入境动植物检疫、进出口食品安全、认证认可、标准化、行政执法等工作。

(2) 商品检验证书

检验证书是商品检验机构出具的具有法律效力的文件。在对进出口货物的质量、数量、包装或产地等实施检验检疫后，根据检验检疫结果，商检机构可以出具符合申请人要求的证明。在进出口业务中，进出口报关、银行付款或相关索赔等环节可能需要提交商检证书。最常用的商检证书如下：质量/重量/数量/包装检验证书；兽医检验证书；卫生检验证书；消毒检验证书；原产地证书；普惠制原产地证书格式 A；价值检验证书；货物残损检验证书；油罐或货舱检验证书。

(3) 检验标准

商检机构应当按照下列标准进行检验。

商品检验应当按照法律、法规规定的标准进行，这些标准是强制性的。

没有强制性商品检验标准的，按照交易合同约定的检验标准执行。如果（进出口）贸易是凭样品成交的，则应当按照所提供样品的相关标准进行检验。

如果强制性标准低于交易合同所约定的标准，那么应当按照交易合同规定的标准进行检验。

如果没有强制性标准，或者合同中没有规定检验标准或者规定不明确的，应按照制造国标准、相关国际标准或者国家检验机构指定的标准进行检验。

(4) 商检地点、时间的规定

合同中对于商检地点和时间的规定会在一定程度上影响买卖双方的利益，一般有如下四种规定方法。

① 在出口国进行检验。这意味着在卖方工厂或装运港进行的商品检验及其结论是对于商品品质及数量等的最终判定。买方可以在目的港复验货物，但不能索赔。因此这种方式对卖方有利。

② 在进口国进行检验。这意味着在目的港进行的商品检验是关于商品品质及数量等的最终判定。显然，这种安排对买方有利。

③ 重量检验在装运港或装运地进行，而质量检验则在目的港或目的地进行。

④ 在出口国进行检验，在进口国进行复验。这意味着在装运港进行检验后，买方保留复验和索赔的权利。显然，这种方式对双方都有利。因此，该方式被经常使用。

9.1.2 检验检疫程序

对于对外贸易合同规定应由检验机构检验的进口商品，收货人或其代理人（货代）在进口商品抵达时，应当及时向到货口岸的检验机构提出商检申请。商检后，检验机构将向申请人出具检验报告或检验证书。海关凭（进口货物）报关单上加盖的商检机构专用章查验和放行货物。

对于贸易合同或者法律规定必须检验的出口商品，出口商或其代理人（货代）应当在装运前申请检验。经检验合格的，检验机构在报关单上加盖商检机构专用章或者出具检验证书，以便出口商办理出口报关手续。如果船舶和集装箱是用于运输易腐烂的出口货物，如谷物、油、食品和冷冻产品等，承运人或者装箱机构应当向检验机构申请对货舱、油轮、集装箱进行检验，以确保申报的货舱、集装箱符合运输技术条件。

进出口商品检验检疫程序如图 9.1 所示。

我国出入境商品检验检疫的范围包括：

1）我国《出入境检验检疫机构实施检验检疫的进出境商品目录》中所列的商品以及其他国际公约、法律法规规定商检的商品，包括各种动植物以及动植物产品等；

2）出口危险货物包装容器的性能及使用记录；

3）运载出口易腐烂变质食品、冷冻食品的船舱、容器、集装箱等；

4）运载动植物、动植物产品的运输工具及包装、铺垫材料、饲养工具等；

5）动物疫苗、血清、诊断液、动植物性废弃物；

6）出口食品卫生检疫；

7）进口食品、食品添加剂、食品容器、包装材料和食品用工具设备。

9.1.3 办理进口商品检验检疫的要点

实践中，在办理进口商品检验检疫时，应注意以下几点。

1）入境货物检验检疫所需单证有：对外贸易合同、商业发票、提单（空运提单、铁路运单等）、装箱单、重量单、进口许可证（动物入境检疫许可证、进口废料作为原料的环保

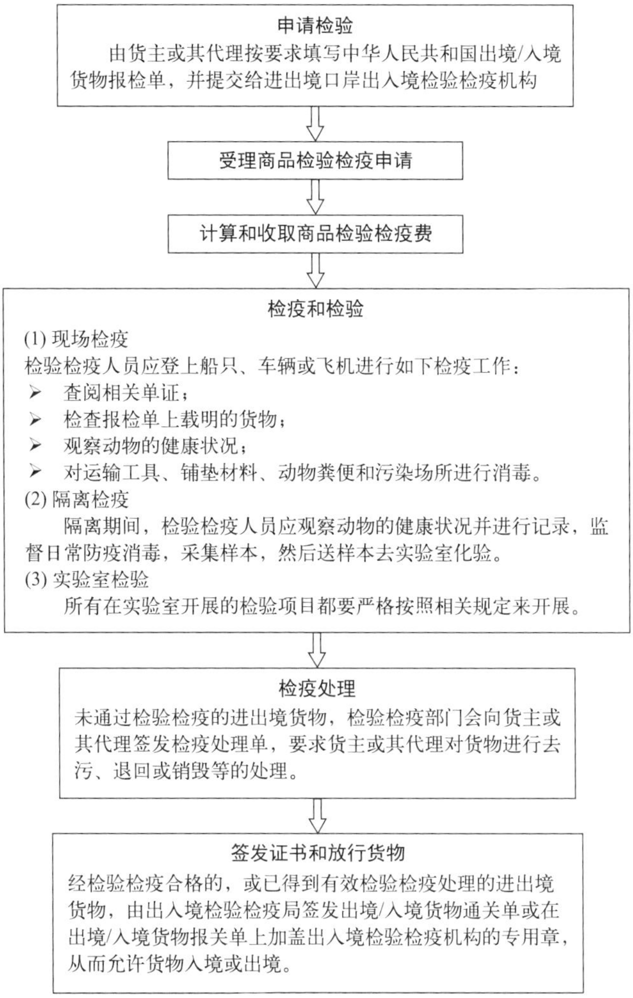

图 9.1 进出口商品检验检疫程序

证明）、出口国出具的检疫报告和原产地证明。

2）进口检验检疫程序应在进口合同规定的索赔期限内完成。

3）对于重要的进口商品或成套设备，按照进出口合同约定的条款，进口商可以去往出口国进行装运前的预检验检疫和监督。必要时，我国出入境检验检疫机构可以派出检验检疫人员前往参加检验和监督。

9.1.4 办理出口商品检验检疫的要点

实践中，在办理出口商品检验检疫时，应注意以下几点。

1）出境货物检验检疫所需单证为：出口销售合同（销售确认书）、信用证、许可证（出口商品质量证明、卫生登记证）、工厂检验清单。

2）出口商品检验检疫程序应在装运前完成。因此，我国规定出口商至少要在装运日前7天向出入境检验检疫机构提交出境货物报检表。

3）出口商品通过检验检疫并经出入境检验检疫机构出具检验证书的，应当在规定的期限内报关装运出境，否则须在装运前再次进行检验。不同货物规定的时间期限会有所不同，且会在商检证书中注明。

4）列入我国《出入境检验检疫机构实施检验检疫的进出境商品目录》的出口商品，海关凭出入境检验检疫机构签发的检验证书，或者出境货物通关单，或者出入境检验检疫机构加盖在出境货物报关单上的专用章，进行货物放行、允许货物出口。

9.1.5 动植物检疫

根据《中华人民共和国进出口商品检验法》及其实施条例、《中华人民共和国进出境动植物检疫法》及其实施条例、《中华人民共和国国境卫生检疫法》及其实施细则、《中华人民共和国食品安全法》等有关法律、法规规定，下列动物、植物必须接受动植物检疫才能入境。

1）进口动植物、动植物产品和其他检疫物；

2）出口或者转口货物；

3）装载动植物、动植物产品和其他检疫物的容器、包装件和垫舱物；

4）来自疫区的交通工具；

5）因救助目的入境的废旧船舶；

6）有关法律、行政法规、国际条约、贸易合同规定应当检疫的货物、物品。

下列动物和植物禁止进入中国国境：

1）动植物的病原微生物（包括细菌、病毒种子）、害虫和其他有害生物；

2）动植物疫情发生国家或者地区的有关动植物、动植物产品和其他检疫物；

3）动物尸体和土壤。

9.2 Tariff and Clearance

9.2.1 Introduction to Tariff

Tariff is one of the taxes imposed on goods when they are moved across a country's customs territory, where the customs authorities levy a duty on the exporter or importer. Customs duties are levied by the Customs according to law. The consignee of import goods and the consignor of export goods are duty payers. Customs territory is different from national territory, and the customs duty takes place in customs territory. It has three characteristics: compulsory, gratuitous, preordained.

Generally speaking, there are four ways of imposing tariff.

(1) Specific Tariff /Duty

It refers to the tariff/duty calculated and levied based on the weight, quantity, length, volume and other measuring units of the goods. The duty payable can be calculated by multiplying the quantity (volume, weight) of the goods by the taxable amount per unit. Typically, a country, according to its import and export tariff, sets the taxable amount per unit for commodities under different tax headings according to the domestic common measuring units.

The calculation formula for Specific Tariff is:

Duty Payable = Quantity of Goods × Unit Duty (taxable amount per unit of the goods)

(2) Ad Valorem Tariff /Duty

Ad valorem tariff refers to the tariff/duty levied on the basis of the price of the goods, and the tariff rate is a certain percentage of the price of the goods. Ad valorem tariff is equal to the total customs value of the goods multiplied by Ad valorem tariff rate.

The calculation formula for Ad Valorem Duty is:

Duty Payable=Customs Value of the goods × Ad Valorem Tariff Rate

(3) Compound (or Mixed) Tariff

It is the combination of Ad Valorem Tariff and Specific Rate Tariff.

(4) Selective Tariff

Both Ad Valorem Tariff and Specific Tariff are used to calculate the tariff. Usually, the higher of the two is chosen.

9.2.2 Types of Tariff

There are four major customs duties:

(1) Import Duty

This is the most common form of tariff. Import duty is the main source of a country's tariff revenue. In China, tariff rates on import goods are composed of the most-favored-nation (MFN) tariff rate, conventional tariff, preferential tariff rate, ordinary tariff rate, tariff quota duty rate, etc. Temporary duty rates may apply to import goods within a specific time limit.

MFN tariff rate shall apply to imported goods originating from members of the World Trade Organization (WTO) that jointly apply the most-favored-nation (MFN) treatment clause, imported goods originating from countries or regions with which the People's Republic of China has concluded bilateral trade agreements containing provisions for granting mutual most-favored-nation treatment, and imported goods originating in the territory of the People's Republic of China.

Conventional tariff shall apply to imported goods originating from countries or regions with which the People's Republic of China has concluded regional trade agreements containing preferential tariff terms.

Preferential tariff rate shall apply to imported goods originating from countries or regions with which the People's Republic of China has concluded trade agreements containing special preferential tariff terms.

Ordinary tariff rate shall apply to imported goods originating from countries or regions other than those above-mentioned countries or regions or to imported goods of undetermined origins.

(2) Export Duty

It is rarely adopted in the developed countries, but is occasionally adopted in the developing countries so as to increase government revenue. In some cases, tariff rates on export goods are designed to restrict the export of strategic materials and resources like rare earth minerals. Temporary rates may be applied to export goods within a specified period of time.

(3) Transit Duty

Transit taxes are duties imposed by a country on foreign goods passing through its borders.

(4) Import Surcharge/Surtax

Import surcharge refers to the additional import duties levied by a country on some import goods in addition to normal import tariff according to a certain purpose. Imposing Import surtaxes is usually a special temporary measure, and the commonly used import surtaxes include countervailing duty and anti-dumping duty.

9.2 关税及通关

9.2.1 关税的介绍

关税是指进出口商品在经过一国关境时，由政府设置的海关向进出口商所征收的税收。海关依据相关法律征收关税。进口货物的收货人和出口货物的发货人是关税的纳税义务人。关境不同于国境，关税征收发生在关境而不是国境。关税具有三个重要特点：强制性、无偿性和预定性。

关税有四种计算方法。

(1) 从量关税

它是指以货物的重量、数量、长度、体积、容积等计量单位为计征标准而计算征收的关税。计税时以货物的数量（体积、重量）乘以每单位应纳税金额即可得出该货物的关税税额。一般情况下，一国根据其进出口税则，分别对不同税目下的商品按本国通用的计量单位制订出其每单位应纳税金额。

从量关税的计算公式为：从量关税税额＝货物数量×每单位关税税费（每单位应纳税金额）。

(2) 从价关税

从价关税是指按照货物的价格为标准征收的税种，其关税税率为货物价格的一定百分比。从价关税税额等于货物总值乘以从价关税税率。

从价关税的计算公式为：从价关税税额＝进口完税价格/出口完税价格×从价关税税率。

(3) 复合关税

复合税是对某种进口商品混合使用从价关税和从量关税的一种关税计征方法。

(4) 选择关税

即选择从量关税和从价关税两者中的较高者来征收。

9.2.2 关税的种类

关税一般可分为四种。

(1) 进口税

进口税是最普遍的一种关税，也是一个国家关税收入的主要来源。在我国，进口关税设置有最惠国税率、协定税率、特惠税率、普通税率、关税配额税率等多种税率。对进口货物在一定期限内可以实行暂定税率。

原产于共同适用最惠国待遇条款的世界贸易组织成员国或地区的进口货物，原产于与中华人民共和国签订含有相互给予最惠国待遇条款的双边贸易协定的国家或者地区的进口货物，以及原产于中华人民共和国境内的进口货物，适用最惠国税率。

原产于与中华人民共和国签订含有关税优惠条款的区域性贸易协定的国家或者地区的进口货物，适用协定税率。

原产于与中华人民共和国签订含有特殊关税优惠条款的贸易协定的国家或者地区的进口

货物，适用特惠税率。

原产于非上述国家或地区进口货物以及原产地不明的进口货物，适用普通税率。

(2) 出口税

发达国家很少采用，但发展中国家偶尔会采用，以增加政府收入。在某些情况下，征收出口关税旨在限制战略物资和资源（如稀土）的出口。在特定期限内，对出口货物可实行暂定税率。

(3) 过境税

过境税是一国对通过其边境的外国货物征收的关税。

(4) 进口附加税

进口附加税是指一个国家根据一定的目的，对某些进口货物在征收正常进口关税的基础上另行加征的进口关税。征收进口附加税通常是一种特殊的临时措施，进口附加税通常包括反补贴税和反倾销税。

9.3 China Customs

9.3.1 Introduction to the General Administration of Customs

The General Administration of Customs of the People's Republic of China (GACC), the headquarters of China Customs, is a key border agency of the nation. Following government restructuring in 2018, China Customs has 100000 staff nationwide, mainly responsible for traditional customs supervision, border health checks, inspection and quarantine for imported and exported animals and plants and their products, import and export food safety, and commodity inspection. Besides GACC in Beijing, Customs offices are also set up at international ports and at places where customs control operations are concentrated. GACC oversees 42 Customs districts which operate through a total of 678 Customs units nationwide. GACC has a Guangdong branch located in Guangzhou, responsible for regional coordination.

Under the General Administration of Customs, there are 17 departments and 6 directly subordinate service or coordinating agencies. GACC manages 2 associations (Customs Institute of China, China Society for Import and Export Biosafety), and has offices in the EU, Russia and the US.

China Customs exercises a centralized management structure. The Customs offices exercise their functions and powers independently in accordance with the law, and are responsible for GACC. Customs districts report to GACC instead of local governments.

9.3.2 Main Responsibilities of China Customs

(1) Customs Revenue Collection

Customs levies duties and taxes on Entry-exit goods and articles in accordance with the Customs Law of the People's Republic of China and the Import & Export tariff schedule.

(2) Cracking Down on Smuggling

Customs anti-smuggling refers to the law enforcement of the Customs, using both criminal and administrative means to curb, repress and dispose of smuggling activities and crimes at Customs control areas and prescribed coastal or border areas where Customs office is established.

(3) Customs Supervision

Broadly, Customs has specific rules and regulations on the supervision and control over the transportation vehicles, goods and articles entering or leaving China's customs territory.

These rules and regulations mainly include the following contents:

The Entry-exit goods must enter or leave the territory through places established by the Customs and be subject to the supervision and control of the Customs.

The customs clearance formalities for Entry-exit goods must be gone through by a declarant authorized by the Customs. The declarant must be hired by a Customs-registered declaration company.

Unless specially approved by the Customs, exported goods must be declared to the Customs 24 hours before being shipped out. The imported goods must be declared to the Customs within 14 days from the date on which the transportation vehicle is declared to the Customs to enter the territory. The Customs may impose a fee for delayed declaration on the import goods declared in an overdue period.

The licenses for Entry-exit goods and other approval documents must be submitted for those goods restricted by the nation.

The Import & Export goods must be checked and verified by the Customs.

During the period of supervision and control over the I&E goods by the Customs, any corporation or individual is prohibited to load, unload, move, deliver, take out, open, refit, switch, mortgage, transfer the goods or change any signs without the permission of the Customs.

The operators in charge of Customs supervision warehouses must go through the formalities of receiving, storage and shipping. If goods under Customs control are stored outside the scope of Customs control, Customs approval must be obtained.

All kinds of bonded, duty-free, temporarily I& E goods must be filed for record, examined and approved by the Customs.

(4) Audit-based Customs Control

① Time limit of Audit-based Customs control.

within 3 years upon the release of general I&E goods;

within the time limit of Customs control over bonded goods;

within the time limit of Customs control over import goods with reduced or exempted duties.

② Customs verification

Customs has the right to verify the accounting books, accounting documents, Customs declaration documents, and relevant I&E goods of the legal entities so as to supervise the truthfulness and legitimacy of their import & export activities.

(5) Customs Statistics

Customs conducts statistics compilation and comprehensive analysis of such items as the description, quantity, weight, price, country (region) of origin, legal entity, destination, domestic place of origin, trade method, transport means and relevant Customs districts (offices) of the import and export goods. Customs collects, sorts and processes Import & Export declaration documents so as to accurately reflect the tendency of foreign trade, conduct early warning and monitoring, and provide information for national macro-economic decision-making and the development of foreign trade.

(6) Port Management

Currently, there are 253 first-class ports across our country, the opening of which must be approved by the central government. According to the statistics of the Integrated Clearance Project (involving such nodes as Customs, quarantine, shipment, loading and unloading), the clearance time for import and export sea cargo is usually about 24 hours, for air freight around a dozen hours and for urgent goods such as fresh or perishable commodities several hours on average. For vehicles and passengers traveling between Guangdong and Hong Kong as well as between Guangdong and Macao, the total clearance time is normally no more than 1 hour for vehicles and no more than 30 minutes for passengers.

(7) Customs Legal Framework

China Customs has strengthened Customs protection of domestic independent intellectual property rights and supported export of products to promote the overseas development of enterprises with independent brands. In addition, China Customs adopts such means as arbitration and mediation to settle the administrative and enforcement disputes.

(8) Science and Technology

The application of science and technology is an important foundation of Customs' operations. "Building a smart Customs with science and technology" in its daily work has become the crucial strategy of China Customs. It has basically established an application pattern of E-Customs, E-Port and E-General Administration.

9.3.3 Essential Missions of China Customs

China Customs takes on four main missions in the supervision and control over the Import & Export goods:

1) To exercise supervision and control over inward and outward goods and transport vehicles, passenger's luggage and personal postal articles.

2) To collect Customs duties, taxes and fees.

3) To prevent and suppress smuggling.

4) To compile Customs statistics and deal with other Customs matters.

Customs supervision and control is the basic mission of the Customs, and other missions are carried out on this basis.

9.3 中国海关

9.3.1 中国海关总署简介

中华人民共和国海关总署（GACC）是中国海关的总部，是国家重要的边境管理机构。2018 年，中国海关在全国范围内拥有 10 万名工作人员，主要负责传统海关监管、边境卫生检查、进出口动植物及其产品检验检疫、进出口食品安全、商检等工作。除北京海关总署外，国家在对外开放口岸和海关监管业务集中的地点设立海关。目前，海关总署下辖 42 个关区，在全国设有 678 个海关单位，在广州设有广东分署，负责区域协调工作。

海关总署下设 17 个部门和 6 个直属服务或协调机构，管理着 2 个协会（中国海关研究所、中国进出口生物安全学会），并在欧盟、俄罗斯和美国设有办事机构。

中国海关（机构运行）实行垂直领导体制。海关机构依法独立行使职权，对海关总署负责。关区不向地方政府申报，而是向海关总署申报。

9.3.2 中国海关总署的工作职责

(1) 征收关税

海关对进出口货物及物品，依照《中华人民共和国海关法》和进出口关税表规定征收关税。

(2) 打击走私

海关缉私是指海关在海关管制区和沿海沿边海关规定地区，采取刑事、行政手段，遏制、制止和处置走私活动和犯罪的执法活动。

(3) 海关监管

广义上讲，海关对进出境运输工具、货物、物品的监督管理有具体的规章制度。这些规章制度主要包括以下内容：

进出口货物必须通过海关设立的场所进出境，接受海关监管。

进出口货物必须由海关授权的报关员办理报关手续。报关员必须受雇于海关注册的报关公司。

出口货物除海关特准外，必须在装船前 24 小时向海关申报。进口货物应当自运输工具向海关申报进境之日起 14 日内向海关申报。海关可以对逾期申报的进口货物征收滞报费。

属于国家限制进出口货物的，应当提交进出口许可证和其他批准文件。

进出口货物必须经海关查验、核销。

在进出口货物接受海关监管期间，未经海关许可，任何单位或者个人不得装卸、搬运、交付、携带、打开、改装、调换、抵押、转让货物或者改变货物标志。

海关监管仓库负责人必须办理接收、储存、发货手续。在海关监管范围以外存放海关监管货物的，必须经海关同意。

各类保税、免税、临时进出口货物必须经海关备案记录、检查和批准。

(4) 基于审计的海关监管

① 海关稽核管制时限

进出口货物放行后 3 年内；

在海关保税货物监管期限内；

在海关减征或者免征进口货物监管期限内。

② 海关核查

海关有权对被稽查人的会计账簿、会计凭证、报关单证及有关进出口货物进行核查，以监督被稽查人进出口活动的真实性和合法性。

(5) 海关统计

海关需对进出口货物的品名、数量、重量、价格、原产国（地区）、法人、国内目的地、国内原产地、贸易方式、运输方式及有关关区（所）等项目进行统计汇编和综合分析。海关对核定的进出口报关单进行收集、整理、加工，用以全面、准确地反映外贸走势，进行早期预警监测，并为国家宏观经济决策和外贸发展提供信息服务。

(6) 港口管理

目前，全国有 253 个一级口岸，其口岸开放必须经过中央政府批准。根据一体化清关方案（涉及的节点有海关、检疫、装卸），海运进出口货物的清关时间通常是 24 小时，空运清关大约十几个小时（鲜活商品等的紧急货物平均几小时）。来往粤港、粤澳两地的车辆和旅客，正常通关时间车辆不超过 1 小时，旅客不超过 30 分钟。

(7) 海关法律框架

中国海关加强对国内自主知识产权的海关保护，支持产品出口以促进自主品牌企业的海外发展。此外，中国海关还采用仲裁、调解等方式解决行政执法纠纷。

(8) 科学与技术

科学技术的应用是海关业务的重要基础。在日常工作中“用科技构建智慧海关”已成为中国海关的战略，基本形成了“电子海关、电子口岸、电子总局”的应用模式。

9.3.3 中国海关总署的工作使命

中国海关在对进口货物的监管中担负着四大任务：

1）监督管理进出境货物和运输工具，旅客行李及个人邮递物品。

2）征收关税、税费。

3）防止、制止走私活动。

4）编制海关统计和办理其他海关事务。

海关监管是海关的核心任务，其他使命均在此基础上履行。

9.4 Procedures of Import and Export Clearance

9.4.1 Declaration

The term “declaration” means that consignees or consignors of the I&E goods or their designated customs declaration agents are required to declare to Customs about the actual situation of the I&E goods and accept the verification of Customs in the specified period and location by submitting electronic or paper Customs declaration forms in accordance with the Customs Law and other relevant administrative regulations.

The consignees of Import goods or their customs declaration agents shall declare to Customs within 14 days after the date when customs declaration is made for the arrival of conveyance. Customs may, in accordance with the Measures of the General Administration of Customs of the People's Republic of China for Charging Delayed Declaration Fees for Import Goods, charge a delayed declaration fee against the party who fails to declare to Customs within the specified period. The consignors of Export goods or their customs declaration agents shall declare to Customs after the goods arrive at the Customs control area but 24 hours before being loaded on board the vessel.

The date of declaration refers to the day when the declared data is accepted by Customs. No matter in what form the declaration is submitted, either electronically or in paper form, the date when the declared data is accepted by Customs is deemed as the date of declaration.

In the case of electronic declaration, the date of declaration shall be the day when the declared data is accepted by the computer system of Customs with the acceptance date recorded automatically, which is then notified to the enterprise that presents the data, or published at the operational site of the Customs or through public information system.

In the case of paper declaration, the date of declaration shall be the day when Customs accepts the paper declaration form and makes a record of the declaration.

The declaration is regarded as being refused by Customs when the electronic declaration form is returned by the computer system of Customs after examination. Consignees or Consignors of the I&E goods or their customs declaration agents shall immediately modify the declaration forms and make the re-declaration as is required, with the date of declaration being the day when the Customs accepts the re-declaration.

If it is necessary to modify part of the electronic data of the declaration forms which has been accepted by the Customs after the forms are sent to manual examination, consignees or consignors of the I&E goods or their customs declaration agents shall adjust and re-submit the electronic data as is required, and the declaration date shall be the date on which the Customs originally accepted the declaration.

When consignees or consignors of the I&E goods or their customs declaration agents go to the operational sites of Customs for procedures including declaration, payment of customs duties and other taxes and fees, as well as examination and release of goods, they need to submit paper declaration forms consistent with the contents of electronic declaration forms, Import and Export Licenses and other documents required by the Customs.

The documents attached to the customs declaration form for the I&E goods include:

1) Contract;

2) Commercial Invoice;

3) Packing List;

4) Manifest;

5) Bill of Lading (air waybill, railway bill, etc.);

6) Power of Attorney for Customs declaration;

7) Import License or Export License;

8) Manual for Processing Trade required by Customs (in the form of paper or electronic data) and other documents relating to import and export.

9.4.2 Customs Inspection

All import and export goods are subject to customs inspection, and more often in the form of sampling inspection. While the examination is being carried out, the consignees of import goods, the consignors of export goods, or their forwarders have to be present and be responsible for moving the goods and opening and restoring the package. The Customs is entitled to examine or re-examine the goods or take samples from them without the presence of the consignee or the consignor whenever Customs considers this necessary.

(1) Customs Inspection

The inspection is jointly conducted by two or more Customs officials/inspectors. The inspectors ought to wear customs uniforms when conducting the inspection. The inspection is conducted within an area under Customs' supervision. If the inspection is unfit to be conducted within Customs control areas because the goods can be easily affected by temperature, static electricity, dust or any other natural factor, or the inspection needs to be conducted outside Customs control areas due to any other special factor, Customs may assign officials to carry out inspection outside Customs control area upon written application of the consignee/consignor or his forwarder. When carrying out the inspection, Customs officials may conduct either thorough inspection or selective inspection. The inspection may be divided into manual inspection and machine inspection, and the former can be further divided into inspection of the exterior packing and inspection by package opening. Customs may determine the specific inspection methods to be used according to the conditions of the goods and the actual enforcement requirements.

Customs, before carrying out the inspection, usually asks the consignees or consignors or their forwarders thereof to be present. They are responsible for moving goods, removing and re-sealing the package of goods as requested by Customs, and to faithfully answer the inquiries of inspectors and provide necessary materials.

(2) Customs Re-inspection

In any of the following circumstances, Customs may re-inspect those goods that have been inspected:

1) The true nature of goods has not been identified upon the first inspection, and it is necessary to further determine some characteristics of the goods that have been inspected;

2) The goods are suspected of being involved in a case of smuggling, and it is necessary to conduct a new inspection;

3) The consignee or consignor of the I&E goods holds objection to the inspection conclusion issued by Customs and requests re-inspection and the requests have been approved by Customs;

4) Any other circumstance under which a new inspection is necessary as required by Customs.

The re-inspection follows the above-mentioned steps, and Customs officials will mark "re-inspection" on the inspection records. Those officials who participated in the first inspection are not allowed to take part in the reinspection of the same goods.

9.4.3 Duty Payment

The duty payer shall pay the duties at a designated bank within 15 days after the date of issuance of the Memorandum of Duty Payment by Customs. In case of any payment in arrears, 0.05% of the total amount of the overdue duties shall be charged as a fine for late payment per day from the date when the delayed payment occurs.

The Customs may publish the information about the arrearages on duties by duty payers.

The Customs shall issue a duty-memo for duties collected or receipt for fines for late payment. The format of the duty-memo or receipt is prescribed by the General Administration of Customs.

The customs value of import goods is the CIF price based on normal transaction price approved by the Customs, which contains the value of the goods, the costs of international transport, charges associated with international transport, and the cost of international insurance incurred prior to the unloading of such goods at the port or place of entry within the Customs territory of the People's Republic of China.

As for export goods, the customs value shall be the FOB price of the goods sold abroad as determined by the Customs after deducting the export duty/tax. The calculation formula is as follows.

Customs value of export goods＝FOB price/(1＋export duty rate)

9.4.4 Customs Release

Except the special approval of Customs, import and export goods shall be released only after the passing of Customs inspection, the payment of customs duties or the provision of guarantees. Take import goods as an example: The importer needs to pay duties and taxes to the bank designated by the Customs; The bank should stamp on the duty memorandum testifying the payment; At the Customs hall, the importer should present the duty memorandum stamped by the bank, and the Customs shall return to the importer the customs declaration form stamped with the customs release seal and the accompanying documents after careful verification.

As far as common goods are concerned, Customs release means the end of customs supervision. The consignees can dispose import goods freely while export goods can be shipped on board the vessels. But as for goods released under guarantee, bonded goods, temporarily imported goods as well as goods of duty reduction or exemption, Customs release does not mean the completion of Customs clearance formalities. Only after going through the formalities, including verification, close of declaration, and payment of customs duties, is the Customs clearance of the above-mentioned special types of import goods accomplished.

9.4 进出口通关业务程序

9.4.1 申报

申报指进出口货物的收、发货人或其报关代理向海关呈送规定的单证（可以书面或电子交换方式）以申报进出口货物的真实信息，并在特定时间和区域接受海关查验、放行的手续。

进口货物的收货人或其报关代理人应在运输工具进境之日期 14 天之内向海关申请报关。据海关总署的相关规定，海关对延期申报进口的货主征收滞报金。出口货物的发货人或其报关代理人应当在货物运抵海关监管区后，装船前 24 小时向海关申请出口报关。

申报日期指的是海关接受申报的日期。不管是纸质申报还是电子申报，均以海关接受申报数据的时间作为申报日期。电子申报时，申报日期为海关计算机系统接受申报数据时记录的日期，将该日期反馈给原数据发送单位，或公布于海关业务现场，或通过公共信息系统发布。纸质申报时，申报日期是海关接受纸质申报单并对申报进行登记的日期。

若电子数据报关单经过海关计算机检查并被退回，视为海关不接受申报。进出口收发货人、受委托的报关代理应当按照要求修改后重新申报，申报日期为海关接受重新申报的日期。

海关已接受申报的报关单电子数据送人工审核后，需要对部分内容进行修改的，进出口货物收发货人或其报关代理人应当按照海关规定进行修改并重新发送，申报日期为海关原接受申报的日期。

进出口货物的收、发货人或其报关代理去海关办理申报、交纳关税及其他税费，查验货物、放行货物手续时，需要提交纸质申报单，进出口许可证及海关需要的其他文件。

进出口货物申报时需要提交的单据如下：

1）合同；

2）发票；

3）装箱单；

4）载货单；

5）海运提单（或航空运单、铁路运单等）；

6）代理报关委托书；

7）进口许可证或出口许可证；

8）加工贸易手册（纸质或电子）以及其他相关单证。

9.4.2 海关查验

所有的进出口货物都要接受海关的查验，更多的是抽检形式。查验时，进口货物的收货人、出口货物的发货人或其货运代理必须在现场，并负责搬运货物、打开和恢复包装。海关认为必要时，可以在收、发货人不在场的情况下，对货物进行复验或者提取货样。

(1) 海关查验

海关查验由至少2名海关人员共同完成，查验一般在海关监管场所进行。检查人员进行检查时，应当身着海关制服。在特殊情况下，经进出口收、发货人或其货代申请，海关审核同意，也可派员到规定的时间和场所以外的工厂、仓库或施工工地查验货物。海关实施查验可以是彻底查验，也可以是抽查。查验操作可以分为人工查验和设备查验，其中人工查验又可分为外形查验和开包验货。海关可以根据货物情况以及实际执法需要，确定具体的查验方式。

海关查验时，货物的收、发货人或其货代必须到场，并按海关的要求负责办理货物的搬移、拆装箱和重封货物的包装等工作。他们还需如实回答海关的提问并提供必要的材料。

(2) 海关复验

在下列任何情况发生时，海关可对查验过的货物进行复验。

1）经初次查验未能查明货物的真实属性，需要对已查验货物的某些性状做进一步确认的；

2）货物涉嫌走私违规，需要重新查验的；

3）进出口货物收发货人对海关查验结论有异议，提出复验要求并经海关同意的；

4）海关要求重新检验的其他情形。

复检按照上述查验步骤进行，海关人员将在检查记录上标注“复检”字样。参加初检的官员不得参加同一批货物的复检。

9.4.3 交纳关税

纳税义务人应当自海关填发税款缴款书之日起15日内向指定银行缴纳税款。纳税义务人未按期缴纳税款的，从滞纳税款之日起，按日加收滞纳税款万分之五的滞纳金。海关可以对纳税义务人欠缴税款的情况予以公告。

海关征收关税、滞纳金等，应当制发缴款凭证，缴款凭证格式由海关总署规定。

进口货物的完税价格是以海关审定的正常交易价格为基础的到岸价格（即CIF价），包括货物的货价，货物运抵我国境内输入地点起卸前的国际运输费及其相关费用、国际保险费。

对于出口货物，应当以海关审定的货物售予境外的离岸价格（即FOB价），扣除出口税后，作为其完税价格。计算公式如下。

出口货物完税价格＝FOB价/(1＋出口税率)

9.4.4 海关放行

除经海关特别批准的外，进出口货物在通过海关查验、缴纳完关税或提供担保后将被放行。以进口货物为例：进口商需要向海关指定的银行缴纳关税，银行应在关税专用缴款书上盖章；在海关大厅，进口商应出示银行盖章的关税专用缴款书，海关经仔细查证后返给进口商盖有海关放行章的报关单及随附单据。

对于一般贸易货物来说，放行表示海关监管结束，进境货物可以由收货人自由处置，出境货物可以由发货人装船出运。但是，对于担保放行货物、保税货物、暂时进口货物和海关给予减免税进口的货物来说，放行并不等于办结海关手续，还要在办理核销、结案或者补办进出口和纳税手续后，才能结关。

Part B Vocabulary and Terminology 词汇和术语

commodity inspection 商品检验
Customs declaration 申报
Customs inspection 海关查验
Customs release 海关放行
Customs value 完税价格
import duty 进口税
export duty 出口税
transit duty 过境税
import surcharge surtax 进口附加税
specific tariff 从量税
Ad valorem tariff 从价税
compound (or mixed) tariff 复合税
selective tariff 选择税

Part C Exercise 练习

Ⅰ. 某贸易公司于 2007 年 5 月 11 日周五申报进口一批货物，海关于当日开出税款缴款书。其中关税税款为人民币 24000 元，增值税税款为人民币 35100 元，消费税税款为人民币 18900 元。该公司实际缴纳税款日期为 6 月 7 日周四。计算该公司应缴纳的滞纳金。

Ⅱ. 杭州市某中外合资企业向其合资外方在境外的母公司进口属自动许可管理的纺织机械设备 10 台，成交总价为每台 1200 美元 CIFD Less 3% SHANGHAI，即 3%数量折扣价。合同规定折扣款在买方付款时自行扣除，若买方将该进口设备转售给其他企业则应从获取的利润中返回 10%给卖方。装载该货物的船舶于 2007 年 12 月 2 日申报进境，进口货物收货人于 12 月 8 日向海关申报。海关在审核完税价格时认为买卖双方存在特殊关系，不能用成交价格作为完税价格，决定采用上个月进口的与该货物型号完全相同的机械设备的成交价格每台 1320 美元作为完税价格。该进口货物按从价税征收进口关税税率为 10%，进口环节增值税税率为 17%，海关计征汇率为 1 美元=7.48 人民币元。根据上述情况请回答下列问题。

1. 若进口货物收货人在（ ）之后向海关申报，则海关应当加收滞报金。

A. 12 月 14 日 B. 12 月 15 日 C. 12 月 16 日 D. 12 月 17 日

2. 根据我国《进出口关税条例》的规定这批货物应按（ ）征收进口关税。

A. 一般进口货物 B. 特殊进口货物 C. 法定免税进口货物 D. 外资设备物品

3. 海关对纳税义务人所申报的价格表示怀疑应当首先采用（ ）要求纳税义务人提供资料以证明其申报价格的真实性。

A. 司法程序 B. 仲裁程序 C. 价格质疑程序 D. 价格磋商程序

4. 假如该进口货物确实以“每台 1200 美元 CIFD Less 3% SHANGHAI”成交，除买方向其代理人支付了 360 美元的购货佣金外无其他任何瓜葛。海关决定以该成交价格来估定完税价格，估价时不应计入的是（ ）。

A. 保险费 B. 购货佣金 C. 海运运费 D. 折扣款

5. 若海关以“相同货物成交价格法”审定完税价格，纳税义务人对该批进口货物总计应缴纳的进口税额是（ ）。

A. 8736.00 元 B. 9873.60 元 C. 8463.63 元 D. 28337.23 元

Ⅲ. Translate the following passages into Chinese.

The term “declaration” means that consignees or consignors of the I&E goods or their designated customs declaration agents are required to declare to Customs about the actual situation of the I&E goods and accept the verification of Customs in the specified period and location by submitting electronic or paper Customs declaration forms in accordance with the Customs Law and other relevant administrative regulations.

The consignees of import goods or their customs declaration agents shall declare to Customs within 14 days after the date when customs declaration is made for the arrival of conveyance. Customs may, in accordance with the Measures of the General Administration of Customs of the People's Republic of China for Charging Delayed Declaration Fees for import Goods, charge a delayed declaration fee against the party who fails to declare to Customs within the specified period.

Ⅳ. Answer the following questions.

1. What are the major ways of imposing tariff?

2. What is the definition of MFN tariff rate? What goods does it apply to?

3. Please describe how to calculate the customs value of import goods.

4. What are the commonly used ways of stipulating the place and time of inspection in the contract?

5. What is Customs Declaration? What is the time limit for Customs Declaration of export goods?

Chapter Ten

International Cargo Insurance 国际货物保险

Part A Text 课文

10.1 A Brief Introduction to International Cargo Insurance

10.1.1 Development of International Insurance

International insurance is a new mechanism, which combines, diversifies, and shifts risk by scientific calculation in global scope. Meanwhile, international insurance is also involved in insurance cooperation and loss sharing.

The limited insurance technique and risk bearing ability in contrast to relative market surplus and saturation is a distinct characteristic of international insurance market.

The overall development of insurance industry is comprehensively reflected by: design and adjustment of insurance coverage; financing method and loss control; coinsurance, insurance integration, cooperation, merger and restructuring in international insurance market; risk and obligation assumption, and so on. Insurance market is also constrained by law of supply and demand, together with competition within the industry. The clauses and premium taken by developed countries are often used as references in the industry. The insurance principles of fairness, timeliness, reasonableness and stabilization are perquisites on which premium rate is determined.

International insurance provides long term and stable services for international investment, international trade, international shipping, and international credit, helping to minimize the risks in these industries. As one of the business domains in global economy, international insurance develops together with other industries such as international shipping. In summary, international insurance is closely interlinked with international trade and transportation.

10.1.2 Insurable Risk and Insurable Interest

From law viewpoint, insurance is a compensatory contract behavior, i. e. , the insurer is responsible for indemnifying the insured for any possible future loss within the insurance coverage, at premium paid by the insured. In international logistics, cargo is subject to various risks and losses, insurance companies are not to insure all the risks or indemnify for all the losses. Therefore, the risk and loss in international logistics insurance have specified meaning. Only after the applicant comprehends the content of risk and loss involved can he understand the obligations incurred in various coverages and consequently arrange appropriate insurance coverage.

(1) Insurable Risk

Risk is a probability or threat of damage, injury, liability, loss, or any other negative occurrence that is caused by external or internal vulnerabilities, and that may be avoided through preemptive action. There are pure risk and speculative risk.

Pure risk is a category of risk in which loss is the only possible outcome; there is no beneficial result. Pure risk is related to events that are beyond the risk taker's control, e. g., stranding of the vessel and fire to the cargo, where owner of vessel and cargo are only subject to loss.

Speculative risk, on the other hand, could lead to loss or benefit. This risk induces some people to take possible risk of loss in expectation for possible future financial gains.

Not every risk could be safeguarded in the way of insurance. Insurable risk is the risk acceptable to the insurer. For a risk to be insurable, several things need to be true:

1) The insurer must be able to charge a premium high enough to cover not only claims expenses, but also his expenses. In other words, the risk cannot be catastrophic, or so large that no insurer would like to pay for the loss.

2) The nature of the loss must be definite and financially measurable. That is, there should be no room for argument of payment or amount of payment.

3) The loss should be random in nature, else the insured may engage in adverse selection (anti-selection).

(2) Insurable Interest

Insurable interest is true, valid, determinable, and direct economic stake of an insurance policy holder (or beneficiary of the policy) in the continued existence or safety of the insured property or person. An insurable interest means that the policy holder (or the beneficiary) must stand to suffer a direct financial loss if the event (against which the insurance cover was bought) does occur. A person has an insurable interest in something when loss of or damage to that thing would cause the person to suffer a financial or other kind of loss. Typically, insurable interest is established by ownership, possession, or direct relationship. In marine cargo insurance, the owner, carrier and other parties who have real interest in the goods are all parties with insurable interest. That is to say, the value in cargo, freight, premium, expected profit, seller's interest, and commission can all be insured as insurance benefit by insurance company.

10.1.3 Function of International Logistics Insurance

The fundamental function of international logistics insurance is to set up insurance fund and compensate economic loss. In long distance transport, cargo is subject to loss from natural calamities or fortuitous accidents. The Owner of the cargo needs to arrange cargo transport insurance to transfer risk of such loss. Therefore, cargo insurance arrangement is an economic method for cargo owners to fight against natural calamities and fortuitous accidents. The cargo transport insurance is:

(1) Beneficial to Smooth Operation

Under market economy, companies independently bear all risks and obligations rising from their operation. When organizing international transport for cargo, a company may have to face greater risks due to calamities and/or accidents, which could lead to loss in great amount. Without appropriate compensation method, the company's operation will be greatly endangered. To insure the cargo in international transport is in essence to convert uncertain risk to certain expenditure (i. e. insurance premium), which is beneficial to the company's smooth operation.

(2) Helpful to International Logistics and Trade Promotion

In international trade, the importer and exporter are in great distance. During the transport, goods are exposed to loss from calamities. For this reason, all transactions should be covered by cargo insurance, which assists in promoting international logistics and international trade.

(3) Beneficial to Foreign Currency Revenue Increase

When seller is responsible for arranging insurance in an export, foreign currency earnings are increased. The premium income in foreign exchange is one important non-trade foreign exchange earnings for one independent country. In an import transaction, on the other hand, foreign exchange is saved if the buyer is to arrange insurance.

(4) Helpful to Calamities and Loss Prevention

For sake of his own benefit, insurance company is willing to participate in preventing calamities and loss. In handling the cases of compensation, insurance company may find out the reasons for and laws of calamities and thereby more effectively manage risks in international logistics. Furthermore, in some insurance contract, it is regulated that insurer be entitled to scrutinizing the safety of cargo. The insured should immediately apply countermeasures to eradicate potential hazard should any vulnerability be found out, failing to do so will incur corresponding responsibility on the part of the insured. This practice will subjectively improve the work of calamities and loss prevention.

10.1 国际货物保险概述

10.1.1 国际保险的发展

在全球范围内通过科学测算，从而起到组合、分散、转嫁经济风险作用并成为一种新的机制被称之为“国际保险”，同时国际保险又承担着保险合作、损失分担的义务。

保险技术、承担能力的局限和市场相对过剩、饱和成为当前国际保险业市场的显著特征。国际保险险种设计、调整；融资方式、损失控制等环节；国际保险中联合承保以及保险一体化、保险市场融通、合作、跨国性兼并、重组；保险活动中风险承担、责任划分等方面都是保险业内部整体发展水平的综合性反映。同时，保险市场又时刻受制于市场供需矛盾和业内之间的相互竞争，发达国家保险条款和费率通常作为行业间参照的依据所在。公平、适时、合理、稳定的保险原则成为制定费率的基本要素与条件。

国际保险的发展伴随着相关产业和行业以及保险业内部的同步成长和发展，因而它是一种非独立性的，与外界保持紧密关系的发展。国际保险为国际投资、国际贸易、国际航运、国际信用等方面提供长期、稳定的服务，从而使这些行业风险降低至最低程度。作为全球经济领域的一个分支，国际保险的发展伴随着其他行业的发展，比如国际贸易及国际航运业等。由此可见，国际保险与国际贸易、国际运输具有不可分割的紧密关系。

10.1.2 可保风险与可保利益

从法律角度看，保险是一种补偿性的契约行为，即保险人向被保险人提供一定的保险费，保险人则对被保险人将来可能遭受的承保范围内的损失负有赔偿责任。货物在国际物流和运输过程中可能遭遇各种风险和各种损失，保险公司并不是对所有风险都给予承保，也不是对一切损失都予以赔偿。因此国际物流保险中的“风险”和“损失”有特定的含义，投保人只有先弄清“风险”和“损失”的内容，才能正确理解各种险别的责任，而后方能有针对性地办理投保业务。

(1) 可保风险

风险是由于外部或内部的不确定性而导致的损坏、伤害、责任、损失或其他负面结果发生的可能性或威胁。风险可能通过预防性措施得以避免。风险分为纯粹风险和投机风险两类。

纯粹风险是指只有损失可能而无获利机会的风险。该风险超出承担人的控制范围，例如海轮发生触礁、货物遭受火灾的风险，船东和货主只会遭受经济损失，而不会有利益可得。

投机风险是指既可能遭受损失，也可能产生收益的风险。这种风险带有一定的诱惑性，可能会使某些人为了获利而甘冒这种可能损失的风险。

风险的种类有很多，但并不是说所有的风险都可以通过保险进而转嫁并取得保障的。可保风险是指保险人可以接受承保的风险。一般情况下，保险人接受承保的风险必须具备如下的条件。

1）保险人需能收取高额保费以弥补索赔费用及保险人的开支。换句话说，风险不能太过严重或巨大，否则没有人愿意对损失进行偿付。

2）损失必须确定并且可衡量。也就是说是否该偿付以及偿付多少的问题上双方不应有争议。

3）损失需是随机的，否则被保险人可能进行逆向选择。

(2) 可保利益

可保利益是保单持有人（或受益人）在被保险财产或被保险人持续存在或安全的情况下而拥有的真实、有效、可确定的直接经济利益。可保利益意味着保单持有人（或受益人）在意外事件（凭此意外购买保险）发生时要蒙受直接财物损失。当某物的丢失或损坏会对某人造成财务或其他方面的损失时，此人对此事物便拥有可保利益。一般地说，可保利益来自对事物的所有权、占有权或其他直接关系。在海洋运输保险中，对货物拥有实际利益的货主、承运人或其他参与方都对货物拥有可保利益。也就是说，货物的价值、运费、保费、预期利润、卖方的利息以及佣金都可以作为保险利益而通过保险公司进行保险。

10.1.3 国际货物保险的作用

建立保险基金，补偿经济损失，是国际货物运输保险的基本职能。由于国际货物都要经过长途运输，在整个运输过程中，货物可能遭遇自然灾害或意外事故而遭受损失，货主为了转嫁货物在运输过程中的风险损失，就需要办理货物运输保险。可见，办理货物运输保险，是货主同自然灾害和意外事故做斗争的经济措施。在国际物流中，货物运输保险的作用主要表现在以下几个方面。

(1) 有利于企业经营的正常进行

在市场经济条件下，企业独立承担经营活动中的一切风险和责任。企业在组织货物的国际运输过程中，通常存在较大的风险，很可能因自然灾害和意外事故的发生而遭受损失。若没有适当的补救措施，就可能影响企业经营的正常进行，甚至危及企业的生存。企业对国际物流运输中的货物进行保险实际上是将由此产生的不确定性的风险转化为确定的费用开支(保险费)，从而有利于企业经营的正常进行。

(2) 有助于国际物流和国际贸易的顺利开展

在国际贸易和国际物流中，买卖双方所在的国家相距遥远，进出口货物在运输过程中，容易因灾害事故的发生而遭受损失，所以，每笔交易都必须办理货物运输保险。提供货物运输保险有助于推动国际物流和国际贸易的顺利开展。

(3) 可以为国家增加外汇收入

在出口贸易中，尤其是在卖方负责办理保险的交易中，还可以增加出口创汇的能力。就世界范围来看，外汇保费的收入已经成为一个国家一项重要的非贸易外汇收入。在进口贸易中，如由买方在本国自行办理保险，可以为国家节省外汇支出。

(4) 有利于防灾防损工作的开展

防灾防损是减少国际物流成本、提高国际物流效率的有效途径，也是企业与保险公司的共同任务。保险公司从自身利益出发，一般都愿意参与这项工作，因为防灾防损工作做得好，灾害事故就容易减少，经济补偿也随之减少。同时，保险公司在处理为数众多的赔偿案件中，可以找出灾害产生的原因和发生的规律，从而更有力的对国际物流中风险加以管理，并提出改进的建议。此外，有的保险合同还规定，保险人有权对货物的安全情况进行检查，如发现有不安全因素，投保人应及时采取措施消除灾害隐患，否则后果由投保人自行负责，这种做法客观上也能促进防灾防损工作。

10.2 Main Insurance Coverage for International Cargo Insurance

Various transport modes can be adopted in international trade, including ocean transport, inland transport, air transport, and parcel post transport. Accordingly, there are insurance coverages for different modes of transport.

10.2.1 Ocean Transport Cargo Insurance

(1) Scope of Ocean Transport Cargo Insurance Coverage

1) Peril of the Sea: Peril of the sea refers to the risks happening peculiar to the sea, or to where sea meets land, inland water or barge. According to the *Ocean Marine Cargo Insurance Clauses* revised by People's Insurance Company of China in Jan 1st, 1981, the peril of sea includes general perils and extraneous risks.

① General perils of the sea: Natural calamities are one type of general perils of the sea, and accidents are the other.

Natural Calamities are disasters as a result of natural changes, e.g., the loss to the cargo caused by bad weather, lightning, tsunami, earthquake, and flood and so.

Accidents are the result of unforeseeable factors or force majeure, e. g. , stranding, grounding, submergence, collision with vessel or other objects, fire, and explosion and so on.

② Extraneous risks: Extraneous risks refer to the risks caused by reasons other than perils of the sea, which include general extraneous risks and special extraneous risks. General extraneous risks are risks due to theft, rain, leakage, shortages, breakage, dampness, mildewing, heating, taint of odor, hooking and rusting. Special extraneous risks are risks such as wars, hostilities, strikes, rejection of import or confiscation of goods, etc.

2) Maritime Loss and Charges

① Maritime loss: Maritime loss is direct or indirect loss of insured cargo caused by perils of sea during the shipment. Maritime loss includes total loss and partial loss.

(a) Total loss includes actual total loss and constructive total loss. Actual total loss means the insured goods are totally damaged or have been lost or found valueless upon arrival. Constructive total loss occurs when the actual loss of the insured goods is unavoidable, or when the ship or the consignment must be abandoned because the cost of salvage or recovery will exceed the value of the ship and the consignment upon arrival.

(b) Partial loss refers to partial loss of or damage to the insured object, which includes General Average (G. A.) and Particular Average.

General Average (G. A.) is the partial loss resulting from a deliberate act of the ship's master, such as throwing overboard all or part of the cargo to save the ship. In this case, all beneficial parties will share the loss of the specific consignor.

The following premises have to be met to make it a G. A.

Firstly, the vessel is indeed in calamity, which endangers the safety of the vessel and the cargo. The risk is indeed unavoidable rather than from subjective assumption. When losses are caused due to wrong judgment of the ship master or any predictable common events, it doesn't make it a G. A.

Secondly, G. A. sacrifice has to be caused by voluntary and conscious action of human being, rather than accidental loss due to perils of the sea.

Thirdly, the sacrifice and expenses made in G. A. must be reasonable, which should be to the extent that the danger is removed, and the safety is guaranteed. Any power misuse and expansion of expenses are forbidden.

Fourthly, the purpose of G. A. sacrifice and expenses caused is only to protect the safety of ship and cargo.

Fifthly, loss must be directly resulted from General Average actions. For instance, when the vessel is in danger and the action of throwing overboard is taken, there might be water splashing into the cabin, the loss from which belongs to General Average too. G. A. sacrifice and expenses are made for sake of the whole vessel and cargo; consequently, they should be shared pari passu on the value of rescued cargo, which is called G. A. contribution.

Particular Average is the partial loss suffered by the party whose consignment is partially lost or damaged. When the loss or damage occurs, no cargo of other parties has to be sacrificed to save the voyage. An example is the partial damage to the goods caused by water splashing in when the vessel encounters violent storm and roaring waves.

Apart from the above mentioned losses, extraneous risks, such as theft and war, may also lead to loss.

② Maritime charges: Maritime Charges refer to expenses incurred for the rescue of the insured cargo when the ship is in danger, which include sue and labor charges and salvage charges.

Sue and labor charges is the expenses paid to prevent loss expansion when the insured, his agent or employee tries to rescue insured cargo in the event of insurance covered natural calamities and accidents. The insurer is responsible for the remuneration of sue and labor charges.

According to maritime law, salvage charges is the remuneration or reward payable by the saved party to savers who voluntarily and independently of contract render services to successfully rescue or save property at sea. The insurer is responsible for the remuneration of salvage charges. No reward for services or payments for loss or expenses can be claimed by savers where the services were unsuccessful and the property was totally lost. This is called the Principle of "No Cure, No Pay".

(2) Insurance Coverages in Ocean Transport Cargo

Insurance coverages define the obligation of the insurer to bear risks and loss. It is the basis on which the insurer and the insured perform their duties and calculate premium. According to *the Ocean Marine Cargo Clauses of China*, the covers of Chinese ocean marine cargo insurance include basic coverage and additional coverage.

1) Basic coverage: Basic coverage can be independently arranged, instead of being attached to other insurance coverages. There are three basic coverages, namely, Free from Particular Average (FPA), With Particular Average (WA/WPA) and All Risks.

① Free from particular average (FPA): This insurance covers the following loss except particular average loss:

(a) Total or constructive total loss of the whole consignment hereby insured caused in the course of transit by natural calamities: heavy weather, lightning, tsunami, earthquake and flood.

(b) Total or partial loss caused by accidents to the carrying conveyance such as grounding, stranding, sinking or collision with other conveyance, floating ice or other objects, fire or explosion.

(c) Partial loss of the insured goods attributable to heavy weather, lightning and/or tsunami, where the conveyance has been grounded, stranded, sunk or burnt, irrespective of whether the event or events take place before or after such accidents.

(d) Partial or total loss consequent to falling of entire package or packages into sea during loading, transshipment or discharge.

(e) Reasonable cost incurred by the insured on salvaging the goods or averting or minimizing a loss recoverable under the Policy, provided that such cost shall not exceed the sum insured of the consignment.

(f) Losses attributable to discharge of the insured goods at a port of distress following a sea peril as well as special charges arising from loading, warehousing and forwarding of the goods at an intermediate port of call or refuge.

(g) Sacrifice in and contribution to general average and salvage charges.

(h) The loss sustained by the ship owners is to be reimbursed by the Cargo Owner under the Contract of Affreightment Both to Blame Collision Clause.

② With particular average (WA/WPA): WPA covers wider risk than FPA, including particular average loss. Aside from the risks covered under FPA condition as above, this insurance also covers partial losses of the insured goods caused by heavy weather, lightning, tsunami, earthquake and/or flood.

③ All risks: This insurance covers the most widely in these three basic coverages. Aside from the risks covered under FPA and WPA conditions as above, this insurance also covers all risks of loss of or damage to the insured goods, whether partial or total, arising from external causes in the course of transit.

The insured is free to choose from any coverages mentioned above.

2) Additional coverage: Additional coverage makes complement to basic coverages. Different from basic coverages, additional coverage cannot be applied for independently, but has to be attached to at least one of the basic coverages. It covers losses from extraneous risks and involves general additional risks coverage and special additional risks coverage.

① General additional risks coverage: It covers losses caused by general extraneous risks including risk of theft, pilferage and non-delivery (TPND), risk of fresh and/or rain water damage (wetting), risk of shortage in weight/quantity, risk of inter-mixture and contamination, risk of leakage, risk of clash and breakage, risk of taint of odor, risk of sweating and/or heating, risk of hook damage, risk of packing breakage, and risk of rust.

As General Additional Risks coverage is contained in All Risks, no such coverage is needed if All Risks is arranged.

② Special additional risks coverage: Special Additional Risks Coverage deals with risks related to national administrative measure, regulations, and trade conventions, which is excluded from basic coverages and is gained by additional insurance. People's Insurance Company of China covers the following 8 special additional risks coverages:

(a) War risk insurance. War risk insurance is a type of insurance which covers damage due to acts of war, including invasion, insurrection, rebellion and hijacking. Some policies also cover damage due to weapons of mass destruction. It is most commonly used in shipping and aviation industries. War risk insurance generally has two components: War Risk Liability, which covers people and items inside the craft and is calculated based on the indemnity amount; and War Risk Hull, which covers the craft itself and is calculated based on value of the craft. The premium varies based on the expected stability of the countries to which the vessel will travel.

(b) Strike risk insurance. It covers direct losses due to actions taken by strikers and workers forced to suspend working or involved in labor disturbance, riot, or public struggle, and direct losses for reasons of malicious actions, as well as the General Average sacrifice, sharing, and salvage charges.

(c) On deck risk insurance. It covers the losses to the cargo on deck due to insured accidents, throwing overboard or falling into sea.

(d) Failure to deliver risk insurance. This insurance covers the losses caused by failure to deliver the cargo, already loaded on board the vessel, at the destination within six months of scheduled date for arrival due to whatever cause it might be.

(e) Import duty risk insurance. It covers the losses occurring when the insured is still required to pay import duty on the basis of full value of goods after the goods suffered from insured accidents and consequent loss.

(f) Rejection risk insurance. It covers the losses caused when import government or related authorities reject or confiscate the goods for various reasons.

(g) Aflatoxin risk insurance. Within the validity of insurance, if the insured goods are inspected at import port by local health authorities and proved to contain excessive aflatoxin than that limited by import country, they could be rejected, confiscated, or forced to alter their use. The loss caused in this situation is covered by Aflatoxin Risk insurance.

(h) Fire risk extension clause-for storage of cargo at destination Hongkong (including Kowloon) or Macao. If the insured cargo is directly stored in the warehouse named by transfer bank and clarified in the insurance policy after its arrival in Hongkong (including Kowloon) or Macao and unloading from the vessel, the losses from fire in the warehouse is covered by this insurance, till the bank recoups the mortgage and removes his interests on the cargo or 30 days after the expiry of transport liability.

(3) Differences between Institute Cargo Clauses and China Insurance Clauses

At present, China Insurance Clause (C. I. C.) stipulated by the People's Insurance Company of China (PICC) is usually adopted in China's import and export cargo transportation insurance business. However, insurance companies in many countries and regions in the world usually adopt the Institute Cargo Clause (ICC) formulated by the Association of British Insurers in their international Cargo insurance business. There are also three basic insurance covers in Institute Cargo Clauses, namely ICC (A), ICC (B) and ICC (C). According to Institute Cargo Clause (ICC), the obligations covered by the three basic insurance coverages are summarized as following:

1) ICC (A): ICC (A) is basically the same to All Risks, except that it regulates Clauses of Exclusions, meaning that the insurance doesn't cover situation of unseaworthiness or war, or strike.

2) ICC (B): It covers total or partial losses caused by listed natural calamities and accidents, General Average sacrifice, throwing overboard, and splashing of water into vessel, lighter, shipping conveyance, container, large sea-chest, or storage places. The cargo originally covered by FPA is presently covered by ICC (B), if any total loss of the whole piece is incurred when cargo falls into the sea or to the ground during unloading.

3) ICC (C): It only covers the loss caused by accidents (including total loss and partial loss), throwing goods overboard and General Average sacrifice.

The coverage of marine cargo insurance differs between different insurance companies;

the obligation covered may be different too even in the same company. Therefore, when signing an insurance policy, the insured must make sure the name of the insurance company before deciding on appropriate coverage.

The scope and coverages of ocean transport insurance is shown in Figure 10. 1.

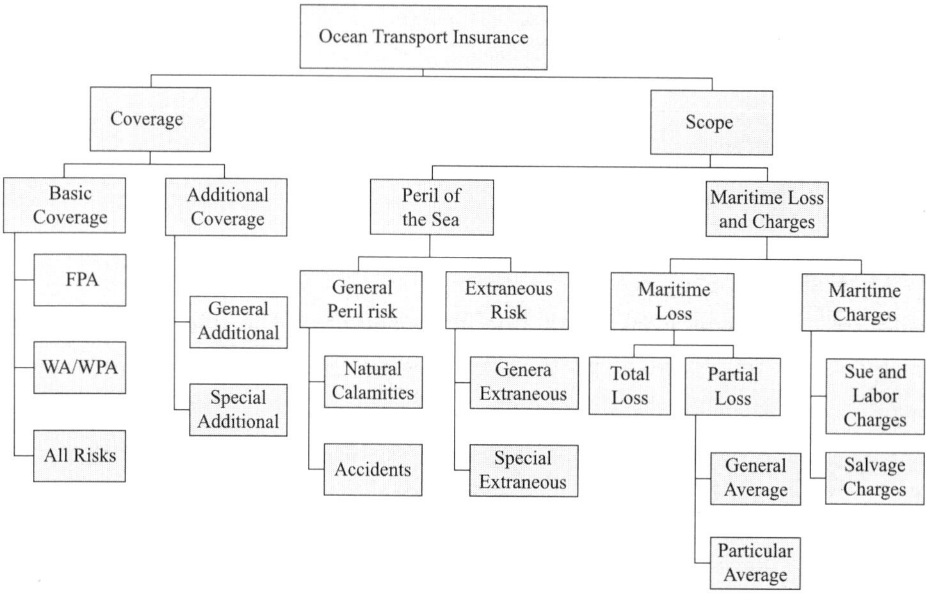

Figure 10. 1 The scope and coverages of ocean transport insurance

10. 2. 2 Cargo Insurance under Other Transport Mode

(1) Overland Transportation Cargo Insurance

In China, it includes Overland Transportation Risks and Overland Transportation All Risks, which are only applicable to railway and roadway transportation.

1) Overland Transportation Risks: This insurance covers the following:

① Total or partial loss of or damage to the insured goods caused in the course of transportation by natural calamities-windstorm, lightning, earthquake, flood, etc. or by accidents, collision, overturning or derailment of the conveyance; or by grounding, stranding, sinking or collision of the craft in case crafts are employed and/or collapse of tunnel, landslide, fire, explosion, etc.

② Reasonable cost incurred by the insured in salvaging the goods or averting or minimizing a loss recoverable under the policy, provided that such cost shall not exceed the sum insured of the consignment so saved.

2) Overland Transportation All Risks: This insurance coverage is similar to that of All Risks in Marine Cargo Transportation Insurance Clause. Aside from the risks covered under the Overland Transportation Risks as above, this insurance also covers all risks of loss of the insured goods, whether partial or total, arising from external causes in the course of transit (e. g. shortage, theft, leakage).

Overland Transportation Risks and Overland Transportation All Risks use Warehouse to Warehouse Clause (W/W Clause) to define the commencement and termination of obligation. These insurance coverages attach from the time the goods hereby insured leave the warehouse or place of storage named in the Policy for the commencement of the transit and continues in force in the ordinary course of transit including incidental transit by craft until the insured goods are delivered to the Consignee's final warehouse or place of storage at the destination named in the Policy or to any other place used by the insured for allocation or distribution of the goods. These insurances shall, however, be limited to sixty (60) days upon arrival of the insured goods at the final station of discharge before they reach the Consignee's warehouse.

The exclusions of the two insurance coverages are the same with that of Marine Cargo Transportation Insurance. The time validity of a claim shall not exceed two years counting from the completion of discharge of the insured goods from the train/truck at the station of final destination.

In addition, there is one additional insurance called Overland Transportation Cargo War Risks, which is accessible only after Overland Transportation Risks or Overland Transportation All Risks is arranged and which is only suitable to railway transportation.

(2) International Air Freight Cargo Insurance

According to the Air Transportation Cargo Insurance Clauses amended on January 1st, 1981 by People's Insurance Company of China, basic air transportation cargo insurance is classified into two conditions-Air Transportation Risks and Air Transportation All Risks. Additionally, Air Transportation Cargo War Risks works as additional coverage.

Air Transportation Risks insurance covers:

1) Total or partial loss of the insured goods caused in the course of transportation by lightning, fire, explosion, jettison due to bad weather or other perils, collision, overturning, crashing or missing of the aircraft and other accidents.

2) Reasonable cost incurred by the insured in salvaging the goods or averting or minimizing a loss recoverable under the policy, provided that such cost shall not exceed the value of the consignment so saved.

Aside from the risks covered under the Air Transportation Risks conditions as above, Air Transportation All Risks insurance also covers all risks of loss of or damage to the insured goods, whether partial or total, arising from external causes in the course of transit.

These two insurances also use "warehouse to warehouse" clause to define the commencement and termination of obligation, with the period limited to thirty (30) days after completion of discharge of the insured goods from the aircraft at the final airport of discharge.

Air Transportation Cargo War Risks is an additional coverage, which must be attached to Air Transportation Risks or Air Transportation All Risks. It covers the loss of or damage to the insured goods caused directly by or consequent upon war, warlike operations, hostile acts, armed conflicts, or conventional weapons and bombs, but the loss caused by atomic or nuclear weapons are excluded.

(3) Postal Parcel Transportation Insurance

The Parcel Post Insurance Clauses amended by People's Insurance Company of China on January 1st, 1981 involves Parcel Post Risks, Parcel Post All Risks, and Parcel Post War Risks as additional coverage.

Parcel Post Risks undertakes to indemnify for total or partial loss of the insured parcel caused by:

1) Natural calamities such as heavy weather, lightning, tsunami, earthquake, and flood;

2) Grounding, stranding, sinking, collision, overturning, derailing, crashing or missing of the carrying conveyance;

3) Fire or explosion;

4) Reasonable cost incurred by the insured in salvaging the insured parcel or averting or minimizing a loss recoverable under the Policy, provided that such cost shall not exceed the sum insured of the parcel so saved.

Aside from the liability covered under the aforesaid Parcel Post Risks, Parcel Post All Risks shall also indemnify for total or partial loss of the insured parcel arising from external causes in the course of transit.

This insurance attaches from the time the insured parcel leaves the premises or place of business of the sender for transit to the post office and continues in force until the expiry of fifteen (15) days counting from midnight of the day of issuance of the notice of arrival by the post office at the destination named in the policy when the parcel arrives, or until delivery of the parcel to the premises or place of business of the recipient if such delivery takes place prior to the expiry of the aforesaid fifteen (15) days.

Parcel Post War Risks covers loss of or damage to the insured goods caused directly by or consequent upon war, hostile acts, armed conflicts or conventional weapons of war including explosion of mines or torpedoes, as well as reasonable cost incurred by the insured in salvaging the insured parcel or averting or minimizing a loss recoverable under the Policy. However, the loss, damage or expenses arising from any hostile use of atomic or nuclear weapons of war are excluded from this insurance.

10.2 国际货物保险的主要险别

国际货物采取的运输方式很多，其中包括海洋运输、陆上运输、航空运输和邮包运输等，因此，国际货物运输保险也相应地分为海洋运输货物保险、陆上运输货物保险、航空运输货物保险和邮包运输保险。

10.2.1 海洋运输货物保险

(1) 海洋运输货物保险承保的范围

1) 海上风险：海上风险是指保险人承保的在海上和海与陆上、内河或与驳船相连接的地方所发生的风险。根据中国人民保险公司1981年1月1日修订的“海洋运输货物保险条款”的规定，海上风险主要分两类，一类是一般海上风险；另一类是外来风险。

① 一般海上风险：一般海上风险包括自然灾害和意外事故。

自然灾害（Natural Calamities），是指由于自然界的变化产生的破坏力量所造成的灾害。如被保险货物在运输途中遭遇恶劣气候、雷电、海啸、地震、洪水等造成的损失。

意外事故（Accidents），是指由于不能预料的原因或者说由于不可抗力的原因所造成的事故。如船舶搁浅、触礁、沉没、互撞与流冰或其他物体碰撞、火灾、爆炸等造成货物的损失。

② 外来风险：外来风险（Extraneous Risks），是指海上风险以外的其他外来原因所造成的风险。外来风险可分为一般外来风险和特殊外来风险。

一般外来风险是指被保险货物在运输途中遭遇意外的外来因素导致的事故。通常包括偷窃、雨淋、渗漏、短量、破碎、受潮、发霉、受热、串味、钩损、锈损等外来原因造成一定的损失。特殊外来风险是指除一般外来风险以外的其他原因导致的风险，如货物在运输过程中还可能遭受由于战争、敌对行为、罢工、进口国拒绝进口或没收等特殊外来原因造成的损失。

2）海上损失和费用

① 海上损失：海上损失，是指被保险的货物在运输过程中，由于发生海上风险导致保险标的直接或间接的损失。海上损失分为全部损失和部分损失。

(a) 全部损失（Total Loss），又称全损，全部损失分为实际全损和推定全损。实际全损（Actual Total Loss），是指保险标的全部损坏或丢失，或到岸后已毫无价值。推定全损（Constructive Total Loss），是指被保险的货物的实际全损已经不可避免，或者恢复、修复受损货物以及运送货物到原定目的地所花费的费用超过该货物运往目的地的货物价值。

(b) 部分损失（Partial Loss），是指保险标的一部分毁损或灭失，部分损失可以分为共同海损和单独海损。

共同海损（General Average，简称 G. A.）是由于船主的故意行为而造成的部分海损，如将全部或部分货物抛入大海以挽救船只。在此情况下，所有因此受益的货主将共同承担特定发货人的损失。

共同海损的成立，一般应具备以下几个条件。

第一，载货船舶必须确实遭遇危及货、船等共同安全的风险，载货船舶处在危难之中。风险必须实际存在并且是不可避免地产生，而不是主观臆断。如果因船长判断错误，采取了某些措施，或因可以预测的常见事故所造成的损失，不能构成共同海损。

第二，共同海损牺牲必须是自愿的和有意识的行动所造成的。共同海损牺牲的产生是由于人为的故意行动，而不是遭遇海上风险造成的意外损失。

第三，共同海损牺牲和费用的支出必须是合理的。共同海损牺牲和费用的支出必须以解除危难局面为限，船长不能滥用职权，任意扩大物资牺牲和费用的支出。

第四，共同海损牺牲和费用支出的目的仅限于为保船、货等各方面的共同安全。

第五，损失必须是共同海损行为的直接结果。例如，当载货船舶遇到危难，开始往海中抛货，在抛货时海水溅入或冲入船舱，造成其他货物损失，此项损失也属于共同海损。共同海损牺牲和费用支出都是为使船舶、货物和运费免于损失，因而应该由船舶、货物或运费等方面按最后获救的价值共同按比例分摊，通常称为共同海损分摊（G. A. Contribution）。

单独海损（Particular Average），是指被保险货物受损后，尚未达到全损程度，仅为部分损失，而这种部分损失不属于共同海损，是由各受损者单独负担损失。例如，载货船舶在航行中遇到狂风巨浪，海水入舱造成部分货物受损。

除上述损失外，货物在运输途中，还有由于外来风险引起的种种损失。例如，由于偷窃行为所遭受的损失和因战争所遭受的损失等。

② 海上费用：海上费用（Maritime Charges），是指船只遭遇风险时为对被保险货物进行施救而产生的费用，包括施救费用和救助费用。

施救费用（Sue and Labor Charges），又称单独海损费用，是指当被保险货物遭受保险责任范围内的自然灾害和意外事故时，被保险人或其代理人或其受雇人等为抢救被保险货物，防止损失继续扩大所支付的费用。保险人对这种施救费用负责赔偿。

救助费用（Salvage Charges），是指被保险货物遭受承保范围内的灾害事故时，除保险人和被保险人以外的无契约关系的第三者采取救助措施，获救成功，依据国际上的法律，被救方应向救助的第三者支付的报酬。救助费用应由保险人负责赔偿。保险人在赔付时，必须要求救助成功。国际上，一般称为“无效果-无报酬”。

（2）海洋运输货物保险的险别

保险险别是保险人对风险和损失的承保责任范围，它是保险人与被保险人履行权利与义务的基础，也是保险人承保责任大小和被保险人缴付保险费多少的依据。根据我国现行的《海洋货物运输保险条款》的规定，我国海洋货物运输保险的险别分为基本险别和附加险别两大类。

1）基本险别：基本险，又称主险，是可以独立投保，不必依附于其他险别项下的险别。我国海洋运输货物保险的基本险别分为平安险、水渍险和一切险三种。

① 平安险：平安险是我国保险公司使用的险别名称，其英文原文是“Free Particular Average，FPA”，意指不负责单独海损。当前平安险的责任范围包括：

（a）被保险货物在运输途中由于恶劣气候、雷电、海啸、地震、洪水等自然灾害造成整批货物的全部损失或推定全损。

（b）由于运输工具遭受搁浅、触礁、沉没、互撞、与流冰或其他物体碰撞以及失火、爆炸意外事故造成货物的全部或部分损失。

（c）在运输工具已经发生搁浅、触礁、沉没、焚毁意外事故的情况下，货物在此前后又在海上遭受恶劣气候、雷电、海啸等自然灾害所造成的部分损失。

（d）在装卸或转运时由于一件或数件货物落海造成的全部损失或部分损失。

（e）被保险人对遭受承保责任内危险的货物采取抢救、防止或减少货损的措施而支付的合理费用，但以不超过该批被救货物的保险金为限。

（f）运输工具遭遇自然灾害或者意外事故，在中途港或者在避难港停靠，因此而引起的卸货、装货、存仓以及运送货物所产生的特别费用。

（g）共同海损的牺牲、分摊和救助费用。

（h）运输契约订有“船舶互撞条款”，根据该条款规定由货方偿还船方的损失。

② 水渍险：水渍险的责任范围比平安险大，其英文原文是“With Particular Average，W. A/W. P. A”，意思是包括单独海损。根据现行条款的规定，水渍险除承保平安险的全部责任外，还承保被保险货物由于恶劣气候、雷电、海啸、地震、洪水自然灾害所造成的部分损失。

③ 一切险：一切险是三个基本险中责任范围最大的险种，英文名称是“All Risks”。一切险除包括平安险和水渍险的各项责任外，还包括货物在运输途中由于一般外来原因所致的全部或部分损失。

上述三种基本险别，被保险人可以从中选择一种投保。

2）附加险别：附加险别是对基本险别的补充和扩大。附加险不能单独投保，只能在投保一种基本险的基础上才能加保一种或数种附加险，它投保的是外来风险引起的损失。按承保风险的不同，附加险又可分为一般附加险和特殊附加险。

① 一般附加险：一般附加险是承保由于一般外来风险所造成的损失，一般附加险有以下 11 种：偷窃提货不着险；淡水雨淋险；短量险；混杂、沾污险；渗漏险；碰损、破碎险；串味险；受潮受热险；钩损险；包装破裂险；锈损险。

由于一般附加险已包含在一切险的责任范围内，所以，如果已投保了一切险，就不需要再加保一般附加险。

② 特殊附加险：特别附加险所承保的风险大多与国家的行政措施、政策法令、航海贸易习惯有关，它并不包括在基本险中，必须另行加保才能获得保障。中国人民保险公司承保的特殊附加险有以下八种。

(a) 海运战争险。该险种承保由于战争行为而造成的损失，包括入侵、暴动、叛乱或劫持，有些保单还承保由于大规模破坏性武器所导致的损失，通常被用在船运与航空运输中。战争险包括战争责任险和战争船体险：战争责任险对船内的人员与货物承担保险责任，保费计算的依据是赔偿金额；战争船体险承保船体本身，依据船体价值计算保费。保费随一国的稳定性的不同而有所不同。

(b) 罢工险。承保货物由于罢工者、被迫停工工人或参加工潮、暴动、民众斗争的人员的行为或任何人的恶意行为所造成的直接损失和上述行动和行为引起的共同海损的牺牲、分摊和救助费用。

(c) 舱面险。承保载于舱面的货物因遭受保险事故而导致的损失，以及抛弃和浪击落海的损失。

(d) 交货不到险。承保货物装上船后，不论任何原因，如果在预定抵达目的地日期起满六个月仍未运到目的地交货的损失。

(e) 进口关税险。承保货物由于遭受保险事故损失，但被保险人仍需按完好货物价值缴纳进口关税所造成的损失。

(f) 拒收险。承保货物在进口时由于各种原因被进口国政府或有关当局拒绝进口或没收所造成的损失。

(g) 黄曲霉素险。承保货物在保险责任有效期内，在进口港或进口地经当地卫生当局检验，证明黄曲霉素的含量超过进口国对该毒素的限制标准，因而被拒绝进口、没收或强制改变用途的损失。

(h) 货物出口到香港（包括九龙）或澳门存仓火险责任扩展条款。承保被保险货物到达目的地卸离运输工具后，如直接存放在于保险单载明的过户银行所指定的仓库所造成的存仓火险损失，直至银行收回押款解除货物的权益为止或运输责任终止时期满 30 天为止。

海洋运输货物保险的承保范围与保险险种如图 10.1 所示。

(3) 协会货物条款和中国保险条款的区别

目前，在我国进出口货物运输保险业务中，通常采用中国人民保险公司（PICC）规定的“中国保险条款”（China Insurance Clause，C. I. C. ），而世界上许多国家和地区的保险公司在其国际货物运输保险业务中往往采用英国保险业协会制定的《协会货物条款》（Institute Cargo Clause，简称 I. C. C. ）。《协会货物条款》也有三种基本保险险别，即 ICC（A）险、ICC（B）险以及 ICC（C）险。

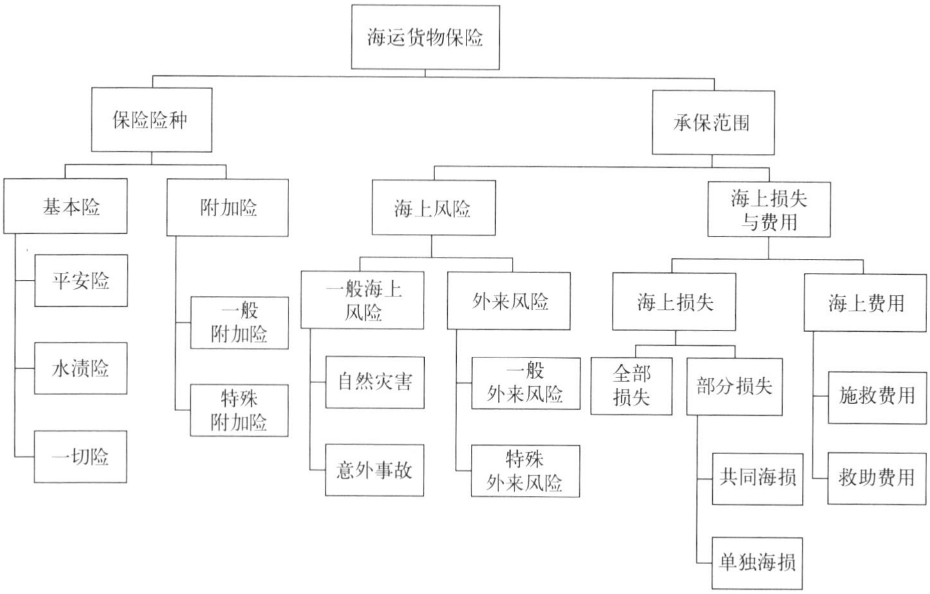

图 10.1 海洋运输货物保险的承保范围与保险险种

按照《协会货物条款》的规定，三种基本险的责任范围可归纳如下。

1）ICC（A）险：它基本上与原来的一切险相同，但在表述上采用“除外责任”的提法，即除不适航、不适货、战争、罢工外，对其他一切风险所造成的损失（包括共同海损和救助费用）都予以承保。

2）ICC（B）险：承保由于所列举的自然灾害和意外事故所造成的全部或部分损失以及共同海损牺牲，抛货或浪击落海，海水、潮水或河水进入船舶、驳船、运输工具、集装箱、大型海运箱或储存处所造成的损失。原来属于平安险责任范围的货物在船舶或驳船装卸时落海或跌落所造成任何整件的全损，也包括在 ICC（B）险之内。

3）ICC（C）险：只承保由于意外事故所造成的损失（包括全部损失和部分损失）以及抛货和共同海损牺牲。

海上货物运输保险的险别可因保险公司的不同而不同，即使是同一个保险公司，其承保的责任范围也会因险别的不同而有很大的差别。所以买卖双方在签订合同的保险条款时，必须首先明确保险公司的名称，然后才商订适当的险别和是否加保附加险。

10.2.2 其他运输方式的货物保险

（1）陆上运输货物保险险别

目前，我国陆上运输货物保险的基本险别分为陆运险和陆运一切险。两种险别的责任范围仅限于铁路和公路运输。

1）陆运险：陆运险包括以下几种。

① 被保险货物在运输途中遭受暴风、雷电、地震、洪水等自然灾害；或由于运输工具遭受碰撞、倾覆、出轨；或因在驳运过程中驳运工具遭受搁浅、触礁、沉没、碰撞；或由于遭受隧道坍塌、崖崩或失火、爆炸等意外事故所造成的全部或部分损失；

② 被保险人对遭受承保责任内危险的货物采取抢救，防止或减少货损的措施而支付的合理费用，但以不超过该批被救货物的保险金额为限。

2）陆运一切险：陆运一切险的承保责任范围与海洋运输货物保险条款中的“一切险”相似，除包括上列陆运险的责任外，还对被保险货物在运输途中由于外来原因所造成的货物短少、短量、偷窃、渗漏等全部或部分损失负责赔偿。

陆运险与陆运一切险的责任起讫采用“仓至仓”条款，即保险责任自被保险货物运离保险单所载明的起运地仓库或储存处所开始运输时生效，包括正常运输过程中的陆上和与其有关的水上驳运在内，直至该项货物运达保险单所载目的地收货人的最后仓库或储存处所，或被保险人用作分配、分派的其他储存处所为止，如未运抵上述仓库或储存处所，则以被保险货物运抵最后卸载的车站满 60 天为止。

陆运险与陆运一切险的除外责任与海洋运输货物险的除外责任相同。陆运险与陆运一切险的索赔时效为从被保险货物在最后目的地车站全部卸离车辆后起算，最多不超过两年。

此外，还有陆上运输货物战争险，它是陆上运输货物险的一种附加险，只有在投保了陆运险或陆运一切险的基础上才能加保，且仅适用于铁路运输。

(2) 国际航空运输货物保险险别

根据中国人民保险公司 1981 年 1 月 1 日修订的《航空运输货物保险条款》规定，航空运输保险的基本险别分为航空运输险和航空运输一切险两类，此外，还有航空运输货物战争险作为附加险。

航空运输险的责任范围如下。

1）被保险货物在运输途中遭受雷电、火灾、爆炸或由于飞机遭受恶劣气候或其他危难事故而被抛弃；或由于飞机遭受碰撞、倾覆、坠落或失踪等意外事故所造成的全部或部分损失；

2）被保险人对遭受承保责任内危险的货物采取抢救、防止或减少货损的措施而支付的合理费用，但以不超过该批被救货物的保险金额为限。

航空一切险的责任范围除包括航空运输险的责任外，还负责赔偿被保险货物由于外来原因所造成的全部或部分损失。

航空运输险与航空一切险的责任起讫也采用“仓至仓”条款，其最长责任期间为到达卸载地卸离飞机后满 30 天为止。

航空运输货物战争险是一种附加险，只有在投保了航空运输险或航空一切险的基础上才能加保。加保航空运输货物战争险后，保险公司承担赔偿在航空运输途中由于战争、敌对行为或武装冲突以及各种常规武器和炸弹所造成的货物损失，但不包括因使用原子或热核制造的武器所造成的损失。

(3) 邮政包裹运输保险险别

根据中国人民保险公司 1981 年 1 月 1 日修订的《邮包保险条款》规定，邮包保险的基本险别分为邮包险和邮包一切险两种，此外，还有邮包战争险作为附加险。

邮包险的责任范围包括被保险邮包在运输途中由于以下原因所造成的全部或部分损失。

1）恶劣气候、雷电、海啸、地震、洪水等自然灾害；

2）运输工具遭受搁浅、触礁、沉没、碰撞、倾覆、出轨、坠落、失踪；

3）失火、爆炸；

4）被保险人对遭受承保责任内危险的货物采取抢救、防止或减少货损的措施而支付的合理费用，但以不超过该批被救货物的保险金额为限。

邮包一切险的责任范围除承担邮包险的各项责任外，还承担被保险邮包在运输途中由于外来原因所造成的全部或部分损失。

邮包险和邮包一切险的保险责任是自被保险邮包离开保险单所载起运地点寄件人的处所运往邮局时开始生效，直至被保险邮包运达保险单所载明的目的地邮局，自邮局签发到货通知书当日午夜起算满 15 天终止。但在此期限内邮包一经递交至收件人的处所时，保险责任即告终止。

加保邮包战争险后，保险公司负责赔偿在邮包运输过程中由于战争、敌对行为或武装冲突以及各种常规武器包括水雷、鱼雷爆炸所造成的损失。此外，保险公司还负责被保险人对遭受以上承保责任内危险的物品采取抢救、防止或减少损失的措施而支付的合理费用。但保险公司不承担因使用原子或热核制造的武器所造成的损失的赔偿。

10.3 Operations of International Cargo Insurance

Cargo transport insurance is needed in the transit of cargo from export country to import country. It involves the insured applying to the insurer for insurance, on the value of goods and appropriate coverage, and the insurer collecting insurance premium and issuing Insurance Policy (or Insurance Certificate). If the insured cargo suffers loss covered in the Policy in the transit, the holder of the certificate who is of insurance interest is entitled to filing a claim.

In arranging international cargo insurance, the parties should choose coverage, determine insurance amount, calculate premium, and so on. The general procedure is illustrated in Figure 10.2.

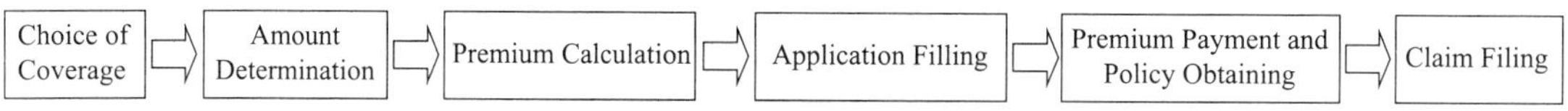

Figure 10.2 General Procedure of Insurance Arrangement

10.3.1 Choice of Coverage

The following factors will influence the choice of coverage:

(1) Nature of Goods

Goods of different nature may face different risks and probabilities of loss. Therefore, nature of goods must be considered before determining insurance coverage. For instance, All Risks is needed for product of brittle glass but not product of durable iron. For special goods (e. g. refrigerated goods and bulk commodities such as wood oil in bulk), particular or specified insurance clauses are in need according to the nature of goods.

(2) Packing of Goods

Packing is important in safeguarding the goods in transport. When applying for insurance and choosing coverage, the applicant should take into consideration the possible damage to the package and subsequently to the goods in the transit. However, damage to the goods arising from poor or unsuitable packing is not covered in the Insurance Policy but has to be undertaken by the consignor.

(3) Route of Shipping and Port of Call

Goods may face different risks and loss when different route of shipping and port of call are chosen. Loss of goods will increase in route of hot weather and possibility of accidental loss rises if the vessel passes turbulent or martial sea area. Apart from that, ports of call differ in their facilities, handling capacity and security, which may lead to different damage to or missing of goods in the handling. Therefore, careful investigation is needed before choosing appropriate coverage.

(4) Shipping Season

Different seasons have different impact on the risk to cargo shipment. Carrying vessel is in great exposure to risk of collision with moving icebergs when shipping in cold ocean areas in winter, but to risk of mildew or worm when shipping grains and vegetables in summer.

(5) Trade Customs and International Conventions

If goods are exported under CIF terms, the coverage applied by the seller should be clearly defined in the trade contract. Any different insurance requirement by one party after the entrance of contract should be submitted to the counter party for modification of contract or L/C. If no such provision is provided in the contract, international trade conventions and relative national laws should be followed in insurance arrangement. For instance, according to the *Revised American Foreign Trade Definitions 1941*, under CIF terms the seller is responsible for arranging war risk insurance on behalf of and at the cost of the buyer. Under CIF terms, the seller is supposed to apply for WPA in Belgium but for WPA and war risk insurance in Australia.

To summarize, one should consider many factors when choosing an insurance coverage. Generally speaking, the basic risk covered by cargo transport insurance is the loss of and damage to the goods in transit arising from natural calamities and accidents. Therefore, WPA or FPA should be the prior choice, and additional coverage could be arranged as needed. If the nature, packing and transport of the goods imply that they are exposed to wider extraneous risks and greater possibilities of loss, the goods need to be covered by All Risks.

10.3.2 Amount Determination

The applicant should declare insured amount when applying for insurance. The insured amount is the actual amount insured to the goods by the insurer and the basis on which premium is calculated and the maximum amount indemnified in a claim. The insured amount is determined on the insured value which is the monetary expression of the insurable interest of the insured object held by the insured (usually including price of goods, freight, premium and expected profit, and so on).

Under CIF and CIP terms, the contract usually defines insured amount, generally invoice amount plus a percentage of it which is called Insured Markon Percentage. If no such specific amount is provided in the contract, the Incoterms 2020, *Uniform Customs and Practice for Documentary Credits* (International Chamber of Commerce Publication No. 600th), and regular practices in international insurance market should be followed and thereby the seller should use invoice amount plus 10 percent as insured amount. If the buyer requires increasing insured markon percentage and applying for insurance on higher insured amount, the seller may choose to accept upon agreement of insurance company, with additional premium undertaken by the buyer. The insured amount is calculated as:

$$\text{Insured Amount} = \text{CIF(or CIP)} \times (1 + \text{Insured Markon Percentage})$$

If the FOB or CFR price is known, the CIF or CIP price can be calculated according to the following formula:

$$\text{CIF(or CIP)} = \frac{\text{FOB(or FCA)} + \text{Freight}}{1 - [\text{Insurance Premium} \times (1 + \text{Insured Markon Percentage})]}$$

$$\text{CIF(or CIP)} = \frac{\text{CFR(or CPT)}}{1 - [\text{Insurance Premium} \times (1 + \text{Insured Markon Percentage})]}$$

In China, the insured amount of imported goods is calculated on CIF or CIP. If the contract is under FOB (or FCA) or CFR (or CPT) terms, export companies and People's Insurance Company of China should negotiate an average freight rate and average insurance premium, and then calculate insured amount as:

$$\text{Insured amount} = \text{FOB(or FCA)} \times (1 + \text{average freight rate} + \text{average insurance premium})$$

Or

$$\text{Insured amount} = \text{CFR(or CPT)} \times (1 + \text{average insurance premium})$$

The aforesaid estimated CIF (or CIP) doesn't need additional markon percentage, however, the insurance company may choose to accept it if required by the applicant.

10.3.3 Premium Calculation

An insurance premium is the amount of money charged by the insurer for bearing indemnity and payment liability, which is the main source of insurance fund. The act of premium payment by the applicant is the prerequisite of an effective insurance contract and the basic obligation of the applicant.

The applicant calculates premium as:

$$\text{Insurance Premium} = \text{Insured Amount} \times \text{Premium Rate}$$

Premium rate is the rate of premium charged to insured amount, which is the basis on which the insurer calculates the premium. It is determined by the insurer after considering possible risk to the insured cargo, loss ratio, claim ratio, and operation expenses, as well as nature of commodity, different destination, and different insurance coverage. Higher loss ratio usually accompanies higher premium.

The insurance premium rate for export cargo formulated by People's Insurance Company of China has two categories, namely general premium rate and named premium rate. Cargo not listed into the table of named premium rate will apply general premium rate. Cargo using named premium rate will, apart from calculating premium on the basis of general premium rate, add named additional premium rate. There are Promissory Insurance Rate Sheet and Import Cargo Insurance Rate Sheet. Promissory Insurance Rate Sheet is only suitable for foreign trade companies who have signed Open Cover with People's Insurance

Company of China. It is actually a preferential average premium rate, which employs a fixed rate to a broad category of commodity, irrespective of country or region, cargo or coverage. Import Cargo Insurance Rate Sheet has general rate and special rate. General rate is formulated according to different mode of transport, coverage and area, irrespective of cargo type, and is suitable to any goods except those listed in special rate sheet. Special rate, however, is applicable to insuring All Risks to named cargo.

10.3.4 Application Filling

When applying for cargo transport insurance, the applicant needs to make an insurance offer in writing by filling in an application form. With the signature and seal of the insurer on the form, or a Policy issued by the insurer, the contractual relationship between the parties is confirmed. According to the Principle of Insurable Interest, the insured must have insurable interest in the cargo when filing a claim; however, he is not required to hold the interest when applying for the insurance. Therefore, the applicant should arrange insurance before the shipment, in order that each party's interest won't suffer from accidents to the cargo in the transit.

The application form involves the applicant informing the insurer of facts of the insured object, on which the insurer issues Insurance Policy and determines the insurance premium. Therefore, the application form must be explicitly and honestly filled in. The Policy should contain the following items: name of the insured, invoice number, contract number, packing and quantity, insured cargo, insured amount, conveyance, voyage or flight number, departure date, shipping route, insurance coverage, place of indemnity, signature, name, address, telephone of the applicant and date of insurance.

The distance between seller and buyer may lead to error in information transmission. It is possible that the date of loading or goods reception by the carrier precedes the date of insurance application, or loss already occurred to the goods in the transit at the time of insurance application. In such cases, the consequent policy should be theoretically deemed ineffective. However, in international cargo insurance practice, the insurer needs to make indemnity as regulated in the policy should the insurance application by the importer be out of good attention and the applicant has no idea about the loss, despite the loss happening before the application. On the other hand, if the applicant knows about the loss before application, that act of application is seemed to be insurance fraud and correspondingly the Policy is deemed to be ineffective. Of course, the insurer will not accept the insurance should he know the truth. If the insured and the insurance company have signed an open policy, the insurer will automatically cover the insurance from the moment the shipping notice is sent/forwarded to the insurance company.

Insurance means a contractual relationship established on Principle of Utmost Good Faith. The insurer's acceptance of insurance application and the calculation of premium is primarily based on what is reported by the applicant. Therefore, the applicant should provide true report and correct declaration of the insured object to the insurer.

10.3.5 Premium Payment and Policy Obtaining

The applicant (the insured) obtains the Policy only after he pays premium. In international trade, two forms of Policy are widely used.

(1) Insurance Policy (or Policy)

Insurance policy (or Policy) is a formal certificate proving the contractual relationship between the insurer and the insured, which has different coverage and form. In marine insurance, the widely used forms of policy include Hull Policy, Cargo Policy, Freight Policy, Ship Owner's Liability Policy, and so on.

The basic content of a Policy includes name of the insurer and the insured, Policy and insurance certificate, Marks & No., packing and quantity, insured amount and currency denominated, premium and premium rate, shipping clauses (name of the ship, voyage number, departure date, origin and destination, etc.), insurance coverage, indemnity place (usually located in import country), date of insurance (at least earlier than date of shipment), and so on. Additionally, detailed clauses concerning the rights and duties of the insurer and the insured should be formulated. Any supplement or removal of the rights and duties required by the parties should be attached in added clause or note. See Appendix 10-1 for details.

The Policy is a formal document with which the insured could file a claim and the insurer could settle the claim. The Policy is transferable and usually used as one of the collateral documents by the insured to his bank. Under CIF contract, the seller must provide the buyer with Policy.

(2) Insurance Certificate

Insurance Certificate (also called Small Policy) is actually a kind of simplified insurance policy. The insurance certificate only indicates the name of the insured, name of the insured cargo, quantity, marks, conveyance, place of destination, insurance cover, and insurance amount. But the rights and obligations of two parties are omitted. Generally speaking, the insurance certificate has the same legal validity as the insurance policy. However, when an L/C regulates the submission of a Policy, the insurance certificate can not substitute the insurance policy.

Besides the above two forms of Policy, Open Policy is adopted in some cases. An Open Policy is a long-term insurance contract for the carriage of goods. It stipulates coverage, types of risks, rates, liability treatment and other items. Cargoes covered under an open policy are automatically covered during the validity of the open policy. The advantage of an open policy is that it simplifies the procedure of signing the insurance contract one by one and protects against irreparable losses caused by missed or delayed insurance. The insurance company generally offers more favorable premium to the insured who has concluded an open policy with it, thus attracting many applicants. If the importer and the insurance company have signed an open policy, every time after loading the goods, the exporter is responsible for immediately sending the shipping advice (including name of the commodity, quantity, weight, amount, means of transport, shipping date and open policy number stated in the L/C, etc.) to the insurance company and the importer, with the shipping advice acting as a sign that the policy has become effective.

10.3.6 Claim Filing

The insured is entitled to filing a claim to the insurer against the loss of goods on regulated formalities. Insurance claim refers to the act of the insured lodging a claim to the insurer for compensation against the loss of insured goods caused by insured risks. After receiving the claim requirement, the insurer should handle the compensation requirement from the insured, which is called settlement of claim.

When filing a claim, the insured must have insurable interest on the insured goods. Take ocean shipment for example, under CIF term, it is the seller who should file a claim should the loss occur in the transit before the goods are loaded on the vessel at port of departure; whereas if the loss occurs after loading on board the vessel, it is the buyer who should file a claim to the insurer, as stipulated by the Principle of Insurable Interest.

When filing a claim, the insured should follow the following steps:

(1) Notification of Loss

When shortage of or damage to the goods is observed, the insured should immediately notify the insurance company or his local agent of inspection or claim settlement listed in the Policy, which is one indispensable step in lodging a claim. The notification implies that a claim commences and therefore is not confined by time of claim validity.

(2) Inspection Application

When notifying the insurer or his agent of the loss, the insured should apply for goods inspection. The inspection is essential for discovering the cause of loss and determining accountability. Therefore, the insured should make timely inspection application once the loss is observed. Insurance company strictly limits the time of loss notification and inspection application, which is no more than ten (10) days after the termination of insurance coverage in China, except when the reasons for late inspection application is out of the control of the insured.

(3) Submission of Claims Document

When lodging a claim to the insurer or his agent, the insured should submit various documents needed, which according to China's Cargo Transportation Insurance Clauses includes original Insurance Policy, Bill of Lading, invoice, Packing List, Weight Memo, Certificate of Loss or Damage, Inspection Report, and Statement of Claim. If third party liability is involved, necessary documents or certificates filed for Recovery from the third party should also be submitted.

Apart from the above mentioned certificates and documents, the insurer could require the insured to provide certificates proving the nature of insured accidents and loss severity. All the documents and certificates are the basis on which the insured files a claim. How the insurer will perform indemnity obligation depends primarily on the submission of these documents, apart from the on-site observation.

(4) Collection of Claim Indemnity and Conduction of Subrogation

The insured is entitled to timely collecting claim indemnity. However, he is forbidden to double benefit from one loss if the loss is caused by negligence of a third party (with ship owner included); and the third party cannot deny his compensation liability for reason of indemnity made by the insurer. After total or partial loss indemnity, the insurer could require the insured to transfer his right to claim for total or partial compensation, within the limit of his indemnity, from the third responsible party. This is called Right of Subrogation. In practice, the right of subrogation could be exerted only after the insurer's compensation has been performed. After the indemnity, the insured signs a Letter of Subrogation to the insurer as a proof of subrogation right transfer, with which the insurer could file a Recovery from the third responsible party.

In a claim, the exporter and importer should:

1) Actively salvage and organize the damaged goods. When goods are found damaged, the insured should, apart from notifying the insurer and applying for inspection, conduct necessary salvage and appropriate organization to the damaged goods together with the insurer and his agent to prevent loss expansion. The reasonable expenses incurred to salvage goods and minimize loss should be covered by insurance within the limit of the insured amount of the goods so saved. The insured mustn't standby and watch indifferently the loss of the goods because of the insurance made. The insurance laws and clauses regulate that the insurer not be responsible for loss expansion arising from non-salvage or non-organization by the insured.

In addition, the insured is obliged to resell, fix, and alter the use of the damaged goods, for he is more familiar with the nature of the goods and can thus make better use of the damaged goods. In China, the damaged goods are in principle handled by the insured at his discretion with the notification to or permission from the insurer.

2) If a third responsible party is involved, the insured should in the first place raise an objection to the party in order to retain right of recourse before he files a claim to the insurer.

When the insured or his agent inspects the goods and finds obvious damage to the package, shortage in entire package, or damage to bulk commodity, they should immediately require Certificate of Loss or Damage from the carrier, trustee, customs and port authority. If the loss and damage are to be answered for by carrier, port, or stevedoring company, a claim should be filed in writing to retain the right of recourse. Sometimes the insured needs to apply for extension of claim, for the transport contract and relative transport authority regulate that if claim is not filed immediately, the goods are considered to be in good condition and no claim should be filed later. The validity of claim regulated by People's Insurance Company of China is 2 years, beginning from the moment the insured goods are discharged from the vessel at port of destination. However, once the claim is filed, the insured is not confined by the time validity.

10.3 国际货物保险实务

国际物流中的货物在从出口国到进口国的运输过程中，一般均需要办理货物运输保险。办理货物运输保险，是指被保险人就其货物按一定的金额和险别向保险公司提出投保申请，经保险人同意后，保险人便按照投保金额和险别的费率收取保险费，并出具保险单证。如所保货物在运输过程中遭受保险责任范围内的损失，享有保险利益的单证持有人即可向保险公司提出赔偿要求。

投保国际货物保险，应选择险种，确定保险金额、计算保费等，大致程序如图 10.2 所示。

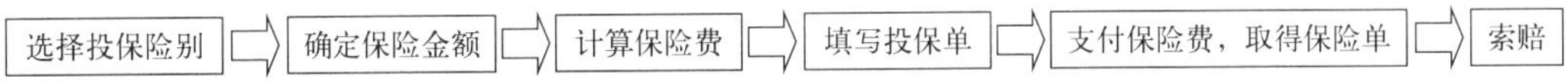

图 10.2 投保的大致程序

10.3.1 选择投保险别

对保险险别的选择，一般应考虑以下因素。

(1) 货物的性质

不同种类的货物所具有的性质和特点有所不同，在运输途中遭遇的风险和发生的损失往往有很大的不同，因此，在投保时必须充分考虑货物的特点，据以确定适当的险别。例如：易碎的玻璃制品要保一切险；不易损失、损坏的钢铁制品就不必投保一切险。对于某些特殊的货物则要投保特种险，如冷藏货物以及某些大宗货物，如散装桐油，需按不同的货物特点选择保险人提供的特定的或专门的保险条款进行投保。

(2) 货物的包装

货物的包装对货物的安全运输具有重要作用。在办理投保和选择险别时，应把货物包装在运输过程中可能发生的损坏及其对货物可能造成的损害考虑在内。但值得注意的是，因货物包装不良或由于包装不适应国际贸易运输的一般要求而致货物遭受损失，属于发货人的责任，保险人一般不予负责。

(3) 运输路线及停靠港口

海运中船舶的航行路线和停靠的港口不同，货物可能遭受的风险和损失也有很大的不同。某些航线途经气候炎热地区，如果载货船舶通风不良，就会增大货损。而在政局动荡不定或在已经发生战争的海域内航行，货物遭受意外损失的可能性自然增大。同时，由于不同停靠港口在设备、装卸能力以及安全等方面有很大差异，进出口货物在港口装卸时发生货损、货差的情况也就不同。因此，在投保前应做好调查了解工作，以便选择适当的险别。

(4) 运输季节

货物运输季节不同，也会对运输货物带来不同风险和损失。例如，载货船舶冬季在寒冷海域航行，极易发生与流动冰山碰撞的风险；夏季装运粮食、果品，极易出现发霉腐烂或生虫的现象。

(5) 各国的贸易习惯和国际惯例

如果货物按 CIF 条件出口，卖方应负责投保何种险别，须在贸易合同中加以明确规定。

合同订立后，一方有不同的保险要求，就只能向对方提出修改合同或信用证。如果合同中对此没有规定，便需按照国际贸易惯例及有关国家的法律规定办理。例如，按美国《1941 年美国对外贸易定义修正本》的规定，CIF 条件下卖方有义务代买方投保战争险，但费用由买方负担；在比利时，CIF 条件下卖方通常要负责投保水渍险；在澳大利亚，按许多行业习惯，CIF 条件下卖方须负责投保水渍险和战争险等。

总之，在选择投保险别时，要根据多方面的因素进行考虑。一般来说，由于进出口货物运输保险承保的基本风险是在运输途中因自然灾害和运输工具遭受意外事故所造成的货物损失，所以选择投保险别应首先在基本险别中选择水渍险或平安险，然后再根据需要加保必要的附加险别。如果根据商品特点、包装和运输等情况，发现货物遭受外来原因风险的范围较广，遭受损失的可能性较大，则可投保一切险。

10.3.2 确定保费金额

投保人在投保货物运输保险时应向保险人申报保险金额。保险金额是被保险人对保险标的的实际投保金额，是保险人计算保险费的依据，也是发生损失时保险人赔偿的依据和最高限额。保险金额是根据保险价值确定的。保险价值是被保险人对保险标的所具有的可保利益的货币表现形式，一般包括货价、运费、保险费以及预期利润等。

国际贸易采用 CIF 或 CIP 贸易术语成交，买卖合同一般均规定保险金额，而且保险金额通常还需在发票金额的基础上增加一定的百分率，即“投保加成率”。如合同未作规定，按 Incoterms 2020 和《跟单信用证统一惯例》（国际商会第 600 号出版物）以及国际保险市场的习惯做法，卖方应按 CIF 或 CIP 价格的总值另加 10%作为保险金额。如买方要求适当提高投保加成率，按较高保险金额投保，在保险公司同意承保的前提下，卖方可考虑接受，但因此而增加的保险费原则上应由买方支付。保险金额的计算公式是：

$$\text{保险金额}=\text{CIF(或 CIP)}\times(1+\text{投保加成率})$$

在实际工作中，如已有成本价或运费加成本价，要计算 CIF 或 CIP 的价格，可按下列公式计算出 CIF 或 CIP 价格：

$$\begin{aligned}\text{CIF(或 CIP)}&=\frac{\text{FOB(或 FCA)}+\text{运费}}{1-[\text{保险费率}\times(1+\text{投保加成率})]}\\&=\frac{\text{CFR(或 CPT)}}{1-[\text{保险费率}\times(1+\text{投保加成率})]}\end{aligned}$$

我国进口货物的保险金额，原则上按进口货物的 CIF 或 CIP 价格计算。若进口合同采用 FOB（或 FCA）或 CFR（或 CPT）条件，为简化手续、方便计算，各外贸企业与中国人民保险公司共同议订平均运费率和平均保险费率，其保险金额的计算公式如下：

$$\text{保险金额}=\text{FOB(或 FCA)}\times(1+\text{平均运费率}+\text{平均保险费率})$$

或

$$\text{保险金额}=\text{CFR(或 CPT)}\times(1+\text{平均保险费率})$$

上述进口保险金额即估算的 CIF（或 CIP）价不另外加成，如投保人要求在 CIF 或 CIP 价基础上加成投保，保险公司也可接受。

10.3.3 计算保险费

保险费是保险人因承担特定的赔偿或给付责任而向投保人收取的费用，它是保险基金的主要来源。投保人交付保险费是保险合同生效的前提条件，也是投保人的基本义务。

保险人按下列公式计算保险费：保险费＝保险金额×保险费率

保险费率指收取的保险费占保险金额的比例值。保险费率是保险人计算保险费的依据，是由保险人根据保险标的可能遇到的危险性大小、损失率、赔付率高低和经营费用多少等因素，并按不同商品、不同目的地以及不同的投保险别加以规定的。一般情况下，损失率越高，保险费率也越高。

目前，中国人民保险公司制定的出口货物保险费率分为“一般货物费率”和“指明货物费率”两大类。凡是未列入“指明货物费率”中的货物，统属“一般货物费率”的范围。凡指明货物费率的商品，除应按一般商品费率计算外，再加上指明货物加费费率计算。进口货物保险费率有“特约费率表”和“进口货物保险费率表”两种。“特约费率表”仅适用于同中国人民保险公司签订有预约保险合同的外贸企业，它不分国别和地区，对某一大类商品只订一个费率，有的也不分货物和险别，实际上是一种优惠的平均费率。“进口货物保险费率表”分一般货物费率和特价费率两项。一般货物费率按不同的运输方式，分险别和地区制定，但不分商品，除特价费率中列出的商品以外，适用于其他一切货物；而特价费率，是对一些指定的商品投保一切险时采用。

10.3.4 填写投保单

无论在进口或出口业务中，投保货物运输保险时，投保人通常需以书面方式做出投保要约，即填写货物运输保险投保单，经保险人在投保单上签章承诺，或是出立保险单，保险双方即确定了合同关系。按照保险利益原则的规定，在货物运输保险中，被保险人必须在索赔时对保险货物具有保险利益，但并不要求其在投保时便具有保险利益，因此，为保障贸易双方的利益不会因货物在运输途中发生事故而遭受损失，投保人应在货物开始运输之前办理保险。

投保单是投保人在投保时对保险标的及与有关事实的告知和陈述，也是保险人签发保险单和确定保险费的依据，因此，投保单的填写必须准确、真实。进出口货物运输保险投保单的具体内容主要有以下几项：被保险人，发票号码和合同号码，包装数量，保险货物项目，保险金额，装载运输工具，航次、航班，开航日期，运输路线，承保险别，赔款地，投保人签章及企业名称、电话地址、投保日期等。

保险人承保的是未来可能发生的风险，由于买卖双方处于不同的国家，距离遥远，如果出现信息传递失误，买方投保的日期可能在货物装船以后或货物交承运人接管以后，甚至可能出现投保时货物已经在运输途中发生损失的情形。按理保险应当是无效的。但按照国际货运保险的习惯，如果投保时货物已经发生损失，只要进口方的投保是善意的，事先并不知情，保险仍然有效，保险人仍需按保险合同的规定予以赔偿。反之，如果进口方在投保时已经知道货损事件，则该投保行为属于保险欺诈，保险无效。如果保险人已经知情，则不会接受承保。如果被保险人和保险公司签订了预约保单，一经启运，即从装船通知发送到保险公司的那一刻起，保险人即自动承保。

保险是建立在最高诚信原则的基础之上的契约关系。保险人对投保人的投保是否接受，按什么费率承保主要是以投保人所申报的情况为依据来确定的。因此，投保人在办理投保时，应当将有关被保险货物的重要事项向保险人作真实地申报和正确地陈述。

10.3.5 支付保险费，取得保险单

投保人（被保险人）交付保险费后，即可取得保险单。在国际贸易业务中，常用的保险单据主要有两种形式。

（1）保险单（Insurance Policy 或 Policy）

保险单（俗称大保单），是保险人和被保险人之间成立保险合同关系的正式凭证，因险别的内容和形式有所不同，海上保险最常用的形式有船舶保险单、货物保险单、运费保险单和船舶所有人责任保险单等。

保险单的基本内容：保险人（又称承保人，Insurer）、被保险人（Insured）、保险单和保险凭证、唛头和号码、包装及数量、保险金额与货币、保费及费率、运输条款（船名、航次、开航日期、运输起讫点等）、承保险别、赔付地点（一般是在进口国内的地点）和日期（至少应早于提单日期）等。此外，还附有关于保险人责任范围以及保险人和被保险人的权利和义务等方面的详细条款。如当事人双方对保险单上所规定的权利和义务需要增补或删减时，可在保险单上加贴条款或加注字句。详见附录 10-1。

保险单是被保险人向保险人索赔的正式文件，也是保险人理赔的主要依据。保险单可转让，通常是被保险人向银行进行押汇的单证之一。在 CIF 合同中，保险单是卖方必须向买方提供的单据。

（2）保险凭证（Insurance Certificate）

保险凭证（也称小保单）实际上是一种简化的保险单。保险凭证仅记载被保险人名称、被保险货物名称、数量、唛头、运输工具、目的地、保险范围和保险金额等，但省略了双方的权利和义务。总体而言，保险凭证与保险单具有相同的法律效力。但如果信用证规定提交保险单时，不能以保险凭证代替保险单。

除了上述两种保单外，有时会采用预约保险单。预约保险单（Open Policy）是一种长期性的货物运输保险合同。保单上规定了承保范围、险别、费率、责任赔款处理等项目。凡属于预约保单约定的运输货物，在保单有效期内自动承保。预约保单的优点是减少了逐笔签订保险合同的手续，并可以防止因漏保或迟保而造成的无法弥补的损失。保险公司一般对使用预约保单的投保人提供更优惠的保险费用，因而也吸引了不少投保人。如果进口商和保险公司订有长期的预约保单，每当货物装船后，出口商承担将装船通知（内容包括商品名称、数量、重量、金额、运输工具、运输日期和信用证中列明的预约保单号码等）立即发送给保险公司及进口商的责任，并以此作为保险单正式生效的标志，即以装船通知送达保险公司的时刻作为保险合同生效的时点。

10.3.6 索赔

被保险货物遭受损失后，被保险人应按规定办理索赔手续，向保险人提出赔偿要求。保险索赔，是指被保险货物遭受承保责任范围内的风险而造成损失时，被保险人向保险人提出赔偿要求的行为。保险人在接到被保险人的索赔要求后，对被保险货物的损失赔偿要求的处理称为理赔。

索赔时，被保险人对保险标的必须具有保险利益，以海运为例，若以 CIF 条件成交，货物的损失若是发生在起运港装上海轮之前的运输途中，应由卖方向保险公司索赔；如果货物的损失发生在装上海轮之后，根据保险利益原则的规定，应由买方向保险公司进行索赔。

被保险人在索赔时必须履行如下手续。

(1) 发出损失通知

当被保险人发现被保险的货物有短损情况，应立即通知保险公司或保险单上所载明的保险公司在当地的检验、理赔代理人。及时发出损失通知，是向保险人请求赔偿的必备手续。因为一经通知，便表明已知开始索赔行为而不再受索赔时效的限制。

(2) 申请检验

被保险人在向保险人或其代理人发出损失通知的同时，应向其申请货物检验。货物的检验对查清损失原因、审定责任归属是极其重要的，因此，被保险人在发现保险货物受损后，应立即申请检验。各国的保险机构对货物的损失通知和申请检验均有严格的时间限制，我国的保险公司一般要求申请检验的时间最迟不能超过保险责任终止后10天。当然，如果导致申请检验的时间超过规定期限的原因是被保险人无法控制的，保险人还是应根据实际情况予以受理。

(3) 提交索赔单证

索赔人员在向保险人或其代理人索赔时，应提交索赔必需的各种单证，按照我国货物运输保险条款的规定，索赔人员在索赔时应提供保险单正本、提单、发票、装箱单、磅码单、货损货差证明、检验报告及索赔清单。如果涉及第三者责任，还须提供向责任方追偿的有关函电及其他必要单证或文件。

除上述各种证明和单据外，保险人还可根据损失情况和理赔需要，要求被保险人提供与确认保险事故性质和损失程度有关的证明材料。所有这些证明和资料是被保险人索赔的依据，保险人是否承担赔偿责任，除根据现场调查搜集的资料外，主要是依据这些证明和资料进行判断。

(4) 领取保险赔款与代位追偿

被保险人有权及时获得保险赔偿。但是如果损失是由于其他第三者（包括船方在内）的疏忽或过失所致，被保险人不能双重获益，任何第三者也不能因保险人负责赔偿而推卸责任。保险人在履行全损赔偿或部分损失赔偿后，在其赔偿金额内，要求被保险人转让其对造成损失的第三者责任方要求全损赔偿或相应部分赔偿的权利。这种权利称为代位求偿或称为代位追偿权或简称代位权。在实际业务中，保险人需首先向被保险人赔付，才能取得代位追偿权。其具体做法是被保险人在获得赔偿时，签署一份权益转让书，作为保险人取得代位权的证明。保险人便可凭此向第三者责任方进行追偿。

无论是在出口或进口的索赔工作中，必须特别注意下列问题。

1）对受损失货物应积极采取措施进行施救和整理。被保险货物受损后，作为被保险人，除了应及时通知保险公司的代理人请求对受损货物进行联合检验之外，还应会同保险公司及其他代理人对受损的货物采取必要的施救和整理措施，以防止损失的扩大，因施救、阻止或减少货损的措施而支付的合理费用，可由保险公司补偿，但以不超过该批被救货物的保险金额为限。被保险人绝不能因为货物已经投保便袖手旁观。根据各国保险法令或保险条款的规定，对于被保险人没有采取必要的施救、整理措施所造成的继续扩大的损失，保险人不负赔偿的责任。

另外，被保险人还负有处理受损货物的转售、修理、改变用途等义务。这是因为被保险人对于货物的性能、用途比保险公司更为熟悉，能更好地利用物资。在我国，无论是进口货物或国内运输的货物受损后，原则上都应由被保险人自行处理。当然，被保险人必须在通知保险公司或征得保险公司的同意下才能对受损货物进行上述转售、修理、改变用途等处理。

2）如果涉及第三者责任，虽然赔款一般先由保险人赔付，但被保险人应首先向责任方提出异议，以保留追偿权利。

被保险人或其代理人在提取货物时，如果发现被保险货物的包装有明显的受损痕迹，或者整件短少，或者散装货物已经残损等情况，除了要向保险公司发出损失通知外，还应立即向承运人、受托人以及海关、港务局等索取货损货差证明。尤其是这些货损货差涉及承运人、码头、装卸公司等某一方或多方面的责任时，还应立即以书面形式向他们提出索赔，保留追偿权利。有时还要申请延长索赔时效。因为，按照运输合同及有关运输部门的规定，如果收货人不在当时提出异议索赔，即视为所交货物完好，事后就不能再行提出赔偿。中国人民保险公司规定的索赔时效为 2 年，即从被保险货物在最后卸港全部卸离海轮后起算，最多不超过 2 年。但被保险人一经提出赔偿要求后，即不受时效限制。

10.4 Tactics Taken in International Cargo Insurance

How to use insurance to avoid cargo transport risk in foreign trade is a specialized work. International cargo transport insurance is complicated in its coverages, with basic coverage and additional coverage. The choice of basic coverage and the mixed use of it and additional coverage all need specialized knowledge.

10.4.1 Five Considerations in the Choice of Insurance Coverage

When applying for insurance, the applicant would like to make a trade-off between insurance coverage and premium. To do this, he should in the first place evaluate the risks and identify the greatest one, and take premium in different coverages into consideration to make a trade-off.

The exporter should take the following factors into consideration:

① the type, nature and characteristics of the goods.

② the packing of goods.

③ the transportation (including mode, conveyance and route of transportation).

④ the loss and damage happening at the port or in the course of stevedoring.

⑤ the political situation in place of destination.

10.4.2 When to Choose All Risks

All Risks is the most widely used and the most convenient coverage, for its insurance scope includes that of FPA, WPA and 11 additional coverages. The L/C issued by the buyer usually requires the exporter to arrange All Risks. However, All Risks costs more for its convenience, the premium of which is twice that of WPA and three times that of FPA.

Goods such as wool, cotton, linen, silk, silk fabric, apparel, and chemical fiber are in greater exposure to loss from instances such as contamination, hook damage, rain damage, shortage and theft and so on; in this case, All Risks is necessary. However, for lower valued and non-packaged bulk cargo such as iron ore, steel and cast iron products, FPA is fine.

For goods that are less likely to break or goods that tend to rust but are still usable (e. g. hardware products such as nail, wire, screw), or used commodity such as cars or machines, the applicant could arrange WPA as basic coverage.

Some goods need additional coverage. Take food containing aflatoxin for example, food such as peanuts, rapeseed and rice usually contains this microbial toxin. If rejected, expropriated or forced to alter usage by import country for reason of excessive aflatoxin, the exporter will have to endure great loss. In this case, Aflatoxin Risk should be arranged as additional coverage.

10. 4. 3 Flexible Use of Basic Coverage and Additional Coverage

When settling a claim, insurance company will identify cause of the loss in the first place and make indemnity only if the loss is covered in the insurance. Therefore, when applying for additional coverage, the applicant should consider the risks more likely to happen. For instance, fragile products such as glassware and ceramic artwork need to be covered by basic coverage (FPA or WPA) as well as Clash & Breakage Risks as additional coverage. Linen products will emit heat, mildew or self-ignite when exposed to damp, and thus need to be covered by basic coverage and Sweat and Heating Risk. The applicant should also take destination market into consideration. For instance, in market with disordered wharf, Theft, Pilferage and Non-Delivery (TPND) and Shortage Risk should be applied as additional coverage, or the applicant could buy All Risks.

10. 4. 4 Risk Prevention is Important

Insurance is a way to transfer and diversify risk. Though the loss caused could be compensated by the insurer, it is costly for the cargo owner to file a claim both financially and mentally. Therefore, the consciousness and method of risk prevention is important.

Damaged container has led to more and more cargo loss and damage. To prevent this risk, one should choose shipping company with good reputation and better equipment and carefully check the empty container for any breakage or poor seals on the door. Besides, the applicant should conjecture the cargo last shipped if any peculiar smell is sensed. If the cargo to be shipped is food or medicine but the last cargo has strong smell, the cargo is in great risk of odor.

For sake of convenient claim, the insured better requires Master Bill of Lading instead of House Bill of Lading, for the former is issued to the consignor in strict accordance with the actual condition of shipment whereas the latter may have the problem of anti-dated bill or different name of the vessel, which brings great trouble to the claim.

10. 4 国际物流货物保险策略

如何灵活运用保险，规避进出口货物的运输风险，是技巧性很强的专业工作。国际货物运输险就业务内容来讲是最复杂的。它的品种多，有基本险和附加险，基本险的选择、基本险和附加险的搭配运用都需要专业知识。

10.4.1 险别选择五要素

在投保时，都希望在保险范围和保险费之间寻找到一个平衡点。要做到这一点，首先要对自己所面临的风险做出评估，甄别哪种风险最大、最可能发生，并结合不同险种的保险费率来加以权衡。

出口商投保时，通常要对以下几个因素进行综合考虑。

① 货物的种类、性质和特点；

② 货物的包装情况；

③ 货物的运输情况（包括运输方式、运输工具、运输路线）；

④ 发生在港口和装卸过程中的损耗情况等；

⑤ 目的地的政治局势。

10.4.2 何时选用一切险

“一切险”是最常用的一个险种，投保一切险最方便，因为它的责任范围包括了平安险、水渍险和11种一般附加险。买方开立信用证通常会要求出口方投保一切险。然而一切险因其方便性而成本更高，其保费是水渍险的两倍，是平安险的三倍。

是否选择一切险作为主险要视实际情况而定。例如，毛、棉、麻、丝、绸、服装类和化学纤维类商品，遭受损失的可能性较大，如玷污、钩损、偷窃、短少、雨淋等，有必要投保一切险。有的货品则确实没有必要投保一切险，像低值、裸装的大宗货物如矿砂、钢材、铸铁制品，主险投保平安险就可以了。

对于不大可能发生碰损、破碎或容易生锈但不影响使用的货物，如铁钉、铁丝、螺丝等小五金类商品，以及旧汽车、旧机床等二手货，可以投保水渍险作为主险。

有的货物投保了一切险作为主险可能还不够，还需投保特别附加险。某些含有黄曲霉素的食物，如花生、油菜籽、大米等食品，往往含有这种毒素，会因超过进口国对该毒素的限制标准而被拒绝进口、没收或强制改变用途，从而造成损失，那么，在出口这类货物的时候，就应将黄曲霉素险作为特别附加险予以承保。

10.4.3 基本险与附加险灵活使用

保险公司在理赔的时候，首先要确认导致损失的原因，只有在投保险种的责任范围内导致的损失才会被赔偿，因此，附加险的选择要针对易出险因素来加以考虑。例如，玻璃制品、陶瓷类的日用品或工艺品等产品，会因破碎造成损失，投保时可在平安险或水渍险的基础上加保破碎险；麻类商品，受潮后会发热、引起霉变、自燃等而带来损失，应在平安险或水渍险的基础上加保受热受潮险；投保人还应考虑市场因素，如所销往的市场码头秩序混乱，则应加保偷盗、提货不着与短量险作为附加险，或干脆投保一切险。

10.4.4 防险比保险更重要

保险是转移和分散风险的工具。虽然风险造成的损失由保险公司负责理赔，但货主在索赔的过程中费时费力，会付出不小的代价，所以，预防风险的意识和投保基础上的预防措施都非常必要。

现在，因集装箱的破漏而导致货物受损的案例越来越多。要防止这种风险，一是尽量选择实力强、信誉好的船公司，他们的硬件设备相对好一些；二是装货前要仔细检查空柜，查看有无破漏，柜门口的封条是否完好。还要查看是否有异味，推测前一段装了什么货物。如果现在要装的货是食品或药品，而以前装的是气味浓烈的货物的话，就可能导致串味，甚至使货物根本不能使用。

为了日后办理索赔更方便，提单最好选择船东提单，而不是货代提单。因为船东提单是严格按照装运实际情况出具给发货人的，而货代提单则存在倒签装船日期、提单上船名与实际船名不符这样的情况，这会给将来的索赔取证工作带来麻烦。

Part B Vocabulary and Terminology 词汇和术语

insurable risk 可保风险
insurable interest 可保利益
coverage 险种
the insurer 保险人
the insured 被保险人
the applicant 投保人
beneficiary 受益人
perils of the sea 海上风险
general perils of the sea 共同海上风险
extraneous risk 外来风险
total loss 全损
actual total loss 实际全损
constructive total loss 推断全损
General Average 共同海损
Particular Average 单独海损
G. A. Contribution 共同海损分担
maritime charges 海上费用
sue and labor charges 施救费用
salvage charges 救助费用
Free from Particular Average (FPA) 平安险
With Particular Average (WA/WPA) 水渍险
All Risks 一切险
port of call 停靠港
policy 保单
Overland Transportation Risks 陆运险
Overland Transportation All Risks 陆运一切险
premium 保费
insured markon percentage 保险加成率
right of subrogation 代位求偿权
Letter of Subrogation 权益转让书

claim 索赔

Part C Exercise 练习

Ⅰ. Answer the following questions.

1. Please briefly describe the roles of international logistics insurance.

2. What strategies should be taken when applying for international cargo transport insurance?

3. What is General Average? Under what condition does GA apply?

4. What are the Basic Covers in marine cargo transport insurance? Please make comparison by their obligation scope.

5. What are the coverages of air transport insurance and their obligation scope?

6. Please describe the basic procedure of international logistics insurance.

7. What are the considerations of filing a claim in import/export?

Ⅱ. Translate the following passages into Chinese.

1. Insurable interest is true, valid, determinable, and direct economic stake of an insurance policy holder (or beneficiary of the policy) in the continued existence or safety of the insured property or person. An insurable interest means that the policy holder (or the beneficiary) must stand to suffer a direct financial loss if the event (against which the insurance cover was bought) does occur.

2. Insurance policy (or Policy) is a formal certificate proving the contractual relationship between the insurer and the insured, which has different coverage and form. In marine insurance, the widely used forms of policy include Hull Policy, Cargo Policy, Freight Policy, Ship Owner's Liability Policy, and so on.

3. Insurance claim refers to the act of the insured lodging a claim for compensation to the insurer against the loss of insured goods caused by insured risks. After receiving the claim requirement, the insurer should handle the compensation requirement from the insured, which is called settlement of claim.

4. Basic coverage can be independently arranged, instead of being attached to other insurance covers. There are three basic coverages, namely, Free from Particular Average, With Particular Average and All Risks.

Ⅲ. Translate the following passages into English.

1. 附加险不能单独投保，只能在投保一种基本险的基础上才能加保一种或数种附加险，它投保的是外来风险引起的损失。

2. 保险索赔，是指被保险货物遭受承保责任范围内的风险而造成损失时，被保险人向保险人提出赔偿要求的行为。

3. 虽然风险造成的损失由保险公司负责理赔，但货主在索赔的过程中费时费力，会付出不小的代价，所以，预防风险的意识和投保的基础上的预防措施都非常必要。

4. 单独海损费用，是指当被保险货物遭受保险责任范围内的自然灾害和意外事故时，被保险人或其代理人或其受雇人等为抢救被保险货物，防止损失继续扩大所支付的费用。

Appendix Insurance Policy
附录 保险单

××××保险公司

××××INSURANCE COMPANY ××××

总公司设于北京　　一九四九年创立

Head Office: BEIJING　　Established in 1949

保险单　号次

INSURANCE POLICY　　No. SH02/304246

×××× 保 险 公 司（以 下 简 称 本 公 司）

This Policy of Insurance witnesses that The People's Insurance Company of China (hereinafter called "the Company"),

根据

at the request of ______

（以下简称被保险人）的 要 求，由 被 保 险 人 向 本 公 司 缴 付 约 定 的 保 险 费，

(hereinafter called "the Insured") and in consideration of the agreed premium paid to the Company by the Insured,

按 照 本 保 险 单 承 保 险 别 和 背 面 所 载 条 款 与 下 列 条 款

undertakes to insure the undermentioned goods in transportation subject to the conditions of this Policy

承 保 下 述 货 物 运 输 保 险，特 立 本 保 险 单。

as per the Clause printed overleaf and other special clauses attached hereon.

标　记 Marks & Nos.	包装及数量 Quantity	保险货物项目 Description of Goods	保险金额 Amount Insured
As per Invoice No.			

总保险金额：

Total Amount Insured: ______

保　费　　费率　　装载运输工具

Premium: as arranged　　Rate as arranged　　Per conveyance S. S. ______

开行日期　　自　　至

Slg. on or abt. As Per B/L　　From ______ to ______

承保险别

Conditions

所保货物，如遇出险，本公司凭本保险单及其他有关证件给付赔款。

Claims, if any, payable on surrender of this Policy together with other relevant documents.

所保货物，如发生本保险单项下负责赔偿的损失或事故，

In the event of accident whereby loss or damage may result in a claim under this Policy

应立即通知本公司下述代理人查勘。

immediate notice applying for survey must be given to the Company's Agent as mentioned

hereunder:
赔款偿付地点
Claim payable at ____________________

日期 上海
Date ____________________ Shanghai
地址：中国上海中山东一路××号。
Address: ×× Zhongshan Dong Yi Lu Shanghai, China.
Cables: 42001 Shanghai.
Telex: ×××× PICCS CN

××××公司上海分公司
××××INSURANCE CO. ××××
SHANGHAI BRANCH

____
General Manager

(1/1/2009) ××××××× INSURANCE COMPANY ××××
OCEAN MARINE CARGO CLAUSES

Ⅰ. Scope of Cover:

This insurance is classified into the following three Conditions-Free Particular Average (F. P. A.). With Average (W. A.) and All Risks. Where the goods insured hereunder sustain loss or damage, the Company shall undertake to indemnify therefore according to the Insured Condition specified in the Policy and the Provisions of these Clauses: 1. Free From Particular Average (F. P. A.) This insurance covers: 1) Total or Constructive Total Loss of the whole consignment hereby insured caused in the course of transit by natural calamities-heavy weather, lightning, tsunami, earthquake and flood. In case a constructive total loss is claimed for, the Insured shall abandon to the Company the damaged goods and all his rights and title pertaining thereto. The goods on each lighter to or from the seagoing vessel shall be deemed a separate risk. "Constructive Total Loss" refers to the loss where an actual total loss appears to be unavoidable or the cost to be incurred in recovering or reconditioning the goods together with the forwarding cost to the destination named in the policy would exceed their value on arrival. 2) Total or Partial Loss caused by accidents-the carrying conveyance being grounded, sunk or in collision with floating ice or other objects as well as fire or explosion. 3) Partial loss of the insured goods attributable to heavy weather, lightning and/or tsunami, where the conveyance has been grounded, stranded, sunk or burnt, irrespective of whether the event or events took place before or after such accidents. 4) Partial or total loss consequent on falling of entire package or packages into sea during loading, transshipment or discharge. 5) Reasonable cost incurred by the Insured in salvaging the goods or minimizing a loss recoverable under the Policy, provided that such cost shall not exceed the sum insured of the consignment so saved. 6) Losses attributable to discharge of the insured goods at a port of distress following a sea peril as well as special charges arising from loading, warehousing and forwarding of the goods at an intermediate port of call or refuge. 7) Sacrifice in and Contribution to General Average and Salvage Charges. 8) Such proportion of losses sustained by the ship owners as is to be reimbursed by the Cargo Owner under the Contract of Affreightment "Both to Blame Collision" clause. 2. With Average (W. A.) Aside from the risks covered under F. P. A. condition as above, this insurance also covers partial losses of the insured goods caused by heavy weather, lightning, tsunami, earthquake and/or flood. 3. All Risks Aside from the risks covered under the F. P. A. and W. A. conditions as above, this insurance also covers all risks of loss of or damage to the insured goods whether partial or total, arising from external causes in the course of transit.

Ⅱ. Exclusions:

This insurance does not cover: 1. Loss or damage caused by the intentional act or fault of the Insured. 2. Loss or damage falling under the liability of the consignor. 3. Loss or damage arising from the inferior quality or shortage of the insured goods prior to the attachment of this insurance. 4. Loss or damage arising from normal loss inherent vice or nature of the insured goods, loss of market and/or delay in transit and any expenses arising therefrom. 5. Risks and liabilities covered and excluded by the ocean marine (cargo) war risks clauses and strike, riot and civil commotion clauses of this Company

Ⅲ. Commencement and Termination of Cover:

1. Warehouse to Warehouse Clause: This insurance attaches from the time the goods hereby insured leave the warehouse or place of storage named in the Policy for the commencement of the transit and continues in force in the ordinary course of transit including sea, land and inland waterway transits and transit in lighter until the insured goods are delivered to the consignee's final warehouse or place of storage at the destination named in the Policy or to any other place used by the Insured for allocation or distribution of the goods or for storage other than in the ordinary course of transit. 2. If owing to delay, deviation forced discharge, reshipment or transshipment beyond the control of the Insured or any change or termination of the voyage arising from the exercise of a liberty granted to the shipowners under the contract of affreightment, the insured goods arrive at a port or place other than that named in the Policy, subject to immediate domain in force and shall terminate as hereunder: 1) If the insured goods are sold at port or place not named in the Policy, this insurance shall terminate on delivery of the goods sold, but in no event shall this insurance extend beyond sixty (60) days after completion of discharge of the insured goods from the carrying vessel at such port or place. 2) If the insured goods are to be forwarded to the final destination named in the Policy or any other destination, this insurance shall terminate in accordance with Section 1 above.

Ⅳ. Duty of the Insured:

It is the duty of the Insured to attend to all matters as specified hereunder, failing which the Company reserves the right to reject his claim for any loss if and when such failure prejudice the rights of the Company: 1. The Insured shall take delivery of the insured goods in good time upon their arrival at the port of destination named in the Policy. In the event of any damage to the goods, the INSURED SHALL IMMEDIATELY APPLY FOR SURVEY TO THE survey and/or settling agent stipulated in the Policy. If the insured goods are found short in entire package or packages or to show apparent traces of damage, the Insured shall obtain from the carrier, bailee or other relevant authorities (Customs and Port Authorities etc.) certificate of loss or damage and/or shortloading memo. Should the carrier, bailee or the other relevant authorities be responsible for such shortage or damage, the Insured shall lodge a claim with them in writing and, if necessary, obtain their confirmation of an extension of the time limit of validity of such claim. 2. The Insured shall, and the Company may also, take reasonable measures immediately in salvaging the goods or preventing or minimizing a loss or damage thereto. The measures so taken by the Insured or by the Company shall not be considered respectively, as a waiver of abandonment hereunder, or as an acceptance thereof. 3. In case of a change of voyage or any omission or error in the description of the interest, the name of the vessel or voyage this insurance shall remain in force only upon prompt notice to this Company when the Insured becomes aware of the same and payment of an additional premium if required. 4. The following documents should accompany any claim hereunder made against the Company: Original Policy, Bill of Lading, Invoice Packing List, Tally Sheet, Weight Memo. Certificate of Loss or Damage and/or Shortloading Memo. Survey Report. Statement of Claim. If any third party is involved, documents relative to pursuing of recovery from such party should also be included. 5. Immediate notice should be given to the Company when the Cargo Owner's actual responsibility under the Contract of Affreightment "Both to Blame Collision" Clause becomes known.

Ⅴ. The Time of Validity of A Claim: The time of validity of a claim under this insurance shall not exceed a period of two years counting from the time of completion of discharge of the insured goods from the seagoing vessel at the final port of discharge.

(1/1/2009)

×××××× INSURANCE COMPANY ××××

OCEAN MARINE CARGO WAR RISK CLAUSES

Ⅰ. Scope of Cover:

This insurance covers: 1. Loss of or damage to the insured goods caused directly by or consequent upon WAR. WARLIKE OPERATIONS. HOSTILE ACTS. ARMED CONFLICTS OR PIRACY: 2. Loss or damage caused by CAPTURE, SEIZURE. ARREST. RESTRAINT OR DETAINMENT arising from the events in Section 1. 1 above. 3. Loss or damage caused by conventional weapons of war including mines, torpedoes and bombs. 4. Sacrifice in and contribution to General Average and Salvage Charges arising from the risks covered hereunder.

Ⅱ. Exclusions:

This insurance does not cover: 1. Loss damage or expenses arising from any hostile use of atomic or nuclear weapons of war. 2. Any claim based upon Loss of, or frustration of, the insured voyage caused by arrest, restraint or detainment by any executive authorities, authorities in power or any other armed groups.

Ⅲ. Commencement and Termination:

1. This insurance shall attach from the time the insured goods are loaded on the seagoing vessel or lighter at the port of shipment named in the Policy until discharged overside from the seagoing vessel or lighter at the port of destination named in the Policy If the insured goods are not discharged therefrom. The longest duration at the port of discharge shall be limited to fifteen (15) days counting from midnight of the day of the vessel's arrival. In the absence of such berth or place, the vessel's arrival refers to the vessel's first anchoring, mooring or securing either at or off the intended port or at or neat the place of discharge.

2. In case of transshipment at an intermediate port, regardless of whether or not the in-

sured goods are unloaded, the longest duration of this insurance at such port of transshipment shall be limited to fifteen (15) days counting from midnight of the day of the vessel's arrival at such port or place of discharge. However, this insurance shall reattach when the insured goods are loaded on the on-carrying seagoing vessel.

3. If the contract of affreightiment is terminated at a port or place other than the destination named in the Policy, such port or place shall be deemed the destination under the Policy and this insurance shall terminate according to Section Ⅲ. I above If the insured goods are to be reshipped to the original or any other destination, this insurance shall attach when the goods are loaded on the on-carrying vessel or lighter provided notice is given to the Company and an additional premium is paid prior to the commencement of such further transit.

4. This insurance shall remain in force during any deviation, change of voyage, variation of adventure arising from the exercise of a liberty granted to the shipowners under the contract of affreightment subject to immediate notice to the Company and payment of an additional premium, when such event comes to the knowledge of the Insured.

Note:

These clauses are the clauses of an additional insurance to the Ocean Marine Cargo Insurance of the Company. In case of conflict between any clauses of these clauses and the ocean marine cargo clauses, these clauses shall prevail.

Chapter Eleven

International Freight Forwarder 国际货运代理

Part A Text 课文

11.1 Basic Knowledge of Freight Forwarder

11.1.1 Agency

(1) Definition of Agency

There are general and narrow concepts of agency.

The general concept of agency is a fiduciary relationship between two parties in which one (the agent) is under the control of (is obligated to) the other (the principal). The agent is authorized by the principal to perform certain acts, for and on behalf of the principal. The principal is bound by the acts of the agent. This general concept of agent is adopted by Anglo-American law system.

General concept of agency includes indirect agency and direct agency. Indirect agency means that the agent performs civil juristic acts in his own name, the legal consequence of which is indirectly assumed by the principal. In contrast, in direct agency, the agent performs civil juristic acts in the principal's name within the scope of the power of agency, with the consequence directly taken by the principal.

Narrow concept of agency refers to direct agency, which is accepted by countries of civil law system such as Germany, Japan, and China.

In China, agency refers to its narrow concept, more specifically direct agency.

(2) Characteristics of Agency

In China, agency has the following characteristics:

1) The agent must act in name of the principal.

2) The agent must act within the scope of power of agency.

3) The act by the agent must be of legal significance.

4) The legal consequence of agent's act is upon the principal.

(3) Types of Agency

Article 64 in *General Principles of the Civil Law of the People's Republic of China* regulates that agency shall include entrusted agency, statutory agency and appointed agency. Entrusted agency means that the agent acts upon the delegation of the principal. Statutory agency involves the agent acting according to the law and regulations, and appointed agency means that the agent acts according to the appointment from law court or related entities. Transport agency (or cargo agency) falls into category of entrusted agency.

When it comes to type of business, there are commodity agency, foreign trade agency, insurance agency, real estate agency, securities agency, culture agency, law agency, advertisement agency, transport agency, bidding agency, etc. According to the exclusive right of agency, we have exclusive agency and nonexclusive agency.

11.1.2 International Freight Forwarder

(1) Freight Forwarder

A freight forwarder, also referred to as a forwarder or a forwarding agent, is a person or company that organizes shipments for individuals or corporations to get goods from manufacturer or producer to a market, customer or final point of distribution. Forwarders contract with a carrier or often multiple carriers to transit the goods. A forwarder does not ship the goods but acts as an expert in logistics network. These carriers can use a variety of shipping modes, including ships, airplanes, trucks, and railroads, and often multiple modes for a single shipment. For example, the freight forwarder may arrange to have cargo moved from a plant to an airport by truck, flown to destination city, and then moved from airport to a customer's building by another truck.

International freight forwarders typically handle international shipments. They have additional expertise in preparing and processing customs and other documentation and performing activities pertaining to international shipments.

Information typically reviewed by a freight forwarder includes commercial invoice, shipper's export declaration, bill of lading and other documents required by the carrier or country of export, import, and/or transshipment.

The relationship between freight forwarder and cargo owner is that of the trustee and the principal. In forwarding business, the trustee as an agent of the owner answers to the cargo owner and provides service upon request of the owner in order to get agent commission.

(2) Nature of International Freight Forwarding Agency

International freight forwarding agency has the meaning of both international freight forwarder and international freight forwarding business.

1) The Nature of International Freight Forwarder: The freight forwarder in nature is the agent of interested parties in cargo transport and works as an intermediary for consignor, consignee and carrier.

As agent for consignor and consignee, the forwarder is responsible for selecting transport route and carrier, booking cargo space from the carrier, preparing shipping documents, arranging short-distance transport, warehousing, weighing and inspection of the cargo, applying for insurance, customs inspection, declaration and clearance, and paying the carrier, warehouse keeper and related authorities. Sometimes he needs to receive and examine shipping documents, perform above mentioned relative activities and then pick up the goods on behalf of the consignee.

When working as agent of carrier, the forwarder is, on behalf of the carrier, responsible for goods collection and stowage, container stuffing, assembling and devanning, and shipping documents issuance. Sometimes, a forwarder works as an independent operator to conduct warehousing and transport, even issue shipping document and bill of lading as a contracting carrier. In this case, the nature of transport agent is not affected.

2) The Nature of International Freight Forwarding Business: International freight forwarding business in social structure belongs to tertiary industry; it is of service industry in nature.

(3) Function of International Freight Forwarder

International freight forwarders thoroughly understand international trade process and various transport businesses, are familiar with relative law and regulations, and have access to update and accurate information. They have developed close relationship with various carriers, warehouse operators, insurers, ports, airports, stations, depots, banks, and governmental agencies such as Customs, commodity inspection department, sanitary quarantine department, animal and plant inspection and quarantine department, import and export control department. They play significant role in connecting the consignor, consignee, carrier, port, airport, station, warehouse and operator. For the principal, the forwarder's function can be summarized as follows.

1) Coordinating and organizing. The forwarder is to organize transport activities, design transport route, and choose transport mode and carrier. He will coordinate various parties such as the cargo owner, the carrier, the insurer, the depot operator and so on, which will greatly save time and cost of the shipper.

2) Providing specialized service. By providing various specialized services, the forwarder saves time and energy of the principal and accordingly increases the efficiency of the latter.

3) Controlling communication. Equipped with wide business relations and advanced information technique, the forwarder can keep effective communication with interested parties involved in cargo shipment, conduct accurate tracking and control of the goods, in order to guarantee the safe and timely arrival of the goods.

4) Consulting. With the understanding of international trade and international shipment, the forwarder is able to provide explicit and detailed advises for the principal in order to assist the principal in designing appropriate scheme and avoiding unnecessary waste and loss.

5) Reducing cost. By choosing optimal transport route and mode, the best warehouse operator, stevedoring company, and the insurer, and arranging reasonable premium, the forwarder helps in reducing the cost of interested parties and thus increasing their main business income.

6) Fund financing. Having developed good relationship with interested parties, the forwarder may help the consignor and consignee to pay related charges and taxes, settle pay-

ment with the carrier, warehouse operator and stevedoring company, even provide guarantee to the carrier, warehouse operator, stevedoring company, banks, and Customs authorities on expenses and taxes.

11.1 国际货运代理的基本知识

11.1.1 代理

(1) 代理的概念

代理（agency）这一概念，各国法律规定各有不同，总的来说，可以分为广义和狭义两种。

广义的代理：广义的代理是双方之间的信托关系，指一方（代理人）受制于另一方（委托人）或对另一方负责。代理人经委托人授权，代表委托人实施某种行为，而这种行为的法律后果直接由委托人承担。这种广义的代理概念为英美法系所采纳。

广义的代理又包括两种：直接代理和间接代理。间接代理，即代理人以自己的名义，代替委托人（被代理人）实施民事法律行为，而其法律后果间接地由委托人承担。直接代理指代理人以委托人的名义，代替委托人实施民事法律行为，其法律后果直接地由委托人承担。

狭义的代理仅指直接代理而不包括间接代理。这一种概念为德国、日本、中国等大陆法系的国家所采纳。

在我国，代理的概念就是上述的狭义代理（直接代理）的概念。

(2) 代理的特点

我国的代理具有以下特点。

1）代理人必须以委托人（被代理人）的名义进行活动。

2）代理人必须在代理权限内进行活动。

3）代理人所进行的必须是具有法律意义的活动。

4）代理人代理行为的法律后果归属于委托人。

(3) 代理的种类

根据我国《民法通则》第64条的规定，代理包括委托代理、法定代理和指定代理。

代理人根据委托人（被代理人）的委托而进行代理活动，称为委托代理。法定代理是指代理人根据法律的直接规定进行代理活动。指定代理是指代理人根据法院或其他有关单位的指定进行代理活动。运输代理（货运代理）属于委托代理的范畴。

另外根据代理业务的不同，代理可以分为商品代理、外贸代理、保险代理、房地产代理、证券代理、文化代理、法律代理、广告代理、运输代理、投标代理等；按代理商有无独家代理权来划分，可分为独家代理和多家（佣金）代理。

11.1.2 国际货运代理

(1) 货运代理

货运代理是指为个体或公司组织运输，将货物从制造商运往市场、顾客或最终分销地的个人或公司。货运代理与一个或多个承运人签订合约以运输货物，其本身不对货物进行运输，而是在物流网络中起到组织协调的作用；这些实际承运人使用包括海运、空运、陆运、铁路运输等多种运输方式，并常常使用多式联运方式。例如，货运代理可安排货物从工厂陆运至机场，再空运至目的地城市，而后再次陆运至最终客户处。

国际货运代理通常安排国际运输，他们在准备并办理结关手续和其他单证，以及从事国际运输活动方面，有着特殊专长。

国际货代审查的信息通常包括商业发票、发货方报关手续、货运提单及承运人或出口/进口/转口国要求的其他单证。

货运代理和货主之间是受托人和委托人的关系。在货代行业，受托人作为货主的代理对货主负责，并按照委托人的要求提供货代服务，以获取代理佣金。

（2）国际货运代理的性质

“国际货运代理”一词具有两种含义：其一是指国际货运代理人，其二是指国际货运代理行业。

1）国际货运代理人的性质：货运代理本质上属于货物运输关系人的代理人，是联系发货人、收货人和承运人的货物运输中介人。

作为收、发货人的代理，国际货运代理负责选择运输路线、承运人，向承运人订舱，编制运输单据，安排货物的短途运输、仓储、称重、检测，办理货物的保险、报检、报验和通关手续，向承运人、仓储保管人及有关当局支付有关费用。有时代表收货人接收、检查运输单据，办理货物的保险、报检报验和通关手续，提取货物，安排仓储和短途运输，支付运费及其他相关费用，协助收货人向责任方索赔。

作为承运人的代理，国际货运代理负责代表承运人揽货、配载、装箱、拼箱、拆箱，签发运输单据。国际货代有时也以独立经营人的身份从事货物的仓储、运输，甚至以缔约承运人身份出具运单、提单，但这并不影响其作为运输代理人的本质特征。

2）国际货运代理行业的性质：国际货运代理行业在社会结构中属于第三产业，性质上属于服务行业。

（3）国际货运代理的作用

国际货运代理企业通晓国际贸易环节，精通各种运输业务，熟悉有关法律、法规，业务关系广泛，信息来源准确、及时，与各种承运人、仓储经营人、保险人、港口、机场、车站、堆场、银行等相关企业，海关、商检、卫检、动植物检、进出口管制等有关政府部门存在着密切的业务关系，不论对于进出口货物的收、发货人，还是对于承运人和港口、机场、车站、仓库经营人都有着重要的桥梁和纽带作用。对于委托人来说，国际货运代理的作用概括如下。

1）组织协调作用。国际货运代理人组织运输活动，设计运输路线，选择运输方式和承运人（或货主），协调货主、承运人及其与仓储保管人、保险人、银行、港口等各方关系，可以节省托运人/货主的时间，减少许多不必要的麻烦，使货主专心致力于主营业务。

2）专业服务作用。国际货运代理人通过向委托人提供各种专业服务，可以节约委托人的时间和精力，提高委托人的工作效率。

3）沟通控制作用。国际货运代理人拥有广泛的业务关系、发达的服务网络、先进的信息技术手段，可以随时保持货物运输关系人之间的有效沟通，对货物运输的全过程进行准确的跟踪和控制，保证货物安全、及时运抵目的地。

4）咨询顾问作用。国际货运代理人通晓国际贸易和国际运输知识，可以向委托人提出明确、具体的咨询意见，协助委托人设计、选择适当处理方案，避免、减少不必要风险、周折和浪费。

5）降低成本作用。国际货运代理人通过选择货物的最佳运输路线、运输方式，最佳仓储保管人、装卸作业人和保险人，争取公平、合理的费率，从而降低货物运输关系人的业务成本，提高其主营业务效益。

6）资金融通作用。国际货运代理人与相关方关系密切，长期合作，可以代替收、发货人支付有关费用、税金，提前与承运人、仓储保管人、装卸作业人结算有关费用，向承运人、仓储保管人、装卸作业人及银行、海关当局提供费用、税金担保或风险担保。

11.2 Business Scope of International Freight Forwarder

11.2.1 Business Scope of International Transport Freight Forwarder

According to the *Provisions of the People's Republic of China on Administration of the International Goods Shipping Agency Industry*, *Measures for the Management of Foreign-Funded International Forwarding Agents of the People's Republic of China*, and *Detailed Rules for Implementing the Regulation of the People's Republic of China on the Administration of the International Freight Forwarding Industry (for Trial Implementation)*, an international freight forwarder may engage in management activities as an agent or an independent operator. Its scope of business shall include:

1) Canvassing cargo, booking space (including ship renting, plane chartering and cabin booking), consignment for shipment, warehousing and packing;

2) Supervision on cargo loading and discharging, container stuffing and devanning, distribution, transit, and related short-distance transport services;

3) Custom declaration, commodity inspection and checking, and insurance purchases;

4) Making, signing and issuing of relevant documents and bills, payment of transport fees, settlement and payment of incidental charges;

5) Freight forwarding of international items for display, personal belongings and cargo passing through the territory of a country;

6) International multi-modal transport, and container transport (including container assembling);

7) International express delivery (personal letters excluded);

8) Consultation and other international freight forwarding businesses.

However, not every forwarder conducts all the businesses listed above. The actual operation business should be in accordance with those approved by and registered in department of foreign economic relations and trade and other relevant departments. In addition, a forwarder is allowed to expand his business scope if needed. Other businesses must be investigated and approved by department in charge and registered in industry and commerce administration authorities.

11.2.2 Business Contents of International Freight Forwarder

The business scope of international freight forwarder is a summary of businesses a forwarder could conduct by law. The forwarder can detail his business scope into specified business content according to the client, category and mode of service.

A forwarder could work as an agent of cargo owner or carrier, or as an independent operator. The role of a forwarder in international logistics is summarized in Figure 11.1.

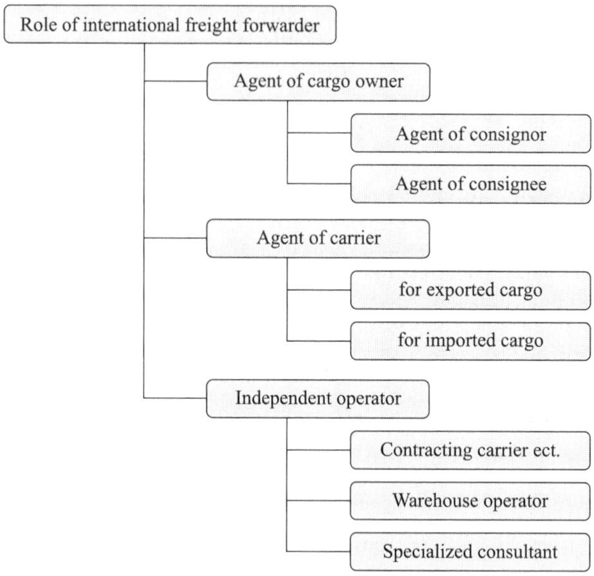

Figure 11.1 Role of international freight forwarder in international logistics

(1) Business Content a Forwarder Provides When He Works as Agent of Cargo Owner

1) Working as agent of consignor, an international freight forwarder provides the following services:

① Providing information on train number, shipping date, flight number, freight rate, Customs declaration, commodity inspection and checking, loading and unloading regulations at port of shipment, transit and destination.

② Choosing transport route, transport mode and appropriate carrier upon request of the consignor, arranging transport and transit of the goods, negotiating for preferential freight rate, and confirming freight charge and other related expenses.

③ Accepting and examining the certificates and documents provided by the consignor and reminding the latter to prepare transport files, certificates and documents as required by export/import country or region.

④ Filling in and making out cargo transportation documents for purpose of Customs declaration, commodity inspection and checking.

⑤ Renting conveyance from chosen carrier and booking vessel and cargo space.

⑥ Arranging short-distance transport of goods from place of consignor or other place named by the consignor to the departure station, port or airport, and handing over the goods to the carrier or his agent.

⑦ Arranging the packing, warehousing, weighing, tallying, labeling and marking of the goods, and station, port and airport entrance formalities.

⑧ Arranging the stuffing and assembling of container, tallying of cargo and supervising the loading.

⑨ Processing transport insurance formalities.

⑩ Arranging formalities of Customs declaration, commodity inspection and checking and paying relevant charges.

⑪ Inquiring and mastering shipping condition and time of departure and timely informing the principal of shipment information.

⑫ Collecting shipping document, bill of lading and other certificates of cargo receipt from carrier or his agent and handing them over to the consignor or handling on his instruction.

⑬ Making payment with the carrier or his agent and relative authorities for freight, incidental charges, taxes and government fees, etc.

⑭ Contacting the carrier or his agent at place of departure or destination for shipping condition, supervising the shipping process, and making timely notification to the consignor.

⑮ Recording damage to, shortage and loss of the goods, collecting relevant proofs, and assisting consignor in filing a claim to responsible parties and insurance company.

⑯ Conducting other activities commissioned by the consignor.

2) Working as agent of consignee, an international freight forwarder provides the following services:

① Contacting the carrier or his agent at the place of departure or destination for shipping condition, supervising the shipping process, and making timely notification to the consignee.

② Keeping in contact with the consignee, accepting and examining his documents, assisting him in preparing goods pick-up and acceptance.

③ Paying the carrier, his agent and other parties on freight and incidental charges.

④ Arranging customs declaration, taxation, and clearance, commodity inspection and checking, and making payment on relative tax and charges.

⑤ Arranging formalities of goods pick-up, acceptance, container devanning, unloading and checking.

⑥ Arranging movement, warehousing, transit and distribution of goods.

⑦ Arranging short-distance transport of goods from place of unloading to place of consignee or other place named by the consignee.

⑧ Handing over required goods and related documents to the consignee or his named party.

⑨ Recording damage to, shortage and loss of the goods, collecting relevant proofs, and assisting the consignee in filing claim to responsible parties and insurance company.

⑩ Other activities commissioned by consignee.

(2) Business Content a Forwarder Provides When He Works as Agent of Carrier

1) As agent of carrier for exported cargo, a forwarder can conduct the following activities:

① Replying the shipper information on number of vehicle, shipping date and number of airplane, freight rate, shipping condition, etc.

② Canvassing cargo and organizing stowage, accepting the rent of train, vessel and airplane and the space booking of train and cabin from the consignor, and concluding shipping contract.

③ Making entry documents of goods and arranging the entry of goods into warehouse, station, port, airport or container.

④ Assisting the carrier, station, port or airport in assigning conveyance and loading of goods.

⑤ Examining bill of goods gathered in the station, port or depot, making out export shipping documents, bill of lading and etc., and making Customs declaration.

⑥ Issuing notice of demurrage or notice of dispatch to the charter.

⑦ Issuing shipping document and bill of lading to the consignor and charging freight and incidental fees.

⑧ Arranging transit of cargo and container.

⑨ Gathering export cargo shipping documents and settling payment.

⑩ Turning the shipping documents and materials over to the principal and reporting the cargo load, container usage, expenses and charges.

⑪ Transiting shipping documents and information to the carrier at destination.

⑫ Conducting other activities commissioned by the carrier.

2) As the agent of carrier for imported cargo, a forwarder can serve in:

① Obtaining, organizing and examining import cargo shipping documents.

② Providing information of goods arrival to the consignee or Notify Party and notifying of goods pick-up.

③ Making import cargo shipping documents and arranging import Customs declaration of container, unit load device and cargo.

④ Notifying the station, port or airport of goods unloading.

⑤ Arranging container devanning, goods transit, checking and acceptance.

⑥ Collecting freight, incidental charges and other related fees and arranging goods release.

⑦ Gathering import cargo shipping documents, examining related expenses and settling payment.

⑧ Other services commissioned by the carrier.

(3) Forwarder Could Also Work as An Independent Operator

1) When working as contracting carrier, non-vessel operating common carrier and multimodal transport operator, an international freight forwarder could provide the following services:

① Accepting goods from consignor or his agent at place of departure or other place and issuing certificate of good acceptance, bill of lading and shipping documents.

② Confirming route and mode of transport and entering into cargo transport contract with actual carrier and sub-carrier.

③ Arranging and tracking the shipment.

④ Ensuring the container to be used if necessary and applying for carrier's liability risk insurance.

⑤ Notifying the agent at place of transit and sub-carrier of the transit, reloading and transshipment of goods.

⑥ Periodically informing the consignor, consignee or their agents of goods location and condition.

⑦ Arranging stoppage in transit upon request of cargo owner.

⑧ Informing the consignee or his agent of time of arrival and arranging the agent at destination to send notification of goods pickup/transfer.

⑨ Settling and collecting freight and incidental charges from cargo owner or his agent and making settlement.

⑩ Arranging claim filing and settlement.

2) When working as warehouse operator, the business content of an international freight forwarder includes:

① Tallying goods, inspecting package and label, and arranging goods acceptance with cargo owner or shipping staff.

② Examining quality of goods on behalf of the cargo owner upon his request.

③ Arranging entry of goods into the warehouse according to examination result.

④ Making reasonable storage, stacking, covering and padding of the goods according to the nature, characteristics and storage requirements of the goods.

⑤ Establishing storage record, making periodic or occasional count of the goods and making inventory record.

⑥ Storing goods properly and conducting timely maintenance.

⑦ Organizing original packing and assembling odd-lot goods upon request of cargo owner.

⑧ Examining exit certificate of goods filled in by cargo owner such as bill of lading and allocation order of goods and updating inventory record.

⑨ Dispatching, packing and marking the goods and moving the goods to tallying spot for shipping.

⑩ Reexamining exit certificate of goods, handing over the goods to cargo owner or his carrier, and writing off the stored goods.

3) Working as a specialized consultant, the forwarder could provide information on related law, regulations, conventions and transportation, and suggest on:

① Route, mode and scheme of transport;

② Packing of goods and means of loading;

③ Customs clearance, commodity inspection, animal and plant quarantine, and sanitary inspection;

④ Shipping documents and bank request;

⑤ Transport insurance coverage and insurance scope;

⑥ The filing and settlement of a claim;

⑦ Other issues consulted by the principal.

11.2 国际货运代理的经营范围及业务内容

11.2.1 国际货物运输代理企业的经营范围

根据《中华人民共和国国际货物运输代理业管理规定》《中华人民共和国外商投资国际货运代理业管理办法》和《中华人民共和国国际货物运输代理业管理规定实施细则（试

行)》的有关规定，国际货运代理企业可以接受委托，作为代理人或者独立经营人从事下列全部或部分经营活动。

1）揽货、订舱（含租船、包机、包舱)、托运、仓储、包装；

2）货物的监装、监卸、集装箱拆箱、分拨、中转及相关的短途运输服务；

3）报关、报检、报验、保险；

4）缮制签发有关单证、交付运费、结算及交付杂费；

5）国际展品、私人物品及过境货物运输代理；

6）国际多式联运、集运（含集装箱拼箱)；

7）国际快递（不含私人信函)；

8）咨询及其他国际货运代理业务。

但是，这些并不是每个国际货运代理企业都具有的经营范围。各个国际货运代理企业实际经营的国际货运代理业务范围，应当以对外经济贸易主管部门及其他相关部门批准、登记、注册的经营范围为准。此外，国际货运代理企业还可以根据实际需要，扩大经营范围。国际货运代理企业兼营的其他业务，依照有关法律、法规和规章，需要有关主管部门审查、批准，并在工商行政管理机关登记。

11.2.2 国际货物运输代理企业的业务内容

国际货物运输代理企业的经营范围是其依法可以从事的业务活动的原则概括。国际货物运输代理企业可以根据服务对象、服务类别、服务方式等的不同，将其经营范围内的业务活动具体化。

实践中，国际货物运输代理企业可以作为货主或承运人的代理人或独立经营人而从事货代业务。国际货运代理企业在国际物流中的角色作用如图11.1所示。

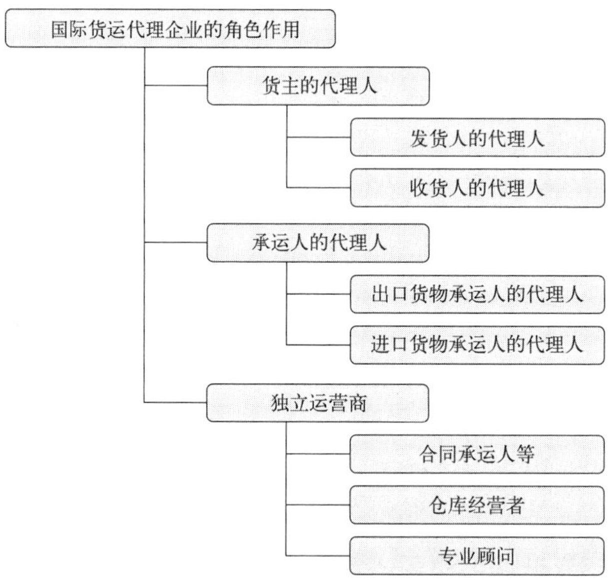

图11.1 国际货运代理企业在国际物流中的角色作用

(1) 作为货主的代理人提供货运代理服务方面

1）国际货物运输代理企业作为出口货物发货人的代理人，其业务内容通常可以分为以下具体项目。

① 查询、提供车次、船期、航班、运价信息，以及出口货物的报关、报检、报验、装运港、中转港、目的港装卸、运输规定；

② 根据发货人的货物运输要求，选择运输路线、运输方式和适当的承运人，安排货物运输、转运，争取优惠运价，确认运费及其他相关费用；

③ 接受、审核发货人提供的货物运输资料、单证，提醒发货人准备货物进出口地所属国家或地区要求的货物运输文件、单证；

④ 代为填写、缮制货物运输单据，以备办理通关、报检、报验等出口手续；

⑤ 向选定的承运人租赁运输工具、洽订车辆、舱位；

⑥ 安排货物从发货人处或发货人指定的其他处所到货物起运车站、港口或机场的短途运输，将货物交付承运人或其代理人；

⑦ 办理出运货物的包装、仓储、称重、计量、标记、刷唛、进站、进港、进场手续；

⑧ 办理出运货物的装箱、拼箱、理货、监装事宜；

⑨ 办理货物的运输保险手续；

⑩ 办理货物的通关、报检、报验等手续，支付有关费用；

⑪ 查询、掌握货物装载情况及运输工具离开车站、港口、机场时间，及时向委托人报告货物出运信息；

⑫ 向承运人或其代理人领取运单、提单及其他收货凭证，及时交给发货人或按其指示处理；

⑬ 向承运人、承运人的代理人、其他有关各方、各有关当局结算、交付运费、杂费、税金、政府规费等款项；

⑭ 联系承运人或其在货物起运地、目的地的代理人，掌握运输情况，监管运输过程，及时向发货人通报有关信息；

⑮ 记录货物的残损、短缺、灭失情况，收集有关证据，协助发货人向有关责任方、保险公司索赔；

⑯ 发货人委托办理的其他事项。

2）国际货物运输代理企业作为进口货物收货人的代理人，其业务内容通常可以分为以下具体项目。

① 保持与承运人或其在货物运输目的地的代理人的联系，随时查询，及时掌握货物动态和运抵目的地的信息，及时通报收货人；

② 保持与收货人的联系，接受、审核其提供的运输单据，协助其准备提货文件，办妥相关手续，做好提货、接货准备；

③ 向承运人、承运人的代理人及其他有关各方支付运费、杂费；

④ 办理货物的报关、纳税、结关、报检、报验手续，代为支付有关税金和费用；

⑤ 办理货物的提取、接收、拆箱、监卸、查验手续；

⑥ 安排货物的短倒、仓储、转运、分拨事宜；

⑦ 安排货物从卸货地到收货人处或其指定处所的短途运输；

⑧ 向收货人或其指定的其他人交付货物及有关单据；

⑨ 记录货物的残损、短缺、灭失情况，收集有关证据，协助收货人向有关责任方、保险公司索赔；

⑩ 收货人委托的其他事项。

(2)作为承运人的代理人提供货运代理服务方面

1)国际货物运输代理企业作为出口货物承运人的代理人，其业务内容通常可以分为以下具体项目。

① 回复托运人关于陆运车辆班次、海运船舶船期、空运飞机航班、运价、运输条件等相关事宜的查询；

② 承揽货物，组织货载，接受托运人的包车、租船、包机、订车、订舱要求，与之洽谈、订定车辆、船舶、飞机、舱位，签订运输合同；

③ 填写、缮制货物入仓、进站、进港、进场单据或集装箱、集装器放行单，安排货物入仓、进站、进港、进场或装箱；

④ 协助承运人或车站、码头、机场进行车辆、船舶、飞机配载，装车、装船、装机；

⑤ 审核车站、码头、场站汇总的货物清单，缮制货物出口运单、提单等单证，并向海关申报集装箱、集装器、货物情况；

⑥ 向航次租船的船舶承租人签发滞期或速遣通知；

⑦ 向托运人签发运单、提单，收取运费、杂费；

⑧ 办理货物、集装箱的中转手续；

⑨ 汇总出口货物运输单据，审核有关费用、费收，办理支付、结算手续；

⑩ 向委托人转交货物运输文件、资料，报告出口货载、用箱、费用、费收情况；

⑪ 向货物的目的地车站、港口、机场承运人代理传送货物运输文件、资料，传递运输信息；

⑫ 承运人委托的其他事项。

2)国际货物运输代理企业作为进口货物承运人的代理人，其业务内容通常可以分为以下具体项目。

① 取得、整理、审核进口货物运输单据；

② 向收货人或通知人传达货物到站、到港、运抵信息，通知其提货；

③ 填写、缮制进口货物运输单据，办理集装箱、集装器、货物进口申报手续；

④ 通知、协助车站、港口、机场安排卸货作业；

⑤ 安排集装箱的拆箱、货物的转运、查验、交接；

⑥ 收取运费、杂费及其他相关费用，办理放货手续；

⑦ 汇总进口货物运输单据，审核有关费用、费收，办理支付、结算手续；

⑧ 承运人委托的其他事项。

(3)作为独立经营人提供有关服务方面

1)国际货物运输代理企业以缔约承运人、无船承运人、多式联运经营人身份提供货物运输服务，其业务内容通常可以分为以下具体项目。

① 在货物的起运地或其他地点与托运人或其代理人办理货物的交接手续，签发收货凭证、提单、运单；

② 确定运输方式、运输路线，与实际承运人、分包承运人签订货物运输合同；

③ 安排货物运输，跟踪监管货物运输过程；

④ 必要时，对装载货物的集装箱进行保险，对货物的运输投保承运人责任险；

⑤ 通知在货物转运地的代理人，与分包承运人进行联系，申办货物的过境、换装、转运手续，办理相关事宜；

⑥ 定期向发货人、收货人或其代理人发布货物位置、状况信息；

⑦ 在货主提出要求时，安排货物的中途停运；

⑧ 通知收货人或其代理人货物运抵目的地的时间，安排在货物目的地的代理人办理通知提货、交货手续；

⑨ 向货主或其代理人收取、结算运费、杂费；

⑩ 办理货物的索赔、理赔手续。

2）国际货物运输代理企业以仓储保管人身份提供货物仓储服务，其业务内容通常可以分为以下具体项目。

① 清点货物数量，检查货物包装和标志，与货主或运输人员办理货物交接手续；

② 根据货主要求，代为检验货物品质；

③ 根据验收结果，办理货物入库手续；

④ 根据货物的性质、特点、保管要求，分区、分类按货位编号合理存放、堆码、苫垫；

⑤ 编制保管账卡，定期或根据临时需要进行盘点，做好盘点记录；

⑥ 妥善保管货物，及时保养、维护；

⑦ 根据货主要求，整理货物原件包装，进行零星货物的组配、分装；

⑧ 审核货主填制的提货单或调拨单等出库凭证，登记保管账卡；

⑨ 配货、包装、刷唛，集中到理货场所等待运输；

⑩ 复核货物出货凭证，向货主或承运人交付货物，核销储存货量。

3）国际货物运输代理企业以专业顾问身份提供货物运输咨询服务，向客户提供有关法律、法规、规章、惯例和运输信息。其业务内容通常分为以下具体项目。

① 就货物的运输路线、运输方式、运输方案提出意见和建议；

② 就货物的包装、装载形式、方式、方法提出意见和建议；

③ 就货物的进出口通关、清关、领事、商品检验、动植物检疫、卫生检验要求提供咨询意见；

④ 就货物的运输单证和银行要求提出意见和建议；

⑤ 就货物的运输保险险种、保险范围提供咨询意见；

⑥ 就货物的理赔、索赔提出意见和建议；

⑦ 客户提出咨询的其他事项。

11.3 International Tally

Tally involves the ship owner or cargo owner entrusting tally company at the port to conduct cargo tallying, loss and damage examination, stevedoring guidance, related document making and so on when they accept or deliver goods at port of shipping or discharge according to transport contract.

International tally is an indispensable part of foreign trade and ocean cargo transport. Ocean shipping tally company works as intermediary between the consignor and carrier and judges the quantity and condition of cargo delivered. Tally directly influences the interest of ship owner and cargo owner by accurate tallying and clear definition of loss of and damage to the goods. To some degree, tally may influence the safety of ship and cargo. The tally man is responsible for supervising and guiding the cargo stowage on the vessel. Reasonable stowage not only increases shipping volume and capacity utilization rate, but also guarantees the sailing safety.

11. 3. 1 Nature of International Tally

1) Nature of impartiality: The tally company makes independent and authentic judge and confirmation on the quantity and condition of the cargo and issues tally certificate.

2) Nature of service: International tally serves the principal and plays its role in foreign trade and international cargo shipment. However, it is not bound to any restriction or hint from the principal, nor will he discriminate in favor of the principal. Therefore, service provided by tally is restricted by its nature of impartiality.

3) Nature of being international: Tally men often work on foreign vessel and communicate with foreign sailors and merchants, and it is important that they follow foreign customs.

11. 3. 2 Category and Principles of Tally

(1) Category of Tally

Tally could be classified into compulsory tally and entrusted tally according to different foreign trade policy. Compulsory tally means that all the vessels for foreign trade must apply for cargo tally when stevedoring the cargo at a country's port. In many countries, the clause of tally application is included in the stevedoring application from the ship owner, i. e. , while applying for cargo stevedoring, the ship owner is simultaneously applying for tally. Some countries use entrusted tally, meaning that the tallying work could be conducted only after voluntary written application from the ship owner and the agreement from the tallying company. Or else, the tally company won't perform tally or take any related responsibility. Export and import relate to a country's sovereignty, Customs tariff, commodity quality, pollution and epidemic prevention and so on. For this reason, most countries regulate that foreign trade vessel must be exposed to compulsory tally whereas entrusted tally is suitable to domestic trade vessel.

(2) Principle of Tally

Impartial tally must follow the principles of:

1) Authenticity: The work of tally must be conducted on facts of the goods and truly and accurately reflect the actual condition of the goods; any fraud or deliberate concealment is forbidden.

2) Free alongside ship: The goods must be delivered alongside the ship to the consignee for purpose of tally. The delivery alongside the ship is where risk and obligation are divided.

3) One-off certificate signing: It means that the result of tally must be accurately submitted to the principal for one-off signing without any revise. According to international shipping conventions, the ship owner should sign the certificate of tally as a confirmation to the tally result when discharging is completed.

11. 3. 3 Services Provided by Tallying Company

International tallying company works as an independent third party to issue legally binding certificate on the quantity and quality of the goods in export and import. After many years' development, China's international tally companies widen their business scope from ocean shipping tally to domestic shipping tally, container stuffing and devanning tally and on-site tally, etc.

(1) Certificate Issuance Service

1) Provide papers of tallying.

2) Issue certificates of tallying. Tallying company could accept record inquiry and issue the following certificates for the client upon original materials:

① Issue certificate of goods exportation upon original export goods Customs declaration form and copy of B/L.

② Issue certificate of non-export upon original export goods Customs declaration form and certificate of non delivery of goods from ship owner.

③ Issue certificate of over-landed/short-landed and damaged cargo, which should be applied for at the section of container devanning, with the Tally Sheet signed by tallying staff and other documents such as copy of ocean B/L, tally sheet for stuffing, photos of cargo in the container.

3) Provide EDI message for clients. To increase competitiveness, some tally companies provide EDI messages on request of the client, e. g. messages on over-landed container, short-landed container, container damage, and container loading.

(2) Tallying Work performed on Behalf of Ship Owner

1) Counting the number of cargo and examining damage to cargo according to Manifest (for import cargo) or Shipping Order (for export cargo) and main marks shown on the cargo (i. e. contract number, geometric figures, or symbols, similarly hereinafter).

2) Counting the number of containers and examining damage to containers.

3) Sealing containers, examining seals, counting the packages and examining damage to cargo in containers during vanning and/or devanning.

4) Drawing stowage plan and container stowage plan and making cargo hatch list.

5) Assorting mixed-up cargo according to their main marks.

6) Signing of cargo papers delivery of cargo, furnishing relevant tally papers according to the results of tallying.

(3) Tallying Work performed upon Entrustment (Figure 11. 2)

1) Shippers, consignees and/or organizations at home and abroad may entrust tallying company with tally of general cargo, container, and stuffing and devanning of container.

2) Businesses concerning tally papers and formalities when bulk cargo is loaded on and/or unloaded from the vessel, which includes: providing the progress of loading and/or unloading of cargo; examining damage to cargo; signing of cargo papers and delivery of cargo; and drawing stowage plan.

3) Sealing containers, examining seals, counting the packages and examining damage to cargo in containers and making container load plan during vanning and/or devanning in all places.

(4) Tallying Services on Container Stuffing and Devanning

1) Supervise the stuffing and devanning of container.

2) Conduct sealing and seal examination to container.

3) Accept inquiry on container tallying and issue corresponding certificate.

4) Air cargo tallying.

5) Other related services.

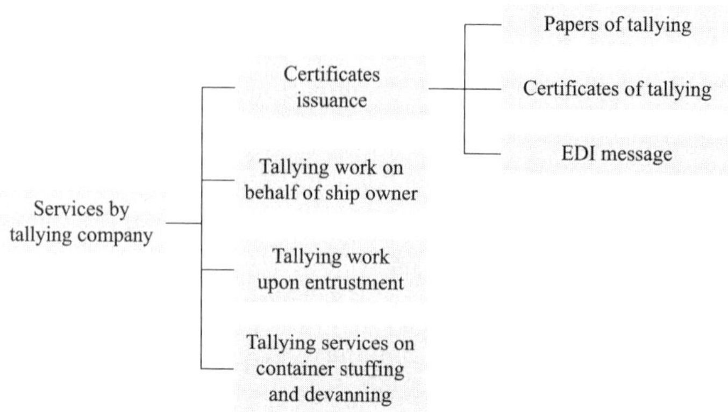

Figure 11.2 Services provided by tallying company

11.3.4 Tallying Certificates

1) Application for Tally. It is a written certificate representing the principal entrusting the tallying company with tallying business. Application for Tally is used in entrusted tally but not compulsory tally.

2) Tally Sheet. Tally Sheet is an original record of tally result and the only basis on which one could tell whether there is over-landed or short-landed cargo in unloading and whether the quantity of cargo is correct in loading. Meanwhile it is the original certificate used in claim arising from over landing or short landing. Therefore, ship owner pays much attention to Tally Sheet and frequently checks whether the number of tally is correct.

3) On-the-spot Record. On-the-spot Record is the original voucher recording abnormal condition of cargo and on-the-spot situation. On the Record, abnormal situation is recorded, e. g. original damage, mixed stowage and indistinct separation of cargo, standing by of workers or handling difficulty caused by ship owner, and so on.

4) Daily Report. Daily Report is a document recorded for daily report to ship owner of handling progress.

5) Stand-by Time Record. It records the standing-by of tallying staff caused by the ship owner.

6) Over-Landed/Short-Landed Cargo List. It is a document made at the time of unloading recording the outnumbered or short numbered cargo than listed in Manifest of cargo. Once signed by the ship owner, it could be used as proof of goods handover. It is the basis on which shipping agent sends Cargo Tracer to related port and the consignee files claim to ship owner against cargo shortage.

7) Damaged Cargo List. It is a record of original damage to the imported cargo, with which the ship owner and port clarify their responsibilities, and ship owner and cargo owner

make damaged goods transfer. With the List, the consignee can file a claim on original damaged goods to cargo owner and commodity inspection agency can make inspection and authentication to the goods and issue correspondent certificates.

8) Cargo Hatch List. It is the list showing the (exact) position by port and cabin for each Bill. On the List, number of packages, mode of packing (packaged or bulk) and weight of cargo are recorded.

9) Discharging Report in Separate Ports. This is a certificate recording the number of packages discharged at the first port when the same shipment of cargo is to be discharged at more than one port.

10) Stowage Plan. Stowage Plan is an exhibition of actual stowage location of export cargo.

11) Tally Certificate. It is a confirmation certificate of tallying work by ship owner (principal).

12) Certificate of Summary on Tally. This certificate summarizes the overall tallying result of the whole cargo load. Apart from that, it could also illustrate the quantity, quality and condition of the cargo in remarks column.

13) Tally Sheet for Containers. This Sheet is an original voucher recording the number of container by tallying staff at loading/unloading. It is a source document on which Chief Tally man makes Outturn List for Containers, Container Stowage Plan, Tally certificate and Certificate of Summary on Tally.

14) Outturn List for Containers. It records the over-landed and short-landed container and damage to containers.

15) Tally Sheet for Stuffing/Devanning. An original record of bill number, and number of and damage to goods in the container. It forms the basis on which Outturn List for Containerized Cargo is made and provides reference for making Container Load Plan at container yard in Containerized cargo export.

16) Outturn List for Containerized Cargo. A certificate recording the over-landed and short-landed cargo and original damaged cargo in the container, against which Customs supervises the cargo in the container and related parties file a claim.

17) Record of Container Sealing/Seal Examining. A record of seal examination and resealing to the container.

18) Container Stowage Plan. The Plan is made up of Bay Plan (a record of number, weight, location, model and size of container), Container Summary and General Stowage Plan (an overall layout plan of container).

19) Notice of Payment and Note on Payment. They are certificates respectively showing agreement to pay and payment of indemnity to the claimant.

20) List of Loading/Unloading Lash Lighters. It lists the number of LASH (Lighter Aboard Ship), number of lighters handled and original damage to the lighters.

21) List of Cargo Measurement. The list of cargo measurement is a record of cargo size, upon which tallying company charges tallying and measurement fees.

22) Rechecking List. Rechecking list is issued after rechecking the original tallying re-

sult and is a certificate of tallying result recheck.

23) Correction List. It is used for correction of original tallying result.

24) List of Marks Assorting. When making mixed discharge to consolidated cargo imported, the tally company should assort marks on the cargo and provide related information to ship owner. This is shown on List of Marks Assorting.

25) Cargo Tracer. It is a document inquiring the over-landed and short-landed cargo.

11.3 国际理货

理货是指船方或货主根据运输合同在装运港和卸货港收受和交付货物时，委托港口的理货公司代理完成的在港口对货物进行计数、检查货物残损、指导装舱积载、制作有关单证等工作。

国际理货是国际贸易和海洋货物运输不可缺少的环节。外轮理货公司处于承、托运双方的中间地位，判断货物交接数量和状态。理货通过准确的计数和对货物残损清晰的区分，影响着船货双方的利益。在一定程度上，理货还会影响船货的安全。理货人员对货物积载负有监督和指导责任，合理的积载既能提高船舶载货量和舱容利用率，又能保证船舶在航行中的安全。

11.3.1 国际理货的性质

1）公正性：理货公司对货物的数量及状况做出独立的真实的判断与确认，并出具理货证明。

2）服务性：国际理货服务于委托人，在国际贸易与国际货物运输中起到重要作用。但又不受制于委托方的限制与暗示，不偏袒委托方的利益。因此，理货的服务性是受公正性制约的。

3）涉外性：国际理货需要理货人员经常登上外轮工作并与外国船员和商人打交道，因而遵守外国风俗习惯就显得很重要。

11.3.2 理货的种类与原则

（1）理货的种类

根据一国对外贸易政策的不同，理货可以分为强制理货和委托理货两种。强制理货是指所有停靠一国港口的外贸船舶在装卸货物时必须申请当地理货机构进行理货，否则不能装卸货物。有许多国家把船方申请理货的条款纳入船方申请码头装卸货物的申请书中，当船方向码头申请装卸货物时，也同时意味着申请理货。有个别国家是委托性理货，即船舶到达某一港口后，船方或其他委托方自愿以书面形式向当地理货机构提出理货申请，经理货机构同意并办理手续后，理货工作才能进行。如船方或其他人不申请理货，理货机构则不派人上船理货，也不承担任何责任。由于进出口贸易涉及国家的主权、海关关税、商品品质、污染和防疫等问题，大多数国家对外贸船舶是进行强制性理货的，而内贸船舶则是通过委托或协议理货。

（2）理货应遵循的原则

公正性理货必须遵循以下三条原则。

1）实事求是原则：实事求是原则是指理货工作必须以货物的事实为依据，理货数据准确、可靠，如实反映货物的本来面目，不能有任何弄虚作假、有意掩盖事实真相的行为。

2）船边交接原则：是指理货工作必须以船边为界限进行交接，船边交接作为划分责任、风险的界限。

3）一次签证原则：理货结果必须准确无误地提交委托方一次签证，不得随意更改签证结果。根据国际航运惯例，在货物卸货完毕时，船方应对理货结果进行签字，以此作为对理货结果的确认。

11.3.3 国际理货服务的业务范围

国际理货以独立的第三方的身份为进出口货物交接的数量和质量出具具有法律效力的证明。国际理货公司在我国历经多年的发展，业务范围从开始的只为外轮理货，发展到为内贸船舶理货、集装箱拆装箱理货、上门理货等。

(1) 国际理货公司为客户提供的出单服务

1）为客户提供理货单证服务。

2）为客户提供出证服务。理货公司可接受进出口业务资料记录查询，根据原始资料为客户出具以下证明。

① 根据向海关申报的出口货物报关单正本、海运提单副本，办理出口货物证明。

② 根据向海关申报的出口货物报关单正本、船公司有关货物未出运证明，办理未出口证明。

③ 办理进口货物溢短装、残损证明。应根据理货公司理货员签署的拆箱理货计数单及有关资料，如海运提单副本、装箱单、集装箱内货物照片，到申请拆箱的理货办事处办理。

3）为客户提供 EDI 信息服务。有些理货公司为提高竞争力，可根据用户要求，为客户提供下列 EDI 报文信息服务，如集装箱溢卸报文、集装箱短卸报文、集装箱残损报文、集装箱装船报文等。

(2) 理货公司代表船方办理的理货业务

1）按舱单（进口货物）、装货单（出口货物）和货物上标明的运输标志（即合同号或几何图形、符号）理清货物数字，分清货物残损。

2）理清集装箱数字，分清集装箱残损。

3）集装箱装拆箱的施封、验封以及理清箱内货物数字，分清箱内货物残损。

4）绘制货物积载图和集装箱积载图，制作货物舱单。

5）分清混装货物的主要标志。

6）依据理货结果，办理交接、签证手续，提供有关理货单证。

(3) 受发货人委托理货公司办理的理货业务（图 11.2）

1）收发货人或国内外各单位可委托理货公司办理件杂货、集装箱、装拆箱等理货业务。

2）办理散装货物装卸船的单证、手续业务：提供货物装卸进度，分清货物残损，办理交接、签证手续，绘制货物积载图。

3）集装箱在各地装拆箱的施封、验封以及理清箱内货物数字，分清箱内货物残损，制作装箱单。

(4) 集装箱装拆箱理货业务

1）集装箱监装监拆业务；

2）集装箱装拆箱的施封、验封业务；

3）集装箱装拆箱理货的查询、出证业务；

4）集装箱装拆箱空运货物理货；

5）其他有关业务。

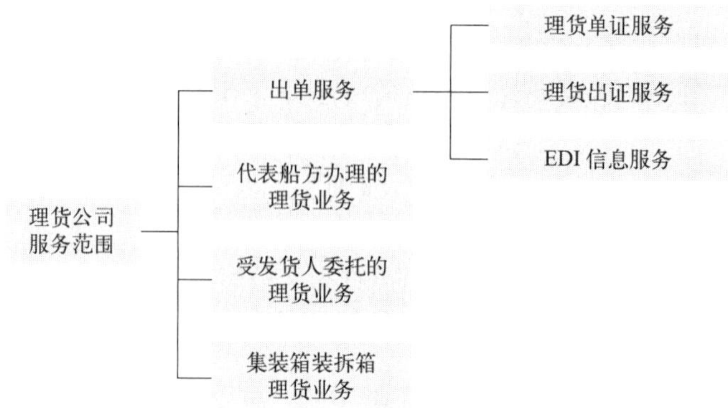

图 11.2　理货公司所提供的服务分类

11.3.4　理货单证

1）委托书：是委托方委托理货机构办理理货业务的书面凭证。属于委托性理货业务的，要使用理货委托书；属于强制性理货业务的，则不需要该委托。

2）计数单：计数单（Tally Sheet）是理货员理货计数的原始记录。它是判断卸船货物数字是否有溢、短装，装船货物数字是否正确的唯一依据。同时，也是处理因货物溢短而引起的索赔案件时的最原始的单据。船方对理货单比较重视，在理货过程中，要经常检查理货员编制的计数单是否准确。

3）现场记录：现场记录（On-the-spot Record）是理货员记载货物异常状态和现场情况的原始凭证。记录货物的原残、混票、隔票不清等情况，船方原因造成的待工或困难作业等情况。

4）日报单：日报单（Daily Report）是每日向船方报告装、卸货物进度的单证。

5）待时记录：待时记录（Stand-by Time Record）是记载由于船方原因造成理货人员停工待时的证明。

6）货物溢短单（Over-Landed/Short-Landed Cargo List）：是记载进口货物实卸件数比舱单所列件数溢出或短少的证明；船方签认后，可作为船、货双方货物交接凭证；是各船舶代理公司向有关港口发出货物查询单的依据；是收货人在货物短少时向船方提出索赔的依据。

7）货物残损单（Damaged Cargo List）：是记载进口货物原残的证明；是船、港双方对残损货物分清责任以及船、货双方对原残货物进行交接的凭证；是收货人向货主对原残货物索赔和商检部门对原残货物进行检验、鉴定和对外出证的重要依据。

8）货物分舱单（Cargo Hatch List）：它是分港分舱记载每票货物装舱部位的清单。货物分舱单上列明货物的件数、包装或散装及相应的重量。

9）分港卸货单（Discharging Report in Separate Ports）：记载同一票货物在两个港口分卸时，第一个卸货港卸货件数的证明。

10）货物积载图（Stowage Plan）：是出口货物实际装卸部位示意图。

11）理货证明书（Tally Certificate）：船方/委托方确认理货工作的证明。

12）理货结果汇总证明（Certificate of Summary on Tally）：是记载全船货物，或集装箱经理货后最终反映全船理货结果的汇总证明。除反映理货结果外，还可对货物的数量、质量及有关情况，在情况说明处加以说明。

13）集装箱理箱单（Tally Sheet for Containers）：是船舶装卸集装箱时理货员记载箱数的原始凭证，是理货组长编制集装箱溢短/残损单、集装箱积载图、理货业务凭证和理货结果汇总证明的原始依据。

14）集装箱溢短/残损单（Outturn List for Containers）：记载集装箱箱数溢短和箱体残损情况的证明。

15）装/拆箱理货单（Tally Sheet for Stuffing/Devanning）：是理货员记载集装箱内货物票号、数字和残损情况的原始记录，是编制集装箱货物溢短/残损单的依据。在集装箱出口过程中，是集装箱堆场填制“装箱单”的参考资料。

16）集装箱货物溢短/残损单（Outturn List for Containerized Cargo）：记载集装箱内货物件数溢短和原残情况的凭证。是海关对箱内货物进行监管和有关方进行索赔的重要依据。

17）集装箱验封/施封记录（Record of Container Sealing/Seal Examining）：记载集装箱铅封完好情况和重新施封情况的单证。

18）集装箱积载图（Container Stowage Plan）：集装箱积载图由三个部分组成，即“排位图”（Bay Plan，记录每个集装箱的箱号、重量、位置、箱型、尺寸等），“综合明细单”（Container Summary）和“总积载图”（General Stowage Plan，是全船总箱位分布图）。

19）认赔通知单（Notice of Payment）和付款单（Note on Payment）：它们是向索赔方承认赔偿和支付赔款的证明。

20）载驳船装/卸驳船清单（List of Loading/Unloading Lash Lighters）：记载载驳船数量、装卸子船计数和驳船原残情况的原始凭证。

21）货物丈量单（List of Cargo Measurement）：是记录货物尺码的单证，同时也是收取理货费、丈量费的依据之一。

22）复查单（Rechecking List）：对原理货经过复查后出具的单证，是复查理货结果的凭证。

23）更正单（Correction List）：更正原理货结果的单证。

24）分标志单（List of Marks Assorting）：是对进口混装货物且卸船当时混卸，卸船后分清标志并向船公司提供有关情况的凭证。

25）查询单（Cargo Tracer）：是指查询货物溢短卸情况的单证。

Part B Vocabulary and Terminology 词汇和术语

freight forwarder 货运代理
fiduciary relationship 信托关系
agent 代理人
principal 被代理人
entrusted agency 委托代理
statutory agency 法定代理
appointed agency 指定代理

exclusive agency 独家代理
contracting carrier 缔约承运人
notice of demurrage 滞期通知
notice of dispatch 速遣通知
multimodal transport operator 多式联运经营人
stoppage in transit 中途停运
international tally 国际理货
ocean shipping tally 外轮理货
entrusted tally 委托性理货
compulsory tally 强制性理货
tally sheet 计数单
container load plan 装箱单
manifest of cargo 舱单，货物清单
shipping order 装货单
stowage plan 货物积载图
container stowage plan 集装箱积载图
consolidated cargo 混装货物
general cargo 件杂货
application for tally 理货委托书
on-the-spot record 现场记录
daily report 日报单
mixed stowage 混票
separation of cargo 隔票
original damage 原残
stand-by time record 待时记录
over-landed/short-landed cargo list 货物溢短单
damaged cargo list 货物残损单
cargo hatch list 货物分舱单
discharging report in separate ports 分港卸货单
tally certificate 理货证明书
certificate of summary on tally 理货结果汇总证明
tally sheet for containers 集装箱理箱单
outturn list for containers 集装箱溢短/残损单
tally sheet for stuffing/devanning 装/拆箱理货单
outturn list for containerized cargo 集装箱货物溢短/残损单
record of container sealing/seal examining 集装箱验封/施封记录
container stowage plan 集装箱积载图
notice of payment 认赔通知单
note on payment 付款单
list of loading/unloading lash lighters 载驳船装/卸驳船清单
list of cargo measurement 货物丈量单

rechecking list 复查单
correction list 更正单
list of marks assorting 分标志单
cargo tracer 查询单

Part C Exercise 练习

Ⅰ. Answer the following questions.

1. What is international freight forwarder? What is the nature and role of international freight forwarder?

2. What businesses does an international freight forwarder cover?

3. What is the obligation of international freight forwarder?

4. What role does international tally play in international trade?

5. What principles should a tally company follow in the tallying of goods?

Ⅱ. Please tell whether the following statements are true or false.

1. In China, agency refers to its general concept, more specifically direct and indirect agency.

2. The agent must act in the name of the principal and therefore the legal consequence of agent's act is upon the principal.

3. A forwarder could work as an agent of cargo owner or carrier, or as an independent operator.

4. A tally company is often bound to the restriction or hint from the principal and thus tend to make decisions in favor of the principal.

5. Compulsory tally is applied in most countries in their foreign trade whereas entrusted tally is suitable to domestic trade vessel.

6. Once signed, the tally result cannot be revised.

Ⅲ. Translate the following passages into Chinese.

1. Equipped with wide business relations and advanced information technique, the forwarder can keep effective communication with interested parties involved in cargo shipment, conduct accurate tracking and control of the goods, in order to guarantee the safe and timely arrival of the goods.

2. To some degree, tally may influence the safety of ship and cargo. The tally clerk is responsible for supervising and guiding the cargo stowage in loading. Reasonable stowage not only increases shipping volume and capacity utilization rate, but also guarantees the sailing safety.

3. Tally involves the ship owner or cargo owner entrusting Tally Company at the port to conduct cargo tallying, loss and damage examination, stevedoring guidance, related document making and so on when they accept or deliver goods at port of shipping or discharge according to transport contract.

4. Tally Sheet is an original record of tally result and the only basis on which one could tell whether there is over-landed or short-landed cargo in unloading and whether the quantity of cargo is correct in loading. Meanwhile it is the original certificate used in claim arising

from over landing or short landing.

5. International freight forwarders have additional expertise in preparing and processing customs and other documentation and performing activities pertaining to international shipments. Information typically reviewed by a freight forwarder includes commercial invoice, shipper's export declaration, bill of lading and other documents required by the carrier or country of export, import, and/or transshipment.

Ⅳ. Translate the following sentences into English.

1. 货运代理本质上属于货物运输关系人的代理人，是联系发货人、收货人和承运人的货物运输中介人。

2. 委托代理是指代理人根据被代理人的委托而进行代理活动，法定代理是指代理人根据法律的直接规定进行代理活动，而指定代理是指代理人根据法院或其他有关单位的指定进行代理活动。

3. 货运代理和货主之间是受托人和委托人的关系。在货代行业，受托人作为货主的代理对货主负责，并按照委托人的要求提供货代服务，以获取代理佣金。

4. 理货工作必须以货物的事实为依据，理货数据准确、可靠，如实反映货物的本来面目，不能有任何弄虚作假、有意掩盖事实真相的行为。

Chapter Twelve

Cross Border E-commerce Logistics 跨境电子商务物流

Part A Text 课文

12. 1 Outline of E-commerce

12. 1. 1 Definition

E-commerce，short for electronic commerce，refers to the buying and selling of goods，information，or services using the internet，and the transfer of money and data to execute these transactions.

E-commerce is a newly sprouting sector in the world of doing business，which however didn't stop us witnessing the tremendously speedy pace of its development. Even during the 1960s，businesses conducted electronic transactions via primitive computer networks. Through Electronic Data Interchange（EDI），they were able to share business documents with other companies' machines. With the wide adoption of the Internet and the introduction of the World Wide Web in 1991 and of the first browser for accessing it in 1993，most e-commerce shifted to Internet. More recently，with the global spread of smartphones and the accessibility of fast broadband connections to Internet，much e-commerce moved to mobile devices which mainly refer to smartphones and also include tablets，laptops，and wearable products such as watches.

12. 1. 2 Pros and Cons of E-commerce

12. 1. 2. 1 Pros of e-commerce

The benefits of e-commerce include its around-the-clock availability，the easiness and speed of access，the cost saving and the personalized service.

1）Availability. Usually，e-commerce sites are available all the hours，allowing visitors to browse and shop anytime and anywhere at their convenience. Apart from that，e-commerce enables brands to make a wide array of products available，which are then shipped from a warehouse after a purchase is made.

2）Easy accessibility. Compared with traditional commerce，customers don't have to spend time finding the physical store that may or may not have what they want and then have a hard time determining which aisle a particular product is in. In e-commerce, visitors can browse product category pages and use the site search function to find the product immediately, without knowing where the product or the store is actually located.

Retailers also benefit from easy accessibility in ways of gaining new customers and new markets. Besides branding and relationships, e-commerce retailers can attract new customers by creating traffic from search engines. It is not unusual for customers to follow a link in search engine results and land on an e-commerce website that they have never heard of. This additional source of traffic is particularly important for newly start e-commerce businesses who are not limited by geographical area any more and have the accessibility to customers beyond their physical reach. Additionally, the advent of m-commerce, i. e. , e-commerce on mobile devices, has broken every remaining limitation of geography. Different from those bricks and mortar businesses who sell to customers physically visiting their stores, e-commerce businesses can serve any customer including those who are located outside the border, as long as they can access the web. As such, e-commerce has the potential to expand a business' customer base globally.

3) Lower cost. One of the most obvious positives of e-commerce is the lowered cost for both customers and retailers.

Customers save time and money in travelling long distances to reach their preferred physical store. E-commerce allows them to visit the same store virtually, with just a few mouse clicks.

For retailers, cost is lowered in aspects of:

① Advertising and marketing: Organic search engine traffic, pay-per-click, and social media traffic are some of the advertising channels that can be cost-effective.

② Personnel: The automation of checkout, billing, payments, inventory management, and other operational processes lowers the number of employees required to run an e-commerce setup.

③ Real estate: This one is a no-brainer. An e-commerce merchant does not need a prominent physical location or eye-catching and expensive inner decoration compared to physical store.

④ Inventory: E-commerce businesses don't need to store high pile and a wide variety of merchandises to cater for the customer's immediate needs, which in great extent saves inventory cost.

A part of the lowered cost could be passed on to customers in the form of discounted prices, which in turn will increase sales. Given the growing sales and lowered cost, e-commerce businesses' profit increases to great extent.

4) Personalization and product recommendations. E-commerce personalization means showing individualized offers, product recommendations, and other content to visitors based on their previous actions, demographics, and other personal data. E-commerce sites can track visitors' browse, search and purchase history. They can leverage this data to present useful and personalized product recommendation. Examples include the sections of Amazon product pages labeled "Frequently bought together" and "Customers who viewed this item also viewed."

Due to the convenience to both buyers and sellers, e-commerce has taken off to dramatic development since its inception. Let's take online retail for example, in 2021, retail e-commerce sales amounted to approximately 4.9 trillion U.S. dollars worldwide. This figure is forecast to grow by 50 percent over the next few years, reaching about 7.4 trillion dollars by 2025. See Figure 12.1.

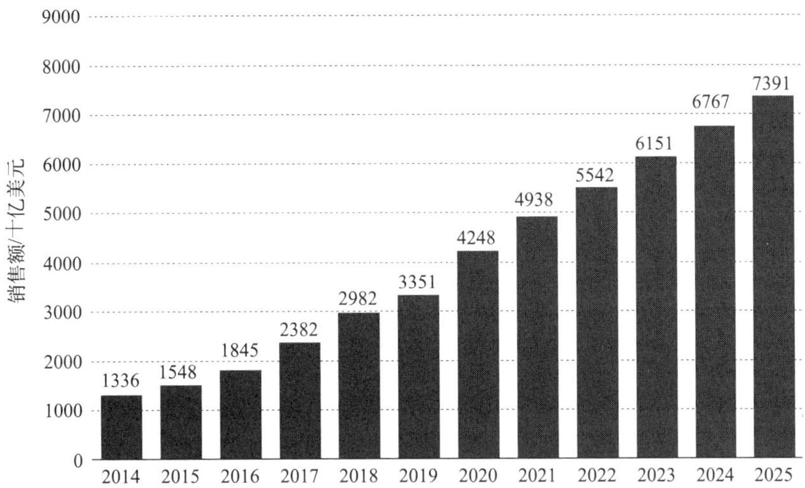

Figure 12.1 Retail e-commerce sales worldwide from 2014 to 2025 (in billion U.S. dollars)

12.1.2.2 Cons of e-commerce

The perceived downsides of e-commerce include security issue, limited customer service, poor experience before purchase and the wait time for product shipping.

1) Security and lack of privacy. The issue of security and lack of privacy has been a concern since the inception of e-commerce and is considered a major disadvantage of it. A customer has to provide his personal details before making a purchase like address, name, and phone number and so on. It may lead to credit card fraud or worse, identity theft due to hacks by cybercriminals and hackers. This is a harsh reality in e-commerce context and a website cannot give this assurance that the financial information cannot be divulged on its portal. The website owner needs to take important steps to change its password so as to stop any data leakages.

2) Limited customer service. If a customer has a question or issue in a physical store, he or she can ask a clerk, cashier or store manager for help. In an e-commerce store, customer service may be limited: the site may only provide support during certain hours of the day, or a call to a customer service phone number may keep the customer on hold.

3) Poor experience before purchase. While images on a web page can provide a good sense about a product, it's different from feeling it directly like what customers usually do in a brick-and-mortar store. Customers miss the tangible feeling and there is always the fear that the product will not meet the standard they are expecting, which makes them a bit hesitant before making a purchase. The chance is not small that customers receive products that differ from their expectations. In this scenario, customers may have to burden the cost of reverse logistics.

4) Longer wait time. Customers consider shipping times to be one of the biggest e-commerce disadvantages. After placing an order, a customer has to wait for the goods to be delivered. It could take days before he receives the parcel depending on the mode of transportation, the inventory status and so on. An exception to this rule is the case of digital goods, e. g. , an eBook or a music file. In this case, e-commerce might be faster than purchasing goods from a physical store.

12. 1. 3 Types of E-commerce

12. 1. 3. 1 Types of e-commerce——based on transaction parties

1) Business-to-Business (B2B) e-commerce. Among the various categories of e-commerce, business-to-business (B2B) commerce is the largest category, which refers to the electronic exchange of products, services or information between businesses rather than between businesses and consumers. B2B companies have an entirely different target audience: they offer the raw materials, finished parts, services or consultation that other businesses need to operate, grow and profit. One of the major purposes why businesses use e-commerce is to lower transaction costs and save time and effort in conducting e-business.

Some of the best and fastest growing top global B2B platforms include Alibaba, DHgate, Global Sources, eWorldTrade and so on.

2) Business-to-Consumer (B2C) e-commerce. It refers to the process of selling products and services via internet directly between a business and consumers who are the end-users of its products or services. Most companies that sell directly to consumers can be referred to as B2C companies. Today, there are innumerable virtual stores and malls on the internet selling all types of consumer goods. The most recognized example of these sites is Amazon, which dominates the B2C market.

3) Consumer-to-Consumer (C2C) e-commerce. This is a type of e-commerce where consumers trade products, services and information with each other online. These transactions are generally conducted through a third party that provides an online platform on which the transactions are carried out.

The main advantage of C2C business is that sellers and buyers are reachable. It is also effortless and handy and does not take much time to use. Moreover, it is possible for one customer to be a seller as well as a buyer. What is more, it provides a rich social linking. Numerous community and forum discussions are available.

Two implementations of C2C markets are auctions and classified advertisements. The most prominent examples of C2C include eBay, an online auction site, and Amazon, which acts as both B2C and C2C marketplace.

4) Consumer-to-Business (C2B) e-commerce. C2B is a type of e-commerce in which consumers make their products and services available online for companies to bid on and purchase. This is the opposite of the traditional commerce model of B2C where businesses offer products or services in the first place to meet the needs of consumers. This is actually a reverse of the traditional model, with those who would normally be end-users creating products and services that are consumed by the businesses and organizations they themselves buy from. The famous C2B model in e-commerce is Hiring Websites where businesses pay to get

a service and consumers decide whether the salary is acceptable or not.

5) Business-to-Administration (B2A) e-commerce, also referred to as B2G e-commerce. It is generally defined as e-commerce between companies and the public sector. It refers to the use of the Internet for public procurement, licensing procedures, and other government-related operations. A major difference as compared to B2B and B2C is that in B2G model, companies generally respond to requirements published by a certain government entity through a structured bidding process. This bidding process can take place online in real time and can be highly competitive. These types of services have increased considerably in recent years with investments made in e-government.

6) Consumer-to-Administration (C2A), also known as consumer-to-government (C2G). It refers to connection conducted online between individual consumers and public administration or government bodies. C2A e-commerce doesn't assist the government in procuring products or services from citizens but helps consumers to request information or post various feedback regarding public sectors directly to the government authorities or administration. This provides an easy and instant solution or way to establish communication between the consumers and the government. C2A e-commerce is applied in areas such as education, social security, taxes, and health.

Both B2A and C2A are strongly associated to the idea of efficiency and easy usability of the services provided to citizens/business by the government, with the support of information and communication technologies.

7) Mixed e-commerce models. The technological advancement of e-commerce has also made it easier for businesses to follow more than one model at a time, such as by combining B2C and B2B sales on a single website. This could be illustrated by the official website of Lenovo which is accessible to personal consumer, SME customer, and government client. It presents satisfactory shopping experience for personal consumers, and yet still offers bulk wholesaling or other B2B as well as B2G specific services in different parts of the website without confusing things for either set of customers. B2B and B2G customers can get different pricing, different options, and even different products than B2C customers.

The 6 types of e-commerce are exhibited in Figure 12. 2.

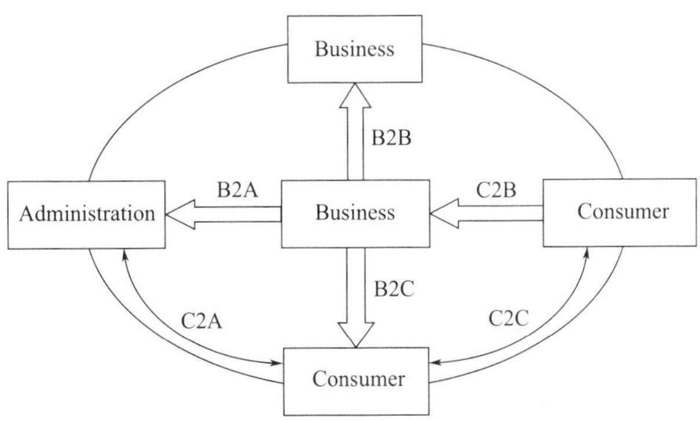

Figure 12. 2 Types of e-commerce based on transaction parties

12. 1. 3. 2 Types of e-commerce——based on type of e-commerce website

There are three main parties involved in e-commerce, seller, operator (e-commerce company) and buyer. Based on who owns the transaction website and whether there is an e-commerce operator working as a middleman, we classify e-commerce into the following three categories:

(1) Online storefront model

Having an online storefront is one of the most straightforward ways to conduct e-commerce. In this model, instead of using a 3rd party operator's website, the seller creates a website of its own and uses it to sell products and services using shopping carts and e-commerce solutions. Most online stores fall into this category. The website belongs completely to the seller who has much better control over the functionality and outlook and the like of the website. The seller can build and enhance its brand and create customer loyalty as well by providing better customer shopping experience. Other sellers sell commodity purchased from their suppliers and make profit from the spreads of the commodity. However, this model requires much effort and initial investment from the seller. Dell, Huawei and lots of other companies have their own online storefront. With respect to the complexity of website setting up and management, we also have e-commerce platform such as SaaS (Software as a Service), open source, licensed, proprietary, PaaS (Platform as a Service), the technical issues of which are not discussed further.

(2) Online marketplace model

Online marketplace model of e-commerce means provision of an information technology platform by an e-commerce entity on a digital and electronic network to act as a facilitator between buyer and seller. In this model, there is a 3rd party operator (also called platform e-commerce company) who sets up an online mall, integrates service resources such as logistics, payment and operation, invites merchants to settle in the platform, and provides transaction services for them. The platform operator collects commissions and value-added service fees (such as advertising fees) from the merchants as its main profit. Widely known examples of this pattern include eBay, AliExpress, BestBuy, Etsy, DHgate, Global Sources, and the like. The characteristics presented by this pattern are: 1) the platform e-commerce company only working as middleman who doesn't directly participate in the transaction as seller or buyer; 2) the platform attracting brand owner, manufacturer, distributor and online shop and organizing commodity exhibition and sales activities; 3) the platform gathering many merchants and having a wide variety of trading commodities. Using online marketplace brings sellers huge exposure to potential customers. Even sellers that have their own websites already, or sell on other websites, can benefit by placing their products for sale on a marketplace where customers are likely to find them.

(3) Mixed model

This type of e-commerce website belongs to an e-commerce company who not only sells product of its own brand, but also invites other sellers to station in its website to conduct business. Amazon is a great example of this type. Amazon itself sells products as seller on one hand, but on the other hand works as an operator and allows qualified third-party sellers to participate. In fact, Amazon basically evolved from an online storefront who sold books to an online marketplace platform. Amazon employs three administration platforms: Seller Central, Vendor Express and Vendor Central. Seller Central is open to all merchants for registration and the products sold are displayed as from third-party sellers. Vendor Central implements invitation entry system with the most stringent entry standards to the vendors who could enjoy the strongest promotion. Vendor Express, however, permits application from companies of different sizes in the United States. The products sold via Vendor Central and Vendor Express are displayed as products from Amazon. In standard online storefront sales, Amazon gets quotations from its vendors, and determines the order quantity and ordering time based on big data analysis and calculation results. The subsequent work of consumer order placement, payment, logistics, and after-sales service are all the sole responsibility of Amazon. Suppliers are only responsible for production.

12.1.3.3 Types of e-commerce——based on categories of products served

There are online marketplaces that focus exclusively on electronics, while some others focus on clothing and apparel. There are also a number of such platforms that cater to almost all the categories. According to the width of product line an online marketplace sells, we classify e-commerce into horizontal and vertical e-commerce.

(1) Horizontal e-commerce

The horizontal e-commerce model implies selling all and everything reaching the broadest audience possible. Basically, the horizontal e-commerce is a digital one-stop shop from where customers can buy anything they need in one place without problems of finding the product category they are looking for. Amazon exhibits a standard horizontal e-commerce. Having started as a bookseller, the company expanded its product range to an unbelievable range over time. Customers can buy literally everything on Amazon. Example seen in Figure 12.3(a).

(2) Vertical e-commerce

Unlike horizontal online marketplaces, vertical marketplace aims at a single market sector to serve some specific category of products to the targeted audience. Etsy is one rich example that follows the vertical marketplace concept of the e-commerce business model. This US Brooklyn-based online artisanal marketplace typically focuses on art & crafts to sell. Thus, it now becomes one of the leading marketplaces for handcrafts & vintage items. Example is seen in Figure 12.3(b).

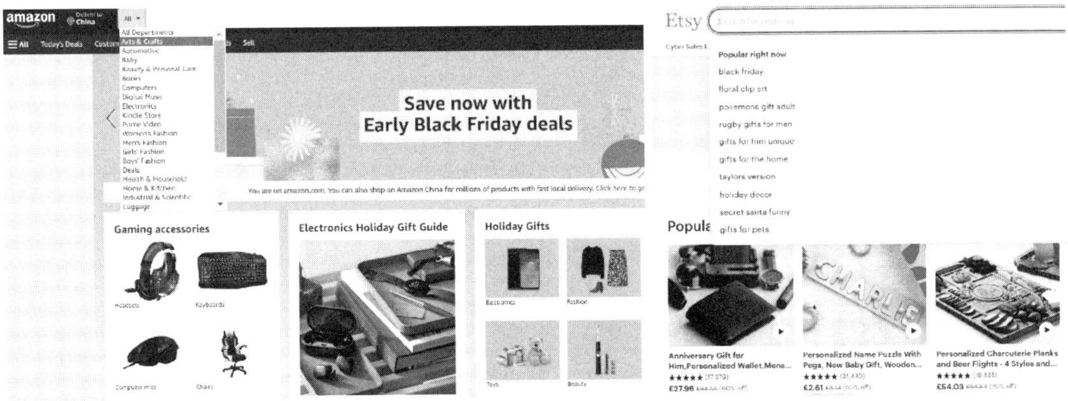

(a) Horizontal e-commerce (b) Vertical e-commerce

Figure 12.3 Horizontal and vertical e-commerce

12.1 电子商务概述

12.1.1 概念

电子商务（E-commerce，全称 electronic commerce），是指使用互联网实现对商品、信息或服务的买卖，以及对这些交易的资金和数据的转移。

电子商务是一个新兴的商业领域，然而，它仍以极快的速度发展着。早在20世纪60年代，企业已经通过原始计算机网络进行电子交易。通过电子数据交换（EDI），他们能够与其他公司的机器共享业务文档。随着Internet的广泛采用和1991年万维网的引入以及1993年第一个用于访问Internet的浏览器的引入，大多数电子商务都转移到了Internet进行。近来，随着智能手机在全球范围内的普及以及快速宽带连接Internet，许多电子商务转移到了移动设备上，主要指手机，也包括平板电脑、笔记本电脑和手表等可穿戴产品。

12.1.2 电子商务的优缺点

12.1.2.1 电子商务的优点

电子商务的优点包括其全天候可用性，访问的便捷性和速度，成本的节约和个性化服务。

1）利用性高。通常，电子商务网站会全天候开放，从而使访问者可以在任何时间，任何地点方便地浏览和购物。除此之外，电子商务使商家可以提供多种产品，并在购买后从仓库发货。

2）易于访问。与传统商业相比，客户不必花时间去寻找实体商店，而实体店里也可能没有他们想要的商品，且进店之后他们还需费力地寻找商品的位置。在电子商务中，访问者可以浏览产品类别页面并使用站点搜索功能立即查找产品，而无需知道产品或商店的实际位置。

零售商还可以通过电子商务更便捷地获得新客户和进入新市场。除了品牌效应和长期客户关系，电子商务零售商还可以通过创建搜索引擎的流量来吸引新客户。客户跟随搜索引擎结果中的链接并登录他们从未听说过的电子商务网站，这一现象并不少见。对于新成立的电子商务企业而言，这种额外的流量来源尤其重要，因为它们不再受地理区域的限制，并且可以接触到超出其实际覆盖范围的客户。另外，移动电子商务（即移动设备上的电子商务）的出现消除了地理上的所有剩余限制。与只能销售给来店顾客的实体企业不同，电子商务企业可以服务于任何顾客，也包括国界外的顾客，只要他们可以访问网络即可。因此，电子商务有潜力在全球扩展企业的客户群。

3）节约成本。电子商务最明显的好处之一就是降低了客户和零售商的成本。

客户不必耗时耗财长途跋涉到达他们首选的实体店。电子商务使他们仅需单击几下鼠标即可虚拟访问同一家商店。

对于零售商而言，可在以下方面降低成本。

① 广告和营销：自然搜索引擎流量，按点击数付费和社交媒体流量是一些更有成本效益的广告渠道。

② 人员：结账、开票、付款、库存管理和其他操作流程的自动化减少了运行电子商务设置所需的员工数量。

③ 店面：理所当然地，与实体商店不同，电子商务企业不需要突出的地理位置或醒目

且昂贵的内部装饰。

④ 库存：电子商务企业无需存储大量及种类繁多的商品来满足客户的即时需要，从而在很大程度上节省了库存成本。

降低的成本中，一部分可以以折扣价的形式转移给客户，这反过来会增加销售量。考虑到销售的增长和成本的降低，电子商务业务的利润将大大增加。

4）个性化及产品推介。个性化意味着电商企业能根据访问者的先前行为、人口统计信息和其他个人数据，向访问者推送个性化的报价、产品推荐和其他内容。电子商务网站可以追踪访问者的浏览、搜索和购买历史，可以利用这些数据来提供有用的个性化产品推荐。比如 Amazon 产品页面上标有“经常一起购买”和“查看过此商品的客户也看到过”的部分。

由于给买卖双方带来的便利性，电子商务自诞生之日起就得到了飞速发展。以在线零售为例，2021 年，全球零售电子商务销售额达到约 4.9 万亿美元，这一数字在未来几年预计将以每年 50%的速度攀升，于 2025 年达到约 9.4 万亿美元。如图 12.1 所示。

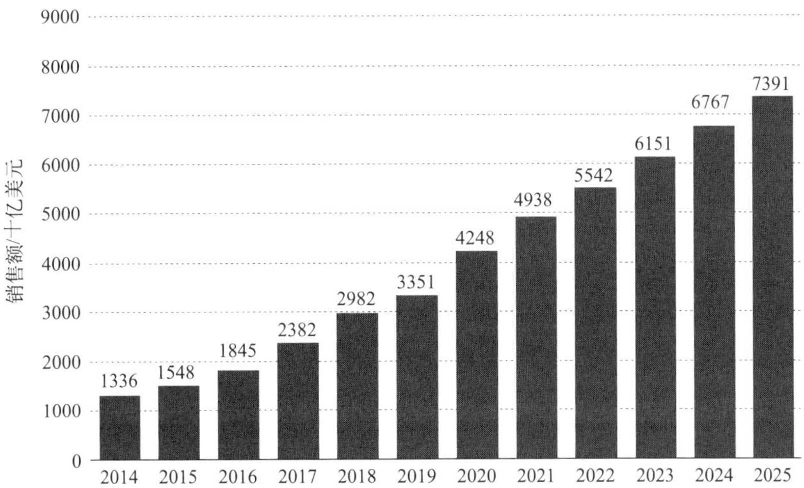

图 12.1 2014—2025 年全球零售电子商务销售额

（图片来源：www. statista. com）

12. 1. 2. 2 电子商务的缺点

电子商务明显的缺点包括安全问题、顾客服务受限、购前体验较差，以及收货时间长等。

1）安全性与隐私性。自电子商务诞生以来，安全性和缺乏隐私一直是人们关注的问题，并且被认为是电子商务的主要缺点。客户在购买之前必须提供其个人详细信息，例如地址、姓名和电话号码等。由于网络犯罪分子和黑客的入侵，这可能导致信用卡欺诈或更严重的身份盗用。这是电子商务环境下的严酷现实，并且网站无法保证财务信息不会在其门户网站上泄露。网站所有者需要采取重要步骤来更改其密码，以阻止任何数据泄露。

2）客户服务受限。如果客户在实体店中有疑问或问题，则可以向店员、收银员或经理寻求帮助。在电子商务商店中，客户服务可能会受到限制：网站可能仅在一天中的某些时段提供客服在线支持，或者客服电话一直无法接通。

3）购买前体验不足。网页上的图片虽然可以很好地说明产品，但仍与实体店中的直接体验不同。顾客不能亲身体验，因而总是担心产品与期望不符，这使他们在购买之前有些犹豫。客户收到的产品与期望不符屡见不鲜，在这种情况下，客户可能还得负担退换货成本。

4)收货时间长。大多数客户认为收货时间长是电子商务的最大缺陷之一。下订单后，客户必须等待货物交付。根据运输方式、库存状态等，他可能需要等上好几天才能收到包裹。数字商品(例如，电子书或音乐文件)则是一个例外，网上购买此类商品能比从实体店购买更快买到。

12.1.3 电子商务的类型

12.1.3.1 按照交易方进行分类

1)企业对企业(B2B)电子商务。在电子商务的各种类别中，企业对企业(B2B)贸易是最大的类别，是指企业之间(而非企业与消费者之间)以电子方式交换产品、服务或信息。B2B公司拥有完全不同的目标受众，他们提供其他企业运营、增长和获利所需的原材料、成品、服务或咨询。企业使用电子商务的主要目的之一是降低交易成本，节省时间和精力。

全球最佳、发展最快的顶级B2B平台包括阿里巴巴、DHgate、Global Sources、eWorldTrade等。

2)企业对消费者(B2C)电子商务。这种类型是指企业通过Internet将产品和服务直接销售给作为其最终用户的消费者的过程。直接向消费者销售产品的大多数公司都可以称为B2C公司。如今，互联网上有无数的虚拟店铺和购物中心出售各种类型的消费品。这些网站中最受认可的是在B2C市场上占主导地位的亚马逊公司。

3)消费者对消费者(C2C)电子商务。它是指消费者之间可以在线交易产品、服务和信息。这些交易通常通过第三方在线平台进行。

C2C业务的主要优势是买卖双方的可达性。这种方式毫不费力，而且方便省时。另外，一个顾客有可能既是卖方又是买方，而且，它提供了丰富的社交联系，如社区和论坛等。

C2C市场的两种实现方式是拍卖和分类广告。C2C最突出的例子包括在线拍卖网站eBay和同时开展B2C和C2C业务的亚马逊。

4)消费者对企业(C2B)电子商务模式下，消费者在线提供其产品和服务，由公司进行投标和购买。这与传统的B2C商业模式正好相反，在传统的B2C商业模式中，企业首先提供产品或服务来满足消费者的需求。这种变化完全逆转了传统模式，由通常作为最终消费者的用户创造产品和服务，而由他们原本从之采购的商家或组织进行消费。大家较为熟知的C2B电子商务模式就是招聘网站，企业在这里付费以获取服务，而消费者则决定是否接受薪水。

5)企业对管理当局(B2A)电子商务，也称为B2G电子商务，通常定义为公司与公共部门之间的电子商务。它是指使用Internet进行公共采购、颁发许可以及其他与政务相关的程序。与B2B和B2C的主要区别在于，B2G模式中，公司通常通过结构化的招标流程来响应某个政府实体发布的要求。该招标过程可以实时在线进行，并且竞争激烈。近年来，随着对电子政务的投资，这种类型的服务已大大增加。

6)消费者对政府(C2A)电子商务，也称为C2G。它是指个人消费者与公共管理部门或政府机构之间在线进行的联系。C2A电子商务并非协助政府从公民处购买产品或服务，而是帮助消费者直接向政府当局或行政部门索取有关公共部门的信息或发布各种反馈。这为建立消费者与政府之间的沟通提供了一种简便、即时的解决方案或方式。C2A电子商务可应用在教育、社会保障、税收和健康等领域。

在信息和通信技术的支持下，B2A和C2A都与政府向公民/企业提供服务的效率和易用性理念紧密相关。

7）混合电子商务模式。电子商务技术的进步还使企业更容易同时开展多种模式，例如在同一个网站上同时进行 B2C 和 B2B 销售。联想官方网站就可以很好地说明这一混合模式的运作。个体消费者、中小型企业客户和政府机构均可访问联想官方网站。它不仅能为个体消费者提供满意的购物体验，且其网站仍可提供批发或其他 B2B 业务以及 B2G 特定服务，却不会给任何一组客户造成困扰。与 B2C 消费者相比，B2B 企业客户和 B2G 政府机构客户可以得到不同的价格、不同的选择方案甚至不同的产品。

电子商务的前六种类型见图 12.2。

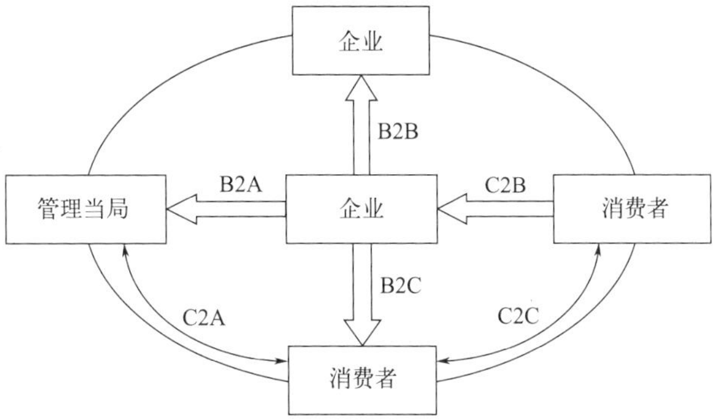

图 12.2 根据交易双方划分的电子商务类型

12.1.3.2 按照电子商务网站进行分类

电子商务的核心主体有三类：卖方、运营商（电子商务公司）和买方。根据谁拥有交易网站，以及是否有电子商务运营商作为中间人，我们将电子商务分为三类。

（1）网上店面模式

拥有网上店面是进行电子商务的最直接的方式之一。在此模式中，卖方并非使用第三方运营商的网站，而是创建自己的网站，并使用该网站通过购物车和电子商务解决方案来销售产品和服务。大多数网店都属于这种模式。该网站完全属于卖方，该卖方可以更好地控制网站的功能和外观等。卖方可以通过提供更好的客户购物体验来建立和强化其品牌并建立客户忠诚度。还有的卖方利用自己的网站出售从供应商那里购买的商品，并从商品的价差中获利。但是，该模式需要卖方付出大量的精力和初始投资。戴尔、华为和许多其他公司都有自己的网上店面。根据网站建立和管理的复杂性，我们还可分成 SaaS（软件即服务）、开源、许可、专有、PaaS（平台即服务）等不同的平台，此类技术问题我们在此不作深入介绍。

（2）网上商城模式

电子商务的网上商城模式是指电子商务实体企业在数字和电子网络上提供信息技术平台，以促进买卖双方之间的交易。这种模式下，第三方运营商也被称为平台型电商，通过线上搭建商城，整合物流、支付、运营等服务资源，吸引商家入驻，并为其提供电商交易服务，由入驻的商家和买方进行交易。同时，平台以收取商家佣金以及增值服务费（如广告费）作为主要盈利模式。代表企业有 eBay、速卖通、BestBuy、Etsy、敦煌网、环球资源等。这种模式的特点是，平台型电商本身不作为买方或卖方直接参与商品交易环节，而是作为中间人；平台吸引国内外品牌商、制造商、经销商、网店等多种从事商品交易的企业，由平台组织商品展示和销售活动；电商平台云集众多商家，交易商品种类丰富。使用网上商城模式能给卖家带来大量的潜在客户。即使已经拥有自己的网站或在其他网站上销售，卖家也可以通过网上商城出售产品给顾客而受益。

(3) **混合模式**

这种类型的电子商务网站属于一家电子商务公司，该公司不仅销售自己品牌的产品，而且还邀请其他卖家入驻其网站开展业务。亚马逊就是一个很好的例子。亚马逊本身一方面以卖方的身份出售产品，但另一方面以运营商的身份运作，并允许合格的第三方卖方参与。实际上，亚马逊就是从销售图书的网上店面发展为网上商城模式的。亚马逊网站主要使用三个管理平台，分别为 Seller Central、Vendor Express、Vendor Central。其中只有 Seller Central 是面向所有商户开放注册，并且其售卖商品显示为第三方卖家。Vendor Central 的入驻标准最为严格，实行邀请入驻制度，但获得推广力度最强。Vendor Express 主要面向于美国本土不同规模企业，实行申请制度。Vendor Central 和 Vendor Express 两个平台上的商品同样都标注为自营。在标准自营流程中，亚马逊向供应商获取报价，根据大数据分析及计算结果决定下单量和订货时间，后续一系列包括消费者下单、支付、物流、售后服务都由亚马逊全权负责，供应商只负责生产产品。

12.1.3.3 按照所售产品进行分类

有些在线商城仅专注于出售电子产品，而另一些则专注于服装。也有许多此类平台可满足几乎所有类别商品的出售。根据网上商城销售产品的种类，我们将电子商务分为横向和垂直电子商务。

(1) **横向电子商务**

横向电子商务模式意味着可面向尽可能广泛的受众群体出售所有商品。从根本上说，横向电子商务是一个一站式数字商城，客户可以从网上商城毫不费力地搜索所需产品类目，并且一站式地购买所需的任何物品。亚马逊就是一个标准的横向电子商务平台，该公司最初经营图书，但随着时间的推移，其产品品类扩大到了令人难以置信的范围。客户几乎可以在亚马逊网站上购买任何商品。见图 12.3(a)。

(2) **垂直电子商务**

与横向网上商城不同，垂直市场针对单个市场，旨在向目标受众提供某些特定类别的产品。Etsy 就是一个很好的例子，它实践了电子商务商业模型的垂直市场概念。这个位于美国布鲁克林的网上手工艺品商城专注于出售手工艺品。因此，它成了手工艺品和古董的主要卖场之一。见图 12.3(b)。

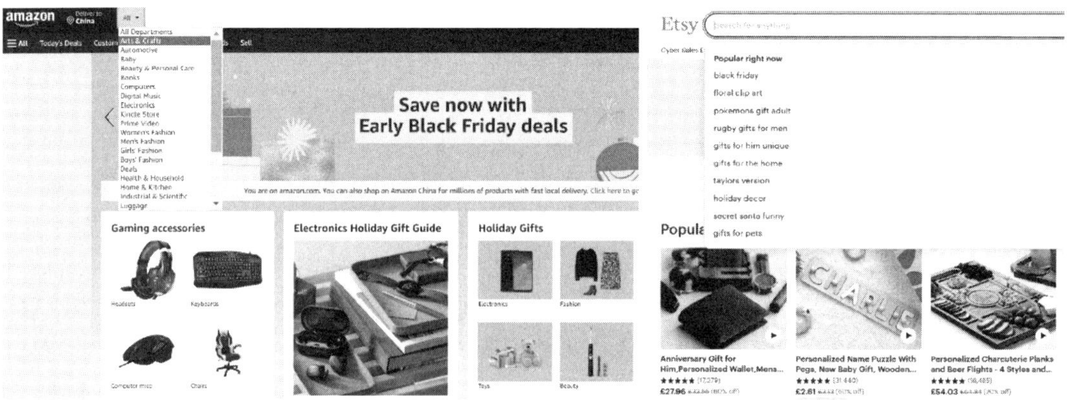

(a) 横向电子商务　　(b) 垂直电子商务

图 12.3　横向与垂直电子商务

12.2 Logistics in the Context of E-commerce

12.2.1 Impact of E-commerce on Logistics

According to the Market Analysis Report by Grand View Research, the global e-commerce market size was valued at USD 9.09 trillion in 2019 and is expected to grow at a compound annual growth rate (CAGR) of 14.7% from 2020 to 2027. The growth of sales and other influences of e-commerce have changed the composition of consumer buying behavior and expectations, as consumers now expect fast, free shipping, and competitive pricing, which will undoubtedly impact the logistics and transportation industry as they will need to be prepared to manage increased volume and delivery expectations. These expectations challenge traditional logistics and supply chain models, and logistics service providers are now forced to adjust their strategies to provide the low-cost and on-demand delivery service.

The impact of e-commerce on logistics can be summarized as the following:

(1) Providing new opportunities for the development of logistics industry

The thriving development of e-commerce enforces the role of logistics. In e-commerce, consumers purchase in vitual stores and make online payment but leave the job of distribution to logistics company. The function of brick-and-mortar stores and banks could be weakened in E-shopping, but not the role of logistics which on the contrary will assume much more work than ever. Logistics companies will not only deliver the goods ordered from online store to consumers, but also make timely replenishment of the goods from producers and store the goods in their warehouses for later delivery. In this process, logistics companies serve producers, sellers, and consumers.

In e-commerce context, informatization facilitates business transaction. Logistics industry has become one of the core industries in the entire market and logistics companies have proved to be the most centralized and comprehensive service providers who deliver tangible goods to customers on behalf of the manufacturers and suppliers, and the only entities who distribute physical goods to market. E-commerce has facilitated logistics industry to great extent and offered new opportunities for the development of the industry.

(2) Expanding the service domain of logistics

What E-commerce company needs is not ordinary shipping or warehousing but logistics services. Logistics differs greatly from warehousing and transportation. Traditional warehousing providers incur much complaint from e-commerce operators that logistics services offered in the 21st century fail to meet the requirement of e-commerce. What e-commerce operators need is far beyond traditional logistics services, but value-added services featured, primarily because they still provide services under traditional logistics service standard as convenient, quick response, cost efficiency, extendibility, and so on.

(3) Promoting the advancement of logistics technique

Traditional logistics technique mainly refers to transportation and circulation technique applied in the transfer of supplies from manufacturers to consumers, which involves the needed hardware such as material, machine and facility at each stage of stoppage and movement, as well as software technique used in planning, application, and appraisal. Modern logistics technique, however, includes various operation methods and management techniques such as processing, packing, identification, and real-time tracing, as well as planning, appraisal, design, and strategy of logistics. The application and popularity of computer network technology, coupled with the rapid development of e-commerce, has equipped logistics with more modern techniques such as Geographic Information System (GIS), Global Positioning System (GPS), Electronic Data Interchange system (EDI) and bar code.

12. 2. 2 The Role of Logistics in E-commerce

Unarguably, with Internet related technology advancement, e-commerce has been experiencing drastic proliferation since its inception, which on one hand creates new growth opportunities and on the other hand presents challenges for businesses. Along with issues such as identity verification, product returns and refunds, fierce competition, logistics is undoubtedly one of the top challenges e-commerce businesses must face to. E-commerce attaches even greater importance to logistics and distribution.

Logistics is one undetachable function of e-commerce business that needs precise treatment, observation, and supervision. No matter what type of e-commerce a firm adopts, how fantastic the website looks and how competitive the price is, the goods have to be delivered on a timely and safe basis to the buyer by means of logistics activities.

(1) Logistics works to guarantee production process

Production is the start of merchandise circulation either in traditional trade or in e-commerce transaction. The merchandise production needs support of various logistics activities which virtually constitutes the entire production process.

① Supply logistics starts from material procurement, where needed materials are procured and shipped to ensure the production.

② Production logistics involves the flow of material and semi-finished products through various processes to realize the flow of production.

③ Reverse logistics is responsible for recycling those residual and recyclable materials produced in the production process.

④ Waste material logistics handles the disposal of waste produced.

In the production process, modern logistics activities are employed to decrease production cost, reduce capital occupation, and shorten production cycle to guarantee efficient production. Without the support of modern logistics, commodity production will be difficult and consequently e-commerce will lose its advantage.

(2) The circulation of commodity is implemented by logistics activities

The result of commodity circulation is the transfer of property right from supplier to buyer. However, the commodity is not physically transferred right after the transaction agreement is reached. In traditional trade, the transaction will be finalized only by means of various logistics activities.

Under e-commerce, internet consumer completes the transfer of property right by means of online shopping. However, the transaction process doesn't end accordingly until the goods or services are eventually transferred to the consumer by means of logistics. As such, logistics plays the role of servicer in the commodity circulation in an e-commerce transaction. Without modern logistics, the commodity transaction in e-commerce will lead to nowhere.

E-commerce, as a brand-new transaction mode in internet epoch, is a revolution against traditional transaction. However, it must be supported by modern logistics techniques to exhibit its unparalleled advancement and superiority and thus benefit transaction parties to the greatest extent. Therefore, the advancement of e-commerce must be accompanied by the development of modern logistics.

12.2.3 E-commerce Logistics and its Characteristics

E-commerce logistics, also called e-logistics, is the use of web-based technologies to support the material acquisition, warehousing, and transportation. By closely incorporating route optimization and inventory-tracking with distribution, e-commerce logistics aims to increase efficiency, reduce operating costs, build strong customer relationship, and enhance brand reputation. It represents the latest driver of change in logistics and physical distribution networks, which have evolved substantially over the past 40 years.

E-commerce logistics manifests unique characteristics as following:

(1) Informatization

With traditional logistics, the frequently mentioned characteristics are paper-based documentation, scanned PDFs, manually input data, different IT systems along supply chain. There's little or no interchangeability between the various software systems used by supply chain members, and most of the coordination and communication is done over the phone. Clearly, this is not cost or time efficient. In comparison, e-logistics gathers information through Internet, Electronic Data Interchange (EDI), Radio Frequency Identification (RFID) and Integrated IS, making information sharing more reliable and faster than traditional logistics. E-logistics is a new cloud-based method which enables optimization and collaboration between all stakeholders in the supply chain. All data can be shared electronically between different management systems and applications and be reused repeatedly once input.

Logistics informatization is the requirement of e-commerce which is represented by the commercialization of logistics information, the datamation and coding in logistics information collection, the electronization and computerization of logistics information processing, the standardization and real-timeness of logistics information transmission, and the digitization of logistics information storage. Therefore, technology and concept such as Bar Code, Database, Electronic Ordering System (EOS), Electronic Data Interchange (EDI), Quick Response (QR), Effective Customer Response (ECR), and Enterprise Resource Planning (ERP) will be widely applied in logistics. Informatization is the foundation of everything in logistics. The application of information and computer technology in logistics will completely change the status of global logistics.

(2) automation

Informatization based automation focuses on mechatronics and is represented by unmanned technique. The effect of automation is saving of labor, increase of operation capacity and labor productivity, and reduction of errors in logistics operation. There are many automatic logistics equipment such as bar code/voice/ radio frequency automatic identification system, automatic sorting system, automatic storage retrieval system, automatically guided vehicle, automatic cargo tracing system and so on. These equipment have been widely employed in many countries.

(3) networking

Networking, one of the primary characteristics of logistics in e-commerce context, is also based on informatization. One implication of networking is the computerized communication network employed in logistics distribution system, including the computer network between distribution center and supplier (or manufacturer) and the network between distribution center and downstream customer. For instance, with the help of Electronic Ordering System (EOS) and EDI on Value-Added Network (VAN), the order placement from distribution center to supplier can be automatically realized by means of computerized communication, so can the order collection by distribution center from downstream customers. The other implication of networking refers to organizational network, or the so-called intranet. Let's take the global operational production and sale model created by Taiwan computer industry in 1990s for example. This model will utilize global computer resources, organize production on customers' order and outsource the production of all the parts, components and chips to manufacturers located across the world. This model then, by using global logistics network, ship these parts, components and chips to the same distribution center for assembly, from where the assembled computers are distributed to customers. The whole process needs support from efficient logistics network which is certainly based on information and computer network.

(4) intellectualization

Intellectualization is a higher level application of automation and informatization. There are lots of planning and decision-making issues in logistics operation such as the determination of inventory level, the choice of shipment/movement route, the moving trajectory and control of automatically guided vehicle, the operation of automatic sorter, and the decision-making support in the operation and management of distribution center, all of which need professional knowledge. In the process of logistics automation, logistics intelligence is an unavoidable technical problem. Fortunately, expert systems, robots and other related technologies have made great advancement. Intellectualization will be a new development direction for logistics in the context of e-commerce to increase logistics service level.

(5) flexibility

Flexibility was originally proposed in the field of production to realize the customer-centered management. However, without the support of flexible logistics system, it is impossible to truly adjust production process flexibly to meet the change of consumer's demand. 1990s witnessed the global introduction of concepts and technologies such as Flexible

Manufacturing System (FMS), Computer Integrated Manufacturing System (CIMS), Manufacturing Requirement Planning (MRP-Ⅱ), Enterprise Resource Planning (ERP), and supply chain management, which virtually helped to integrate production and circulation, organize production, and arrange logistics activities according to the end users' demand. Therefore, flexible logistics is a new logistics model to meet the needs of production, circulation, and consumption. It requires the distribution center to flexibly organize and perform logistics operation to cater for consumers' needs of various items in small lot to be delivered in multi-batch and shorter cycle.

12.2 电子商务背景下的物流

12.2.1 电子商务对物流的影响

根据Grand View研究的市场分析报告，全球电子商务市场规模在2019年达到了9.09万亿美元，预计将在2020年至2027年间实现14.7%的复合年增长率。销售额的增长及电子商务的其他影响，改变了消费者的购买行为和期望，因为消费者现在期望快速发货、免运费和低价。这无疑将对物流和运输业产生影响，因为它们需要做好准备以应对运货数量的增加以及消费者对送货的期望。这些期望挑战了传统的物流和供应链模式，迫使物流服务提供商调整其策略以提供低价的按需送货服务。

电子商务对物流产生了如下影响。

(1) 电子商务为物流业的发展提供了新的机遇

电子商务的蓬勃发展必将导致物流业逐渐强化。这是因为，在电子商务的环境里，消费者在网上的虚拟商店购物，并完成网上支付，配送的功能就交由物流公司承担。也就是说，实体店和银行都可以省略，但是物流公司非但不能省略掉，反而任务加重了。物流公司不但要把消费者从虚拟店铺订购的货物配送到用户手上，而且还要从各个生产企业及时进货，存放到物流企业的仓库中。物流公司既为生产企业服务，又为销售店铺服务，还要为具体的消费者服务。

在电子商务环境下，商务事务处理实现了信息化，物流成了整个市场运行的核心之一。物流企业成了代表所有生产企业、供应商向用户进行实物供应的唯一最集中、最广泛的服务提供者，是进行市场实物供应配送的唯一主体。电子商务把物流业提升到了前所未有的高度。可以说，电子商务为物流业的发展提供了新的机遇。

(2) 电子商务促使物流服务空间的拓展

电子商务需要的不是普通的运输和仓储服务，它需要的是物流服务，而物流与仓储运输存在比较大的差别。正是因为传统的储运经营者用传统物流服务的要求和标准为电子商务服务，才使得电子商务经营者在21世纪初的今天仍然抱怨物流服务跟不上电子商务的要求。电子商务经营者需要的是增值性的物流服务，而不仅仅是传统的物流服务。增值性的物流服务要具有便利性、快速响应性、低成本性及延展性等特征。

(3) 电子商务促进物流技术水平的提高

传统的物流技术主要是指物资运输技术或者物资流通技术，也就是说物流技术是各种流通物资从生产者转移给消费者时，实现各种流通形态的停顿与流动功能所需要的材料、机械、设施等硬件环境和计划、运用、评价等软件技术。现代的物流技术包括各种操作方法、管理技能等，如流通加工技术、物品包装技术、物品标识技术、物品实时跟踪技术等。物流技术也包括物流规划、物流评价、物流设计、物流策略等。在计算机网络技术得到应用并普及后，尤其随着电子商务的飞速发展，物流技术涉及许多现代技术，例如，地理信息系统、全球卫星定位系统、电子数据交换系统、条码技术等。

12.2.2 物流在电子商务中的作用

毫无疑问，自出现以来，随着互联网相关技术的发展，电子商务一直在经历着急剧的增长。虽然随之而来的新增长机会令人振奋，但这也给企业带来了挑战。除了身份验证、产品退货和退款、激烈的竞争之外，物流无疑是电子商务企业必须高度重视的最大挑战之一，并且物流和分销在电子商务中显得更加重要。

物流是电子商务业务必不可少的功能，必须对其进行精确的处理和监管。无论采取何种类型的电子商务，无论网站的外观多么吸睛以及价格如何具有竞争力，都必须通过物流及时、安全地将货物交付给买方。

(1) 物流是生产过程的保障

无论是传统的贸易环境还是在电子商务的环境下，生产都是商品流通的开始，而商品生产的顺利进行需要各类物流活动支持，整个生产过程实际上就是一系列的物流活动。

① 供应物流从生产全过程的原材料采购开始，将生产所需的材料采购到位，保证生产的进行。

② 生产物流涉及的原材料、半成品的物流贯穿于生产的各工艺流程之间，以实现生产的流动性。

③ 回收物流对生产过程中的部分余料和可重复利用的物资进行回收。

④ 废弃物流完成对生产过程中废弃物的处理。

在商品生产的过程中，现代化的物流活动可以降低生产成本、减少资金占压和缩短生产周期，最终保障了生产的高效进行。相反，如果没有现代物流的支持，商品的生产将难以顺利进行，电子商务交易模式将会先天不足，优势不复存在。

(2) 商流的结果由物流完成

商流活动的最终结果是将商品所有权由供方转移到买方，但是实际上在交易合同签订后，商品实体并没有立即移动。在传统交易环境下，商流的结果必须由相应的物流活动来执行完成。

在电子商务的环境下，网络消费者虽然通过上网订购完成了商品所有权的交割过程，但必须通过物流的过程将商品和服务真正转移到消费者手中，电子商务的交易活动才告以终结。因此，物流在电子商务交易的商流中起到了后续者和服务者的作用，没有现代化物流，电子商务的商流活动将是一纸空文。

综上所述，电子商务作为网络时代的一种全新的交易模式，相对于传统交易方式是一场革命。但是，电子商务必须有现代化的物流技术的支持，才能体现出其所具有的无可比拟的先进性和优越性，在最大程度上使交易双方得到便利，获得效益。因此，只有大力发展作为电子商务重要组成部分的现代化物流，电子商务才能得到更好的发展。

12.2.3 电子商务物流及其特点

电子商务物流是利用基于 Web 的技术，以支持物料的获取、仓储和运输过程，它使配送能够将路径优化与库存跟踪信息结合在一起，目的是提高效率，降低运营成本，建立牢固的客户关系并提高品牌声誉。它是物流和物流网络变化的最新推动力，在过去 40 年中，物流配送网络已经发生了重大变化。

电子商务物流表现出以下独特特征。

(1) 信息化

在传统物流中，关于纸质文档、扫描的 PDF、手动输入数据、供应链中的企业使用不同 IT 系统这些特征人们耳熟能详。供应链成员使用的各种软件系统之间几乎没有互换性，大多数的协调和通信都是通过电话完成的。显然，无论从成本还是时间上看，传统物流缺乏效率。相比之下，电子物流通过互联网、电子数据交换（EDI），射频识别（RFID）和集成信息系统收集并交换数据，这使得电子物流比传统物流在信息共享方面更可靠、更快捷。电子物流是一种新的基于云的方法，可实现供应链中所有利益相关者之间的优化与协作。所有数据可以在不同的管理系统和应用程序之间以电子方式共享，并且一旦输入即可重复利用。

电子商务时代，物流信息化是电子商务的必然要求。物流信息化表现为物流信息的商业化、物流信息收集的数据库化和代码化、物流信息处理的电子化和计算机化、物流信息传递的标准化和实时化、物流信息存储的数字化等。因此，条码技术（Bar Code)、数据库技术(Database)、电子订货系统 EOS：Electronic Ordering System)、电子数据交换 Electronic Data Interchange，EDI)、快速响应（Quick Response，QR）及有效的客户响应（Effective Customer Response，ECR)、企业资源计划（Enterprise Resource Planning，ERP）等技术与观念在物流中将会得到普遍的应用。信息化是一切的基础，信息技术及计算机技术在物流中的应用将会彻底改变世界物流的面貌。

(2) 自动化

自动化的基础是信息化，自动化的核心是机电一体化，自动化的外在表现是无人化，自动化的效果是省力化，另外还可以扩大物流作业能力、提高劳动生产率、减少物流作业的差错等。物流自动化的设施非常多，如条码/语音/射频自动识别系统、自动分拣系统、自动存取系统、自动导向车、货物自动跟踪系统等。这些设施在许多国家已普遍用于物流作业流程中。

(3) 网络化

物流领域网络化的基础也是信息化，是电子商务下物流活动主要特征之一。这里指的网络化有两层含义：一是物流配送系统的计算机通信网络，包括物流配送中心与供应商或制造商之间、物流配送中心与下游顾客之间的计算机网络通信。比如物流配送中心向供应商提出订单这个过程，就可以使用计算机通信方式，借助于增值网（Value-Added Network，VAN）上的电子订货系统（EOS）和电子数据交换技术（EDI）来自动实现，物流配送中心通过计算机网络收集下游客户的订货的过程也可以自动完成；二是组织的网络化，即所谓的企业内部网（Intranet)。比如，台湾的电脑业在 20 世纪 90 年代创造出了"全球运筹式产销模式"，这种模式的基本点是按照客户订单组织生产，生产采取分散形式，即将全世界的电脑资源都利用起来，采取外包的形式将一台电脑的所有零部件、元器件、芯片外包给世界各地的制造商去生产，然后通过全球的物流网络将这些零部件、元器件和芯片发往同一个物流配送中心进行组装，由该物流配送中心将组装的电脑迅速发给客户。这一过程需要有高效的物流网络支持，当然物流网络的基础是信息和电脑网络。

(4) 智能化

这是物流自动化、信息化的一种高层次应用。物流作业过程大量的运筹和决策，如库存水平的确定、运输（搬运）路径的选择、自动导向车的运行轨迹和作业控制、自动分拣机的运行、物流配送中心经营管理的决策支持等问题都需要借助于大量的知识才能解决。在物流自动化的进程中，物流智能化是不可回避的技术难题。好在专家系统、机器人等相关技术在国际上已经有比较成熟的研究成果。为了提高物流现代化的水平，物流的智能化已成为电子商务下物流发展的一个新趋势。

（5）柔性化

柔性化本来是为实现“以顾客为中心”的理念而在生产领域提出的，但要真正做到柔性化，即真正地能根据消费者需求的变化来灵活调节生产工艺，没有配套的柔性化的物流系统是不可能达到目的的。20 世纪 90 年代，国际生产领域纷纷推出柔性制造系统（Flexible Manufacturing System，FMS）、计算机集成制造系统（Computer Integrated Manufacturing System，CIMS）、制造资源系统（Manufacturing Requirement Planning，MRP-Ⅱ）、企业资源计划（Enterprise Resource Planning，ERP）以及供应链管理的概念和技术。这些概念和技术的实质是要将生产、流通进行集成，根据需求端的需求组织生产，安排物流活动。因此，柔性化的物流正是适应生产、流通与消费的需求而发展起来的一种新型物流模式。这就要求物流配送中心要根据消费需求“多品种、小批量、多批次、短周期”的特色，灵活组织和实施物流作业。

12. 3 Cross Border E-Commerce Logistics

12. 3. 1 Cross Border E-commerce

E-commerce has helped businesses establish a wider market presence by providing cheaper and more efficient distribution channels for their products or services. More importantly, it facilitates the transaction across border and enables consumers to shop globally. That model of conducting business across the world by means of internet and computerized communication technology is known as cross border e-commerce, global e-commerce, or international e-commerce. It entails the sale or purchase of products via online shops across national borders. Buyer and seller are situated in different countries, ruled by different jurisdiction, use different currencies, and speak different languages. The increasing popularity of tablets and smart phones, allows consumers worldwide to compare prices, connect with other consumers via social media, discuss products and services, select a cross border online shop and make payment via their PC, laptop, mobile phone or tablet anytime and anywhere. The oppotunities presented by global e-commerce will benefit not only consumers, but also merchants and payment service providers such as banks. The Asia Pacific region dominated by China will be the largest e-commerce cross border region in both import and export.

12. 3. 2 Characteristics of Cross Border E-commerce Logistics

In cross border e-commerce, the fulfilment of transaction between e-business and consumers is based on non-virtual international logistics, the efficiency and cost of which influences consumers' purchase experience. High costs, slow delivery, and low service level have impeded the development of e-commerce. Unlike domestic logistics, cross border logistics inherently faces the problem of longer distance and shipping time, higher costs, as well as customs clearance in destination country, all of which pose great challenges on international seller. As such, more attention has been paid to cross border e-commerce logistics. It refers to a set of international business activities by which transaction parties located in different customs territory reach a deal and make payment via e-commerce platform and then ship the commodity and complete the deal through cross border logistics.

Companies conducting cross border e-commerce must take logistics issues seriously and give great priority to the following functions if they want to succeed in the fierce competition.

(1) Inventory management

Some businesses opt to establish warehouses or distribution facilities in the countries where their global e-commerce markets are targeted. This can shorten shipping time and reduce costs significantly for both the company and its customers. However, it adds a layer of complexity to inventory management that is best handled with an integrated software solution that tracks sales and delivers data to the appropriate departments in real time. More importantly, in global e-commerce, traditional warehouses are being replaced by mega e-fulfillment centers where the merchandise is stocked and picked at item level. These facilities, which are either operated by the retailer or a logistics service provider, typically cover 500 thousand to one million sq ft in size, or even larger. They often operate 24/7.

(2) Payment and shipping solutions

Consumers prefer to pay using the most popular options in their countries. Therefore, companies marching into global e-commerce must be sensitive to various prevailing payment options in different parts of the world. Hassle-free payment is critical to making sales in an e-commerce context and avoiding high abandonment rate that may occur during the checkout process. Shipping is another critical piece of the puzzle. Delivering to a global audience means factoring in customs and duties, potential wait times and differences in shipping rates.

(3) Optimizing fulfillment

Managing localized warehouses and offering popular shipping options ensures quick delivery to customers, but it can pose some tricky budget problems for businesses. To preserve profits while providing positive customer experience, e-businesses must work with suppliers and shipping companies to strike a balance between these variables. The goal is always to deliver goods to customers in the easiest and cheapest way possible without weakening profitability in the process.

(4) Parcel sortation and last mile delivery

Parcel hubs/sortation centers are in need where orders are sorted by zip code so that they can be shipped to the relevant parcel delivery center for final delivery to customer's home or designated collection point. Parcel delivery centers which handle the 'last mile' delivery to customer is also critical especially in B2C.

(5) Real time information updating

Seamlessly integrated technology is crucial where shopping carts connect to transportation management system via API, web xml or some other connection, so that shoppers can get the exact price quote of shipping by various modes. These technology products for logistics, such as Transportation Management System (TMS), must be accessible along with the shopping cart and provide real time information functions such as:

① Ability to organize and trace shipment no matter under what modes;

② Online order status and documentation;

③ Online dispatch documentation and invoice, such as a bill of lading and freight invoice;

④ Auto reminder for payments;

⑤ Seamless interface with existing SCM or ERP system;

⑥ Online alerts for critical information via text or mobile;

⑦ Information systems reports on past data analysis, delivery history, etc.

12.3.3 Popular Cross Border E-commerce Logistics Patterns

(1) International postal parcel

This pattern resolves the distribution and other logistics issues mainly in the form of personal parcel through Universal Postal Union. Universal Postal Union is an international postal organization with about 200 member countries who handle their international postal affairs within the Union. The postal network basically covers every part of the world, wider than any other logistics channel. Besides, postal service providers are generally state-owned businesses who can enjoy state tax subsidies, which results in much lower freight rate. As such, by using international postal parcel, one can enjoy lower cost and easier customs clearance. However, one must bear the disadvantages of higher loss rate, lower security, and longer delivery time, as well as the limitation on the shape, size, weight of the parcel, which to some extent affects the efficiency and customer experience.

(2) International Express

International express, like international postal parcel, is also a traditional logistics channel in global e-commerce. It gets the distribution and other logistics issues handled by international express companies. Internationally renowned express companies include UPS, USPS, FedEx, DHL, etc. who use their own global network, powerful IT systems and localized services all over the world to bring excellent logistics experience to overseas online customers. Lately, some express companies in China, such as SF Express and YTO Express, are also marching into cross border e-commerce. The pattern of international express can meet the requirement of customers from all over the world with its merits of shorter time and better service. However, its higher cost and lack of dedicated line somehow influence customers' experience.

(3) Dedicated line logistics

Cross border dedicated line logistics usually by means of cabin chartering ships the commodity to other territory where a partner local company is responsible for the final delivery. This pattern has its dedicated transportation vehicle, route, point of departure and destination, transportation cycle and timetable. Most importantly the dedicated line is designed in accordance with the characteristics of cross border logistics in different countries/regions. Examples are Sino-Europe Railway and e-ulink. These characteristics enable the dedicated line logistics to avoid risk in customs clearance and commodity inspection. Another advantage lies in its lower costs achieved by economies of scales, for it is able to centralize a large quantity of commodity and make consolidated shipment to a specified country/region. As a result, the freight rate is lower than that in international express. With respect to delivery speed, it is faster than postal parcel but slower than international express.

(4) Overseas warehousing

Overseas warehousing is an emerging cross border e-commerce logistics pattern. It involves cross border e-commerce company building or leasing a warehouse located in a destination territory to where the cargo is to be shipped by sea/land/air. After the order is placed online, the e-commerce company will make direct distribution and shipment by use of the overseas warehouse or with the help of a third-party logistics entity. Overseas warehousing includes three stages:

① First leg transportation: seller ships commodity to overseas warehouse by sea, land, air, or multimodal transportation.

② Warehousing management: seller remotely handles overseas warehousing and makes real time inventory management by using logistics information system.

③ Local distribution: the overseas warehouse uses local postal service or express to deliver the commodity to customer according to order information.

E-commerce sellers benefit a lot from this pattern. With overseas warehouse, it is easier to adjust price in foreign market and lower logistics costs. In this scenario, with the commodity being distributed from buyer's country, the order cycle will be shortened, customer experience be enhanced, and rate of repurchase be increased. Meanwhile, the issues like commodity inspection and return can be resolved more efficiently.

On the other hand, despite its solution to lower cost and shorten delivery cycle, cross border e-commerce seller should know that this pattern is not suitable to all products, but to hot sale products with higher inventory turnover; for other commodities, there might be overstock. Furthermore, this pattern needs huge investment and poses higher requirement on supplier's supply chain management, inventory management and so on.

(5) Border warehousing

Like overseas warehousing, border warehousing is also an emerging cross border e-commerce logistics pattern with warehouse set up beyond the seller's territory. But it differs from overseas warehousing in that the warehouse is situated in a country adjacent to the import country, while overseas warehouse is in the destination country. Based on specific location, border warehouse could be classified into relative and absolute border warehouse, with the former set up in territory not adjacent to the importing country and the latter set up in neighboring country. In practice, border warehousing manifests the benefits such as avoiding political, law and tax risks arising from destination country, making the most use of logistics politics in free trade zone, and consequently reducing logistics costs and increasing logistics efficiency.

(6) Free trade zone or bonded zone logistics

As the term suggests, the goods are shipped to the warehouse located in free trade zone or bonded zone where they are sorted, quarantined, packed and concentratedly dispatched, while the cross border e-commerce company is responsible for the sale of the goods. The biggest benefit of this model is that it can take full advantages of free trade zone and bonded zone to ensure the rapid operation of international logistics for cross border e-commerce.

12.3 跨境电商物流

12.3.1 跨境电子商务

电子商务通过为其产品或服务提供更低价、更有效的分销渠道，帮助企业扩展了市场范围。更重要的是，它促进了跨境交易，使消费者能够在全球采购。这种通过互联网和计算机化通信技术在全球开展业务的模式被称为跨境电子商务、全球电子商务或国际电子商务。它是指在跨越国界的网店进行买卖活动，买卖双方不在同一国家/地区，通常不受同一司法管辖区的管辖，使用不同的货币及不同的语言。平板电脑和智能手机的日渐普及，使全球范围内的消费者可以比较价格，通过社交媒体与其他消费者联系，讨论产品和服务，选择一个其境外的网点，并随时随地通过个人电脑、笔记本电脑、移动设备或平板进行支付。全球电子商务不仅给消费者，给商人和银行等支付服务提供商都带来了获利机会。知名的技术和市场调研公司 Forrester 预测，到 2022 年，跨境采购将占全球电子商务的 20%，销售额将达到 6270 亿美元。以中国为主导的亚太地区将成为进出口最大的电子商务跨境地区。

12.3.2 跨境电商物流的特点

跨境电子商务之中，企业与消费者合约践行的基础就在于非虚拟性的“国际物流”，而影响消费者消费体验的因素也在于物流的效率及成本。物流成本过高、配送速度慢、服务水平低等已成为发展电子商务进程中亟待解决的问题。不同于国内物流，跨境物流距离远、时间长、成本高，不仅如此，中间还涉及目的国清关（办理出关手续）等相关问题，这中间的种种难题为卖家带来了巨大的挑战。因此，越来越多的人开始关注跨境电商物流。跨境电商物流是指分属不同关境的交易主体通过电子商务平台达成交易，进行支付结算，并通过跨境物流送达商品、完成交易的一种国际商业活动。

在激烈的市场竞争中取胜，从事跨境电商的企业必须将物流纳入考虑范围，着重考虑以下物流功能。

(1) 库存管理

一些企业倾向于在跨境电商目标市场建立仓库或配送中心，此法虽能为公司和顾客极大地缩短运输时间并节约成本，却增加了库存管理的复杂性。此时的库存管理需要使用综合软件解决方案随销售进行跟踪并即时地将数据传输至相应部门。更重要的是，在全球电子商务中，传统仓库被大型电子履约中心所取代，在那里商品在单品级别进行库存和拣选。这些中心可由零售商或物流服务商运营，面积至少可达 50～100 万平方英尺，常年运营。

(2) 支付与运输解决方案

消费者更乐于采用其所在国最受欢迎的方式进行支付。因而，从事跨境电商的公司必须知晓世界各地所流行的支付方式有所不同。在电子商务环境下，为促成销售并避免结账过程中出现较高的放弃率，实现无障碍支付至关重要。运输是另一个关键的难题。为全球各地的客户送货意味着要考虑关税、潜在的等待时间和运费差异。

(3) 优化履约

管理当地仓并提供受欢迎的运输方案能够确保产品尽快送抵顾客，但另一方面也为公司预算增加了负担。为了能在为顾客提供良好购物体验的同时保证利润的实现，公司需会同供应商与运输公司在这些因素之间进行平衡，终极目标在于保证盈利的同时采用最简单最节约的方式将订货送抵顾客。

(4) 包裹分拣

需要建立包裹枢纽或包裹分拣中心，在该中心，订单将按照邮政编码进行分拣进而被运至相关的包裹运输中心，并最终上门运送至客户或指定的包裹收集站。旨在处理最后一公里运输的包裹运输中心也至关重要，尤其是在 B2C 电子商务模式中。

(5) 实时信息更新

无缝集成技术至关重要，使用该技术，购物车通过 API、WEB XML 或其他连接与运输管理系统相连，从而购物者可获得不同运输模式的确切报价。这些用于物流的技术，如 TMS（运输管理系统），必须与购物车一起实现并提供实时信息，如：

① 无论何种模式都能组织并跟踪发货；

② 在线订单状态和文档；

③ 在线调度文档和发票，例如提单和运输发票；

④ 付款提醒；

⑤ 与现有 SCM 或 ERP 系统的无缝界面连接；

⑥ 以信息或电话的方式就关键信息进行在线警报；

⑦ 就过去的数据分析及交付历史等生成信息系统报告。

12.3.3 跨境电商国际物流模式

(1) 国际邮政小包

主要通过万国邮政联盟来解决商品配送及物流问题，以个人邮包的形式进行发货；而万国邮政联盟是世界邮政国际组织，它是加入其中的成员国处理邮政事务的国际组织，目前其成员国在 200 个左右。邮政网络基本覆盖全球，比其他任何物流渠道都要广。而且，由于邮政一般为国营，有国家税收补贴，价格非常便宜。因而，国际邮政小包具有成本低、通关容易等优势。但在实际运营过程中，国际邮政小包的丢包率高、安全性低、时效性不强等劣势较为突出；同时使用国际邮政小包进行物流运输，还受制于包裹形状、体积、重量等因素，国际邮政小包在一定程度上影响物流效率及物流体验。

(2) 国际快递模式

国际快递跟国际邮政小包一样，也是用于跨境电子商务物流服务的一种传统模式，它主要是通过国际快递公司来解决跨境电子商务之中商品配送及物流的问题。在国际上知名的国际快递公司包括 UPS、USPS、FedEx、DHL 等，他们通过自建的全球网络，利用强大的 IT 系统和遍布世界各地的本地化服务，为网购的海外用户带来极好的物流体验。而我国一些快递公司如顺丰、圆通等也纷纷在时代驱使之下涉足跨境电子商务。国际快递这种传统的物流模式在快递时效性及服务质量上占据着优势，可以满足世界各地客户的需求；但是其也存在着价格高、特色专线快递未开通等劣势，进而影响客户物流体验。

(3) 专线物流模式

跨境专线物流一般是通过包舱方式运输到国外，再通过合作公司进行目的国的派送。专线物流有其专门使用的物流运输工具、物流线路、物流起点与终点、物流运输周期及时间等，同时它还是根据特定国家或地区跨境电商物流特点所推出的物流专线；比如现在已开通的中欧班列、e-ulink 专线等。由于其特点，使得国际物流专线此种物流模式能够有效规避通关及商检风险。专线物流的另一优势在于其能够集中大批量到某一特定国家或地区的货物，通过规模效应降低成本。因此，其价格一般比商业快递低。在时效上，专线物流稍慢于商业快递，但比邮政包裹快很多。

(4) 海外仓储模式

海外仓是最近几年兴起的新型跨境电商国际物流模式，它是指经营跨境电商的企业在境外目的地建立或租赁仓库，采用海陆空等运输方式将货物运输至境外目的地，通过跨境电商的方式进行线上销售，消费者成功下订单之后，企业再利用境外目的地仓库或境外第三方物流机构直接进行商品配送及运输。海外仓储应该包括头程运输、仓储管理和本地配送三个部分。

① 头程运输，即卖家通过海运、空运、陆运或者联运将商品运送至海外仓库。

② 仓储管理：卖家通过物流信息系统，远程操作海外仓储货物，实时管理库存。

③ 本地配送：海外仓储中心根据订单信息，通过当地邮政或快递将商品配送给客户。

选择这类模式的好处在于，仓库置于海外不仅有利于海外市场价格的调配，同时还能降低物流成本。拥有自己的海外仓库，能从买家所在国发货，从而缩短订单周期，完善客户体验，提升重复购买率，同时还能有效解决商品检验及退换货等诸多问题。

然而，这种海外仓储的模式虽然解决了小包时代成本高昂、配送周期漫长的问题，但是，跨境电商需要知道，不是任何产品都适合使用海外仓。库存周转快的热销单品最为适合此类模式，否则，极容易压货。同时，这种方式基础设施的投资巨大，且对卖家在供应链管理和库存管控等方面提出了更高的要求。

(5) 边境仓

边境仓与海外仓都是新型跨境电商国际物流模式，都是将物流仓库设立在远离国境的国家。而边境仓与海外仓的区别就在于，海外仓位于境外目的国，而边境仓则位于商品输入国的邻国。同时，根据仓库的位置，边境仓可以分为相对边境仓及绝对边境仓两种。相对边境仓也就是仓库设立在与商品输入国不相邻却相近的国家，而绝对边境仓则是仓库设立在与商品输入国相邻的国家。在实际运作中，边境仓的优势主要体现在可以有效规避商品目的国的政治、法律、税收等风险，同时设立边境仓还能够充分利用“自由贸易区”区域物流政策，从而降低物流成本及提升物流效率。

(6) 自贸区或保税区物流

自贸区或保税区物流模式也是跨境电子商务之下的产物。这种模式下，将货物运输至自贸区或保税区仓库，仓库负责货物分拣、检疫、包装以及集中配送，并由跨境电商企业负责商品销售。其最大优势是可以在最大程度上利用自贸区及保税区自身优势，为跨境电子商务国际物流的快速运行提供保障。

12.4 Cross Border E-commerce Supervision Modes in China

Till now, China makes the biggest B2C cross border e-commerce transaction market, handling 26 percent of the global deals. Other modes of e-commerce also grow dramatically.

Cross border e-commerce started as Daigou which is a channel of commerce, in which a Chinese individual living abroad sells foreign products to a customer in mainland China. China's fast growing middle-class group rapidly accelerated this cross-border shopping phenomenon in such a pace that China's customs didn't have a stable clearance system or service method to support its fast development, causing huge loss of tax and higher logistics costs.

In response to the outburst of these semi-legal cross-border shipments from overseas individuals, Chinese government began to designate some areas in cross border e-commerce comprehensive pilot cities. Generally near large trading ports, these areas provide favorable business environments, bonded warehouses, and key infrastructure support for cross-border e-commerce. Till 2020, China has 105 cross border e-commerce pilot areas in total under the supervision of China customs. The pilot areas differ slightly in terms of regulations and infrastructure, as they further specialize in particular product categories or businesses.

Cross border e-commerce, as a new international trade mode, has brought great challenges to China's customs supervision. Since 2014, customs authorities have regularly introduced new trade supervision methods, exploring innovative ways to help the industry develop in a well-regulated and systematic way.

12. 4. 1 Cross Border E-commerce Retail Import Supervision Methods

Currently, there are two main import modes for cross border e-commerce trade, namely direct purchase import and bonded import.

(1) Direct purchase import mode

The General Administration of Customs of China (GACC) issued the No. 12 announcement in 2014 to promote the development of cross border e-commerce retail import and export and facilitate the customs clearance process. On February 10, 2014, the customs supervision mode code "9610" was added. It applies to transactions made via e-commerce platforms by domestic individual consumers, e-commerce companies, and platforms that carry out e-commerce retail imports.

Chinese consumers will firstly place an order on a registered cross border e-commerce website/platform. Once the order is received, the platform will submit the records of the order, shipment, and payment to customs. All products sold via cross border e-commerce platform must be pre-registered with customs. Figure 12. 4 shows the procedure of this mode.

VAT and customs duties are recorded at the time of dispatch of the goods from an overseas warehouse (supplier) via direct post. Overseas commodities are imported through logistics methods such as post and express to special sites supervised for cross border e-commerce, and cross border e-commerce companies or their agents declare entry to the customs and dispatch the commodities on a one-by-one basis. The standard delivery time, from order submission to customer reception, for direct purchase import mode is between 10～15 days.

This mode is featured as the following:

Firstly, it is a direct import mode. Imported commodities are declared for entry right after being unloaded from conveyance. There is no storage period in bonded warehouse before declaration under this mode, which fundamentally differs from bonded import mode.

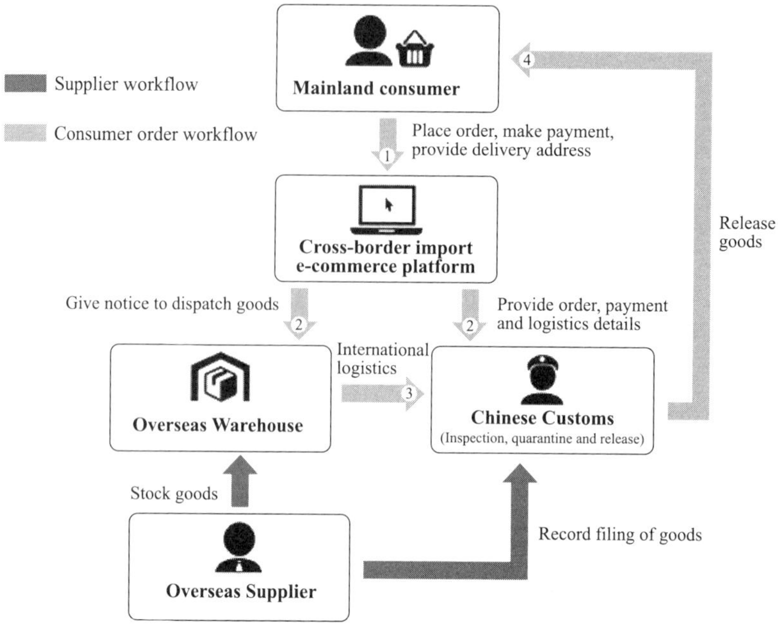

Figure 12.4　Direct purchase import mode

(Source: hkmb. hktdc. com)

Secondly, direct purchase is an order triggered mode. Imported commodities cannot be stored in customs supervised area for a long time and therefore cannot be prepared before order is placed like in bonded imported mode. Import transportation is arranged only after orders are placed by domestic individual consumers.

Thirdly, direct purchase is not a bulk import mode. It generally cannot realize the centralized import of a single commodity in batches, for transportation is arranged after order is placed.

Fourthly, it is a pre-registry mode. As required by customs, e-commerce companies and the direct purchase commodities should be pre-registered before import and e-commerce platform should send real time data of order, payment and logistics to customs.

(2) Bonded import mode

In recent years, online shopping bonded import has flourished, accounting for over 80% of cross border e-commerce retail import. Under this mode, products are shipped in bulk into approved cross border e-commerce warehouses within the pilot zones in China. Products on the Positive List can be stored in bonded warehouses and enjoy faster product registration and simplified customs clearance procedures.

When a Chinese consumer places an order on a registered e-commerce platform, the order is prepared for dispatch from the bonded warehouse, cleared with customs, and delivered to the customer directly. Import duties and VAT are paid at the time of actual sale. The standard delivery time from order submission to customer reception to is between 3—7 days.

This mode has two customs supervision codes of 1210 and 1239, which are slightly different in application area and commodity import requirement.

Bonded import follows the steps shown in Figure 12.5.

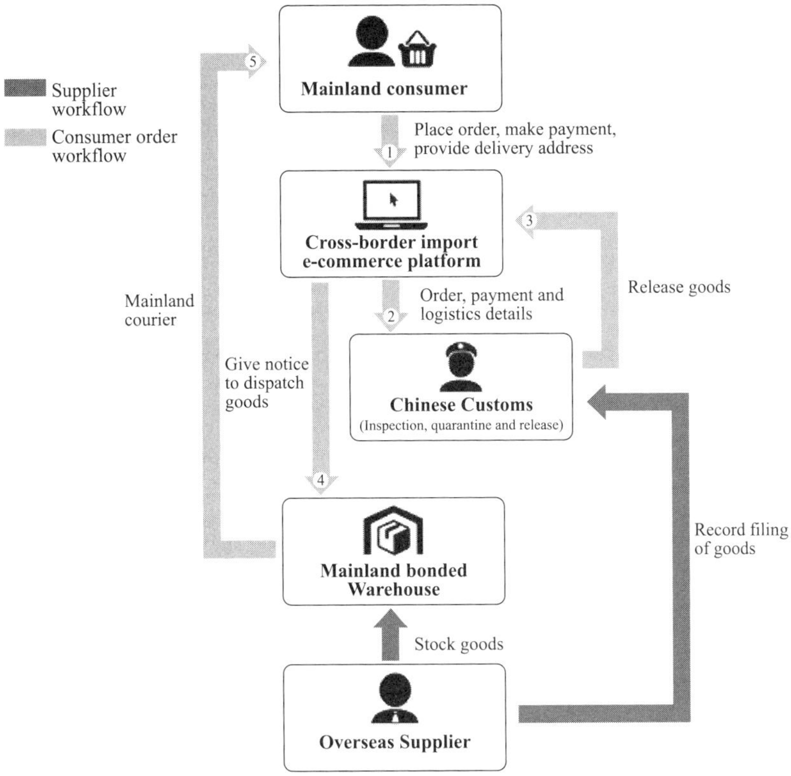

Figure 12.5 Bonded import mode

(Source: hkmb.hktdc.com)

(3) Differences between the two modes

Direct purchase mode covers more commodity options. Commodities are shipped from overseas suppliers or warehouses and therefore cover wider range of products, especially newly listed ones, which can be timely traded across borders. Under the bonded mode however, the products for sale are limited to those approved to be stored in bonded warehouses.

Direct purchase mode takes longer logistics time. It takes extra days for international transportation when commodities are shipped from overseas. Once the order is placed, the whole chain of logistics should be integrated immediately, posing higher requirement on logistics than bonded import mode does. The bonded mode, however, operates logistics activities virtually like domestic logistics, for imported retail products are shipped to domestic warehouses in the first place and then dispatched from specialized sites supervised by customs once orders placed by domestic individuals.

Difference in cost incurred. In bonded mode, commodities are prepared previously, relieving the stress on international shipment time and making the cheaper maritime transportation a better choice. Besides, bulk transportation lowers average logistics cost. In comparison, direct purchase mode requires shipment by order, thus causing higher average logistics cost.

Difference in customs clearance. In direct purchase mode, the imported goods are supervised as goods for personal use. Goods, when meeting certain conditions, are not required to follow the requirement of license approval, registration or filing for the first time of import, except when the import of products from epidemic areas has been banned by relevant authorities or when emergency response measures are initiated for products that present major quality and safety risks. The direct purchase import in non-pilot cities shall be implemented with reference to relevant regulations. In contrast, for the bonded import mode in non-pilot cities, the entry of overseas commodities into the specialized supervised areas should follow the requirements of goods supervision. Therefore, the direct purchase mode offers more convenient customs clearance.

12.4.2 Cross Border E-commerce Export Supervision Modes

According to China customs regulation, cross border e-commerce export has four modes, each denoted by a specific supervision code, including 9610 general export, 1210 bonded export, 9710 cross border e-commerce B2B direct export, and 9810 cross border e-commerce export overseas warehousing. 9610 and 1210 aim to handle B2C transactions while the other two are designed to facilitate B2B transactions.

(1) 9610——General Export Mode

The general export mode (9610 export) adopts the method of "Checking and Releasing on List, Declaration on Summary". The e-commerce export goods are transported in batches by post or express. The customs will release the goods based on the checklist and regularly summarize the data of the approved checklists to form customs declaration.

(2) 1210——Bonded Export Mode

On August 1 2014, the customs supervision code "1210" was introduced, which is called "bonded cross border e-commerce". When applied in export, it is referred to as "bonded export mode", commonly known as "stocking" mode.

In 1210 bonded export mode, domestic companies pre-ship goods into bonded warehouses in advance based on overseas market forecast, and then put them on e-commerce platform for sale and export in batches. When an order is placed, the e-commerce company handles customs clearance procedures for each item according to the order, completes the veneer and packaging in the bonded warehouse, and entrusts logistics companies to make delivery to the foreign consumer after customs inspection and release. The 1210 bonded export mode can realize tax refund upon the entry of the goods into the zone and has the advantages of simplified tax refund, short cycle, and high efficiency. It is especially suitable for manufacturing enterprises who sell goods globally online.

Figure 12.6 and Figure 12.7 exhibit the procedure of general export and bonded export mode.

(3) 9710——Cross Border E-commerce B2B Direct Export

After reaching transaction agreement with overseas enterprises via cross border e-commerce platform, domestic exporters will directly export goods to overseas enterprises through cross border logistics and transit relevant data to customs.

(4) 9810——Cross Border E-commerce Export Overseas Warehousing

Domestic exporters will ship the export goods to overseas warehouses through cross

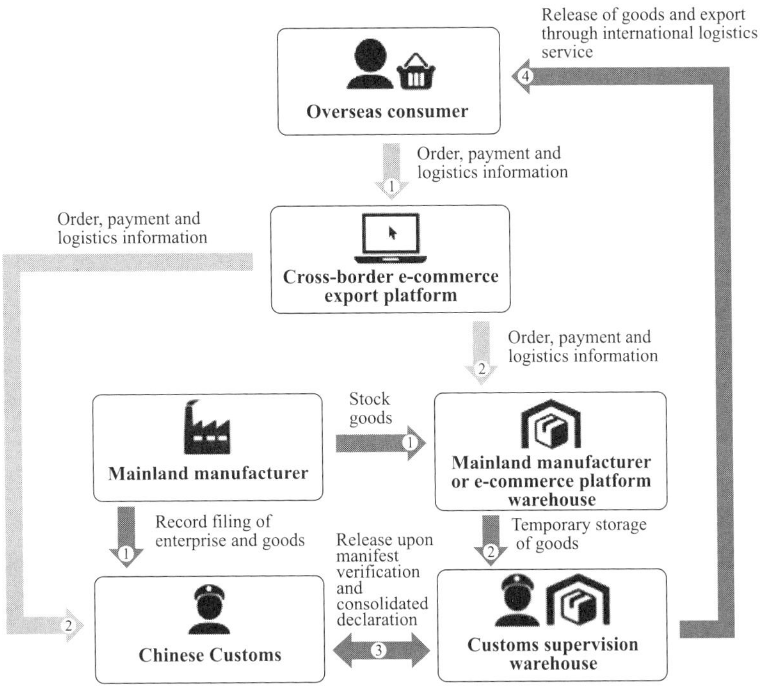

Figure 12.6 General export mode

(Source: hkmb. hktdc. com)

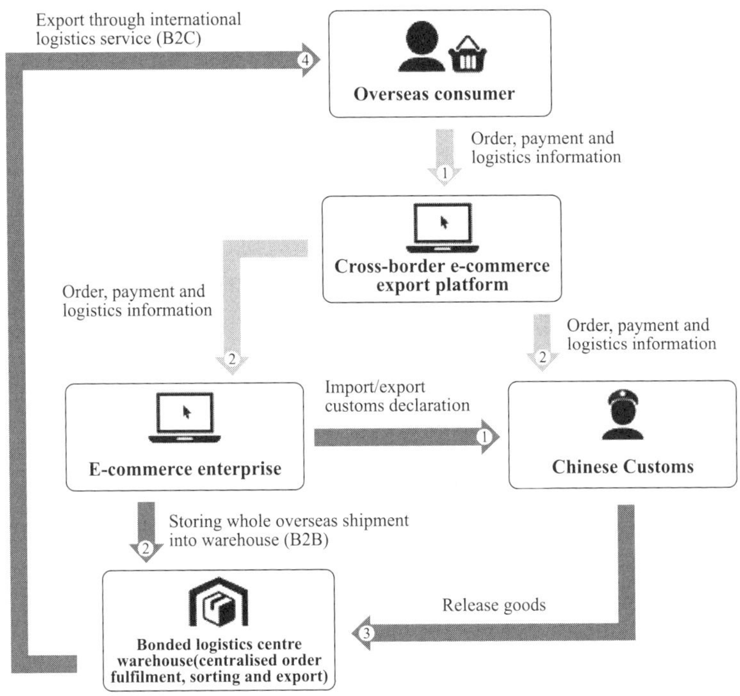

Figure 12.7 Bonded export mode

(Source: hkmb. hktdc. com)

border logistics, and then deliver them from overseas warehouses to buyers after the transaction is made through cross border e-commerce platform. Domestic exporters should transmit relevant electronic data on customs requirements and accept customs supervision.

With the application of more emerging cross border e-commerce customs supervision modes, companies planning to expand cross border e-commerce business can choose suitable mode and operate under rule.

12.4 我国跨境电商监管模式

目前,中国是全球最大的B2C跨境电商交易市场,全球26%的交易发生于此,其他电子商务模式也迅速增长。

跨境电子商务始于代购,是居住在国外的中国人向中国大陆客户销售外国产品的商业渠道。中国快速增长的中产阶级加速了跨境购物这一现象的发展。事实上,这一现象增长如此之快,中国的海关清关当时尚没有一个稳定的系统和服务方式来对此进行立即处理,因此产生了大量的税收损失及高昂的物流成本。

为应对这些来自海外个人的半合法跨境货运的爆发,中国政府开始在跨境电子商务综合试点城市设立指定区域。这些区域通常靠近大型贸易港口,为跨境电子商务提供有利的商业环境、保税仓库和关键基础设施支持。截至2020年,中国共有105个跨境电子商务试点区,由中国海关监管。试点区在法规和基础设施方面都略有不同,因为它们进一步专门针对特定的产品类别或业务。

跨境电子商务作为一种新的国际贸易模式,也给我国海关监管带来了巨大挑战。自2014年以来,海关经常采用新的贸易监管方法,探索创新的方式,帮助该行业以规范和系统的方式发展。

12.4.1 跨境电商零售进口监管模式

目前,我国跨境电商进口存在两种模式,即直购进口模式和保税进口模式。

(1)直购进口模式

2014年,中国海关总署(GACC)发布第12号公告,促进跨境电子商务零售进出口业务的发展,方便海关通关手续。2014年2月10日,增加了“9610”这一海关监管模式代码。它适用于通过电子商务平台进行的国内个人订单交易,以及从事电子商务零售进口的电子商务公司和平台。

中国消费者首先要在注册的跨境电子商务网站/平台下单。一旦收到订单,平台将提交订单、装运和支付记录至海关。所有经跨境电商平台销售的产品必须事先向海关登记。直购进口模式的流程如图12.4所示。

增值税和关税是通过直接邮寄方式从海外仓库(供应商)发货时记账的。境外商品通过邮件、快件等物流运输方式进口至跨境电商专门的监管场所,跨境电商或其代理人向海关申报入境,逐个核发配送。从订单提交至顾客收货,直购进口模式的标准交货期为10~15天。

该模式有以下特点。

首先,是一种直接进口模式。进口商品从运输工具卸下后报关入境,不存在报关前保税仓储期间,这是与保税模式的根本区别。

其次,是一种订单发起模式。由于没有保税仓储期间,直购模式下的进口商品一般不能在海关监管区域内长期储存,因而不能像保税模式那样进行事先备货,而只能在境内消费者

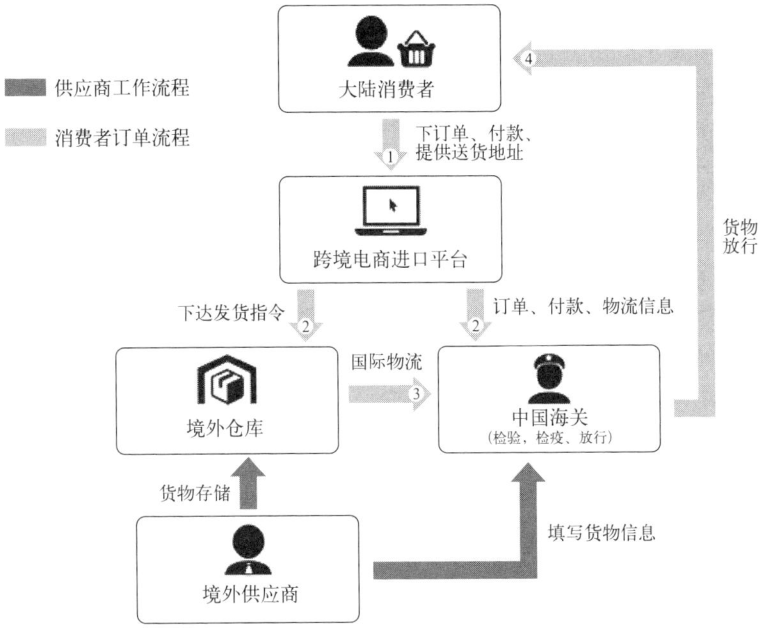

图 12.4 直购进口模式（来源：hkmb.hktdc.com）

订单形成后启动进口运输。

第三，是一种非批量进口模式。由于只能在订单形成后进行运输，直购模式一般不能实现单一商品批量集中进口。

第四，是一种事先备案模式。根据海关监管要求，直购模式商品进口前，须已完成电商企业及商品海关备案手续，且电商平台应将订单、支付、物流数据实时传送给海关。

(2) 保税进口模式

近年来网购保税进口蓬勃发展，业务量占跨境电商零售进口 80%以上。在保税进口模式下，产品批量进口到中国跨境电商试验区内经批准的跨境电商仓库。列在准许进口清单上的产品可储存在保税仓库，并可享受更快的产品登记和简化的清关流程。

当我国消费者在注册的电商平台上下订单时，订单准备从保税仓库发货，经海关清关，并直接交付给客户。进口关税和增值税在实际销售时缴纳。从客户下订单到收到订单的标准交货时间为 3～7 天。

此模式下有海关监管代码，分别是 1210 和 1239，两种监管在实施范围和商品进口要求上略有不同。

保税进口模式的流程见图 12.5。

(3) 直购模式与网购保税模式之区别

直购模式具有更多的商品选择。直购模式直接从境外供应商或海外仓发运，因此可充分利用离岸货源优势，提供更多商品选择，尤其是新上柜商品，可以第一时间进行跨境销售；而保税模式下，商品的销售种类仅限于保税存储的范围之内。

直购模式的物流时间较长。直购模式从境外发货，额外增加了国际物流时间；而且，由于订单一经形成，直购模式需要具备物流全链条迅速整合能力，物流要求高于保税模式。而保税模式实质上是将境外零售商品先运至境内储存，本国消费者发出订单后，商品直接从海关特殊监管区发货，相当于国内物流。

二者成本不同。保税模式采用事前备货，因此在国际物流段不存在物流时间压力，可以

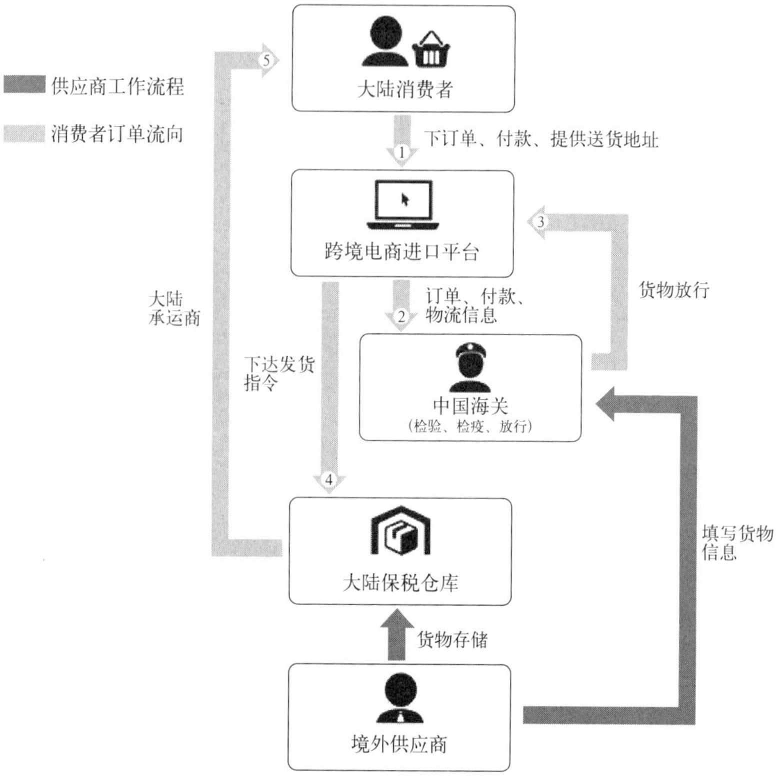

图 12.5 保税进口模式（来源：hkmb.hktdc.com）

采用物流成本较低的海运方式。同时，由于是批量进口备货，又可以摊薄单位商品的物流成本。而直购模式是订单送货，因此，相对而言每单位物流成本要高于保税模式。

清关方面的不同。直购模式按照个人自用进境物品监管。满足一定条件的商品不执行有关商品首次进口许可批件、注册或备案要求。但对相关部门明令暂停进口的疫区商品，和对出现重大质量安全风险的商品启动风险应急处置时除外。非试点城市的直购进口业务，参照相关规定执行。相较而言，对于非试点城市的保税进口模式，“一线”进区时需按货物监管要求执行。因而，直购模式通关便利性更高。

12.4.2 跨境电商出口业务模式

按照海关规定，跨境电商出口目前有四种模式，分别以四种监管代码表示，包括“9610 一般出口”“1210 保税出口”“9710 跨境电商 B2B 直接出口”以及“9810 跨境电商出口海外仓”模式，其中 9610 和 1210 针对的是 B2C 出口，而 9710 和 9810 针对的是 B2B 出口。

(1) 9610 一般出口模式

一般出口方式（9610 出口）采用“清单核放、汇总申报”的方式。电子商务出口货物通过邮政或快递批量运输。海关将根据清单放行货物，并定期汇总核定清单的数据，形成报关单。

(2) 1210 保税出口模式

自 2014 年 8 月 1 日起，新增海关监管代码“1210”，称为“保税跨境贸易电子商务”。应用于出口时，称为“保税出口模式”，俗称“备货”模式。

在 1210 保税出口模式下，国内企业根据海外市场预期，将货物提前备入海关监管下的保税仓库，然后在电商平台上批量销售出口。消费者下单后，电商企业根据订单为每件商品办理海关通关手续，在保税仓库完成贴面单和打包，经海关查验放行后，由电商企业委托物流配送至消费者手中。1210 保税出口模式可实现入区即退税，具有退税流程简单、周期短、效率高、减轻生产企业经营压力等优点，特别适合制造企业销售全球电子商务商品。

两种模式的流程如图 12.6 和图 12.7 所示。

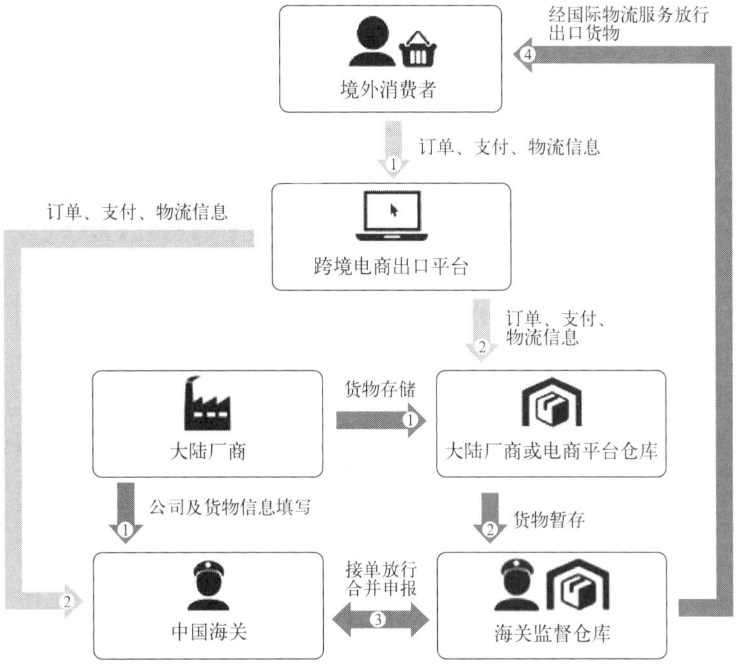

图 12.6 一般出口模式（来源：hkmb. hktdc. com）

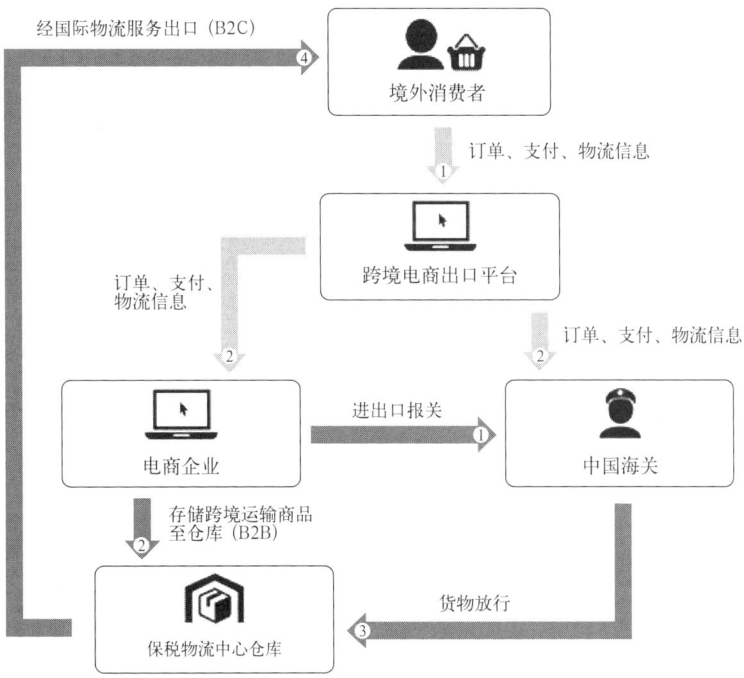

图 12.7 保税出口模式（来源：hkmb. hktdc. com）

(3) 9710 跨境电商 B2B 直接出口模式

境内企业通过跨境电子商务平台与境外企业达成交易后，通过跨境物流直接向境外企业出口货物，并向海关传输相关电子数据。

(4) 9810 跨境电商出口海外仓模式

国内企业将出口的货物通过跨境物流运送到海外仓，通过跨境电商平台实现交易后，再从海外仓发货给买家。境内企业应按照海关要求传输相关电子数据，接受海关监管。

随着跨境电商各种海关监管模式越来越丰富，计划拓展跨境电商业务的企业可选择适合自己的跨境电商业务模式，并合规经营。

Part B Vocabulary and Terminology 词汇和术语

electronic commerce 电子商务
Electronic Data Interchange（EDI） 电子数据交换
m-commerce 移动商务
brick-and-mortar store 实体店
online storefront model 网上店面模式
online marketplace model 网上商城模式
horizontal e-commerce 横向电子商务
vertical e-commerce 纵向电子商务
Universal Postal Union 万国邮政联盟
dedicated line logistics 专线物流
first leg transportation 头程运输
border warehouse 边境仓
overseas warehouse 海外仓
Positive List 准许进口商品清单
direct purchase import mode 直购进口模式
bonded import mode 保税进口模式

Part C Exercise 练习

Ⅰ. Answer the following questions.

1. What impact do e-commerce and logistics have on each other?
2. What are the pros and cons of e-commerce?
3. What are the types of e-commerce considering the transaction parties?
4. In what way could logistics promote the development of cross border e-commerce?
5. What are the differences between overseas warehouse and border warehouse?
6. Please make comparison between 9610 and 1210 import supervision?
7. What cross border e-commerce export supervision modes do we have now in China?

Please make brief comparison between them.

Ⅱ. Translate the following passages into Chinese.

1. Overseas warehousing is an emerging cross-border e-commerce logistics pattern. It involves cross-border e-commerce company building or leasing a warehouse located in a destination territory to where the cargo is to be shipped by sea/land/air. After the order is placed online, the e-commerce company will make direct distribution and shipment by use of the overseas warehouse or with the help of a third-party logistics entity.

2. Cross border dedicated line logistics usually by means of cabin chartering ships the commodity to other territory where a partner local company is responsible for the final delivery. This pattern has its dedicated transportation vehicle, route, point of departure and destination, transportation cycle and timetable. Most importantly the dedicated line is designed in accordance with the characteristics of cross border logistics in different countries/regions. Examples are Sino-Europe Railway and e-ulink.

3. Goods, when meeting certain conditions, are not required to follow the requirement of license approval, registration or filing for the first time of import except when the import of products from epidemic areas has been banned by relevant authorities or when emergency response measures are initiated for products that present major quality and safety risks.

Ⅲ. Translate the following sentences into English.

1. 除了身份验证、产品退货和退款、激烈的竞争之外，物流无疑是电子商务企业必须高度重视的最大挑战之一，并且物流和分销在电子商务中显得更加重要。

2. 电子商务经营者需要的是增值性的物流服务，而不仅仅是传统的物流服务。增值性的物流服务要具有便利性、快速响应性、低成本性及延展性等特征。

3. 跨境电商物流是指分属不同关境的交易主体通过电子商务平台达成交易，进行支付结算，并通过跨境物流送达商品、完成交易的一种国际商业活动。

4. 在实际运营过程中，国际邮政小包的丢包率高、安全性低、时效性不强等劣势较为突出；同时使用国际邮政小包进行物流运输，还受制于包裹形状、体积、重量等因素，国际邮政小包在一定程度上影响物流效率及物流体验。

Chapter Thirteen

Information Technology Applied in International Logistics 国际物流信息技术

Part A Text 课文

13.1 Brief Introduction

In recent years, the development of business model, logistics operation mode, big data and other technologies promotes the rapid development of smart logistics. On the basis of logistics automation technology, a new generation of information technology such as Internet of Things (IoT), big data, artificial intelligence and cloud computing has been widely used in the field of international logistics. These technologies endow international logistics system with wisdom, significantly improving the effectiveness of the system as well as generating cost savings.

Smart logistics is a kind of modern logistics system with certain intelligent capabilities. It improves the abilities of analysis, decision-making and intelligent execution of the logistics system and raises the level of intelligence and automation of the whole logistics system through intelligent technologies and means such as sensor network, Internet, IoT, and big data. Smart logistics integrates a variety of technologies and service functions, reflecting the new requirements of modern business operations. That is, It emphasizes the rapid, cost-effective and smooth operations of information flow and physical flow, so as to achieve the purposes of reducing social costs, improving production efficiency and integrating social resources.

The intellectualization of international logistics has become a mainstream direction of logistics development under e-commerce. Intellectualization is a high-level application of logistics automation and informationization. In the process of logistics operation, abundant operational and decision-making problems, such as the determination of inventory level, the selection of transportation route, the control of track and operation for Automatic Guide Vehicles (AGVs), the operation of automatic sorters, the decision support of logistics distribution center management and so on, can be solved with the aid of expert system, artificial intelligence, robot and other related technologies. In addition to intelligent transportation, modern logistics technologies such as AGVs, robot stacking, unmanned forklifts, and automatic sorting system have greatly improved the mechanization, automation and intelligence of logistics. At the same time, the supply chain management of virtual warehouses and virtual banks has emerged, which will push the international logistics to a new development stage-smart international logistics.

According to the technical framework of smart logistics, the main information technologies applied in international logistics mainly include tag and automatic identification technology, positioning and tracking technology, data processing technology, network communication technology and system simulation technology.

13.1 概述

近年来，商业模式、物流运作模式、大数据等技术的发展促使智慧物流迅速发展。在物流自动化技术基础之上，诸如物联网、大数据、人工智能、云计算等新一代信息技术开始广泛应用于国际物流领域。这些技术的应用赋予物流系统以智慧，从而显著提高了系统的效益，并降低了总成本。

智慧物流是具有智能化运营能力的现代物流系统，它通过传感网、互联网、物联网、大数据等智慧化技术与手段，提高物流系统分析决策和智能执行的能力，提升整个物流系统的智能化、自动化水平。智慧物流集多种技术和服务功能于一体，体现了现代商业运作的新需求，即强调信息流与实物流快速、高效、通畅地运转，从而实现降低社会成本、提高生产效率、整合社会资源的目的。

国际物流的智能化已经成为电子商务下物流发展的一个主流方向。智能化是物流自动化、信息化的一种高层次应用。物流作业过程中大量的运筹和决策问题，如库存水平的确定，运输路线的选择，自动导向车的运行轨迹和作业控制，自动分拣机的运行，以及物流配送中心经营管理的决策支持等问题，都可以借助专家系统、人工智能和机器人等相关技术加以解决。除了智能化交通运输外，无人搬运车、机器人堆码、无人叉车、自动分类分拣系统等现代物流技术，都大大提高了物流的机械化、自动化和智能化水平。同时，还出现了虚拟仓库、虚拟银行的供应链管理，这些必将把国际物流推向一个崭新的发展阶段——国际智慧物流。

根据智慧物流的技术架构，国际物流中主要应用的物流信息技术主要包括标签与自动识别技术、定位跟踪技术、数据处理技术、网络通信技术以及系统仿真技术等。

13.2 Label and Automatic Identification Technology

Modern logistics information system is inseparable from automatic identification and data acquisition technology, which is an integral part of modern logistics information system. These technologies include bar code technology, label technology, magnetic stripe card technology, radio frequency identification and data transfer technology, biometric identification method, etc.

13.2.1 Barcode Technology

13.2.1.1 Brief Introduction to Barcode

Barcode technology is one of the most typical and popular application technologies of automatic identification and data acquisition technology. Barcode is a kind of information code, with special graphics to represent numbers, letters, and some symbols. It is composed of a group of combined black bars and blanks with different widths and reflectance according to the specified code rules to represent a group of data.

The common bar codes are one-dimensional bar code and two-dimensional bar code. One-dimensional bar code is composed of a set of regularly arranged bars, blanks and corresponding characters. "Bar" refers to the part with low reflectance to light, while "blank" means the part with high reflectance to light. The data composed of these bars and blanks expresses certain information and can be read by special devices and converted into binary and decimal information compatible with computers.

With the development of modern high technology, bar code technology is required to express more information in the limited geometric space, so as to meet the ever-changing information needs. For instance, two-dimensional bar code is a new bar code which makes full use of the redundancy of one-dimensional bar code in the vertical direction and expands to the two-dimensional direction. Two-dimensional bar code records the information of data symbols with some specific geometric figures distributed in the plane (two-dimensional direction) according to a certain rule. It shares the common characteristics of bar code technology, with each code system having its own specific character set and each character occupying a certain width and performing a certain verification function. Two-dimensional bar code is divided into two types: stacked bar code and dot matrix bar code.

Two-dimensional barcode is an ideal method for storing, carrying and automatically reading large capacity and high reliability information of various certificates and cards. Its application level and application field are more advantageous than one-dimensional bar code. Symbol company in the US officially launched a two-dimensional bar code named PDF417 in 1991. Actually, this code is a type of layered two-dimensional bar code and up till now it has become relatively mature and widely used.

13. 2. 1. 2 Logistics Barcode

Currently, there are many bar code systems. Logistics barcode is a special code used to identify specific objects in the field of logistics. It is the shared data for all the links of the entire logistics process, including manufacturers, distributors, transportation service providers, consumers and so on. It runs through the whole trade process and completes the collection and feedback of data, making the information transmission more convenient, fast and accurate, so as to improve the economic benefits of the whole logistics system. Compared with commodity bar code, logistics barcode has the following characteristics:

1) It serves as the unique identification of the storage and transportation unit;

2) It serves the whole process of logistics;

3) It is able to store a large amount of information;

4) It is highly variable.

Logistics barcode is a bar code developed by EAN and UCC for trade unit identification, including EAN / UPC, ITF-14, UCC / EAN-128, location code, etc. There are three commonly used and recognized kinds of logistics barcode systems in the world: EAN-13 barcode, ITF-14 barcode and UCC/EAN-128 barcode.

Different bar code systems should be adopted according to different goods and packaging. EAN-13 barcode is often used on the packaging cartons of single large commodities, such as TV sets, refrigerators, washing machines and so on. The ITF-14 barcode or UCC/EAN-128 barcode is often adopted in case of transport package. Inside a transport package, there may be one item, or different items or multiple small packages.

In the field of logistics, barcode technology is like a link, which connects the information generated at all stages of product life cycle, and can track the whole process of products from production to sales. Through the handheld barcode terminal, the functions of data acquisition, data transmission, data deletion and system management can be well realized. The main application fields of logistics barcode are: ①the application in warehouses and Distribution Centers, including receiving, sorting, storage, stock-taking, shipping, etc.; ②the application in retailing stores, including automatic replenishment, arrival confirmation and inventory management.

13.2.2 Label Technology

13.2.2.1 Wired Electronic Label Technology

Electronic label system is a network computer-aided picking system composed of a series of devices installed on the shelf. The electronic labeling has the functions of flexible control over picking process, real-time on-site control and emergency order processing, and can reduce the error rate of picking, speed up picking process, eliminate form-making operation and save human resources.

The main functions of the electronic label system can be summarized as follows: ①upload and download of picking data; ②real-time monitoring of picking data; ③self-monitoring of hardware; ④discrete order picking; ⑤early exit; ⑥emergency order; ⑦conformance of product number and label; ⑧stock-out notice; ⑨stock query; ⑩report generation.

13.2.2.2 RFID Technology

Radio Frequency Identification (RFID) Technology is a kind of automatic identification technology, also known as wireless tracking system, which began to rise in the 1990s. It uses radio frequency to carry out non-contact two-way communication in order to identify and exchange data. Different from the barcode, IC card and other contact identification technologies, RFID is a non-contact automatic identification technology, which has the advantages of waterproof, antimagnetic, high temperature resistance, long service life, long reading distance, large amount of information, etc. Furthermore, RFID can realize multi-target simultaneous recognition and moving-target recognition, and thus can be applied in a wider range of occasions.

RFID technology enables customers to make faster check-out, retailers to master the situation of stock, make real-time replenishment, and prevent theft. Additionally, by using RFID technology, suppliers get to know the sales of their products and formulate appropriate plans for production and replenishment.

At present, there are three main problems in RFID Technology: high cost, privacy, and security. In addition, there are also concerns about the impact of electromagnetic waves.

13.2 标签与自动识别技术

现代物流信息系统离不开自动识别与数据采集技术，这些技术是现代物流信息系统的重要组成部分。这些技术包括条形码技术、标签技术、磁条磁卡技术、射频识别和数据传递技术、光学字符识别技术、生物统计识别方法等。

13.2.1 条形码技术

13.2.1.1 条形码概述

条形码技术是自动识别与数据采集技术最典型和最普及的应用技术之一。条形码是一种信息代码，用特殊的图形来表示数字、字母信息和某些符号，由一组宽度不同、反射率不同的条和空按规定的编码规则组合起来，用以表示一组数据。

常见的条形码有一维条形码和二维条形码。一维条形码是由一组规则排列的条、空以及对应的字符组成的标记。“条”指的是对光线反射率较低的部分，而“空”指的是对光线反射率较高的部分，这些条、空组成的数据表达一定的信息，并能够用特定的设备识读，转换成与计算机兼容的二进制和十进制信息。

随着现代高新技术的发展，要求条形码技术做到在有限的几何空间内表示更多的信息，从而满足千变万化的信息需求。其中二维条形码就是一种充分利用一维条形码在垂直方向上的冗余，向二维方向扩展而形成的新的条形码。二维条形码用某种特定的几何图形按一定规律在平面（二维方向）上分布的条、空相间的图形来记录数据符号信息，它具有条形码技术的共性，即每种码制有其特定字符集，每个字符占有一定的宽度，具有一定的校验功能等。二维条形码分为层排式二维条形码和矩阵式二维条形码两大类型。

二维条形码是各种证件及卡片等大容量、高可靠性信息实现存储、携带并自动识读的最理想的方法。其应用水平和应用领域都比一维条形码有更大的优越性。美国 Symbol 公司于 1991 年正式推出名为 PDF417 的二维条形码，简称为 PDF417 条形码，它是一种层排式二维条形码，是目前技术比较成熟，应用比较广泛的二维条形码。

13.2.1.2 物流条码

目前的条形码码制有许多，物流条码是用于标识物流领域中具体实物的一种特殊代码，是在整个物流过程中，包括制造商、分销商、运输服务商、消费者等所有环节的共享数据。它贯穿整个贸易过程，并通过物流条码完成数据的采集和反馈，使信息的传递更加方便、快捷、准确，从而提高整个物流系统的经济效益。与商品条码相比较，物流条码有以下特点：

1）是储运单元的唯一标识；

2）服务于物流的整个过程；

3）信息量大；

4）可变性强。

物流条码是由 EAN（国际物品编码协会）和 UCC（美国统一代码委员会）制定的用于贸易单元标识的条码，包括商品条码（EAN/UPC）、储运单元条码（ITF-14）、贸易单元 128 条码（UCC/EAN-128）、位置码等。国际上通用且公认的物流条码码制主要有三种：EAN-13 条码、ITF-14 条码和 UCC/EAN-128 条码。

根据货物的不同和商品包装的不同，应采用不同的条码码制。单个大件商品，如电视机、电冰箱、洗衣机等商品的包装箱往往采用 EAN-13 条码。（集合包装的）运输包装常常采用 ITF-14 条码或 UCC/EAN-128 条码，其包装箱内可以是单一商品，也可以是不同的商品或多件商品小包装。

在物流领域，条形码技术就像一条纽带，把产品生命周期各阶段产生的信息连接在一起，可跟踪产品从生产到销售的全过程。通过手持式条形码终端，可以实现数据采集、数据传送、数据删除和系统管理等功能。主要应用领域有：①仓储及配送中心中的应用，包括商品的入库验收、出库发货和库存盘点等；②商品卖场中的应用，包括自动补充订货、到货确认和盘点管理等。

13. 2. 2 标签技术

13. 2. 2. 1 有线电子标签技术

电子标签系统是指装置于货架上的由一系列设备构成的网络化计算机辅助拣货系统。电子标签具有弹性控制拣货流程、即时现场控制、紧急订单处理功能，并能降低拣货错误率，加快拣货速度，免除表单作业，节省人力资源。

电子标签系统的主要功能可以归纳为：①拣货资料的上传与下载；②拣货资料即时监控；③硬件自我监测；④跳跃式拣货；⑤提早离开；⑥紧急插单；⑦货号与标签对应维护；⑧缺货通知；⑨查询作业；⑩报表作业。

13. 2. 2. 2 射频识别技术

射频识别（RFID）技术是自动识别技术的一种，也称为无线追踪系统，是从 20 世纪 90 年代开始兴起的。它利用无线射频方式进行非接触双向通信，以达到识别并交换数据的目的。与条形码、IC 卡等接触式识别技术不同，RFID 是非接触式的自动识别技术，它能够识别单品，具有防水、防磁、耐高温、使用寿命长、读取距离远、信息量大等优点。RFID 还可实现多目标的同时识别以及移动目标的识别，可在更广泛的场合中应用。

使用 RFID 技术，顾客可以迅速结账，零售商可以掌握库存实况、快速进行补货和防止商品被盗，供应商可以了解产品的真实销售情况并制定恰当的生产和补货计划。

当前 RFID 技术存在的问题主要有三点：一是成本相对较高，二是隐私问题，三是安全问题。此外，还有人担心会受到电磁波的冲击。

13. 3 Positioning and Tracking Technology

13. 3. 1 Global Positioning System

13. 3. 1. 1 Brief Introduction to Global Positioning System

Global Positioning System (GPS) is the third largest space project in the United States after Apollo landing and space shuttle. It is a global, all-weather and continuous satellite radio navigation system, which can provide real-time 3D position, three-dimensional speed and high-precision time information. The United States has developed GPS since 1970s, which lasted 20 years and cost 20 billion dollars. It was built in 1994. It is a new generation of satellite navigation and positioning system with the ability of all-round real-time three-dimensional navigation and positioning at the same time in the sea, land and air.

GPS is the second generation of satellite navigation system in the United States. It is developed on the basis of the meridian instrument satellite navigation system, and has adopted the successful experience of the meridian system. The GPS system consists of three parts: outer space part-GPS satellite constellation, ground control part-ground monitoring system, user equipment part-GPS signal receiver.

(1) Outer space part

The outer space part of GPS, working 20200 kilometers away from the earth, consists of 24 satellites distributed evenly over 6 orbit surfaces (4 satellites for each surface), with each orbit working at a 55-degree angle. In addition, there are four active backup satellites in orbit. The distribution of satellites ensures that more than 4 satellites can be observed anywhere and at any time in the world, and the geometric images with good positioning accuracy can be obtained, and the continuous global navigation capability can be provided.

(2) Ground control part

The ground control part consists of 1 main control station, 5 global monitoring stations and 3 ground control stations. The monitoring stations are equipped with a precise cesium clock and receivers capable of continuously measuring all visible satellites. The satellite observation data (including ionosphere and meteorological data) received by the monitoring station are transmitted to the main control station after being preliminarily processed. The main control station collects tracking data from each monitoring station, calculates the orbit and clock parameters of the satellite, and then sends the results to three ground control stations. When each satellite is running above, the ground control station injects the navigation data and the command of the master control station into the satellite. Each GPS satellite is injected once a day and the final injection is made before the satellite leaves the range of the station. If a certain ground station breaks down, the navigation information stored in the satellite can be used for a while, but the navigation accuracy will gradually decrease.

(3) User equipment part

The user equipment part refers to the GPS signal receiver. Its major function is to capture the signals of the satellites to be measured according to the cut-off angle of certain satellites and to track the operation of these satellites. When the receiver captures the signals of the tracking satellite, the pseudo distance and distance variation rate from the receiving antenna to the satellite can be measured, and the satellite orbit parameters and other data can be demodulated. According to these data, the micro processing computer in the receiver can calculate the location according to the location solution method, and acquire the longitude, latitude, height, speed, time and other information of the user's geographical location.

The receiver hardware, in-machine software and the post-processing software package of GPS data constitute a complete GPS user equipment. GPS receiver is divided into antenna unit and receiving unit. The receiver generally adopts two kinds of DC power supply, internal and external. The purpose of setting the internal power supply is to replace the external power supply without interrupting the observation. The internal power supply charges automatically when the external power supply is used. After power-off, the internal power supply powers the RAM memory to prevent data loss. At present, the volume of various types of receivers has become smaller and lighter, which is convenient for field observation.

13.3.1.2 Application of GPS in Logistics

GPS can monitor the location of moving targets such as vehicles in real time in logistics field, and send out real-time dispatching instructions to mobile targets according to road traffic conditions. GPS is mainly used in the arena of logistics distribution, such as precise navigation, urban traffic guidance, vehicle tracking, cargo distribution route planning, fixed point positioning measurement, information inquiry, emergency assistance, and integrated application of GPS/GIS.

13.3.2 Geographic Information System

13.3.2.1 Brief Introduction to Geographic Information System

Geographic Information System (GIS) was born in the early 1960s. When computer technology is widely used in the branch fields of data automatic collection, data analysis and display technology, the GIS eventually came into being.

GIS can be defined as a system composed of computer system, geographic data, and users, which, through the inheritance, storage, retrieval, operation and analysis of geographic data, inputs and generates various geographic information, provides new knowledge to the fields of land use, resource management, environment monitoring, transportation, economic construction, urban planning, and administration of various government departments, and serves engineering design, planning, and decision. It can also be defined as a computer information system dedicated to the collecting, simulating, processing, retrieving, analyzing and expressing of geographic spatial data. Its main functions are spatial data management and spatial information analysis.

A typical GIS should include three parts: computer system (hardware+software), geographic database system, application personnel and organization.

Computer system can be divided into hardware system, software system, GIS development tool, standard system for the selection of hardware and network platform.

The geographic database system is composed of database and database management system (DBMS). The geographic database system is mainly used for operation, data maintenance, as well as query and retrieval.

The personnel required for the smooth operation of GIS includes system project manager, technical group, database manager, digital operator, system operator, application analysis software manager and program editor. According to different classification standards, GIS can be divided into different categories. For example, according to the function, GIS can be divided into thematic GIS, regional GIS and GIS tools; according to the content, it can be divided into urban information system, natural resources inquiry information system, planning and evaluation information system, land management information system, etc.; according to the application field, it can be divided into land information system, resource management information system, geoscience information system, etc.; according to the data model, it can be divided into vector, grid and hybrid information system. Its main functions are as follows:

1) Data collection, inspection and editing;

2）Data formatting and conversion，usually referred to as data operation；

3）Organization and storage of data；

4）Query，search，statistics and calculation；

5）Spatial analysis（the core function of GIS）.

13. 3. 2. 2 Application of GIS in Logistics Field

The application of GIS in the field of logistics mainly includes vehicle route model，network logistics model，distribution area division model，facility positioning model，spatial query model and so on.

When GIS is applied to logistics information system，it can automatically determine the customer's geographic location（longitude and latitude）and the customer's central station and substation through the customer's zip code and detailed address string. Through the query based on GIS and the assistant decision of map representation，the reasonable scheduling of delivery route and the proper arrangement of customer delivery order can be achieved. Its work sequence is customer address location，organization area division，site selection，delivery sequencing，delivery route in turn.

GIS，GPS and wireless communication technology，when combined effectively and supported by vehicle route model，shortest path model，network logistics model，distribution set model and facility positioning model，etc. can be helpful to establish a powerful logistics information system and realize real-time information sharing and transportation route optimization. At present，the technology combining GPS，GIS and 5G has been developed，which can carry out real-time positioning，tracking，alarm and communication for vehicles in transit. This integrated technology helps to grasp the real transportation state of vehicles in transit and implement effective remote management of vehicles，so as to effectively prevent the phenomenon of empty return vehicles. At the same time，customers can also access to the real-time information on the transportation status of their goods with the aid of the Internet and the IoT technologies.

13. 3 定位跟踪技术

13. 3. 1 全球定位系统

13. 3. 1. 1 全球定位系统概述

全球定位系统 GPS 是美国继阿波罗登月计划、航天飞机之后的第三大航天工程，是一种全球性、全天候、连续的卫星无线电导航系统，可提供实时的三维位置、三维速度和高精度的时间信息。美国从 20 世纪 70 年代开始研制 GPS，历时 20 年，耗资 200 亿美元，于 1994 年全面建成，它是具备在海、陆、空同时进行全方位实时三维导航和定位能力的新一代卫星导航与定位系统。

GPS 是美国第二代卫星导航系统，它是在子午仪卫星导航系统的基础上发展起来的，并采纳了子午仪系统的成功经验。与子午仪系统相同，GPS 系统包括 3 大部分：空间部分——GPS 卫星星座，地面控制部分——地面监控系统，用户设备部分——GPS 信号接收机。

（1）空间部分

GPS 的空间部分由 24 颗工作卫星组成，它位于距地表 20200km 的上空均匀分布在 6 个轨道面上（每个轨道面4颗），轨道倾角55°。此外，还有4颗有源备份卫星在轨运行。卫星的分布保证了在全球任何地方、任何时间都可观测到4颗以上的卫星，并能保持得到具有良好定位解算精度的几何图像，提供在时间上连续的全球导航能力。

（2）地面控制部分

地面控制部分由1个主控站、5个全球监测站和3个地面控制站组成。监测站均配装有精密的铯钟以及能够连续测量到所有可见卫星的接收机。监测站将收到的卫星观测数据（包括电离层和气象数据）经过初步处理后传送到主控站。主控站从各监测站收集跟踪数据，计算出卫星的轨道和时钟参数，然后将结果送到3个地面控制站。地面控制站在每颗卫星运行至上空时，把这些导航数据及主控站指令注入卫星。每天对每颗GPS卫星进行一次注入，并在卫星离开注入站作用范围之前进行最后的注入。如果某地面站发生故障，那么在卫星中预存的导航信息还可用一段时间，但导航精度会逐渐降低。

（3）用户设备部分

用户设备部分即GPS信号接收机。其主要功能是捕获按一定卫星截止角所选择的待测卫星的信号，并跟踪这些卫星的运行。当接收机捕获到跟踪的卫星信号后，即可测量出接收天线至卫星的伪距离和距离的变化率，解调出卫星轨道参数等数据。根据这些数据，接收机中的微处理计算机就可按定位解算方法进行定位计算，计算出用户所在地理位置的经纬度、高度、速度、时间等信息。

接收机硬件和机内软件以及GPS数据的后处理软件包构成完整的GPS用户设备。GPS接收机分为天线单元和接收单元两部分。接收机一般采用机内和机外两种直流电源。设置机内电源的目的在于更换外电源时不中断观测。在用机外电源时机内电池自动充电。关机后，机内电池为RAM存储器供电，以防止数据丢失。目前各种类型的接收机体积越来越小，质量越来越轻，便于野外观测使用。

13.3.1.2 GPS在物流领域的应用

在物流领域GPS可以实时监控车辆等移动目标的位置，根据道路交通状况向移动目标发出实时调度指令。GPS在物流配送中的应用主要有精确导航、城市交通疏导、车辆跟踪、货物配送路线规划、固定点的定位测量、信息查询、紧急援助以及GPS/GIS在物流领域的集成应用等。

13.3.2 地理信息系统

13.3.2.1 地理信息系统概述

地理信息系统（GIS）萌芽于20世纪60年代初。当计算机技术广泛应用于数据自动采集、数据分析和显示技术等分支领域时，最终导致了GIS的产生。

GIS可定义为由计算机系统、地理数据和用户组成的，通过对地理数据的继承、存储、检索、操作和分析，生成并输入各种地理信息，从而为土地利用、资源管理、环境监测、交通运输、经济建设、城市规划以及政府各部门行政管理提供新的知识，为工程设计和规划、决策服务的系统。也可定义为用于采集、模拟、处理、检索、分析和表达地理空间数据的计算机信息系统。它是进行空间数据管理和空间信息分析的计算机系统。

一个典型的GIS应包括三个部分：计算机系统（硬件、软件）、地理数据库系统、应用人员与组织机构。

1）计算机系统可分为硬件系统、软件系统、GIS的开发工具、硬件和网络平台的选择标准体系。

2）地理数据库系统由数据库和数据库管理系统组成。地理数据库系统主要用于操作、数据维护和查询检索。

3）GIS的人员配置有系统项目经理、技术组、数据库经理、数字化操作员、系统操作员、应用分析软件经理和程序编写员。按照不同的分类标准，GIS可以分成不同的类别。例如，按照功能划分，GIS可分为专题GIS、区域GIS和GIS工具；按内容划分，可分为城市信息系统、自然资源查询信息系统、规划与评估信息系统、土地管理信息系统等；依据其应用领域可分为土地信息系统、资源管理信息系统、地学信息系统等；按照其使用的数据模型，可分为矢量、栅格和混合型信息系统。其主要功能如下：

1）数据采集、检验与编辑；

2）数据格式化、转换，通常称为数据操作；

3）数据的组织与存储；

4）查询、检索、统计及计算；

5）空间分析（GIS的核心功能）。

13.3.2.2 GIS在物流领域的应用

GIS在物流领域的应用主要有车辆路线模型、网络物流模型、配送区域划分模型、设施定位模型、空间查询模型等。

当GIS应用于物流信息系统时，它可以通过客户的邮编和详细地址字符串，自动确定客户的地理位置（经纬度）和客户所在的中心站和分站。通过基于GIS的查询、地图表现辅助决策，实现对配送路线的合理调度以及客户投递排序的安排。其工作顺序是按照客户地址定位、机构区域划分、站点选址、投递排序、投递路线依次进行的。

GIS、GPS和无线通信技术有效结合，再辅以车辆路线模型、最短路径模型、网络物流模型、分配集合模型和设施定位模型等，可以建立功能强大的物流信息系统，实现信息的实时共享以及运输路径优化。目前，已开发出把GPS、GIS以及5G技术结合起来对在途车辆进行实时定位、跟踪、报警、通信等的技术。该集成技术有助于掌握在途车辆的真实运输状态，对车辆实施有效的远程管理，从而有效防止车辆的回程空驶。同时，客户也能借助互联网和物联网技术，实时获取自己商品的运输状况信息。

13.4 Data Processing Technology

13.4.1 Electronic Data Interchange

13.4.1.1 Definition of Electronic Data Interchange

Electronic Data Interchange（EDI） refers to using an internationally recognized standard format to translate the information of trade，transportation，insurance，banking，Customs and other industries or departments into structured transaction processing message data format. And through computer communication network，data exchange and processing can be carried out efficiently between relevant departments，companies and enterprises，and the whole business process with the center of trade can be completed. EDI includes data exchange between buyers and sellers，and data exchange within enterprises，etc.

EDI can be understood from the following five aspects：

1）EDI is the electronic information transmission between computer systems.

2）EDI is the exchange of standard format and structured electronic data.

3) EDI is the exchange of electronic data according to the standard and structure agreed upon by the sender and receiver.

4) EDI is the exchange of electronic data automatically read by computer without manual intervention.

5) EDI is the exchange of electronic data for commercial purposes.

From a technical perspective, we can generalize the concept of EDI as follows: EDI is the transmission and automatic processing of standard business information with certain structure between participants' computers through data communication network according to the agreement reached between two or more involved parties. Its advantages are as follows.

Firstly, it greatly reduces the consumption of paper, also known as paperless trade. According to the survey organized by the United Nations, an import or export trade requires the exchange of nearly 200 documents and forms, and the total cost of paper, writing, printing and checking errors may be about 7 percent of the price of the goods. EDI can greatly reduce transaction costs. According to statistics, after the adoption of EDI by General Motors, the savings were \$250 per vehicle produced, or \$1.25 billion per year based on 5 million vehicles produced each year.

Secondly, it reduces repetitive work and improves work efficiency. Without EDI, even highly informationized companies often need to re-enter external data into their own computers. Surveys show that as much as 70 percent of the output from one computer needs to be inputted into other computers, which is time-consuming and error-prone. After the application of EDI, Digital Equipment in the US reduced inventory period from 5 days to 3 days and cost per order from US \$125 to US \$32. With the adoption of EDI trade network in Singapore, the Customs procedures for trade were shortened from 3～4 days to 10～15 minutes.

13.4.1.2 EDI Application in Logistics Industry

Modern logistics is a logistics information and e-commerce service based on many modern information technology platforms such as Internet and EDI. In the enterprise logistics activities, cargo owners, carriers and other relevant units exchange logistics data through EDI system, and implement logistics activities on this basis. EDI system effectively connects enterprises engaged in cargo transportation, processing, trade, and circulation with departments of customs, inspection and quarantine, tax, environment protection, border inspection and banking, resulting in the coordination and synchronization of the whole supply chain and its related links and consequently the efficiency improvement of modern logistics management.

13.4.2 Cloud Computing

13.4.2.1 Concept of Cloud Computing

The concept of "cloud computing" was first proposed by Eric Schmidt, CEO of Google, at the "Search Engine Strategy Conference" in 2006. Subsequently, Microsoft, Amazon, IBM, Cisco, HP, Oracle, EMC and many other Internet giants all followed up. And IT giants also regarded it as the "decisive battle place" in the future.

Cloud computing is a supercomputing mode based on the Internet. In the remote data center, thousands of computers and servers are connected into a computer cloud. Users can access the data center through computers, laptops, mobile phones and other means, and experience the computing capacity of more than 10 trillion times per second.

13. 4. 2. 2 Advantages of Cloud Computing

The advantages of applying cloud services in the field of logistics lie in the following aspects.

1) Cost saving: Enterprises do not need to invest heavily on Intranet connections, computer servers and support, etc. And secure computing capacity is provided on a rental basis without capital investment. It usually provides complex technical support for enterprises in the form of services, which attracts innovative enterprises and small and medium-sized enterprises to a large extent.

2) Access speed and availability: It offers flexibility, allowing enterprises to quickly develop new markets or new products, so that enterprises can achieve expansion in the shortest time with the least investment. Through cloud computing, enterprises can quickly implement and run secure and cost-effective applications with low IT maintenance and upgrade costs.

3) Reliability and fault tolerance: To ensure higher reliability, cloud computing systems need to be exceptionally fault tolerant. Fault Tolerance (FT) is the ability of a system to deliver the desired services even when failures and errors happen in the system.

4) Operation support and upgrade services: Suppliers are responsible for providing operation support and upgrade services for the server and network.

For example, Keyfort, a cloud computing service provider located in Hull, England, has developed a cloud-based logistics management information system called Keyfort Data Interchange Service (KDIS). It can be used to capture and store data, generate reports, perform data analysis, and query information on demand. Any company can use KDIS system. The company has also developed a specific optional app, namely KeyPOD, to improve traceability by monitoring the status, location and other information of the goods in transit by monitoring the smartphone of the driver carrying out the delivery task. By means of the KeyPOD, distribution centers and carriers are able to work together effectively and share real-time delivery information.

In short, mobile technology and cloud computing applications are providing companies with the online and real-time benifit. In a logistics supply chain environment, the timeliness and reliability of the system are crucial to the development of the enterprise, so this benefit is even more significant.

13. 4. 2. 3 Application of Cloud Computing Technology in Modern Logistics

Due to the above advantages of cloud computing, the application of cloud computing to improve the logistics service ability has become the first choice of logistics enterprises, and building the logistics information platform based on cloud computing has naturally become an important service of cloud service providers. The service provided by a cloud service provider includes the application layer, platform layer, infrastructure layer, and virtualization layer.

1) Application layer. In the construction of cloud computing information platform, the application layer is mainly used to provide the software services required by logistics enterprises. Based on their actual needs, logistics enterprises consider which software services they need in the operation process, and then pay the corresponding service fees to cloud computing service providers according to the service time and mode they obtained. Logistics enterprises do not need to purchase and maintain application software by themselves, and it is cloud service providers who are responsible for the management and maintenance of software.

2) Platform layer. In the construction of cloud computing information platform, the platform layer is the development environment used to provide software services. The hardware resources needed in the software and service of the server platform are provided to logistics enterprises through the platform layer, and logistics service enterprises provide customer service through the establishment of secondary Internet service system on the basis of this platform layer.

3) Infrastructure layer. At the infrastructure layer of the cloud computing information platform, IT infrastructure is provided to customers in the form of services, including resources such as servers, network equipment, etc.

4) Virtualization layer. This layer is the key to the construction of cloud computing information platform, which can provide services such as server cluster and hardware detection, as well as the maintenance and management of hardware. This layer includes physical resources and virtual resources of the server, middleware management part of the service platform and the service interface for logistics enterprises to connect.

The cloud computing logistics information platform builds an informationized logistics service platform through the construction and setting of application layer, platform layer, infrastructure layer and virtualization layer, and provides a safe service environment for logistics enterprises to offer their customers fast, safe and reliable information services. The main application modes are as follows.

1) Business platform based on cloud computing mode. Logistics enterprises use the processed perceptual data to provide their customers with rich specific applications and services through Web browser, including monitoring services (logistics monitoring, pollution monitoring), query services (intelligent search, information query), scanning services (information code scanning, goods transport transfer scanning) and so on.

2) Data storage center based on cloud computing mode. This mode aims to provide specific data services needed by logistics enterprises, including the storage, query, and analysis of massive data, so as to achieve complete sharing, automatic deployment, allocation and dynamic adjustment of resources.

3) Basic service platform based on cloud computing mode. The introduction of cloud computing mode on the basis of traditional data center can provide logistics enterprises with servers needed for various Internet applications, so that logistics enterprises have advantages in data storage and network resource utilization. The service price of cloud computing service

platform is more advantageous, which can reduce the operating cost of logistics enterprises. In addition, it implements dynamic resource allocation and automatic installation and deployment during application, providing users with on-demand response, pay-per-use, and high-quality infrastructure services.

13.4.3 Big Data

According to Gartner Group, "big data" is the massive, high-growth, and diversified information assets that require new modes of processing for better decision making, insight discovery, and process optimization. The significance of big data technology is not to master and possess a large amount of data, but to professionally process meaningful data to realize the added value of data. At present, a large number of new technologies have emerged in the field of big data, and these new technologies are becoming a powerful weapon for the collection, storage, processing and presentation of big data.

Logistics big data refers to the data and information involved in logistics links such as transportation, warehousing, material handling, packaging, distribution and circulation processing. Although big data technology has wide application value in various fields, logistics field is one of the main application fields of big data. It is because of the development of bar code and other technologies that the logistics department can use the front-end PC system to collect and store a large amount of data, such as the historical record of goods in and out, the status of goods in and out and service records, etc. The logistics industry, like other data-intensive enterprises, has accumulated a vast amount of data, which is the basis of big data. Big data technology helps identify transportation behavior, discover new distribution patterns and trends, improve transportation efficiency, so that logistics enterprises can achieve higher core competitiveness and lower logistics costs.

From the current research, the support of big data to the development of intelligent logistics is mainly reflected in several aspects.

Firstly, it helps to promote the transformation of the competition concept of logistics enterprises. The era of big data has changed business competitive environment, realizing the sharing of information data and other resources. At the same time, the mining of information value by big data technology improves the decision-making ability of enterprises and impacts the competitiveness of enterprises from the aspects of environment, resources and ability.

Secondly, it helps to optimize the resources and capabilities of logistics enterprises. Big data not only realizes the full development and utilization of human and material resources in logistics transportation, such as the selection of talents with the help of big data information technology, but also improves the adaptability of logistics enterprises to the environment and enables them to obtain valuable resources.

Thirdly, the application of big data technology in logistics activities can make logistics activities more intelligent, and thus improves the competitiveness of enterprises.

To be specific, the typical application of big data technology in the field of logistics mainly includes the following aspects.

1) Demand forecast. By collecting big data such as users' consumption characteristics

and merchants' historical sales, the algorithm is used to predict demand in advance, and arrange the warehousing and transportation ahead of time. Currently, some applications have emerged in this area, but there is still a lot of potential for improving the forecast accuracy, which needs to expand the data amount and optimize the algorithm.

2) Equipment maintenance forecast. Through the application of the Internet of Things, chips can be installed on the equipment to monitor the real-time operation data, and pre-maintenance can be achieved through big data analysis to increase the service life of the equipment. With the use of robots in logistics, there will be a very wide range of applications in the future.

3) Supply chain risk prediction. Through the collection of abnormal data, supply chain risks such as trade risks and goods damage caused by force majeure can be predicted.

4) Supply chain system management. Suppliers and manufacturers can achieve better supply coordination and reduce the loss of stock-out by establishing VMI (Vendor Managed Inventory) cooperation mechanism and realizing the sharing of inventory and demand information. In addition, the supply chain management system can be built with the support of supplier data, quality data, transaction data, resource data and other data to track and control the cost and efficiency of the supply chain system, and on this basis the control of quality and reliability can be further improved.

5) Network and route planning. Using historical data, timeliness and coverage to build analysis models, businesses can optimize the layout of storage, transportation and distribution networks. For example, through the analysis of consumer data, enterprises are able to prepare goods in the warehouse nearest to consumers in advance. It can even realize real-time routing optimization to guide vehicles to use the optimal routes for cross-city transportation and same-city distribution.

In addition, big data technology has a broad application prospect in understanding the overall situation of transportation, optimizing inventory management, and conducting customer segmentation.

At present, the scale of online shopping in China is expanding unprecedently, which puts forward a high demand for logistics and information. With logistics big data analysis, transportation and distribution efficiency can be improved, logistics costs can be reduced, customer satisfaction can be improved, and customer service requirements can be more effectively met. Taking the "double eleven" precision marketing of Jingdong Mall with the aid of big data and cloud computing as an example: According to a large amount of historical sales data information, combined with climate, promotion conditions and other factors, the best-selling commodities are selected, and the sales of these best-selling commodities in various cities are predicted, so that the commodities are transported in advance to the front warehouses nearest to consumers; According to the analysis of the big data related to users, the demand for mainstream commodities in each region of the core city can be predicted more accurately, and the goods can be delivered in advance to the regional warehouses; According to historical sales data and forecast of future market, businesses are able to formulate accurate production plans and carry out reasonable division of regional warehouses. Big data plays a crucial role in intelligent logistics activities. Reasonable use of big data enables enterprises to seize more innovation opportunities, which will play a significant role in promoting logistics enterprises' management and decision-making, customer relationship maintenance, resource allocation and so on.

13.4.4 Artificial Intelligence

Artificial intelligence (AI) is a technical science that researches and develops theories, methods, technologies and application systems for simulating, extending and expanding human intelligence. The intelligence relating to other animals or man-made systems is also generally considered as its related research area.

We often say that the Internet has built a global village, so the development of artificial intelligence can be said to light up the smart global village. Artificial intelligence is the core driving force of a new round of technological and industrial transformation. It can be seen as accumulating the energy of previous technological and industrial transformation and then conducting a superimposed release, thus rapidly giving rise to a series of new products, services and business structures in the field of logistics. Driven by its innovation, there are many new technologies that lead to a new round of intelligent logistics industry reform, such as automatic cargo sorting system, intelligent distribution robot, intelligent customer service and so on. Artificial intelligence technology will become a highly competitive technology field in the future logistics industry. The reason why "artificial intelligence+logistics" can be quickly accepted and absorbed by the industry is that artificial intelligence enables businesses to achieve cost reduction and efficiency improvement in logistics industry, which can effectively solve the problem of high logistics cost in China. The era of intelligent logistics 2.0 is fully opened.

AI technology mainly has the following five logistics application scenarios.

1) Intelligent operation rule management. In the future, the operating rules engine will be equipped with self-learning and adaptive abilities through machine learning, and can make autonomous decisions after sensing business conditions. For example, in the future, artificial intelligence will be able to independently set operation rules such as order production mode, delivery time, freight, abnormal order processing and so on for orders in different scenarios between e-commerce peak and normal times according to commodity categories and other conditions to realize artificial intelligence processing.

2) Warehouse location. Artificial intelligence technology can sufficiently do the optimizing and learning according to various constraints of the real environment, such as the geographical location of customers, suppliers and manufacturers, transportation economy, labor availability, construction cost, tax system, etc., so as to provide site selection recommendations that are close to the optimal solution.

3) Decision support. Machine learning and other technologies are used to automatically identify the state of people, objects, equipment and vehicles inside and outside the yard, and learn command and scheduling experiences as well as decision-making from excellent managers and operation personnel, in order to gradually achieve auxiliary decision and auto-

matic decision.

4) Image recognition. Computer image recognition, address database and convolutional neural network are used to improve the effective recognition rate and accuracy of handwritten waybills, thus greatly reducing the workload and error rate of manual order entry.

5) Intelligent scheduling. Through the analysis of the fundamental data such as quantity and measurement of cargo, the intelligent scheduling of various links such as packaging and transportation vehicles is carried out. For example, by measuring the volume and carton size of millions of SKU, the system intelligently calculates and recommends packaging materials and packing sequence by using deep learning algorithm technology, and consequently the scheme of carton type and commodity placement is well arranged.

13.4 数据处理技术

13.4.1 电子数据交换

13.4.1.1 电子数据交换的概念

电子数据交换（EDI）是将贸易、运输、保险、银行和海关等行业或部门的信息，用一种国际公认的标准格式形成结构化的事务处理报文数据格式，通过计算机通信网络，使各有关部门、公司与企业之间进行数据交换与处理，并完成以贸易为中心的全部业务过程。EDI包括买卖双方数据交换、企业内部数据交换等。

对 EDI 可以从以下 5 个方面进行理解：

1）EDI 是计算机系统之间所进行的电子信息传输。

2）EDI 是标准格式和结构化的电子数据的交换。

3）EDI 是按发送者和接收者达成一致的标准和结构所进行的电子数据的交换。

4）EDI 是由计算机自动读取而无须人工干预的电子数据的交换。

5）EDI 是为了满足商业用途的电子数据的交换。

从一般技术角度，我们可以将 EDI 的概念概括为：EDI 是参加商业运作的双方或多方按照协议，对具有一定结构的标准商业信息，通过数据通信网络在参与方计算机之间所进行的传输和自动处理。其优势主要有以下两点。

第一，降低了纸张的消耗（无纸贸易）。根据联合国组织的调查，进行一次进出口贸易，双方约需交换近 200 份文件和表格，其纸张、行文、打印及查错可能引起的总开销大约为货物价格的 7%。使用 EDI 可以大幅降低交易成本。据统计，美国通用汽车公司采用 EDI 后，每生产一辆汽车可节约成本 250 美元，按每年生产 500 万辆汽车计算，每年可以节约 12.5 亿美元的成本。

第二，减少了重复劳动，提高了工作效率。如果没有 EDI 系统，即使是高度信息化的公司，也需要经常将外来的资料重新输入本公司的计算机。调查表明，从一台计算机输出的资料中有多达 70%的数据需要再输入其他的计算机，既费时又容易出错。美国数字设备公司（DEC）应用 EDI 后，库存周期由 5 天缩短为 3 天，每笔订单费用从 125 美元降到 32 美元。新加坡采用 EDI 贸易网络之后，国际贸易的海关手续从原来的 3～4 天缩短到 10～15 分钟。

13.4.1.2 EDI 在物流业中的应用

现代物流是建立在互联网和 EDI 等众多现代信息技术平台基础上的物流资讯和电子商务服务。在企业物流活动中，货主、承运人以及其他相关方之间通过 EDI 系统进行物流数据交换，并以此为基础实施物流作业活动。EDI 系统把货物运输企业、加工贸易企业、流通领域企业，以及海关、检验检疫、税务、环保、边检和银行等部门有效地连接起来，使整个供应链以及相关的各个环节协调同步，从而促进现代物流管理效率的提高。

13.4.2 云计算

13.4.2.1 云计算的概念

"云计算"概念最早由 Google 首席执行官埃里克·施密特在 2006 年的"搜索引擎战略大会"上首次提出，随后微软、亚马逊、IBM、思科、惠普、甲骨文、EMC 等众多行业巨头全部跟进，IT 巨头们也把它看作未来的"决战之地"。

云计算是一种基于互联网的超级计算模式，在远程的数据中心中，成千上万台电脑和服务器连接成一片电脑云，用户可以通过计算机、笔记本电脑、手机等方式接入数据中心，体验每秒超过 10 万亿次的运算能力。

13.4.2.2 云计算的优势

将云服务应用于物流领域的优势在于以下方面。

1）成本节约：企业不需要大量投资于内网连接、计算机服务器和支持等相关费用，节省了成本，且安全计算能力以租赁的方式提供，不占用企业资金。它通常以服务形式为企业提供复杂技术支持，会很大程度吸引创新企业和中小企业。

2）接入速度和可用性：云计算能提供一种弹性，允许企业快速地开发新市场或者新产品，使得企业能够在最短的时间以最少的投资实现扩张。通过云计算方式，企业可以快速实施和运行安全且经济的应用程序，并且享受低 IT 维护和升级成本。

3）可靠性和容错性：为了确保更高的可靠性，云计算系统需要具有异常的容错能力。容错性是即使系统发生故障和错误时仍能提供所需服务的能力。

4）服务器与网络的运营支持和升级：云服务提供商负责提供运营和网络的支持和升级服务。

例如，位于英格兰赫尔的云计算服务提供商 Keyfort 公司开发了一个云应用环境下的物流管理信息系统，称作 KDIS 系统。通过它可以获取和存储数据，并利用数据生成报告、进行数据分析、按需查询信息等。任何公司都可以应用 KDIS 系统。同时该公司还开发了一种特定的手机应用软件 KeyPOD，通过监测执行配送任务司机的智能手机实现对产品状态、位置等信息的追踪，提高产品的可追踪性。使用 KeyPOD，配送中心和承运人能够协同运作，共享实时交付信息。

总而言之，移动技术和云计算的应用为公司提供了全程在线且实时监控的收益。在物流供应链环境下，系统的及时性和可靠性对企业的发展至关重要，因此这种收益的意义就更加重大。

13.4.2.3 云计算技术在现代物流中的应用

由于云计算具有上述多项优点，应用云计算提升物流服务能力就成为物流企业的首选，而利用云计算为物流企业构建物流信息平台自然也成为云服务提供商的重要服务。云服务提供商提供的服务，按照其服务层次，分别包括应用层、平台层、基础设施层和虚拟化层。

1）应用层。在云计算信息平台的构建中，应用层主要用于向物流企业提供其所需的软件服务。物流企业从自己的实际需要出发，考虑在运营过程中需要哪些软件服务，然后按服务时间和方式向云计算服务提供商支付相应的服务费用，而不必自行购买、维护这些软件，软件的管理、维护交由云服务提供商来解决。

2）平台层。在云计算信息平台的构建中，平台层用来提供服务的开发环境。服务器平台的软件和服务中所需要的硬件资源通过平台层提供给物流企业，而物流公司在此平台层的基础上，通过建立次级互联网服务系统向其客户提供服务。

3）基础设施层。在云计算信息平台的基础设施层，将 IT 基础设施以服务形式提供给客户，包括服务器、网络设备等资源。

4）虚拟化层。这个层次是云计算信息平台构建的关键，可提供服务器集群及硬件检测等服务，以及硬件的维护管理。该层包括服务器的物理资源、虚拟化资源、服务平台的中间件管理以及供物流公司连接的服务接口。

云计算物流信息平台正是通过应用层、平台层、基础设施层、虚拟化层的层层构建和设置，搭建起一个信息化的物流服务平台，提供安全的服务环境为物流企业提供快速、安全、可靠的信息服务。其主要的应用模式如下：

1）基于云计算模式的业务平台。物流企业利用经过分析处理的感知数据，通过 Web 浏览器为其客户提供丰富的特定应用与服务，包括监控型服务（物流监控、污染监控）、查询型服务（智能检索、信息查询）、扫描型服务（信息码扫描、物品的运输传递扫描）等。

2）基于云计算模式的数据存储中心。提供物流企业所需要的具体数据服务，包括数据的海量存储、查询、分析，实现资源完全共享，资源自动部署、分配和动态调整。

3）基于云计算模式的基础服务平台。在传统数据中心的基础上引入云计算模式，能够为物流企业提供各种互联网应用所需的服务器，这样物流企业便在数据存储及网络资源利用方面具备了优越性。云计算服务平台的服务价格更具优势，能够减少物流企业的经营成本；还可在应用时实现动态资源调配，自动安装部署，提供给用户按需响应、按使用收费和高质量的基础设施服务。

13.4.3 大数据

根据 Gartner 集团的定义，“大数据”是需要新处理模式才能具有更强的决策力、洞察发现力和流程优化能力的海量、高增长率和多样化的信息资产。大数据技术的意义并不是掌握和拥有大量数据，而是通过对含有意义的数据进行专业化的处理实现数据的价值增值。目前大数据领域已经涌现出大量新技术，这些新技术正在成为大数据采集、存储、处理和呈现的有力武器。

物流大数据指的是在运输、仓储、装卸搬运、包装、配送及流通加工等物流环节中涉及的数据和信息。虽然大数据技术在各种领域都存在广泛的应用价值，但是物流领域是大数据的主要应用领域之一。这是因为条形码等技术的发展，使得物流部门可以利用前端 PC 系统收集、存储大量的数据，如货物进出历史记录、货物进出状态和服务记录等。物流业同其他数据密集型企业一样积累了大量的数据，这些数据正是大数据的基础。大数据技术有助于识别运输行为，发现配送新模式和趋势，改进运输效率，从而取得更高的核心竞争力，减少物流成本。

从目前的研究看，大数据对于智慧物流发展的助力作用主要表现在以下几个方面。

第一，促进物流企业竞争观念的转变。大数据时代改变了商业竞争环境，实现了信息数据等多种资源的共享，同时大数据技术对信息价值的最大程度地挖掘提高了企业的决策等方面的能力，从环境、资源和能力等方面影响企业的竞争力。

第二，优化物流企业的资源和能力。大数据不仅实现了对物流运输中的人力、物力资源的充分开发利用，如借助大数据信息技术进行人才甄选等活动，并且可以提升物流企业对环境的适应能力，同时使得企业能够获取有价值的资源。

第三，在物流活动中应用大数据技术，能够使物流活动变得更加灵活和“智能”，随之也会提升企业的竞争能力。

具体来讲，大数据技术在物流领域中的典型应用主要有以下几个方面。

1）需求预测。通过收集用户消费特征、商家历史销售等大数据，利用算法提前预测需求，前置仓储与运输环节。这方面目前已经有了一些应用，但在预测精度上仍有很大提升空间，需要扩充数据量，优化算法。

2）设备维护预测。通过物联网的应用，在设备上安装芯片，可实时监控设备运行数据，并通过大数据分析做到预先维护，增加设备使用寿命。机器人在物流环节的使用将成为未来应用的一个主要方向。

3）供应链风险预测。通过对异常数据的收集，可以对诸如贸易风险、不可抗力引起的货物损坏等供应链风险进行预测。

4）供应链系统管理。供应商和生产商在建立 VMI（供应商管理库存）合作机制以及实现库存与需求信息共享的情况下，可以实现更好的供需匹配，减少因缺货而造成的损失。此外，在供应商数据、质量数据、交易数据、资源数据等数据的支持下构建供应链管理系统可以对供应链系统的成本以及效率进行跟踪和掌控，在此基础上实现对质量与可靠性的控制。

5）网络及路线规划。利用历史数据、时效、覆盖范围等构建分析模型，对仓储、运输、配送网络进行优化布局，如通过对消费者数据的分析，提前在离消费者最近的仓库进行备货。甚至可实现实时路径优化，指导车辆采用最佳路径进行跨城运输与同城配送。

此外，大数据技术在了解运输全局、优化库存管理、客户细分等方面也具有广阔的应用前景。

当前中国的网络购物规模空前扩大，这对物流提出了很高的要求，信息需求量也越来越大。而借助物流大数据分析，可以提高运输配送效率、降低物流成本并且提高客户满意度，更有效地满足客户服务要求。以借助大数据和云计算所进行的京东平台“双十一”精准营销为例：根据大量的历史销售商品数据信息，结合气候、促销条件等因素，选取火爆商品，同时对火爆商品在各个城市的销量进行预测，从而提前将商品转移到距离消费者最近的前置仓；根据对用户相关大数据进行分析，可以实现对核心城市的各个区域的主流商品需求量的准确预测，提前发往相应的物流分站；根据历史销售数据以及对未来市场的预测，在制订精准生产计划方面为商家提供帮助，帮助他们进行合理的区域分仓等。大数据在此智慧化物流活动中起到的作用是至关重要的。合理地运用大数据可以为企业带来更多创新机遇，这将对物流企业的管理与决策、维护客户关系、配置资源等起到相当大的推动作用。

13.4.4 人工智能

人工智能（AI）是研究、开发用于模拟、延伸和扩展人的智能的理论、方法、技术及应用系统的一门技术科学。而其他关于动物或人造系统的智能也普遍被认为是其相关的研究课题。

我们经常说互联网构建了地球村，那么人工智能的发展可以说是点亮了智慧地球村。人工智能是新一轮科技与产业变革的核心驱动力，它可以看成是正在积累历次科技与企业变革的能量，并将其叠加释放，从而快速催生一系列的物流领域新型产品、服务与业态结构。在其创新驱动作用下，出现了很多引发新一轮物流智慧化行业变革的新型技术，如自动货物分拣系统、智能配送机器人、智能客服等。人工智能技术将成为未来物流行业极具竞争力的技术领域。"人工智能+物流"之所以可以被业界快速接受和吸收，是因为人工智能能够实现物流行业的降本增效，这可以有效解决我国社会物流成本过高的问题，智慧物流 2.0 时代正全面开启。

人工智能技术主要有以下 5 个物流应用场景。

1）智能运营规则管理。未来将会通过机器学习，使运营规则引擎具备自学习、自适应的能力，能够在感知业务条件后进行自主决策。如未来人工智能将可对电商高峰期与常态不同场景订单，依据商品品类等条件自主设置订单生产方式、交付时间、运费、异常订单处理等运营规则，实现人工智能处理。

2）仓库选址。人工智能技术能够根据现实环境的种种约束条件，如顾客、供应商和生产商的地理位置、运输经济性、劳动力可获得性、建设成本、税收制度等，进行充分的优化与学习，从而给出接近最优解决方案的选址建议。

3）决策辅助。利用机器学习等技术来自动识别场站内外的人、物、设备、车的状态，学习优秀的管理和操作人员的指挥调度经验、决策等，逐步实现辅助决策和自动决策。

4）图像识别。利用计算机图像识别、地址库和卷积神经网络提升手写运单的机器有效识别率和准确率，大幅减少人工输单的工作量和差错率。

5）智能调度。通过对商品数量、体积等基础数据分析，对物流各环节如包装、运输车辆等进行智能计算及调度。例如，将上万种库存单品的体积数据和包装箱尺寸输入系统，系统将利用深度学习算法技术，进行智能地计算并推荐包装耗材和打包排序，从而合理安排箱型和商品摆放方案。

13.5 Network and Communication Technology

13.5.1 Mobile Internet

Mobile Internet is an emerging technology formed by the integration of Internet and mobile communication after their independent development. With the rapid development of the logistics industry, the downstream customer demands and development modes are constantly changing, and logistics informatization should also move in response to the needs and further improve the level of development. The rapid popularization and application of mobile Internet in the logistics industry has provided important technical support for the upgrading and development of logistics informatization, and accelerated its progress towards smart logistics.

Mobile Internet plays a supporting role in the development of smart logistics in the following aspects.

1) Smart cloud platform helps to open up the supply chain. Due to the era of supply chain competition, each stage/link of supply chain needs to break through the boundary between enterprises to realize mutual cooperation, occupy favorable market positions, and obtain competitive advantages. Mobile Internet platform can provide logistics enterprises with a cloud resource pool with high performance, on-demand allocation and dynamic adjustment, which saves enterprises from the massive input of information hardware resources, the capital tied up in the maintenance and upgrade. It can also provide enterprises with tailored service solutions and facilitate the integration of supply chain.

2) Dynamic tracking of goods can be realized through real-time collection of mobile information. By locating the movement of drivers or vehicles, enterprises can accurately determine the location of goods in transit. Meanwhile, customers can also query and determine the real-time location of their goods by phone, mobile Internet App and other means.

3) Smart logistics mobile Internet platform can build information communication bridge among different participating enterprises and help them to conduct high-quality and effective communication. The platform also has data interface with enterprises' existing application systems and procedures, allowing the existing systems to work better.

13. 5. 2 Internet of Things

In 1999, Auto-ID Labs at the MIT first proposed the concept of "Internet of things". In the same year, the mobile computing and network conference held in the United States proposed that "the Internet of things is another development opportunity facing mankind in the next century. " In 2003, the US "Technical Review" proposed that sensor network technology would be the top ten technologies to change people's life in the future. On November 17th, 2005, at World Summit on the Information Society (WSIS) held in Tunisia, the International Telecommunication Union (ITU) issued the "ITU Internet Report 2005: Internet of Things", formally proposing the concept of "Internet of Things" (IoT). The Internet of Things is a network that connects all objects to the Internet through information sensing devices such as Radio Frequency Identification (RFID), infrared sensors, Global Positioning Systems (GPS), and laser scanners. The Internet of Things can realize intelligent identification, location, tracking, monitoring and management.

Literally, the Internet of things is "Internet of things connected". There are two implications:

Firstly, the core and foundation of the IoT is still the Internet, and the IoT is an extended and expanded network on the basis of the Internet.

Secondly, the client/user equipment has been extended and expanded compared to the Internet. While the user equipment of the Internet mainly includes such electronic devices as computers and mobile phones, the Internet of Things extends the user equipment to any object.

The basic principle of IoT is to construct an Internet of Things covering everything in the world by using RFID, wireless data communication and other technologies on the basis of computer Internet. In this network, objects can communicate with each other without human intervention. Its essence is to use RFID technology, through the computer Internet, to realize the automatic identification of things (commodities) as well as information interconnection and sharing. The steps are as follows: ①identifying object attributes; ②completing the reading of the object attributes, and transforming the information into a data format suitable for network transmission; ③The information of the object is transmitted to the information processing center through the network, and the processing center completes the relevant calculation of object communication.

The conditions for an "object" to enter the Internet of things are: There should be receivers for corresponding information; There should be data transmission channels; Must have certain storage function; Have the CPU; Have an operating system; Have a dedicated app; Have a data transmitter; Follow the communication protocols of the Internet of Things; Have a unique number that can be identified in the world network.

The Internet of things applies the sensing technology and network technology to all things, manages human's production and life in a fine and dynamic way, improves the utilization rate and productivity of resources, and improves the relationship between human and nature. With the use of various devices and technologies such as information sensors, RFID, GPS, infrared sensors, and laser scanners, the real world is fully connected to the virtual "Internet" and thereby information about any object or process needed to be monitored, connected, and interacted could be collected. In this process, information on sound, light, heat, electricity, mechanics, chemistry, biology, location, etc. , is collected and connected to various possible networks, In this way, the connection between objects can be achieved, as well as the connection between objects and people, and the intelligent perception, identification and management to object and process can be realized.

The IoT industry chain is divided into four parts: identification, perception, processing and information transmission. The key technologies of each link are RFID, sensor, intelligent chip and wireless transmission network. The three main products of IoT are: electronic labels (storage chips, antennas, various sensors, etc.), readers and writers (intelligent chips, read antennas, information transmission modules, etc.), system integration products (system middleware, database software, PC terminal, data server, router, switch, transmission network, etc.).

The IoT is a highly integrated and comprehensive application of the new generation of information technologies, which is of great significance to the new round of industrial reform and the green, intelligent and sustainable development of economy and society. At present, the Internet of things is mainly used in business offices, automobile industry, logistics, consumption, resource environment, households, plants and cities. The global IoT is worth \$4 trillion to \$12 trillion and involves every aspect of life and work. Among them, smart city, smart transportation, smart wearable, smart medical market are the most promising. With the advent of 5G, the Internet of everything is getting closer, and the Internet of Things has undoubtedly become the hottest keyword. The Internet of Things is replacing the mobile Internet as the main driver of the information industry.

In the field of logistics, enterprises applying the Internet of things to improve business operations need to take improving efficiency and reducing human errors as the goal. By using the IoT technology to analyze and inspect business processes, sense and collect logistics information, and automatically process data, etc. , enterprises can make better decisions and further optimize business processes. Details are as follows.

(1) Intelligent Transportation

Logistics enterprises that use the IoT technology to upgrade their transportation business need to provide fast, punctual, safe and high-quality standardized services based on the transportation network platform that extensively covers the service area. By integrating internal and external logistics resources, business provides "one-stop" comprehensive logistics services to meet customers' personalized needs for transportation business applications. The Internet of Things technology is applied to optimize each operation link of the transportation business, realize the information and intelligence of the transportation management process, and carry out logistics resource integration and seamless connection with upstream and downstream enterprises.

(2) Automatic Storage

The application of the Internet of Things technology in the storage management business can realize the automatic sorting of goods, intelligent receiving and shipping, automatic inventory management and "virtual warehouse" management, so as to form the automatic warehousing. Through intelligent and automatic warehousing, costs can be effectively reduced, operations can be visible and transparent, and service level can be improved.

(3) Dynamic Distribution

In traditional distribution processes, the changes of traffic conditions, price factors, the number and distribution of users as well as user demands impact the distribution scheme and distribution process. The introduction of the Internet of things solves this problem well. Through the information collection and effective feedback of the objects involved in the above factors, the dynamic distribution scheme can be formulated, so as to improve the distribution efficiency and service quality. In addition, it can also provide customers with real-time distribution status.

(4) Information Service

As the third revolution in the field of information technology, the Internet of things can play a greater role in improving the speed of information transmission, the ability of information acquisition and processing, and controlling the direction of information transmission, so as to upgrade the information flow activities of logistics enterprises, improve the response speed and accuracy of the whole logistics, and realize the leap of logistics information management and control. The information interaction, information feedback control, and external information transmission of each business process can be optimized through the Internet of things technology, which greatly improves the operation efficiency of the logistics system, improves the information level of logistics enterprises and the service level based on information feedback.

13.5 网络与通信技术

13.5.1 移动互联网

移动互联网是互联网与移动通信各自独立发展后，互相融合形成的新兴技术。随着物流业的快速发展，下游客户需求和发展模式不断变化，物流信息化也要应需而动，进一步提升发展水平。而移动互联网在物流行业的快速普及应用，给物流信息化的升级发展提供了重要技术支撑，促使其加速向智慧物流迈进。

移动互联网在智慧物流发展中起到的支持作用表现在以下几方面。

1）智慧云平台助力打通供应链。由于进入供应链竞争时代，各环节需要打通企业间的边界以实现相互协作，占据主动，获得竞争优势。移动互联平台可以为物流企业提供高性价比、按需分配且动态调整的云资源池，免去了企业对信息化硬件资源的大量投入、维护以及升级的资金成本，还可以为企业提供个性化物流解决方案，帮助打通供应链。

2）通过移动信息的实时采集，实现货物的动态跟踪。企业通过对司机或车辆进行移动定位，就能够掌握在途货物所处位置；同时，客户通过电话、移动互联网 App 等方式，也可以查到自己货物的实时位置。

3）智慧物流移动互联平台可以在不同参与企业之间搭建信息沟通桥梁，协助参与企业之间高质量、高效率地交流。它还提供与企业现有应用系统和程序的数据接口，让现有系统发挥出更好的应用效果。

13.5.2 物联网

1990 年，美国麻省理工学院的自动识别实验室（Auto-ID Labs）首先提出“物联网”的概念。同年，在美国召开的移动计算和网络会议提出，“物联网是下一个世纪人类面临的又一个发展机遇。”2003 年，美国《技术评论》提出传感网络技术将是未来改变人们生活的十大技术之首。2005 年 11 月 17 日，在突尼斯举行的信息社会世界峰会 WSIS 上，国际电信联盟 ITU 发布《国际电信联盟互联网报告 2005：物联网》，正式提出“物联网”这一概念。物联网是把所有物品通过射频识别（RFID）、红外感应器、全球定位系统、激光扫描器等信息传感设备与互联网连接起来，进行信息交换的网络。物联网可实现智能化识别、定位、跟踪、监控和管理。

从字面解释，物联网就是“物物相连的互联网”。具体有两层意思：

第一，物联网的核心和基础仍然是互联网，是在互联网基础上延伸和扩展的网络。

第二，用户端相比互联网进行了延伸和扩展。互联网的用户端是计算机、手机等电子设备，物联网则扩展到了任何物体。

物联网的基本原理是在计算机互联网的基础上，利用 RFID、无线数据通信等技术，构造一个覆盖世界上万事万物的 Internet of Things。在这个网络中，物品能够彼此进行“交流”，无须人的干预。其实质是利用 RFID 技术，通过计算机互联网实现物品（商品）的自动识别和信息的互联与共享。其操作步骤为：①标识物体属性；②完成对物体属性的读取，并将信息转换为适合网络传输的数据格式；③将物体的信息通过网络传输到信息处理中心，由处理中心完成物体通信的相关计算。

“物品”进入物联网的条件为：要有相应信息的接收器；要有数据传输通路；要有一定的存储功能；要有 CPU；要有操作系统；要有专门的应用程序；要有数据发送器；要遵循物联网的通信协议；要在世界网络中有可被识别的唯一编号。

物联网把感知技术、网络技术运用于万物，以精细动态方式管理人类生产生活，提高资源利用率和生产力水平，改善人与自然的关系。现实的世间万物与虚拟的“互联网”充分结合，通过各种信息传感器、射频识别技术、全球定位系统、红外感应器、激光扫描器等装置与技术，实时采集任何需要监控、连接、互动的物体或过程，采集其声、光、热、电、力学、化学、生物、位置等各种需要的信息，接入各类可能的网络，实现物与物、物与人的泛在连接从而实现对物品和过程的智能化感知、识别和管理。物联网是一个基于互联网、传统电信网等信息承载体，让所有能够被独立寻址的普通物理对象实现互联互通的网络。

物联网产业链细分为四个环节：标识、感知、处理、信息传送。每个环节对应的关键技术分别为：RFID、传感器、智能芯片、无线传输网络。物联网的三大类产品主要为：电子标签（存储芯片、天线、各种传感器等）、读写器（智能芯片、识读天线、信息传输模块等）、系统集成产品（系统中间件、数据库软件、PC 终端、数据服务器、路由器、交换机、传输网络等）。

物联网是新一代信息技术的高度集成和综合运用，对新一轮产业变革和经济社会绿色、智能、可持续发展具有重要意义。目前，物联网主要应用于办公、汽车业、物流、消费领域、资源环境、家庭、工厂和城市九大方面。全球物联网产值 4 万亿～12 万亿美元，涉及生活与工作方方面面。其中，智能城市、智能交通、智能穿戴、智能医疗市场最为可期。随着 5G 的到来，万物互联渐近，物联网无疑成了最热的关键词，物联网正在取代移动互联网成为信息产业的主要驱动。

在物流领域中，企业应用物联网完善业务，需要以提高效率、减少人为错误为目标，利用物联网技术分析研究业务流程、物流感知与信息采集、进行数据的自动化处理等，以做出更好的决策，进一步优化业务流程。

(1) 智能运输

利用物联网技术实施运输业务升级的物流企业，需以广泛覆盖所服务区域的运输网络平台为基础，提供快捷、准时、安全、优质的标准化服务。通过整合内、外物流资源，提供“一站式”综合物流服务，以满足客户对运输业务的个性化需求。应用物联网技术，可优化运输业务的各个作业环节，实现运输管理过程的信息化、智能化，并与上、下游业务进行物流资源整合和无缝连接。

(2) 自动仓储

将物联网技术应用于仓储管理业务中，可实现仓储管理中的货物自动分拣、智能化出入库管理、货物自动盘点及“虚拟仓库”管理，从而形成自动仓储业务。通过智能及自动化的仓储管理，可有效降低仓储成本，实现仓储作业的可视化和透明化管理，以及提高仓储服务水平。

(3) 动态配送

在传统的配送过程中，交通条件、价格因素、用户数量及分布和用户需求等因素的变化会对配送方案、配送过程产生影响。物联网的引入很好地解决了这一问题，通过对以上影响因素涉及的物体利用物联网感知布点进行信息采集并有效反馈就可形成动态的配送方案，从而提高配送效率，提升服务质量。此外，还可为客户提供实时的配送状态。

(4) 信息服务

物联网作为信息技术领域的第三次革命，可在物流企业提高信息传输速度、信息获取能力和信息处理能力，把控信息传输方向等方面发挥较大作用，实现物流企业的信息流活动升级，从而提高整个物流的反应速度和准确度，实现物流信息管理与控制的飞跃。各业务流程的信息交互、信息反馈控制、企业与外部信息传递都可以通过物联网技术进行优化，极大地提高物流系统的运转效率，提升物流企业的信息化水平和基于信息反馈的服务水平。

13. 6 Simulation Technology of Logistics System

13. 6. 1 System Simulation

System simulation is a process of experimental research on the system in a specific time by establishing the actual system model. With the development of computer technology, system simulation has gradually evolved into a new subject. To be specific, system simulation is a comprehensive and practical method, based on control theory, similarity theory, information processing technology and computer technology and assisted by computer and other special logistics equipment, to carry out experiments on real or hypothetical system models and make analysis on experimental results with the aid of expert experience, statistical data and information for further decision making.

Generally speaking, system simulation can be divided into the following nine steps.

1) Defining the problem. The more general the statement that defines the problem is, the better. We should consider the possible causes of the problem in detail and make appropriate assumptions.

2) Setting goals and defining system effectiveness measures. When defining goals, the performance measures that influence the realization of goals should be described in detail, and the prerequisites for the simulation results should be listed.

3) Describing the system and listing assumptions. Simulation divides real system resources into four categories: processor, queue, transport and shared resources (such as operators). In the process of establishing the simulation model, it is necessary to describe the real system first, abstract and accurately express its essential attributes through reasonable assumptions.

4) Listing possible alternatives. Alternatives should be considered at the beginning of the simulation so that the designed model can be easily converted to the replacement system.

5) Collecting data and information. Data can be obtained through historical records, experience and calculation. These crude data will provide the basis for the input parameters of the model. In addition to inputting data for model parameters, the actual data can be compared with the performance measurement data of the model in the validation phase.

6) Building a computer model. Generally, the modeling process is phased. Before the next stage of modeling, the model of this stage should be verified to be normal, and the model of each stage should be run and debugged during the modeling process.

7) Verifying and validating the model. The content of "verification" includes whether the function of the model is consistent with the assumed system function, and whether the model is consistent with the model to be built. The scope of "validation model" includes whether the validation model can correctly reflect the real system, and how reliable the simulation results are.

8) Running alternative experiments. When the system is stochastic, the experiment needs to be run several times. As far as possible, the confidence interval for each of the defined performance measures is calculated in step (2).

9) Analyzing the outcomes. Reports, graphs, and tables are usually used to analyze the output results, while statistical techniques are applied to analyze the simulation results of different scenarios. Once conclusions are drawn, they should be able to interpret the results in terms of the objectives of the simulation and propose implementation or optimization schemes.

13.6.2 Logistics System Simulation

System simulation technology is widely used in logistics system, such as logistics system facilities planning and design, material control, material transportation scheduling, logistics cost estimation and so on.

(1) Logistics system facilities planning and design

Suppose that there is a complex logistics system composed of automated warehouses, AGVs, buffer stations, etc. The content of the system design includes: determining the number of goods in the automatic warehouse; determining the speed and quantity of AGV; determining the number of buffer stations; determining loading capacity (running speed and quantity) of the stacker; planning the layout of logistics equipment; designing AGV transport route, etc. The important indexes that should be considered in the system design include production capacity, production efficiency and system investment, etc. These indexes are contradictory to each other to some extent. Logistics system facilities planning and design require the selection of the best combination of technology and economy.

(2) Material control

The supply and demand relationship between material supply department and manufacturing department is contradictory, and the processing rhythm of each working procedure in manufacturing is generally not coordinated. In order to ensure the timely and accurate supply of materials, the most effective way is to set up material warehouses at the plants and workshops, and set up buffer material warehouses between working procedures to coordinate the production rhythm.

(3) Material transportation scheduling

For a complex logistics system with a variety of transportation vehicles and routes, it is very necessary to use reasonable scheduling tools to plan transportation routes to ensure the smooth and efficient transportation. Due to the complexity and dynamic nature of transportation scheduling in logistics system, system simulation has become an effective method to solve the problem. Through the transportation system model established by dynamic operation, it vividly presents the running state, road congestion, material supply, and meanwhile presents the data of various simulation results including vehicle running time, utilization rate and so on.

(4) Logistics cost estimation

Logistics cost accounting is directly related to the time spent. In order to ensure the economy of the system, cost accounting results are usually used to evaluate various schemes of logistics system. Typically, total logistics cost includes transportation cost, inventory cost, material handling cost, etc. Logistics process is a very complex dynamic process. In the actual simulation, the estimation of logistics cost can be obtained simultaneously with other statistical performance of logistics system.

13.6 物流系统仿真技术

13.6.1 系统仿真

系统仿真是通过建立实际的系统模型，在特定的时间内对系统进行实验研究的过程。随着计算机技术的发展，系统仿真已逐步形成一门新兴学科。具体来说、系统仿真是以控制理论、相似理论、信息处理技术和计算机技术等理论为基础，以计算机和其他专用物流设备为工具，对真实或假设的系统模型进行实验，并借助于专家经验、统计数据和信息资料对实验结果进行分析研究，进而作出决策的一门综合性、实验性的学科。

一般而言，系统仿真可以分为以下 9 个步骤。

1）界定问题。界定问题的陈述越通用越好，应详细考虑引起问题的可能原因，做出恰当的假设。

2）制定目标和定义系统效能测度。在制定目标时，应详细说明影响目标实现的性能测度，并列出仿真结果的先决条件。

3）描述系统和列出假设。仿真将现实系统资源分成 4 类：处理器、队列、运输和共享资源（如操作员）。在建立仿真模型时，首先需要对现实系统作模型描述，通过合理假设，抽象并准确表达其本质属性。

4）列举可能的替代方案。应在仿真初期考虑替代方案，使设计的模型能够非常容易地转换到替换系统。

5）收集数据和信息。数据可以通过历史记录、经验和计算得到。这些粗糙的数据将为模型输入参数提供基础。除了为模型参数输入数据外，在验证模型阶段还可以把实际数据与模型的性能测度数据进行比较。

6）建立计算机模型。一般建模过程是呈阶段性的，在进行下一阶段建模之前，首先验证本阶段的模型工作是否正常，并应在建模过程中运行和调试每一阶段的模型。

7）验证和确认模型。“验证”的内容包括模型的功能是否与设想的系统功能相符合，模型是否与设想构建的模型一致。“确认模型”的范围包括确认模型是否能够正确反映现实系统，模型仿真结果的可信度有多大等。

8）运行可替代实验。当系统具有随机性时，就需要多次运行实验。尽可能在第 2）步中计算出已定义的每一性能测度的置信区间。

9）输出分析。通常使用报表、图形和表格进行输出结果的分析，同时应用统计技术分析不同方案的模拟结果。一旦得出结论，就要能够根据模拟的目标来解释这些结果，并提出实施或优化方案。

13.6.2 物流系统仿真

系统仿真技术在物流系统中的应用非常普遍，例如物流系统设施规划与设计、物料控制、物料运输调度、物流成本估算等，具体如下。

(1) 物流系统设施规划与设计

假设一个由自动化立体仓库、AGV、缓冲站等组成的复杂物流系统。系统设计的内容包括确定：自动化立体仓库的货位数；AGV 的速度、数量；缓冲站的个数；堆垛机的装载能力（运行速度和数量）以及规划物流设备的布局；设计 AGV 的运送路线等。系统设计应该考虑的重要指标包括生产能力、生产效率和系统投资等，这些指标在某种程度上是相互矛盾的，物流系统设施规划与设计要求选择技术性与经济性的最佳结合点。

(2) 物料控制

物料供应部门与生产加工部门的供求关系存在着矛盾，且生产加工中各个工序的加工节奏一般不可协调。为确保物料的及时、准确供应，最有效的办法是在工厂、车间设置物料仓库，在生产工序间设置缓冲物料库来协调生产节奏。

(3) 物料运输调度

对于拥有多种运输车辆和多种运输路线的复杂物流系统来说，应用合理的调度工具来规划运输路线，对于保障运输的通畅和高效是非常必要的。由于物流系统运输调度的复杂、动态性，系统仿真已成为解决问题的有效方法。它通过动态运行所建立的运输系统模型，生动呈现运行状态、道路堵塞情况、物料供应情况，并呈现包括车辆的运行时间、利用率等各种仿真结果的数据。

(4) 物流成本估算

物流成本的核算与花费的时间直接相关，为保证系统的经济性，通常用成本核算结果来评价物流系统的各种方案。一般而言，物流总成本包括运输成本、库存成本、装卸成本等。物流过程是非常复杂的动态过程，在实际仿真中，物流成本的估算可以与物流系统其他统计性能同时得到。

Part B Vocabulary and Terminology 词汇和术语

Smart Logistics 智慧物流
Internet of Things (IoT) 物联网
Artificial Intelligence 人工智能
cloud computing 云计算
bar code/barcode technology 条形码技术
two-dimensional bar code 二维条形码
stacked bar code 层排式二维条形码
dot matrix bar code 矩阵型二维条形码
EAN 国际物品编码协会
UCC 美国统一代码委员会
wired electronic label technology 有线电子标签技术
Radio Frequency Identification (RFID) Technology 射频识别技术
Global Positioning System (GPS) 全球定位系统
Geographic Information System (GIS) 地理信息系统
Database Management System (DBMS) 数据库管理系统
Electronic Data Interchange (EDI) 电子数据交换
Vender Managed Inventory (VMI) 供应商管理库存
World Summit on the Information Society (WSIS) 信息协会世界峰会
International Telecommunication Union (ITU) 国际电信联盟
logistics system simulation 物流系统仿真

Part C Exercise 练习

Ⅰ. True or false.

1. One-dimensional bar code is composed of a set of regularly arranged bars, blanks and

corresponding characters.

2. RFID uses laser scanners, which can read data through external data, while barcode reads data by radio RF.

3. The ground monitoring system of GPS working satellite consists of three parts, including one main control station, three injection stations and four monitoring stations.

4. Big data technology and cloud computing technology are two completely unrelated technologies.

5. One prominent drawback to RFID involves privacy concerns.

6. EDI is no longer an important logistics technology in the twenty-first century.

7. The Internet of Things refers to the sensors and data-communication technology that is built into physical objects that enables them to be tracked and controlled over the Internet.

Ⅱ. Choose the right answer from the four choices below.

1. How do data and information differ? ________.

A. Data is a body of facts in a format suitable for decision-making whereas information is simply facts.

B. Data and information are the same.

C. Data is simply facts; Information is a body of facts in a format suitable for decision-making.

D. Data is associated with decision support system; information is associated with enterprise resource planning system.

2. Internationally recognized bar code used in the field of logistics does not include ________.

A. EAN-13　　B. Cross 25 yards　　C. QR Code　　D. UCC/EAN-128

3. ________ refers to a collection of large amounts of near-real-time data collected through a variety of sources such as sensors and smartphones.

A. Cloud Computing　　B. Big Data

C. Data Warehousing　　D. Decision Support System

4. Which of the following refers to a network of satellites that transmit signals that pinpoint exact location of an object.

A. Global Positioning System.　　B. Cloud Computing.

C. Internet of Things.　　D. Electronic Data Interchange.

5. The most popular automatic identification system currently in use is ________.

A. Voice-data entry Contact　　B. Radio frequency identification

C. Magnetic strips　　D. Bar code scanners

Ⅲ. Answer the following questions.

1. Please tell the main difference between bar code and RFID.

2. What are the components of GPS system?

3. Please briefly describe the main functions of GIS system.

4. How do you define EDI?

5. What are the advantages of cloud computing in the field of logistics?

6. Please tell the main applications of Internet of Things in the field of logistics.

7. What are the general steps of system simulation?

参考文献

[1] 丁立言，张铎. 国际物流学［M］. 北京：清华大学出版社，2000.

[2] 赵可培. 运筹学［M］. 上海：上海财经大学出版社，2000.

[3] 刘北林. 国际物流实务［M］. 北京：中国物资出版社，2006.

[4] 周哲，申雅君. 国际物流［M］. 北京：清华大学出版社，2006.

[5] 率功兵，王慧玲. 国际物流［M］. 北京：中国物资出版社，2006.

[6] 王昭凤. 国际物流组织与管理［M］. 北京：电子工业出版社，2006.

[7] 杨霞芳. 国际物流管理［M］. 上海：同济大学出版社，2004.

[8] 张清，杜杨. 国际物流与货运代理［M］. 北京：机械工业出版社，2004.

[9] 杨占林. 国际物流操作实物［M］. 北京：中国商务出版社，2004.

[10] 张海燕，吕明哲. 国际物流［M］. 大连：东北财经大学出版社，2005.

[11] 杨志刚. 国际货运物流实务、法规与案例［M］. 北京：化学工业出版社，2003.

[12] 邵作仁. 国际物流［M］. 大连：东北财经大学出版社，2005.

[13] 葛承群，韩刚，沈兴龙. 物流运作典型案例诊断［M］. 北京：中国物资出版社，2006.

[14] 王子训. 我国外贸运输与国际物流问题［M］. 北京：对外经济贸易大学出版社，2001.

[15] 马丁·克里斯托弗 著. 物流竞争——后勤与供应链管理［M］. 马越，马月才 译. 北京：北京出版社，2001.

[16] 詹姆士·斯托克. 战略物流管理［M］. 邵晓峰 等译. 北京：中国财政经济出版社，2002.

[17] 安德鲁·伯杰，约翰·加托纳 著. 网际时代的供应链管理［M］. 马士华 等译. 北京：电子工业出版社，2001.

[18] 李长霞，罗兴武. 国际物流［M］. 北京：电子工业出版社，2005.

[19] 王任祥. 国际物流［M］. 杭州：浙江大学出版社，2004.

[20] 顾丽亚. 国际货运代理与报关实务［M］. 北京：电子工业出版，2004.

[21] 龙桂先. 国际物流与货运代理实务［M］. 北京：机械工业出版社，2005.

[22] 刘树密. 国际货运代理［M］. 南京：东南大学出版社，2004.

[23] 张清，杜杨. 国际物流与货运代理［M］. 北京：机城工业出版社，2006.

[24] 霍红. 国际货运代理与海上运输［M］. 北京：化学工业出版社，2004.

[25] 克里斯托弗 著. 物流与供应链管理：降低成本与改善服务的战略［M］. 2 版. 北京：电子工业出版社，2003.

[26] 杨鹏强，林青. 电子口岸实务［M］. 北京：中国海关出版社，2010.

[27] "关务通. 电子口岸系列"编委会. 电子口岸实用功能［M］. 北京：中国海关出版社，2012.

[28] 傅龙海，丛晓明. 国际贸易实务双语教程［M］. 北京：对外经济贸易大学出版社，2011.

[29] 中国国际货运代理协会. 国际货运代理专业英语 2005 版［M］. 北京：中国商务出版社，2005.

[30] 中国国际货运代理协会. 国际货运代理专业英语 2009 版［M］. 北京：中国商务出版社，2009.

[31] Donald J. Browersox，David J. Closs，M. Bixby Cooper 著，供应链物流管理［M］. 马士华 译. 北京：机械工业出版社，2006.

[32] 谢国娥. 海关报关实务［M］. 上海：华东理工大学出版社，2007.

[33] 孙家庆. 集装箱运输实务［M］. 北京：北京大学出版社，2013.

[34] 易露霞，陈新华，尤彧聪. 国际贸易实务双语教程［M］. 5 版. 北京：清华大学出版社，2020.

[35] International Chamber of Commerce.（2019）. Incoterms 2020. ICC Rules for the Use of Domestic and International Trade Terms. ICC Services.

[36] 朱长征. 物流信息技术［M］. 2 版. 北京：清华大学出版社，2020.

[37] 黄新祥，宋娟娟，陈雅萍. 国际物流［M］. 2 版. 北京：清华大学出版社，2020.

[38] 陈言国. 国际物流实务［M］. 2 版. 北京：清华大学出版社，2020.